INVESTIGATION OF
THE ASSASSINATION OF PRESIDENT JOHN F. KENNEDY

HEARINGS

Before the President's Commission

on the Assassination

of President Kennedy

Pursuant To Executive Order 11130, an Executive order creating a Commission to ascertain, evaluate, and report upon the facts relating to the assassination of the late President John F. Kennedy and the subsequent violent death of the man charged with the assassination and S.J. Res. 137, 88th Congress, a concurrent resolution conferring upon the Commission the power to administer oaths and affirmations, examine witnesses, receive evidence, and issue subpoenas.

I0359569

Volume

I

UNITED STATES GOVERNMENT PRINTING OFFICE

WASHINGTON, D.C.

Published by Michigan Legal Publishing Ltd.
www.michlp.com
ISBN 978-1-64002-101-3

PRESIDENT'S COMMISSION ON THE ASSASSINATION OF PRESIDENT KENNEDY

Chief Justice Earl Warren, *Chairman*

Senator Richard B. Russell
Senator John Sherman Cooper
Representative Hale Boggs
Representative Gerald R. Ford
Mr. Allen W. Dulles
Mr. John J. McCloy

J. Lee Rankin, *General Counsel*

Assistant Counsel

Francis W. H. Adams
Joseph A. Ball
David W. Belin
William T. Coleman, Jr.
Melvin Aron Eisenberg
Burt W. Griffin
Leon D. Hubert, Jr.
Albert E. Jenner, Jr.
Wesley J. Liebeler
Norman Redlich
W. David Slawson
Arlen Specter
Samuel A. Stern
Howard P. Willens[*]

Staff Members

Phillip Barson
Edward A. Conroy
John Hart Ely
Alfred Goldberg
Murray J. Laulicht
Arthur Marmor
Richard M. Mosk
John J. O'Brien
Stuart Pollak
Alfredda Scobey
Charles N. Shaffer, Jr.

Biographical information on the Commissioners and the staff can be found in the Commission's *Report*.

---

[*] Mr. Willens also acted as liaison between the Commission and the Department of Justice.

Foreword

On November 29, 1963, President Lyndon B. Johnson signed Executive Order No. 11130, creating a Commission "to ascertain, evaluate and report upon the facts relating to the assassination of the late President John F. Kennedy and the subsequent violent death of the man charged with the assassination." By the same Executive order, the President appointed seven Commissioners: Earl Warren, Chief Justice of the United States; Richard B. Russell, Democratic Senator from Georgia; John Sherman Cooper, Republican Senator from Kentucky; Hale Boggs, Democratic Congressman from Louisiana and House Majority Whip; Gerald R. Ford, Republican Congressman from Michigan; Allen W. Dulles, former Director of the Central Intelligence Agency; and John J. McCloy, former High Commissioner of Germany. The President designated Chief Justice Warren as the Commission's Chairman. The findings of the Commission, based on an examination of all the facts, are set forth in the separate volume entitled "Report of the President's Commission on the Assassination of President Kennedy."

An essential part of the investigation conducted by this Commission has been the securing of sworn testimony from witnesses possessing information relevant to the inquiry. This testimony has been taken under the authority of Senate Joint Resolution 137 (88th Cong., 1st sess.), enacted by Congress on December 13, 1963, which conferred upon the Commission the power to administer oaths and affirmations, examine witnesses, receive evidence, and issue subpenas. Under the procedures adopted by the Commission, some witnesses have appeared before members of the Commission, others have been questioned under oath on depositions by members of the staff, and others have provided affidavits to the Commission. Beginning with its first witness on February 3, 1964, the Commission under these procedures took the testimony of approximately 550 witnesses and received more than 3,100 exhibits into evidence.

The testimony and exhibits obtained by the Commission are printed in this and the succeeding volumes, organized in the following order:

    (1) Testimony before members of the Commission, in the order in which it was taken.

    (2) Testimony by sworn deposition or affidavit, grouped into four general subject categories; the medical attention given to the President and the Governor, identification of the assassin of President Kennedy, the background of Lee Harvey Oswald, and the killing of Lee Harvey Oswald by Jack L. Ruby on November 24, 1963.

    (3) Exhibits introduced in connection with the testimony before the Commission in numerical order.

    (4) Exhibits introduced in connection with sworn depositions and affidavits, grouped alphabetically by name of witness.

    (5) Other exhibits introduced before the Commission in numerical order.

The transcripts of this testimony, prepared by qualified court reporters, were reviewed by members of the Commission staff and, in most instances, by the witness concerned. Editing of the transcript prior to printing in these volumes was confined to correction of stenographic errors and punctuation, and minor changes designed to improve the clarity and accuracy of the testimony. In the few cases indicated, brief deletions have been made of material which might be considered in poor taste and is clearly irrelevant to any facet of the Commission's investigation. All the original transcripts prepared by the court reporters, of course, have been preserved and will be available for inspection under the same rules and regulations which will apply to all records of this Commission.

vi Each volume contains a brief preface discussing the contents of the volume. In addition, each volume of testimony contains a table of contents with the names of the witnesses whose testimony appears in the volume, and the numbers of the exhibits introduced in connection with that testimony. Each volume of exhibits contains a table of contents with short descriptions of the exhibits reproduced in the volume. Volume XV contains a name index setting forth all references to persons (other than Lee Harvey Oswald) appearing in the Hearings volumes and an index setting forth all references to Commission exhibits and Deposition exhibits in these volumes.

Preface

The testimony of the following witnesses is contained in volume I: Mrs. Marina Oswald, the widow of Lee Harvey Oswald; Mrs. Marguerite Oswald, Oswald's mother; Robert Edward Lee Oswald, Oswald's brother; and James Herbert Martin, who acted for a brief period as Mrs. Marina Oswald's business manager.

Publisher's Note

This reprint of the Warren Commission hearings attempts to retain the original page numbers by including them in the text. The reader will notice numbers appearing in front of lines of testimony.

For instance, the reader will notice a line that looks like the following: "2 The Chairman. Mrs. Oswald, do you have an attorney, a lawyer?" This means that the line of text quoted begins page two in the original printed volumes. This is to assist readers with the many external references to the Warren Commission hearings volumes.

Contents

Testimony of Mrs. Lee Harvey Oswald 1
Testimony of Mrs. Marguerite Oswald 135
Testimony of Robert Edward Lee Oswald 281
Testimony of James Herbert Martin 502

Hearings Before the President's Commission on the Assassination of President Kennedy

Monday, February 3, 1964

Testimony of Mrs. Lee Harvey Oswald

The President's Commission met at 10:35 a.m. on February 3, 1964, at 200 Maryland Avenue NE., Washington, D.C.

Present were Chief Justice Earl Warren, Chairman; Senator John Sherman Cooper, Representative Hale Boggs, Representative Gerald R. Ford, and Allen W. Dulles, members.

Also present were J. Lee Rankin, general counsel; John M. Thorne, attorney for Mrs. Lee Harvey Oswald; William D. Krimer and Leon I. Gopadze, interpreters.

The Chairman. Well, Mrs. Oswald, did you have a good trip here?

The Commission will come to order, and at this time, I will make a short statement for the purpose of the meeting. A copy of this statement has been given to counsel for Mrs. Oswald, but for the record, I should like to read it.

On November 29, 1963, President Lyndon B. Johnson issued Executive Order No. 11130 appointing a Commission "to ascertain, evaluate, and report upon the facts relating to the assassination of the late President John F. Kennedy, and the subsequent violent death of the man charged with the assassination."

On December 13, 1963, Congress adopted Joint Resolution S.J. 137 which authorizes the Commission, or any member of the Commission or any agent or agency designated by the Commission for such purpose to administer oaths and affirmations, examine witnesses, and receive evidence.

Mr. Rankin. Mr. Chairman, excuse me, the interpreter——

The Chairman. I understood they have a copy and if they want to at the end he may do that.

On January 21, 1964, the Commission adopted a resolution authorizing each member of the Commission and its General Counsel, J. Lee Rankin, to administer oaths and affirmations, examine witnesses, and receive evidence concerning any matter under investigation by the Commission.

The purpose of this hearing is to take the testimony of Mrs. Marina Oswald, the widow of Lee Harvey Oswald who, prior to his death, was charged with the assassination of President Kennedy. Since the Commission is inquiring fully into the background of Lee Harvey Oswald and those associated with him, it is the intention of the Commission to ask Mrs. Marina Oswald questions concerning Lee Harvey Oswald and any and all matters relating to the assassination. The Commission also intends to ask Mrs. Marina Oswald questions relating to the assassination of President Kennedy and the subsequent violent death of Lee Harvey Oswald.

Mrs. Marina Oswald has been furnished with a copy of this statement and a copy of the rules adopted by the Commission for the taking of testimony or the production of evidence. Mrs. Marina Oswald has also been furnished with a copy of Executive Order No. 11130 and Congressional Resolution S.J. Res. 137 which set forth the general scope of the Commission's inquiry and its authority for the examining witnesses and the receiving of evidence.

2 The Chairman. Mrs. Oswald, do you have an attorney, a lawyer?

Mrs. Oswald. Yes.

The Chairman. And your lawyer is Mr. Thorne?
Mrs. Oswald. Yes.
The Chairman. He is the only lawyer you wish to represent you here?
Mrs. Oswald. Yes.
The Chairman. And may I ask you, Mr. Thorne, if you have received a copy of this?
Mr. Rankin. Mr. Chairman, that is the copy he received there.
Mr. Thorne. I have read a copy of it, Mr. Chief Justice, yes, sir.
The Chairman. Are there any questions about it?
Mr. Thorne. There are no questions.
The Chairman. Very well.
Very well, we will proceed to swear Mrs. Oswald as a witness.
Will you please rise, Mrs. Oswald.
(The Chairman administered the oath to the witness, Mrs. Oswald, through the interpreter.)
The Chairman. Mr. Reporter, will you rise, please, and be sworn.
(The Chairman administered the oath to the interpreter and the stenotype reporter, following which all questions propounded to the witness and her answers thereto, were duly translated through the interpreter.)
The Chairman. Now, Mr. Thorne and Mrs. Oswald, I want to say to you that we want to see that Mrs. Oswald's rights are protected in every manner and you are entitled to converse with her at any time that you desire. You are entitled to give her any advice that you want, either openly or in private; if you feel that her rights are not being protected you are entitled to object to the Commission and have a ruling upon it, and at the conclusion of her testimony if you have any questions that you would like to ask her in verification of what she has said you may feel free to ask them.

After her testimony has been completed, a copy will be furnished to you so that if there are any errors, corrections or omissions you may call it to our attention, is that satisfactory to you?

Mr. Thorne. Very satisfactory, Mr. Chairman.

The Chairman. I might say also to her we propose to ask her questions for about 1 hour, and then take a short recess for her refreshment, and then we will convene again until about 12:30. At 12:30 we will recess until 2 o'clock, and then we may take her to her hotel where she can see her baby and have a little rest, and we will return at 2 o'clock, and we will take evidence until about 4:30. If at any time otherwise you should feel tired or feel that you need a rest, you may feel free to say so and we will take care of it.

Mrs. Oswald. Thank you.

The Chairman. The questions will be asked of you by Mr. J. Lee Rankin, who is the general counsel of the Commission.

I think now we are ready to proceed, are we not, Mr. Rankin?

Mr. Rankin. Mrs. Oswald, you be at your ease, and the interpreter will tell you what I ask and you take your time about your answers.

Will you state your name, please?

Mrs. Oswald. Marina, my name is Marina Nikolaevna Oswald. My maiden name was Prussakova.

Mr. Rankin. Where do you live, Mrs. Oswald?
Mrs. Oswald. At the present time I live in Dallas.
Mr. Rankin. And where in Dallas?
Mrs. Oswald. Mr. Thorne knows my address.
Mr. Thorne. 11125 Ferrar Street, Dallas, Dallas County, Tex.
Mr. Rankin. Do you live with friends there?
Mrs. Oswald. I live with Mr. Jim Martin and his family.
Mr. Rankin. Mrs. Oswald, do you have a family?

Mrs. Oswald. I have two children, two girls, June will be 2 years old in February, and Rachel is 3 months old.

Mr. Rankin. Are you the widow of the late Lee Harvey Oswald?

Mrs. Oswald. Yes.

3 Mr. Rankin. Mrs. Oswald, did you write in Russian a story of your experiences in the United States?

Mrs. Oswald. Yes, I have. I think that you are familiar with it.

Mr. Rankin. You furnished it to the Commission, did you not, or a copy of it?

Mrs. Oswald. Yes.

Mr. Rankin. Will you describe for the Commission how you prepared this document in Russian that you furnished to us?

Mrs. Oswald. I wrote this document not specifically for this Commission, but merely for myself. Perhaps there are, therefore, not enough facts for your purpose in that document. This is the story of my life from the time I met him in Minsk up to the very last days.

Mr. Rankin. And by "him" who did you mean?

Mrs. Oswald. Lee Harvey Oswald.

Mr. Rankin. Did you have any assistance in preparing this document in Russian?

Mrs. Oswald. No, no one.

Mr. Rankin. Are all the statements in that document true insofar as you know?

Mrs. Oswald. Yes.

Mr. Rankin. Since your husband's death and even back to the time of the assassination of President Kennedy, you have had a number of interviews with people from the Secret Service and the FBI, have you not?

Mrs. Oswald. Yes, I did.

Mr. Rankin. We have a record of more than 46 such interviews, and I assume you cannot remember the exact number or all that was said in those interviews, is that true?

Mrs. Oswald. I don't know how many there were.

Mr. Rankin. As far as you can recall now, do you know of anything that is not true in those interviews that you would like to correct or add to?

Mrs. Oswald. Yes, I would like to correct some things because not everything was true.

Mr. Rankin. Will you tell us——

Mrs. Oswald. It is not just that it wasn't true, but not quite exact.

Mr. Rankin. Do you recall some of the information that you gave in those interviews that was incorrect that you would like to correct now? Will you tell us that?

Mrs. Oswald. At the present time, I can't remember any specific instance, but perhaps in the course of your questioning if it comes up I will say so.

Mr. Rankin. Do you recall the date that you arrived in the United States with your husband, Lee Harvey Oswald?

Mrs. Oswald. On the 13th of June, 1962—I am not quite certain as to the year—'61 or '62, I think '62.

Mr. Rankin. How did you come to this country?

Mrs. Oswald. From Moscow via Poland, Germany, and Holland we came to Amsterdam by train. And from Amsterdam to New York by ship, and New York to Dallas by air.

Mr. Rankin. Do you recall the name of the ship on which you came?

Mrs. Oswald. I think it was the SS Rotterdam but I am not sure.

Mr. Rankin. What time of the day did you arrive in New York?

Mrs. Oswald. It was—about noon or 1 p.m., thereabouts. It is hard to remember the exact time.

Mr. Rankin. How long did you stay in New York at that time?

Mrs. Oswald. We stayed that evening and the next 24 hours in a hotel in New York, and then we left the following day by air.

Mr. Rankin. Do you recall the name of the hotel where you stayed?

Mrs. Oswald. I don't know the name of the hotel but it is in the Times Square area, not far from the publishing offices of the New York Times.

Mr. Rankin. What did you do during your stay in New York?

Mrs. Oswald. That evening we just walked around the city to take a look at it. In the morning I remained in the hotel while Lee left in order to arrange for tickets, and so forth.

4 Mr. Rankin. Did you visit anyone or have visitors at your hotel during that period?

Mrs. Oswald. We didn't have any visitors but I remember that with Lee we visited some kind of an office, on official business, perhaps it had something to do with immigration or with the tickets. Lee spoke to them in English and I didn't understand it.

Mr. Rankin. Would that be a Travelers' Aid Bureau or Red Cross?

Mrs. Oswald. I don't know.

Mr. Rankin. Do you know whether or not you or your husband received any financial assistance for the trip to Texas at that time?

Mrs. Oswald. I don't know exactly where Lee got the money, but he said that his brother Robert had given him the money. But the money for the trip from the Soviet Union to New York was given to us by the American Embassy in Moscow.

Mr. Rankin. Do you recall what time of the day you left on the flight to Texas?

Mrs. Oswald. I think that by about 5 p.m. we were already in Texas.

Mr. Rankin. Did you go to Dallas or Fort Worth at that time?

Mrs. Oswald. In Dallas we were met by the brother, Robert, he lived in Fort Worth, and he took us from Dallas to Fort Worth and we stopped at the house.

Mr. Rankin. Who else stayed at Robert's house at that time besides your family?

Mrs. Oswald. His family and no one else.

Mr. Rankin. What did his family consist of at that time?

Mrs. Oswald. He and his wife and two children, a boy and a girl.

Mr. Rankin. How long did you stay at Robert's?

Mrs. Oswald. About 1 to 1½ months—perhaps longer, but no longer than 2 months.

Mr. Rankin. Were your relations and your husband's with Robert pleasant at that time?

Mrs. Oswald. Yes, they were very good. His brother's relationship to us was very good.

Mr. Rankin. Would you briefly describe what you did during that time when you were at Robert's?

Mrs. Oswald. The first time we got there we were, of course, resting for about a week, and I was busy, of course, with my little girl who was then very little. And in my free time, of course, I helped in the household.

Mr. Rankin. Did your husband do anything around the house or did he seek work right away?

Mrs. Oswald. For about a week he was merely talking and took a trip to the library. That is it.

Mr. Rankin. Then did he seek work in Fort Worth?

Mrs. Oswald. Yes.

Mr. Rankin. And when did he find his first job there?

Mrs. Oswald. While we were with Robert. It seems it was at the end of the second month that Lee found work. But at this time I don't remember the date exactly but his mother who lived in Fort Worth at that time rented a room and she proposed that we spend some time with her, that we live with her for some time.

Mr. Rankin. Did you discuss with your husband this proposal of your mother-in-law to have you live with her?

Mrs. Oswald. Well, she made the proposal to my husband, not to me. Of course, I found out about it.

Mr. Rankin. Did you and he have any discussion about it after you found out about it?
Mrs. Oswald. Yes, of course.
Mr. Rankin. You recall that discussion?
Mrs. Oswald. No. I only remember the fact.
Mr. Rankin. Did he find work after you left Robert's then?
Mrs. Oswald. Yes.
Mr. Rankin. You did move to be with your mother-in-law, lived with her for a time?
5 Mrs. Oswald. Yes, about 3 weeks. And then after 3 weeks Lee did not want to live with her any more and he rented an apartment.
Mr. Rankin. Do you know the reason why he did not want to live there any more?
Mrs. Oswald. It seemed peculiar to me and didn't want to believe it but he did not love his mother, she was not quite a normal woman. Now, I know this for sure.
Mr. Rankin. Did he tell you that at the time?
Mrs. Oswald. He talked about it but since he spoke in English to his mother, I didn't understand it. There were quite a few scenes when he would return from work he didn't want to talk to her. Perhaps she thought I was the reason for the fact that Lee did not want to talk to her. And, of course, for a mother this is painful and I told him that he should be more attentive to his mother but he did not change. I think that one of the reasons for this was that she talked a great deal about how much she had done to enable Lee to return from Russia, and Lee felt that he had done most of—the greatest effort in that respect and didn't want to discuss it.
Mr. Rankin. Where did he find work at that time?
Mrs. Oswald. Of course, if I had been told now I would have remembered it because I have learned some English but at that time I didn't know, but Lee told me that it wasn't far from Mercedes Street where we lived, and it was really common labor connected with some kind of metal work, something for buildings.
Mr. Rankin. Did he ever say whether he enjoyed that work?
Mrs. Oswald. He didn't like it.
Mr. Rankin. Do you recall how long he stayed at that job?
Mrs. Oswald. I don't know but it seemed to me that he worked there for about 3 or 4 months. Perhaps longer. Dates are one of my problems.
Mr. Rankin. Do you know whether he left that job voluntarily or was discharged?
Mrs. Oswald. He told me that he had been discharged but I don't know why.
Mr. Rankin. When you left the mother-in-law's house where did you go?
Mrs. Oswald. I have already said that we moved to Mercedes Street.
Mr. Rankin. Did you have an apartment there?
Mrs. Oswald. Yes, we rented an apartment in a duplex.
Mr. Rankin. Do you recall the address on Mercedes Street?
Mrs. Oswald. No, I don't remember the exact number.
Mr. Rankin. Will you describe the apartment, how many rooms it had?
Mrs. Oswald. Living room, kitchen, bath, and one bedroom.
Mr. Rankin. This was the first time since you had come to this country then that you had an opportunity to have a home of your own, is that right?
Mrs. Oswald. No, we had our own home in Russia.
Mr. Rankin. Did your husband work a full day at that time on this job?
Mrs. Oswald. Yes, sometimes he even worked on Saturdays.
Mr. Rankin. What did you do when he came home, did he help you with housework?
Mrs. Oswald. Yes. He frequently went to a library. He read a great deal.
Mr. Rankin. Do you recall any of the books that he read at that time?
Mrs. Oswald. No. I only know that they were books more of a historical nature rather than fiction or literature.

Mr. Rankin. In your story in Russian you relate the fact that he read a great deal of the time. Could you describe to the Commission just how that was? Did he go off by himself to read or how did he handle that?

Mrs. Oswald. He would bring a book from a library, sit in the living room and read. I was busy with housework, and that is the way it happened.

Mr. Rankin. Did you have differences between you about the time that he spent reading rather than devoting it to you or the other members of the family?

Mrs. Oswald. No. We did have quarrels about his relationship to his mother, the fact that he didn't want to change his relationship to his mother. I know that he read so much that when we lived in New Orleans he used to read sometimes all night long and in order not to disturb me he would be sitting in the bathroom for several hours reading.

6 Mr. Rankin. Did your quarrels start at that time when you were at Mercedes Street the first time.

Mrs. Oswald. Yes, we didn't have many quarrels.

Mr. Rankin. When you were at Mercedes Street did you have Robert visit you or did you visit him?

Mrs. Oswald. No, he came to us sometimes.

Mr. Rankin. Do you recall seeing any guns at Mercedes Street while you were there?

Mrs. Oswald. No.

Mr. Rankin. Did your mother-in-law come to see you at Mercedes Street?

Mrs. Oswald. Yes.

Mr. Rankin. Will you describe the relationship between your husband and your mother-in-law while he was at Mercedes Street?

Mrs. Oswald. She did not want us to move away to Mercedes Street, and Lee did not want to remain with her and did not even want her to visit us after that. Lee did not want her to know the address to which we were moving and Robert helped us in the move. I felt very sorry for her. Sometime after that she visited us while Lee was at work and I was quite surprised wondering about how she found out our address. And then we had a quarrel because he said to me, "Why did you open the door for her, I don't want her to come here any more."

Mr. Rankin. During this period did your husband spend much time with the baby, June?

Mrs. Oswald. Yes. He loved children very much.

Mr. Rankin. Did you obtain a television set at that time?

Mrs. Oswald. Lee wanted to buy a television set on credit. He then returned it. Should I speak a little louder?

Mr. Rankin. Did Robert help any with the money or just in guaranteeing the payments?

Mrs. Oswald. I think that he only guaranteed the payments.

Mr. Rankin. Do you recall how much the television set cost?

Mrs. Oswald. No.

Mr. Rankin. So far as you know it was paid for out of your husband's income?

Mrs. Oswald. Yes.

Mr. Rankin. Were you still at Mercedes Street when he lost his job with the welding company?

Mrs. Oswald. Yes.

Mr. Rankin. Did he try to find another job in Fort Worth then?

Mrs. Oswald. Yes.

Mr. Rankin. Do you know how much he looked for jobs before he found one then?

Mrs. Oswald. He looked for work for some time but he could not find it and then some Russian friends of ours helped him find some work in Dallas.

Mr. Rankin. How long was he out of work?

Mrs. Oswald. It seems to me it was about 2 weeks; hard to remember, perhaps that long.

Mr. Rankin. Where did he find work in Dallas, do you remember the name?

Mrs. Oswald. I know it was some kind of a printing company which prepares photographs for newspapers.

Mr. Rankin. Was he working with the photographic department of that company?

Mrs. Oswald. Yes.

Mr. Rankin. Was he an apprentice in that work trying to learn it?

Mrs. Oswald. Yes, at first he was an apprentice and later he worked.

Mr. Rankin. Do you know what his income was when he was working for the welding company?

Mrs. Oswald. I think it was about $200 a month, I don't know. I know it was a dollar and a quarter an hour.

Mr. Rankin. Did he work much overtime at that time?

Mrs. Oswald. Not too much but sometimes he did work Saturdays.

7 Mr. Rankin. Do you recall how much he received as pay at the printing company?

Mrs. Oswald. A dollar forty an hour.

Mr. Rankin. How many hours did he work a week, do you recall?

Mrs. Oswald. He usually worked until 5 p.m. But sometimes he worked later, and on Saturdays, too.

Mr. Rankin. The ordinary work week at that time was the 5-day week then, and the Saturdays would be an overtime period?

Mrs. Oswald. Yes.

Mr. Rankin. Who were the Russian friends who helped your husband find this job in Dallas?

Mrs. Oswald. George Bouhe.

Mr. Rankin. Did this friend and other Russian friends visit you at Mercedes Street?

Mrs. Oswald. Yes. When we lived at Fort Worth we became acquainted with Peter Gregory, he is a Russian, he lives in Fort Worth and through him we became acquainted with others.

Mr. Rankin. Will you tell us insofar as you recall, the friends that you knew in Fort Worth?

Mrs. Oswald. Our first acquaintance was Gregory. Through him I met Gali Clark, Mrs. Elena Hall. That is all in Fort Worth. And then we met George Bouhe in Dallas, and Anna Meller, and Anna Ray and Katya Ford.

Mr. Rankin. By your answer do you mean that some of those people you met in Dallas and some in Fort Worth?

Mrs. Oswald. George De Mohrenschildt—this was both in Fort Worth and Dallas, the names of my recital but they were well acquainted with each other, even though some lived in Dallas and some lived in Fort Worth.

Mr. Rankin. Will you please sort them out for us and tell us those you met in Dallas?

Mrs. Oswald. You mean by the question, who out of these Russians lives in Dallas?

Mr. Rankin. Or which ones you met in Dallas as distinguished from those you had already met in Fort Worth?

Mrs. Oswald. In Fort Worth I met the people from Dallas. There was George Bouhe, George De Mohrenschildt—no. Anna Meller and George Bouhe only, they were from Dallas, but I met them in Fort Worth.

Mr. Rankin. Did these friends visit you at your home in Fort Worth?

Mrs. Oswald. Yes, sometimes they came to visit us when they were in Dallas, they came to us. Sometimes they made a special trip to come and see us.

Mr. Rankin. Did you ever visit them in their homes?

Mrs. Oswald. Yes, when we lived in Fort Worth we went to Dallas several times to visit them.

Mr. Rankin. When you made these visits did you go to spend an evening or a considerable part of the time or were they short visits? Can you describe that?

Mrs. Oswald. We used to come early in the morning and leave at night. We would spend the entire day with them. We went there by bus.

Mr. Rankin. Did you have an automobile of your own at any time during this period?

Mrs. Oswald. No.

Mr. Rankin. Did any of these people have meals in your home when they visited you?

Mrs. Oswald. No. They usually brought—they usually came for short visits and they brought their own favorite vegetables such as cucumbers, George liked cucumbers.

Mr. Rankin. When you moved to Dallas, where did you live the first time?

Mrs. Oswald. I did not move to Dallas together with Lee. Lee went to Dallas when he found the job, and I remained in Fort Worth and lived with Elena Hall.

Mr. Rankin. For how long a period did you live with Mrs. Hall?

Mrs. Oswald. I think that it was about a month and a half.

Mr. Rankin. During that month and a half what did your husband do?

8 Mrs. Oswald. He had a job. He was working. He would call me up over the telephone but how he spent his time, I don't know.

Mr. Rankin. Do you know during that month and a half where he lived?

Mrs. Oswald. At first, I know that he rented a room in the YMCA but very shortly thereafter he rented an apartment. But where I don't know.

Mr. Rankin. During that month and a half did he come and see you and the baby?

Mrs. Oswald. Yes, two or three times he came to see us because he had no car. It was not very easy.

Mr. Rankin. Were these trips to see you on the weekends?

Mrs. Oswald. Yes.

Mr. Rankin. When he came did he also stay at the Hall's?

Mrs. Oswald. Yes.

Mr. Rankin. When you were staying at the Hall's did you pay them for your room and your meals?

Mrs. Oswald. No. No, she was very friendly toward us and she tried to help us.

Mr. Rankin. What did you and your husband do when he came to see you? Did he spend his time with you there in the home or did you go some place?

Mrs. Oswald. No, we didn't go anywhere.

Mr. Rankin. Did he do any reading there?

Mrs. Oswald. No. I remember that it was only a couple of times that he came for a weekend. Generally, he only came for a very short period of time, because he would come together with our friends, and they could not stay very long.

Mr. Rankin. When he came during that period did he discuss what he had been doing in Dallas, his work and other things?

Mrs. Oswald. He liked his work very much.

Mr. Rankin. After this month and a half did he find a place for you all to live together?

Mrs. Oswald. Yes, but it wasn't a problem there to find a place, no problem there to find a place.

Mr. Rankin. Did you then move to a home in Dallas?

Mrs. Oswald. Yes, on Elsbeth, Elsbeth Street in Dallas.

Mr. Rankin. Do you remember the number?

Mrs. Oswald. No.

Mr. Rankin. How did you move your things from Mrs. Hall's to the place on Elsbeth Street?

Mrs. Oswald. A friend who had a car helped us—I don't remember his name, Taylor, Gary Taylor.

The Chairman. Suppose we take a recess now for about 10 minutes to allow Mrs. Oswald to refresh herself.

(Short recess.)

The Chairman. The Commission may be in order.

Mr. Rankin. Did that require one or more trips to move your things from Fort Worth to Dallas when you went to Elsbeth Street?

Mrs. Oswald. One trip was enough.

Mr. Rankin. Did you observe any guns in your things when you moved?

Mrs. Oswald. No.

Mr. Rankin. What kind of place did you have at Elsbeth Street, was it rooms or an apartment?

Mrs. Oswald. An apartment.

Mr. Rankin. How many rooms in the apartment?

Mrs. Oswald. One living room, a bedroom, a kitchen, and the bathroom. It sounds very small for all of you but for us it was quite sufficient.

Mr. Rankin. Did you have a telephone there?

Mrs. Oswald. No.

Mr. Rankin. Do you recall what rent you paid?

Mrs. Oswald. It seems to me that it was $60, plus the utilities.

Mr. Rankin. That would be $60 a month?

Mrs. Oswald. Yes, and electricity and gas but the water was free. Sixty dollars a month including water.

Mr. Rankin. Did your husband help you with the housework at that address?

9 Mrs. Oswald. Yes, he always helped.

Mr. Rankin. What about his reading habits there, were they the same?

Mrs. Oswald. Yes, about the same.

Mr. Rankin. Can you tell us a little more fully about his reading? Did he spend several hours each evening in this reading?

Mrs. Oswald. Yes.

Mr. Rankin. Do you recall any of the books that he read at Elsbeth Street?

Mrs. Oswald. No. He had two books, two thick books on the history of the United States.

Mr. Rankin. Did your husband come home for a midday meal?

Mrs. Oswald. No.

Mr. Rankin. Did you go out in the evenings?

Mrs. Oswald. Yes.

Mr. Rankin. Where did you go?

Mrs. Oswald. Sometimes we went shopping to stores, and movies, though Lee really went to the movies himself. He wanted to take me but I did not understand English. Then on weekends we would go to a lake not far away or to a park or to a cafe for some ice cream.

Mr. Rankin. When you went to the lake or the park did you take food with you and have a picnic?

Mrs. Oswald. Yes.

Mr. Rankin. How did you get to the lake or the park, by bus or car, or what means of transportation?

Mrs. Oswald. It was only 10 minutes away, 10 minutes walking time from us.

Mr. Rankin. Were either you or your husband taking any schooling at that time?

Mrs. Oswald. Lee took English courses or typing courses.

Mr. Rankin. During what days of the week were these typing courses?

Mrs. Oswald. It was three days a week. I don't remember exactly what the days were. It seems to me it was 1 day at the beginning of the week and 2 days at the end of the week that he took these night courses.

Mr. Rankin. Would it help you to recall if I suggested they were Monday, Tuesday, and Thursday?

Mrs. Oswald. It seems to me that is the way it was. I know it was on Monday.

Mr. Rankin. Do you recall what hours of the evening he was supposed to be at these classes?
Mrs. Oswald. It seems that it was from 7 until 9.
Mr. Rankin. About what time would he get home from work?
Mrs. Oswald. About 5 to 5:30.
Mr. Rankin. Then would you eat your evening meal?
Mrs. Oswald. Yes.
Mr. Rankin. How soon after that would he leave for the class?
Mrs. Oswald. When Lee took his courses he generally did not come home for dinner, usually he didn't.
Mr. Rankin. Did he practice his typewriting at home at all?
Mrs. Oswald. At home, no. But he had a book, a textbook on typing which he would review when he was at home.
Mr. Rankin. How soon after the class was over did he come home ordinarily?
Mrs. Oswald. Nine o'clock.
Mr. Rankin. Did he tell you anything about friends that he met at these classes?
Mrs. Oswald. No.
Mr. Rankin. While you were at Elsbeth Street do you recall seeing any guns in your apartment?
Mrs. Oswald. No.
Mr. Rankin. Do you remember exhibiting any guns to the De Mohrenschildt's while you were at Elsbeth Street?
Mrs. Oswald. That was on Neely Street, perhaps you are confused, this was on Neely Street.
Mr. Rankin. When did you move to Neely Street from the Elsbeth Street apartment?
10 Mrs. Oswald. In January after the new year. I don't remember exactly.
Mr. Rankin. Do you remember why you moved from Elsbeth to Neely Street?
Mrs. Oswald. I like it better on Neely Street. We had a porch there and that was more convenient for the child.
Mr. Rankin. What size apartment did you have on Neely Street?
Mrs. Oswald. The same type of apartment.
Mr. Rankin. Was the only difference the terrace then?
Mrs. Oswald. Yes, except that it was on the second floor. It was a second-floor apartment.
Mr. Rankin. Was the Elsbeth Street apartment a first-floor apartment?
Mrs. Oswald. Yes.
Mr. Rankin. What about the rent? Was there a difference in rent between the two places?
Mrs. Oswald. No, it was the same rent. It is perhaps even less. It seems to me it was $55.
Mr. Rankin. Did you have any differences with your husband while you were at Neely Street?
Mrs. Oswald. No. Well, there are always some reasons for some quarrel between a husband and wife, not everything is always smooth.
Mr. Rankin. I had in mind if there was any violence or any hitting of you. Did that occur at Neely Street?
Mrs. Oswald. No. That was on Elsbeth Street.
Mr. Rankin. Do you recall what brought that about?
Mrs. Oswald. Not quite. I am trying to remember. It seems to me that it was at that time that Lee began to talk about his wanting to return to Russia. I did not want that and that is why we had quarrels.
Mr. Rankin. Did you have discussions between you about this idea of returning to Russia?

Mrs. Oswald. Yes. Lee wanted me to go to Russia. I told him that that—Lee wanted me to go to Russia, and I told him that if he wanted me to go then that meant that he didn't love me, and that in that case what was the idea of coming to the United States in the first place. Lee would say that it would be better for me if I went to Russia. I did not know why. I did not know what he had in mind. He said he loved me but that it would be better for me if I went to Russia, and what he had in mind I don't know.

Mr. Rankin. Do you know when he first started to talk about your going to Russia?

Mrs. Oswald. On Elsbeth Street.

Mr. Rankin. Do you remember any occasion which you thought caused him to start to talk that way?

Mrs. Oswald. No, I don't.

Mr. Rankin. Do you know why he started to hit you about that?

Mrs. Oswald. Now, I think that I know, although at that time I didn't. I think that he was very nervous and just this somehow relieved his tension.

Mr. Rankin. Did you observe sometime when you thought he changed?

Mrs. Oswald. I would say that immediately after coming to the United States Lee changed. I did not know him as such a man in Russia.

Mr. Rankin. Will you describe how you observed these changes and what they were as you saw them?

Mrs. Oswald. He helped me as before, but he became a little more of a recluse. He did not like my Russian friends and he tried to forbid me to have anything to do with them.

He was very irritable, sometimes for a trifle, for a trifling reason.

Mr. Rankin. Did he tell you why he did not like your Russian friends?

Mrs. Oswald. I don't know why he didn't like them. I didn't understand. At least that which he said was completely unfounded. He simply said some stupid or foolish things.

Mr. Rankin. Will you tell us the stupid things that he said?

Mrs. Oswald. Well, he thought that they were fools for having left Russia; they were all traitors. I would tell him he was in the same position being an American in America but there were really no reasons but just irritation. He said that they all only like money, and everything is measured by money. It11 seems to me that perhaps he was envious of them in the sense they were more prosperous than he was. When I told him, when I would say that to him he did not like to hear that.

Perhaps I shouldn't say these foolish things and I feel kind of uncomfortable to talk about the foolish things that happened or what he said foolish things.

This is one of the reasons why I don't know really the reasons for these quarrels because sometimes the quarrels were just trifles. It is just that Lee was very unrestrained and very explosive at that time.

Mr. Rankin. Mrs. Oswald, we will ask you to be very frank with us. It isn't for the purpose of embarrassing you or your husband that we ask you these things but it might help us to understand and even if you will tell us the foolish and stupid things it may shed some light on the problem. You understand that?

Mrs. Oswald. I understand you are not asking these questions out of curiosity but for a reason.

Mr. Rankin. Did your husband indicate any particular Russian friends that he disliked more than others?

Mrs. Oswald. He liked De Mohrenschildt but he—because he was a strong person, but only De Mohrenschildt. He did not like Bouhe or Anna Meller.

Mr. Rankin. Did you ever tell him you liked these people?

Mrs. Oswald. Yes, I told him all the time that I liked these people and that is why he was angry at me and would tell me that I was just like they were. At one time I left him and went to my friends because he put me into—put me on the spot by saying, "Well, if you like your friends so much then go ahead and live with them," and he left me no choice.

Mr. Rankin. When was this, Mrs. Oswald?
Mrs. Oswald. On Elsbeth Street.
Mr. Rankin. How long were you gone from him then?
Mrs. Oswald. One week.
Mr. Rankin. Did he ask you to return?
Mrs. Oswald. Yes. I took June and I went to Anna Meller, took a cab and went there. I spent several days with her. Lee didn't know where I was but he called up and about 2 or 3 days after I came to and we met at De Mohrenschildt's house and he asked me to return home. I, of course, did not want a divorce but I told him it would be better to get a divorce rather than to continue living and quarreling this way. After all this is only a burden on a man if two people live together and fight. I simply wanted to show him, too, that I am not a toy. That a woman is a little more complicated. That you cannot trifle with her.
Mr. Rankin. Did you say anything at that time about how he should treat you if you returned?
Mrs. Oswald. Yes. I told him if he did not change his character, then it would become impossible to continue living with him. Because if there should be such quarrels continuously that would be crippling for the children.
Mr. Rankin. What did he say to that?
Mrs. Oswald. Then he said that it would be—it was very hard for him. That he could not change. That I must accept him, such as he was. And he asked me to come back home with him right on that day but he left feeling bad because I did not go and remained with my friend.
Mr. Rankin. What did you say about accepting him as he was?
Mrs. Oswald. I told him I was not going to. Of course, such as he was for me he was good, but I wanted simply for the sake of the family that he would correct his character. It isn't that I didn't mean to say he was good for me, I meant to say that I could stand him, but for the sake of the children I wanted him to improve his behavior.
Mr. Rankin. Then did he get in touch with you again?
Mrs. Oswald. At that time there was very little room at Anna Meller's and it was very uncomfortable and I left and went to Katya Ford whose husband at that time happened to be out of town on business. I spent several days with Katya Ford but then when her husband returned I did not want to remain with her. And it was on a Sunday morning then when I moved over to Anna Ray. Lee called me and said he wanted to see me, that he had come by bus and he wanted to see me and he came that evening and he cried and said that he12 wanted me to return home because if I did not return he did not want to continue living. He said he didn't know how to love me in any other way and that he will try to change.
Mr. Rankin. While you were at Mrs. Ford's did she go to the hospital?
Mrs. Oswald. No. I think that you are confused—this was Elena Hall in Fort Worth, she was ill and went to the hospital. It is not very interesting to hear all that. Somewhat boring.
Mr. Rankin. Do you recall the manner in which Lee brought up the idea of your going to Russia alone?
Mrs. Oswald. Quite simply he said it was very hard for him here. That he could not have a steady job. It would be better for me because I could work in Russia. That was all.
Mr. Rankin. Did you understand when he suggested it that he proposed that you go and he stay?
Mrs. Oswald. Yes. Now, I think I know why he had in mind to start his foolish activity which could harm me but, of course, at that time he didn't tell me the reason. It is only now that I understand it. At that time when I would ask him he would get angry because he couldn't tell me.
Mr. Rankin. What would you say to him at that time?

Mrs. Oswald. I told him at that time that I am agreeable to going if he could not live with me. But he kept on repeating that he wanted to live with me but that it would be better for me, but when I wanted to know the reason he would not tell me.

Mr. Rankin. Is there something that you have learned since that caused you to believe that this suggestion was related to trying to provide for you or to be sure that you wouldn't be hurt by what he was going to do?

Mrs. Oswald. At that time I didn't know this. I only saw that he was in such a state that he was struggling and perhaps did not understand himself. I thought that I was the reason for that.

Mr. Rankin. Did he have a job then?

Mrs. Oswald. Yes.

Mr. Rankin. Did you feel that you were getting along on what he was earning?

Mrs. Oswald. Of course.

Mr. Rankin. Were you urging him to earn more so that he could provide more for the family?

Mrs. Oswald. No. We had enough.

Mr. Rankin. You were not complaining about the way you were living?

Mrs. Oswald. No. I think that my friends had thought, and it was also written in the newspapers that we lived poorly because for Americans $200 appears to be very little. But I have never lived in any very luxurious way and, therefore, for me this was quite sufficient. Some of the others would say, "well here, you don't have a car or don't have this or that." But for me it was sufficient. Sometimes Lee would tell me I was just like my friends, that I wanted to have that which they had. That I preferred them to him because they give me more, but that is not true.

Mr. Rankin. Did you understand when he suggested you return to Russia that he was proposing to break up your marriage?

Mrs. Oswald. I told him that I would go to Russia if he would give me a divorce, but he did not want to give me a divorce.

Mr. Rankin. Did he say why?

Mrs. Oswald. He said that if he were to give me a divorce that that would break everything between us, which he didn't want. That he wanted to keep me as his wife, but I told him that if he wants to remain in the United States I want to be free in Russia.

Mr. Rankin. During this period did he appear to be more excited and nervous?

Mrs. Oswald. Not particularly, but the later time he was more excited and more nervous but it was quite a contrast between the way he was in Russia.

Mr. Rankin. By the later time that you just referred to what do you mean? Can you give us some approximate date?

Mrs. Oswald. When we went to Neely Street.

13 The Chairman. I think this is a good time to take our luncheon recess now. So, we will adjourn until 2 o'clock.

Mrs. Oswald. Thank you.

(Whereupon, at 12:30 p.m., the President's Commission recessed.)

Afternoon Session
TESTIMONY OF MRS. LEE HARVEY OSWALD RESUMED
The President's Commission reconvened at 2 p.m.

The Chairman. All right. Let us proceed.

(The Chairman administered the oath to Alvin I. Mills, Stenotype Reporter.)

Mr. Rankin. Mr. Reporter, do you have the last questions?

In the future, would you do that, so we can refresh the witness about the last couple of questions on her testimony? I think it will make it easier for her, if she doesn't have to try to remember all the time.

Mr. Rankin. Mrs. Oswald, as I recall you were telling us about these developments at Neely Street when you found that your husband was suggesting that you go back to Russia alone and you discussed that matter, and you thought it had something to do with the idea he had, which I understood you have discovered as you looked back or thought back later but didn't know at the time fully. Is that right?

Mrs. Oswald. That is correct.

Mr. Rankin. Could you tell us those things that you observed that caused you to think he had something in mind at that time, and I will ask you later, after you tell us, those that you discovered since or that you have obtained more light on since.

Mrs. Oswald. At that time I did not think anything about it. I had no reasons to think that he had something in mind. I did not understand him at that time.

Mr. Rankin. Do you recall the first time that you observed the rifle?

Mrs. Oswald. That was on Neely Street. I think that was in February.

Mr. Rankin. How did you learn about it? Did you see it some place in the apartment?

Mrs. Oswald. Yes, Lee had a small room where he spent a great deal of time, where he read—where he kept his things, and that is where the rifle was.

Mr. Rankin. Was it out in the room at that time, as distinguished from in a closet in the room?

Mrs. Oswald. Yes, it was open, out in the open. At first I think—I saw some package up on the top shelf, and I think that that was the rifle. But I didn't know. And apparently later he assembled it and had it in the room.

Mr. Rankin. When you saw the rifle assembled in the room, did it have the scope on it?

Mrs. Oswald. No, it did not have a scope on it.

Mr. Rankin. Did you have any discussion with your husband about the rifle when you first saw it?

Mrs. Oswald. Of course I asked him, "What do you need a rifle for? What do we need that for?"

He said that it would come in handy some time for hunting. And this was not too surprising because in Russia, too, we had a rifle.

Mr. Rankin. In Russia did you have a rifle or a shotgun?

Mrs. Oswald. I don't know the difference. One and the other shoots. You men. That is your business.

The Chairman. My wife wouldn't know the difference, so it is all right.

Mrs. Oswald. I have never served in the Army.

Mr. Rankin. Did you discuss what the rifle cost with your husband?

Mrs. Oswald. No.

Mr. Rankin. Was the rifle later placed in a closet in the apartment at Neely Street?

14 Mrs. Oswald. No, it was always either in a corner, standing up in a corner or on a shelf.

Mr. Rankin. Do you know what happened to the gun that you had in Russia? Was it brought over to this country?

Mrs. Oswald. No, he sold it there. I did not say so when I had the first interviews. You must understand this was my husband. I didn't want to say too much.

Mr. Rankin. Is this rifle at Neely Street the only rifle that you know of that your husband had after you were married to him?

Mrs. Oswald. Yes.

Mr. Rankin. Did you ever show that rifle to the De Mohrenschildts?

Mrs. Oswald. I know that De Mohrenschildts had said that the rifle had been shown to him, but I don't remember that.

Mr. Rankin. Do you recall your husband taking the rifle away from the apartment on Neely Street at any time?

Mrs. Oswald. You must know that the rifle—it isn't as if it was out in the open. He would hang a coat or something to mask its presence in the room. And sometimes when he walked out, when he went out in the evening I didn't know, because I didn't go into that room very often. I don't know whether he took it with him or not.

Mr. Rankin. Did you ever see him clean the rifle?

Mrs. Oswald. Yes. I said before I had never seen it before. But I think you understand. I want to help you, and that is why there is no reason for concealing anything. I will not be charged with anything.

Mr. Gopadze. She says she was not sworn in before. But now inasmuch as she is sworn in, she is going to tell the truth.

Mr. Rankin. Did you see him clean the rifle a number of times?

Mrs. Oswald. Yes.

Mr. Rankin. Could you help us by giving some estimate of the times as you remember it?

Mrs. Oswald. About four times—about four or five times, I think.

Mr. Rankin. Did your husband ever tell you why he was cleaning the—that is, that he had been using it and needed to be cleaned after use?

Mrs. Oswald. No, I did not ask him, because I thought it was quite normal that when you have a rifle you must clean it from time to time.

Mr. Rankin. Did you ever observe your husband taking the rifle away from the apartment on Neely Street?

Mrs. Oswald. Now, I think that he probably did sometimes, but I never did see it. You must understand that sometimes I would be in the kitchen and he would be in his room downstairs, and he would say bye-bye, I will be back soon, and he may have taken it. He probably did. Perhaps he purely waited for an occasion when he could take it away without my seeing it.

Mr. Rankin. Did you ever observe that the rifle had been taken out of the apartment at Neely Street—that is, that it was gone?

Mrs. Oswald. Before the incident with General Walker, I know that Lee was preparing for something. He took photographs of that house and he told me not to enter his room. I didn't know about these photographs, but when I came into the room once in general he tried to make it so that I would spend less time in that room. I noticed that quite accidentally one time when I was cleaning the room he tried to take care of it himself.

I asked him what kind of photographs are these, but he didn't say anything to me.

Mr. Rankin. That is the photographs of the Walker house that you were asking about?

Mrs. Oswald. Yes. Later, after he had fired, he told me about it.

I didn't know that he intended to do it—that he was planning to do it.

Mr. Rankin. Did you learn at any time that he had been practicing with the rifle?

Mrs. Oswald. I think that he went once or twice. I didn't actually see him take the rifle, but I knew that he was practicing.

Mr. Rankin. Could you give us a little help on how you knew?

Mrs. Oswald. He told me. And he would mention that in passing—it isn't15 as if he said, "Well, today I am going"—it wasn't as if he said, "Well, today I am going to take the rifle and go and practice."

But he would say, "Well, today I will take the rifle along for practice."

Therefore, I don't know whether he took it from the house or whether perhaps he even kept the rifle somewhere outside. There was a little square, sort of a little courtyard where he might have kept it.

When you asked me about the rifle, I said that Lee didn't have a rifle, but he also had a gun, a revolver.

Mr. Rankin. Do you recall when he first had the pistol, that you remember?

Mrs. Oswald. He had that on Neely Street, but I think that he acquired the rifle before he acquired the pistol. The pistol I saw twice—once in his room, and the second time when I took these photographs.

Mr. Rankin. What period of time was there between when he got the rifle and you learned of it, and the time that you first learned about the pistol?

Mrs. Oswald. I can't say.

Mr. Rankin. When you testified about his practicing with the rifle, are you describing a period when you were still at Neely Street?

Mrs. Oswald. Yes.

Mr. Rankin. Do you know where he practiced with the rifle?

Mrs. Oswald. I don't know where. I don't know the name of the place where this took place. But I think it was somewhere out of town. It seems to me a place called Lopfield.

Mr. Rankin. Would that be at the airport—Love Field?

Mrs. Oswald. Love Field.

Mr. Rankin. So you think he was practicing out in the open and not at a rifle range?

Mrs. Oswald. Yes.

Mr. Rankin. Do you recall seeing the rifle when the telescopic lens was on it?

Mrs. Oswald. I hadn't paid any attention initially.

I know a rifle was a rifle. I didn't know whether or not it had a telescope attached to it. But the first time I remember seeing it was in New Orleans, where I recognized the telescope. But probably the telescope was on before. I simply hadn't paid attention.

I hope you understand. When I saw it, I thought that all rifles have that.

Mr. Rankin. Did you make any objection to having the rifle around?

Mrs. Oswald. Of course.

Mr. Rankin. What did he say to that?

Mrs. Oswald. That for a man to have a rifle—since I am a woman, I don't understand him, and I shouldn't bother him. A fine life.

Mr. Rankin. Is that the same rifle that you are referring to that you took the picture of with your husband and when he had the pistol, too?

Mrs. Oswald. Yes. I asked him then why he had dressed himself up like that, with the rifle and the pistol, and I thought that he had gone crazy, and he said he wanted to send that to a newspaper. This was not my business—it was man's business.

If I had known these were such dangerous toys, of course—you understand that I thought that Lee had changed in that direction, and I didn't think it was a serious occupation with him, just playing around.

Mr. Rankin. Do you recall the day that you took the picture of him with the rifle and the pistol?

Mrs. Oswald. I think that that was towards the end of February, possibly the beginning of March. I can't say exactly. Because I didn't attach any significance to it at the time. That was the only time I took any pictures.

I don't know how to take pictures. He gave me a camera and asked me—if someone should ask me how to photograph, I don't know.

Mr. Rankin. Was it on a day off that you took the picture?

Mrs. Oswald. It was on a Sunday.

Mr. Rankin. How did it occur? Did he come to you and ask you to take the picture?

Mrs. Oswald. I was hanging up diapers, and he came up to me with the rifle and I was even a little scared, and he gave me the camera and asked me to press a certain button.

16 Mr. Rankin. And he was dressed up with a pistol at the same time, was he?

Mrs. Oswald. Yes.

Mr. Rankin. You have examined that picture since, and noticed that the telescopic lens was on at the time the picture was taken, have you not?

Mrs. Oswald. Now I paid attention to it. A specialist would see it immediately, of course. But at that time I did not pay any attention at all. I saw just Lee. These details are of great significance for everybody, but for me at that time it didn't mean anything. At the time that I was questioned, I had even forgotten that I had taken two photographs. I thought there was only one. I thought that there were two identical pictures, but they turned out to be two different poses.

Mr. Rankin. Did you have anything to do with the prints of the photograph after the prints were made? That is, did you put them in a photographic album yourself?

Mrs. Oswald. Lee gave me one photograph and asked me to keep it for June somewhere. Of course June doesn't need photographs like that.

Mr. Rankin. Do you recall how long after that the Walker matter occurred?

Mrs. Oswald. Two, perhaps three weeks later. I don't know. You know better when this happened.

Mr. Rankin. How did you first learn that your husband had shot at General Walker?

Mrs. Oswald. That evening he went out, I thought that he had gone to his classes or perhaps that he just walked out or went out on his own business. It got to be about 10 or 10:30, he wasn't home yet, and I began to be worried. Perhaps even later.

Then I went into his room. Somehow, I was drawn into it—you know—I was pacing around. Then I saw a note there.

Mr. Rankin. Did you look for the gun at that time?

Mrs. Oswald. No, I didn't understand anything. On the note it said, "If I am arrested" and there are certain other questions, such as, for example, the key to the mailbox is in such and such a place, and that he left me some money to last me for some time, and I couldn't understand at all what can he be arrested for. When he came back I asked him what had happened. He was very pale. I don't remember the exact time, but it was very late.

And he told me not to ask him any questions. He only told me that he had shot at General Walker.

Of course I didn't sleep all night. I thought that any minute now, the police will come. Of course I wanted to ask him a great deal. But in his state I decided I had best leave him alone—it would be purposeless to question him.

Mr. Rankin. Did he say any more than that about the shooting?

Mrs. Oswald. Of course in the morning I told him that I was worried, and that we can have a lot of trouble, and I asked him, "Where is the rifle? What did you do with it?"

He said, that he had left it somewhere, that he had buried it, it seems to me, somewhere far from that place, because he said dogs could find it by smell.

I don't know—I am not a criminologist.

Mr. Rankin. Did he tell you why he had shot at General Walker?

Mrs. Oswald. I told him that he had no right to kill people in peacetime, he had no right to take their life because not everybody has the same ideas as he has. People cannot be all alike.

He said that this was a very bad man, that he was a fascist, that he was the leader of a fascist organization, and when I said that even though all of that might be true, just the same he had no right to take his life, he said if someone had killed Hitler in time it would have saved many lives. I told him that this is no method to prove your ideas, by means of a rifle.

Mr. Rankin. Did you ask him how long he had been planning to do this?

Mrs. Oswald. Yes. He said he had been planning for two months. Yes—perhaps he had planned to do so even earlier, but according to his conduct I could tell he was planning—he had been planning this for two months or perhaps a little even earlier.

The Chairman. Would you like to take a little recess?

Mrs. Oswald. No, thank you. Better to get it over with.

17 Mr. Rankin. Did he show you a picture of the Walker house then?

Mrs. Oswald. Yes.

Mr. Rankin. That was after the shooting?

Mrs. Oswald. Yes. He had a book—he had a notebook in which he noted down quite a few details. It was all in English, I didn't read it. But I noticed the photograph. Sometimes he would lock himself in his room and write in the book. I thought that he was writing some other kind of memoirs, as he had written about his life in the Soviet Union.

Mr. Rankin. Did you ever read that book?

Mrs. Oswald. No.

Mr. Rankin. Do you know of anything else he had in it besides this Walker house picture?

Mrs. Oswald. No. Photographs and notes, and I think there was a map in there.

Mr. Rankin. There was a map of the area where the Walker house was?

Mrs. Oswald. It was a map of Dallas, but I don't know where Walker lived. Sometimes evenings he would be busy with this. Perhaps he was calculating something, but I don't know. He had a bus schedule and computed something.

After this had happened, people thought that he had a car, but he had been using a bus.

Mr. Rankin. Did he explain to you about his being able to use a bus just as well as other people could use a car—something of that kind?

Mrs. Oswald. No. Simply as a passenger. He told me that even before that time he had gone also to shoot, but he had returned. I don't know why. Because on the day that he did fire, there was a church across the street and there were many people there, and it was easier to merge in the crowd and not be noticed.

Mr. Rankin. Did you ask him about this note that he had left, what he meant by it?

Mrs. Oswald. Yes—he said he had in mind that if in case he were arrested, I would know what to do.

Mr. Rankin. The note doesn't say anything about Walker, does it?

Mrs. Oswald. No.

Mr. Rankin. Did you ask him if that is what he meant by the note?

Mrs. Oswald. Yes, because as soon as he came home I showed him the note and asked him "What is the meaning of this?"

Mr. Rankin. And that is when he gave you the explanation about the Walker shooting?

Mrs. Oswald. Yes.

I know that on a Sunday he took the rifle, but I don't think he fired on a Sunday. Perhaps this was on Friday. So Sunday he left and took the rifle.

Mr. Rankin. If the Walker shooting was on Wednesday, does that refresh your memory as to the day of the week at all?

Mrs. Oswald. Refresh my memory as to what?

Mr. Rankin. As to the day of the shooting?

Mrs. Oswald. It was in the middle of the week.

Mr. Rankin. Did he give any further explanation of what had happened that evening?

Mrs. Oswald. When he fired, he did not know whether he had hit Walker or not. He didn't take the bus from there. He ran several kilometers and then took the bus. And he turned on the radio and listened, but there were no reports.

The next day he bought a paper and there he read it was only chance that saved Walker's life. If he had not moved, he might have been killed.

Mr. Rankin. Did he comment on that at all?

Mrs. Oswald. He said only that he had taken very good aim, that it was just chance that caused him to miss. He was very sorry that he had not hit him.

I asked him to give me his word that he would not repeat anything like that. I said that this chance shows that he must live and that he should not be shot at again. I told him that I would save the note and that if something like that18 should be repeated again, I would go to the police and I would have the proof in the form of that note.

He said he would not repeat anything like that again.

By the way, several days after that, the De Mohrenschildts came to us, and as soon as he opened the door he said, "Lee, how is it possible that you missed?"

I looked at Lee. I thought that he had told De Mohrenschildt about it. And Lee looked at me, and he apparently thought that I had told De Mohrenschildt about it. It was kind of dark. But I noticed—it was in the evening, but I noticed that his face changed, that he almost became speechless.

You see, other people knew my husband better than I did. Not always—but in this case.

Mr. Rankin. Was De Mohrenschildt a friend that he told—your husband told him personal things that you knew of?

Mrs. Oswald. He asked Lee not because Lee had told him about it, but I think because he is smart enough man to have been able to guess it. I don't know—he is simply a liberal, simply a man. I don't think that he is being accused justly of being a Communist.

Mr. Rankin. That is De Mohrenschildt that you refer to?

Mrs. Oswald. Yes.

Mr. Rankin. Did you tell the authorities anything about this Walker incident when you learned about it?

Mrs. Oswald. No.

Mr. Rankin. You have told the Secret Service or the FBI people reasons why you didn't. Will you tell us?

Mrs. Oswald. Why I did not tell about it?

First, because it was my husband. As far as I know, according to the local laws here, a wife cannot be a witness against her husband. But, of course, if I had known that Lee intended to repeat something like that, I would have told.

Mr. Rankin. Did he ask you to return the note to him?

Mrs. Oswald. He forgot about it. But apparently after that he thought that what he had written in his book might be proof against him, and he destroyed it.

Mr. Rankin. That is this book that you have just referred to in which he had the Walker house picture?

Mrs. Oswald. There was a notebook, yes, that is the one.

Mr. Rankin. What did you do with the note that he had left for you after you talked about it and said you were going to keep it?

Mrs. Oswald. I had it among my things in a cookbook. But I have two—I don't remember in which.

Mr. Rankin. Did your relations with your husband change after this Walker incident?

Mrs. Oswald. Yes.

Mr. Rankin. Will you describe to us the changes as you observed them?

Mrs. Oswald. Soon after that, Lee lost his job—I don't know for what reason. He was upset by it. And he looked for work for several days. And then I insisted that it would be better for him to go to New Orleans where he had relatives. I insisted on that because I wanted to get him further removed from Dallas and from Walker, because even though he gave me his word, I wanted to have him further away, because a rifle for him was not a very good toy—a toy that was too enticing.

Mr. Rankin. Did you say that you wanted him to go to New Orleans because of the Walker incident?

Mrs. Oswald. No. I simply told him that I wanted to see his home town. He had been born there.

Mr. Rankin. When he promised you that he would not do anything like that again, did you then believe him?

Mrs. Oswald. I did not quite believe him inasmuch as the rifle remained in the house.

Mr. Rankin. Did you ask him to get rid of the rifle at that time?

Mrs. Oswald. Yes.

19 Mr. Rankin. After he shot at Walker, did you notice his taking the rifle out any more to practice?

Mrs. Oswald. No.

Mr. Rankin. Do you recall when you went to New Orleans?

Mrs. Oswald. I think it was in May. Lee went there himself, by himself. At that time, I became acquainted with Mrs. Paine, and I stayed with her while he was looking for work. In about one week Lee telephoned me that he had found a job and that I should come down.

Mr. Rankin. When did you first get acquainted with Mrs. Paine?

Mrs. Oswald. I think it was a couple of months earlier—probably in January.

Mr. Rankin. How did you happen to go to Mrs. Paine's house to stay? Did she invite you?

Mrs. Oswald. Yes; she invited me. I had become acquainted with her through some Russian friends of ours. We had visited with some people, and she was there. Inasmuch as she was studying Russian, she invited me to stay with her.

Mr. Rankin. Did you pay her anything for staying with her?

Mrs. Oswald. No, I only repaid her in the sense that I helped her in the household and that I gave her Russian language lessons. This, in her words, was the very best pay that I could give her. And she wanted that I remain with her longer.

But, of course, it was better for me to be with my husband.

Mr. Rankin. How did your husband let you know that he had found a job?

Mrs. Oswald. He telephoned me.

Mr. Rankin. Did you then leave at once for New Orleans?

Mrs. Oswald. Yes.

Mr. Rankin. And how did you get to New Orleans from Dallas?

Mrs. Oswald. Mrs. Paine took me there in her car. She took her children and my things and we went there.

Mr. Rankin. Did you have much in the way of household goods to move?

Mrs. Oswald. Everything—we could put everything into one car. But, in fact, most of the things Lee had taken with him. Because he went by bus.

Mr. Rankin. Did he take the gun with him to New Orleans?

Mrs. Oswald. I don't remember exactly, but it seems to me that it was not among my things.

Mr. Rankin. Where did you live at New Orleans?

Mrs. Oswald. Magazine Street. By the time I arrived there Lee already had rented an apartment.

Mr. Rankin. When Mrs. Paine brought you down to New Orleans, did she stay with you for any period of time?

Mrs. Oswald. Yes, she was there for two days.

Mr. Rankin. How did Mrs. Paine and your husband get along? Were they friendly?

Mrs. Oswald. She was very good to us, to Lee and to me, and Lee was quite friendly with her, but he did not like her. I know that he didn't like her.

Mr. Rankin. Did he tell you why he didn't like her?

Mrs. Oswald. He considered her to be a stupid woman. Excuse me—these are not my words.

Mr. Rankin. Were you and Mrs. Paine good friends?

Mrs. Oswald. Yes, so-so. I tried to help her as much as I could. But I also—I was—I did not like her too well. I also considered her not to be a very smart woman.

Mr. Rankin. I think it is about time for a recess, Mr. Chairman.

The Chairman. Very well. We will take a recess for 10 minutes.

(Brief recess.)

The Chairman. The Committee will be in order.

Mr. Rankin, you may continue.

Mr. Rankin. Mrs. Oswald, did you discuss the Walker shooting with Mrs. Paine?

Mrs. Oswald. No. I didn't tell anyone. Apart from the FBI. That is after—that is later.

Mr. Rankin. When was it that you told the FBI about the Walker shooting?

Mrs. Oswald. About 2 weeks after Lee was killed.

Mr. Rankin. Before you went to New Orleans, had you seen anyone from the FBI?
Mrs. Oswald. The FBI visited us in Fort Worth when we lived on Mercedes Street.
Mr. Rankin. Was that in August 1962?
Mrs. Oswald. Probably.
Mr. Rankin. Do you know the names of the FBI agents that visited you then?
Mrs. Oswald. No, I don't remember that Lee had just returned from work and we were getting ready to have dinner when a car drove up and man introduced himself and asked Lee to step out and talk to him.

There was another man in the car. They talked for about 2 hours and I was very angry, because everything had gotten cold. This meant more work for me. I asked who these were, and he was very upset over the fact that the FBI was interested in him.

Mr. Rankin. Did that interview take place in the car?
Mrs. Oswald. Yes.
Mr. Rankin. Did your husband tell you what they said to him and what he said to them?
Mrs. Oswald. I don't know to what extent this was true, but Lee said that the FBI had told him that in the event some Russians might visit him and would try to recruit him to work for them, he should notify the FBI agents. I don't know to what extent this was true. But perhaps Lee just said that.
Mr. Rankin. Did our husband say anything about the FBI asking him to work for them?
Mrs. Oswald. No, he didn't tell me.
Mr. Rankin. Did he say anything more about what they said to him in this interview?
Mrs. Oswald. No, he didn't tell me verbatim, but he said that they saw Communists in everybody and they are very much afraid and inasmuch as I had returned from Russia.
Mr. Rankin. Did he tell you that they had asked him whether he had acted as an agent or was asked to be an agent for the Russians?
Mrs. Oswald. No.
Mr. Rankin. Do you recall any other——
Mrs. Oswald. Excuse me. They did ask him about whether the Russians had proposed that he be an agent for them.
Mr. Rankin. Did he tell you what he said to them in that regard?
Mrs. Oswald. He told me that he had answered no.
Mr. Rankin. After this interview by the FBI agents, do you recall any later interview with them and yourself or your husband before you went to New Orleans?
Mrs. Oswald. No, there were no other interviews.

The next time was in Irving, when I lived with Mrs. Paine. But that is after I returned from New Orleans.

Mr. Rankin. At New Orleans, who did your husband work for?
Mrs. Oswald. He worked for the Louisiana Coffee Co. But I don't know in what capacity. I don't think that this was very good job, or perhaps more correctly, he did not—I know that he didn't like this job.
Mr. Rankin. Do you know what he received in pay from that job?
Mrs. Oswald. $1.35 an hour, I think. I am not sure.
Mr. Rankin. How long did he work for this coffee company?
Mrs. Oswald. I think it was from May until August, to the end of August.
Mr. Rankin. Was he discharged?
Mrs. Oswald. Yes.
Mr. Rankin. And then was he unemployed for a time?
Mrs. Oswald. Yes.
Mr. Rankin. After you had discussed with your husband your going to Russia, was anything done about that?

Mrs. Oswald. Yes, I wrote a letter to the Soviet Embassy with a request to be permitted to return. And then it seems to me after I was already in New Orleans, I wrote another letter in which I told the Embassy that my husband wants to return with me.

21 Mr. Rankin. Do you recall the date of the first letter that you just referred to?

Mrs. Oswald. No. But that is easily determined.

Mr. Rankin. Were you asking for a visa to return to Russia?

Mrs. Oswald. Yes.

Mr. Rankin. Did you discuss with your husband his returning with you before you wrote the second letter that you have described?

Mrs. Oswald. I didn't ask him. He asked me to do so one day when he was extremely upset. He appeared to be very unhappy and he said that nothing keeps him here, and that he would not lose anything if he returned to the Soviet Union, and that he wants to be with me. And that it would be better to have less but not to be concerned about tomorrow, not to be worried about tomorrow.

Mr. Rankin. Was this a change in his attitude?

Mrs. Oswald. Towards me or towards Russia?

Mr. Rankin. Towards going to Russia.

Mrs. Oswald. I don't think that he was too fond of Russia, but simply that he knew that he would have work assured him there, because he had—after all, he had to think about his family.

Mr. Rankin. Did you know that he did get a passport?

Mrs. Oswald. It seems to me he always had a passport.

Mr. Rankin. While he was in New Orleans, that he got a passport?

Mrs. Oswald. Well, it seems to me that after we came here, he immediately received a passport. I don't know. I always saw his green passport. He even had two—one that had expired, and a new one.

Mr. Rankin. Do you know when the new one was issued?

Mrs. Oswald. No. It seems to me in the Embassy when we arrived. I don't know. But please understand me correctly, I am not hiding this. I simply don't know.

Mr. Rankin. Do you know about a letter from your husband to the Embassy asking that his request for a visa be considered separately from yours?

Mrs. Oswald. No, I don't.

Mr. Rankin. When you were at New Orleans, did your husband go to school, that you knew of?

Mrs. Oswald. No.

Mr. Rankin. Did he spend his earnings with you and your child?

Mrs. Oswald. Most of the time, yes. But I know that he became active with some kind of activity in a pro-Cuban committee. I hope that is what you are looking for.

Mr. Rankin. When did you first notice the rifle at New Orleans?

Mrs. Oswald. As soon as I arrived in New Orleans.

Mr. Rankin. Where was it kept there?

Mrs. Oswald. He again had a closet-like room with his things in it. He had his clothes hanging there, all his other belongings.

Mr. Rankin. Was the rifle in a cover there?

Mrs. Oswald. No.

Mr. Rankin. Did you notice him take it away from your home there in New Orleans at any time?

Mrs. Oswald. No. I know for sure that he didn't. But I know that we had a kind of a porch with a—screened-in porch, and I know that sometimes evenings after dark he would sit there with his rifle. I don't know what he did with it. I came there by chance once and saw him just sitting there with his rifle. I thought he is merely sitting there and resting. Of course I didn't like these kind of little jokes.

Mr. Rankin. Can you give us an idea of how often this happened that you recall?

Mrs. Oswald. It began to happen quite frequently after he was arrested there in connection with some demonstration and handing out of leaflets.

Mr. Rankin. Was that the Fair Play for Cuba demonstration?

Mrs. Oswald. Yes.

Mr. Rankin. From what you observed about his having the rifle on the back porch, in the dark, could you tell whether or not he was trying to practice with the telescopic lens?

22 Mrs. Oswald. Yes. I asked him why. But this time he was preparing to go to Cuba.

Mr. Rankin. That was his explanation for practicing with the rifle?

Mrs. Oswald. Yes. He said that he would go to Cuba. I told him I was not going with him—that I would stay here.

Mr. Rankin. On these occasions when he was practicing with the rifle, would they be three or four times a week in the evening, after the Fair Play for Cuba incident?

Mrs. Oswald. Almost every evening. He very much wanted to go to Cuba and have the newspapers write that somebody had kidnapped an aircraft. And I asked him "For God sakes, don't do such a thing."

Mr. Rankin. Did he describe that idea to you?

Mrs. Oswald. Yes.

Mr. Rankin. And when he told you of it, did he indicate that he wanted to be the one that would kidnap the airplane himself?

Mrs. Oswald. Yes, he wanted to do that. And he asked me that I should help him with that. But I told him I would not touch that rifle.

This sounds very merry, but I am very much ashamed of it.

Mr. Rankin. Did you tell him that using the rifle in this way, talking about it, was not in accordance with his agreement with you?

Mrs. Oswald. Yes.

Mr. Rankin. What did he say about that?

Mrs. Oswald. He said that everything would go well. He was very self-reliant—if I didn't want to.

Mr. Rankin. Was there any talk of divorce during this period?

Mrs. Oswald. No. During this time, we got along pretty well not counting the incidents with Cuba. I say relatively well, because we did not really have—generally he helped me quite a bit and was good to me. But, of course, I did not agree with his views.

Mr. Rankin. At this time in New Orleans did he discuss with you his views?

Mrs. Oswald. Yes.

Mr. Rankin. What did he say about that?

Mrs. Oswald. Mostly—most of the conversations were on the subject of Cuba.

Mr. Rankin. Was there anything said about the United States—not liking the United States.

Mrs. Oswald. No. I can't say—he liked some things in Russia, he liked some other things here, didn't like some things there, and didn't like some things here.

And I am convinced that as much as he knew about Cuba, all he knew was from books and so on. He wanted to convince himself. But I am sure that if he had gone there, he would not have liked it there, either. Only on the moon, perhaps.

Mr. Rankin. Did he tell you what he didn't like about the United States?

Mrs. Oswald. First of all, he didn't like the fact that there are fascist organizations here. That was one thing.

The second thing, that it was hard to get an education and hard to find work. And that medical expenses were very high.

Mr. Rankin. Did he say who he blamed for this?

Mrs. Oswald. He didn't blame anyone.

Mr. Rankin. Did he ever say anything about President Kennedy?

Mrs. Oswald. No. At least—I was always interested in President Kennedy and had asked him many times to translate articles in a newspaper or magazine for me, and he always had something good to say. He translated it, but never did comment on it. At least in Lee's behavior—from Lee's behavior I cannot conclude that he was against the President, and therefore the thing is incomprehensible to me. Perhaps he hid it from me. I don't know. He said that after 20 years he would be prime minister. I think that he had a sick imagination—at least at that time I already considered him to be not quite normal—not always, but at times. I always tried to point out to him that he was a man like any others who were around us. But he simply could not understand that.

I tried to tell him that it would be better to direct his energies to some more practical matters, and not something like that.

23 Mr. Rankin. Can you tell us what you observed about him that caused you to think he was different?

Mrs. Oswald. At least his imagination, his fantasy, which was quite unfounded, as to the fact that he was an outstanding man. And then the fact that he was very much interested, exceedingly so, in autobiographical works of outstanding statesmen of the United States and others.

Mr. Rankin. Was there anything else of that kind that caused you to think that he was different?

Mrs. Oswald. I think that he compared himself to these people whose autobiographies he read. That seems strange to me, because it is necessary to have an education in order to achieve success of that kind. After he became busy with his pro-Cuban activity, he received a letter from somebody in New York, some Communist—probably from New York—I am not sure from where—from some Communist leader and he was very happy, he felt that this was a great man that he had received the letter from.

You see, when I would make fun of him, of his activity to some extent, in the sense that it didn't help anyone really, he said that I didn't understand him, and here, you see, was proof that someone else did, that there were people who understood his activity.

I would say that to Lee—that Lee could not really do much for Cuba, that Cuba would get along well without him, if they had to.

Mr. Rankin. You would tell that to him?

Mrs. Oswald. Yes.

Mr. Rankin. And what would he say in return?

Mrs. Oswald. He shrugged his shoulders and kept his own opinion. He was even interested in the airplane schedules, with the idea of kidnapping a plane. But I talked him out of it.

Mr. Rankin. The airplane schedules from New Orleans?

Mrs. Oswald. New Orleans—but—from New Orleans—leaving New Orleans in an opposite direction. And he was going to make it turn around and go to Cuba.

Mr. Rankin. He discussed this with you?

Mrs. Oswald. Yes.

Mr. Rankin. When did his Fair Play for Cuba activity occur—before or after he lost his job?

Mrs. Oswald. After he lost his job. I told him it would be much better if he were working, because when he didn't work he was busy with such foolishness.

Mr. Rankin. What did he say about that?

Mrs. Oswald. Nothing. And it is at that time that I wrote a letter to Mrs. Paine telling her that Lee was out of work, and they invited me to come and stay with her. And when I left her, I knew that Lee would go to Mexico City. But, of course, I didn't tell Mrs. Paine about it.

Mr. Rankin. Had he discussed with you the idea of going to Mexico City?

Mrs. Oswald. Yes.

Mr. Rankin. When did he first discuss that?

Mrs. Oswald. I think it was in August.

Mr. Rankin. Did he tell you why he wanted to go to Mexico City?
Mrs. Oswald. From Mexico City he wanted to go to Cuba—perhaps through the Russian Embassy in Mexico somehow he would be able to get to Cuba.
Mr. Rankin. Did he say anything about going to Russia by way of Cuba?
Mrs. Oswald. I know that he said that in the embassy. But he only said so. I know that he had no intention of going to Russia then.
Mr. Rankin. How do you know that?
Mrs. Oswald. He told me. I know Lee fairly well—well enough from that point of view.
Mr. Rankin. Did he tell you that he was going to Cuba and send you on to Russia?
Mrs. Oswald. No, he proposed that after he got to Cuba, that I would go there, too, somehow.
But he also said that after he was in Cuba, and if he might go to Russia, he would let me know in any case.
Mr. Rankin. Did he discuss Castro and the Cuban Government with you?
24 Mrs. Oswald. Yes.
Mr. Rankin. When did he start to do that?
Mrs. Oswald. At the time that he was busy with that pro-Cuban activity. He was sympathetic to Castro while in Russia, and I have also a good opinion of Castro to the extent that I know. I don't know anything bad about him.
Mr. Rankin. What did he say about Castro to you?
Mrs. Oswald. He said that he is a very smart statesman, very useful for his government, and very active.
Mr. Rankin. What did you say to him?
Mrs. Oswald. I said, "Maybe." It doesn't make any difference to me.
Mr. Rankin. Did you know he was writing to the Fair Play for Cuba organization in New York during this latter period in New Orleans?
Mrs. Oswald. Yes.
Mr. Rankin. Did he show you that correspondence?
Mrs. Oswald. No.
Mr. Rankin. How did you learn that?
Mrs. Oswald. He told me about it. Or, more correctly, I saw that he was writing to them.
Mr. Rankin. Did you write the Russian Embassy in regard to your visa from New Orleans.
Mrs. Oswald. Yes.
Mr. Rankin. Do you recall what address you gave in New Orleans when you wrote?
Mrs. Oswald. No, I don't remember. Sometimes I would write a letter, but Lee would insert the address and would mail the letters. That is why I don't remember.
Mr. Rankin. Did you get your mail in New Orleans at your apartment or at a post office box?
Mrs. Oswald. No, we had a post office box, and that is where we received our mail.
Mr. Rankin. Did your husband have any organization in his Fair Play for Cuba at New Orleans?
Mrs. Oswald. No, he had no organization. He was alone. He was quite alone.
Mr. Rankin. When did you learn about his arrest there?
Mrs. Oswald. The next day, when he was away from home overnight and returned, he told me he had been arrested.
Mr. Rankin. What did he say about it?
Mrs. Oswald. He was smiling, but in my opinion he was upset. I think that after that occurrence—he became less active, he cooled off a little.
Mr. Rankin. Less active in the Fair Play for Cuba?
Mrs. Oswald. Yes. He continued it, but more for a person's sake. I think that his heart was no longer in it.

Mr. Rankin. Did he tell you that the FBI had seen him at the jail in New Orleans?
Mrs. Oswald. No.
Mr. Rankin. Did he complain about his arrest and say it was unfair, anything of that kind.
Mrs. Oswald. No.
Mr. Rankin. Did you know he paid a fine?
Mrs. Oswald. Yes.
Mr. Rankin. Did you have anything to do with trying to get him out of jail?
Mrs. Oswald. No.
He was only there for 24 hours. He paid his fine and left. He said that the policeman who talked to him was very kind, and was a very good person.
Mr. Rankin. While you were in New Orleans, did you get to know the Murrets?
Mrs. Oswald. Yes. They are his relatives. I think that Lee engaged in this activity primarily for purposes of self-advertising. He wanted to be arrested. I think he wanted to get into the newspapers, so that he would be known.
Mr. Rankin. Do you think he wanted to be advertised and known as being in support of Cuba before he went to Cuba?
25 Mrs. Oswald. Yes.
Mr. Rankin. Do you think he thought that would help him when he got to Cuba?
Mrs. Oswald. Yes.
Mr. Rankin. Did he tell you anything about that, or is that just what you guess?
Mrs. Oswald. He would collect the newspaper clippings about his—when the newspapers wrote about him, and he took these clippings with him when he went to Mexico.
Mr. Rankin. Did the Murrets come to visit you from time to time in New Orleans?
Mrs. Oswald. Yes—sometimes they came to us, and sometimes we went to them.
Mr. Rankin. Was that a friendly relationship?
Mrs. Oswald. I would say that they were more of a family relationship type. They were very good to us. His uncle, that is the husband of his aunt, was a very good man. He tried to reason with Lee after that incident. Lee liked them very much as relatives but he didn't like the fact that they were all very religious.
When his uncle, or, again, the husband of his aunt would tell him that he must approach things with a more serious attitude, and to worry about himself and his family, Lee would say, "Well, these are just bourgeois, who are only concerned with their own individual welfare."
Mr. Krimer. The word Mrs. Oswald used is not quite bourgeois, but it is a person of a very narrow viewpoint who is only concerned with his own personal interests, inclined to be an egotist.
Mr. Rankin. Did you hear the discussion when the uncle talked about this Fair Play for Cuba and his activities?
Mrs. Oswald. Yes.
Mr. Rankin. What did the uncle say to your husband about that?
Mrs. Oswald. At that time. I did not know English too well, and Lee would not interpret for me. He only nodded his head. But I knew that he did not agree with his uncle. His uncle said that he condemned that kind of activity.
Mr. Rankin. What was your husband's attitude about your learning English?
Mrs. Oswald. He never talked English to me at home, and did not give me any instruction. This was strictly my own business. But he did want me to learn English. But that was my own concern. I had to do that myself somehow. That is the truth.
Mr. Rankin. Did any of your Russian friends visit you at New Orleans?
Mrs. Oswald. No.
Mr. Rankin. Outside of the Murrets, were there some people from New Orleans that visited you at your home in New Orleans?

Mrs. Oswald. Once or twice a woman visited who was a friend of Ruth Paine's. Ruth Paine has written her. She had written to Ruth Paine to find out whether she knew any Russians there. And once or twice this woman visited us. But other than that, no one.

Mr. Rankin. What was the name of this woman?

Mrs. Oswald. I don't remember. I only remember that her first name is also Ruth.

Mr. Rankin. Did your husband have friends of his that visited you there at New Orleans?

Mrs. Oswald. No, never.

Once some time after Lee was arrested, on a Saturday or a Sunday morning, a man came early and questioned Lee about the activity of the allegedly existing organization, which really did not exist. Because in the newspaper accounts Lee was described as a member and even the leader of that organization, which in reality did not exist at all.

Mr. Rankin. Do you know who that was?

Mrs. Oswald. No, I don't. I asked Lee who that was, and he said that is probably some anti-Cuban, or perhaps an FBI agent. He represented himself as a man who was sympathetic to Cuba but Lee did not believe him.

26 Mr. Rankin. Did your husband ever tell you what he told the FBI agent when they came to the jail to see him?

Mrs. Oswald. No.

Mr. Rankin. After you wrote Mrs. Paine, did she come at once in response to your letter to take you back to Dallas?

Mrs. Oswald. Not quite at once. She came about a month later. She apparently was on vacation at that time, and said that she would come after her vacation.

Mr. Rankin. Didn't she indicate that she was going to come around September 30, and then came a little before that?

Mrs. Oswald. No. In her letter to me she indicated that she would come either the 20th or the 21st of September, and she did come at that time.

Mr. Rankin. Did you move your household goods in her station wagon at that time?

Mrs. Oswald. Yes.

Mr. Rankin. Do you know whether or not the rifle was carried in the station wagon?

Mrs. Oswald. Yes, it was.

Mr. Rankin. Did you have anything to do with loading it in there?

Mrs. Oswald. No. Lee was loading everything on because I was pregnant at the time. But I know that Lee loaded the rifle on.

Mr. Rankin. Was the rifle carried in some kind of a case when you went back with Mrs. Paine?

Mrs. Oswald. After we arrived. I tried to put the bed, the child's crib together, the metallic parts, and I looked for a certain part, and I came upon something wrapped in a blanket. I thought that was part of the bed, but it turned out to be the rifle.

Mr. Rankin. Do you remember whether the pistol was carried back in Mrs. Paine's car too?

Mrs. Oswald. I don't know where the pistol was.

Mr. Rankin. Before you went back to Mrs. Paine's house, did you discuss whether you would be paying her anything for board and room?

Mrs. Oswald. She proposed that I again live with her on the same conditions as before. Because this was more advantageous for her than to pay a school. She received better instruction that way.

In any case, she didn't spend any extra money for me—she didn't spend any more than she usually spent.

Mr. Rankin. Did you give her lessons in Russian?

Mrs. Oswald. No, these were not quite lessons. It was more in the nature of conversational practice. And then I also helped her to prepare Russian lessons for the purpose of teaching Russian.

Mr. Rankin. When you found the rifle wrapped in the blanket, upon your return to Mrs. Paine's, where was it located?

Mrs. Oswald. In the garage, where all the rest of the things were.

Mr. Rankin. In what part of the garage?

Mrs. Oswald. In that part which is closer to the street, because that garage is connected to the house. One door opens on the kitchen, and the other out in the street.

Mr. Rankin. Was the rifle lying down or was it standing up on the butt end?

Mrs. Oswald. No, it was lying down on the floor.

Mr. Rankin. When your husband talked about going to Mexico City, did he say where he was going to go there, who he would visit?

Mrs. Oswald. Yes. He said that he would go to the Soviet Embassy and to the Cuban Embassy and would do everything he could in order to get to Cuba.

Mr. Rankin. Did he tell you where he would stay in Mexico City?

Mrs. Oswald. In a hotel.

Mr. Rankin. Did he tell you the name?

Mrs. Oswald. No, he didn't know where he would stop.

Mr. Rankin. Was there any discussion about the expense of making the trip?

Mrs. Oswald. Yes. But we always lived very modestly, and Lee always had some savings. Therefore, he had the money for it.

Mr. Rankin. Did he say how much it would cost?

Mrs. Oswald. He had a little over $100 and he said that that would be sufficient.

Mr. Rankin. Did he talk about getting you a silver bracelet or any presents before he went?

Mrs. Oswald. It is perhaps more truth to say that he asked me what I would like, and I told him that I would like Mexican silver bracelets. But what he did buy me I didn't like at all. When he returned to Irving, from Mexico City, and I saw the bracelet, I was fairly sure that he had bought it in New Orleans and not in Mexico City, because I had seen bracelets like that for sale there. That is why I am not sure that the bracelet was purchased in Mexico.

Lee had an identical bracelet which he had bought in either Dallas or New Orleans. It was a man's bracelet.

Mr. Rankin. The silver bracelet he gave you when he got back had your name on it, did it not?

Mrs. Oswald. Yes.

Mr. Rankin. Was it too small?

Mrs. Oswald. Yes, I was offended because it was too small, and he promised to exchange it. But, of course, I didn't want to hurt him, and I said, thank you, the important thing is the thought, the attention.

Mr. Rankin. Did he discuss other things that he planned to do in Mexico City, such as see the bullfights or jai alai games or anything of that kind?

Mrs. Oswald. No, I was already questioned about this game by the FBI, but I never heard of it. But I had asked Lee to buy some Mexican records, but he did not do that.

Mr. Rankin. Do you know how he got to Mexico City?

Mrs. Oswald. By bus.

Mr. Rankin. And did he return by bus, also?

Mrs. Oswald. It seems, yes. Yes, he told me that a round-trip ticket was cheaper than two one-way tickets.

Mr. Rankin. Did you learn that he had a tourist card to go to Mexico?

Mrs. Oswald. No.

Mr. Rankin. If he had such a card, you didn't know it then?

Mrs. Oswald. No.

Mr. Rankin. After he had been to Mexico City, did he come back to Irving or to Dallas?

Mrs. Oswald. When Lee returned I was already in Irving and he telephoned me. But he told me that he had arrived the night before and had spent the night in Dallas, and called me in the morning.
Mr. Rankin. Did he say where he had been in Dallas?
Mrs. Oswald. It seems to me at the YMCA.
Mr. Rankin. Did he come right out to see you then?
Mrs. Oswald. Yes.
Mr. Rankin. Did he tell you anything about his trip to Mexico City?
Mrs. Oswald. Yes, he told me that he had visited the two embassies, that he had received nothing, that the people who are there are too much—too bureaucratic. He said that he has spent the time pretty well. And I had told him that if he doesn't accomplish anything to at least take a good rest. I was hoping that the climate, if nothing else, would be beneficial to him.
Mr. Rankin. Did you ask him what he did the rest of the time?
Mrs. Oswald. Yes, I think he said that he visited a bull fight, that he spent most of his time in museums, and that he did some sightseeing in the city.
Mr. Rankin. Did he tell you about anyone that he met there?
Mrs. Oswald. No.
He said that he did not like the Mexican girls.
Mr. Rankin. Did he tell you anything about what happened at the Cuban Embassy, or consulate?
Mrs. Oswald. No. Only that he had talked to certain people there.
Mr. Rankin. Did he tell you what people he talked to?
28 Mrs. Oswald. He said that he first visited the Soviet Embassy in the hope that having been there first this would make it easier for him at the Cuban Embassy. But there they refused to have anything to do with him.
Mr. Rankin. And what did he say about the visit to the Cuban Embassy or consulate?
Mrs. Oswald. It was quite without results.
Mr. Rankin. Did he complain about the consular or any of the officials of the Cuban Embassy and the way they handled the matter?
Mrs. Oswald. Yes, he called them bureaucrats. He said that the Cubans seemed to have a system similar to the Russians—too much red tape before you get through there.
Mr. Rankin. Is there anything else that he told you about the Mexico City trip that you haven't related?
Mrs. Oswald. No, that is all that I can remember about it.
Mr. Rankin. Do you recall how long he was gone on his trip to Mexico City?
Mrs. Oswald. All of this took approximately 2 weeks, from the time that I left New Orleans, until the time that he returned.
Mr. Rankin. And from the time he left the United States to go to Mexico City to his return, was that about 7 days?
Mrs. Oswald. Yes. He said he was there for about a week.
Mr. Rankin. When you were asked before about the trip to Mexico, you did not say that you knew anything about it. Do you want to explain to the Commission how that happened?
Mrs. Oswald. Most of these questions were put to me by the FBI. I do not like them too much. I didn't want to be too sincere with them. Though I was quite sincere and answered most of their questions. They questioned me a great deal, and I was very tired of them, and I thought that, well, whether I knew about it or didn't know about it didn't change matters at all, it didn't help anything, because the fact that Lee had been there was already known, and whether or not I knew about it didn't make any difference.
Mr. Rankin. Was that the only reason that you did not tell about what you knew of the Mexico City trip before?
Mrs. Oswald. Yes, because the first time that they asked me I said no, I didn't know anything about it. And in all succeeding discussions I couldn't very well have said I

did. There is nothing special in that. It wasn't because this was connected with some sort of secret.

Mr. Rankin. Did your husband stay with you at the Paines after that first night when he returned from Mexico?

Mrs. Oswald. Yes, he stayed overnight there.
And in the morning we took him to Dallas.

Mr. Rankin. And by "we" who do you mean?

Mrs. Oswald. Ruth Paine, I and her children.

Mr. Rankin. Do you know what he did in Dallas, then?

Mrs. Oswald. He intended to rent an apartment in the area of Oak Cliff, and to look for work.

Mr. Rankin. Do you know whether he did that?

Mrs. Oswald. Yes, I know that he always tried to get some work. He was not lazy.

Mr. Rankin. Did he rent the apartment?

Mrs. Oswald. On the same day he rented a room, not an apartment, and he telephoned me and told me about it.

Mr. Rankin. Did you discuss the plans for this room before you took him to Dallas?

Mrs. Oswald. No. I asked him where he would live, and he said it would be best if he rented a room, it would not be as expensive as an apartment.

Mr. Rankin. Did he say anything about whether you would be living with him, or he would be living there alone?

Mrs. Oswald. No, I did not really want to be with Lee at that time, because I was expecting, and it would have been better to be with a woman who spoke English and Russian.

Mr. Rankin. Do you know where your husband looked for work in Dallas at that time?

29 Mrs. Oswald. No. He tried to get any kind of work. He answered ads, newspaper ads.

Mr. Rankin. Did he have trouble finding work again?

Mrs. Oswald. Yes.

Mr. Rankin. How long after his return was it before he found a job?

Mrs. Oswald. Two to three weeks.

Mr. Rankin. When he was unemployed in New Orleans, did he get unemployment compensation?

Mrs. Oswald. Yes.

Mr. Rankin. Do you know how much he was getting then?

Mrs. Oswald. $33 a week. It is possible to live on that money. One can fail to find work and live. Perhaps you don't believe me. It is not bad to rest and receive money.

Mr. Rankin. When he was unemployed in Dallas, do you know whether he received unemployment compensation?

Mrs. Oswald. We were due to receive unemployment compensation, but it was getting close to the end of his entitlement period, and we received one more check.

Mr. Rankin. Did you discuss with him possible places of employment after his return from Mexico?

Mrs. Oswald. No. That was his business. I couldn't help him in that. But to some extent I did help him find a job, because I was visiting Mrs. Paine's neighbors. There was a woman there who told me where he might find some work.

Mr. Rankin. And when was this?

Mrs. Oswald. I don't remember. If that is important, I can try and ascertain date. But I think you probably know.

Mr. Rankin. Was it shortly before he obtained work?

Mrs. Oswald. As soon as we got the information, the next day he went there and he did get the job.

Mr. Rankin. And who was it that you got the information from?

Mrs. Oswald. It was the neighbor whose brother was employed by the school book depository. He said it seemed to him there was a vacancy there.

Mr. Rankin. What was his name?

Mrs. Oswald. I don't know.

The Chairman. Well, I think we have arrived at our adjournment time. We will recess now until tomorrow morning at 10 o'clock.

(Whereupon, at 4:30 p.m., the President's Commission recessed.)

Tuesday, February 4, 1964

TESTIMONY OF MRS. LEE HARVEY OSWALD RESUMED

The President's Commission met at 10 a.m. on February 4, 1964, at 200 Maryland Avenue NE., Washington, D.C.

Present were Chief Justice Earl Warren, Chairman; Senator John Sherman Cooper, Representative Hale Boggs, Representative Gerald R. Ford, John J. McCloy, and Allen W. Dulles, members.

Also present were J. Lee Rankin, general counsel; Norman Redlich, assistant counsel; Leon I. Gopadze and William D. Krimer, interpreters; and John M. Thorne, attorney for Mrs. Lee Harvey Oswald.

The Chairman. The Commission will be in order.

Mr. Rankin, will you proceed with the questioning of Mrs. Oswald.

Mr. Rankin. Mrs. Oswald, there are a number of things about some of the material we have been over, the period we have been over, that I would like30 to ask you about, sort of to fill in different parts of it. I hope you will bear with us in regard to that.

Were you aware of the diary that your husband had written and the book that he had typed?

Mrs. Oswald. Yes.

Mr. Rankin. Did he hire a public stenographer to help him with his book?

Mrs. Oswald. No, he wrote his in longhand. He started it in Russia. But he had it retyped here because it had been in longhand.

Mr. Rankin. And do you know about when he started to have it retyped here?

Mrs. Oswald. We arrived in June. I think it was at the end of June.

Mr. Rankin. Do you know what happened to that book, or a copy of it?

Mrs. Oswald. At the present time it is—I don't know where—the police department or the FBI.

Mr. Rankin. And what was done with the diary? Do you know that?

Mrs. Oswald. I don't know where it is now. I know that it was taken. But where it is now, I don't know.

Mr. Rankin. It was taken by either the FBI or the Secret Service or the police department?

Mrs. Oswald. I don't know that, because I was not at home when all these things were taken.

Mr. Rankin. Would you tell us about what you know about their being taken. Were you away from home and someone else was there when various things belonging to you and your husband were taken from the house?

Mrs. Oswald. I don't know where this book was, whether it was at Mrs. Paine's or in Lee's apartment, because I did not see it there. I was not at Mrs. Paine's because I lived in a hotel at that time in Dallas.

Mr. Rankin. What hotel was that?

Mrs. Oswald. I don't know.

Mr. Rankin. Was this diary kept by your husband daily, so far as you know?

Mrs. Oswald. In Russia?

Mr. Rankin. Well, Russia first.

Mrs. Oswald. It seems to me that he did not continue it here, that he had completed it in Russia. Not everything, but most of the time.

Mr. Rankin. And was it in his own handwriting?

Mrs. Oswald. Yes.

Mr. Rankin. You have told us about an interview with the FBI, when your husband went out into the car and spent a couple of hours, in August of 1962. Do you recall whether there was an FBI interview earlier than that?

Mrs. Oswald. No, there wasn't. At least I don't know about it. Perhaps there was such a meeting, perhaps at the time we were in Fort Worth somebody had come, when we lived with Robert. One reporter wanted to interview Lee but Lee would not give the interview, and perhaps the FBI came, too.

Mr. Rankin. The particular interview that I am asking you about was June 26, according to information from the FBI.

Mrs. Oswald. I don't know about it. The first time I knew about the FBI coming was when we lived in Fort Worth.

Mr. Rankin. What rental did you pay on Mercedes Street?

Mrs. Oswald. I don't remember.

Mr. Rankin. Did you have any difficulties while you were on Mercedes Street with your husband—that is, any quarreling there?

Mrs. Oswald. Only in connection with his mother, because of his mother.

Mr. Rankin. Were you having any problems about finances there, on Mercedes Street?

Mrs. Oswald. Of course we did not live in luxury. We did not buy anything that was not absolutely needed, because Lee had to pay his debt to Robert and to the government. But it was not particularly difficult. At least on that basis we had not had any quarrels.

Mr. Rankin. Could you tell us about De Mohrenschildt? Was he a close friend of your husband?

Mrs. Oswald. Lee did not have any close friends, but at least he had—here in America—he had a great deal of respect for De Mohrenschildt.

31 Mr. Rankin. Could you describe that relationship. Did they see each other often?

Mrs. Oswald. No, not very frequently. From time to time.

Mr. Rankin. Did your husband tell you why he had so much respect for De Mohrenschildt?

Mrs. Oswald. Because he considered him to be smart, to be full of joy of living, a very energetic and very sympathetic person.

Mr. Rankin. We had a report that——

Mrs. Oswald. Excuse me. It was pleasant to meet with him. He would bring some pleasure and better atmosphere when he came to visit—with his dogs—he is very loud.

Mr. Rankin. Did you like him?

Mrs. Oswald. Yes. Him and his wife.

Mr. Rankin. Did you understand any of the conversations between your husband and De Mohrenschildt?

Mrs. Oswald. Yes, they were held in Russian.

Mr. Rankin. Did they discuss politics or the Marxist philosophy or anything of that kind?

Mrs. Oswald. Being men, of course, sometimes they talked about politics, but they did not discuss Marxist philosophy. They spoke about current political events.

Mr. Rankin. Did they have any discussions about President Kennedy or the Government in the United States at that time?

Mrs. Oswald. No, only George said that before she got married he knew Jackie Kennedy, that she was a very good, very sympathetic woman. Then he was writing a book, that is George, and with reference to that book he had written a letter to President

Kennedy. This was with reference to the fact that John Kennedy had recommended physical exercise, walking and so on, and De Mohrenschildt and his wife had walked to the Mexican border. And he hoped that John Kennedy would recommend his book.

I don't know—perhaps this is foolishness.

Mr. Rankin. Did he say anything, or either of them say anything about President Kennedy at that time?

Mrs. Oswald. Nothing bad.

Mr. Rankin. When you referred to George, did you mean Mr. De Mohrenschildt?

Mrs. Oswald. Yes. I generally didn't believe him, that he had written a book. Sometimes he could say so, but just for amusement.

Mr. Rankin. Did De Mohrenschildt have a daughter?

Mrs. Oswald. He had several daughters, and many wives.

Mr. Rankin. Was one of his daughters named Taylor, her last name?

Mrs. Oswald. Yes. That is a daughter of his first marriage. At the present time, I think he has—that is his fourth wife.

Mr. Rankin. And what was her——

Mrs. Oswald. It seems that that is the last one.

Mr. Rankin. What was her husband's name—the Taylor daughter?

Mrs. Oswald. Gary Taylor.

Mr. Rankin. Did you have anything to do with the Gary Taylors?

Mrs. Oswald. Yes, at one time when I had to visit the dentist in Dallas, and I lived in Fort Worth, I came to Dallas and I stayed with them for a couple of days.

Mr. Rankin. Do you know about when that was?

Mrs. Oswald. October or November, 1962.

Mr. Rankin. Did Gary Taylor help you to move your things at one time, move you and your daughter?

Mrs. Oswald. Yes, he moved our things from Fort Worth to Dallas, to Elsbeth Street.

Mr. Rankin. Did he help you to move to Mrs. Hall's at any time, anyone else?

Mrs. Oswald. No, he did not move me to Mrs. Hall. But sometimes he came for a visit. Once or twice I think he came when we lived—to Mrs. Hall's, and once when we lived on Mercedes Street.

Mr. Rankin. What did he do when he came? Were those just visits?

32 Mrs. Oswald. Yes, just visits. Just visits, with his wife and child.

Mr. Rankin. When the De Mohrenschildts came to the house and you showed them the rifle, did you say anything about it?

Mrs. Oswald. Perhaps I did say something to him, but I don't remember.

Mr. Rankin. Did you say anything like "Look what my crazy one has done? Bought a rifle" or something of that kind?

Mrs. Oswald. This sounds like something I might say. Perhaps I did.

Mr. Rankin. In the period of October 1962, you did spend some time with Mrs. Hall, did you not, in her home?

Mrs. Oswald. Yes.

Mr. Rankin. Will you tell us about how that happened?

Mrs. Oswald. When Lee found work in Dallas, Elena Hall proposed that I stay with her for some time, because she was alone, and I would be company.

Mr. Rankin. Did that have anything to do with any quarrels with your husband?

Mrs. Oswald. No.

Mr. Rankin. During that period of October of 1962, when your husband went to Dallas to get work, do you know where he lived?

Mrs. Oswald. I know that for—at first, for some time he stayed at the YMCA, but later he rented an apartment, but I don't know at what address. Because in the letters which he wrote me, the return address was a post office box.

Mr. Rankin. Do you know whether he stayed during that period part of the time with Gary Taylor?

Mrs. Oswald. No.

Mr. Rankin. Where did you live while your husband was looking for work and staying at the YMCA and at this apartment that you referred to?

Mrs. Oswald. When he stayed at the YMCA he had already found work, and I was in Fort Worth.

Mr. Rankin. And where in Fort Worth were you staying then?

Mrs. Oswald. With Mrs. Hall.

Mr. Rankin. Did you notice a change, psychologically, in your husband during this period in the United States?

Mrs. Oswald. Yes.

Mr. Rankin. When did you first notice that change?

Mrs. Oswald. At—at Elsbeth Street, in Dallas. After the visit of the FBI, in Fort Worth. He was for some time nervous and irritable.

Mr. Rankin. Did he seem to have two different personalities then?

Mrs. Oswald. Yes.

Mr. Rankin. Would you describe to the Commission what he did to cause you to think that he was changing?

Mrs. Oswald. Generally he was—usually he was quite as he always was. He used to help me. And he was a good family man. Sometimes, apparently without reason, at least I did not know reasons, if any existed, he became quite a stranger. At such times it was impossible to ask him anything. He simply kept to himself. He was irritated by trifles.

Mr. Rankin. Do you recall any of the trifles that irritated him, so as to help us to know the picture?

Mrs. Oswald. It is hard to remember any such trifling occurrences, sometimes such a small thing as, for example, dinner being five minutes late, and I do mean five minutes—it is not that I am exaggerating—he would be very angry. Or if there were no butter on the table, because he hadn't brought it from the icebox, he would with great indignation ask, "Why is there no butter?" And at the same time if I had put the butter on the table he wouldn't have touched it.

This is foolishness, of course. A normal person doesn't get irritated by things like that.

Mr. Rankin. Mrs. Oswald, I do not ask these questions to pry into your personal affairs, but it gives us some insight into what he did and why he might have done the things he did.

I hope you understand that.

Mrs. Oswald. I understand.

Mr. Rankin. Could you tell us a little about when he did beat you because33 we have reports that at times neighbors saw signs of his having beat you, so that we might know the occasions and why he did such things.

Mrs. Oswald. The neighbors simply saw that because I have a very sensitive skin, and even a very light blow would show marks. Sometimes it was my own fault. Sometimes it was really necessary to just leave him alone. But I wanted more attention. He was jealous. He had no reason to be. But he was jealous of even some of my old friends, old in the sense of age.

Mr. Rankin. When he became jealous, did he discuss that with you?

Mrs. Oswald. Yes, of course.

Mr. Rankin. What did he say?

Mrs. Oswald. I don't remember.

Basically, that I prefer others to him. That I want many things which he cannot give me. But that was not so. Once we had a quarrel because I had a young man who was a boyfriend—this was before we were married, a boy who was in love with me, and I liked him, too. And I had written him a letter from here. I had—I wrote him that I was very lonely here, that Lee had changed a great deal, and that I was sorry that I had not married him instead, that it would have been much easier for me. I had mailed that letter showing the post office box as a return address. But this was just the time when the postage rates went up by one cent, and the letter was returned. Lee brought that letter and asked me what it was and forced me to read it. But I refused. Then he sat down across from me and started to read it to me. I was very much ashamed of my foolishness. And, of course, he hit me, but he did not believe that this letter was sincere. He asked me if it was true or not, and I told him that it was true. But he thought that I did it only in order to tease him. And that was the end of it. It was a very ill-considered thing.

Mr. Rankin. Do you recall anything more that he said at that time about that matter?

Mrs. Oswald. Of course after he hit me, he said that I should be ashamed of myself for saying such things because he was very much in love with me. But this was after he hit me.

Generally, I think that was right, for such things, that is the right thing to do. There was some grounds for it.

Please excuse me. Perhaps I talk too much.

Mr. Rankin. When you had your child baptized, did you discuss that with your husband?

Mrs. Oswald. I knew that Lee was not religious, and, therefore, I did not tell him about it. I lived in Fort Worth at that time, while he lived in Dallas.

But when June was baptized, I told him about it, and he didn't say anything about it. He said it was my business. And he said, "Okay, if you wish." He had nothing against it. He only took offense at the fact that I hadn't told him about it ahead of time.

Mr. Rankin. Are you a member of any church?

Mrs. Oswald. I believe in God, of course, but I do not go to church—first because I do not have a car. And, secondly, because there is only one Russian Church. Simply that I believe in God in my own heart, and I don't think it is necessary to visit the church.

Mr. Rankin. While your husband—or while you were visiting the Halls, did your husband tell you about getting his job in Dallas?

Mrs. Oswald. Yes. I knew about it before he left for Dallas, that he already had work there.

Mr. Rankin. Do you recall whether your husband rented the apartment in Dallas about November 3, 1962?

Mrs. Oswald. For him?

Mr. Rankin. Yes.

Mrs. Oswald. He had told me that he rented a room, not an apartment. But that was in October.

What date I don't know.

Mr. Rankin. And had he obtained an apartment before you went to Dallas to live with him?

Mrs. Oswald. Yes. Cleaned everything up.

34 Mr. Rankin. So that you would have gone to Dallas to live with him some time on or about the date that he rented that apartment?

Mrs. Oswald. Yes.

Mr. Rankin. After you went to live with him in the apartment at Dallas, did you separate from him again and go to live with somebody else?

Mrs. Oswald. Only after this quarrel. Then I stayed with my friends for one week. I had already told you about that.

Mr. Rankin. That is the Meller matter?

Mrs. Oswald. Yes.

Mr. Rankin. Do you recall that you called Mrs. Meller and told her about your husband beating you and she told you to get a cab and come to stay with her?

Mrs. Oswald. Yes, but he didn't beat me.

Mr. Rankin. And you didn't tell her that he had beat you, either?

Mrs. Oswald. I don't think so. Perhaps she understood it that he had beaten me, because it had happened.

Mr. Rankin. Can you give us any more exact account of where your husband stayed in the period between October 10 and November 18, 1962?

Mrs. Oswald. I don't remember his exact address. This was a period when I did not live with him.

I am asking about which period is it. I don't remember the dates.

Mr. Rankin. The period that he rented the apartment was November 3, so that shortly after that, as I understood your testimony, you were with him, from November 3, or about November 3 on to the 18th. Is that right?

Mrs. Oswald. From November 3 to November 18, 1962? On Elsbeth Street? No, I was there longer.

Mr. Rankin. And do you recall the date that you went to Mrs. Hall's, then?

Mrs. Oswald. No, I don't remember. The day when he rented the apartment was a Sunday. But where he lived before that, I don't know.

Mr. Rankin. After you went to live with him in the apartment, around November 3, how long did you stay before you went to live with your friend?

Mrs. Oswald. Approximately a month and a half. Perhaps a month. I am not sure.

Mr. Rankin. And when you were at Fort Worth, and he was living in Dallas, did he call you from time to time on the telephone?

Mrs. Oswald. Yes, he called me and he wrote letters and sometimes he came for a visit.

Mr. Rankin. And during that time, did he tell you where he was staying?

Mrs. Oswald. Yes, he said that he had rented a room, but he did not tell me his address.

I want to help you, but I don't know.

Mr. Rankin. Did you think there was something in your husband's life in America, his friends and so forth, that caused him to be different here?

Mrs. Oswald. No, he had no friends who had any influence over him. He himself had changed by comparison to the way he was in Russia. But what the reason for that was, I don't know.

Am I giving sufficient answers to your questions?

Mr. Rankin. You are doing fine.

Did your consideration of a divorce from your husband have anything to do with his ideas and political opinions?

Mrs. Oswald. No. The only reasons were personal ones with reference to our personal relationship, not political reasons.

Mr. Rankin. In your story you say that what was involved was some of his crazy ideas and political opinions. Can you tell us what you meant by that?

Mrs. Oswald. This was after the case, after the matter of the divorce. I knew that Lee had such political leanings.

Mr. Rankin. With regard to your Russian friends, did you find the time when they came less to see you and didn't show as much interest in you?

Mrs. Oswald. Yes.

Mr. Rankin. Can you give us about the time, just approximately when you noticed that difference?

Mrs. Oswald. Soon after arriving in Dallas. Mostly it was De Mohrenschildt[35] who visited us. He was the only one who remained our friend. The others sort of removed themselves.

Mr. Rankin. Do you know why that was?

Mrs. Oswald. Because they saw that Lee's attitude towards them was not very proper, he was not very hospitable, and he was not glad to see them. They felt that he did not like them.

Mr. Rankin. Will you describe what you observed that caused you to think this, or how your husband acted in regard to these friends?

Mrs. Oswald. He told me that he did not like them, that he did not want them to come to visit.

Mr. Rankin. Did he show any signs of that attitude towards them?

Mrs. Oswald. Yes, he was not very talkative when they came for a visit. Sometimes he would even quarrel with them.

Mr. Rankin. When he quarreled with them, was it in regard to political ideas or what subjects?

Mrs. Oswald. Yes, they would not agree with him when he talked on political matters.

Mr. Rankin. Do you recall any conversation that you can describe to us?

Mrs. Oswald. Of course it is difficult to remember all the conversations. But I know that they had a difference of opinion with reference to political matters. My Russian friends did not approve of everything. I am trying to formulate it more exactly. They did not like the fact that he was an American who had gone to Russia. I think that is all. All that I can remember.

Mr. Rankin. What did they say about——

Mrs. Oswald. Excuse me. Simply I would be busy, and I didn't listen to the conversation.

Mr. Rankin. Can you recall anything else about the conversation or the substance of it?

Mrs. Oswald. No.

Mr. Rankin. When did you first consider the possibility of returning to the Soviet Union?

Mrs. Oswald. I never considered that, but I was forced to because Lee insisted on it.

Mr. Rankin. When you considered it, as you were forced to, by his insistence, do you know when it was with reference to your first request to the Embassy, which was February 17, 1963?

Mrs. Oswald. February 17?

Mr. Rankin. Yes.

Mrs. Oswald. I think it was a couple of weeks before that, at the beginning of February.

Mr. Rankin. Did your husband know about the letter you sent to the Embassy on February 17?

Mrs. Oswald. Of course. He handed me the paper, a pencil, and said, "Write."

Mr. Rankin. Did he tell you what to put in the letter, or was that your own drafting?

Mrs. Oswald. No, I knew myself what I had to write, and these were my words. What could I do if my husband didn't want to live with me? At least that is what I thought.

Mr. Rankin. Did you ever have arguments with your husband about smoking and drinking wine, other things like that?

Mrs. Oswald. About drinking wine, no. But he didn't like the fact that I smoked, because he neither smoked nor drank. It would have been better if he had smoked and drank.

Mr. Rankin. Can you tell us approximately when you first met Ruth Paine?

Mrs. Oswald. Soon after New Years—I think it was in January.

Mr. Rankin. Would that be 1963?

Mrs. Oswald. Yes.

Mr. Rankin. Can you describe the circumstances when you met her?

Mrs. Oswald. We were invited, together with George De Mohrenschildt and his wife, to the home of his friend, an American. And Ruth was acquainted with that American. She was also visiting there. And there were a number of other people there, Americans.

36 Mr. Rankin. Who was this friend? Do you recall?

Mrs. Oswald. I don't remember his last name. If you would suggest, perhaps I could say.
Mr. Rankin. Was that Mr. Glover?
Mrs. Oswald. What is his first name?
Mr. Rankin. Everett.
Mrs. Oswald. Yes. I don't know his last name.
Mr. Rankin. Did you talk to Mrs. Paine in Russian at that time?
Mrs. Oswald. A little, yes.
Mr. Rankin. Did Mrs. Paine ever visit you at Elsbeth Street?
Mrs. Oswald. At Neely, on Neely Street.
Mr. Rankin. But not at Elsbeth?
Mrs. Oswald. We moved soon after that acquaintance.
Mr. Rankin. How did your husband treat June? Was he a good father?
Mrs. Oswald. Oh, yes, very good.
Mr. Rankin. Did you notice any difference in his attitude towards your child after you saw this change in his personality?
Mrs. Oswald. No.
Mr. Rankin. Will you describe to the Commission how your husband treated the baby, and some of his acts, what he did?
Mrs. Oswald. He would walk with June, play with her, feed her, change diapers, take photographs—everything that fathers generally do.
Mr. Rankin. He showed considerable affection for her at all times, did he?
Mrs. Oswald. Yes. If I would punish June, he would punish me.
Mr. Rankin. When did you first meet Michael Paine?
Mrs. Oswald. After I became acquainted with Ruth and she visited me for the first time, she asked me to come for a visit to her. This was on a Friday. Her husband, Michael, came for us and drove us to their home in Irving.
Mr. Rankin. They were living together at that time, were they?
Mrs. Oswald. No.
Mr. Rankin. Did Michael Paine know Russian?
Mrs. Oswald. No.
Mr. Rankin. At the time of the Walker incident, do you recall whether your husband had his job or had lost it?
Mrs. Oswald. You had said that this had happened on a Wednesday, and it seems to me that it was on a Friday that he was told that he was discharged. He didn't tell me about it until Monday.
Mr. Rankin. But it was on the preceding Friday that he was discharged, was it not?
Mrs. Oswald. No, not the preceding Friday—the Friday after the incident. That is what he told me.
Mr. Rankin. If he had lost his job before the Walker incident, you didn't know it then?
Mrs. Oswald. No.
Mr. Rankin. On the day of the Walker shooting did he appear to go to work as usual?
Mrs. Oswald. Yes.
Mr. Rankin. And when did he return that day, do you recall?
Mrs. Oswald. Late at night, about 11.
Mr. Rankin. He did not come home for dinner then, before?
Mrs. Oswald. Yes, he had come home, and then left again.
Mr. Rankin. Did you notice any difference in his actions when he returned home and had dinner?
Mrs. Oswald. No.
Mr. Rankin. Did he appear to be excited, nervous?
Mrs. Oswald. No, he was quite calm. But it seemed to me that inside he was tense.
Mr. Rankin. How could you tell that?

Mrs. Oswald. I could tell by his face. I knew Lee. Sometimes when some thing would happen he wouldn't tell me about it, but I could see it in his eyes, that something had happened.

Mr. Rankin. And you saw it this day, did you?

37 Mrs. Oswald. Yes.

Mr. Rankin. When did he leave the home after dinner?

Mrs. Oswald. I think it was about 7. Perhaps 7:30.

Mr. Rankin. Did you observe whether he took any gun with him?

Mrs. Oswald. No. He went downstairs. We lived on the second floor. He said, "Bye-bye."

Mr. Rankin. Did you look to see if the gun had been taken when he did not return?

Mrs. Oswald. No, I didn't look to see.

Mr. Rankin. Mr. Chairman, we have gone our hour.

The Chairman. Yes. I think we will take a 10 minute recess now, so you might refresh yourself.

Mrs. Oswald. Thank you.

(Brief recess.)

The Chairman. The Commission will be in order. Mr. Rankin, you may continue.

Mr. Rankin. Mrs. Oswald, you told us about your knowledge about the trip to Mexico and said that you were under oath and were going to tell us all about what you knew.

Did your husband ever ask you not to disclose what you knew about the Mexican trip?

Mrs. Oswald. Yes.

Mr. Rankin. And when was that?

Mrs. Oswald. Before he left. I had remained and he was supposed to leave on the next day, and he warned me not to tell anyone about it.

Mr. Rankin. After he returned to Dallas from his Mexico trip, did he say anything to you then about not telling he had been to Mexico?

Mrs. Oswald. Yes, he asked me whether I had told Ruth about it or anyone else, and I told him no, and he said that I should keep quiet about it.

Mr. Rankin. I will hand you Exhibit 1 for identification, and ask you if you recall seeing that document before.

Mrs. Oswald. Yes, this is the note that I found in connection with the Walker incident.

Mr. Rankin. That you already testified about?

Mrs. Oswald. Yes.

Mr. Rankin. And there is attached to it a purported English translation.

The Chairman. Do you want that marked and introduced at this time, Mr. Rankin?

Mr. Rankin. Yes, I would like to offer the document.

The Chairman. The document may be marked Exhibit 1 and offered in evidence.

(The document referred to was marked Commission Exhibit No. 1, and received in evidence.)

Mr. Rankin. Can you tell us what your husband meant when he said on that note, "The Red Cross also will help you."

Mrs. Oswald. I understand that if he were arrested and my money would run out, I would be able to go to the Red Cross for help.

Mr. Rankin. Had you ever discussed that possibility before you found the note?

Mrs. Oswald. No.

Mr. Rankin. Do you know why he left you the address book?

Mrs. Oswald. Because it contained the addresses and telephone numbers of his and my friends in Russia and here.

Mr. Rankin. And you had seen that book before and knew its contents, did you?

Mrs. Oswald. Yes.

Mr. Rankin. I will hand you Exhibit 2 for identification and ask you if you know what that is.

Mrs. Oswald. No.

Mr. Rankin. Do you know whether or not that is a photograph of the Walker house in Dallas?

Mrs. Oswald. I didn't see it—at least—taken from this view I can't recognize38 it. I know that the photograph of Walker's home which I saw showed a two-story house. But I don't recognize it from this view. I never saw the house itself at any time in my life.

Mr. Rankin. Does Exhibit 2 for identification appear to be the picture that you described yesterday of the Walker house that you thought your husband had taken and put in his book?

Mrs. Oswald. No. Perhaps this was in his notebook. But I don't remember this particular one.

The Chairman. Mr. Rankin, do you want this in the record?

Mr. Rankin. Mr. Chairman, she hasn't been able to identify that sufficiently.

Mrs. Oswald. Excuse me. Perhaps there are some other photographs there that I might be able to recognize.

Mr. Rankin. I will present some more to you, and possibly you can then pick out the Walker house.

Mrs. Oswald. I know these photographs.

Mr. Rankin. I now hand you a photograph which has been labeled Exhibit 4 for identification. I ask if you can identify the subject of that photograph, or those photographs.

Mrs. Oswald. All of them?

Mr. Rankin. Whichever ones you can.

Mrs. Oswald. I know one shows Walker's house. Another is a photograph from Leningrad. P-3—this is probably New Orleans. P-4—Leningrad. It is a photograph showing the castle square in Leningrad.

Mr. Rankin. Can you point out by number the photograph of the Walker house?

Mrs. Oswald. P-2.

Mr. Rankin. Do you know whether the photographs on Exhibit 4 for identification were part of your husband's photographs?

Mrs. Oswald. Yes.

Mr. Rankin. Mr. Chairman, I offer Exhibit 4 for identification in evidence.

The Chairman. It may be admitted.

(The document referred to was marked Commission Exhibit 2, and received in evidence.)

Mr. Dulles. What is being offered—the whole of it, or just P-2?

Mr. Rankin. No, all of it—because she identified the others, too, as a part of the photographs that belonged to her husband. And she pointed out P-2 as being the Walker residence.

When did you first see this photograph of the Walker residence, P-2, in this Exhibit 2?

Mrs. Oswald. After the Walker incident Lee showed it to me.

Mr. Rankin. And how did you know it was a photograph of the Walker residence?

Mrs. Oswald. He told me that.

Mr. Rankin. I hand you Exhibit 3 for identification. I ask you if you can identify the photographs there.

Mrs. Oswald. Yes, these are all our photographs. P-1 is Walker's house. P-4 and P-3 is a photograph showing me and a girlfriend of mine in Minsk, after a New Year's party, on the morning, on January 1. Before I was married. This was taken early in the morning, after we had stayed overnight in the suburbs. P-5 shows Paul—Pavel

Golovachev. He is assembling a television set. He sent us this photograph. He is from Minsk. He worked in the same factory as Lee did.

Mr. Rankin. Can you tell us which one is the picture of the Walker house on that exhibit?

Mrs. Oswald. P-1.

Mr. Rankin. And when did you first see that exhibit, P-1, of Exhibit 3?

Mrs. Oswald. Together with the other one. P-2 and P-6, I know that they are Lee's photographs, but I don't know what they depict.

Mr. Rankin. Were you shown the P-1 photograph of that Exhibit 3 at the same time you were shown the other one that you have identified regarding the Walker house?

39 Mrs. Oswald. It seems to me that that is so. I don't remember exactly. It is hard to remember.

Mr. Rankin. And was that the evening after your husband returned from the Walker shooting?

Mrs. Oswald. No. This was on one of the succeeding days.

Mr. Rankin. By succeeding, you mean within two or three days after the shooting?

Mrs. Oswald. Yes.

Mr. Rankin. Mr. Chairman, I offer in evidence Exhibit 3.

The Chairman. It may be admitted.

(The document referred to was marked Commission Exhibit No. 3, and was received in evidence.)

Mrs. Oswald. I don't remember the photograph, the first one that you showed me. I only assumed that was Walker's house.

Mr. Rankin. But the other ones, you do remember those photographs?

Mrs. Oswald. Yes, the others I do.

Mr. Rankin. When you say you do not remember the picture of the Walker house, you are referring to the Exhibit 2 for identification that we did not offer in evidence, that I will show you now?

Mrs. Oswald. Yes.

Mr. Rankin. Do you recall that your husband showed you any other exhibits that were pictures of the Walker house at the time he discussed the Walker shooting with you, beyond those that I have shown you?

Mrs. Oswald. Yes.

Mr. Rankin. I shall hand you Exhibit——

Mrs. Oswald. There was some railroad—not just a photograph of a house. Perhaps there were some others. There were several photographs.

Mr. Rankin. I shall hand you Exhibit 4 for identification——

Mrs. Oswald. One photograph with a car.

Mr. Rankin. ——if you can recall the photographs on that exhibit.

Mrs. Oswald. As for P-1 and P-2, I don't know what they are.

P-3, that is Lee in the Army.

P-4, I don't know what that is.

P-5, I did see this photograph with Lee—he showed it to me after the incident.

Mr. Rankin. When your husband showed you the photograph P-5, did he discuss with you what that showed, how it related to the Walker shooting?

Mrs. Oswald. No. I simply see that this is a photograph of a railroad. It was in that book. And I guessed, myself, that it had some sort of relationship to the incident.

Mr. Rankin. I offer in evidence photographs P-3 and P-5 on this exhibit.

The Chairman. They may be admitted, and take the next number.

(The document referred to was marked Commission Exhibit No. 4, and received in evidence.)

Mr. Rankin. Now, I shall hand you Exhibit 6 for identification and ask you if you recognize those two photographs.

Mrs. Oswald. Yes. These photographs I know, both of them. They seem to be identical. Walker's house.

Mr. Rankin. When did you first see those exhibits?

Mrs. Oswald. After the incident.

Mr. Rankin. About the same time that you saw the other pictures of the Walker house that you have described?

Mrs. Oswald. Yes.

Mr. Rankin. Did your husband tell you why he had these photographs?

Mrs. Oswald. He didn't tell me, but I guessed, myself—I concluded myself that these photographs would help him in that business.

Mr. Rankin. That is the business of the shooting at the Walker house?

Mrs. Oswald. Yes.

Mr. Rankin. I offer in evidence the two photographs in this exhibit.

The Chairman. They may be admitted and take the next number.

(The documents referred to were marked Commission Exhibit No. 5, and received in evidence.)

40 Mr. Rankin. Before you told the Commission about the Walker shooting, and your knowledge, did you tell anyone else about it?

Mrs. Oswald. Yes, to the members of the Secret Service and the FBI.

Mr. Rankin. Did you tell your mother-in-law?

Mrs. Oswald. Yes, I also told his mother about it.

Mr. Rankin. When did you tell his mother about the incident?

Mrs. Oswald. After Lee was arrested, on Saturday—he was arrested on Friday. I don't remember when I met with his mother—whether it was on the same Friday—yes, Friday evening. I met her at the police station. From there we went to Ruth Paine's where I lived at that time. And she remained overnight, stayed overnight there. I had a photograph of Lee with the rifle, which I gave. At that time I spoke very little English. I explained as best I could about it. And that is why I showed her the photograph. And I told her that Lee had wanted to kill Walker.

Mr. Rankin. Now, turning to the period when you were in New Orleans, did you write to the Russian Embassy about going to Russia, returning to Russia at that time?

Mrs. Oswald. Yes.

Mr. Rankin. Was that about the first part of July, that you wrote?

Mrs. Oswald. Probably.

Mr. Rankin. And then did you write a second letter to follow up the first one?

Mrs. Oswald. Yes.

Mr. Rankin. I hand you Exhibit 6 for identification and ask you if that is the first letter that you sent to the Embassy. Take your time and look at it.

Mrs. Oswald. This was not the first letter, but it was the first letter written from New Orleans.

Mr. Rankin. Will you examine the photostat that has just been handed to you, and tell us whether or not that was the first letter that you wrote to the Embassy about this matter?

Mrs. Oswald. No, this is a reply to my first letter.

Mr. Rankin. Will you examine the one that you now have, and state whether that is the first letter?

Mrs. Oswald. Yes, this was the first. This was only the declaration. But there was a letter in addition to it.

Mr. Rankin. The declaration was a statement that you wished to return to the Soviet Russia?

Mrs. Oswald. Yes, about granting me a visa.

Mr. Rankin. And what date does that bear?

Mrs. Oswald. It is dated March 17, 1963.

Mr. Rankin. And did you send it with your letter about the date that it bears?

Mrs. Oswald. Yes.
I don't know—perhaps a little later, because I was not very anxious to send this.
Mr. Rankin. But you did send it?
Mrs. Oswald. Yes.
Mr. Rankin. And it might have been within a few days or a few weeks of that time?
Mrs. Oswald. Yes.
Mr. Dulles. Do we have the date of the second letter?
Mr. Rankin. I want to go step by step.
Mr. Dulles. Yes, I understand. That is not introduced yet.
Mr. Rankin. It might be confusing if we get them out of order.
Mrs. Oswald. Yes, this is the first letter.
Mr. Rankin. Now, the photostatic document that you have just referred to as being the first letter, does it bear a date?
Mrs. Oswald. Yes.
Mr. Rankin. Do you recall the date?
Mrs. Oswald. It says there the 17th of February.
Mr. Rankin. And do you know that that letter had attached to it your declaration that you just referred to?
Mrs. Oswald. Yes, it seems to me. Perhaps it was attached to the next letter. I am not sure.
41 Mr. Rankin. This letter of February 17 that you referred to as the first letter is in your handwriting?
Mrs. Oswald. Yes.
Mr. Rankin. Will you examine the translation into English that is attached to it and inform us whether or not that is a correct translation?
Mrs. Oswald. I can't do that, because——
Mr. Rankin. Mr. Interpreter, can you help us in that regard, and tell her whether it is a correct translation?
Mr. Krimer. If I may translate it from the English, she could check it.
Mr. Rankin. Would you kindly do that?
Mrs. Oswald. That is a quite correct translation. I didn't want to, but I had to compose some such letters.
Mr. Rankin. I offer in evidence the photostatic copy of the letter in Russian as Exhibit 6.
The Chairman. Together with the translation that is attached to it?
Mr. Rankin. Together with the translation that is attached to it as Exhibit 7.
The Chairman. It may be admitted and take the next number.
(The documents referred to were marked Commission Exhibit Nos. 6 and 7, respectively, and received in evidence.)
Mr. Rankin. I hand you again the declaration, Exhibit 8, and ask you if that accompanied the first letter, Exhibit 6, that you have referred to?
Mrs. Oswald. I don't remember whether it accompanied the first letter or the second letter with which I had enclosed some photographs and filled out questionnaires.
Mr. Rankin. I hand you Exhibit 9 and ask you if that is the second letter that you have just referred to.
Mrs. Oswald. No, this was perhaps the third. Perhaps I could help you, if you would show me all the letters, I would show you the sequence.
Mr. Rankin. I hand you Exhibit 9, dated March 8, 1963, and ask you if you can tell whether that is the letter which accompanied the declaration.
Mrs. Oswald. This is a reply from the Embassy, a reply to my first letter.
Mr. Rankin. Mr. Chairman, may we have a short recess to get the original exhibits that we have prepared, and I think we can expedite our hearing.
The Chairman. Very well. We will have a short recess.
(Brief recess.)

The Chairman. The Commission will come to order. We will proceed.

Mr. Rankin. Mrs. Oswald, we will see if we have these in proper order now.

I will call your attention to the photostats of the declaration and the accompanying papers that I shall now call Exhibit 8 to replace the references to Exhibit 8 and 9 that we made in prior testimony, and ask you to examine that and see if they were sent together by you to the Embassy.

Mrs. Oswald. I sent this after I received an answer from the Embassy, an answer to my first letter. This is one and the same. Two separate photostats of the same declaration. All of these documents were attached to my second letter after the answer to my first.

Mr. Rankin. I call your attention to Exhibit 9, and ask you if that is the answer to your first letter that you have just referred to.

Mrs. Oswald. Yes, this is the answer to that letter.

Mr. Rankin. Will you compare the translation?

Mrs. Oswald. The only thing is that the address and the telephone number of the Embassy are not shown in the Russian original. They are in the translation.

Mr. Rankin. Otherwise the translation is correct, is it?

Mrs. Oswald. Otherwise, yes.

Mr. Rankin. Mr. Chairman, I ask leave to substitute the Exhibit No. 8 for what I have called 9, as the reply of the Embassy, so that we won't be confused about the order of these.

The Chairman. The correction may be made.

Mr. Rankin. I offer in evidence the original and the translation of Exhibit 8, except for the address of the Embassy, which was not on the original.

The Chairman. It may be admitted, and take the next number.

42 (The documents referred to were marked Commission Exhibit No. 8, and received in evidence.)

Mr. Rankin. Now, as I understand, what I will call Exhibit 9 now, to correct the order in which these letters were sent to the Embassy, was your response to the letter of the Embassy dated March 8, is that correct?

Mrs. Oswald. Yes, sir.

Mr. Rankin. Will you compare the translation with the interpreter and advise us if it is correct?

Mr. Krimer. It says, "Application" in the translation; the Russian word is "Declaration".

Mr. Rankin. Will you note that correction, Mr. Krimer, please?

Mr. Krimer. In pencil?

Mr. Rankin. Yes.

Mr. Krimer. Crossing out the word "application".

Mrs. Oswald. That is correct.

Mr. Krimer. Sir, this was a printed questionnaire, and there is a translator note on here which states that since printed questions are given both in Russian and English translation, only the answer portion of the document is being translated.

Mrs. Oswald. That is correct.

Mr. Rankin. You have now examined Exhibit 9 and the translation into English from that exhibit where it was in Russian and compared them with the interpreter, have you?

Mrs. Oswald. Yes, correct.

Mr. Rankin. Do you find the translation is correct?

Mrs. Oswald. Yes.

Mr. Rankin. I offer in evidence Exhibit 9, being the Russian communications, and the English translations.

The Chairman. The documents may be admitted with the next number.

(The documents referred to were marked Commission Exhibit No. 9, and received in evidence.)

Mr. Rankin. Mrs. Oswald, do you recall that in the letter from the Embassy of March 8, which is known as Commission's Exhibit 8, that you were told that the time of processing would take 5 to 6 months?
Mrs. Oswald. Yes.
Mr. Rankin. Did you discuss that with your husband?
Mrs. Oswald. Yes.
Mr. Rankin. And about when did you do that?
Mrs. Oswald. What is the date of that letter?
Mr. Rankin. March 8.
Mrs. Oswald. At that time we did not discuss it. We discussed it in New Orleans. Or more correctly, we thought that if everything is in order, I would be able to leave before the birth of my second child.
Mr. Rankin. And did you discuss that idea with your husband?
Mrs. Oswald. Yes.
Mr. Rankin. And you think that you discussed it with him while you were at New Orleans?
Mrs. Oswald. Yes.
Mr. Rankin. Do you recall that it is also requested in the letter of March 8 from the Embassy, Commission's Exhibit 8, that you furnish one or two letters from relatives residing in the Soviet Union who were inviting you to live with them?
Mrs. Oswald. Yes, but I didn't have any such letters and I did not enclose any.
Mr. Rankin. You never did send such letters to the Embassy, did you?
Mrs. Oswald. No.
Mr. Rankin. After you sent Exhibit 9 to the Embassy, did you have further correspondence with them?
Mrs. Oswald. Yes.
Mr. Rankin. I will hand you Exhibit 10, a letter purporting to be from the Embassy dated April 18, and ask you if you recall that.
Mrs. Oswald. Yes, I remember that.
Mr. Rankin. Will you please compare the translation with the Russian?
43 Mrs. Oswald. Yes, the translation is correct.
Mr. Rankin. We offer the exhibit in evidence, together with the translation.
The Chairman. It may be admitted with the next number.
(The documents referred to were marked Commission Exhibit No. 10, and received in evidence.)
Mr. Rankin. Did you note that the Embassy invited you to come and visit them personally?
Mrs. Oswald. Yes.
Mr. Rankin. Did you ever do that?
Mrs. Oswald. No.
Mr. Rankin. I hand you a letter purporting to be from the Embassy, dated June 4, marked Exhibit 11, and ask you if you recall receiving that?
Mrs. Oswald. Yes. This is a second request to visit the Embassy.
Mr. Rankin. Will you please compare the translation with the Russian?
Mrs. Oswald. Correct.
Mr. Rankin. We offer in evidence Exhibit 11, being the Russian letter from the Embassy together with the English translation.
The Chairman. It may be admitted and take the next number.
(The documents referred to were marked Commission Exhibit No. 11, and received in evidence.)
The Chairman. We will now recess for lunch.
The Commission will reconvene at 2 o'clock.
(Whereupon, at 12:30 p.m., the Commission recessed.)

Afternoon Session
TESTIMONY OF MRS. LEE HARVEY OSWALD RESUMED

The President's Commission reconvened at 2 p.m.
The Chairman. The Commission will convene.
Mr. Rankin, you may continue.
Mr. Rankin. Mrs. Oswald, I will now give you Exhibit 12 to examine and ask you to compare the Russian with the English translation.
Mrs. Oswald. The translation is correct.
Mr. Rankin. I offer in evidence Exhibit 12, being the Russian letter, and the English translation.
The Chairman. The documents are admitted under that number.
(The documents referred to were marked Commission Exhibit No. 12, and received in evidence.)
Mr. Rankin. Now, this Exhibit 13 that you have just examined in Russian, is that your letter, Mrs. Oswald, to the Embassy?
Mrs. Oswald. Is that No. 12?
Mr. Rankin. Yes.
Mrs. Oswald. Yes, it is.
Mr. Rankin. And is it in your handwriting?
Mrs. Oswald. Yes.
Mr. Rankin. Did you find any date on the letter? I didn't.
Mrs. Oswald. I probably didn't date it. No. I wrote this from New Orleans.
Mr. Rankin. Can you tell the Commission the approximate date you wrote it?
Mrs. Oswald. What was the date of the preceding letter, No. 11—Exhibit No. 11?
Mr. Rankin. June 4, 1963.
Mrs. Oswald. This was probably in July, but I don't know the date.
Mr. Rankin. Do you notice there was a "P.S." on Exhibit 12?
Mrs. Oswald. Yes.
Mr. Rankin. Referring to an application by your husband?
Mrs. Oswald. Yes.
Mr. Rankin. And was an application for your husband for a visa included or enclosed with Exhibit 12 when you sent it?
44 Mrs. Oswald. Lee told me that he had sent an application, but it was he who put this letter in an envelope and addressed it, so I don't know whether it was there or not.
Mr. Rankin. And when you say that it was he that put the letter into the envelope and addressed it, you mean this Exhibit 12, that was a letter that you had written?
Mrs. Oswald. Yes.
Mr. Rankin. Do I understand you correctly that you do not know whether his application was included because he handled the mailing of it?
Mrs. Oswald. Yes.
Mr. Rankin. I will hand you Exhibit 13 and ask you if you recall that?
Mrs. Oswald. I don't remember this. He did not write this in my presence. But it is Lee's handwriting.
Mr. Rankin. Mr. Krimer, will you please translate it for her so she will know the contents.
Mrs. Oswald. Why "separately"—the word "separately" here is underlined.
Mr. Rankin. I was going to ask you. But since you have not seen it before, I guess you cannot help us.
Is this the first time that you knew that he had ever asked that his visa be handled separately from yours?
Mrs. Oswald. Yes, I didn't know this. Because I hadn't seen this letter.
Mr. Rankin. I offer in evidence Exhibit 13.
The Chairman. It may be admitted.

(The document referred to was marked Commission Exhibit No. 13, and received in evidence.)

Mr. Rankin. Is the word "separately" the last word of the letter that you are referring to—that is the word that you asked about?

Mrs. Oswald. Yes. Was that underlined by Lee?

Mr. Rankin. That is the way we received it, Mrs. Oswald. We assume it was underlined by your husband. We know that it was not underlined by the Commission, and no one in the Government that had anything to do with it has ever told us that they had anything to do with underlining it.

Mrs. Oswald. I think that perhaps he asked for that visa to be considered separately because the birth of the child might complicate matters, and perhaps he thought it would speed it up if they do consider it separately.

Mr. Rankin. In connection with that thought, I will hand you Exhibit 14, and ask you to examine that and tell us whether you have seen that before.

Mrs. Oswald. Yes.

Mr. Rankin. Will you please compare the translation in English?

Mrs. Oswald. Yes, the translation is all right.

Mr. Rankin. I offer in evidence the letter in Russian, Exhibit 14, and the English translation.

The Chairman. It may be admitted under that number.

(The documents referred to were marked Commission Exhibit No. 14, and received in evidence.)

Mr. Rankin. Did you have any impression that your husband may not have planned to go back to Russia himself, but was merely trying to arrange for you and your daughter to go back?

Mrs. Oswald. At that time I did not think so, but now I think perhaps. Because he planned to go to Cuba.

Mr. Rankin. By that you mean you think he may have planned to go to Cuba and never go beyond Cuba, but stay in Cuba?

Mrs. Oswald. I think that in time he would have wanted to come and see me.

Mr. Rankin. I hand you Exhibit 15 and ask you whether you remember having seen that before.

Mrs. Oswald. No.

Mr. Rankin. Can you tell whether your husband's handwriting is on that exhibit?

Mrs. Oswald. The signature is his, yes. I would like to have it translated.

Mr. Rankin. Would you translate it for her, please, Mr. Krimer?

Mrs. Oswald. A crazy letter. Perhaps from this I could conclude that he did want to go to the Soviet Union—but now I am lost, I don't know. Because—45perhaps because nothing came out of his Cuban business, perhaps that is why he decided to go to the Soviet Union. The letter is not too polite, in my opinion.

Mr. Rankin. I offer in evidence Exhibit 15.

The Chairman. It may be admitted.

(The document referred to was marked Commission Exhibit No. 15, and received in evidence.)

Mr. Rankin. Mr. Chief Justice, I think in the examination about this letter, if I would circulate it to the Commission it would be a little clearer what it is all about—if you could have a moment or two to examine it, I think it would help in your understanding of the examination.

Mrs. Oswald. This was typed on the typewriter belonging to Ruth.

Mr. Rankin. You can tell that by the looks of the typing, can you, Mrs. Oswald?

Mrs. Oswald. No, I don't know, but I know that he was typing there. I don't know what he was typing.

Mr. Rankin. And it is Ruth Paine's typewriter that you are referring to, when you say Ruth?

Mrs. Oswald. Ruth Paine. Because Lee did not have a typewriter, and it is hardly likely that he would have had it typed somewhere else.

Mr. Rankin. I hand you Exhibit 16, which purports to be the envelope for the letter, Exhibit 15. Have you ever seen that?

Mrs. Oswald. The envelope I did see. I did not see the letter, but I did see the envelope. Lee had retyped it some 10 times or so.

Mr. Rankin. Do you recall or could you clarify for us about the date on the envelope—whether it is November 2 or November 12?

Mrs. Oswald. November 12.

Mr. Rankin. I offer in evidence Exhibit 16.

The Chairman. It may be admitted.

(The document referred to was marked Commission Exhibit No. 16, and received in evidence.)

Mr. Rankin. I might call your attention, Mrs. Oswald, to the fact that Exhibit 15, the letter, is dated November 9. Does that help you any?

Mrs. Oswald. Yes. Then this must be 12.

Mr. Rankin. That is the only way you can determine it, is it?

Mrs. Oswald. Yes.

Mr. Rankin. Did you have anything to do with the mailing of this letter, Exhibit 15?

Mrs. Oswald. No.

Mr. Rankin. Yesterday you testified to the fact that your husband told you about his trip to Mexico when he returned, is that right?

Mrs. Oswald. Yes.

Mr. Rankin. Where were you when he told you about it?

Mrs. Oswald. In the home of Mrs. Paine, in my room.

Mr. Rankin. Was there anyone other than yourself and your husband present when he told you about it?

Mrs. Oswald. No.

Mr. Rankin. Will you tell us in as much detail as you can remember just what he said about the trip at that time?

Mrs. Oswald. Everything that I could remember I told you yesterday. I don't remember any more about it.

Mr. Rankin. At that time——

Mrs. Oswald. But I asked him that we not go to Russia, I told him that I did not want to, and he said, "Okay."

Mr. Rankin. That was in this same conversation, after he had told you about the trip to Mexico?

Mrs. Oswald. Yes.

Mr. Rankin. When he asked you not to tell anyone about the trip to Mexico, did he tell you why he asked you to do that?

Mrs. Oswald. No. I knew that he was secretive, and that he loved to make secrets of things.

Mr. Rankin. Did you know the Comrade Kostin that is referred to in this letter of November 8, Exhibit 15?

46 Mrs. Oswald. I never wrote to him. I don't know. I don't know where he got that name from.

Mr. Rankin. Did your husband say anything about Comrade Kostin and his visit with him at the embassy in Mexico City, when he told you about the trip?

Mrs. Oswald. He did not name him. He didn't tell me his name. But he told me he was a very pleasant, sympathetic person, who greeted him, welcomed him there.

Mr. Rankin. Did your husband say anything to you about what he meant when he said he could not take a chance on requesting a new visa unless he used a real name, so he returned to the United States?

Mrs. Oswald. No, he didn't tell me about it.

Mr. Rankin. Did you understand that he had used any assumed name about going to Mexico?

Mrs. Oswald. No.

Mr. Rankin. He never told you anything of that kind?

Mrs. Oswald. No. After Lee returned from Mexico, I lived in Dallas, and Lee gave me his phone number and then when he changed his apartment—Lee lived in Dallas, and he gave me his phone number. And then when he moved, he left me another phone number.

And once when he did not come to visit during the weekend, I telephoned him and asked for him by name—rather, Ruth telephoned him and it turned out there was no one there by that name. When he telephoned me again on Monday, I told him that we had telephoned him but he was unknown at that number.

Then he said that he had lived there under an assumed name. He asked me to remove the notation of the telephone number in Ruth's phone book, but I didn't want to do that. I asked him then, "Why did you give us a phone number, when we do call we cannot get you by name?"

He was very angry, and he repeated that I should remove the notation of the phone number from the phone book. And, of course, we had a quarrel. I told him that this was another of his foolishness, some more of his foolishness. I told Ruth Paine about this. It was incomprehensible to me why he was so secretive all the time.

Mr. Rankin. Did he give you any explanation of why he was using an assumed name at that time?

Mrs. Oswald. He said that he did not want his landlady to know his real name because she might read in the paper of the fact that he had been in Russia and that he had been questioned.

Mr. Rankin. What did you say about that?

Mrs. Oswald. Nothing. And also he did not want the FBI to know where he lived.

Mr. Rankin. Did he tell you why he did not want the FBI to know where he lived?

Mrs. Oswald. Because their visits were not very pleasant for him and he thought that he loses jobs because the FBI visits the place of his employment.

Mr. Rankin. Now, if he was using an assumed name during the trip in Mexico, you didn't know about it, is that correct?

Mrs. Oswald. I didn't know, that is correct.

Mr. Rankin. Before the trip to Mexico, did your husband tell you that he did not expect to contact the Soviet Embassy there about the visa?

Mrs. Oswald. He said that he was going to visit the Soviet Embassy, but more for the purpose of getting to Cuba, to try to get to Cuba. I think that was more than anything a masking of his purpose. He thought that this would help.

Mr. Rankin. You mean it was a masking of his purpose to visit the Soviet Embassy in Mexico, or to write it in this letter?

Mrs. Oswald. I don't understand the question.

Mr. Rankin. You noticed where he said in this letter "I had not planned to contact the Soviet Embassy in Mexico," did you not?

Mrs. Oswald. Why hadn't he planned that?

Mr. Rankin. That is what I am trying to find out from you.

Did he ever tell you that he didn't plan to visit the Soviet Embassy?

Mrs. Oswald. This is not the truth. He did want to contact the embassy.

Mr. Rankin. And he told you before he went to Mexico that he planned to visit the Soviet Embassy, did he?

Mrs. Oswald. Yes.

Mr. Rankin. Did he ever say to you before he went to Mexico that he planned to communicate with the Soviet Embassy in Havana?

Mrs. Oswald. Yes, he said that if he would be able to get to Cuba, with the intention of living there, he would get in touch with the Soviet Embassy for the purpose of bringing me there. Or for him to go to Russia. Because sometimes he really sincerely wanted to go to Russia and live and sometimes not. He did not know, himself. He was very changeable.

Mr. Rankin. But in Exhibit 15, Mrs. Oswald, he refers to the fact that he hadn't been able to reach the Soviet Embassy in Havana as planned, and then he says, "The Embassy there would have had time to complete our business."

Now, did he discuss that at all with you before he went to Mexico?

Mrs. Oswald. Yes. If he said in Mexico City that he wanted to visit the Soviet Embassy in Havana, the reason for it was only that he thereby would be able to get to Cuba.

Is this understandable? Does this clarify the matter or not?

Mr. Rankin. The difficulty, Mrs. Oswald, with my understanding of Exhibit 15 is that he purports to say, as I read the letter, that if he had been able to reach the Soviet Embassy in Havana, he would have been able to complete his business about the visa, and he wouldn't have had to get in touch with the Soviet Embassy in Mexico City at all.

Mrs. Oswald. The thing is that one cannot go to Cuba—that the only legal way is via Mexico City. And, therefore, he went to the Soviet Embassy there in Mexico City and told them that he wanted to visit the Soviet Embassy in Havana, but only for the purpose of getting into Cuba.

I don't think he would have concluded his business there. I don't think that you understand that Lee has written that letter in a quite involved manner. It is not very logical. I don't know whether it is clear to you or not.

Mr. Rankin. I appreciate, Mrs. Oswald, your interpretation of it.

I was trying to find out also whether your husband had told you anything about what he meant or what he did or whether he had tried to contact the Embassy in Havana, as he says in this letter.

Mrs. Oswald. Yes. I don't know of this letter. I only know that Lee wanted to get to Cuba by any means.

Mr. Rankin. Then he next proceeds to say, "Of course the Soviet Embassy was not at fault. They were, as I say, unprepared". As I read that, I understand that he was trying to let the Embassy in Washington know that the Mexico City Embassy had not been notified by him, and, therefore, was unprepared.

Now, did he say anything like that to you after his return to Mexico?

Mrs. Oswald. Why did the Embassy in Washington have to notify the Embassy in Mexico City that Lee Oswald was arriving?

It is not that I am asking. It seems to me that this is not a normal thing.

Mr. Rankin. The question is did he say anything to you about it when he got back?

Mrs. Oswald. He said that when he went to the Soviet Embassy in Mexico City they had promised him that they would write a letter to the Embassy in Washington.

Please excuse me, but it is very difficult for me to read the involved thoughts of Lee. I think that he was confused himself, and I certainly am.

Mr. Rankin. Is that all that you can recall that was said about that matter?

Mrs. Oswald. Yes.

Mr. Rankin. Then he goes on to say——

Mrs. Oswald. Excuse me. I only know that his basic desire was to get to Cuba by any means, and that all the rest of it was window dressing for that purpose.

Mr. Rankin. Then in this Exhibit 15 he proceeds to say, "The Cuban Consulate was guilty of a gross breach of regulations." Do you know what he meant by that?

48 Mrs. Oswald. What regulations—what are the regulations?

Mr. Rankin. I am trying to find out from you.

Mrs. Oswald. I don't know about that. I don't know what happened.

Mr. Rankin. Did he ever say what regulations he thought were breached, or that the Cuban Embassy didn't carry out regulations when he returned from his trip and told you about what happened there?

Mrs. Oswald. I don't know.

Mr. Rankin. Then he goes on to say in the Exhibit, "I am glad he has since been replaced."

Do you know whom he was referring to?

Mrs. Oswald. I have no knowledge of it. I think that if the person to whom this letter was addressed would read the letter he wouldn't understand anything, either.

Mr. Rankin. Your husband goes on in Exhibit 15 to say, "The Federal Bureau of Investigation is not now interested in my activities in the progressive organization 'Fair Play for Cuba Committee' of which I was secretary in New Orleans (State of Louisiana) since I no longer reside in that state."

Do you know why he would say anything like that to the Embassy?

Mrs. Oswald. Because he was crazy.

He wrote this in order to emphasize his importance. He was no secretary of any—he was not a secretary of any organization.

Mr. Rankin. Do you know that he had received any inquiry from the Embassy or anyone of the Soviet Union about the matters that he is telling about here?

Mrs. Oswald. No. I don't know.

Mr. Rankin. Then he goes on to say, "However, the FBI has visited us here in Dallas, Texas, on November 1. Agent James P. Hosty"—do you know whether there was such a visit by that man?

Mrs. Oswald. Yes.

Mr. Rankin. And was he referring to the man that you know as James P. Hosty?

Mrs. Oswald. I don't know his last name. He gave us his telephone number, but it seems to me that his name was different.

Mr. Rankin. After you received the telephone number, what did you do with it?

Mrs. Oswald. He gave the telephone number to Ruth, and she, in turn, passed it on to Lee.

Mr. Rankin. Do you know whether he put it in a book or did anything with it?

Mrs. Oswald. He took the note with him to Dallas. I don't know what he did with it.

Mr. Rankin. Did the agent also give his license number for his car to Mrs. Paine or to you or to your husband?

Mrs. Oswald. No. But Lee had asked me that if an FBI agent were to call, that I note down his automobile license number, and I did that.

Mr. Rankin. Did you give the license number to him when you noted it down?

Mrs. Oswald. Yes.

Mr. Rankin. Now, he goes on to say that this agent, James P. Hosty "warned me that if I engaged in FPCC activities in Texas the FBI will again take an 'interest' in me."

Do you remember anything about anything like that?

Mrs. Oswald. I don't know why he said that in there, because if he has in mind the man who visited us, that man had never seen Lee. He was talking to me and to Mrs. Paine. But he had never met Lee. Perhaps this is another agent, not the one who visited us.

But I don't know whether Lee had talked to him or not.

Mr. Rankin. Do you know whether any FBI agent had ever warned your husband that if he engaged in any Fair Play for Cuba activities in Texas, the FBI would be again interested in him?

Mrs. Oswald. No, I didn't know that.

Mr. Rankin. Then in the exhibit he goes on to say, "This agent also 'suggested' to Marina Nichilyeva that she could remain in the United States under FBI protection."

49 Did you ever hear of anything like that before?

Mrs. Oswald. I had not been proposed anything of the sort at any time.

The only thing the agent did say is that if I had ever any kind of difficulties or troubles in the sense that someone would try to force me to do something, to become an agent, then I should get in touch with him, and that if I don't want to do this, that they would help me. But they never said that I live here and that I must remain here under their protection.

Mr. Rankin. Then in this Exhibit 15 he goes on to explain what he means by the word "protection", saying "That is, she could defect from the Soviet Union, of course." Do you remember anybody saying anything like that to you?

Mrs. Oswald. No, no one said anything like that.

Mr. Rankin. Did anyone at any time, while you were in the United States, suggest that you become an agent of any agency of the United States?

Mrs. Oswald. No, never.

Mr. Rankin. Did anyone from the Soviet Union suggest that you be an agent for that government, or any of its agencies?

Mrs. Oswald. No.

Mr. Rankin. Now, in this Exhibit 15, your husband goes on to say, "I and my wife strongly protested tactics by the notorious FBI."

Do you know of any protest of that kind, or any action of that kind?

Mrs. Oswald. I don't know of any protests, but simply that I said that I would prefer not to get these visits, because they have a very exciting and disturbing effect upon my husband. But it was not a protest. This was simply a request.

Mr. Rankin. And you never made any protests against anyone asking you to act as an agent or to defect to the United States because no one asked you that, is that right?

Mrs. Oswald. No one ever asked me.

Mr. Rankin. Do you know of anything that you could tell the Commission in regard to these matters in this letter, Exhibit 15, that would shed more light on what your husband meant or what he was trying to do, that you have not already told us?

Mrs. Oswald. Everything that I could tell you with reference to this letter I have told you.

The Chairman. I think we will take a short recess now, about 10 minutes.

Mrs. Oswald. I would like to help you, but I simply don't know, I cannot.

(Brief recess)

The Chairman. The Commission will be in order.

Mr. Rankin, you may proceed.

Mr. Rankin. Mrs. Oswald, I will hand you again Exhibit 14 and the translation from the Russian and call your attention to the urgency of your request there. I ask you, was that your idea to press for help from the Embassy in regard to the visa, or your husband's?

Mrs. Oswald. Of course my husband.

Mr. Rankin. At the time of Exhibit 14, then, you were not anxious to return to Russia?

Mrs. Oswald. I never wanted to return but Lee insisted and there is nothing else I could do. But sometimes when I wrote these letters, I felt very lonely—since my husband didn't want me, I felt perhaps this would be the best way.

Mr. Rankin. Do you know the Spanish language?

Mrs. Oswald. Perhaps five words.

Mr. Rankin. Have you given it any study?

Mrs. Oswald. No. I have a Spanish textbook of the Spanish language and I had intended to study even while I was still in Russia, but I never did.

Mr. Rankin. Did your husband ever study Spanish that you know of?

Mrs. Oswald. He didn't study it, but before his trip to Mexico he would sit down with the textbook and look at it.

Mr. Rankin. I hand you Exhibit 17 and ask you if you recall having seen that before.

Mrs. Oswald. May I take it out?

Mr. Rankin. Yes.

50 Mrs. Oswald. June seems to have played with it. This was Lee's study of Spanish perhaps because this was all photographed, it is soiled. Here I helped Lee. I wrote some Spanish words.

Mr. Rankin. Does that Exhibit 17 have any of your husband's handwriting on it?

Mrs. Oswald. Some of it is my handwriting and some of it is Lee's handwriting.

Mr. Rankin. Can you tell us when he was trying to study Spanish? Was it at any time with regard to the time when he planned to go to Cuba?

Mrs. Oswald. Yes.

Mr. Rankin. About when did he start?

Mrs. Oswald. In August, in New Orleans, 1963.

Mr. Rankin. And whatever he did in this notebook, Exhibit 17, he did at that time or thereafter?

Mrs. Oswald. No, this was in September.

Mr. Rankin. Did he do whatever writing he did in connection with the study of the Spanish language in Exhibit 17 at New Orleans in August or after that date?

Mrs. Oswald. Yes.

Do you want to know whether this was earlier than August or later?

Mr. Rankin. Yes.

Mrs. Oswald. No, not earlier. This was in September, not in August.

Mr. Rankin. And did he do anything in the writing of what is in Exhibit 17 in the study of the Spanish language at Dallas, that you know of?

Mrs. Oswald. No.

Mr. Rankin. I offer in evidence Exhibit 17.

The Chairman. It may be marked with the next number and received in evidence.

(The document referred to was marked Commission Exhibit No. 17, and received in evidence.)

Mrs. Oswald. How a simple notebook can become a matter of material evidence—the Spanish words in it, and June's scribbling on it.

Mr. Rankin. Returning to the time that your husband came back from Mexico City to Dallas, can you tell us what type of luggage he brought back with him?

Mrs. Oswald. He had a military type raincoat with him and a small bag with a zipper, blue in color.

Mr. Rankin. As far as you recall he did not have two bags that he brought back with him from Mexico?

Mrs. Oswald. No.

Mr. Rankin. Did he spend the first weekend of October 4 to 6 with you at the Paines?

Mrs. Oswald. No, not the whole weekend. When he returned he stayed overnight and then he went to Dallas. But he returned on Saturday or Friday evening. And he remained until Monday.

Mr. Rankin. Did you notice any change in your husband after this trip to Mexico?

Mrs. Oswald. In my opinion, he was disappointed at not being able to get to Cuba, and he didn't have any great desire to do so any more because he had run into, as he himself said—into bureaucracy and red tape. And he changed for the better. He began to treat me better.

Mr. Rankin. Will you tell us how he treated you better?

Mrs. Oswald. He helped me more—although he always did help. But he was more attentive. Perhaps this was because he didn't live together with me but stayed in Dallas. Perhaps, also because we expected a child and he was in somewhat an elated mood.

Mr. Rankin. Did your husband have any money with him when he returned from Mexico?

Mrs. Oswald. Yes, he had some left. But I never counted how much money he had in his wallet. That is why I don't know.

Mr. Rankin. Was it a small or a large amount or do you know that?

Mrs. Oswald. What would be a large amount for me would not be a large amount for you.

51 Mr. Rankin. Well, can you give us any estimate of what you think he had?

Mrs. Oswald. He might have had $50 or $70, thereabouts. It is necessary sometimes to make a joke. Otherwise, it gets boring.

Mr. Rankin. After the first weekend, after your husband returned, which he spent at the Paines, as you have described, where did he live in Dallas?

Mrs. Oswald. He said that he rented a room in Oak Cliff, but I don't know the address. I didn't ask, because I didn't need it.

Mr. Rankin. Do you know that he lived with a Mrs. Bledsoe at any time in Dallas?

Mrs. Oswald. In what sense do you mean "lived with"?

Mr. Rankin. I mean roomed in her home.

Mrs. Oswald. No.

Mr. Rankin. That was a place on Marsallis Street?

Mrs. Oswald. I don't know about it.

Mr. Rankin. How did he return from Irving to Dallas at that time?

Mrs. Oswald. Ruth met him at the bus station at that time and drove him home. By bus.

Mr. Rankin. You said before that you learned about the depository job at some neighbor's home, is that right?

Mrs. Oswald. Yes.

Mr. Rankin. In whose home was that?

Mrs. Oswald. I don't know her last name. When you walk out of the Paine house, it is the first house to the right. I am trying to remember. Perhaps later I will.

Mr. Rankin. Was it the lady of that house who told you, or someone that was a guest there?

Mrs. Oswald. Perhaps you know the name.

Mr. Rankin. We don't know the name of the lady next door. We know a number of names, but not by the location.

Mrs. Oswald. Her first name is Dorothy. And there was another woman there, another neighbor, who said that her brother worked at the depository, and that as far as she knew, there was a vacancy there.

Mr. Rankin. And what was the name of that neighbor whose brother worked at the depository?

Mrs. Oswald. I don't know.

Mr. Rankin. Was that Mrs. Randle?

Mrs. Oswald. I don't know. I might know her first name if you mention it.

Mr. Rankin. Is there a Linnie Mae Randle that you remember?

Mrs. Oswald. No.

Mr. Rankin. Was she a sister of Mr. Frazier?

Mrs. Oswald. I don't know such people.

Mr. Rankin. Do you know a Mr. Frazier that had a job at the depository?

Mrs. Oswald. I didn't know his name. I knew that it was a young man. I don't think he was 18 yet.

Mr. Rankin. And was he the brother of this friend who was at the neighbor's house?

Mrs. Oswald. Yes.

Mr. Rankin. And he was the one that your husband rode from Irving into Dallas from time to time to go to work, did he?

Mrs. Oswald. Yes, after Lee was already working this boy would bring Lee and take him back with him to Dallas.

Mr. Rankin. And when did he take him, ordinarily?

Mrs. Oswald. 8 o'clock in the morning.

Mr. Rankin. And did he take him on Monday morning?

Mrs. Oswald. Yes.

Mr. Rankin. Usually each week he would take him on Monday morning?

Mrs. Oswald. When Lee came for a weekend, yes.

Mr. Rankin. And then when did he bring him back from Dallas?

Mrs. Oswald. At 5:30 on Friday.

Mr. Rankin. Did your husband ever come in the middle of the week?

Mrs. Oswald. No, only during the last week when all of this happened with reference to the assassination of the President—he came on a Thursday.

52 Mr. Rankin. Did Mrs. Paine have anything to do with your husband getting this job at the depository?

Mrs. Oswald. She had no direct connection with it, but an indirect connection, of course. I lived with her and she talked to a neighbor and mentioned that Lee was out of work.

Mr. Rankin. Was it Mrs. Paine that found out about the job, then?

Mrs. Oswald. Yes. And she telephoned there and asked whether they had a job available. They didn't say anything specific but they asked that Lee come there on the following day.

Mr. Rankin. Did you find out whether your husband did go there the following day?

Mrs. Oswald. On the following day he went there, had a talk with them, and he telephoned that he had already received the job.

Mr. Rankin. Did he telephone to you or to Mrs. Paine about getting the job?

Mrs. Oswald. He telephoned me. But, of course, he thanked Ruth.

Mr. Rankin. And when did he start on the job? Was there two or three days before he got the job and started, or more than that?

Mrs. Oswald. I think that he started on the day following being accepted for the job. I think it was either on the 14th, 15th, or 16th of October.

Mr. Rankin. When he was staying at Mrs. Bledsoe's rooming house, did he call you and give you the number there?

Mrs. Oswald. Yes.

Mr. Rankin. Do you recall where he was when he gave this fictitious name?

Mrs. Oswald. What do you mean where he was? From where he telephoned?

Mr. Rankin. Yes, or the number that he gave you—that is the rooming house that he was at when he used this fictitious name, and you told us you called there.

Mrs. Oswald. He lived at first in one place, and then he changed. It was the last place where he had given a fictitious name. I don't know what name he lived under in the first place, because I never telephoned him.

Mr. Rankin. Do you know the name that he lived under in the second place, when you did call him?

Mrs. Oswald. No.

Mr. Rankin. You don't remember the fictitious name that he gave you?

Mrs. Oswald. I read in the paper after everything happened, but at that time I didn't know. He said that his last name was Lee. He didn't say that. I read that in the paper.

Mr. Rankin. Did that remind you, then, that that was the name they gave you when you called and he answered the telephone?

Mrs. Oswald. No, no one told me anything. I didn't know under what name he lived there.

Mr. Rankin. But you found out that he was not living under his own name, is that what you meant before?

Mrs. Oswald. Yes.

Mr. Rankin. After he got his job, did he return the next weekend to see you?

Mrs. Oswald. Yes.

Mr. Rankin. Do you remember whether that time he returned was on Friday or Saturday?

Mrs. Oswald. It was on Friday, October 18. It was his birthday.

He stopped with Ruth. On Sunday I went to the hospital, and he stayed overnight from Monday until Tuesday.

Mr. Rankin. After your husband returned from Mexico, did you examine the rifle in the garage at any time?

Mrs. Oswald. I had never examined the rifle in the garage. It was wrapped in a blanket and was lying on the floor.

Mr. Rankin. Did you ever check to see whether the rifle was in the blanket?

Mrs. Oswald. I never checked to see that. There was only once that I was interested in finding out what was in that blanket, and I saw that it was a rifle.

Mr. Rankin. When was that?

Mrs. Oswald. About a week after I came from New Orleans.

Mr. Rankin. And then you found that the rifle was in the blanket, did you?

53 Mrs. Oswald. Yes, I saw the wooden part of it, the wooden stock.

Mr. Rankin. On the weekend before your husband got his job at the depository, did he spend that with you at the Paines?

Mrs. Oswald. Yes.

Mr. Rankin. Did he come home Friday or Saturday?

Mrs. Oswald. On a Friday.

Mr. Rankin. When he returned to Dallas on Monday, the 14th of October, did he tell you he was going to change his room?

Mrs. Oswald. No.

Mr. Rankin. Do you remember what your husband's pay was at the depository?

Mrs. Oswald. It seems to me that it was also $1.25.

Mr. Rankin. About how much a month did it run?

Mrs. Oswald. It seems to me it was $210 to $230.

Mr. Rankin. Do you recall the hours that he worked?

Mrs. Oswald. It seems that—it seems to me that it was from 8:30 a.m. to 5 p.m.

Mr. Rankin. And did he work the weekend or any overtime?

Mrs. Oswald. No. It does happen in that depository that they work overtime. But he did not have to work any.

Mr. Rankin. During the week when he was in Dallas and you were at Irving, did he call you from time to time?

Mrs. Oswald. Daily, twice.

Mr. Rankin. Did he leave his telephone number in Dallas with you?

Mrs. Oswald. Yes.
I don't have it, it was in Paine's notebook.

Mr. Rankin. Did he speak to you in Russian when he called you on the telephone?

Mrs. Oswald. Yes. Sometimes he would try to speak in English when someone was listening, and he didn't want them to know he spoke Russian—then he would try to speak in English.

Mr. Rankin. Did he ever speak in Spanish when he was talking to you from Dallas?

Mrs. Oswald. No. He doesn't speak Spanish. I don't either. His landlady heard him say "Adios" and she decided that he spoke Spanish, because she didn't understand that he had spoken Russian all that time.

Mr. Rankin. Did you have a special celebration for your husband's birthday?

Mrs. Oswald. Yes.

Mr. Rankin. When was that?

Mrs. Oswald. On October 18th.

Mr. Rankin. Who was there?

Mrs. Oswald. Ruth and her children, I, Lee, and Paine's husband, Michael.

Mr. Rankin. Did Wesley Frazier bring your husband home at that time?

Mrs. Oswald. Frazier is the last name? Wesley was that boy's name. I now remember.

Mr. Rankin. Did he bring him home that weekend?

Mrs. Oswald. I don't remember.

It seems to me, yes. It is hard to remember now which weekend was which.

Mr. Rankin. On these weekends, did you ever observe your husband going to the garage, practicing with the rifle in any way?

Mrs. Oswald. No.

Mr. Rankin. Did you see him leave the house when he could have been going to the garage and practicing with his rifle?

Mrs. Oswald. No, he couldn't have practiced while we were at the Paine's, because Ruth was there. But whenever she was not at home, he tried to spend as much time as he could with me—he would watch television in the house. But he did go to the garage to look at our things that were there.

Mr. Rankin. And you don't know when he went there what he might have done with the rifle? Is that what you mean?

54 Mrs. Oswald. At least I didn't notice anything.

Mr. Rankin. Now, you have described your husband's——

Mrs. Oswald. Excuse me. I think that it takes considerable time to practice with a rifle. He never spent any great deal of time in the garage.

Mr. Rankin. You have described your husband's practicing on the back porch at New Orleans with the telescopic scope and the rifle, saying he did that very regularly there.

Did you ever see him working the bolt, that action that opens the rifle, where you can put a shell in and push it back—during those times?

Mrs. Oswald. I did not see it, because it was dark, and I would be in the room at that time.

But I did hear the noise from it from time to time—not often.

Mr. Rankin. Do you recall the weekend that you went to the hospital for your baby?

Mrs. Oswald. Very well.

Mr. Rankin. Did your husband go with you at that time?

Mrs. Oswald. No. Ruth drove me at that time. He remained with June because June was crying and we could not leave her with strangers. He wanted to go with me, but we couldn't arrange it any other way.

Mr. Rankin. After the baby was born, did he come and see you?

Mrs. Oswald. Yes.

Mr. Rankin. Did he say anything to you about the baby?

Mrs. Oswald. Every father talks a lot.

Mr. Rankin. Did he talk about the baby?

Mrs. Oswald. About me and the child—he was very happy. He even had tears in his eyes.

Mr. Rankin. Did he call you from Irving when you were in the hospital?

Mrs. Oswald. No, he was working at that time, and he called me from work. But I didn't talk to him. He merely asked the nurse how I was doing.

Mr. Rankin. And those conversations would be reported to you by the nurse, then?

Mrs. Oswald. No, she didn't tell me about them. Because he telephoned to find out when I should be brought home, and he telephoned Ruth and asked her to let him know. But the nurse did tell me that my husband had called.

Mr. Rankin. Now, the weekend of October 25th to the 27th, did your husband return to Irving that weekend?

Mrs. Oswald. There were some weekends when he did not come. But this was at my request. It happened twice, I think. One such weekend was the occasion of the birthday of Mrs. Paine's daughter. And I knew that Lee didn't like Michael, Mrs. Paine's husband, and I asked him not to come.

This was one occasion.

The other I don't recall. I don't recall the date of this. But I remember that the weekend before he shot at the President, he did not come on Saturday and Sunday. Because we had a quarrel—that incident with the fictitious name.

No, I am confused.

It would be easier for me to remember if I knew the birthday of that girl. Perhaps you know. Perhaps you have it noted down somewhere.

Mr. Rankin. You are asking me the birthday of Mrs. Paine's daughter?

Mrs. Oswald. Because I know that the FBI questioned me about it, and they had made a note about it. Because they wanted to determine each time when he did come and when did not.

Mr. Rankin. Now, if it was the weekend of November 16th and 17th that he remained in Dallas, would that help you as to the time of the birthday?

Mrs. Oswald. Yes. This was the weekend before the 21st, and he had not come home that weekend.

Mr. Rankin. Now, the neighbor next door that you referred to, where you learned about the job with the depository, could that have been Dorothy Roberts?

55 Mrs. Oswald. Yes.

Mr. Rankin. Do you recall that your husband went to some meeting with Michael Paine in October of 1963?

Mrs. Oswald. Yes.

It seems to me—I know for sure that this was one of the Fridays. It seems to me that this was the birthday—it was after dinner. They talked in English. I don't know about what. I know that they got together and went to some kind of a meeting.

Mr. Rankin. Was that a meeting of the American Civil Liberties Union?

Mrs. Oswald. Ruth said something about that, but I didn't understand anything. This was right after the incident with Stevenson, who was hit.

Mr. Rankin. Was that in the weekend of October 25th?

Mrs. Oswald. Yes, probably. This was not Lee's birthday. It was the week after that, the following Friday.

Mr. Rankin. Now, on October 26th, Saturday, was your husband with you all day?

Mrs. Oswald. Yes. All day. Whenever he came, he never went anywhere else.

Mr. Rankin. We had some information that a telescopic sight was fitted to a gun for your husband on that date, and that is why I am asking you if there was any time that he could have left to have that done.

Mrs. Oswald. How is it about the telescope? He always had the telescope. Were there two?

Mr. Rankin. We are trying to find out.

Someone says that they mounted a sight.

Mrs. Oswald. This is not the truth, if they say that. Simply people talking. Perhaps someone who looked like Lee.

Mr. Rankin. Someone may be mistaken and thought that he had mounted a telescopic sight when he did it for someone else. And that is why we want to check with you.

When your husband went back to work on Monday, October 28th, did he drive with Wesley Frazier at that time?

Mrs. Oswald. It seems—it seems that he had overslept and that someone else had picked him up. But, no—no, I remember that he did not come to get him, but Lee met him near his house. Lee told me that. Or his sister. I don't remember. Lee told me about it. But I have forgotten.

Mr. Rankin. But he did not go in by bus that day?

Mrs. Oswald. No. He said his sister drove him to the bus. I only know that this boy did not come to get him that day.

Mr. Rankin. As far as you know, he may have gone all the way into Dallas in a car, or he may have gone in a bus?

Mrs. Oswald. Perhaps he hadn't told him to pick him up on that day. I don't know. I only know the fact that the boy did not pick him up on that day.

Mr. Rankin. We have reports of FBI interviews the last part of October, that is October 29, and also November 1, and November 5. We would like to ask you about them, since some of them may have been with Mrs. Paine in your presence or with you. Do you recall one on October 29th?

Mrs. Oswald. I don't remember the interview. Ruth interpreted—she talked to them.

Mr. Rankin. In order that the Commission will understand, whenever the FBI would try to ask you any questions, Mrs. Paine would interpret for you?

Mrs. Oswald. Yes.

Mr. Rankin. And would she at the same time answer things in English, too, herself?

Mrs. Oswald. Yes.

Mr. Rankin. So, in effect, the FBI was——

Mrs. Oswald. Excuse me—she loves to talk.

Mr. Rankin. The FBI was interviewing both of you at the same time, to some extent, is that right?

56 Mrs. Oswald. Yes. They asked her about Lee, as far as I know.

Mr. Rankin. Do you recall that you did have such an interview at Mrs. Paine's house when she acted as interpreter on November 1, 1963?

Mrs. Oswald. Yes.

Mr. Rankin. Were you present on November 5, 1963, when FBI agents Hosty and Wilson interviewed Mrs. Paine at her home?

Mrs. Oswald. I was in my room at that time busy with little Rachel, and I heard voices which I thought were voices of the FBI. I came out of the room and they were in a hurry to leave. They did not talk to me at that time, other than just a greeting.

Mr. Rankin. Do you know whether or not they had been talking to Mrs. Paine about you or your husband?

Mrs. Oswald. Yes. She told me about it, but I was not especially interested. She does not interpret quite exactly. She is hard to understand. But she told me that in general terms.

Mr. Rankin. You have told us about the fact that you got the telephone number of the FBI agent and gave it to your husband. Was that the November 1 interview when that happened?

Mrs. Oswald. Yes.

Mr. Rankin. I will hand you Exhibit 18, and ask you if you can identify that for us, and tell us what it is.

Mrs. Oswald. Lee's notebook.

Mr. Rankin. Is your handwriting in that Exhibit 18?

Mrs. Oswald. It must be, yes, I will find mine. There are many different handwritings in here. Different people have written in this notebook. Sometimes Russian friends in Russia would note their address in this notebook.

This is mine.

Mr. Rankin. Will you tell us—is it a long notation by you?

Mrs. Oswald. No. That is my aunt's address when Lee would remain in Minsk while I went on vacation.

Mr. Rankin. Is much of that notebook, Exhibit 18, in your husband's handwriting?

Mrs. Oswald. The majority, mostly.

Mr. Rankin. Except for the page with your handwriting on it and the notations of other friends that you referred to, is it generally in your husband's handwriting?

Mrs. Oswald. I can tell exactly which is noted down by Lee and which is noted down by others.

Mr. Rankin. And it is a regular notebook that he kept for all types of notes?

Mrs. Oswald. This is from Russia.

Mr. Rankin. He started it in Russia?

Mrs. Oswald. Yes.

Mr. Rankin. And there are a number of notations that were made after you returned to this country, is that right?

Mrs. Oswald. Yes.

Mr. Rankin. We offer in evidence Exhibit 18.

The Chairman. It may be admitted with that number.

(The document referred to was marked Commission Exhibit No. 18, and received in evidence.)

Mrs. Oswald. There is a Russian term for "wedding ring" noted in there. Before we were married I wrote that down for him, because he didn't know the Russian expression for it. I didn't tell him. He looked it up in the dictionary himself and translated it.

Mr. Rankin. I would like to hand this back to you and call your attention to the page of Exhibit 18 where the little white slip is.

I ask you if you recognize the handwriting there, where it refers to Agent Hosty.

Mrs. Oswald. Lee wrote that. And this is the license number.

Mr. Rankin. And the telephone number?

57 The license number, the name, and the telephone number are all in your husband's——

Mrs. Oswald. The date when he visited him, FBI agent, telephone, name, license number, and probably the address.

Mr. Rankin. Are all in your husband's handwriting?

Mrs. Oswald. Yes.

Mr. Rankin. Do you know when they were entered in that notebook, Exhibit 18?

Mrs. Oswald. After the first visit.

Mr. Rankin. Did you note the notation "November 1" on that page?

Mrs. Oswald. Yes.

Mr. Rankin. You think that is about the date of the first visit, then?

Mrs. Oswald. Yes.

Mr. Rankin. Now, did you report to your husband the fact of this visit, November 1, with the FBI agent?

Mrs. Oswald. I didn't report it to him at once, but as soon as he came for a weekend, I told him about it.

By the way, on that day he was due to arrive.

Mr. Rankin. That is on November 1?

Mrs. Oswald. Yes. Lee comes off work at 5:30—comes from work at 5:30. They left at 5 o'clock, and we told them if they wanted to they could wait and Lee would be here soon. But they didn't want to wait.

Mr. Rankin. And by "they" who do you mean? Do you recall the name of the other man beside Agent Hosty?

Mrs. Oswald. There was only one man during the first visit. I don't remember his name. This was probably the date because there is his name and the date.

Mr. Rankin. Now, what did you tell your husband about this visit by the FBI agent and the interview?

Mrs. Oswald. I told him that they had come, that they were interested in where he was working and where he lived, and he was, again, upset.

He said that he would telephone them—I don't know whether he called or not—or that he would visit them.

Mr. Rankin. Is that all you told him at that time about the interview?

Mrs. Oswald. No. I told him about the content of the interview, but now I don't remember.

Mr. Rankin. Do you remember anything else that happened in the interview that you could tell the Commission at this time?

Mrs. Oswald. I told you that I had told them that I didn't want them to visit us, because we wanted to live peacefully, and that this was disturbing to us.

Mr. Rankin. Was there anything else?
Mrs. Oswald. There was more, but I don't remember now.
Mr. Rankin. Now, during this period of time——
Mrs. Oswald. Excuse me. He said that he knew that Lee had been engaged in passing out leaflets for the Committee for Cuba, and he asked whether Lee was doing that here.
Mr. Rankin. Did you answer that question?
Mrs. Oswald. Yes.
Mr. Rankin. What did you say?
Mrs. Oswald. I said that Lee does not engage in such activities here. This was not like an interview. It was simply a conversation. We talked about even some trifles that had no relationship to politics.
Mr. Rankin. Do you know whether or not your husband had any interviews or conversations with the FBI during this period?
Mrs. Oswald. I know of two visits to the home of Ruth Paine, and I saw them each time. But I don't know of any interviews with Lee. Lee had told me that supposedly he had visited their office or their building. But I didn't believe him. I thought that he was a brave rabbit.
Mr. Rankin. Did your husband continue to call you daily from Dallas after he got his job?
58 Mrs. Oswald. Yes.
Mr. Rankin. Did he tell you what he was doing?
Mrs. Oswald. Usually he would call me during the lunch break, and the second time after he was finished work, and he told me that he was reading, that he was watching television, and sometimes I told him that he should not stay in his room too much, that he should go for a walk in the park.
Mr. Rankin. What did he say in answer to that?
Mrs. Oswald. Or I would tell him to go out and eat, and he said that he would listen to me. I don't know to what extent he fulfilled my requests.
Mr. Rankin. Did your husband come back from Dallas on November 8th?
Mrs. Oswald. I don't remember.
Mr. Rankin. Do you know whether he came back on Saturday of that week?
Mrs. Oswald. I remember that there was one weekend when he didn't come on a Friday, but said that he would come on a Saturday. And he said that that was because he wanted to visit another place—supposedly there was another job open, more interesting work.
Mr. Rankin. Did he say where this other job was that he thought was more interesting?
Mrs. Oswald. He said that this was also based upon an ad in a newspaper, and that it was connected—that it was related to photography. And he went there in the morning and then—on a Saturday—and then came to us, still during the morning.
Mr. Rankin. He came home, then, on Saturday, some time before noon of that day?
Mrs. Oswald. Yes, before noon.
It seems to me that there was a holiday on that day, on the 8th—elections—were there elections on that day?
Mr. Rankin. Are you thinking of November 11th, Veterans Day?
Mrs. Oswald. I remember that day exactly. We didn't go anywhere on that Saturday.
Mr. Rankin. Did you and your husband buy groceries in Irving some place?
Mrs. Oswald. Not always. Sometimes we would go together with Ruth and buy a few things.
Mr. Rankin. Do you remember the Hutch's Supermarket, owned by Mr. Hutchison?
Mrs. Oswald. No.
Mr. Rankin. Did you ever shop there with your husband?
Mrs. Oswald. We never went just Lee and I.

Mr. Rankin. Did the three of you—Mrs. Paine and you and your husband go together to shop?

Mrs. Oswald. And her children.

Mr. Rankin. Did your husband try to cash checks at the Hutch's market?

Mrs. Oswald. He may have tried to cash checks sometimes when he received unemployment compensation.

Mr. Rankin. Do you recall that he tried to cash a check of $189 at this market?

Mrs. Oswald. He didn't have such a check.

Mr. Rankin. As far as you know, he didn't try to cash a check of that size at this market?

Mrs. Oswald. I don't remember this market. I do remember one time when Lee wanted to cash a check, but it was $33.

Mr. Rankin. Is that the only time that you recall he tried to cash a check?

Mrs. Oswald. Yes.

Are you speaking of a store in Dallas or in Irving?

Mr. Rankin. It is in Irving.

Mrs. Oswald. Then I understand it. Because in Dallas I could not have been with him.

The Chairman. The hour of adjournment has arrived. So we will adjourn now until tomorrow morning at 10 o'clock.

(Whereupon, at 4:30 p.m., the President's Commission adjourned.)

Wednesday, February 5, 1964

TESTIMONY OF MRS. LEE HARVEY OSWALD RESUMED

The President's Commission met at 10 a.m., on February 5, 1964, at 200 Maryland Avenue NE., Washington, D.C.

Present were Chief Justice Earl Warren, Chairman; Senator Richard B. Russell, Senator John Sherman Cooper, Representative Hale Boggs, Representative Gerald R. Ford, Allen W. Dulles, members.

Also present were J. Lee Rankin, general counsel; Norman Redlich, assistant counsel; Leon I. Gopadze and William D. Krimer, interpreters; John M. Thorne, attorney for Mrs. Lee Harvey Oswald; and Ruben Efron.

The Chairman. The Commission will be in order. We will continue with the examination. Mr. Rankin, you may proceed.

Mr. Rankin. Mrs. Oswald, have you become familiar with the English language to some extent?

Mrs. Oswald. I have never studied it, but simple language I do understand.

Mr. Rankin. We had reports that you made some study at the Southern Methodist University. Is there anything to that?

Mrs. Oswald. No.

Mr. Rankin. How about Mr. Gregory? Did you study English with him?

Mrs. Oswald. No.

Mr. Rankin. Did you have any formal aid or teaching of English by anyone?

Mrs. Oswald. I had no formal instructions in it, but a Russian acquaintance, Mr. Bouhe, wrote down some Russian phrases, and I would try to translate them into English.

Mr. Rankin. Now, since you have been living with the Martins, I assume you haven't had any Russian friends to try to translate English for you, is that right?

Mrs. Oswald. If you do not count Mr. Gopadze and the FBI interpreter, I have not been in contact with any Russians.

Mr. Rankin. And there were considerable periods during the time you have been living with the Martins when neither Mr. Gopadze or the FBI agent or translator were present, is that right?

Mrs. Oswald. Yes.

Mr. Rankin. So have you been able to learn a little more English while you have been with the Martins than you had before, because of that experience?

Mrs. Oswald. Only a little, I think.

At least it is very useful for me to live with an American family who do not speak Russian.

Mr. Rankin. That has helped you to learn some English, more than when you were living with Mrs. Paine, who could speak Russian to you, I take it.

Mrs. Oswald. Of course.

Mr. Rankin. Do you know any French?

Mrs. Oswald. No. Other than Russian, I don't know any other language.

Mr. Rankin. Now, when you were with the Martins the Secret Service people were there, too, were they not?

Mrs. Oswald. Yes, they helped me a great deal.

Mr. Rankin. Did you object to the Secret Service people being there?

Mrs. Oswald. No.

Mr. Rankin. Did they treat you properly?

Mrs. Oswald. Excellently—very well.

Mr. Rankin. Did you object to their being around and looking out for you as they did?

Mrs. Oswald. No.

Mr. Rankin. How did the Martins treat you during the time you have been with them?

Mrs. Oswald. Better than I—could have been expected.

Mr. Rankin. Have you been pleased with the way they have treated you?

Mrs. Oswald. I am very pleased and I am very grateful to them.

Mr. Rankin. Now, Mr. Thorne is your attorney. I understand that he told the Civil Liberties Union people of Dallas it was all right for the Secret Service60 people to be there with you and that you liked that arrangement and did not want to be interfered with. Was that satisfactory to you?

Mrs. Oswald. Yes, that is correct.

Mr. Rankin. Was he speaking for you when he said that?

Mrs. Oswald. Yes, because I received a letter from Mr. Olds, a leader of that union. In that letter he said that he sympathizes with my situation, that he supposed that the Secret Service treated me very badly and stopped me from doing something.

I answered him in a letter written in Russian which was later translated into English that all of this was not the truth.

Mr. Rankin. Did you feel any restraint or that you were being forced to do anything there while you were at the Martins that was not satisfactory to you?

Mrs. Oswald. No, I was not forced to do anything that I did not want to.

Mr. Rankin. Anybody that tried to see you that you wanted to see during that time or from that time up to the present—I withdraw that.

Was anyone who you wished to see or wanted to see you that you were willing to see kept from seeing you at that time or up to the present?

Mrs. Oswald. Generally some people wanted to talk to me but they couldn't do so simply because I did not want to.

Mr. Rankin. And was that always the case, whenever you didn't talk to someone during that period of time?

Mrs. Oswald. Yes.

Everything depended only on me.

Mr. Rankin. And whenever you did want to talk to someone or see someone, you were always able to do that, were you?

Mrs. Oswald. Yes, I did meet with Katya Ford, my former Russian friend.

Mr. Rankin. And you were always able to meet with anyone that you wanted to, is that right?
Mrs. Oswald. Yes.
Mr. Rankin. Now, it has been claimed that Mrs. Ruth Paine tried to see you at various times and was unable to do so. Can you tell us about that?
Mrs. Oswald. She is trying very hard to come to see me, but I have no desire to meet with her. I think that she is trying to do that for herself, rather than for me.
Mr. Rankin. And whenever you have refused to see her when she tries to see you, that is because you didn't want to see her yourself, is that right?
Mrs. Oswald. Yes.
Mr. Rankin. What about the newspaper and television and radio people? Have some of those tried to see you while you were at the Martins?
Mrs. Oswald. Yes, they have tried.
Mr. Rankin. And have you done anything about their efforts to see you?
Mrs. Oswald. I never wanted to be popular in such a bad sense in which I am now, and therefore I didn't want to see them. But I did have a television interview in which I said that I am relatively satisfied with my situation, that I am not too worried and I thanked people for their attention towards me.
Mr. Rankin. Will you describe to us your relationship with your mother-in-law now?
Mrs. Oswald. After all of this happened I met with her at the police station. I was, of course, very sorry for her as Lee's mother. I was always sorry for her because Lee did not want to live with her.
I understood her motherly concern. But in view of the fact of everything that happened later, her appearances in the radio, in the press, I do not think that she is a very sound thinking woman, and I think that part of the guilt is hers. I do not accuse her, but I think that part of the guilt in connection with what happened with Lee lies with her because he did not perhaps receive the education he should have during his childhood, and he did not have any correct leadership on her part, guidance. If she were in contact with my children now, I do not want her to cripple them.
Mr. Rankin. Has she tried to see you since the assassination?
Mrs. Oswald. Yes, all the time.
Mr. Rankin. And have you seen her since that time?
Mrs. Oswald. Accidentally we met at the cemetery on a Sunday when I visited61 there, but I didn't want to meet with her, and I left. She didn't understand that I didn't want to meet with her and she accused the Secret Service personnel of preventing her from seeing me.
Mr. Rankin. Except for the time at the jail and at the cemetery, have you seen her since the assassination?
Mrs. Oswald. No.
Mr. Rankin. At the time you did see your mother-in-law, did you observe any difference in her attitude towards you?
Mrs. Oswald. Yes, of course.
Mr. Rankin. Will you describe that difference that you observed?
Mrs. Oswald. At first I said that I didn't see her any more. But after Lee was in jail I lived with her for some time at that inn.
Mr. Rankin. The Six Flags?
Mrs. Oswald. The Six Flags. And inasmuch as I lived with her and met with her every day I could see—I was able to see the change. At least if her relationship with me was good, it was not sincere. I think that she does not like me. I don't think that she simply is able to like me.
There were some violent scenes, she didn't want to listen to anyone, there were hysterics. Everyone was guilty of everything and no one understood her.
Perhaps my opinion is wrong, but at least I do not want to live with her and to listen to scandals every day.

Mr. Rankin. Did she say anything to indicate that she blamed you in connection with the assassination?

Mrs. Oswald. No, she did not accuse me of anything.

Mr. Rankin. In your presence, at any time, did she accuse Ruth Paine of being involved in causing the assassination or being directly involved?

Mrs. Oswald. No, she never accused Ruth Paine. She simply did not like her.

Mr. Rankin. Did she tell you why she didn't like Ruth Paine?

Mrs. Oswald. She told me but I didn't understand it because it was in English. She expresses more by rather stormy mimicry, thinking that that would get across and I would understand.

Mr. Rankin. You said that you didn't want to see Ruth Paine because you thought she wanted to see you for her own interests. Will you tell us what you meant by that?

Mrs. Oswald. I think that she wants to see me in her own selfish interests. She likes to be well known, popular, and I think that anything that I should write her, for example, would wind up in the press.

The reason that I think so is that the first time that we were in jail to see Lee, she was with me and with her children, and she was trying to get in front of the cameras, and to push her children and instructed her children to look this way and look that way. And the first photographs that appeared were of me with her children.

Mr. Rankin. Do you recall that in the note your husband left about the Walker incident, that there was a reference to the Red Cross, and that you might get help there? Did you ever obtain any help from the Red Cross before that date?

Mrs. Oswald. No, never.

Mr. Rankin. Do you know any reason why your husband put that in the note?

Mrs. Oswald. Well, because the Red Cross is an organization in all countries which helps people who need help, and in case I needed help, since I have no relatives here, I would be able to obtain it from this organization.

Mr. Rankin. Do you know whether or not your husband received any help from the Red Cross in money payments while he was in Russia?

Mrs. Oswald. No, I don't.

Mr. Rankin. In that note you remember that there was a reference to an embassy—it didn't say which embassy. Do you know what embassy your husband was referring to?

Mrs. Oswald. He had in mind the Soviet Embassy.

Mr. Rankin. You told about the incident of De Mohrenschildt coming to the house and saying something about how your husband happened to miss, and your husband looked at you and looked at him, and seemed to think that you might have told. You have described that.

62 Now, did you have any cause to believe at that time that De Mohrenschildt knew anything about the Walker incident?

Mrs. Oswald. De Mohrenschildt didn't know anything about it. Simply he thought that this was something that Lee was likely to do. He simply made a joke and the joke happened to hit the target.

Mr. Rankin. Do you conclude that from what you knew about the situation or from something that De Mohrenschildt said at some time?

Mrs. Oswald. No, I know this, myself. I know that Lee could not have told him. And, otherwise, how would he have known?

Mr. Rankin. From your knowledge, were they close enough so that your husband would have made De Mohrenschildt a confidant about anything like that?

Mrs. Oswald. No matter how close Lee might be to anyone, he would not have confided such things.

Mr. Rankin. Do you recall the money that your husband borrowed from the Embassy in Moscow to come to this country? Do you know where he got the money to repay that amount?

Mrs. Oswald. He worked and we paid out the debt. For six or seven months we were paying off this debt.

Mr. Rankin. Some of the payments were rather large during that period. Do you remember that?

Mrs. Oswald. Yes. And no one will believe it—it may appear strange. But we lived very modestly. Perhaps for you it is hard to imagine how we existed.

Mr. Rankin. Did you handle the finances——

Mrs. Oswald. Of course we were economizing.

No, Lee always handled the money, but I bought groceries. He gave me money and I bought groceries, or more correctly, together.

Mr. Rankin. You would usually go to the grocery store together to buy what you needed?

Mrs. Oswald. Yes.

Mr. Rankin. And then did he give you any funds separately from that, for you to spend alone?

Mrs. Oswald. Yes, he would give it to me, but I would not take it.

Mr. Rankin. How much were those amounts?

Mrs. Oswald. Excuse me, I want to add something.

You asked me yesterday to make a list of how much we spent during a month—I forgot. Excuse me—I will do it today.

For example, when we paid $60 to $65 rent per month, we would spend only about $15 per week for groceries. As you see, I didn't die and I am not sick.

Mr. Rankin. Did you buy clothing for yourself?

Mrs. Oswald. Not everything. At first some of our Russian friends would occasionally give us some clothes. But Lee would also buy clothes for me. But in America this is no problem.

Mr. Rankin. What do you mean by that?

Mrs. Oswald. In my opinion life is not very expensive here. Everyone buys according to his financial status, and no one walks around undressed. You can buy for $20 and at a sale you might buy for $2, clothes for an entire season.

Mr. Rankin. What about clothing for your child? Did you handle the buying of that?

Mrs. Oswald. Yes.

Mr. Rankin. Returning to the——

Mrs. Oswald. Excuse me. Some of the things for children were given to us by friends who had children. But I didn't like them and I bought some.

Mr. Rankin. Returning to the date of November 11, 1963, did you recall that that was a holiday?

Mrs. Oswald. November 11?

Mr. Rankin. Yes.

Mrs. Oswald. I don't remember that it was a holiday. We did not celebrate it. But something, I remember, was closed. Perhaps there were elections.

Mr. Rankin. That is Veterans Day in this country, and it was a Monday—refreshing your memory in that regard.

Do you recall whether or not your husband went to work that day?

Mrs. Oswald. No. I remember that he remained at the Paine's.

63 Mr. Rankin. Can you tell us what he did during that day?

Mrs. Oswald. As always, he played with June and he helped me a little with preparation of lunch, and he sat around, watched television.

Mr. Rankin. Was he doing any reading at that time?

Mrs. Oswald. He didn't read. It seems to me that on that day he was typing. I don't know.

Mr. Rankin. And you don't know what he was typing?

Mrs. Oswald. It seems to me it was the envelope——

Mr. Rankin. Which you have identified?

Mrs. Oswald. You remember you had a letter which mentioned Mexico and Kostin, it was that envelope.

Mr. Rankin. Is this Exhibit 16 that you are referring to?

Mrs. Oswald. Yes. You see the date is the 12th. You see, I can't remember a specific date, but some event I can connect with it brings it back.

Mr. Rankin. Do you remember whether your husband returned from Dallas to Irving at any time during that week?

Mrs. Oswald. It seems he came on Saturday or Friday for the weekend.

Perhaps he didn't come. I am mixed up as to which weekends he did and didn't come.

Mr. Rankin. We have a statement from a Mr. Hutchison of the supermarket that I referred to yesterday that you and your husband were in his supermarket on November 13. Do you recall anything like that?

Mrs. Oswald. If the 12th was a Monday and the 13th a Tuesday, Lee was at work. He couldn't have been there.

Mr. Rankin. In one of your statements that you have given the FBI and the Secret Service you indicated that this particular weekend your husband stayed in Dallas—that is the 15th through the 17th of November. Does that refresh your memory?

Mrs. Oswald. Yes—the 15th to the 17th he remained in Dallas. That is, he didn't come that weekend.

But on the 13th he was not in Irving.

Mr. Rankin. That would be the weekend before the assassination, to refresh your memory again.

Mrs. Oswald. You see, this is why I was not surprised that he didn't come—that he came, rather, he had not come on Friday and Saturday, and on Sunday I called him over the telephone and this is when he had a quarrel over the fictitious name.

By the way, he didn't come because I told him not to come. He had wanted to come, he had telephoned.

Mr. Rankin. What did you tell him about not coming?

Mrs. Oswald. That he shouldn't come every week, that perhaps it is not convenient for Ruth that the whole family be there, live there.

Mr. Rankin. Did he say anything about that?

Mrs. Oswald. He said, "As you wish. If you don't want me to come, I won't."

Mr. Rankin. Were you quite angry with him about the use of the fictitious name?

Mrs. Oswald. Yes. And when he called me over the phone a second time I hung up and would not talk to him.

Mr. Rankin. Did you tell him why you were so angry?

Mrs. Oswald. Yes, of course.

Mr. Rankin. What did you say?

Mrs. Oswald. I said, "After all, when will all your foolishness come to an end? All of these comedies. First one thing then another. And now this fictitious name."

I didn't understand why. After all, it was nothing terrible if people were to find out that he had been in Russia.

Mr. Rankin. What did he say when you said that?

Mrs. Oswald. That I didn't understand anything.

Mr. Rankin. Do you remember an incident when he said you were a Czechoslovakian rather than a Russian?

Mrs. Oswald. Yes. We lived on Elsbeth Street, and he had told the landlady that I was from Czechoslovakia. But I didn't know about it, and when the64 landlady asked me, I told her I was from Russia. I told Lee about it that evening, and he scolded me for having said that.

Mr. Rankin. What did you say to him then?

Mrs. Oswald. That the landlady was very nice and she was very good to me and she was even pleased with the fact that I was from Russia.

Mr. Rankin. Did you object to your husband saying that you were from some country other than Russia?
Mrs. Oswald. Of course.
Mr. Rankin. What did you say to him about that?
Mrs. Oswald. I am not ashamed of the fact that I am from Russia. I can even be proud of the fact that I am Russian. And there is no need for me to hide it. Every person should be proud of his nationality and not be afraid or ashamed of it.
Mr. Rankin. What did he say in response to that?
Mrs. Oswald. Nothing.
Mr. Rankin. When he gave the fictitious name, did he use the name Hidell?
Mrs. Oswald. Where?
Mr. Rankin. When you called him that time.
Mrs. Oswald. Where?
Mr. Rankin. On the weekend, when you called him, you said there was a fictitious name given.
Mrs. Oswald. I don't know what name he had given. He said that he was under a fictitious name, but he didn't tell me which.
Mr. Rankin. Have you ever heard that he used the fictitious name Hidell?
Mrs. Oswald. Yes.
Mr. Rankin. When did you first learn that he used such a name?
Mrs. Oswald. In New Orleans.
Mr. Rankin. How did you learn that?
Mrs. Oswald. When he was interviewed by some anti-Cubans, he used this name and spoke of an organization. I knew there was no such organization. And I know that Hidell is merely an altered Fidel, and I laughed at such foolishness. My imagination didn't work that way.
Mr. Rankin. Did you say anything to him about it at that time?
Mrs. Oswald. I said that it wasn't a nice thing to do and some day it would be discovered anyhow.
Mr. Rankin. Now, the weekend of November 15th to 17th, which was the weekend before the assassination, do you know what your husband did or how he spent that weekend while he was in Dallas?
Mrs. Oswald. No, I don't.
Mr. Rankin. Do you know whether he took the rifle before he went into Dallas, that trip, for that weekend?
Mrs. Oswald. I don't know. I think that he took the rifle on Thursday when he came the next time, but I didn't see him take it. I assume that. I cannot know it.
Mr. Rankin. Except for the time in New Orleans that you described, and the time you called to Dallas to ask for your husband, do you know of any other time your husband was using an assumed name?
Mrs. Oswald. No, no more.
Mr. Rankin. Did you think he was using that assumed name in connection with this Fair Play for Cuba activity or something else?
Mrs. Oswald. The name Hidell, which you pronounced Hidell, was in connection with his activity with the non-existing organization.
Mr. Rankin. Did you and your husband live under the name Hidell in New Orleans?
Mrs. Oswald. No.
Mr. Rankin. You were never identified as the Hidells, as far as you knew, while you were there?
Mrs. Oswald. No. No one knew that Lee was Hidell.
Mr. Rankin. How did you discover it, then?
Mrs. Oswald. I already said that when I listened to the radio, they spoke of that name, and I asked him who, and he said that it was he.
Mr. Rankin. Was that after the arrest?

65 Mrs. Oswald. I don't remember when the interview took place, before the arrest or after.

Mr. Rankin. But it was in regard to some interview for radio transmission, and he had identified himself as Hidell, rather than Oswald, is that right?

Mrs. Oswald. No—he represented himself as Oswald, but he said that the organization which he supposedly represents is headed by Hidell.

Mr. Rankin. He was using the name Hidell, then, to have a fictitious president or head of the organization which really was he himself, is that right?

Mrs. Oswald. Yes.

Mr. Rankin. You have told us about his practicing with the rifle, the telescopic lens, on the back porch at New Orleans, and also his using the bolt action that you heard from time to time.

Will you describe that a little more fully to us, as best you remember?

Mrs. Oswald. I cannot describe that in greater detail. I can only say that Lee would sit there with the rifle and open and close the bolt and clean it. No, he didn't clean it at that time.

Yes—twice he did clean it.

Mr. Rankin. And did he seem to be practicing with the telescopic lens, too, and sighting the gun on different objects?

Mrs. Oswald. I don't know. The rifle was always with this. I don't know exactly how he practiced, because I was in the house, I was busy. I just knew that he sits there with his rifle. I was not interested in it.

Mr. Rankin. Was this during the light of the day or during the darkness?

Mrs. Oswald. During darkness.

Mr. Rankin. Was it so dark that neighbors could not see him on the porch there with the gun?

Mrs. Oswald. Yes.

Mr. Rankin. Now, during the week of the assassination, did your husband call you at all by telephone?

Mrs. Oswald. He telephoned me on Monday, after I had called him on Sunday, and he was not there.

Or, rather, he was there, but he wasn't called to the phone because he was known by another name.

On Monday he called several times, but after I hung up on him and didn't want to talk to him he did not call again. He then arrived on Thursday.

Mr. Rankin. Did he tell you he was coming Thursday?

Mrs. Oswald. No.

Mr. Rankin. Did you learn that he was using the assumed name of Lee as his last name?

Mrs. Oswald. I know it now, but I did not ever know it before.

Mr. Rankin. Thursday was the 21st. Do you recall that?

Mrs. Oswald. Yes.

Mr. Rankin. And the assassination was on the 22d.

Mrs. Oswald. This is very hard to forget.

Mr. Rankin. Did your husband give any reason for coming home on Thursday?

Mrs. Oswald. He said that he was lonely because he hadn't come the preceding weekend, and he wanted to make his peace with me.

Mr. Rankin. Did you say anything to him then?

Mrs. Oswald. He tried to talk to me but I would not answer him, and he was very upset.

Mr. Rankin. Were you upset with him?

Mrs. Oswald. I was angry, of course. He was not angry—he was upset. I was angry. He tried very hard to please me. He spent quite a bit of time putting away diapers and played with the children on the street.

Mr. Rankin. How did you indicate to him that you were angry with him?
Mrs. Oswald. By not talking to him.
Mr. Rankin. And how did he show that he was upset?
Mrs. Oswald. He was upset over the fact that I would not answer him. He tried to start a conversation with me several times, but I would not answer. And he said that he didn't want me to be angry at him because this upsets him.

On that day, he suggested that we rent an apartment in Dallas. He said that66 he was tired of living alone and perhaps the reason for my being so angry was the fact that we were not living together. That if I want to he would rent an apartment in Dallas tomorrow—that he didn't want me to remain with Ruth any longer, but wanted me to live with him in Dallas.

He repeated this not once but several times, but I refused. And he said that once again I was preferring my friends to him, and that I didn't need him.

Mr. Rankin. What did you say to that?
Mrs. Oswald. I said it would be better if I remained with Ruth until the holidays, he would come, and we would all meet together. That this was better because while he was living alone and I stayed with Ruth, we were spending less money. And I told him to buy me a washing machine, because two children it became too difficult to wash by hand.
Mr. Rankin. What did he say to that?
Mrs. Oswald. He said he would buy me a washing machine.
Mr. Rankin. What did you say to that?
Mrs. Oswald. Thank you. That it would be better if he bought something for himself—that I would manage.
Mr. Rankin. Did this seem to make him more upset, when you suggested that he wait about getting an apartment for you to live in?
Mrs. Oswald. Yes. He then stopped talking and sat down and watched television and then went to bed. I went to bed later. It was about 9 o'clock when he went to sleep. I went to sleep about 11:30. But it seemed to me that he was not really asleep. But I didn't talk to him.

In the morning he got up, said goodbye, and left, and that I shouldn't get up—as always, I did not get up to prepare breakfast. This was quite usual.

And then after I fed Rachel, I took a look to see whether Lee was here, but he had already gone. This was already after the police had come. Ruth told me that in the evening she had worked in the garage and she knows that she had put out the light but that the light was on later—that the light was on in the morning. And she guessed that Lee was in the garage.

But I didn't see it.

Mr. Rankin. Did she tell you when she thought your husband had been in the garage, what time of the day?
Mrs. Oswald. She thought that it was during the evening, because the light remained on until morning.
Mr. Rankin. Why did you stay awake until 11:30? Were you still angry with him?
Mrs. Oswald. No, not for that reason, but because I had to wash dishes and be otherwise busy with the household—take a bath.
Mr. Rankin. This is a good place for a recess, Mr. Chairman.
The Chairman. All right. We can take a recess now.
We will recess now for 10 minutes.
(Brief recess.)
The Chairman. The Commission will be in order.
Mr. Rankin?
Mr. Rankin. Mrs. Oswald, why did the use of this false name by your husband make you so angry? Would you explain that a little bit?

Mrs. Oswald. It would be unpleasant and incomprehensible to any wife if her husband used a fictitious name. And then, of course, I thought that if he would see that I don't like it and that I explained to him that this is not the smart thing to do, that he would stop doing it.

Mr. Rankin. Did you feel that you were becoming more impatient with all of these things that your husband was doing, the Fair Play for Cuba and the Walker incident, and then this fictitious name business?

Mrs. Oswald. Yes, of course. I was tired of it.

Every day I was waiting for some kind of a new surprise. I couldn't wait to find out what else would he think of.

Mr. Rankin. Did you discuss that with your husband at all?

Mrs. Oswald. Yes, of course.

Mr. Rankin. What did you say about that?

Mrs. Oswald. I said that no one needed anything like that, that for no67 reason at all he was thinking that he was not like other people, that he was more important.

Mr. Rankin. And what did he say?

Mrs. Oswald. He would seem to agree, but then would continue again in two or three days.

Mr. Rankin. Did you sense that he was not intending to carry out his agreement with you to not have another Walker incident or anything like that?

Mrs. Oswald. I generally didn't think that Lee would repeat anything like that. Generally, I knew that the rifle was very tempting for him. But I didn't believe that he would repeat it. It was hard to believe.

Mr. Rankin. I wasn't clear about when Mrs. Paine thought that your husband might have been in the garage and had the light on. Can you give us any help on the time of day that she had in mind?

Mrs. Oswald. In the morning she thought about it. But she didn't attach any significance to it at that time. It was only after the police had come that this became more significant for her.

Mr. Rankin. So she thought it was in the morning after he got up from his night's rest that he might have gone to the garage, turned on the light?

Mrs. Oswald. In my opinion, she thought that it was at night, or during the evening that he had been in the garage and turned on the light. At least that is what she said to me. I don't know.

Mr. Rankin. Did she indicate whether she thought it was before he went to bed at 9 o'clock?

Mrs. Oswald. I don't know. At first it seems it wasn't nine, it was perhaps ten o'clock when Lee went to bed. And first, Ruth went to her room and then Lee went. He was there after her.

Mr. Rankin. So he might have been in the garage sometime between 9 and 10? Was that what you thought?

Mrs. Oswald. Yes. But I think that he might have even been there in the morning and turned on the light.

Mr. Rankin. On this evening when you were angry with him, had he come home with the young Mr. Frazier that day?

Mrs. Oswald. Yes.

Mr. Rankin. When was the last time that you had noticed the rifle before that day?

Mrs. Oswald. I said that I saw—for the first and last time I saw the rifle about a week after I had come to Mrs. Paine.

But, as I said, the rifle was wrapped in a blanket, and I was sure when the police had come that the rifle was still in the blanket, because it was all rolled together. And, therefore, when they took the blanket and the rifle was not in it, I was very much surprised.

Mr. Rankin. Did you ever see the rifle in a paper cover?

Mrs. Oswald. No.

Mr. Rankin. Could you describe for the Commission the place in the garage where the rifle was located?

Mrs. Oswald. When you enter the garage from the street it was in the front part, the left.

Mr. Rankin. By the left you mean left of the door?

Mrs. Oswald. It is an overhead door and the rifle was to the left, on the floor.
It was always in the same place.

Mr. Rankin. Was there anything else close to the rifle that you recall?

Mrs. Oswald. Next to it there were some—next to the rifle there were some suitcases and Ruth had some paper barrels in the garage where the kids used to play.

Mr. Rankin. The way the rifle was wrapped with a blanket, could you tell whether or not the rifle had been removed and the blanket just left there at any time?

Mrs. Oswald. It always had the appearance of having something inside of it. But I only looked at it really once, and I was always sure the rifle was in it. Therefore, it is very hard to determine when the rifle was taken. I only68 assumed that it was on Thursday, because Lee had arrived so unexpectedly for some reason.

Mr. Rankin. Did you believe that the reason for his coming out to see you Thursday was to make up?

Mrs. Oswald. I think there were two reasons. One was to make up with me, and the other to take the rifle. This is—this, of course, is not irreconcilable.

Mr. Rankin. But you think he came to take the rifle because of what you learned since. Is that it?

Mrs. Oswald. Yes, of course.

Mr. Rankin. Before this incident about the fictitious name, were you and your husband getting along quite well?

Mrs. Oswald. Yes.

Mr. Rankin. Did he seem to like his job at the depository?

Mrs. Oswald. Yes, because it was not dirty work.

Mr. Rankin. Had he talked about getting any other job?

Mrs. Oswald. Yes. When he went to answer some ads, he preferred to get some work connected with photography rather than this work. He liked this work relatively speaking—he liked it. But, of course, he wanted to get something better.

Mr. Rankin. Did you like the photographic work?

Mrs. Oswald. Yes. It was interesting for him. When he would see his work in the newspaper he would always point it out.

Mr. Rankin. He had a reference in his notebook to the word "Microdot". Do you know what he meant by that?

Mrs. Oswald. No.

Mr. Rankin. How did your husband get along with Mrs. Paine?

Mrs. Oswald. He was polite to her, as an acquaintance would be, but he didn't like her. He told me that he detested her—a tall and stupid woman. She is, of course, not too smart, but most people aren't.

Mr. Rankin. Did he ever say anything to indicate he thought Mrs. Paine was coming between him and you?

Mrs. Oswald. No.

Mr. Rankin. Did Mrs. Paine say anything about your husband?

Mrs. Oswald. She didn't say anything bad. I don't know what she thought. But she didn't say anything bad.
Perhaps she didn't like something about him, but she didn't tell me. She didn't want to hurt me by saying anything.

Mr. Rankin. I have understood from your testimony that you did not really care to go to Russia but your husband was the one that was urging that, and that is why you requested the visa, is that correct?

Mrs. Oswald. Yes.

Mr. Rankin. And later he talked about not only you and your child going, but also his going with you, is that right?

Mrs. Oswald. Yes.

Mr. Rankin. Do you know what caused him to make that change?

Mrs. Oswald. At one time—I don't remember whether he was working at that time or not—he was very sad and upset. He was sitting and writing something in his notebook. I asked him what he was writing and he said, "It would be better if I go with you."

Then he went into the kitchen and he sat there in the dark, and when I came in I saw that he was crying. I didn't know why. But, of course, when a man is crying it is not a very pleasant thing, and I didn't start to question him about why.

Mr. Rankin. Did he say to you that he didn't want you to leave him alone?

Mrs. Oswald. Yes.

Mr. Rankin. Did you at that time say anything to him about your all staying in this country and getting along together?

Mrs. Oswald. I told him, of course, that it would be better for us to stay here. But if it was very difficult for him and if he was always worried about tomorrow, then perhaps it would be better if we went.

Mr. Rankin. On the evening of the 21st, was anything said about curtain rods or his taking curtain rods to town the following day?

69 Mrs. Oswald. No, I didn't have any.

Mr. Rankin. He didn't say anything like that?

Mrs. Oswald. No.

Mr. Rankin. Did you discuss the weekend that was coming up?

Mrs. Oswald. He said that he probably would not come on Friday, and he didn't come—he was in jail.

Mr. Rankin. Did the quarrel that you had at that time seem to cause him to be more disturbed than usual?

Mrs. Oswald. No, not particularly. At least he didn't talk about that quarrel when he came. Usually he would remember about what happened. This time he didn't blame me for anything, didn't ask me any questions, just wanted to make up.

Mr. Rankin. I understood that when you didn't make up he was quite disturbed and you were still angry, is that right?

Mrs. Oswald. I wasn't really very angry. I, of course, wanted to make up with him. But I gave the appearance of being very angry. I was smiling inside, but I had a serious expression on my face.

Mr. Rankin. And as a result of that, did he seem to be more disturbed than usual?

Mrs. Oswald. As always, as usual. Perhaps a little more. At least when he went to bed he was very upset.

Mr. Rankin. Do you think that had anything to do with the assassination the next day?

Mrs. Oswald. Perhaps he was thinking about all of that. I don't think that he was asleep. Because, in the morning when the alarm clock went off he hadn't woken up as usual before the alarm went off, and I thought that he probably had fallen asleep very late. At least then I didn't think about it. Now I think so.

Mr. Rankin. When he said he would not be home that Friday evening, did you ask him why?

Mrs. Oswald. Yes.

Mr. Rankin. What did he say?

Mrs. Oswald. He said that since he was home on Thursday, that it wouldn't make any sense to come again on Friday, that he would come for the weekend.

Mr. Rankin. Did that cause you to think that he had any special plans to do anything?

Mrs. Oswald. No.

Mr. Rankin. Did you usually keep a wallet with money in it at the Paines?

Mrs. Oswald. Yes, in my room at Ruth Paine's there was a black wallet in a wardrobe. Whenever Lee would come he would put money in there, but I never counted it.

Mr. Rankin. On the evening of November 21st, do you know how much was in the wallet?

Mrs. Oswald. No. One detail that I remember was that he had asked me whether I had bought some shoes for myself, and I said no, that I hadn't had any time. He asked me whether June needed anything and told me to buy everything that I needed for myself and for June—and for the children.

This was rather unusual for him, that he would mention that first.

Mr. Rankin. Did he take the money from the wallet from time to time?

Mrs. Oswald. No, he generally kept the amount that he needed and put the rest in the wallet.

I know that the money that was found there, that you think this was not Lee's money. But I know for sure that this was money that he had earned. He had some money left after his trip to Mexico. Then we received an unemployment compensation check for $33. And then Lee paid only $7 or $8 for his room. And I know how he eats, very little.

Mr. Rankin. Do you know what his ordinary lunch was?

Mrs. Oswald. Peanut butter sandwich, cheese sandwich, some lettuce, and he would buy himself a hamburger, something else, a coke.

Mr. Rankin. And what about his evening meal? Do you know what he ate in the evening meal?

Mrs. Oswald. Usually meat, vegetables, fruit, dessert.

Mr. Rankin. Where would he have that?

70 Mrs. Oswald. He loved bananas. They were inexpensive.

The place where he rented a room, he could not cook there. He said that there was some sort of a cafe across the street and that he ate there.

Mr. Rankin. Did he ever tell you what he paid for his evening meal?

Mrs. Oswald. About a dollar, $1.30.

Mr. Rankin. What about his breakfast? Do you know what he had for breakfast ordinarily?

Mrs. Oswald. He never had breakfast. He just drank coffee and that is all.

Not because he was trying to economize. Simply he never liked to eat.

Mr. Rankin. Mr. Reporter, will you note the presence of Mr. Ruben Efron in the hearing room. He also knows Russian.

On November 21, the day before the assassination that you were describing, was there any discussion between you and your husband about President Kennedy's trip or proposed trip to Texas, Dallas and the Fort Worth area?

Mrs. Oswald. I asked Lee whether he knew where the President would speak, and told him that I would very much like to hear him and to see him. I asked him how this could be done.

But he said he didn't know how to do that, and didn't enlarge any further on that subject.

Mr. Rankin. Had there ever been——

Mrs. Oswald. This was also somewhat unusual—his lack of desire to talk about that subject any further.

Mr. Rankin. Can you explain that to us?

Mrs. Oswald. I think about it more now.

At that time, I didn't pay any attention.

Mr. Rankin. How did you think it was unusual? Could you explain that?

Mrs. Oswald. The fact that he didn't talk a lot about it. He merely gave me—said something as an answer, and did not have any further comments.

Mr. Rankin. Do you mean by that usually he would discuss a matter of that kind and show considerable interest?

Mrs. Oswald. Yes, of course, he would have told who would be there and where this would take place.

Mr. Rankin. Did you say anything about his showing a lack of interest at that time?

Mrs. Oswald. I merely shrugged my shoulders.

Mr. Rankin. Now, prior to that time, had there been any discussion between you concerning the proposed trip of President Kennedy to Texas?

Mrs. Oswald. No.

Mr. Rankin. While you were in New Orleans, was there any discussion or reference to President Kennedy's proposed trip to Texas?

Mrs. Oswald. No.

Mr. Rankin. Did your husband make any comments about President Kennedy on that evening, of the 21st?

Mrs. Oswald. No.

Mr. Rankin. Had your husband at any time that you can recall said anything against President Kennedy?

Mrs. Oswald. I don't remember any—ever having said that. I don't know. He never told me that.

Mr. Rankin. Did he ever say anything good about President Kennedy?

Mrs. Oswald. Usually he would translate magazine articles. They were generally good. And he did not say that this contradicted his opinion. I just remembered that he talked about Kennedy's father, who made his fortune by a not very—in a not very good manner. Disposing of such funds, of course, it was easier for his sons to obtain an education and to obtain a government position, and it was easier to make a name for themselves.

Mr. Rankin. What did he say about President Kennedy's father making his fortune?

Mrs. Oswald. He said that he had speculated in wine. I don't know to what extent that is true.

Mr. Rankin. When he read these articles to you, did he comment favorably upon President Kennedy?

71 Mrs. Oswald. I have already said that he would translate articles which were good, but he would not comment on them.

Mr. Rankin. Can you recall——

Mrs. Oswald. Excuse me. At least when I found out that Lee had shot at the President, for me this was surprising. And I didn't believe it. I didn't believe for a long time that Lee had done that. That he had wanted to kill Kennedy—because perhaps Walker was there again, perhaps he wanted to kill him.

Mr. Rankin. Why did you not believe this?

Mrs. Oswald. Because I had never heard anything bad about Kennedy from Lee. And he never had anything against him.

Mr. Rankin. But you also say that he never said anything about him.

Mrs. Oswald. He read articles which were favorable.

Mr. Rankin. Did he say he approved of those articles?

Mrs. Oswald. No, he didn't say anything. Perhaps he did reach his own conclusions reading these articles, but he didn't tell me about them.

Mr. Rankin. So apparently he didn't indicate any approval or disapproval as far as he was concerned, of President Kennedy?

Mrs. Oswald. Yes, that is correct. The President is the President. In my opinion, he never wanted to overthrow him. At least he never showed me that. He never indicated that he didn't want that President.

Mr. Rankin. Did you observe that his acts on November 21st the evening before the assassination, were anything like they were the evening before the Walker incident?

Mrs. Oswald. Absolutely nothing in common.

Mr. Rankin. Did he say anything at all that would indicate he was contemplating the assassination?

Mrs. Oswald. No.

Mr. Rankin. Did he discuss the television programs he saw that evening with you?

Mrs. Oswald. He was looking at TV by himself. I was busy in the kitchen. At one time when we were—when I was together with him they showed some sort of war films, from World War II. And he watched them with interest.

Mr. Rankin. Do you recall films that he saw called "Suddenly," and "We were Strangers" that involved assassinations?

Mrs. Oswald. I don't remember the names of these films. If you would remind me of the contents, perhaps I would know.

Mr. Rankin. Well, "Suddenly," was about the assassination of a president, and the other was about the assassination of a Cuban dictator.

Mrs. Oswald. Yes, Lee saw those films.

Mr. Rankin. Did he tell you that he had seen them?

Mrs. Oswald. I was with him when he watched them.

Mr. Rankin. Do you recall about when this was with reference to the date of the assassination?

Mrs. Oswald. It seems that this was before Rachel's birth.

Mr. Rankin. Weeks or months? Can you recall that?

Mrs. Oswald. Several days. Some five days.

Mr. Rankin. Did you discuss the films after you had seen them with your husband?

Mrs. Oswald. One film about the assassination of the president in Cuba, which I had seen together with him, he said that this was a fictitious situation, but that the content of the film was similar to the actual situation which existed in Cuba, meaning the revolution in Cuba.

Mr. Rankin. Did either of you comment on either film being like the attempt on Walker's life?

Mrs. Oswald. No. I didn't watch the other film.

Mr. Rankin. Was anything said by your husband about how easy an assassination could be committed like that?

Mrs. Oswald. No. I only know that he watched the film with interest, but I didn't like it.

Mr. Rankin. Do you recall anything else he said about either of these films?

72 Mrs. Oswald. Nothing else. He didn't tell me anything else. He talked to Ruth a few words. Perhaps she knows more.

Mr. Rankin. By Ruth, you mean Mrs. Paine?

Mrs. Oswald. They spoke in English.
Yes.

Mr. Rankin. And did Mrs. Paine tell you what he said to her at that time?

Mrs. Oswald. No.

Mr. Rankin. Do you recall your husband saying at any time after he saw the film about the Cuban assassination that this was the old-fashioned way of assassination?

Mrs. Oswald. No.

Mr. Rankin. Do you recall anything being said by your husband at any time about Governor Connally?

Mrs. Oswald. Well, while we were still in Russia, and Connally at that time was Secretary of the Navy, Lee wrote him a letter in which he asked Connally to help him obtain a good character reference because at the end of his Army service he had a good characteristic—honorable discharge—but that it had been changed after it became known he had gone to Russia.

Mr. Rankin. Had it been changed to undesirable discharge, as you understand it?

Mrs. Oswald. Yes. Then we received a letter from Connally in which he said that he had turned the matter over to the responsible authorities. That was all in Russia.

But here it seems he had written again to that organization with a request to review. But he said from time to time that these are bureaucrats, and he was dissatisfied.

Mr. Rankin. Do you know when he wrote again?

Mrs. Oswald. No.

Mr. Rankin. Was that letter written from New Orleans?

Mrs. Oswald. I don't know. I only know about the fact, but when and how, I don't know.

Mr. Rankin. Did your husband say anything to you to indicate he had a dislike for Governor Connally?

Mrs. Oswald. Here he didn't say anything.

But while we were in Russia he spoke well of him. It seems to me that Connally was running for Governor and Lee said that when he would return to the United States he would vote for him.

Mr. Rankin. That is all that you remember that he said about Governor Connally then?

Mrs. Oswald. Yes.

Mr. Rankin. With regard to the Walker incident, you said that your husband seemed disturbed for several weeks. Did you notice anything of that kind with regard to the day prior to the assassination?

Mrs. Oswald. No.

Mr. Rankin. On November 22, the day of the assassination, you said your husband got up and got his breakfast. Did you get up at all before he left?

Mrs. Oswald. No. I woke up before him, and I then went to the kitchen to see whether he had had breakfast or not—whether he had already left for work. But the coffee pot was cold and Lee was not there.

And when I met Ruth that morning, I asked her whether Lee had had coffee or not, and she said probably, perhaps he had made himself some instant coffee.

But probably he hadn't had any breakfast that morning.

Mr. Rankin. Then did he say anything to you that morning at all, or did he get up and go without speaking to you?

Mrs. Oswald. He told me to take as much money as I needed and to buy everything, and said goodbye, and that is all.

After the police had already come, I noticed that Lee had left his wedding ring.

Mr. Rankin. You didn't observe that that morning when your husband had left, did you?

Mrs. Oswald. No.

73 Mr. Rankin. Do you know approximately what time your husband left that morning?

Mrs. Oswald. I have written it there, but I have now forgotten whether it was seven or eight. But a quarter to eight—I don't know. I have now forgotten.

Mr. Rankin. What time was he due for work?

Mrs. Oswald. He was due at work at 8 or 8:30. At 7:15 he was already gone.

Mr. Rankin. Do you know whether he rode with Wesley Frazier that morning?

Mrs. Oswald. I don't know. I didn't hear him leave.

Mr. Rankin. Did you ever see a paper bag or cover for the rifle at the Paine's residence or garage?

Mrs. Oswald. No.

Mr. Rankin. Did you ever see a bag at any time?

Mrs. Oswald. No.

Mr. Rankin. Where did your husband have his lunch? Did he take a sandwich to the depository, or did he go home to his rooming house for lunch? Do you know?

Mrs. Oswald. He usually took sandwiches to lunch. But I don't know whether he would go home or not.

Mr. Rankin. Had your husband ever left his wedding ring at home that way before?

Mrs. Oswald. At one time while he was still at Fort Worth, it was inconvenient for him to work with his wedding ring on and he would remove it, but at work—he would not leave it at home. His wedding ring was rather wide, and it bothered him.

I don't know now. He would take it off at work.

Mr. Rankin. Then this is the first time during your married life that he had ever left it at home where you live?

Mrs. Oswald. Yes.

Mr. Rankin. Do you know whether your husband carried any package with him when he left the house on November 22nd?

Mrs. Oswald. I think that he had a package with his lunch. But a small package.

Mr. Rankin. Do you know whether he had any package like a rifle in some container?

Mrs. Oswald. No.

Mr. Rankin. What did you do the rest of the morning, after you got up on November 22d?

Mrs. Oswald. When I got up the television set was on, and I knew that Kennedy was coming. Ruth had gone to the doctor with her children and she left the television set on for me. And I watched television all morning, even without having dressed. She was running around in her pajamas and watching television with me.

Mr. Rankin. Before the assassination, did you ever see your husband examining the route of the parade as it was published in the paper?

Mrs. Oswald. No.

Mr. Rankin. Did you ever see him looking at a map of Dallas like he did in connection with the Walker shooting?

Mrs. Oswald. No.

Mr. Rankin. How did you learn of the shooting of President Kennedy?

Mrs. Oswald. I was watching television, and Ruth by that time was already with me, and she said someone had shot at the President.

Mr. Rankin. What did you say?

Mrs. Oswald. It was hard for me to say anything. We both turned pale. I went to my room and cried.

Mr. Rankin. Did you think immediately that your husband might have been involved?

Mrs. Oswald. No.

74 Mr. Rankin. Did Mrs. Paine say anything about the possibility of your husband being involved?

Mrs. Oswald. No, but she only said that "By the way, they fired from the building in which Lee is working."

My heart dropped. I then went to the garage to see whether the rifle was there, and I saw that the blanket was still there, and I said, "Thank God." I thought, "Can there really be such a stupid man in the world that could do something like that?" But I was already rather upset at that time—I don't know why. Perhaps my intuition.

I didn't know what I was doing.

Mr. Rankin. Did you look in the blanket to see if the rifle was there?

Mrs. Oswald. I didn't unroll the blanket. It was in its usual position, and it appeared to have something inside.

Mr. Rankin. Did you at any time open the blanket to see if the rifle was there?

Mrs. Oswald. No, only once.

Mr. Rankin. You have told us about that.

Mrs. Oswald. Yes.

Mr. Rankin. And what about Mrs. Paine? Did she look in the blanket to see if the rifle was there?

Mrs. Oswald. She didn't know about the rifle.

Perhaps she did know. But she never told me about it.

I don't know.

Mr. Rankin. When did you learn that the rifle was not in the blanket?

Mrs. Oswald. When the police arrived and asked whether my husband had a rifle, and I said "Yes."

Mr. Rankin. Then what happened?

Mrs. Oswald. They began to search the apartment. When they came to the garage and took the blanket, I thought, "Well, now, they will find it."

They opened the blanket but there was no rifle there.

Then, of course, I already knew that it was Lee. Because, before that, while I thought that the rifle was at home, I did not think that Lee had done that. I thought the police had simply come because he was always under suspicion.

Mr. Rankin. What do you mean by that—he was always under suspicion?

Mrs. Oswald. Well, the FBI would visit us.

Mr. Rankin. Did they indicate what they suspected him of?

Mrs. Oswald. They didn't tell me anything.

Mr. Rankin. What did you say to the police when they came?

Mrs. Oswald. I don't remember now. I was so upset that I don't remember what I said.

Mr. Rankin. Did you tell them about your husband leaving his wedding ring that morning?

Mrs. Oswald. No, because I didn't know it.

Mr. Rankin. Did you tell them that you had looked for the gun you thought was in the blanket?

Mrs. Oswald. No, it seems to me I didn't say that. They didn't ask me.

Mr. Rankin. Did you watch the police open the blanket to see if the rifle was there?

Mrs. Oswald. Yes.

Mr. Rankin. Did Mrs. Paine also watch them?

Mrs. Oswald. It seems to me, as far as I remember.

Mr. Rankin. When the police came, did Mrs. Paine act as an interpreter for you?

Mrs. Oswald. Yes. She told me about what they had said. But I was not being questioned so that she would interpret. She told me herself. She very much loved to talk and she welcomed the occasion.

Mr. Rankin. You mean by that that she answered questions of the police and then told you what she had said?

Mrs. Oswald. Yes.

75 Mr. Rankin. And what did she tell you that she had said to the police?

Mrs. Oswald. She talked to them in the usual manner, in English, when they were addressing her.

But when they addressed me, she was interpreting.

Mr. Rankin. Do you recall the exact time of the day that you discovered the wedding ring there at the house?

Mrs. Oswald. About 2 o'clock, I think. I don't remember. Then everything got mixed up, all time.

Mr. Rankin. Did the police spend considerable time there?

Mrs. Oswald. Yes.

Mr. Rankin. Do you remember the names of any of the officers?

Mrs. Oswald. No, I don't.

Mr. Rankin. How did they treat you?

Mrs. Oswald. Rather gruff, not very polite. They kept on following me. I wanted to change clothes because I was dressed in a manner fitting to the house. And they would not even let me go into the dressing room to change.

Mr. Rankin. What did you say about that?

Mrs. Oswald. Well, what could I tell them?

I asked them, but they didn't want to. They were rather rough. They kept on saying, hurry up.

Mr. Rankin. Did they want you to go with them?

Mrs. Oswald. Yes.

Mr. Rankin. Did you leave the house with them right soon after they came?

Mrs. Oswald. About an hour, I think.

Mr. Rankin. And what were they doing during that hour?

Mrs. Oswald. They searched the entire house.

Mr. Rankin. Did they take anything with them?

Mrs. Oswald. Yes—everything, even some tapes—Ruth's tapes from a tape recorder, her things. I don't know what.

Mr. Rankin. Did they take many of your belongings?

Mrs. Oswald. I didn't watch at that time. After all, it is not my business. If they need it, let them take it.

Mr. Rankin. Did they give you an inventory of what they took?

Mrs. Oswald. No.

Mr. Rankin. You have never received an inventory?

Mrs. Oswald. No.

Mr. Rankin. Do you now know what they took?

Mrs. Oswald. No. I know that I am missing my documents, that I am missing Lee's documents, Lee's wedding ring.

Mr. Rankin. What about clothing?

Mrs. Oswald. Robert had some of Lee's clothing. I don't know what was left of Lee's things, but I hope they will return it. No one needs it.

Mr. Rankin. What documents do you refer to that you are missing?

Mrs. Oswald. My foreign passport, my immigration card, my birth certificate, my wedding certificate—marriage certificate, June's and Rachel's birth certificates. Then various letters, my letters from friends. Perhaps something that has some bearing—photographs, whatever has some reference—whatever refers to the business at hand, let it remain.

Then my diploma. I don't remember everything now.

Mr. Rankin. What documents of your husband's do you recall that they took?

Mrs. Oswald. I didn't see what they took. At least at the present time I have none of Lee's documents.

Mr. Rankin. The documents of his that you refer to that you don't have are similar to your own that you described?

Mrs. Oswald. Yes. He also had a passport, several work books, labor cards. I don't know what men here—what sort of documents men here carry.

Mr. Rankin. Mr. Chairman, it is now 12:30.

The Chairman. I think we will recess now for lunch.

(Whereupon, at 12:30 p.m., the Commission recessed.)

Afternoon Session
TESTIMONY OF MRS. LEE HARVEY OSWALD RESUMED

The President's Commission reconvened at 2 p.m.

The Chairman. The Commission will be in order. Mr. Rankin, you may continue.

Mr. Rankin. Mrs. Oswald, we will hand you Exhibit 19, which purports to be an envelope from the Soviet Embassy at Washington, dated November 4, 1963, and ask you if you recall seeing the original or a copy of that.

Mrs. Oswald. I had not seen this envelope before, but Lee had told me that a letter had been received in my name from the Soviet Embassy with congratulations on the October Revolution—on the date of the October Revolution.

Mr. Rankin. And you think that that came in that Exhibit 19, do you?

Mrs. Oswald. Yes, because the date coincides, and I didn't get any other letters.

Mr. Rankin. We offer in evidence Exhibit 19.

The Chairman. It may be in the record and given the next number.
(The document referred to was marked Commission Exhibit No. 19, and received in evidence.)
Mr. Rankin. In some newspaper accounts your mother-in-law has intimated that your husband might have been an agent for some government, and that she might have—did have information in that regard.
Do you know anything about that?
Mrs. Oswald. The first time that I hear anything about this.
Mr. Rankin. Did you ever know——
Mrs. Oswald. That is all untrue, of course.
Mr. Rankin. Did you ever know that you husband was at any time an agent of the Soviet Union?
Mrs. Oswald. No.
Mr. Rankin. Did you ever know that your husband was an agent of the Cuban government at any time?
Mrs. Oswald. No.
Mr. Rankin. Did you ever know that your husband was an agent of any agency of the United States Government?
Mrs. Oswald. No.
Mr. Rankin. Did you ever know that your husband was an agent of any government?
Mrs. Oswald. No.
Mr. Rankin. Do you have any idea of the motive which induced your husband to kill the President?
Mrs. Oswald. From everything that I know about my husband, and of the events that transpired, I can conclude that he wanted in any way, whether good or bad, to do something that would make him outstanding, that he would be known in history.
Mr. Rankin. And is it then your belief that he assassinated the President, for this purpose?
Mrs. Oswald. That is my opinion. I don't know how true that is.
Mr. Rankin. And what about his shooting at General Walker? Do you think he had the same motive or purpose in doing that?
Mrs. Oswald. I think that, yes.
Mr. Rankin. After the assassination, were you coerced or abused in any way by the police or anyone else in connection with the inquiry about the assassination?
Mrs. Oswald. No.
Mr. Rankin. Did you see or speak to your husband on November 22d, following his arrest?
Mrs. Oswald. On the 22d I did not see him.
On the 23d I met with him.
Mr. Rankin. And when you met with him on the 23d, was it at your request or his?
77 Mrs. Oswald. I don't know whether he requested it, but I know that I wanted to see him.
Mr. Rankin. Did you request the right to see your husband on the 22d, after his arrest?
Mrs. Oswald. Yes.
Mr. Rankin. And what answer were you given at that time?
Mrs. Oswald. I was not permitted to.
Mr. Rankin. Who gave you that answer?
Mrs. Oswald. I don't know. The police.
Mr. Rankin. You don't know what officer of the police?
Mrs. Oswald. No.
Mr. Rankin. Where did you spend the evening on the night of the assassination?

Mrs. Oswald. On the day of the assassination, on the 22d, after returning from questioning by the police, I spent the night with Mrs. Paine, together with Lee's mother.

Mr. Rankin. Did you receive any threats from anyone at this time?

Mrs. Oswald. No.

Mr. Rankin. Did any law enforcement agency offer you protection at that time?

Mrs. Oswald. No.

Mr. Rankin. When you saw your husband on November 23d, the day after the assassination, did you have a conversation with him?

Mrs. Oswald. Yes.

Mr. Rankin. And where did this occur?

Mrs. Oswald. In the police department.

Mr. Rankin. Were just the two of you together at that time?

Mrs. Oswald. No, the mother was there together with me.

Mr. Rankin. At that time what did you say to him and what did he say to you?

Mrs. Oswald. You probably know better than I do what I told him.

Mr. Rankin. Well, I need your best recollection, if you can give it to us, Mrs. Oswald.

Mrs. Oswald. Of course he tried to console me that I should not worry, that everything would turn out well. He asked about how the children were. He spoke of some friends who supposedly would help him. I don't know who he had in mind. That he had written to someone in New York before that. I was so upset that of course I didn't understand anything of that. It was simply talk.

Mr. Rankin. Did you say anything to him then?

Mrs. Oswald. I told him that the police had been there and that a search had been conducted, that they had asked me whether we had a rifle, and I had answered yes.

And he said that if there would be a trial, and that if I am questioned it would be my right to answer or to refuse to answer.

Mr. Gopadze. She asked me if she talked about that thing, the first evening when I talked to her with the FBI agents, she asked me if she didn't have to tell me if she didn't want to. And warning her of her constitutional rights, telling her she didn't have to tell me anything she didn't want to—at that time, she told me she knew about that, that she didn't have to tell me if she didn't want to.

Mrs. Oswald. And he then asked me, "Who told you you had that right?" And then I understood that he knew about it.

Mr. Gopadze. At that time I did not know.

Mrs. Oswald. I thought you had been told about it because the conversation had certainly been written down. I am sure that while I was talking to Lee—after all, this was not some sort of a trial of a theft, but a rather important matter, and I am sure that everything was recorded.

Mr. Rankin. Let me see if I can clarify what you were saying.

As I understand it, Mr. Gopadze had talked to you with the FBI agents after the assassination, and they had cautioned you that you didn't have to talk, in accordance with your constitutional rights, is that correct?

Mrs. Oswald. Yes, that is right.

78 Mr. Rankin. And you told Mr. Gopadze you already knew that?

Mrs. Oswald. I don't remember what I told him.

Mr. Gopadze. Mrs. Oswald, on her own accord, asked me, or told me that she didn't have to tell us anything she didn't want to.

I said, "That is right."

Mrs. Oswald. I disliked him immediately, because he introduced himself as being from the FBI. I was at that time very angry at the FBI because I thought perhaps Lee is not guilty, and they have merely tricked him.

Mr. Gopadze. Mr. Rankin, may I, for the benefit of the Commission—I would like to mention that I didn't represent myself as being an FBI agent. I just said that I was a government agent, with the FBI. And I introduced both agents to Mrs. Oswald.

Mr. Rankin. And, Mrs. Oswald, you thought he was connected with the FBI in some way, did you?

Mrs. Oswald. He had come with them, and I decided he must have been.

Mr. Rankin. And your ill feeling towards the FBI was——

Mrs. Oswald. He did not tell me that he was with the FBI, but he was with them.

Mr. Rankin. Your ill feeling towards the FBI was due to the fact that you thought they were trying to obtain evidence to show your husband was guilty in regard to the assassination?

Mrs. Oswald. Yes.

Mr. Rankin. But you have said since the assassination that you didn't want to believe it, but you had to believe that your husband had killed President Kennedy, is that right?

Mrs. Oswald. Yes. There were some facts, but not too many, and I didn't know too much about it at that time yet. After all, there are in life some accidental concurrences of circumstances. And it is very difficult to believe in that.

Mr. Rankin. But from what you have learned since that time, you arrived at this conclusion, did you, that your husband had killed the President?

Mrs. Oswald. Yes. Unfortunately, yes.

Mr. Rankin. And you related those facts that you learned to what you already knew about your life with him and what you knew he had done and appeared to be doing in order to come to that conclusion?

Mrs. Oswald. Yes.

Mr. Rankin. When you saw your husband on November 23d, at the police station, did you ask him if he had killed President Kennedy?

Mrs. Oswald. No.

Mr. Rankin. Did you ask him at that time if he had killed Officer Tippit?

Mrs. Oswald. No. I said, "I don't believe that you did that, and everything will turn out well."

After all, I couldn't accuse him—after all, he was my husband.

Mr. Rankin. And what did he say to that?

Mrs. Oswald. He said that I should not worry, that everything would turn out well. But I could see by his eyes that he was guilty. Rather, he tried to appear to be brave. However, by his eyes I could tell that he was afraid.

This was just a feeling. It is hard to describe.

Mr. Rankin. Would you help us a little bit by telling us what you saw in his eyes that caused you to think that?

Mrs. Oswald. He said goodbye to me with his eyes. I knew that. He said that everything would turn out well, but he did not believe it himself.

Mr. Rankin. How could you tell that?

Mrs. Oswald. I saw it in his eyes.

Mr. Rankin. Did your husband ever at any time say to you that he was responsible or had anything to do with the killing of President Kennedy?

Mrs. Oswald. After Kennedy—I only saw him once, and he didn't tell me anything, and I didn't see him again.

Mr. Rankin. And did he at any time tell you that he had anything to do with the shooting of Officer Tippit?

Mrs. Oswald. No.

79 Mr. Rankin. Did you ever ask your husband why he ran away or tried to escape after the assassination?

Mrs. Oswald. I didn't ask him about that.

Mr. Rankin. On either November 22d, or Saturday, November 23d, did anyone contact you and advise you that your husband was going to be shot?

Mrs. Oswald. No.

Mr. Rankin. Where did you spend the evening of November 23d?

Mrs. Oswald. After seeing Lee, we went with some reporters of Life Magazine who had rented a room, but it turned out to be—in a hotel—but it turned out to be inconvenient because there were many people there and we went to another place. We were in a hotel in Dallas, but I don't know the name.

Mr. Rankin. Who was with you at that time?

Mrs. Oswald. Lee's mother.

Mr. Rankin. Anyone else?

Mrs. Oswald. No—June and Rachel.

Mr. Rankin. Was Robert with you at all?

Mrs. Oswald. I saw Robert in the police—at the police station, but he did not stay with us at the hotel.

Mr. Rankin. Now, the evening of November 22d, were you at Ruth Paine's house?

Mrs. Oswald. Yes.

Mr. Rankin. At that time did the reporters come there and the Life reporters, and ask you and your mother-in-law and Mrs. Paine about what had happened?

Mrs. Oswald. Yes.

Mr. Rankin. We have a report that there was quite a scene between Mrs. Paine and your mother-in-law at that time. Was there such an event?

Mrs. Oswald. I did not understand English too well, and I did not know what they were quarreling about. I know that the reporters wanted to talk to me, but his mother made a scene and went into hysterics, and said I should not talk and that she would not talk.

Mr. Rankin. Did she say why she would not talk?

Mrs. Oswald. Perhaps she said it in English. I didn't understand. She talked to the reporters.

Mr. Rankin. Did she say anything about being paid if she was going to tell any story?

Mrs. Oswald. She has a mania—only money, money, money.

Mr. Rankin. Did you understand that she was quarreling with Ruth Paine about something concerning the interview?

Mrs. Oswald. Yes. It appeared to be a quarrel, but what they quarreled about, I don't know.

Mr. Rankin. And after the quarrel, did you leave there?

Mrs. Oswald. I went to my room. But then I showed Lee's mother the photograph, where he is photographed with a rifle, and told her he had shot at Walker and it appeared he might have been shooting at the President. She said that I should hide that photograph and not show it to anyone.

On the next day I destroyed one photograph which I had. I think I had two small ones. When we were in the hotel I burned it.

Mr. Rankin. Did you say anything to her about the destruction of the photographs when she suggested that?

Mrs. Oswald. She saw it, while I was destroying them.

Mr. Rankin. After the assassination, did the police and FBI and the Secret Service ask you many questions?

Mrs. Oswald. In the police station there was a routine regular questioning, as always happens. And then after I was with the agents of the Secret Service and the FBI, they asked me many questions, of course—many questions. Sometimes the FBI agents asked me questions which had no bearing or relationship, and if I didn't want to answer they told me that if I wanted to live in this country, I would have to help in this matter, even though they were often irrelevant. That is the FBI.

Mr. Rankin. Do you know who said that to you?

80 Mrs. Oswald. Mr. Heitman and Bogoslav, who was an interpreter for the FBI.

Mr. Rankin. You understand that you do not have to tell this Commission in order to stay in this country, don't you, now?

Mrs. Oswald. Yes.

Mr. Rankin. You are not under any compulsion to tell the Commission here in order to be able to stay in the country.

Mrs. Oswald. I understand that.

Mr. Rankin. And you have come here because you want to tell us what you could about this matter, is that right?

Mrs. Oswald. This is my voluntary wish, and no one forced me to do this.

Mr. Rankin. Did these various people from the police and the Secret Service and the FBI treat you courteously when they asked you about the matters that they did, concerning the assassination and things leading up to it?

Mrs. Oswald. I have a very good opinion about the Secret Service, and the people in the police department treated me very well. But the FBI agents were somehow polite and gruff. Sometimes they would mask a gruff question in a polite form.

Mr. Rankin. Did you see anyone from the Immigration Service during this period of time?

Mrs. Oswald. Yes.

Mr. Rankin. Do you know who that was?

Mrs. Oswald. I don't remember the name. I think he is the chairman of that office. At least he was a representative of that office.

Mr. Rankin. By "that office" you mean the one at Dallas?

Mrs. Oswald. I was told that he had especially come from New York, it seems to me.

Mr. Rankin. What did he say to you?

Mrs. Oswald. That if I was not guilty of anything, if I had not committed any crime against this Government, then I had every right to live in this country. This was a type of introduction before the questioning by the FBI. He even said that it would be better for me if I were to help them.

Mr. Rankin. Did he explain to you what he meant by being better for you?

Mrs. Oswald. In the sense that I would have more rights in this country. I understood it that way.

Mr. Rankin. Did you understand that you were being threatened with deportation if you didn't answer these questions?

Mrs. Oswald. No, I did not understand it that way.

You see, it was presented in such a delicate form, but there was a clear implication that it would be better if I were to help.

Mr. Rankin. Did you——

Mrs. Oswald. This was only felt. It wasn't said in actual words.

Mr. Rankin. Did you feel that it was a threat?

Mrs. Oswald. This was not quite a threat—it was not a threat. But it was their great desire that I be in contact, in touch with the FBI. I sensed that.

Mr. Rankin. But you did not consider it to be a threat to you?

Mrs. Oswald. No.

Mr. Rankin. Did anyone indicate that it would affect your ability to work in this country if you cooperated?

Mrs. Oswald. Excuse me. No.

Mr. Rankin. Is there anything else about your treatment by law enforcement officials during this period that you would like to tell the Commission about?

Mrs. Oswald. I think that the FBI agents knew that I was afraid that after everything that had happened I could not remain to live in this country, and they somewhat exploited that for their own purposes, in a very polite form, so that you could not say anything after that. They cannot be accused of anything. They approached it in a very clever, contrived way.

Mr. Rankin. Was there anyone else of the law enforcement officials that you felt treated you in that manner?

Mrs. Oswald. No. As for the rest, I was quite content. Everyone was very attentive towards me.

81 Mr. Rankin. Where were you on the morning of November 24th when your husband was killed?

Mrs. Oswald. The night from the 23d to the 24th I spent at a hotel in Dallas, together with the mother. She wanted to make sure that the Life reporters who had taken this room would pay for it, as they had promised. But they disappeared. Then she telephoned Robert, it seems to me, and Gregory—no, Mr. Gregory. And I know that he came with Robert, and Robert paid for the room. And, after that, after we left the hotel, we met with the Secret Service agents. I wanted to see Lee, and we were supposed to go to the police station to see him.

Mr. Rankin. That was on November 24th, on Sunday?

Mrs. Oswald. Yes.

Mr. Rankin. And then what happened?

Mrs. Oswald. I don't remember whether we went to Ruth to take my things or perhaps—in general, I remember that en route, in the car, Mike Howard or Charley Kunkel said that Lee had been shot today.

At first he said that it wasn't serious—perhaps just not to frighten me. I was told that he had been taken to a hospital, and then I was told that he had been seriously wounded.

Then they had to telephone somewhere. They stopped at the house of the chief of police, Curry. From there, I telephone Ruth to tell her that I wanted to take several things which I needed with me and asked her to prepare them. And that there was a wallet with money and Lee's ring.

Soon after that—Robert was no longer with me, but Gregory was there, and the mother, and the Secret Service agents. They said that Lee had died.

After that, we went to the Motel Inn, the Six Flags Inn, where I stayed for several days—perhaps two weeks—I don't know.

Mr. Rankin. Do you recall what time of the day you heard that your husband had been shot?

Mrs. Oswald. Two o'clock in the afternoon, I think.

Mr. Rankin. And where were you at that time?

Mrs. Oswald. I was in a car.

Mr. Rankin. Just riding around, or at some particular place?

Mrs. Oswald. No, not at two o'clock—earlier. Lee was shot at 11 o'clock. It was probably close to 12 o'clock. He died at one.

Mr. Rankin. And where was the car that you were in at that time?

Mrs. Oswald. We were on the way to Chief Curry, en route from the hotel.

Mr. Rankin. What did you do after you went to the motel?

Mrs. Oswald. I left with Robert and we prepared for the funeral. Then Ruth Paine sent my things to me via the agent.

Mr. Gopadze. She would like a recess for a little while. She has a headache.

The Chairman. Yes, we will recess.

(Brief recess)

The Chairman. The Commission will be in order. Do you feel refreshed now, Mrs. Oswald, ready to proceed?

Mrs. Oswald. Yes, thank you.

The Chairman. Very well.

Mr. Rankin?

Mr. Rankin. Mrs. Oswald, I asked you if you asked your husband about his efforts to escape, why he did that. I will ask you now whether in light of what you said about his seeking notoriety in connection with the assassination, in your opinion how you explain his efforts to escape, which would presumably not give him that notoriety.

Mrs. Oswald. When he did that, he probably did it with the intention of becoming notorious. But after that, it is probably a normal reaction of a man to try and escape.

Mr. Rankin. You will recall that in the interviews, after the assassination, you first said that you thought your husband didn't do it, do you?

Mrs. Oswald. I don't remember it, but quite possibly I did say that.

You must understand that now I only speak the truth.

Mr. Rankin. Recently you said that you thought your husband did kill President Kennedy.

82 Mrs. Oswald. I now have enough facts to say that.

Mr. Rankin. Can you give us or the Commission an idea generally about when you came to this latter conclusion, that he did kill President Kennedy?

Mrs. Oswald. Perhaps a week after it all happened, perhaps a little more. The more facts came out, the more convinced I was.

Mr. Rankin. You have stated in some of your interviews that your husband would get on his knees and cry and say that he was lost. Do you recall when this happened?

Mrs. Oswald. That was in New Orleans.

Mr. Rankin. Was it more than one occasion?

Mrs. Oswald. When he said that, that was only once.

Mr. Rankin. And do you know what caused him to say that?

Mrs. Oswald. I don't know.

Mr. Rankin. You don't know whether there was some occasion or some happening that caused it?

Mrs. Oswald. No.

Mr. Rankin. Did your mother-in-law ever indicate that she had some particular evidence, either oral or documentary, that would decide this case?

Mrs. Oswald. Yes, she always said that she has a pile of papers and many acquaintances.

Mr. Rankin. Did you ever ask her to tell you what it was that would be so decisive about the case?

Mrs. Oswald. I would have liked to ask her, but I didn't speak any English. And then I didn't believe her. What documents could she have when she had not seen Lee for one year, and she didn't even know we lived in New Orleans?

I think that is just simply idle talk, that she didn't have anything.

Perhaps she does have something.

But I think that it is only she who considers that she has something that might reveal, uncover this.

Mr. Rankin. Has there been any time that you wanted to see your mother-in-law that you have been prevented from doing so?

Mrs. Oswald. Never.

I don't want to see her, I didn't want to.

Mr. Rankin. Mrs. Oswald, I am going to ask you about differences between you and your mother-in-law, not for the purpose of embarrassing you in any way, but since we are going to ask her to testify it might be helpful to the Commission to know that background.

I hope you will bear with us.

Have you had some differences with your mother-in-law?

Mrs. Oswald. I am sorry that you will devote your time to questioning her, because you will only be tired and very sick after talking to her. I am very much ashamed to have this kind of relationship to my mother-in-law. I would like to be closer to her and to be on better terms with her. But when you get to know her, you will understand why. I don't think that she can help you.

But if it is a formality, then, of course.

Mr. Rankin. Mrs. Oswald, can you describe for the Commission your differences so the Commission will be able to evaluate those differences?

Mrs. Oswald. Well, she asserts, for example, that I don't know anything, that I am being forced to say that Lee is guilty in everything, that she knows more.

This is what our differences are.

Mr. Rankin. And have you responded to her when she said those things?

Mrs. Oswald. She said this by means of newspapers and television.

I haven't seen her.

I would like to tell her that, but it is impossible to tell her that, because she would scratch my eyes out.

Mr. Rankin. Are there any other differences between you and your mother-in-law that you have not described?

Mrs. Oswald. No, there are no more.

Mr. Rankin. Do you know of any time that your husband had money in excess of what he obtained from the jobs he was working on?

Mrs. Oswald. No.

83 Mr. Rankin. He had his unemployment insurance when he was out of work. Is that right?

Mrs. Oswald. Yes.

Mr. Rankin. And then he had the earnings from his jobs, is that right?

Mrs. Oswald. Yes.

Mr. Rankin. Now, beyond those amounts, do you know of any sum of money that he had from any source?

Mrs. Oswald. No.

Mr. Rankin. Do you know whether he was ever acting as an undercover agent for the FBI.

Mrs. Oswald. No.

Mr. Rankin. Do you believe that he was at any time?

Mrs. Oswald. No.

Mr. Rankin. Do you know whether or not he was acting as an agent for the CIA at any time?

Mrs. Oswald. No.

Mr. Rankin. Do you believe that he was?

Mrs. Oswald. No.

Mr. Rankin. Did you know Jack Ruby, the man that killed your husband?

Mrs. Oswald. No.

Mr. Rankin. Before the murder of your husband by Jack Ruby, had you ever known of him?

Mrs. Oswald. No, never.

Mr. Rankin. Do you know whether your husband knew Jack Ruby before the killing?

Mrs. Oswald. He was not acquainted with him. Lee did not frequent nightclubs, as the papers said.

Mr. Rankin. How do you know that?

Mrs. Oswald. He was always with me. He doesn't like other women. He didn't drink. Why should he then go?

Mr. Rankin. Do you know any reason why Jack Ruby killed your husband?

Mrs. Oswald. About that, Jack Ruby should be questioned.

Mr. Rankin. I have to ask you, Mrs. Oswald.

Mrs. Oswald. He didn't tell me.

Mr. Rankin. And do you know any reason why he should?

Mrs. Oswald. I don't know, but it seems to me that he was a sick person at that time, perhaps. At least when I see his picture in the paper now, it is an abnormal face.

Mr. Rankin. Has your husband ever mentioned the name Jack Ruby to you?

Mrs. Oswald. No.

Mr. Rankin. He never at any time said anything about Jack Ruby that you can recall?
Mrs. Oswald. No, never. I heard that name for the first time after he killed Lee. I would like to consult with Mr. Thorne and Mr. Gopadze.
The Chairman. You may.
(Brief recess)
The Chairman. All right.
Mr. Rankin. Mrs. Oswald, would you like to add something to your testimony?
Mrs. Oswald. Yes. This is in connection with why I left the room. I will tell you why I left the room.

I consulted with my attorney, whether I should bring this up. This is not a secret. The thing is that I have written a letter, even though I have not mailed it yet, to the attorney—to the prosecuting attorney who will prosecute Jack Ruby. I wrote in that letter that even—that if Jack Ruby killed my husband, and I felt that I have a right as the widow of the man he killed to say that, that if he killed him he should be punished for it. But that in accordance with the laws here, the capital punishment, the death penalty is imposed for such a crime, and that I do not want him to be subjected to that kind of a penalty. I do not want another human life to be taken. And I don't want it to be believed because of this letter that I had been acquainted with Ruby, and that I wanted to protect him.

84 It is simply that it is pity to—I feel sorry for another human life. Because this will not return—bring back to life Kennedy or the others who were killed. But they have their laws, and, of course, I do not have the right to change them. That is only my opinion, and perhaps they will pay some attention to it.

That is all.
Mr. Rankin. Had you ever been in the Carousel Nightclub?
Mrs. Oswald. I have never been in nightclubs.
Mr. Rankin. Did you know where it was located before your husband was killed by Jack Ruby?
Mrs. Oswald. No, I don't know it now either.
Mr. Rankin. Can you tell us whether your husband was right handed or left handed?
Mrs. Oswald. No, he was right handed.

His brother writes with his left hand and so does—his brother and mother both write with their left hand.

And since I mentioned Jack Ruby, the mother and Robert want Ruby to be subjected to a death penalty. And in that we differ.
Mr. Rankin. Have they told you the reason why they wanted the death penalty imposed?
Mrs. Oswald. In their view, a killing has to be repaid by a killing.

In my opinion, it is not so.
Mr. Rankin. Is there anything more about the assassination of President Kennedy that you know that you have not told the Commission?
Mrs. Oswald. No, I don't know anything.
Mr. Rankin. Is there anything that your husband ever told you about proposing to assassinate President Kennedy that you haven't told the Commission?
Mrs. Oswald. No, I don't know that.
Mr. Rankin. Now, Mrs. Oswald, we will turn to some period in Russia, and ask you about that for a little while.

Can you tell us the time and place of your birth?
Mrs. Oswald. I was born on July 17, 1941, in Severo Dvinsk, in the Arkhangelskaya Region.
Mr. Rankin. Who were your parents?
Mrs. Oswald. Names?
Mr. Rankin. Yes, please.

Mrs. Oswald. My mother was Clogia Vasilyevna Proosakova. She was a laboratory assistant.

Mr. Rankin. And your father?

Mrs. Oswald. And I had a stepfather. I had no father. I never knew him.

Mr. Rankin. Who did you live with as a child?

Mrs. Oswald. With my stepfather, with my mother, and sometimes with my grandmother—grandmother on my mother's side.

Mr. Rankin. Did you live with your grandparents before you went back to live with your mother and your stepfather?

Mrs. Oswald. Yes, I lived with my grandmother until I was approximately five years old.

Mr. Rankin. And then you moved to live with your mother and your stepfather, did you?

Mrs. Oswald. Yes.

Mr. Rankin. And was that in Leningrad?

Mrs. Oswald. After the war, we lived in Moldavia for some time. After the war it was easier to live there, better to live there. And then we returned to Leningrad where we lived with my stepfather's mother—also with my half brother and half sister.

Mr. Rankin. What was your stepfather's business?

Mrs. Oswald. He was an electrician in a power station in Leningrad.

Mr. Rankin. Did you have brothers and sisters?

Mrs. Oswald. Yes.

Mr. Rankin. How many?

Mrs. Oswald. One brother, one sister—from my mother's second marriage.

Mr. Rankin. How old were they?

Mrs. Oswald. How old are they, or were they?

Mr. Rankin. Are they—I mean in comparison with your age. Were they three or four years older than you?

Mrs. Oswald. My brother is 5 years younger than I am. My sister is probably 9 years younger than I am. About four years between brother and sister.

Mr. Rankin. Do you know whether your stepfather was a member of the Communist Party?

Mrs. Oswald. No.

Mr. Rankin. That is, you don't know, or you know he was not?

Mrs. Oswald. No, I know that he was not a member.

Mr. Rankin. Did you live for a period with your mother alone?

Mrs. Oswald. No. After my mother's death, I continued to live with my stepfather, and later went to live in Minsk, with my uncle—my mother's brother.

Mr. Rankin. What was your stepfather's name?

Mrs. Oswald. Alexandr Ivanovich Medvedev.

Mr. Rankin. When did you leave the home of your stepfather?

Mrs. Oswald. In 1961. No—1959.

Mr. Rankin. What was your grandfather's occupation?

Mrs. Oswald. On my mother's side?

Mr. Rankin. Yes.

Mrs. Oswald. He was a ship's captain.

Mr. Rankin. Was he a member of the Communist Party?

Mrs. Oswald. No. He died shortly after the war.

Mr. Rankin. Which war?

Mrs. Oswald. Second.

Mr. Rankin. Did you get along well with your grandparents?

Mrs. Oswald. Yes, I was their favorite.

Mr. Rankin. Did you get along with your stepfather?

Mrs. Oswald. No. I was not a good child. I was too fresh with him.

Mr. Rankin. Did your mother and your stepfather move to Zguritsa?

Mrs. Oswald. That is in Moldavia, where we lived. That is after the war. It was a very good life there. They still had some kulaks, a lot of food, and we lived very well.

After the war, people lived there pretty well, but they were dekulakized subsequently.

By the way, I don't understand all of that, because these people worked with their own hands all their lives. I was very sorry when I heard that everything had been taken away from them and they had been sent somewhere to Siberia where after living in the south it would be very cold.

Mr. Rankin. Did your mother have any occupation?

Mrs. Oswald. Yes, laboratory assistant—I said that.

Mr. Rankin. Was she a member of the Communist Party?

Mrs. Oswald. No.

Mr. Rankin. Do you recall when your mother died?

Mrs. Oswald. In 1957.

Mr. Rankin. Did you receive a pension after your mother's death?

Mrs. Oswald. Yes.

Mr. Rankin. How much was it?

Mrs. Oswald. All children received pensions.

We received for it 3520 rubles, the old rubles.

Mr. Rankin. Was that called a children's pension?

Mrs. Oswald. Yes. It was paid up to majority, up to the age of 18.

Mr. Rankin. And was it paid to you directly or to your stepfather?

Mrs. Oswald. It was paid to me directly.

Mr. Rankin. Did your brother and sister get a similar pension?

Mrs. Oswald. Yes.

Mr. Rankin. Did your stepfather adopt you?

Mrs. Oswald. No, I was not adopted.

Mr. Rankin. What was your relationship with your half brother? Did you get along with him?

86 Mrs. Oswald. I loved them very much, and they loved me.

Mr. Rankin. And your half sister, too?

Mrs. Oswald. Yes. They are very good children. Not like me.

Mr. Rankin. Will you tell us what schools you went to?

Mrs. Oswald. At first I went to school in Moldavia, and later in Leningrad, in a girl's school and then after finishing school I studied in a pharmaceutical institute—pharmaceutical school, rather than institute.

Mr. Rankin. Where was the pharmaceutical school?

Mrs. Oswald. In Leningrad.

Mr. Rankin. Did you go through high school before you went to the pharmaceutical school?

Mrs. Oswald. Yes.

Mr. Rankin. Do you recall the names of any of your teachers?

Mrs. Oswald. Dmitry Rossovsky. I remember the director of the school, Nadelman Matvey Akimovich. It is hard to remember now. I have already forgotten. I have had good teachers. They treated me very well, they helped me after my mother died. Knowing my difficult nature, they approached me very pedagogically. But now I would have changed that nature.

Mr. Rankin. Were you a good student?

Mrs. Oswald. I was capable but lazy. I never spent much time studying. You know, everything came to me very easily. Sometimes my ability saved me. My language, you know—I talk a lot, and get a good grade.

Mr. Rankin. Did you work part-time while you were going to school?

Mrs. Oswald. Yes. The money which I received on the pension was not enough, and therefore I had to work as well as study.

Mr. Rankin. And what did you do in working?

Mrs. Oswald. At first I worked in a school cafeteria, school lunchroom. This was good for me, because I also got enough to eat that way.

And then I felt the work was not for me, that it was too restricted, and then I worked in a pharmacy. Then when I graduated I worked in a pharmacy as a full-fledged pharmacist—as a pharmacist's assistant.

Mr. Rankin. Before you graduated, how much were you paid for your work?

Mrs. Oswald. I think I received 36 per month—this is new rubles—at that time it was still 360 old rubles. But I could eat there three times a day. And then this was a lunchroom that was part of a large restaurant where everyone liked me and I always was treated to all sorts of tidbits and candy. I remember they had some busboys there who always saved something for me.

Mr. Rankin. Did you save any money while you were working before you graduated?

Mrs. Oswald. I don't know how to save money. I like to make presents.

Mr. Rankin. Where did you work after you graduated?

Mrs. Oswald. I was assigned to work in Leningrad, but my stepfather didn't want me to remain with him because he thought perhaps he would marry again, and, therefore, I left.

But he hasn't married up until now.

Mr. Rankin. I hand you Exhibit 20, and ask you if you know what that is.

Mrs. Oswald. This is my diploma. My goodness, what did they do with my diploma? I can't work with it. The government seal is missing. Who will give me a new diploma?

Mr. Rankin. Mrs. Oswald, I want to explain to you—the Commission hasn't done anything to your diploma. We are informed that——

Mrs. Oswald. They should have treated it a little more carefully, though.

Mr. Rankin. The process was trying to determine fingerprints. It wasn't our action.

Mrs. Oswald. There must be many fingerprints on there. All of my teachers and everybody that ever looked at it. I am sorry—it is a pity for my diploma.

Mr. Rankin. We offer in evidence Exhibit 20.

The Chairman. It may be marked.

(The document referred to was marked Commission Exhibit No. 20, and received in evidence.)

87 Mr. Rankin. Do you know why on Exhibit 20 there is no date of admission to the school?

Mrs. Oswald. There is no entrance date on it, but it does show the date of issue and the date of graduation.

Mr. Rankin. Isn't there a place for admission, though?

Mrs. Oswald. Yes, there is a place for it.

Mr. Rankin. Do you know when you were admitted to the school?

Mrs. Oswald. In 1955.

Mr. Krimer. I might mention the place here is for the year only, not for a full date.

Mr. Dulles. 1955, did you say?

Mrs. Oswald. Yes, 1955.

Mr. Rankin. In this job that you obtained after you left the school, what were your duties?

Mrs. Oswald. When I worked in the pharmacy?

Mr. Rankin. Yes.

Mrs. Oswald. I worked in a hospital pharmacy. I prepared prescriptions. After the rounds every day, the doctors prescribed prescriptions, and the nurses of each department of the hospital enter that in a book, and turn it over to the pharmacy for preparation, where we again transcribed it from the nurses' book as a prescription and prepared it.

Mr. Rankin. Were you assigned to a particular job or did you go out and get the job? How was that arranged?

Mrs. Oswald. Generally upon graduation there is an assignment. I was sent to work to a drug warehouse in Leningrad. But this work was not very interesting, because everything was in packages. It is more of a warehousing job. And, therefore, if I had wanted to change I could have changed to any pharmacy. This assignment is only performed in order to guarantee that the graduate has a job. But the graduate can go to work somewhere else.

Mr. Rankin. How long did you stay in this first job?

Mrs. Oswald. I was there for three days, which is a probationary period, intended to have the employee familiarize himself with his duties. I didn't like that work, and I went to Minsk, and worked there. I worked there in my own specialty with pleasure. But the reference which I received after I was going to the United States was not very good, because they were very dissatisfied with the fact that I was going to the United States. They could not understand how could it be that a good worker could leave.

Mr. Rankin. Did you select Minsk as a place to go and work yourself?

Mrs. Oswald. Yes.

Mr. Rankin. You were not assigned there, then?

Mrs. Oswald. No.

Mr. Rankin. Could you have selected other places that you wished to go to and work?

Mrs. Oswald. Yes, but the registration is very difficult. In Russia you cannot settle in a large city if you are not registered.

Mr. Rankin. What do you mean by that?

Mrs. Oswald. If I lived in Leningrad, I had the right to work there. But if someone would come there from a village he would not have the right to work, because he was not registered and he would not be permitted to. But to move from a larger city to a smaller one, then they may register, such as Minsk.

Mr. Rankin. By register, do you mean that if you want to go to a place like Leningrad, you had to be recorded some way in the city?

Mrs. Oswald. Yes, that is, registered in the police department.

Mr. Rankin. And if you were not registered, they would not give you a job, is that what you mean?

Mrs. Oswald. Yes.

No, you would not get a job. There are people who want to come to Leningrad. The housing problem has not been solved.

Mr. Rankin. Can you tell us how you get registered if you would like to be registered in Leningrad from some other point?

Mrs. Oswald. First you must have relatives who might have some spare living88 space for a person. Sometimes people who have money buy that. You know money does a great deal everywhere.

Mr. Rankin. And then after you have shown that you have a place to live, do they register you as a matter of course, or do you have to have something else?

Mrs. Oswald. Not always. One has to have connections, acquaintances.

Mr. Rankin. Were you registered in Leningrad before you left there?

Mrs. Oswald. Yes, of course. But if I had spent one year not living in Leningrad, and were to return, I would not be registered.

Mr. Rankin. But since you were registered there, you could have found a position in some pharmacy or pharmaceutical work there, could you?

Mrs. Oswald. Oh, yes, of course.

Mr. Rankin. Then, can you tell us how you decided to go to Minsk instead of staying in Leningrad?

Mrs. Oswald. I was very sorry to leave Leningrad, but there were family circumstances.

What can one do?

It is not very pleasant to be a sty in the eye of a stepfather.

Mr. Rankin. So it is because you liked to leave your stepfather's home that you sought some other city in which to work?

Mrs. Oswald. Yes. I had no other place to live in Leningrad, and I did not have enough money to pay for an apartment.

I received 45 and I would have had to pay 30 for an apartment.

Mr. Rankin. Could you have gotten a job in Leningrad if you stayed there that would pay you so you could have an apartment?

Mrs. Oswald. Pharmaceutical workers received comparatively little, which is quite undeserved, because they have to study so long, and it is responsible work. Teachers and doctors also receive very little.

Mr. Rankin. Did you conclude that you could not get a job that would pay you enough to live in your own apartment in Leningrad, then?

Mrs. Oswald. If I had an apartment in Leningrad. I would have had to work overtime hours in order to be able to pay for it, because the normal workday is only 6½ hours, because they consider that to be hazardous work.

Mr. Rankin. Did you have a social life while you were in Leningrad?

Mrs. Oswald. What do you mean by social life?

Mr. Rankin. Did you have friends that you went out with in the evening, pleasant times?

Mrs. Oswald. An awful lot.

Mr. Rankin. So that except for the problem of your stepfather, you enjoyed it there?

Mrs. Oswald. Oh, yes, of course.

Mr. Rankin. Did you have any vacations while you were in Leningrad?

Mrs. Oswald. Yes. After working in Minsk for one year I received a vacation and went to a rest home near Leningrad.

Mr. Rankin. How long did you stay there on vacation?

Mrs. Oswald. Three weeks. Three weeks in the rest home, and one week I spent in Leningrad with some friends.

Mr. Rankin. Do you recall the name of the rest home?

Mrs. Oswald. No.

Mr. Rankin. Did you have to ask anyone in Leningrad in order to be able to leave there to go to Minsk, or you just go to Minsk and ask the people there to register you?

Mrs. Oswald. I simply bought a ticket and went to Minsk, to my uncle.

Mr. Rankin. And were you registered there then?

Mrs. Oswald. Yes.

Mr. Rankin. What kind of pay did you get when you worked in Minsk?

Mrs. Oswald. Forty-five, as everywhere.

Mr. Rankin. Was that per week?

Mrs. Oswald. No, that is a month. That is not America.

Mr. Rankin. Is that 45 rubles?

Mrs. Oswald. Yes.

Mr. Rankin. Per month?

89 Mr. Dulles. Old rubles or new rubles?

Mr. Rankin. Is that old rubles?

Mrs. Oswald. New rubles.

Mr. Rankin. What were your hours in this work?

Mrs. Oswald. 10 a.m., to 4:30 p.m.

Mr. Rankin. When you said this same pay was paid all over, did you mean to say that you got the same amount regardless of whether you were in a big city or a small city?

Mrs. Oswald. This is the pharmacists rate everywhere. Unless you work in a specialized sort of an institution, such as a military hospital—there the pay is higher.

Mr. Rankin. What was the nature of your work?

Mrs. Oswald. Preparation of prescriptions.

Mr. Rankin. Did you supervise the preparation of the prescriptions, or did you just put them up yourself?
Mrs. Oswald. I prepared them myself.
Mr. Rankin. Did you have a supervisor?
Mrs. Oswald. I was in charge of myself. If I was working at a table, I was responsible for it.
Of course every institution is in charge of a supervisor who does not prepare medications—he is only an administrator.
Mr. Rankin. How many days of the week did you work on this job?
Mrs. Oswald. Six days. Except if a holiday falls upon a weekday. Then I didn't work.
Mr. Rankin. Were these prescriptions prepared only for patients in the hospital?
Mrs. Oswald. Yes. Sometimes we prepared something for ourselves or for friends, or somebody would ask us.
Mr. Rankin. Did you pay anything to your uncle and aunt for staying there?
Mrs. Oswald. No. They had—they were well provided for, and my uncle wanted that I spend the money on myself.
Mr. Rankin. What was the name of this uncle?
Mrs. Oswald. Ilva Vasilyevich Proosakov.
Mr. Rankin. What was the nature of his work?
Mrs. Oswald. He works in the Ministry of the Interior of the Byelorussian SSR.
Mr. Rankin. Did he have something to do with lumbering?
Mrs. Oswald. He is an engineer. He is a graduate of a forestry institute. Technical institute.
Mr. Rankin. Is he an officer?
Mrs. Oswald. He was a colonel—a lieutenant colonel or colonel, I think.
Mr. Rankin. Did he have a nice apartment compared with the others?
Mrs. Oswald. Yes, very nice.
Mr. Rankin. Did he have a telephone in the apartment?
Mrs. Oswald. Yes.
Mr. Rankin. Were you supporting yourself during this period except for the fact you didn't pay anything for your room and board?
Mrs. Oswald. Yes.
Mr. Rankin. Did you save money?
Mrs. Oswald. No. I would receive my pay and I would spend everything in one day—three days tops.
Mr. Rankin. What would you spend it for?
Mrs. Oswald. First all the necessary things which I had to buy—shoes, an overcoat for winter. It is cold there, and, therefore, you have to wear warm clothes.
Mr. Rankin. Was your uncle a member of the Communist Party?
Mrs. Oswald. Yes, he is a Communist.
Mr. Rankin. Did you belong to any organizations during this period in Minsk?
Mrs. Oswald. First I was a member of the Trade Union. Then I joined the Comsomol, but I was discharged after one year.
Mr. Rankin. Do you know why you were discharged?
Mrs. Oswald. I paid my membership dues regularly, and at first they didn't know who I was or what I was, but after they found out that I had married an American and was getting ready to go to the United States, I was discharged from the Comsomol. They said that I had anti-Soviet views, even though I had no anti-Soviet views of any kind.
Mr. Rankin. Do you think that they thought you had anti-Soviet views because you married an American?
Mrs. Oswald. They didn't say that.
Mr. Rankin. Did they give any reason, other than the fact that you had them?

Mrs. Oswald. They never gave that as a direct reason, because the Soviet Government was not against marrying an American. But every small official wants to keep his place, and he is afraid of any troubles. I think it was sort of insurance.

Mr. Rankin. Was there any kind of a hearing about your being let out of the Comsomol?

Mrs. Oswald. Oh, yes.

Mr. Rankin. Did you attend?

Mrs. Oswald. I didn't go there, and they discharged me without me—I was very glad. There was even a reporter there from Comsomol paper, Comsomol Pravda, I think. He tried to shame me quite strongly—for what, I don't know. And he said that he would write about this in the paper, and I told him "Go ahead and write."

But he didn't write anything, because, after all, what could he write?

Mr. Rankin. Did you make any objection to being removed from the Comsomol?

Mrs. Oswald. No.

Mr. Rankin. Did you belong to any social clubs there?

Mrs. Oswald. No.

Mr. Rankin. Did you belong to any culture groups?

Mrs. Oswald. No.

Mr. Rankin. Did you go out with groups of students in the evening?

Mrs. Oswald. Of course.

Mr. Rankin. After you came to the United States, did you correspond with some of these friends?

Mrs. Oswald. Yes, but these were not the same friends. They were generally some girl friends before I was married and some friends we made later.

Mr. Rankin. Did you have a social life there at Minsk?

Mrs. Oswald. Of course.

Mr. Rankin. What did that social life consist of? Did you go to parties or to the opera or theater, or what?

Mrs. Oswald. Sometimes we met at the home of some friends. Of course we went to the opera, to the theater, to concerts, to the circus. To a restaurant.

Mr. Rankin. When did you first meet Lee Oswald?

Mrs. Oswald. The first time when I went to a dance, to a party. And there I met Lee.

Mr. Rankin. Do you recall the date?

Mrs. Oswald. On March 4th.

Mr. Rankin. What year?

Mrs. Oswald. 1961.

Mr. Rankin. Where did you meet him?

Mrs. Oswald. In Minsk.

Mr. Rankin. Yes—but can you tell us the place?

Mrs. Oswald. In the Palace of Trade Unions.

Mr. Rankin. What kind of a place is that? Is that where there are public meetings?

Mrs. Oswald. Sometimes they do have meetings there. Sometimes it is also rented by some institutes who do not have their own halls for parties.

Mr. Rankin. They have dances?

Mrs. Oswald. Yes. Every Saturday and Sunday.

Mr. Rankin. Did someone introduce you to him?

Mrs. Oswald. Yes.

Mr. Rankin. Who introduced you?

91 Mrs. Oswald. I had gone there with my friends from the medical institute, and one of them introduced me to Lee.

Mr. Rankin. What was his name?

Mrs. Oswald. Yuri Mereginsky.

Mr. Rankin. Do you know by what name Lee Oswald was introduced to you?

Mrs. Oswald. Everyone there called him Alec, at his place of work, because Lee is an unusual, cumbersome name. For Russians it was easier—this was easier.

Mr. Rankin. Is Alec a name close to Lee, as far as the Russian language is concerned?

Mrs. Oswald. A little. Somewhat similar.

Mr. Rankin. Did you know that Lee Oswald was an American when you first met him?

Mrs. Oswald. I found that out at the end of that party, towards the end of that party, when I was first introduced to him, I didn't know that.

Mr. Rankin. Did that make any difference?

Mrs. Oswald. It was more interesting, of course. You don't meet Americans very often.

Mr. Rankin. After this first meeting, did you meet him a number of times?

Mrs. Oswald. Yes.

Mr. Rankin. Can you describe just briefly how you met him and saw him?

Mrs. Oswald. After the first meeting he asked me where he could meet me again. I said that perhaps some day I will come back here again, to the Palace. About a week later I came there again with my girl friend, and he was there.

Mr. Rankin. And did he have a period that he was in the hospital there?

Mrs. Oswald. I had arranged to meet with him again. I had already given him a telephone number. But he went to a hospital and he called me from there. We had arranged to meet on a Friday, and he called from the hospital and said he couldn't because he was in the hospital and I should come there, if I could.

Mr. Rankin. Did you learn what was wrong with him then?

Mrs. Oswald. He was near the ear, nose and throat section and it seems that he had something wrong with his ears and also the glands or polyps.

Mr. Rankin. Did you visit him regularly for some period of time?

Mrs. Oswald. Yes, quite frequently, because I felt sorry for him being there alone.

Mr. Rankin. And did you observe a scar on his left arm?

Mrs. Oswald. He had a scar, but I found that out only after we were married.

Mr. Rankin. What did you find out about that scar?

Mrs. Oswald. When I asked him about it, he became very angry and asked me never to ask about that again.

Mr. Rankin. Did he ever explain to you what caused the scar?

Mrs. Oswald. No.

Mr. Rankin. Did you ever learn what caused the scar?

Mrs. Oswald. I found out here, now, recently.

Mr. Rankin. Did you learn that he had tried to commit suicide at some time?

Mrs. Oswald. I found that out now.

Mr. Rankin. During the time Lee Oswald was courting you, did he talk about America at all?

Mrs. Oswald. Yes, of course.

Mr. Rankin. What do you recall that he said about it?

Mrs. Oswald. At that time, of course, he was homesick, and perhaps he was sorry for having come to Russia. He said many good things. He said that his home was warmer and that people lived better.

Mr. Rankin. Did he talk about returning?

Mrs. Oswald. Then? No.

Mr. Rankin. Did he describe the life in America as being very attractive?

Mrs. Oswald. Yes. At least in front of others he always defended it.

Mr. Rankin. Did he——

Mrs. Oswald. It is strange to reconcile this. When he was there he was saying good things about America.

Mr. Rankin. And when he was talking only to you, did he do that, too?

Mrs. Oswald. Yes.

92 Mr. Rankin. Before you were married, did you find out anything about his plans to return to America?

Mrs. Oswald. No.

Mr. Rankin. Did you learn anything before you were married about the fact that there might be some doubt whether he could return to the United States?

Mrs. Oswald. Once before we were married we had a talk and I asked him whether he could return to the United States if he wanted to, and he said no, he could not.

Mr. Rankin. Did he tell you why?

Mrs. Oswald. No. At that time, he didn't. He said that when he had arrived, he had thrown his passport on a table and said that he would not return any more to the United States. He thought that they would not forgive him such an act.

Mr. Rankin. Before you were married, did you ever say to him you would like to go to the United States?

Mrs. Oswald. No.

Mr. Rankin. Can you tell us what attracted you to him?

Mrs. Oswald. I don't know. First, the fact that he was—he didn't look like others. You could see he was an American. He was very neat, very polite, not the way he was here, not as you know him here. And it seemed that he would be a good family man. And he was good.

Mr. Rankin. Did you talk about many things when you were together, when he was courting you?

Mrs. Oswald. We talked about everything, about the moon and the weather.

Mr. Rankin. Where was he living at that time?

Mrs. Oswald. In Minsk. By the way, on the same street where I lived.

Mr. Rankin. Did he have an apartment?

Mrs. Oswald. Yes. By the way, this was the same apartment where I had dreamed to live. I didn't know about it yet. It had a very beautiful balcony, terrace. I would look at that building sometimes and say it would be good to visit in that building, visit someone there, but I never thought that I would wind up living there.

Mr. Rankin. Can you describe the number of rooms there were in his apartment?

Mrs. Oswald. We had a small room—one room, kitchen, foyer, and bathroom. A large terrace, balcony.

Mr. Rankin. Do you know what he paid for rent?

Mrs. Oswald. For two it was quite sufficient. Seven and a half rubles per month.

Mr. Rankin. Wasn't that pretty cheap for such a nice apartment?

Mrs. Oswald. Yes, it was cheap.

Mr. Rankin. Was this apartment nicer than most in this city?

Mrs. Oswald. No, in that city they have good apartments because the houses are new. That is, on a Russian scale, of course. You cannot compare it to private houses people live in here.

Mr. Rankin. Did he have an automobile?

Mrs. Oswald. Oh, no. In Russia this is a problem. In Russia it is difficult to have an automobile.

Mr. Rankin. Did he have a television set?

Mrs. Oswald. No. Only a radio receiver, a record player.

Mr. Rankin. Did you have a telephone?

Mrs. Oswald. No—I don't like television.

Mr. Rankin. Why?

Mrs. Oswald. The programs are not always interesting, and you can get into a stupor just watching television. It is better to go to the movies.

Mr. Rankin. What was his occupation at this time?

Mrs. Oswald. He worked in a radio plant in Minsk.

Mr. Rankin. Do you know what his work was?

Mrs. Oswald. As an ordinary laborer—metal worker. From that point of view, he was nothing special. I had a greater choice in the sense that many of my friends were engineers and doctors. But that is not the main thing.

Mr. Rankin. Did others with a similar job have similar apartments?

93 Mrs. Oswald. The house in which we lived belonged to the factory in which Lee worked. But, of course, no one had a separate apartment for only two persons. I think that Lee had been given better living conditions, better than others, because he was an American. If Lee had been Russian, and we would have had two children, we could not have obtained a larger apartment. But since he was an American, we would have obtained the larger one. It seems to me that in Russia they treat foreigners better than they should. It would be better if they treated Russians better. Not all foreigners are better than the Russians.

Mr. Rankin. Did he say whether he liked this job?

Mrs. Oswald. No, he didn't like it.

Mr. Rankin. What did he say about it?

Mrs. Oswald. First of all, he was being ordered around by someone. He didn't like that.

Mr. Rankin. Anything else?

Mrs. Oswald. And the fact that it was comparatively dirty work.

Mr. Rankin. Did he say anything about the Russian system, whether he liked it or not?

Mrs. Oswald. Yes. He didn't like it. Not everything, but some things.

Mr. Rankin. Did he say anything about Communists and whether he liked that?

Mrs. Oswald. He didn't like Russian Communists. He said that they joined the party not because of the ideas, but in order to obtain better living conditions and to get the benefit of them.

Mr. Rankin. Did it appear to you that he had become disenchanted with the Soviet system?

Mrs. Oswald. Yes, he had expected much more when he first arrived.

Mr. Rankin. Did he ever tell you why he came to Russia?

Mrs. Oswald. Yes. He said he had read a great deal about Russia, he was interested in seeing the country, which was the first in the Socialist camp about which much had been said, and he wanted to see it with his own eyes. And, therefore, he wanted to be not merely a tourist, who is being shown only the things that are good, but he wanted to live among the masses and see.

But when he actually did, it turned out to be quite difficult.

The Chairman. I think we better adjourn now for the day.

(Whereupon, at 4:30 p.m., the President's Commission recessed.)

Thursday, February 6, 1964

TESTIMONY OF MRS. LEE HARVEY OSWALD RESUMED

The President's Commission met at 10 a.m. on February 6, 1964, at 200 Maryland Avenue NE., Washington, D.C.

Present were Chief Justice Earl Warren, Chairman; Senator John Sherman Cooper, Representative Hale Boggs, Representative Gerald R. Ford, and Allen W. Dulles, members.

Also present were J. Lee Rankin, general counsel; Melvin Aron Eisenberg, assistant counsel; Norman Redlich, assistant counsel; William D. Krimer, and Leon I. Gopadze, interpreters; and John M. Thorne, attorney for Mrs. Lee Harvey Oswald.

The Chairman. The Commission will be in order. We will proceed again. Mr. Rankin?

Mr. Rankin. Mrs. Oswald, if I may return a moment with you to the time that you told us about your husband practicing with the rifle at Love Field. As I recall your testimony, you said that he told you that he had taken the rifle and practiced with it there, is that right?

94 Mrs. Oswald. I knew that he practiced with it there. He told me, later.

Mr. Rankin. And by practicing with it, did you mean that he fired the rifle there, as you understood it?

Mrs. Oswald. I don't know what he did with it there. He probably fired it. But I didn't see him.

Mr. Rankin. And then you said that you had seen him cleaning it after he came back, is that right?

Mrs. Oswald. Yes.

Mr. Rankin. Now, do you recall your husband having any ammunition around the house at any time?

Mrs. Oswald. Yes.

Mr. Rankin. And where do you remember his having it in the places you lived?

Mrs. Oswald. On Neely Street, in Dallas, and New Orleans.

Mr. Rankin. Do you know whether that was rifle ammunition or rifle and pistol ammunition?

Mrs. Oswald. I think it was for the rifle. Perhaps he had some pistol ammunition there, but I would not know the difference.

Mr. Rankin. Did you observe how much ammunition he had at any time?

Mrs. Oswald. He had a box of about the size of this.

Mr. Rankin. Could you give us a little description of how you indicated the box? Was it 2 or 3 inches wide?

Mrs. Oswald. About the size here on the pad.

Mr. Rankin. About 3 inches wide and 6 inches long?

Mrs. Oswald. Probably.

Mr. Rankin. Now, do you recall that you said to your husband at any time that he was just studying Marxism so he could get attention?

Mrs. Oswald. Yes.

Mr. Rankin. In order to cause him not to be so involved in some of these ideas, did you laugh at some of his ideas that he told you about, and make fun of him?

Mrs. Oswald. Of course.

Mr. Rankin. Did he react to that?

Mrs. Oswald. He became very angry.

Mr. Rankin. And did he ask you at one time, or sometimes, not to make fun of his ideas?

Mrs. Oswald. Yes.

Mr. Rankin. Now, returning to the period in Russia, while your husband was courting you, did you talk to him, he talk to you, about his childhood?

Mrs. Oswald. No, not very much. Only in connection with photographs, where he was a boy in New York, in the zoo. Then in the Army—there is a snapshot taken right after he joined the Army.

Mr. Rankin. Did he tell you about anything he resented about his childhood?

Mrs. Oswald. He said it was hard for him during his childhood, when he was a boy, because there was a great age difference between him and Robert, and Robert was in some sort of a private school. He also wanted to have a chance to study, but his mother was working, and he couldn't get into a private school, and he was very sorry about it.

Mr. Rankin. In talking about that, did he indicate a feeling that he had not had as good an opportunity as his brother Robert?

Mrs. Oswald. Yes.

Mr. Rankin. When he talked about his service in the Marines, did he tell you much about what he did?

Mrs. Oswald. He didn't talk much about it, because there wasn't very much there of interest to me. But he was satisfied.

Mr. Rankin. Did he indicate that he was unhappy about his service with the Marines?

Mrs. Oswald. No, he had good memories of his service in the Army. He said that the food was good and that sometimes evenings he had a chance to go out.

Mr. Rankin. Did he say anything about his mother during this period of time?

Mrs. Oswald. This was before we were married. I had once asked Lee whether95 he had a mother, and he said he had no mother. I started to question him as to what had happened, what happened to her, and he said that I should not question him about it.

After we were married, he told me that he had not told me the truth, that he did have a mother, but that he didn't love her very much.

Mr. Rankin. Did he tell you why he didn't love her?

Mrs. Oswald. No.

Mr. Rankin. Do you recall anything more he said about his brother Robert at that time?

Mrs. Oswald. He said that he had a good wife, that he had succeeded fairly well in life, that he was smart and capable.

Mr. Rankin. Did he say anything about having any affection for him?

Mrs. Oswald. Yes, he loved Robert. He said that when Robert married Vada that his mother had been against the marriage and that she had made a scene, and this was one of the reasons he didn't like his mother.

Mr. Rankin. Did he say anything about his half brother, by the name of Pic—I guess the last name was Pic—Robert Pic?

Mrs. Oswald. He said that he had a half brother by the name of Pic from his mother's first marriage, but he didn't enlarge upon the subject. It is only that I knew he had a half brother by that name.

He said that at one time they lived with this John Pic and his wife, but that his wife and the mother frequently had arguments, quarrels. He said it was hard for him to witness these scenes, it was unpleasant.

Mr. Rankin. Did you regard your husband's wage or salary at Minsk as high for the work he was doing?

Mrs. Oswald. No. He received as much as the others in similar jobs.

Mr. Rankin. Did your husband have friends in Minsk when you first met him?

Mrs. Oswald. Yes.

Mr. Rankin. How did he seem to get along with these friends?

Mrs. Oswald. He had a very good relationship with them.

Mr. Rankin. Did he discuss any of them with you?

Mrs. Oswald. Yes.

Mr. Rankin. Will you tell us when you married your husband?

Mrs. Oswald. April 30, 1961.

Mr. Rankin. Was there a marriage ceremony?

Mrs. Oswald. Not in a church, of course. But in the institution called Zags, where we were registered.

Mr. Rankin. Was anyone else present at the ceremony?

Mrs. Oswald. Yes, our friends were there.

Mr. Rankin. Who else was there?

Mrs. Oswald. No one besides my girlfriends and some acquaintances. My uncle and aunt were busy preparing the house, and they were not there for that reason.

Mr. Rankin. After you were married did you go to live in your husband's apartment there?

Mrs. Oswald. Yes.

Mr. Rankin. Did you buy any new furniture?

Mrs. Oswald. Yes.

Mr. Rankin. When was your baby born?

Mrs. Oswald. February 15, 1962.
Mr. Rankin. What is her name?
Mrs. Oswald. June Lee Oswald.
Mr. Rankin. Did you stop working before the birth of the baby?
Mrs. Oswald. Yes.
Mr. Rankin. Did you return to work after the baby was born?
Mrs. Oswald. No.
Mr. Rankin. How did you and your husband get along during the period that you were in Minsk, after you were married?
Mrs. Oswald. We lived well.
Mr. Rankin. Were you a member of the trade union at Minsk?
Mrs. Oswald. Yes.
96 Mr. Rankin. Did you have a membership booklet?
Mrs. Oswald. Yes, a booklet.
Mr. Rankin. I hand you Exhibit 21 and ask you if that is the trade union booklet that you had there.
Mrs. Oswald. I never have a good photograph.
Mr. Rankin. I offer in evidence Exhibit 21.
The Chairman. It may be admitted and take the next number.
(The document referred to was marked Commission Exhibit No. 21 and received in evidence.)
Mr. Rankin. Did you pay dues to the trade union?
Mrs. Oswald. Yes.
Mr. Rankin. We didn't notice any notation of dues payments in this booklet, Exhibit 21. Do you know why that was?
Mrs. Oswald. I forgot to paste the stamps in.
Mr. Rankin. That is for the period between 1956 and 1959, they don't seem to be in there.
Mrs. Oswald. Yes.
Mr. Rankin. But you made the payments—you just didn't put the stamps in, is that right?
Mrs. Oswald. Yes. Simply because this is not important. I got the stamps, but the stubs remained with the person to whom I made the payment.
Mr. Rankin. We noted that the book shows a birth date of 1940 rather than 1941. Do you know how that happened?
Mrs. Oswald. The girl who prepared this booklet thought that I was older and put down 1940 instead of 1941.
Mr. Rankin. The booklet doesn't seem to show any registration in Minsk. Do you know why that would occur?
Mrs. Oswald. Because the booklet was issued in Leningrad.
Mr. Rankin. Is it the practice to record a registration in a city that you move to, or isn't that a practice that is followed?
Mrs. Oswald. No.
Mr. Rankin. Did your husband engage in any Communist Party activities while he was in the Soviet Union?
Mrs. Oswald. Not at all—absolutely not.
Mr. Rankin. Do you know whether he was a member of any organization there?
Mrs. Oswald. I think that he was also a member of a trade union, as everybody who works belongs to a trade union. Then he had a card from a hunting club, but he never visited it. He joined the club, apparently.
Mr. Rankin. Did he go hunting while he was there?
Mrs. Oswald. We only went once, with him and with my friends.
Mr. Rankin. Was that when he went hunting for squirrels?

Mrs. Oswald. If he marked it down in his notebook that he went hunting for squirrels, he never did. Generally they wanted to kill a squirrel when we went there, or some sort of a bird, in order to boast about it, but they didn't.

Mr. Rankin. Were there any times while he was in the Soviet Union after your marriage that you didn't know where he went?

Mrs. Oswald. No.

Mr. Rankin. When did you first learn that he was planning to try to go back to the United States?

Mrs. Oswald. After we were married, perhaps a month after.

Mr. Rankin. Did you discuss the matter at that time?

Mrs. Oswald. We didn't discuss it—we talked about it—because we didn't make any specific plans.

Mr. Rankin. Do you recall what you said about it then?

Mrs. Oswald. I said, "Well, if we will go, we will go. If we remain, it doesn't make any difference to me. If we go to China, I will also go."

Mr. Rankin. Did you and your husband make a trip to Moscow in connection with your plans to go to the United States?

Mrs. Oswald. Yes. We went to the American Embassy.

Mr. Rankin. Did your husband make a trip to Moscow alone before that? About his passport?

97 Mrs. Oswald. He didn't go alone. He actually left a day early and the following morning I was to come there.

Mr. Rankin. I understood that he didn't get any permission to make this trip to Moscow away from Minsk. Do you know whether that is true?

Mrs. Oswald. I don't know about this. I know that he bought a ticket and he made the flight.

Mr. Rankin. According to the practice, then, would he be permitted to go to Moscow from Minsk without the permission of the authorities?

Mrs. Oswald. I don't know whether he had the right to go to Moscow. Perhaps he did, because he had a letter requesting him to visit the Embassy. But he could not go to another city without permission of the authorities.

Mr. Rankin. When the decision was made to come to the United States, did you discuss that with your family?

Mrs. Oswald. First when we made the decision, we didn't know what would come of it later, what would happen further. And Lee asked me not to talk about it for the time being.

Mr. Rankin. Later, did you discuss it with your family?

Mrs. Oswald. Later when I went to visit the Embassy, my aunt found out about it, because they had telephoned from work, and she was offended because I had not told her about it. They were against our plan.

Mr. Rankin. Did you tell your friends about your plans after you were trying to arrange to go to the United States?

Mrs. Oswald. Yes.

Mr. Rankin. Was there some opposition by people in the Soviet Union to your going to the United States?

Mrs. Oswald. Somewhat. You can't really call that opposition. There were difficult times.

Mr. Rankin. Can you tell us what you mean by that?

Mrs. Oswald. First, the fact that I was excluded from the Komsomol. This was not a blow for me, but it was, of course, unpleasant. Then all kinds of meetings were arranged and members of the various organizations talked to me. My aunt and uncle would not talk to me for a long time.

Mr. Rankin. And that was all because you were planning to go to the United States?

Mrs. Oswald. Yes.

Mr. Rankin. Were you hospitalized and received medical treatment because of all of these things that happened at that time, about your leaving?
Mrs. Oswald. No.
What?
Mr. Rankin. Did you have any nervous disorder in 1961 that you were hospitalized for?
Mrs. Oswald. I was nervous, but I didn't go to the hospital. I am nervous now, too.
Mr. Rankin. Then you went to Kharkov on a vacation, didn't you?
Mrs. Oswald. Yes.
If you have a record of the fact that I was in the hospital, yes, I was. But I was in the hospital only as a precaution because I was pregnant. I have a negative Rh factor, blood Rh factor, and if Lee had a positive they thought—they thought that he had positive—even though he doesn't. It turned out that we both had the same Rh factor.
Mr. Rankin. Did you receive a promotion about this time in the work you were doing?
Mrs. Oswald. No, no one gets promoted. You work for 10 years as an assistant. All the assistants were on the same level. There were no sub-managers, except for the manager who was in charge of the pharmacy.
Mr. Rankin. What I am asking is your becoming an assistant druggist. Was that something different?
Mrs. Oswald. At first I was—I have to call it—an analyst. My job was to check prescriptions that had been prepared. There was no vacancy for an assistant, pharmacy assistant at first. But then I liked the work of a pharmacist's assistant better, and I changed to that.
98 Mr. Rankin. I will hand you Exhibit 22 and ask you if that is a book that shows that you were promoted or became an assistant druggist.
Mrs. Oswald. The entry here said, "Hired as chemist analyst of the pharmacy."
The next entry says, "Transferred to the job of pharmacy assistant."
These are simply different types of work. But one is not any higher than the other—not because one is a type of management and the other is not. If someone prepared a prescription and I checked it, that was no different from the other work. There is a difference, of course, but not in the sense of a grade of service.
Mr. Rankin. I offer in evidence Exhibit 22.
The Chairman. It may be admitted and take the next number.
(The document referred to was marked Commission Exhibit No. 22, and received in evidence.)
Mr. Rankin. Mr. Chairman, I ask leave at this time to substitute photostatic copies of any documentary evidence offered, and photographs of any physical evidence, with the understanding that the originals will be held subject to the further order of the Commission.
The Chairman. Very well. That may be done.
Mr. Rankin. Were you aware of your husband's concern about being prosecuted with regard to his returning to the United States?
Mrs. Oswald. Yes, he told me about it. He told me about it, that perhaps he might even be arrested.
Mr. Rankin. Was he fearful of prosecution by the Soviet Union or by the United States?
Mrs. Oswald. The United States.
Mr. Rankin. Do you recall any time that the Soviet authorities visited your husband while you were trying to go to the United States?
Mrs. Oswald. No.
Mr. Rankin. What was the occasion for your traveling to Kharkov in 1961?
Mrs. Oswald. My mother's sister lives there, and she had invited me to come there for a rest because I was on vacation.

Mr. Rankin. Did anyone go with you?
Mrs. Oswald. No.
Mr. Rankin. How long did you stay?
Mrs. Oswald. Three weeks, I think.
Mr. Rankin. Did you write to your husband while you were gone?
Mrs. Oswald. Yes.
Mr. Rankin. Was your aunt's name Mikhilova?
Mrs. Oswald. Mikhilova, yes.
Mr. Rankin. Was there any reason why you took this vacation alone and not with your husband?
Mrs. Oswald. He was working at that time. He didn't have a vacation. He wanted to go with me, but he could not.
Mr. Rankin. Do you know what delayed your departure to the United States?
Mrs. Oswald. No.
Mr. Rankin. There was some correspondence with the Embassy about your husband returning alone. Did you ever discuss that?
Mrs. Oswald. Yes.
Mr. Rankin. What did he say about that, and what did you say?
Mrs. Oswald. He said that if he did go alone, he feared that they would not permit me to leave, and that he would, therefore, wait for me.
Mr. Rankin. What did you say?
Mrs. Oswald. I thanked him for the fact that he wanted to wait for me.
Mr. Rankin. Where did you stay in Moscow when you went there about your visa?
Mrs. Oswald. At first, we stopped at the Hotel Ostamkino. And then we moved to the Hotel Berlin, formerly Savoy.
Mr. Rankin. How long were you there on that trip?
Mrs. Oswald. I think about 10 days, perhaps a little longer.
Mr. Rankin. Did you ever have any status in the armed forces of the Soviet Union?
Mrs. Oswald. No. But all medical workers, military, are obligated—all medical workers have a military obligation. In the event of a war, we would be in first place.
Mr. Rankin. Did you ever learn from your husband how he paid his expenses in Moscow for the period prior to the time you went to Minsk?
Mrs. Oswald. No.
Mr. Rankin. I hand you Exhibit 23 and ask you if that is a booklet that records your military status.
Mrs. Oswald. I didn't work. It is simply that I was obligated. There is an indication there "non-Party member".
Mr. Rankin. I offer in evidence Exhibit 23.
The Chairman. It may be received.
(The document referred to was marked Commission Exhibit No. 23, and received in evidence.)
Mr. Rankin. As I understand you, you did not serve in the armed forces of the Soviet Union, but because of your ability as a pharmacist, you were obligated, if the call was ever extended to you, is that right?
Mrs. Oswald. Yes, that is correct.
Mr. Rankin. Do you know any reason why your husband was permitted to stay in the Soviet Union when he first came there?
Mrs. Oswald. I don't know.
Mr. Rankin. Do you know why——
Mrs. Oswald. Many were surprised at that—here and in Russia.
Mr. Rankin. Do you know why he went to Minsk, or was allowed to go to Minsk?
Mrs. Oswald. He was sent to Minsk.
Mr. Rankin. By that, you mean by direction of the government?
Mrs. Oswald. Yes.

Mr. Rankin. Did your husband do any writing while he was in the Soviet Union that you know of?

Mrs. Oswald. Yes, he wrote a diary about his stay in the Soviet Union.

Mr. Rankin. I hand you Exhibit 24 and ask you if that is a photostatic copy of the diary that you have just referred to.

Mrs. Oswald. Yes, that is Lee's handwriting. It is a pity that I don't understand it. Is that all? It seems to me there was more.

Mr. Rankin. Mrs. Oswald, that is all of the historic diary that we have received. There are some other materials that I will call your attention to, but apparently they are not part of that.

I offer in evidence Exhibit 24.

The Chairman. It may be admitted and take the next number.

(The document referred to was marked Commission Exhibit No. 24, and received in evidence.)

Mrs. Oswald. That is all that only has reference to this? Or is that everything that Lee had written?

Mr. Rankin. No, it is not all that he ever wrote, but it is all that apparently fits together as a part of the descriptive diary in regard to the time he was in Russia.

Do you know when your husband made Exhibit 24, as compared with doing it daily or from time to time—how it was made?

Mrs. Oswald. Sometimes two or three days in a row. Sometimes he would not write at all. In accordance with the way he felt about it.

The Chairman. Mrs. Oswald, you said a few moments ago it was a pity that you could not read this. Would you like to have the interpreter read it to you later, so you will know what is in it?

You may, if you wish.

Mrs. Oswald. Some other time, later, when I know English myself perhaps.

The Chairman. You may see it any time you wish.

Mr. Rankin. Mr. Chairman, I just heard Mr. Thorne ask if there was any reason why they could not have photocopies of the exhibits. I know no reason.

The Chairman. No, there is no reason why you cannot. You may have it.

Mr. Thorne. Thank you.

100 Mr. Rankin. Mrs. Oswald has raised the question about whether this was complete. And this was all that was given us, as Exhibit 24, but we are going to check back on it to determine whether there was anything that may have been overlooked by the Bureau when they gave it to us.

Mrs. Oswald, your husband apparently made another diary that he wrote on some paper of the Holland America Line. Are you familiar with that?

Mrs. Oswald. No.

Mr. Rankin. I will hand you Exhibit 25 and ask you if you recall having seen that.

Mrs. Oswald. I know this paper, but I didn't know what was contained in it. I didn't know this was a diary.

Mr. Rankin. Do you know what it was?

Mrs. Oswald. No.

Mr. Rankin. Possibly I misdescribed it, Mrs. Oswald. It may be more accurately described as a story of his experiences in the Soviet Union.

Mrs. Oswald. I don't know even when he wrote this, whether this was aboard the ship or after we came to the United States. I only know the paper itself and the handwriting.

Mr. Rankin. Do you know whether it is your husband's handwriting?

Mrs. Oswald. Yes.

Mr. Rankin. I offer in evidence Exhibit 25.

The Chairman. It may be admitted.

(The document referred to was marked Commission Exhibit No. 25, and received in evidence.)

Mr. Rankin. Do you recall how much money you and your husband had in savings when you left Moscow for the United States?

Mrs. Oswald. I don't know, because Lee did not tell me how much money he had, because he knew that if he would tell me I would spend everything. But I think that we might have had somewhere about 300 rubles, or somewhat more, 350 perhaps.

Mr. Rankin. How did you travel from Moscow to the United States?

Mrs. Oswald. I told you—from Moscow by train, through Poland, Germany, and Holland, and from Holland by boat to New York. From New York to Dallas by air.

Mr. Rankin. I think you told us by another ship from Holland. I wonder if it wasn't the SS Maasdam. Does that refresh your memory?

Mrs. Oswald. Perhaps. I probably am mixed up in the names because it is a strange name.

Mr. Rankin. Do you recall that you exchanged United States money for Polish money during this trip?

Mrs. Oswald. Yes, in Warsaw, on the black market.

Mr. Rankin. Did you buy food there?

Mrs. Oswald. Yes. Some good Polish beer and a lot of candy.

By the way, we got an awful lot for one dollar, they were so happy to get it. More than the official rate.

Mr. Rankin. Did your husband drink then?

Mrs. Oswald. No. He doesn't drink beer, he doesn't drink anything, he doesn't like beer. I drank the beer. I don't like wine, by the way.

Mr. Rankin. Do you recall that you or your husband were contacted at any time in the Soviet Union by Soviet Intelligence people?

Mrs. Oswald. No.

Mr. Rankin. During the time your husband was in the Soviet Union, did you observe any indication of mental disorder?

Mrs. Oswald. No.

Mr. Rankin. How did he appear to get along with people that he knew in the Soviet Union?

Mrs. Oswald. Very well. At least, he had friends there. He didn't have any here.

Mr. Rankin. How much time did you spend in Amsterdam on the way to the United States?

Mrs. Oswald. Two or three days, it seems to me.

Mr. Rankin. What did you do there?

101 Mrs. Oswald. Walked around the city, did some sightseeing.

Mr. Rankin. Did anybody visit you there?

Mrs. Oswald. No.

Mr. Rankin. Did you visit anyone?

Mrs. Oswald. No.

Mr. Rankin. What hotel did you stay in?

Mrs. Oswald. We didn't stop at a hotel. We stopped at a place where they rent apartments. The address was given to us in the American Embassy.

Mr. Rankin. Do you recall what you paid in the way of rent?

Mrs. Oswald. No, Lee paid it. I don't know.

Mr. Rankin. How did your husband spend his time when he was aboard the ship?

Mrs. Oswald. I was somewhat upset because he was a little ashamed to walk around with me, because I wasn't dressed as well as the other girls. Basically, I stayed in my cabin while Lee went to the movies and they have different games there. I don't know what he did there.

Mr. Rankin. In Exhibit 25, the notations on the Holland American Line stationery, your husband apparently made some political observations. Did he discuss these with you while he was on the trip?

Mrs. Oswald. No.

Mr. Rankin. Mr. Chairman, it is time for a recess.
The Chairman. Yes. We will take a recess now.
(Brief recess.)
The Chairman. The Commission will be in order.
We will continue.
Mr. Rankin. Mrs. Oswald, can you tell us what your husband was reading in the Soviet Union after you were married, that you recall?
Mrs. Oswald. He read the Daily Worker newspaper in the English language.
Mr. Rankin. Anything else?
Mrs. Oswald. It seems to me something like Marxism, Leninism, also in the English language. He did not have any choice of English books for reading purposes.
Mr. Rankin. Was he reading anything in Russian at that time?
Mrs. Oswald. Yes, newspapers, and nothing else.
Mr. Rankin. No library books?
Mrs. Oswald. No. It was very hard for him.
Mr. Rankin. Did he go to any schools while he was in the Soviet Union that you know of?
Mrs. Oswald. No.
Mr. Rankin. I hand you Exhibit 26 and ask you if you can tell us what that is.
Mrs. Oswald. The title of this document is shown here, "Information for those who are departing for abroad. Personal data—name, last name, date of birth, place of birth, height, color of eyes and hair, married or not, and purpose of the trip."
Mr. Rankin. What does it say about the purpose of the trip—do you recall?
Mrs. Oswald. Private exit.
Mr. Rankin. Do you recall what members of your family are referred to there under that question?
Mrs. Oswald. It shows here "none." I think before this was filled out—this was before June's birth.
Mr. Rankin. That doesn't refer then to members of your family, like your uncles or aunts, or anything like that?
Mrs. Oswald. No.
Mr. Rankin. Mr. Chairman, I offer in evidence Exhibit 26.
The Chairman. It may be admitted.
(The document referred to was marked Commission Exhibit No. 26, and received in evidence.)
Mr. Rankin. Now, I hand you Exhibit 27 and ask you if you can recall what that is.
Mrs. Oswald. This is a questionnaire which has to be filled out prior to departure for abroad.
Mr. Rankin. I offer in evidence Exhibit 27.
102 The Chairman. It may be admitted.
(The document referred to was marked Commission Exhibit No. 27, and received in evidence.)
Mr. Rankin. Do you recall what relatives you referred to when they asked for close relatives?
Mrs. Oswald. It must be shown there. I don't remember. Probably my uncle.
Mr. Rankin. Mrs. Oswald, can you tell us the handwriting on this exhibit, No. 27?
Mrs. Oswald. This is my handwriting.
Mr. Rankin. You say it is all your handwriting?
Mrs. Oswald. Yes.
Mr. Rankin. Now, can you tell us what Exhibit 28 is?
Mrs. Oswald. That is the same thing. This was a draft.
Mr. Rankin. You mean a rough draft?
Mrs. Oswald. A rough draft of the same thing.
Mr. Rankin. And the other one is the final?

Mrs. Oswald. I don't know. Perhaps there were several drafts, I don't know whether this is from the Embassy or from some other source. These are drafts, because the original would have had to have my photograph. Lee and I were playing.

Mr. Rankin. Then, Mrs. Oswald, you think both Exhibit 27 and 28 are drafts, since neither one has your photograph on them?

Mrs. Oswald. Yes. We were playing dominoes, and this is the score.

Mr. Rankin. I ask that Exhibit 28 be received in evidence, Mr. Chairman.

The Chairman. It will be admitted.

(The document referred to was marked Commission Exhibit No. 28, and received in evidence.)

Mr. Rankin. I hand you Exhibit 29 and ask you if you can tell us what that is?

Mrs. Oswald. This is a residence permit, passport—a passport for abroad. This is a foreign passport for Russians who go abroad.

Mr. Rankin. Did you understand that you had six months in which to leave under that passport?

Mrs. Oswald. Yes. This all has to be filled out before you are allowed to go abroad.

Mr. Rankin. Whose handwriting is in Exhibit 29?

Mrs. Oswald. I don't know who wrote that. It is not I. Officials who issue the passport.

Mr. Rankin. I offer in evidence Exhibit 29.

The Chairman. It may be admitted.

(The document referred to was marked Commission Exhibit No. 29, and received in evidence.)

Mr. Rankin. Do you know any reason why the passport was made valid until January 11, 1964?

Mrs. Oswald. Because the passport which I turned in and for which I received this one in exchange was valid until 1964.

Mr. Rankin. You had a passport prior to this one, then?

Mrs. Oswald. Yes.

Mr. Rankin. Had you obtained that before you were married?

Mrs. Oswald. All citizens of the U.S.S.R. 16 and over must have a passport. It would be good if everyone had a passport here. It would help the Government more.

Mr. Rankin. Mrs. Oswald, you have told us considerably about your husband's unhappiness with the United States and his idea that things would be much better in Cuba, if he could get there. Do you recall that?

Mrs. Oswald. Yes.

Mr. Rankin. Do you recall what he said about what he didn't like about the United States?

Mrs. Oswald. The problem of unemployment.

Mr. Rankin. Anything else?

Mrs. Oswald. I already said what he didn't like—that it was hard to get103 an education, that medical care is very expensive. About his political dissatisfaction, he didn't speak to me.

Mr. Rankin. Did he ever say anything against the leaders of the government here?

Mrs. Oswald. No.

Mr. Rankin. Mr. Chairman, that is all we have now except the physical exhibits, and I think we could do that at 2 o'clock.

The Chairman. Mrs. Oswald, we are going to recess now until 2 o'clock. You must be quite tired by now. And this afternoon we are going to introduce some of the physical objects that are essential to make up our record.

When we finish with those, I think your testimony will be completed.

And I think we should finish today.

You won't be unhappy about that, will you?

Mrs. Oswald. No. Thank you.

The Chairman. 2 o'clock this afternoon.
(Whereupon, at 11:35 a.m., the President's Commission recessed.)

Afternoon Session
TESTIMONY OF MRS. LEE HARVEY OSWALD RESUMED

The President's Commission reconvened at 2 p.m.
The Chairman. The Commission will be in order. Mr. Rankin, you may continue.
Mr. Rankin. Mr. Chairman, I understand that Mrs. Oswald has examined a considerable volume of correspondence during the recess. In order to be helpful, she has identified it, and she is able to tell, through her counsel, by a number for each exhibit, who the letter was to or from as the case may be.

And, after I offer the exhibits, or as part of the offer, I will ask Mr. Thorne if he will tell the description of the recipient and the writer of the letter in the various cases. These exhibits are Exhibits 30 through 65, inclusive.

Mr. Thorne. Exhibit No. 30 is a telegram from a former fiance's mother.

Exhibit No. 31 is a letter from her friend who studied with her, by the name of Ella Soboleva.

Exhibit No. 32 is a letter from the Ziger family, who are friends.

Exhibit No. 33 is another letter from Alexander Ziger. A friend of the family's.

Exhibit No. 34 is a letter concerning departure to the United States by Marina and her husband. She doesn't know who sent the letter or who received it. It is merely some material that she has.

Exhibit No. 35 is an envelope from a friend which contained a letter which is not shown.

Exhibit No. 36 is a letter from a former fiance's mother, the same one that sent the telegram, and Exhibit No. 30.

Exhibit No. 37 is a letter from Marina to Lee while she was in the hospital, during the birth of June Lee.

Exhibit No. 38 is a letter from Olga Dmovskaya, a friend.

Mr. Rankin. When you say fiance, do you mean she was engaged to someone else?

Mr. Thorne. This is what I understand—prior to her relationship to Lee.

Exhibit No. 39 is another letter from Ella Soboleva.

Exhibit No. 40 is a letter from Lee Harvey to Marina while she was in the hospital with June Lee, during the birth of the baby.

Exhibit No. 41 is a letter from her Aunt Valya.

Exhibit No. 42 is a letter from their friend Pavel.

Exhibit No. 43 is the start of a letter by Marina which was never finished.

Exhibit No. 44 is the start of a letter by Marina which was never finished.

Exhibit No. 45 is a letter from Olga Dmovskaya, the same person who sent a letter in Exhibit No. 38.

104 Exhibit No. 46 is a letter—is another letter from Aunt Valya.

Exhibit No. 47 is a letter from a friend by the name of Tolya.

Exhibit No. 48 is an address of one of Marina's friends.

Exhibit No. 49 is Marina's draft of a letter to the consulate.

May I see Exhibit 49? I am trying to clear up a point.

Mr. Dulles. What is the date of that?

Mrs. Oswald. That is not a letter. That is an autobiography.

Mr. Thorne. Yes, that is correct. It is the draft of an autobiography for the Russian Consulate.

Exhibit No. 50 is a letter from a friend Erick Titovetz.

Exhibit No. 51 is another letter from Aunt Valya.

Exhibit No. 52 is a letter received by Marina while she was in the hospital with June Lee.

Exhibit No. 53 is Lee Harvey Oswald's writing.

Exhibit No. 54 is a letter from a friend, Laliya.

Exhibit No. 55 is a letter from Lee Harvey Oswald to Marina while she was in Kharkov.

Exhibit No. 56 is the same.

Exhibit No. 57 is a letter from Aunt Valya.

Exhibit No. 58 is a letter from Lee Harvey Oswald to Marina while she was in the hospital with June Lee.

Exhibit No. 59 is the same.

Exhibit No. 60 is the same.

Exhibit No. 61 is the same.

Exhibit No. 62 is a letter from Anna Meller, who lives in Dallas, to Marina.

Exhibit No. 63 is a letter from Lee Harvey Oswald to Marina while she was in the hospital, giving birth to June Lee.

Exhibit No. 64 is a letter from Lee Harvey Oswald—is a letter to Lee from Erick Titovetz.

Exhibit No. 65 is the second page of Exhibit No. 62. That completes the exhibits.

Mr. Rankin. We offer in evidence Exhibits 30 through 65, inclusive.

The Chairman. They may be admitted and take the appropriate numbers.

(The documents referred to were marked Commission Exhibit Nos. 30 through 65, inclusive, and received in evidence.)

Mr. Rankin. Mrs. Oswald, you remember I asked you about the diary that your husband kept. You said that he completed it in Russia before he came to this country, do you remember that?

Mrs. Oswald. Yes.

Mr. Rankin. Do you know whether or not the entries that he made in that diary were made each day as the events occurred?

Mrs. Oswald. No, not each day.

Mr. Rankin. Were they noted shortly after the time they occurred?

Mrs. Oswald. Not all events. What happened in Moscow I don't think that Lee wrote that in Moscow.

Mr. Rankin. What about the entries concerning what happened in Minsk?

Mrs. Oswald. He wrote this while he was working.

Mr. Rankin. And you think those entries were made close to the time that the events occurred?

Mrs. Oswald. Yes.

Mr. Rankin. As I understand you, you think that the entries concerning the time he was in Moscow before he went to Minsk were entered some time while he was in Minsk, is that right?

Mrs. Oswald. I think so, but I don't know.

Mr. Rankin. Do you know why your husband was sent to Minsk to work and live after he came to the Soviet Union, instead of some other city?

Mrs. Oswald. He was sent there because this is a young and developing city where there are many industrial enterprises which needed personnel. It is an old, a very old city. But after the war, it had been almost completely built anew, because everything has been destroyed. It was easier in the sense of living space in Minsk—it was easier to secure living space. Many immigrants are sent to Minsk. There are many immigrants there now.

105 Mr. Rankin. Were there many Americans there?

Mrs. Oswald. Americans? No. But from South America, from Argentina, we knew many. Many Argentinians live there—comparatively many.

Mr. Rankin. Did your husband say much about the time he was in Moscow before he went to Minsk and what he did there?

Mrs. Oswald. He didn't tell me particularly much about it, but he said that he walked in Moscow a great deal, that he had visited museums, that he liked Moscow better than Minsk, and that he would have liked to live in Moscow.

Mr. Rankin. Did he say anything about having been on the radio or television at Moscow?

Mrs. Oswald. He said that he was on the radio.

Mr. Rankin. Did he tell you anything about any ceremonies for him when he asked for Soviet citizenship?

Mrs. Oswald. No.

Mr. Rankin. When he was not granted Soviet citizenship, did he say anything about the Soviet Government or his reaction towards their failure to give him citizenship?

Mrs. Oswald. When I read the diary, I concluded from the diary that Lee wanted to become a citizen of the Soviet Union and that he had been refused, but after we were married we talked on that subject and he said it was good that he had refused to accept citizenship. Therefore, I had always thought that Lee had been offered citizenship—but that he didn't want it.

Mr. Rankin. What diary are you referring to that you read?

Mrs. Oswald. The diary about which we talked here previously—in the preceding session.

Mr. Rankin. The one that was completed in Russia that you referred to?

Mrs. Oswald. Yes.

Mr. Rankin. And when did you first read that?

Mrs. Oswald. I had never read it, because I didn't understand English. But when I was questioned by the FBI, they read me excerpts from that diary.

Mr. Rankin. And that was after the assassination?

Mrs. Oswald. Yes.

Mr. Rankin. When you and Lee Oswald decided to get married, was there a period of time you had to wait before it could be official?

Mrs. Oswald. Yes.

Mr. Rankin. Did you file an application and then have a period to wait?

Mrs. Oswald. Yes.

Mr. Rankin. How long was that period of waiting?

Mrs. Oswald. Ten days.

Mr. Rankin. After it was known in Minsk that you were to marry this American, did any officials come to you and talk to you about the marriage?

Mrs. Oswald. No.

Mr. Rankin. Mrs. Oswald, we have Exhibits 66 through 91 that we are going to ask your counsel to show to you, and after you have looked at them and are satisfied that you can identify them, then we will ask you to comment on them.

Mrs. Oswald. This is from Lee when I was in the hospital.

Mr. Rankin. What exhibit is that?

Mr. Thorne. These are all part of Exhibit 66. They are various miscellaneous pieces of writing involved in this particular exhibit.

Mrs. Oswald. It was not in June that I was in the hospital. He didn't know that I was in the hospital.

Mr. Rankin. By "he" do you mean your husband Lee Oswald?

Mrs. Oswald. Yes.

Mr. Rankin. And when did he not know that you were in the hospital?

Mrs. Oswald. Because I was going to work when I began to feel ill, and I was taken to the hospital.

Mr. Rankin. And what time was that?

Mrs. Oswald. In the morning, about 10 a.m.

Mr. Rankin. I mean about what day or month or year?

Mrs. Oswald. September 1961.

Mr. Rankin. Is that before you went to Kharkov?
Mrs. Oswald. Yes.
106 Mr. Rankin. And we have already discussed, or I have asked you about that time you were in the hospital.
Mrs. Oswald. Yes. I was there twice.
Mr. Rankin. By twice, you mean this time you have described before you went to Kharkov and the other time when you had the baby?
Mrs. Oswald. This is a letter from Inesse Yakhliel.
Mr. Rankin. That is Exhibit 67?
Mr. Thorne. No, sir, these are all part of Exhibit 66.
Mr. Dulles. I wonder if these should not be marked in some way, because you won't be able to find out what they are in the future—A, B, C, D, or something of this kind.
Mr. Rankin. Mr. Redlich, will you mark those as 66-A, B, C, and D, or however they run?
Mr. Thorne, when you say the first one marked "A", will you make it clear what that is?
Mr. Thorne. The exhibit marked "A"—let me hasten to point out that all of these pieces of paper have a mark "159R". We are denoting individually these papers by starting with A, B, C, and so on.

"A" represents the first piece of paper that was identified earlier in this testimony by Mrs. Oswald, referring again specifically to Exhibit 66, which is composed of many such pieces of paper.

Exhibit B was the second piece of paper that was identified by Mrs. Oswald.
I believe this is the third.
Mrs. Oswald. This is a letter from Inessa Yakhliel.
Mr. Thorne. This will be identified as C.
Mrs. Oswald. The envelope of a letter that Lee wrote me, to Kharkov.
Mr. Thorne. That is identified as Exhibit D.
Mrs. Oswald. From Inessa Yakhliel.
Mr. Thorne. This is identified as Exhibit E.
Mrs. Oswald. This is from Inessa Yakhliel.
Mr. Thorne. This is identified as Exhibit F.
Mrs. Oswald. This is from Lee.
Mr. Thorne. Identified as Exhibit G.
Mrs. Oswald. From my Aunt Luba.
Mr. Thorne. This is identified as Exhibit H.
Mrs. Oswald. This is a letter from Lee.
Mr. Thorne. Exhibit I.

Now, so there is no confusion, let's state again that these are sub-exhibits, letters, and marked 159, from A through I, all part of Exhibit 66.
Mrs. Oswald. I would like to obtain these letters, to preserve them. I don't mean now.
The Chairman. She may see and have copies of any of the letters she desires connected with her testimony.
Mr. Thorne. This is Exhibit 67.
Mrs. Oswald. A photograph of Galiya Khontooleva.
Mr. Thorne. Exhibit 68. Exhibit 68 is two postcards, and they probably need to be identified as A and B.

Let's identify A.
Mrs. Oswald. That is a letter from Lee from New Orleans to Irving—to the home of Mrs. Paine.

And this is a letter from the mother, Lee's mother.
Mr. Thorne. This will be identified as Exhibit 68-B. Exhibit 69 is composed of two postcards. Exhibit 69-A——

Mrs. Oswald. This is from Lee, from New Orleans, addressed to me, when I lived with Ruth Paine.

Mr. Thorne. And Exhibit 69-B?

Mrs. Oswald. A letter from a girl friend from Russia, Ludmila Larionova.

Mr. Thorne. Exhibit No. 70, a postcard.

Mrs. Oswald. From my grandmother, from the mother of my stepfather.

Mr. Thorne. Exhibit No. 71. Two envelopes. 71-A——

Mrs. Oswald. From Pavel Golovachev, addressed to the address of Ruth Paine. And this is an envelope from Ruth Paine.

Mr. Thorne. That is Exhibit B.

Mrs. Oswald. A letter to me.

Mr. Thorne. Exhibit 72 is a writing. In Russian.

Mrs. Oswald. This is a reply to Lee's letter about the fact that he wanted to study at the University of Peoples Friendship, and he was refused.

Mr. Thorne. Exhibit 73 contains two pieces of paper. 73-A is identified as——

Mrs. Oswald. This is from the time that June was a little baby, a certificate of the fact that she was vaccinated for smallpox.

Mr. Thorne. Exhibit B?

Mrs. Oswald. This is Anna Meller's address and telephone number.

Mr. Thorne. Exhibit 74?

Mrs. Oswald. This is Lee's library card of the State Library. I think in Moscow—the State Library.

Mr. Thorne. Exhibit 75 contains a writing and an envelope.

Mrs. Oswald. A letter from Galiya Khontooleva, and an envelope.

Mr. Thorne. Exhibit 76 contains three pages of writing, together with an envelope.

Mrs. Oswald. This was when Lee and I visited his brother in a city in Alabama, he is studying to be a clergyman. There we met a young man who was studying Russian, and he wrote me this letter.

These are all his letters.

Mr. Thorne. This is three pages of one letter together with the envelope.

Mrs. Oswald. Yes.

Mr. Thorne. Exhibit 77 contains an envelope and two written pages—two separate pages of writing.

Mrs. Oswald. This is from Galiya Khontooleva, and the envelope.

Mr. Thorne. Exhibit 78 contains an envelope and two handwritten pages of writing.

Mrs. Oswald. This is a letter from Ruth Paine to New Orleans.

Mr. Thorne. Exhibit No. 79 contains an envelope and one page of writing.

Mrs. Oswald. This is a letter from Pavel Golovachev, from Minsk.

Mr. Thorne. Exhibit No. 80, two handwritten pages.

Mrs. Oswald. I was forced by the FBI to write an account of how much money I had received through them.

Mr. Thorne. Exhibit 81 contains one page of writing.

Mrs. Oswald. The same.

Mr. Thorne. By the same, you mean what?

Mrs. Oswald. A receipt for the receipt of money through the FBI.

Mr. Thorne. Are these donations?

Mrs. Oswald. Yes.

Mr. Thorne. Exhibit 82 contains a page in handwriting.

Mrs. Oswald. A letter from Ruth.

Mr. Thorne. Exhibit 83 is a photograph.

Mrs. Oswald. The son of Ludmila Larionova.

Mr. Thorne. Exhibit 84 contains an envelope.

Mrs. Oswald. Simply an envelope.

Mr. Thorne. Exhibit 85 contains an envelope.

Mrs. Oswald. Lee wrote to me in Kharkov.
Mr. Thorne. Exhibit 86 contains an envelope.
Mrs. Oswald. From Titovetz, a letter from the Soviet Union.
Mr. Thorne. Exhibit 87 contains an envelope.
Mrs. Oswald. From Pavel Golovachev.
Mr. Thorne. Exhibit 88 contains an envelope and one page of writing.
Mrs. Oswald. A letter from Ella Soboleva.
Mr. Thorne. And the letter arrived in the envelope?
Mrs. Oswald. Yes.
Mr. Thorne. Exhibit 89 contains one sheet of writing.
Mrs. Oswald. Also from Soboleva.
Mr. Thorne. Exhibit No. 90.
Mrs. Oswald. I think from Ruth.
Mr. Thorne. This contains several pages—several sheets—three sheets which seem to be one continuous letter.
Mrs. Oswald. A letter from Ruth Paine.
Mr. Thorne. A three-page letter. Exhibit No. 91 contains an envelope.
Mrs. Oswald. From Erick Titovetz.
Mr. Rankin. We offer in evidence Exhibits 66 through 91, inclusive.
The Chairman. You have looked over all these, have you, Mr. Thorne, and your client has identified them?
Mr. Thorne. Yes, sir.
The Chairman. They may be admitted.
(The documents referred to were marked Commission Exhibit Nos. 66 through 91, inclusive, and received in evidence.)
Mr. Rankin. Mrs. Oswald, we will show you photostatic copies of various writings of your husband. As you look at them, would you tell us what each one is, insofar as you recognize them, please?
Mr. Thorne. This is Exhibit 92, which is a writing, a photocopy of a writing.
Mr. Rankin. Do you recognize that exhibit, Mrs. Oswald?
Mrs. Oswald. Lee's handwriting. But I have never seen this. More correctly, I have seen it, but I have never read it.
Mr. Rankin. So you don't know what it purports to be, I take it.
Mrs. Oswald. Yes.
Mr. Rankin. That is, you do not?
Mrs. Oswald. No.
Mr. Rankin. But you do recognize his handwriting throughout?
Mrs. Oswald. Yes.
Mr. Thorne. May I point out to the Commission, please, this is in English. This is handwritten in English and it is typewritten in English.
Mr. Rankin. We offer in evidence Exhibit 92.
The Chairman. It will be admitted.
(The document referred to was marked Commission Exhibit No. 92, and received in evidence.)
Mr. Rankin. I should like to inform the Commission that Exhibit 92 purports to be the book that Lee Oswald wrote about conditions in the Soviet Union.
The Chairman. The one that was dictated to the stenographer?
Mr. Rankin. Yes, that is right.
Mr. Redlich. He had had written notes, and she transcribed them.
Mr. Thorne. The next exhibit is Exhibit No. 93, many pages, handwritten, in English.
Mr. Rankin. Mrs. Oswald, will you tell us what that is, if you know.
Mrs. Oswald. No, I don't know.
Mr. Rankin. Do you know whether it is in the handwriting of your husband?

Mrs. Oswald. Yes, this is Lee's handwriting. These are all his papers. I don't know about them. Everything is in English. I don't know.

Mr. Rankin. We offer in evidence Exhibit 93.

The Chairman. Exhibit 93 may be admitted.

(The document referred to was marked Commission Exhibit No. 93, and received in evidence.)

Mr. Rankin. I should like to advise the Commission that this Exhibit 93 purports to be a résumé of his Marine Corps experience, and some additional minor notes.

Mr. Thorne. Exhibit No. 94 is photocopies of many pages of handwriting, which is in English.

Mrs. Oswald. I don't know what that is. It is Lee's handwriting.

Mr. Rankin. We offer in evidence Exhibit 94.

The Chairman. It may be admitted.

(The document referred to was marked Commission Exhibit No. 94, and received in evidence.)

Mr. Dulles. Do we know what that is?

Mr. Rankin. Exhibit 94 consists of handwritten pages on which the book about Russia, Exhibit 92, was typewritten.

109 Mr. Thorne. Exhibit No. 95 is a photocopy of many pages of typewriting, typewritten words, which are in English.

Mrs. Oswald. I also don't know.

Mr. Rankin. Mrs. Oswald, I will ask you, on Exhibit 95, can you identify the handwriting on that?

Mrs. Oswald. It is Lee's handwriting.

Mr. Rankin. And did you ever see the pages of that Exhibit 95 as a part of his papers and records?

Mrs. Oswald. No. Perhaps I saw them, but I don't remember them.

Mr. Rankin. But you know it is his handwriting, where the handwriting appears?

Mrs. Oswald. Yes.

Mr. Rankin. We offer in evidence Exhibit 95.

The Chairman. It may be admitted.

(The document referred to was marked Commission Exhibit No. 95, and received in evidence.)

Mr. Thorne. Exhibit 96 is a photocopy of two pages that are handwritten and in English.

Mrs. Oswald. I also don't know what that is. For me, that is a dark forest, a heap of papers.

Mr. Rankin. With regard to Exhibit 95 that has been received in evidence, I should like to inform the Commission that that is also material concerning the book, regarding conditions in Russia.

Mrs. Oswald, will you tell us with regard to Exhibit 96—do you recognize the handwriting on those pages?

Mrs. Oswald. This is all Lee's handwriting.

Mr. Rankin. We offer in evidence Exhibit 96.

The Chairman. It may be admitted.

(The document referred to was marked Commission Exhibit No. 96, and received in evidence.)

Mr. Rankin. Exhibit 96 purports to be notes for a speech or article, on "The New Era."

Mr. Thorne. Exhibit 97 is a photocopy of several pages, both printed and in writing, handwriting.

Mrs. Oswald. It is amazing that Lee had written so well.

Mr. Rankin. Do you recognize the handwriting?

Mrs. Oswald. Yes, I do.

Mr. Thorne. This is also in English.
Mrs. Oswald, you state he had written so well. By that you mean what?
Mrs. Oswald. Neatly. And legibly.
Mr. Rankin. I offer in evidence Exhibit 97.
The Chairman. Exhibit 97 may be admitted.
(The document referred to was marked Commission Exhibit No. 97, and received in evidence.)
Mr. Thorne. Exhibit 98 is three photocopy pages of handwriting in English.
Mrs. Oswald. I don't know what that is.
Mr. Thorne. Do you recognize the handwriting?
Mrs. Oswald. That is Lee's handwriting.
Mr. Rankin. Exhibit 97 appears to be a critique on the Communist Party in the United States by Lee Oswald.
The Chairman. It may be admitted.
Mr. Rankin. We offer in evidence Exhibit 98.
The Chairman. It may be admitted.
(The document referred to was marked Commission Exhibit No. 98, and received in evidence.)
Mr. Rankin. Exhibit 98 purports to be notes for a speech.
Mr. Thorne. Exhibit 99 is one photocopy page of handwriting in English.
Mrs. Oswald. I don't know what that is.
Mr. Thorne. Is this Lee's handwriting?
Mrs. Oswald. Yes.
Mr. Rankin. We offer in evidence Exhibit 99.
The Chairman. It may be admitted.
110 (The document referred to was marked Commission Exhibit No. 99, and received in evidence.)
Mr. Thorne. Exhibit No. 100 purports to be four pages, photocopy pages, of handwriting, in English.
Mrs. Oswald. Lee's handwriting. But what it is, I don't know. I am sorry, but I don't know what it is.
Mr. Rankin. We offer in evidence Exhibit 100.
The Chairman. It may be admitted.
(The document referred to was marked Commission Exhibit No. 100, and received in evidence.)
Mr. Rankin. I wish to inform the Commission that this purports to be answers to questionnaires, and shows two formats, one showing that he is loyal to the country and another that he is not so loyal.
Mr. Thorne. Exhibit 101 is a photocopy of one page which is printed and handwritten in English.
Mrs. Oswald. Lee's handwriting. But what it is, I don't know.
Mr. Rankin. We offer in evidence Exhibit 101.
The Chairman. It may be admitted.
(The document referred to was marked Commission Exhibit No. 101, and received in evidence.)
Mr. Rankin. This purports to be a portion of the diary and relates to his meeting at the Embassy on October 31, 1959.
Mr. Thorne. Exhibit 102 is photocopies of two pages, handwritten, in English.
Mrs. Oswald. Lee's handwriting. I don't know what it is.
Mr. Rankin. We offer in evidence Exhibit 102.
The Chairman. It may be admitted.
(The document referred to was marked Commission Exhibit No. 102, and received in evidence.)

Mr. Rankin. I wish to call the Commission's attention to the fact that Exhibit 102 purports to be a draft of memoranda, at least, for a speech.

Mr. Thorne. Exhibit 103 is two pages, two photocopy pages, of handwriting, in English.

Mrs. Oswald. From the address I see that it is a letter—it is Lee's letter, but to whom, I don't know.

Mr. Rankin. I offer in evidence Exhibit 103.

The Chairman. It may be admitted under that number.

(The document referred to was marked Commission Exhibit No. 103, and received in evidence.)

Mr. Rankin. I wish to call the attention of the Commission to the fact that Exhibit 103 is a purported draft of the letter that Lee Oswald sent to the Embassy, the Soviet Embassy, which you will recall referred to the fact that his wife was asked by the FBI to defect—had such language in the latter part of it. This draft shows that in this earlier draft he used different language, and decided upon the language that he finally sent in the exhibit that is in the record earlier. The comparison is most illuminating.

Mr. Thorne. Exhibit 104 is photocopy pages of a small notebook.

Mrs. Oswald. This is my notebook, various addresses—when I was at the rest home, I simply noted down the addresses of some acquaintants.

Mr. Dulles. Is this in Russia, or the United States?

Mrs. Oswald. In Russia.

Mr. Rankin. We offer in evidence Exhibit 104.

The Chairman. It may be admitted.

(The document referred to was marked Commission Exhibit No. 104, and received in evidence.)

Mr. Thorne. Exhibit 105 is a notebook——

Mr. Rankin. Exhibit 104 purports to be a small notebook of Mrs. Oswald.

Mr. Thorne. Exhibit 105 is the original of a notebook containing various writings in English and in Russian.

Mrs. Oswald. This is when Lee was getting ready to go to Russia, and he made a list of the things that he wanted to buy and take with him.

Further, I don't know what he had written in there.

111 Mr. Dulles. Was this the time he went or the time he didn't go?

Mrs. Oswald. When he didn't—when he intended to.

Mr. Rankin. In Exhibit 105, Mrs. Oswald, I will ask you if you noted that your husband had listed in that "Gun and case, Price 24 REC. 17."

Mrs. Oswald. I don't know what that is. Unfortunately, I cannot help. I don't know what this means.

Mr. Rankin. But you do observe the item in the list in that booklet, do you?

Mrs. Oswald. Yes.

Now I see it.

Mr. Rankin. I offer in evidence Exhibit 105.

The Chairman. That will be received.

(The document referred to was marked Commission Exhibit No. 105, and received in evidence.)

Mr. Rankin. With regard to Exhibit 102, I should like to inform the Commission that as a part of this transcribed record, as soon as we can complete it, we will have photostatic copies of these various exhibits for you, along with photographs of the physical material. But I think you will want to examine some of it very closely.

I call your particular attention to this draft of a proposed speech. One of the items, No. 1, states, "Americans are apt to scoff at the idea that a military coup in the U.S. as so often happens in Latin American countries, could ever replace our government. But that is an idea that has grounds for consideration. Which military organization has the potentialities of exciting such action? Is it the Army? With its many conscripts, its unwieldy size, its score of bases scattered across the world? The case of General Walker shows that the Army at least is not fertile enough ground for a far-right regime to go a very long way, for the size, reasons of size, and disposition."

Then there is an insert I have difficulty in reading.

"Which service, then, can qualify to launch a coup in the U.S.A.? Small size, a permanent hard core of officers and few bases as necessary. Only one outfit fits that description, and the U.S. Marine Corps is a rightwing-infiltrated organization of dire potential consequences to the freedom of the United States. I agree with former President Truman when he said that 'The Marine Corps should be abolished.'"

That indicates some of his thinking.

The Chairman. We will just take a short break.

(Brief recess.)

The Chairman. The Commission will be in order.

Mr. Thorne. Exhibit 106 for identification is a notebook.

Mrs. Oswald. This is my book, some poems by——

Mr. Thorne. It contains handwriting in Russian.

Mr. Rankin. How did you happen to write that, Mrs. Oswald?

Mrs. Oswald. I simply liked these verses. I did not have a book of poems. And I made a copy.

Mr. Rankin. I offer in evidence Exhibit 106.

The Chairman. It may be admitted.

(The document referred to was marked Commission Exhibit No. 106, and received in evidence.)

Mr. Thorne. Exhibit 107 contains a small piece of cardboard with some writing in Russian on it.

Mrs. Oswald. This is Lee's pass from the factory.

Mr. Rankin. I offer in evidence Exhibit 107.

The Chairman. It may be admitted.

(The document referred to was marked Commission Exhibit No. 107, and received in evidence.)

Mr. Thorne. Exhibit 108 is an original one sheet of paper, with handwriting in ink, in Russian, on one page.

Mrs. Oswald. These are the lyrics of a popular song.

Mr. Rankin. A Russian popular song?

Mrs. Oswald. Yes. This is Armenian—an Armenian popular song.

Mr. Rankin. I offer in evidence Exhibit 108.

The Chairman. It is admitted.

112 (The document referred to was marked Commission Exhibit No. 108, and received in evidence.)

Mr. Thorne. Exhibit 109 is one sheet with handwriting in ink on both sides, an original.

Mrs. Oswald. This was simply my recollection of some song lyrics and the names of some songs that people had asked me.

Mr. Rankin. I offer Exhibit 109.

The Chairman. It may be admitted.

(The document referred to was marked Commission Exhibit No. 109, and received in evidence.)

Mr. Thorne. Exhibit 110 is a yellow legal sized sheet with handwriting in Russian which seems to be interpreted in English below it, together with a little stamp. I can explain the stamp. It says FBI Laboratory.

Mrs. Oswald. This is when George Bouhe was giving me lessons. I translated from Russian into English—not very successfully—my first lessons.

Mr. Rankin. I offer Exhibit 110.

The Chairman. It may be admitted.

(The document referred to was marked Commission Exhibit No. 110, and received in evidence.)

Mr. Rankin. When was it that George Bouhe was teaching you English and you wrote this out?

Mrs. Oswald. This was in July 1962. I don't remember when I arrived—in '62 or '61.

Mr. Rankin. Is the handwriting in Exhibit 110 in the Russian as well as the English in your handwriting?

Mrs. Oswald. No. The Russian is written by Bouhe, and the English is written by me.

Mr. Rankin. Did you make the translation from the Russian into the English by yourself?

Mrs. Oswald. Yes, I had to study English.

Mr. Rankin. Did you have a dictionary to work with?

Mrs. Oswald. Yes.

Mr. Rankin. So you were taking a Russian-English dictionary and trying to convert the Russian words that he wrote out into English, is that right?

Mrs. Oswald. Yes.

Mr. Thorne. Exhibit 111 is a book written in Russian, a pocket book.

Mrs. Oswald. This is my book.

Mr. Rankin. Do you notice some of the letters are cut out of that book, Exhibit 111?

Mrs. Oswald. Letters?
I see that for the first time.

Mr. Rankin. Do you know who did that?

Mrs. Oswald. Probably Lee was working, but I never saw that. I don't know what he did that for.

Mr. Rankin. You never saw him while he was working with that?

Mrs. Oswald. No. I would have shown him if I had seen him doing that to my book.

Mr. Rankin. You know sometimes messages are made up by cutting out letters that way and putting them together to make words.

Mrs. Oswald. I read about it.

Mr. Rankin. You have never seen him do that?

Mrs. Oswald. No.

Mr. Rankin. I offer Exhibit 111.

The Chairman. It may be admitted.

(The document referred to was marked Commission Exhibit No. 111, and received in evidence.)

Mr. Thorne. Exhibit 112 is an apparent application—an applicant's driving record.

Mrs. Oswald. I have never seen this.

Mr. Thorne. It is in English.

Mr. Rankin. That is not your driving record, then?

Mrs. Oswald. No.

113 Mr. Rankin. You don't know whether it was your husband's?

Mrs. Oswald. I don't know.

Mr. Thorne. May I clarify the exhibit? It is an application for a Texas driver's license. Standard form application.

Mr. Rankin. We offer in evidence Exhibit 112.

The Chairman. It may be admitted.

(The document referred to was marked Commission Exhibit No. 112, and received in evidence.)

Mrs. Oswald. It is quite possible that Lee prepared that, because Ruth Paine insisted on Lee's obtaining a license.

Mr. Rankin. Did you hear her insist?

Mrs. Oswald. Yes. She said it would be good to have.

Mr. Rankin. And when was that?

Mrs. Oswald. October or November.

Mr. Rankin. 1962?
Mrs. Oswald. '63.
Mr. Thorne. Exhibit 113 is a driver's handbook published by the State of Texas.
Mrs. Oswald. We had this book for quite some time. George Bouhe had given that to Lee if he at some time would try to learn how to drive.
Mr. Rankin. I offer in evidence Exhibit 113.
The Chairman. It may be admitted.
(The document referred to was marked Commission Exhibit No. 113, and received in evidence.)
Mr. Rankin. Was your husband able to drive a car?
Mrs. Oswald. Yes, I think that he knew how. Ruth taught him how.
Mr. Rankin. Did he have a driver's license that you know of?
Mrs. Oswald. No.
This is a Russian camera of Lee's—binoculars.
Mr. Thorne. Exhibit 114 is a leather case containing a pair of binoculars.
Mr. Rankin. Do you remember having seen those binoculars, known as Exhibit 114, before?
Mrs. Oswald. Yes. We had binoculars in Russia because we liked to look through them at a park.
Mr. Rankin. Do you know whether your husband used them in connection with the Walker incident?
Mrs. Oswald. I don't know.
Mr. Rankin. He never said anything about that?
Mrs. Oswald. No.
Mr. Rankin. We offer in evidence Exhibit 114.
The Chairman. It may be admitted.
(The article referred to was marked Commission Exhibit No. 114, and received in evidence.)
Mr. Thorne. Exhibit 115 is a box containing a stamping kit.
Mrs. Oswald. That is Lee's. When he was busy with his Cuba, he used it.
Mr. Rankin. You mean when he was working on the Fair Play for Cuba, he used this?
Mrs. Oswald. Yes.
Mr. Rankin. I offer in evidence Exhibit 115.
The Chairman. It may be admitted.
(The article referred to was marked Commission Exhibit No. 115, and received in evidence.)
Mr. Rankin. How did he use that kit in Exhibit 115 in connection with his Fair Play for Cuba campaign?
Mrs. Oswald. He had leaflets for which he assembled letters and printed his address.
Mr. Rankin. And he used this kit largely to stamp the address on the letters?
Mrs. Oswald. Not letters, but leaflets.
Mr. Rankin. He stamped the address on the leaflets?
Mrs. Oswald. Handbills, rather.
Yes.
114 Mr. Rankin. Do you recall whether he stamped his name on the handbills, too?
Mrs. Oswald. Yes.
Mr. Rankin. What name did he stamp on them?
Mrs. Oswald. Lee Harvey Oswald.
Mr. Rankin. Did he use the name Hidell on those, too?
Mrs. Oswald. I don't remember. Perhaps.
Mr. Thorne. Exhibit 116 is a Spanish to English and English to Spanish dictionary.
Mr. Rankin. Have you seen that before?
Mrs. Oswald. When Lee came from Mexico City I think he had this.
Mr. Rankin. I offer in evidence Exhibit 116.

The Chairman. It may be received.
(The document referred to was marked Commission Exhibit No. 116, and received in evidence.)
Mr. Thorne. Exhibit 117 is one sheet of paper with, some penciled markings on it.
Mrs. Oswald. I don't know what that is. I don't know.
Mr. Rankin. Do you recognize any of the writing on that exhibit?
Mrs. Oswald. Lee's handwriting.
Mr. Rankin. I offer in evidence Exhibit 117.
The Chairman. It may be admitted.
(The document referred to was marked Commission Exhibit No. 117, and received in evidence.)
Mr. Thorne. Exhibit 118 is a clipping from a newspaper. There are some notations on it.
Mr. Rankin. Do you recall seeing that clipping, Exhibit 118, before?
Mrs. Oswald. No.
Mr. Rankin. Do you recognize any of the handwriting on it?
Mrs. Oswald. As far as it is visible, it is similar to Lee's handwriting.
Mr. Rankin. I offer Exhibit 118. The Chairman. 118 may be admitted.
(The document referred to was marked Commission Exhibit No. 118, and received in evidence.)
Mr. Rankin. I call attention to the members of the Commission that Exhibit 118 has a reference to the President, with regard to the income tax, and the position of the Administration as being favorable to business rather than to the small taxpayer in the approach to the income tax.
Mr. Thorne. Exhibit 119 contains a key with a chain.
Mrs. Oswald. I don't know what this is a key to.
Mr. Rankin. It appears to be a key to a padlock. Do you recognize it?
Mrs. Oswald. I can see that it is a key to a padlock, but I have never used such a key.
Mr. Rankin. Have you ever seen your husband use such a key?
Mrs. Oswald. It is hard to remember what key he used. I know he had a key.
(The article referred to was marked as Commission Exhibit No. 119 for identification.)
Mr. Thorne. Exhibit 120 purports to be a telescope—15 power telescope.
Mrs. Oswald. I have never seen such a telescope.
Mr. Rankin. You never saw it as a part of your husband's things?
Mrs. Oswald. No.
(The article referred to was marked for identification as Exhibit No. 120.)
Mr. Thorne. Exhibit 121 is a Russell Stover candy box filled with miscellaneous assortment—medicines of all kinds.
Mr. Rankin. Mrs. Oswald, can you help us in regard to that Exhibit 121? Are those your medicines or are those your husband's?
Mrs. Oswald. These are all my medications.
(The article referred to was marked Commission Exhibit No. 121 and received in evidence.)
Mr. Thorne. Exhibit 122 is a cardboard box containing an assortment of items.
Mrs. Oswald. These are all his things. I think he used this to clean the rifle.
115 Mr. Rankin. You are showing us pipe cleaners that you say your husband used to clean the rifle, as you remember it?
Mrs. Oswald. Yes.
Mr. Rankin. How often did he clean it, do you remember?
Mrs. Oswald. Not too often. I have already told you.
Mr. Rankin. I offer in evidence Exhibit 122.
The Chairman. It will be received.

(The article referred to was marked Commission Exhibit No. 122, and received in evidence.)

Mr. Thorne. Exhibit 123 contains seven small one ounce dark brown bottles.

Mrs. Oswald. Lee's brother is a pharmacist. He gave this to us.

Mr. Thorne. As well as the apparent boxes that they came in.

Mr. Rankin. Which brother is a pharmacist?

Mrs. Oswald. Murret.

Mr. Rankin. You mean his cousin?

Mrs. Oswald. Yes. In the Russian the word cousin is second brother.

Mr. Rankin. We offer in evidence Exhibit 123.

The Chairman. It may be received.

(The article referred to was marked Commission Exhibit No. 123, and received in evidence.)

Mr. Thorne. Exhibit 124 is a hunting knife in a sheath, approximately a 4- or 5-inch blade.

Mrs. Oswald. I have never seen this knife.

It is a new knife. And that telescope is also new.

(The article referred to was marked as Commission Exhibit No. 124 for identification.)

Mr. Thorne. Exhibit 125 is a file cabinet for presumably three by five or five by seven inch cards.

Mrs. Oswald. Lee kept his printing things in that, pencils.

Mr. Rankin. The things that he printed his Fair Play for Cuba leaflets on?

Mrs. Oswald. Yes.

Mr. Rankin. Pencils and materials that he used in connection with that matter?

Mrs. Oswald. Yes.

Mr. Rankin. Did he have any index cards in that metal case?

Mrs. Oswald. Yes, he had some.

Mr. Rankin. You don't know what happened to them?

Mrs. Oswald. No.

Mr. Rankin. Do you know what was on those index cards?

Mrs. Oswald. No.

Mr. Rankin. A list of any people that you know of?

Mrs. Oswald. No. I don't know.

Mr. Rankin. Were those leaflets about Fair Play for Cuba printed?

Mrs. Oswald. Yes.

Mr. Rankin. And then did he stamp something on them after he had them printed?

Mrs. Oswald. He would print his name and address on them.

Mr. Rankin. I will offer in evidence Exhibit 125.

The Chairman. It may be admitted.

(The article referred to was marked Commission Exhibit No. 125, and received in evidence.)

Mr. Rankin. You don't know what happened to the cards that were in that?

Mrs. Oswald. No.

Mr. Thorne. Exhibit 126 is a small hand overnight bag, canvas zipper bag.

Mrs. Oswald. That is Lee's handbag, and he arrived with it from Mexico City.

Mr. Rankin. It is one of the bags that you described when you were telling about his bringing one back from Mexico City?

Mrs. Oswald. He only had this one.

Mr. Rankin. Exhibit 126 was the only bag that he brought back?

Mrs. Oswald. Yes.

Mr. Rankin. We offer in evidence Exhibit 126.

116 The Chairman. It may be admitted.

(The article referred to was marked Commission Exhibit No. 126, and received in evidence.)

Mr. Thorne. Exhibit 127 is a suitcase.

Mrs. Oswald. A Russian suitcase.

Mr. Rankin. You have seen that before, have you?

Mrs. Oswald. Of course.

Mr. Rankin. Do you know whether he took Exhibit 127 to Mexico?

Mrs. Oswald. No.

Mr. Rankin. You don't know, or you don't think he did?

Mrs. Oswald. I know that he did not take it.

Mr. Rankin. Do you know when he used Exhibit 127?

Mrs. Oswald. I don't think that he would have used it.

Was this taken in Lee's apartment?

Mr. Rankin. We cannot tell you that, Mrs. Oswald. We don't know which place it was taken from.

You have seen it amongst his things, though, have you not?

Mrs. Oswald. No. I think these things were in Ruth Paine's garage.

Mr. Rankin. You don't know whether it is his or Mrs. Paine's?

Mrs. Oswald. That is my suitcase.

Mr. Rankin. And did you use it to come from the Soviet Union?

Mrs. Oswald. Yes.

Mr. Thorne. This is not Lee's suitcase, then—this is your personal suitcase?

Mrs. Oswald. Yes. Ours, or mine.

Mr. Rankin. We offer in evidence Exhibit 127.

The Chairman. Do you need that? That is hers. She may want it. Do you think we need it?

Very well. It may be admitted.

(The article referred to was marked Commission Exhibit No. 127, and received in evidence.)

Mr. Thorne. Exhibit 128 is a Humble Oil and Refining Company courtesy map of the Dallas-Fort Worth area.

Mr. Rankin. I call your attention, Mrs. Oswald, to the markings in ink, in the area where the assassination took place.

Mrs. Oswald. This map Lee acquired after returning to Irving. Before that, he had another map.

That doesn't tell me anything. I did not use this map.

Mr. Rankin. Did you ever see your husband use it?

Mrs. Oswald. No. I think that this was in his apartment, where he lived. Perhaps he used it there.

Mr. Rankin. Did you ever see him put those markings on it?

Mrs. Oswald. No, I have never seen him use this specific map. Possibly he marked this place, not because of what happened there, but because this was the place where he worked, I don't know. He had a habit to note down the addresses of all acquaintances where he worked.

Mr. Rankin. Can you tell whether the writing on the side of the map there is in your husband's handwriting?

Mrs. Oswald. It doesn't look like his handwriting.

(The document referred to was marked for identification as Commission Exhibit No. 128.)

Mr. Thorne. Exhibit 129 purports to be some type of an official document in Russian.

Mrs. Oswald. That is my birth certificate.

Mr. Rankin. Do you know why it was issued at that date, rather than presumably the one that was issued when you were born?

Mrs. Oswald. Because mine was lost somewhere, and it was reissued.

Mr. Rankin. Did you have to go there to get it?
Mrs. Oswald. No, simply write a letter.
Mr. Rankin. And they mailed it to you?
Mrs. Oswald. Yes.
Mr. Rankin. I offer that exhibit in evidence.
The Chairman. It may be admitted.
117 (The document referred to was marked Commission Exhibit No. 129, and received in evidence.)
Mr. Thorne. Exhibit 130 seems to be an original instrument in Russian.
Mrs. Oswald. This is a copy of a birth certificate which a notary issues.
Mr. Thorne. Whose certificate?
Mrs. Oswald. Mine.
Mr. Rankin. I offer in evidence Exhibit 130.
The Chairman. It may be admitted.
(The document referred to was marked Commission Exhibit No. 130, and received in evidence.)
Mr. Thorne. Exhibit 131 is a one-sheet document in Russian.
Mrs. Oswald. The same thing.
Mr. Rankin. Why did you have these other copies?
Mrs. Oswald. These documents were needed for regularizing all the documents in connection with the trip abroad.
Mr. Rankin. Do you know why the date was rewritten from July 14 to July 19 on them?
Mrs. Oswald. In which?
Mr. Rankin. In the original.
Mrs. Oswald. I didn't see that.
It says July 17, 1941. The certificate is issued July 19, 1961.
Mr. Krimer. The transcript shows 17th of July 1941.
May I explain it, sir?
Mr. Rankin. You explain it, Mr. Krimer, and then ask her if you are explaining it correctly.
Mr. Krimer. I have explained it correctly, and she says it is correct.
This states she was born on July 17, but that an entry was made in the register about that on August 14, 1961. This accounts for the change in the digit. And this was issued on July 19, 1941.
Mr. Rankin. I offer that in evidence.
The Chairman. That will be admitted.
(The document referred to was marked Commission Exhibit No. 131, and received in evidence.)
Mr. Thorne. 132 is a two-sheet, eight-page letter with an envelope. This is written in Russian.
Mrs. Oswald. The envelope is from Sobolev, and the letter is from Golovachev. I simply kept them together.
Mr. Rankin. There is a reference in the last full paragraph of that letter, Mrs. Oswald, where it said, "By the way, Marina, try to explain to Paul that the basic idea of Pagodzin's play 'A man with a rifle' is contained in words"—and then goes on. Do you know what was meant by that?
It says "Now we do not have to fear a man with a rifle." Who is Paul?
Mrs. Oswald. This is only that the word "rifle" scares you, but it is quite harmless. This is Peter Gregory, Paul. He is also studying Russian. And he had to make a report at the institute about Pagodzin's play "Man with a Rifle". This play is about the revolution in Russia, and there is a film. I helped him with it.
Mr. Rankin. You are satisfied that has nothing to do with the assassination?
Mrs. Oswald. Yes.

Mr. Rankin. I offer in evidence Exhibit 132.
The Chairman. It may be admitted.
(The document referred to was marked Commission Exhibit No. 132, and received in evidence.)
Mr. Thorne. Exhibit 133 contains two photographs.
These are pictures of Lee Harvey Oswald with a rifle and pistol.
Mrs. Oswald. For me at first they appeared to be one and the same, at first glance. But they are different poses.
Mr. Rankin. You took both of those pictures, did you, in Exhibit 133?
Mrs. Oswald. Yes.
Mr. Rankin. And are those the pictures you took when you were out hanging up diapers, and your husband asked you to take the pictures of him?
Mrs. Oswald. Yes.
Mr. Rankin. With the pistol and the rifle?
Mrs. Oswald. Yes.
Mr. Rankin. We offer in evidence Exhibit 133.
The Chairman. It may be admitted.
(The documents referred to were marked Commission Exhibit No. 133, and received in evidence.)
Mr. Rankin. Do you recall whether these pictures in Exhibit 133 were taken before or after the Walker incident?
Mrs. Oswald. Before.
Mr. Thorne. Exhibit 134 is an enlargement of one of these pictures—what purports to be an enlargement.
Mrs. Oswald. Yes, this is an enlargement of that photograph.
Mr. Rankin. Mrs. Oswald, in Exhibit 133, in one of the pictures your husband has a newspaper, it appears.
Mr. Dulles. I think in both of them.
Mr. Rankin. I want to correct that.
In both he appears to have a newspaper. In one of them he has the newspaper in the right hand and in the other in the left hand. Do you know what newspaper that is?
Mrs. Oswald. It says there "Militant." But I don't know what kind of a paper that is—whether it is Communist, anti-Communist.
Mr. Rankin. Do you recall how much earlier than the Walker incident you took these photographs?
Mrs. Oswald. About two weeks.
Mr. Rankin. Was the enlargement of one of those pictures, Exhibit 134, made by you, or by someone else?
Mrs. Oswald. No, I don't know who made the enlargement.
Mr. Rankin. Have you seen Exhibit 134, the enlargement, before this?
Mrs. Oswald. No. I have been shown an enlargement, but I don't know whether this is the one I have been shown.
Mr. Rankin. Who showed that to you?
Mrs. Oswald. Apart from Mr. Gopadze, somebody else showed me an enlargement.
Mr. Rankin. Does this appear to be like the enlargement that you saw?
Mrs. Oswald. Yes. I think it was specially enlarged for the investigation.
Mr. Rankin. I offer in evidence Exhibit No. 134.
The Chairman. It may be admitted.
(The document referred to was marked Commission Exhibit No. 134, and received in evidence.)
Mr. Thorne. Exhibit No. 136 purports to be a clipping from a newspaper. It is a clipping of an advertisement, a mail coupon.
Mrs. Oswald. I don't know what that is.
Mr. Rankin. Do you recognize the handwriting on it?

Mrs. Oswald. Lee's handwriting.

Mr. Rankin. I offer in evidence Exhibit 135.

The Chairman. It will be admitted.

(The document referred to was marked Commission Exhibit No. 135, and received in evidence.)

Mr. Rankin. I call the Commission's attention to the fact that this is the coupon under which it appears the rifle was ordered, showing an enclosed $10 notation—"Check for $29.95, A. G. Hidell, age 28, post office box 2915, Dallas, Texas."

And it is marked, "One—quantity. Point 38 ST. W. 2 inch barrel, 29.95," and underlined is 29.95, and an arrow at that point.

Mr. Thorne. Exhibit 136 is a camera contained within a leather case.

Mrs. Oswald. This is a Russian camera.

Mr. Rankin. Is that the camera you used to take the pictures you have referred to?

Mrs. Oswald. I don't remember exactly whether it was an American camera or this.

Mr. Rankin. But this was one of your cameras, or your husband's cameras?

Mrs. Oswald. My husband's camera.

Mr. Rankin. I offer in evidence Exhibit 136.

119 The Chairman. It may be admitted.

(The article referred to was marked Commission Exhibit No. 136, and received in evidence.)

Mr. Thorne. Exhibit 137 is a camera in a leather case.

Mr. Rankin. Have you ever seen that camera before?

Mrs. Oswald. No.

Mr. Dulles. Is that a Russian camera?

Mrs. Oswald. No.

(The article referred to was marked Commission Exhibit No. 137 for identification.)

Mr. Thorne. Exhibit 138 is a flash attachment for some type of camera. It is an Ansco flash attachment.

Mrs. Oswald. I have never seen it.

(The article referred to was marked Commission Exhibit No. 138 for identification.)

Mr. Rankin. Do you know what happened to the American camera that you referred to?

Mrs. Oswald. I don't know.

Mr. Rankin. Was this Ansco flash equipment an attachment for that camera?

Mrs. Oswald. I have never seen it. It seems to me that it is new.

Mr. Thorne. Exhibit 139.

Mrs. Oswald. This is the fateful rifle of Lee Oswald.

Mr. Rankin. Is that the scope that it had on it, as far as you know?

Mrs. Oswald. Yes.

Mr. Rankin. I offer in evidence Exhibit 139.

The Chairman. It may be admitted.

(The article referred to was marked Commission Exhibit No. 139, and received in evidence.)

Mr. Thorne. Exhibit 140 apparently is a blanket.

Mr. Rankin. Have you seen that before, Mrs. Oswald?

Mrs. Oswald. This is still from Russia. June loved to play with that blanket.

Mr. Rankin. Was that the blanket that your husband used to cover up the rifle?

Mrs. Oswald. Yes. We didn't use this blanket as a cover. He used it for the rifle.

Mr. Rankin. And it was the blanket that you saw and thought was covering the rifle in the garage at the Paine's, is it?

Mrs. Oswald. Yes.

Mr. Rankin. Did he use it as a cover for the rifle at other places where you lived?

Mrs. Oswald. No.

Mr. Rankin. I offer in evidence Exhibit 140.

The Chairman. It may be admitted.
(The article referred to was marked Commission Exhibit No. 140, and received in evidence.)
Mr. Rankin. Did you say that June played with this blanket, Exhibit 140?
Mrs. Oswald. Yes. I would put that on the floor to make it softer—on a balcony, for example, when June was playing on it.
Mr. Rankin. Is that in this country or in Russia?
Mrs. Oswald. She didn't crawl yet in Russia.
Mr. Rankin. What balcony was that—what house?
Mrs. Oswald. On Neely Street, in Dallas.
Mr. Thorne. Exhibit 141 is an envelope that contains a bullet.
Mr. Rankin. Have you ever seen bullets or shells like that that your husband had?
Mrs. Oswald. I think Lee's were smaller.
Mr. Rankin. If that was the size for his gun, would that cause you to think it was the same?
Mrs. Oswald. Probably.
Mr. Rankin. Where did you see his?
Mrs. Oswald. In New Orleans, and on Neely Street.
Mr. Rankin. In the box, or laying loose some place?
Mrs. Oswald. In a box.
Mr. Rankin. I offer in evidence Exhibit 141.
The Chairman. It may be admitted.
(The article referred to was marked Commission Exhibit No. 141, and received in evidence.)
Mr. Thorne. Exhibit 142 is some kraft paper, brown wrapping paper.
Mrs. Oswald. It wasn't brown before.
Mr. Rankin. Did you ever see that before?
Mrs. Oswald. The FBI questioned me about this paper, but I don't know—I have never seen it.
Mr. Rankin. At one time it was kraft color, before they treated it to get fingerprints. Did you ever see anything like that?
Mrs. Oswald. Everybody sees such paper. But I didn't see that with Lee.
Mr. Rankin. You have never seen anything like that around the house, then?
Mrs. Oswald. No. We have wrapping paper around the house.
Mr. Rankin. That Exhibit 142 is more than just wrapping paper. It was apparently made up into a sack or bag.
Mrs. Oswald. I didn't see it.
Mr. Rankin. Did you ever see him make up a bag or sack or anything like that, to hold a rifle?
Mrs. Oswald. No.
(The article referred to was marked Commission Exhibit No. 142, for identification.)
Mr. Thorne. Exhibit 143 is a pistol.
Mrs. Oswald. Lee Oswald's.
Mr. Rankin. You recognize that as a pistol of your husband?
Mrs. Oswald. Yes.
Mr. Rankin. I offer in evidence Exhibit 143.
The Chairman. It may be admitted.
(The article referred to was marked Commission Exhibit No. 143, and received in evidence.)
Mr. Thorne. Exhibit 144 is a leather pistol holster.
Mrs. Oswald. That is a holster for Lee's pistol.
Mr. Rankin. Is Exhibit 144 the same holster that is in those pictures that you took?
Mrs. Oswald. Yes.
Mr. Rankin. And the pistol is the same pistol as in those pictures?

Mrs. Oswald. As much as I can tell.
Mr. Rankin. At least they appear to be, as far as you can tell?
Mrs. Oswald. Yes.
Mr. Rankin. And the rifle is the same, or appears to be, is it not?
Mrs. Oswald. Yes.
The Chairman. It may be admitted.
(The article referred to was marked Commission Exhibit No. 144, and received in evidence.)
Mr. Thorne. Exhibit 145 is a small cardboard box containing two bullets, .38 caliber.
Mr. Rankin. Do you recognize those as appearing to be the size of the bullets that your husband had for the pistol?
Mrs. Oswald. It is hard for me to tell, because I don't understand about this. I never looked at them, because I am afraid.
Mr. Rankin. But you have seen bullets like that, have you, in your husband's apartment or rooming house, or in the Neely apartment or at Mrs. Paine's?
Mrs. Oswald. At Mrs. Paine's I never saw any shells.
On Neely Street, perhaps it is similar—New Orleans. It looks like it. If they fit Lee's pistol, then they must be the right ones.
Mr. Rankin. I offer in evidence Exhibit 145.
The Chairman. Admitted.
(The article referred to was marked Commission Exhibit No. 145, and received in evidence.)
121 The Chairman. We will take a short recess.
(Brief recess.)
The Chairman. We will be in order, please.
Mr. Rankin. Mrs. Oswald, would you step over with the interpreter to this desk and point out the different pieces of clothing as we ask you about it, please?
Do you know the shirt that Lee Oswald wore the morning that he left?
Mrs. Oswald. I don't remember. What else interests you? What do you want?
Mr. Rankin. Can you tell us whether any of this clothing set out on this desk belonged to Lee Oswald?
Mrs. Oswald. These are Lee's shoes.
Mr. Rankin. When you say the shoes, you pointed to Exhibit 149?
Mrs. Oswald. Yes.
Mr. Rankin. This is a pair of shoes of which Exhibit 149 is a photograph.
Mrs. Oswald. These are his bath slippers.
Mr. Rankin. Exhibit 148 are his bath slippers?
Mrs. Oswald. Japanese bath slippers. These shoes I have never seen.
Mr. Rankin. That is Exhibit 147, you say those are shoes you have never seen? How about Exhibit 146?
Mrs. Oswald. These are his, yes. These are all Lee's shirts.
Mr. Rankin. Exhibits 150, 151——
Mrs. Oswald. These are his pajamas.
Mr. Rankin. Exhibits 150, and 151 are Lee Oswald's shirts, is that right?
Mrs. Oswald. Yes.
Mr. Rankin. And Exhibit 152 is a pair of his pajamas?
Mrs. Oswald. Yes.
Mr. Rankin. And Exhibit 153—you recognize that?
Mrs. Oswald. That is his shirt.
Mr. Rankin. And Exhibit 154? Is that one of his shirts?
Mrs. Oswald. Yes.
Mr. Rankin. Exhibit 155?
Mrs. Oswald. Yes, also. Why is it all torn?
Mr. Rankin. We are advised it was when he was hurt, they cut into some of these.

Do you recall whether or not he was wearing Exhibit—the shirt that I point to now, the morning of the 22d of November—Exhibit 150?

Mrs. Oswald. Yes, it was a dark shirt.

Mr. Rankin. You think that was the one?

Mrs. Oswald. Yes.

Mr. Rankin. I call your attention to Exhibit 156. Is that a pair of his pants?

Mrs. Oswald. These are his work pants.

Mr. Rankin. And 157?

Mrs. Oswald. Also work pants. These are all work pants.

Mr. Rankin. 158?

Mrs. Oswald. Why were both of those cut? I don't understand.

Mr. Rankin. I have not been informed, but I will try to find out for you.

Mrs. Oswald. It is not necessary.

Mr. Rankin. Do you recall which of the pants he was wearing on the morning of November 22, 1963?

Mrs. Oswald. I think the gray ones, but I am not sure, because it was dark in the room, and I paid no attention to what pants he put on.

Mr. Rankin. By the gray ones, you are referring to what I point to as Exhibit 157, is that right?

Mrs. Oswald. Yes.

Mr. Rankin. Can you tell us about Exhibit 159, a sweater?

Mrs. Oswald. That was my gift to Lee, a sweater.

Mr. Rankin. 160?

Mrs. Oswald. That is Lee's shirt.

Mr. Rankin. 161?

Mrs. Oswald. This is a pullover sweater. This is his pullover sweater.

Mr. Rankin. 162?

122 Mrs. Oswald. That is Lee's—an old shirt.

Mr. Rankin. Sort of a jacket?

Mrs. Oswald. Yes.

Mr. Rankin. 163?

Mrs. Oswald. Also.

Mr. Rankin. Do you recall which one of the sweaters or jackets he was wearing on the morning of November 22, 1963?

Mrs. Oswald. I don't remember.

Mr. Rankin. When was the last time that you saw this jacket, Exhibit 163?

Mrs. Oswald. I don't remember.

Mr. Rankin. Do you remember seeing it on the morning of November 22, 1963?

Mrs. Oswald. The thing is that I saw Lee in the room, and I didn't see him getting dressed in the room. That is why it is difficult for me to say. But I told him to put on something warm on the way to work.

Mr. Rankin. Do you recall whether the jacket, Exhibit 163, is something that he put on in your presence at any time that day?

Mrs. Oswald. Not in my presence.

Mr. Rankin. And you didn't observe it on him at any time, then?

Mrs. Oswald. No.

Mr. Rankin. Is it possible that Exhibit 163 was worn by him that morning without your knowing about it?

Mrs. Oswald. Quite possible.

Mr. Rankin. Now, at the time you saw him at the Dallas jail, can you tell us what clothing of any that are on this desk he was wearing at that time?

Mrs. Oswald. None of these. He had on a white T-shirt. What trousers he was wearing, I could not tell, because I only saw him through a window.

Mr. Rankin. Would you examine the collar on the shirt?

Mrs. Oswald. This is Lee's shirt.

Mr. Rankin. It has a mark "Brent long tail sanforized."

Mrs. Oswald. Yes, I know this shirt. I gave it to him. The sweater is also his.

Mr. Rankin. Do you recall any of these clothes that your husband was wearing when he came home Thursday night, November 21, 1963?

Mrs. Oswald. On Thursday I think he wore this shirt.

Mr. Rankin. Is that Exhibit 150?

Mrs. Oswald. Yes.

Mr. Rankin. Do you remember anything else he was wearing at that time?

Mrs. Oswald. It seems he had that jacket, also.

Mr. Rankin. Exhibit 162?

Mrs. Oswald. Yes.

Mr. Rankin. And the pants, Exhibit 157?

Mrs. Oswald. Yes. But I am not sure. This is as much as I can remember.

Mr. Rankin. Thank you.

Mr. Thorne. I identify this photograph, which is marked Exhibit 164 as being a true photograph of the shirt displayed to Mrs. Oswald, and recognized by her as being a shirt that she gave to Lee Harvey Oswald.

Mr. Rankin. I offer all of the Exhibits, Nos. 146 to 164, inclusive.

The Chairman. They may be admitted.

(The articles referred to were marked Commission Exhibit Nos. 146 to 164, inclusive, and received in evidence.)

Mr. Rankin. Mrs. Oswald, do you remember any information or documents under your control or in your possession which would relate to or shed any light on the matters we have been examining which you have not presented here?

Mrs. Oswald. I have nothing else. Everything has been taken from me.

Mr. Rankin. Some of the Commissioners have a question or two, or a few questions. If you will permit them, they would like to address them to you.

Representative Boggs. Mrs. Oswald, this question has already been asked you, but I would like to ask it again.

I gather that you have reached the conclusion in your own mind that your husband killed President Kennedy.

Mrs. Oswald. Regretfully, yes.

123 Representative Boggs. During the weeks and months prior to the assassination— and I think this question has also been asked—did you ever at any time hear your late husband express any hostility towards President Kennedy?

Mrs. Oswald. No.

Representative Boggs. What motive would you ascribe to your husband in killing President Kennedy?

Mrs. Oswald. As I saw the documents that were being read to me, I came to the conclusion that he wanted in any—by any means, good or bad, to get into history. But now that I have heard a part of the translation of some of the documents, I think that there was some political foundation to it, a foundation of which I am not aware.

Representative Boggs. By that, do you mean that your husband acted in concert with someone else?

Mrs. Oswald. No, only alone.

Representative Boggs. You are convinced that his action was his action alone, that he was influenced by no one else?

Mrs. Oswald. Yes, I am convinced.

Representative Boggs. Did you consider your husband a Communist?

Mrs. Oswald. He told me when we were in New Orleans that he was a Communist, but I didn't believe him, because I said, "What kind of a Communist are you if you don't like the Communists in Russia?"

Representative Boggs. Did he like the Communists in the United States?

Mrs. Oswald. He considered them to be on a higher level and more conscious than the Communists in Russia.

Representative Boggs. Did you consider your husband a normal man in the usual sense of the term?

Mrs. Oswald. He was always a normal man, but where it concerned his ideas, and he did not introduce me to his ideas, I did not consider him normal.

Representative Boggs. Maybe I used the wrong terminology. Did you consider him mentally sound?

Mrs. Oswald. Yes; he was smart and capable. Only he did not use his capabilities in the proper direction. He was not deprived of reason—he was not a man deprived of reason.

Representative Boggs. Thank you, Mr. Chairman. Thank you.

The Chairman. Senator Cooper, did you have any questions to ask?

Mrs. Oswald. No one knows the truth, no one can read someone else's thoughts, as I could not read Lee's thoughts. But that is only my opinion.

Senator Cooper. Mrs. Oswald, some of the questions that I ask you you may have answered—because I have been out at times.

I believe you have stated that your husband at times expressed opposition to or dislike of the United States or of its political or economic system, is that correct?

Mrs. Oswald. As far as I know, he expressed more dissatisfaction with economic policy, because as to the political matters he did not enlighten me as to his political thoughts.

Senator Cooper. Did he ever suggest to you or to anyone in your presence that the economic system of the United States should be changed, and did he suggest any means for changing it?

Mrs. Oswald. He never proposed that, but from his conversations it followed that it would be necessary to change it. But he didn't propose any methods.

Senator Cooper. Did he ever say to you or anyone in your presence that the system might be changed if officials were changed or authorities of our country were changed?

Mrs. Oswald. No, he never said that to me.

Senator Cooper. Did he ever express to you any hostility towards any particular official of the United States?

Mrs. Oswald. I know that he didn't like Walker, but I don't know whether you could call him an official.

Senator Cooper. May I ask if you ever heard anyone express to him hostility towards President Kennedy?

Mrs. Oswald. No, never.

Senator Cooper. More specifically, I will ask—did you know Mr. Frazier?

124 Representative Boggs. Wesley Frazier.

Mrs. Oswald. Oh, yes, that is the boy who took him to work.

Senator Cooper. You never heard him or anyone else express to your husband any hostility towards President Kennedy?

Mrs. Oswald. No.

Senator Cooper. Mrs. Paine?

Mrs. Oswald. No.

Senator Cooper. That is all I have.

The Chairman. Mr. Dulles, have you anything further you would like to ask?

Mr. Dulles. Mr. Chief Justice, I only have one question. Mr. Rankin has kindly asked several questions I had during the course of this hearing, these hearings the last 3 days.

Apart from trying to achieve a place in history, can you think of any other motive or anything that your husband felt he would achieve by the act of assassinating the President? That he was trying to accomplish something?

Mrs. Oswald. It is hard for me to say what he wanted to accomplish, because I don't understand him.

The Chairman. Congressman Ford, did you have anything further?

Representative Ford. Mrs. Oswald after President Kennedy was assassinated, your husband was apprehended and later questioned by a number of authorities. In the questioning he denied that he kept a rifle at Mrs. Paine's home. He denied shooting President Kennedy. And he questioned the authenticity of the photographs that you took of him holding the rifle and the holster.

Now, despite these denials by your husband, you still believe Lee Oswald killed President Kennedy?

Mrs. Oswald. Yes.

Representative Ford. That is all.

Representative Boggs. Mr. Chairman, just one or two other questions.

The Chairman. Yes.

Representative Boggs. Mrs. Oswald, when you lived in New Orleans with your husband, and he was active in this alleged Cuban committee, did you attend any meetings of any committees—was anyone else present?

Mrs. Oswald. No, never.

Representative Boggs. Were there any members of the committee other than your husband?

Mrs. Oswald. There was no one. There was no one. There was no organization in New Orleans. Only Lee was there.

Representative Boggs. One other question. Did he also dislike Russia when he was in Russia?

Mrs. Oswald. Yes.

Representative Boggs. Thank you.

The Chairman. Well, Mrs. Oswald, you have been a very cooperative witness. You have helped the Commission. We are grateful to you for doing this. We realize that this has been a hard ordeal for you to go through.

Mrs. Oswald. It was difficult to speak all the truth.

The Chairman. We hope you know that the questions we have asked you have—none of them have been from curiosity or to embarrass you, but only to report to the world what the truth is.

Now, after you leave here, you may have a copy of everything you have testified to. You may read it, and if there is anything that you think was not correctly recorded, or anything you would like to add to it, you may do so.

Mrs. Oswald. I unfortunately—I cannot—since it will be in English.

The Chairman. Your lawyer may read it for you, and if he points out something to you that you think you should have changed, you may feel free to do that.

Mrs. Oswald. Yes, he will read it.

The Chairman. And if in the future we should like to ask you some more questions about something that develops through the investigation, would you be willing to come back and talk to us again?

Mrs. Oswald. Yes.

The Chairman. We hope it won't be necessary to disturb you. But if it is, you would be willing to come, would you not?

Mrs. Oswald. Yes.

125 The Chairman. Thank you very much.

Representative Ford. Mr. Chairman—I would just like to suggest that if Mrs. Oswald does wish to revise any of her testimony, that this be called to the attention of the Commission through her attorney, Mr. Thorne.

The Chairman. Yes, of course. That is the proper procedure.

Now, Mr. Thorne, you have been very cooperative with the Commission. We appreciate that cooperation. We hope that if anything new should come to your attention that would be helpful to the Commission, you would feel free to communicate with us.

Mr. Thorne. Certainly, Mr. Chairman.

The Chairman. Do you care to say anything at this time?

Mr. Thorne. Mr. Chairman, if I may, I would like to make a closing statement.

The Chairman. Yes. And may I say, also, if you have any questions you would like to ask Mrs. Oswald before you make your statement, you may do that.

Mr. Thorne. There are none.

Representative Boggs. Mr. Chairman, I would just like to say Mr. Thorne has been very helpful.

Mr. Thorne. During the noon recess, Mrs. Oswald made four requests of me to make before this Commission.

You have anticipated several of them, but I think there are one or two that need to be covered.

To begin with, she wanted me to express to you, Mr. Chairman, and members of your Commission, her extreme gratitude to you for the consideration and kindness that has been shown to her in these proceedings. She feels you have certainly gone out of your way to make her comfortable, and she has been comfortable, in spite of the sad and tragic events we have been discussing.

Point No. 2, she did want to make it quite clear to the Commission that in the event her testimony was needed for rebuttal or whatever on down the line, she would be available, and at your wish would come to Washington as convenient for you when it was again convenient.

The third point you have already covered. She did request that she be given a copy of these proceedings, which I told her she would receive, and, of course, copies of the exhibits would be attached for her identification and examination.

Mrs. Oswald. And copies of some of the letters?

Mr. Thorne. This will all be attached as exhibits.

And the final point was this. She has been, as you know, under protective custody of the Secret Service from shortly after the assassination. She has been most grateful for this protection. The Secret Service have shown her every courtesy, as everyone has in this matter. She is extremely grateful for this protection they have given her.

I haven't had personally enough time to think this thing out myself. I don't know. It is her request, however, that, at this point she feels the protection is no longer necessary. She feels that at this time she can walk among people with her head held high. She has nothing to hide. She is not afraid.

She feels that the Secret Service has performed a noble service to her. And this is not meant by way of saying for some action on their part she wants to get rid of them.

I have noticed that since we have been in Washington she resents being guided. She feels she can find her way by herself.

And, if the Commission would give this matter consideration—we don't know whom to go to. I haven't thought about it. I don't know who has suggested the Secret Service continue protecting her. It is a matter, of course, that ought to be considered.

But it is her request that as soon as it is practical, she would like to be a free agent and out of the confines of this protection.

I point out to you gentlemen that she is living, as you well know, with Mr. and Mrs. Martin. They have a rather modest home. Three bedrooms. It has a den and it has a combination living and dining room. The house is not extremely large, but there are always two men in the house. This does burden the family. This is not a request on the part of the Martins. They welcome this protection. This is something she thinks in terms of herself that she does not want to feel that she is being held back.

126 Is that correct?

Mrs. Oswald. What I wanted to say, Mr. Thorne has said.

Mr. Thorne. For my own part, gentlemen, thank you.

The Chairman. Mr. Thorne, we can understand Mrs. Oswald's desire to live a perfectly normal life with her children. Whatever has been done, as you recognize, has been done for her protection, and for her help during these terrible days that she has been going through.

But she may feel from this moment on that she is under no protection, except what she might ask for. And so you are perfectly free, Mrs. Oswald, to live your normal life without any interference from anyone. And should anyone interfere with you, I hope you would call it to the attention of the Commission.

Mrs. Oswald. Thank you very much.

Mr. Thorne. Mr. Chairman, may I add one point, please?

For our purposes, I would appreciate it if this matter of removal, assuming that it is to be removed shortly, is kept secret, also.

I would prefer generally for the public to feel that—at least temporarily—that this protection is available. I don't feel any qualms myself. I don't feel there are any problems. But I think the matter of Mrs. Marguerite Oswald has come up. There may be some problem from some sources.

The Chairman. Mr. Thorne, I think the correct answer to that would be—and it would be the answer we would give—that Mrs. Oswald, in the future, will be given such assistance and only such assistance as she asks for.

Mr. Thorne. Thank you very much, sir.

The Chairman. I want to say also before the session adjourns that we are indebted to Mr. Krimer for the manner in which he has interpreted. Next to the witness, I am sure he has had the hardest position in this whole hearing. And we appreciate the manner in which he has done it.

Mr. Krimer. Thank you very much, sir.

Mrs. Oswald. He is a very good interpreter.

The Chairman. Very well. If there is nothing further to come before the session, we will adjourn.

Mrs. Oswald. I am very grateful to all of you. I didn't think among Americans I would find so many friends.

The Chairman. You have friends here.

Mrs. Oswald. Thank you.

(Whereupon, at 5:50 p.m., the President's Commission recessed.)

Monday, February 10, 1964

Testimony of Mrs. Marguerite Oswald

The President's Commission met at 10 a.m. on February 10, 1964, at 200 Maryland Avenue NE., Washington, D.C.

Present were Chief Justice Earl Warren, Chairman: Senator Richard B. Russell, Representative Hale Boggs, Representative Gerald R. Ford, and Allen W. Dulles, members.

Also present were J. Lee Rankin, general counsel; Wesley J. Liebeler, assistant counsel; John F. Doyle, attorney for Mrs. Marguerite Oswald; and Leon Jaworski, special counsel to the attorney general of Texas.

The Chairman. The Commission will come to order.

Let the record show that Senator Russell and I are present, and we convened today for the purpose of taking the testimony of Mrs. Oswald.

Mrs. Oswald, would you rise and be sworn, please?

Do you solemnly swear that you will tell the truth, the whole truth, and nothing but the truth, so help you God, throughout this proceeding?

127 Mrs. Oswald. I do—so help me God.

The Chairman. You may be seated.

Now, Mrs. Oswald, you are here represented by an attorney, are you?

Mrs. Oswald. Yes, sir; Mr. Doyle is representing me.

The Chairman. Mr. Doyle is representing you. Mr. Doyle was appointed, was he not, at your request?

Mrs. Oswald. Yes, I asked to be represented by counsel.

The Chairman. Yes. And the record may show that Mr. Doyle was appointed to represent her at the request of Mrs. Oswald by the president of the Bar Association of the District of Columbia, Mr. Pratt.

That is correct, is it not, Mr. Doyle?

Mr. Doyle. It is, sir.

The Chairman. Mrs. Oswald, you are appearing voluntarily before the Commission, are you not?

Mrs. Oswald. Yes, voluntarily.

The Chairman. You requested to do so.

In order that you may have a full opportunity to testify in your own manner, and tell us everything that you know, and particularly because we do not know what you know, I am going to ask you if you would like first, in your own way, and in your own time, to tell us everything you have concerning this case.

You would like to do that, would you?

Mrs. Oswald. Yes, Chief Justice Warren. I would like to very much.

However, there are three things that I have asked that should be brought before the Council, three requests of mine. One has already been granted—that is the counsel, Mr. Doyle. And I do appreciate that fact.

I have stated publicly that I believe in the American way of life and justice for all men, which is our American way of life.

My son, Lee Harvey Oswald, was tried and convicted within a few hours time, without benefit of counsel. And so I am appealing to the Board that my son, Lee Harvey Oswald, be represented by counsel. I am being represented by counsel. My daughter-in-law Marina was represented by counsel. And I understand that all other witnesses will have the privilege of being represented by counsel.

However, the main object of the Commission is Lee Harvey Oswald, in the murder of President Kennedy. So I strongly believe that Lee should be represented by counsel.

Now, my reasons for wanting this done this way is, I will state, that Marina has testified. Marina has testified, according to the papers—and I am assuming that this is correct—that Lee wanted to live in Russia and Cuba, and that is why he went to Mexico.

I happen to know differently—because Marina has told me the first day I was with her, "Mama, I write to Russian consul. I want go back to Russia. I like America. But Lee no get work."

So you see, had a counsel been there in behalf of my son, when Marina said that—it doesn't have to be a court trial or a cross-examination. All I am asking is that this man sit quietly, and when he knows of different facts, then he could say, "Well, Mrs. Oswald, isn't it true that you wrote the Russian consul yourself, wanting to go back to Russia?"

And in this way, gentlemen, I believe you would have both sides and a true picture.

I cannot see how you can come to a true conclusion by taking individual testimony.

Now, I, myself, am here today to testify. I have been sworn in. But that doesn't mean that I can tell the whole story. I may forget something. And the counsel would know.

We have investigators all over the country, the reporters are interested, the public. I have over 1,500 letters, people expressing their opinion of the way this case is being handled. And, believe me, gentlemen, they are not satisfied.

I can produce these documents for you.

They think, like I think, that the American way of life, both sides should be heard.

I don't think that seven men of this Commission can come to a true conclusion.128 What it will be, it will be an analysis of what the FBI and the Secret Service and the Dallas police have—mainly, speculation and opinion of other people.

Now, Mr. Lane has affidavits, I understand, from the same witnesses that have made statements to the Dallas police, which are contrary to those particular statements.

I implore you—I implore you, in the name of justice, to let my son, Lee Harvey Oswald, who is accused of assassinating the President, and I, the mother of this man, who is the accused's mother, be represented by counsel.

We have information pertinent to this case.

My daughter-in-law is the only one who has testified.

The things that came out in the paper—I know, I have documents. I am not asking you to believe me as a mother. I can prove the statements that I say.

And I believe in this way you will have a true picture, and a much better picture, because as you are going along you will be having both sides, and won't have to wait to analyze the situation in the end, as the testimony is being given by each individual, right then and there—you will have the other party's testimony.

Now, there is another——

The Chairman. Before you leave that, Mrs. Oswald, may I say to you, first, that the Commission is not here to prosecute your dead son. It is not here and it was not established to prosecute anyone.

It is the purpose and the province of the Commission to obtain all the facts that it can obtain, and then make an impartial report—not as a prosecutor, but as an impartial Commission—on the manner in which the President came to his death.

We are trying to recognize the individual rights of all persons who are called before the Commission, to let them have their lawyers, and let their lawyers have an opportunity to examine them, as well as the Commission.

You may be sure that if Mr. Lane has any evidence of his own knowledge, or has any accumulation of affidavits from others, to the effect—to any effect, concerning this trial, that he will have an opportunity to come here, just as you are here, in order to present those to the Commission.

But so far as his being here at all times before the Commission to cross-examine or to be present when all witnesses are testifying—that is not in accordance with the procedures of the Commission.

But I assure you that if Mr. Lane has any evidence of any kind bearing upon the assassination of the President, he will be accorded the same opportunity that you have to come here and present them, and we will give him an opportunity in his own way to tell his story, and present his own evidence. And should he want counsel, he may have counsel, also.

Now, you may go to your second point.

Mrs. Oswald. No, I am not finished with my first, please.

I appreciate and I understand exactly what you have told me, Chief Justice Warren.

But there is one thing—and, of course, I will have to accept your decision, and will be most happy to have Mr. Lane present his testimony the way you have suggested.

However, I am not in agreement with you. One point I want to make clear.

We do not know the questions that you are asking of myself or Marina or the other witnesses. And I contend that you cannot ask them the pertinent questions because you don't know what I know, and what Mr. Lane knows. And so you will still have an analysis in the long run, a conclusion.

I am going to go back to Marina. As I say, Marina made her statements——

The Chairman. On that particular thing, may I say this: It is true that we don't know how to examine you at the present time because we don't know what you have to present to this Commission. But we are affording you the opportunity before we ask you any questions to tell your story, in your own way.

Then we should know what questions we want to ask of you.

Mrs. Oswald. Yes, sir; I understand that thoroughly.

But I am a human being, going through a life story from childhood, and I may forget something that my counsel would know. And that applies to witnesses.129 They may forget to testify something that my counsel has facts on. I will have to accept your verdict, but I don't do it graciously.

I want that for record.

The Chairman. Yes. Well, that is all right, Mrs. Oswald. You may state that for the record.

Mrs. Oswald. I have documents, and I would like to ask, please—I will not leave any documents out of my hand. I carry them with me wherever I go. Even Mr. Doyle has been told that the documents stay with me.

I have had documents stolen from me. I have had newspaper clippings stolen from me in my home, by the Secret Service.

I make the statement perfectly plain. And so the documents stay with me.

Now, these are originals. I want, and you will want, copies of every original I have, and I will be more than happy to let you have them. However, I want to be present when these copies are made and the original returned to me.

I will under no circumstances let anyone have my originals for an hour or two, and then return them to me—if I am making myself plain.

I would like to request that, please.

The Chairman. We will accommodate you in that respect.

Mrs. Oswald. Then I have one other stipulation or request.

When I tell my story, I will be including people in my story that possibly you don't know of. I request that I have the privilege, through you, of course, to subpena these people that are in connection with the story that I tell, if you do not have the names already.

And I feel sure that I have some information that you don't know about, and there are some people involved.

I also request that after my testimony, that Marina Oswald will be subpenaed—not subpenaed but will then testify again, if you see fit. And I believe that I have contrary testimony to her testimony that would make it necessary for her to be recalled.

I ask that that be granted.

The Chairman. Well, Mrs. Oswald, of course you have no power of subpena, and we have no power to give you the power of subpena. But you may be sure that if your evidence produces anything that is critical to this investigation, that we will pursue it to the end, in order to determine the weight of the testimony for our final report. You may be sure of that.

Mrs. Oswald. I appreciate that.

The Chairman. But as to how we do it, or when we do it, you will just have to leave that to the Commission.

Mrs. Oswald. You will give me the assurance that these people I name, regardless of title—I am liable to name some very important people——

The Chairman. No, we cannot give you any assurance, because we don't know——

Mrs. Oswald. I see no reason, then, for my testimony.

The Chairman. Well, Mrs. Oswald—you cannot commit us to subpenaing anybody. We don't know. You are talking to us, and we are in the dark. You cannot commit this Commission to doing something that might be improper, it might not even be helpful in any way, shape, or form. The Commission will be reasonable in every respect. We have no desire to protect anyone. We have no desire to injure you or anyone else in this matter. And certainly you ought to have some confidence in a commission that is appointed by the President, and not try to tie our hands in a way that would be contrary to the manner in which commissions normally proceed.

Mrs. Oswald. Now, Mr. Warren, you made a statement that you in no way—I cannot quote your words—intimidate me. But you did not include my son. My son is being accused of the murder of President Kennedy. And I think that my son should be considered in this. He is dead. But we can show cause that my son is not the assassin of

President Kennedy. And so I would like my son—he is the main object of the Presidential Commission, is he not, sir?

The Chairman. No, no, he is not, Mrs. Oswald. The purpose of this Commission is to determine what the facts are in the assassination of President Kennedy.

130 It is not an accusation against your son. There was an accusation against your son in the Texas courts. That is an entirely different proceeding.

We are here to do justice and be fair to everyone concerned in this matter. And I assure you that that is our main and our only purpose in serving on this Commission. None of us cherish this responsibility.

Mrs. Oswald. I am sure, sir.

The Chairman. And the only satisfaction we can derive from it is to be fair to all concerned.

And I assure you that is our objective in the matter.

Mrs. Oswald. I do not mean to imply that this Commission will not be fair. I know about the men on the Commission. And they are all very fine men, including yourself, Chief Justice Warren. If I have implied that, I will—will now say I do not imply. But I do state a fact that I do not think that you can come to a true conclusion. I want that for record.

Now, I am going to produce—and this will be a fact—and this is on the basis——

The Chairman. Now, we have finished the three things that you are talking about, and we are going to your testimony?

Mrs. Oswald. This is in connection with this, Chief Justice Warren. And I think it is very important to present a picture.

And then if you allow me these few minutes, I will be through.

Is that satisfactory, sir?

The Chairman. Yes, go right ahead.

Mrs. Oswald. Now, I believe you mentioned that you would not have the power or give me the power to subpena them. But if I could produce the facts in my story, then I believe we should have these people called.

Now, here is an article in the Washington paper—and the date happens to be torn off, but I can get it—that Senator John G. Tower had made. And I have outlined here——

The Chairman. I wonder, Mrs. Oswald—before we get into any details of this kind, let's settle this situation as to whether the Commission will say to you now that it will subpena anyone you ask.

I must say to you that you cannot put that burden on the Commission. The Commission will have to exercise its own discretion as to who it subpenas and when.

Mr. Doyle. Mr. Chief Justice, may I say something? I was wondering if whether or not what Mrs. Oswald is addressing respectfully to the Commission is her confidence that if in the course of her own testimony and the actual facts that she is producing, she expresses confidence that if those facts recommend the subpena of additional witnesses, or the recall of others, she expresses her confidence that that would be done, if the facts she outlines so require.

The Chairman. She may be very sure of that, as I tried to tell her.

But the only thing—I would not want Mrs. Oswald to leave here and say, "I gave the Commission a list of witnesses and they did not call all of them."

Now, that is a matter that will have to be in the province of the Commission, and not in the province of a witness.

And I say that without any combative—not in a combative spirit. Because, as your counsel states, I think we are not far apart on it, Mrs. Oswald.

Mrs. Oswald. No. And I appreciate the fact——

The Chairman. But fairness will have to judge our actions. And we propose to be fair.

Mrs. Oswald. Now, I guess I am a very stubborn person. I am a very aggressive person, as you know by now.

I would like—this would be just 2 minutes, and it would bring a point, and then I would be through, if I may.

The Chairman. Very well.

Mrs. Oswald. Senator Towner has dates here, and the main part of the article is that he had received a letter from the State Department.

Now, I would like—I have information from the State Department, I have documents from the State Department which is contrary to the dates and contrary to Senator Tower's public statement.

131 And I would like to have the letter that he has from the State Department, and the name of the man that wrote it, because it is contrary to what I have.

He could have been, to use an American slang, shooting his mouth off, because he said if he went to Russia let him stay there, I would not help him—is what he said.

But then again he may have this very important letter from this man in the State Department, which is incorrect, from what I have.

Now, he claims—and if you would like to read that—and that is what I was trying to bring out.

The Chairman. I think you will have to leave that to the wisdom of the Commission and its sense of fair play, and what is necessary, all facts considered.

Mrs. Oswald. Well, I have had my say, gentlemen, and I will most graciously continue.

However. I am not too happy that I will not have counsel for my son, because I believe my son would also be entitled to counsel.

The Chairman. Very well, you may continue.

Mrs. Oswald. Now, I will start——

The Chairman. Mrs. Oswald, may I introduce Congressman Ford, also a member of the Commission.

Now, Mrs. Oswald—Mr. Lee Rankin will be in charge of the hearing from this point on. He is our General Counsel, as you know.

Mrs. Oswald. Yes.

Mr. Rankin. Mrs. Oswald, will you proceed to produce the papers and tell us about them, and then I will ask the Commission after we get them, to permit us to substitute copies, and in accordance with your request we will let you be present at the time we make the photostats.

The Chairman. You may start to tell your story in your own way.

Mrs. Oswald. I have three different stories. I understand from Mr. Rankin's letter that my life is to be told from the very start, and so is Lee's life, from the very start. So which will I start first?

I believe it would be easier for me and of more benefit to the counsel if I would continue with one life, the whole story, and then continue with the—whichever way you would suggest I do it.

Mr. Rankin. If you could start out and tell us within the period that Lee Oswald returned from the Soviet Union on, whatever you know about it, in your own way, and then we will go back to the other matters later.

Is that all right?

Mrs. Oswald. Yes, sir—anything is just fine. I am willing to help in any way possible.

I wanted to state it clearly in the beginning.

I received a speedletter from the State Department stating that Lee would leave Moscow, and how he would leave and arrive in New York—on June 13, 1962. I was on a case in Crowell, Tex. I am a practical nurse. And I was taking care of a very elderly woman, whose daughter lived in Fort Worth, Tex.

So I was not able to leave and meet Lee.

Robert, his brother, met him, and Lee went to Robert's home.

Approximately about a week later—I could not stand it any more—I called the daughter and had her come to take care of her mother, and took 3 days off, and went to Fort Worth to see Lee and Marina.

Marina is a beautiful girl. And I said to Lee, "Marina, she doesn't look Russian. She is beautiful."

He says, "Of course not. That is why I married her, because she looks like an American girl."

I asked her where he had met her, and he said he met her at a social function, a community function.

I said, "You know, Lee, I am getting ready—I was getting ready to write a book on your so-called defection.

"I had researched it and came to Washington in 1961, and, by the way, asked to see President Kennedy, because I had a lot of extenuating circumstances at the time because of the defection."

He said, "Mother, you are not going to write a book."

132 I said, "Lee, don't tell me what to do. I cannot write the book now, because, Honey, you are alive and back."

But, at the time, I had no way of knowing whether my son was living or dead, and I planned to write the book.

"But don't tell me what to do. It has nothing to do with you and Marina. It is my life, because of your defection."

He said, "Mother, I tell you you are not to write the book. They could kill her and her family."

That was in the presence of my son Robert Oswald and his wife.

Mr. Rankin. Can you tell us about what date that was?

Mrs. Oswald. Let's see. Lee arrived in New York on June 13, and—now, I have a letter stating, from Lee, that he is arriving in New York on June 13th. However, he plans to go to Washington for a day or two. So I have no way of knowing, Mr. Rankin, whether he came straight from New York to my son's home, or if he stayed in New York and came to Washington a few days.

But I have the letter stating that.

But I have no way of knowing.

Mr. Rankin. Was this conversation within about a week of the time that he came back?

Mrs. Oswald. Yes, approximately. That is correct.

So I stayed in Fort Worth 2 or 3 days. I did not live at Robert's home. I rented a motel. In fact, the lady of the mother I was taking care of paid my motel expenses while I was in Fort Worth. But I went there every day.

While I was there—Marina is a pharmacist. I have a medical book, and Lee was saying that he was losing his hair, and how he had become bald, because of the cold weather in Texas.

So I got the medical book, looking up baldness, and the treatment for baldness, and Marina came by and she read the prescriptions.

So I said, "Lee, she reads English," and he said, "Mother, that is Latin, of course, that is universal."

So because it was a medical conversation, Lee said he had an operation while in the Soviet Union on his throat.

I am sorry—but all of the confusion of myself being there and the daughter-in-law, the Russian girl—that was never gone into. That is all I know.

But that was also said in the presence of my son Robert—that he had an operation on his throat while in the Soviet Union.

Mr. Rankin. Did he say when that was?

Mrs. Oswald. No, sir; that was all that was said.

As I say, with all the confusion of Marina, we were so thrilled with Marina, with the children and all, there was quite a bit of confusion.

Now, I left, and I went back to Crowell on my job.

While I was in Robert's home, Lee immediately was out job-hunting. And I felt very bad about that, because they had come 10,000 miles by ship, by plane, and by train, which was an awfully hard trip with a young baby, and I thought he should at least have a week or two before he would look for work.

But I want you to know that immediately Lee was out looking for work.

And this is the time that Lee had gone to the public stenographer, made the statement that he was writing a book.

You probably have that information. It was highly publicized.

I, myself, gave him the $10 that he gave the public stenographer.

I bought Marina clothes, and brought clothes to her while at my daughter-in-law's house, bought diapers for the baby. And Marina had more clothes when she arrived in the States than I now have.

So what I am trying to state is as we go further into the story, it has been stated that my son neglected Marina, and that she didn't have any clothes. The Russian people have stated that all throughout Texas in the papers. And that is not true. I happen to know, because I, myself, bought Marina three dresses. And my daughter-in-law bought dresses, and my daughter-in-law's sister, which I would like to have as a witness, bought clothes for Marina. So there is this conflicting testimony.

Mr. Rankin. What daughter-in-law was that?

133 Mrs. Oswald. Robert's wife. And Robert's wife's sister, who is a schoolteacher, bought clothes for Marina.

Mr. Rankin. Is she married?

Mrs. Oswald. No. She is a schoolteacher. She is single.

So that story there is incorrect.

So then I went back to Crowell, Tex., and I was not satisfied in my mind because the way they lived. They only had a two-bedroom house. As you know. Robert has two children. And there was another couple with another child.

So Lee immediately began looking for work.

So I decided that I would quit this job and help the children all I could. So I did. I gave notice. And I came to Fort Worth, and I rented an apartment at the Rotary Apartments, which is on West 7th and Summit. And Lee and Marina then came to live with me.

Mr. Rankin. How long did they stay at Robert's?

Mrs. Oswald. They stayed at Robert's approximately 2 or 3 weeks, sir.

So then they came to live with me.

While there, I said to Lee—I am ahead of my story.

Lee and Marina had sent me wonderful gifts, and I have the gifts, from Russia. A box of tea, very fine tea, a Russian scarf, pure linen napkins, embroidered with my initial, a box of candy for Christmas that has a Russian Santa Claus on it.

I said to Lee. "Lee, I want to know one thing. Why is it you decided to return back to the United States when you had a job in Russia, and as far as I know you seemed to be pretty well off, because of the gifts that you have sent me. And you are married to a Russian girl, and she would be better off in her homeland than here. I want to know."

He said, "Mother, not even Marina knows why I have returned to the United States."

And that is all the information I ever got out of my son.

"Not even Marina knows why I have returned to the United States."

Mr. Rankin. How did you get along when you were there together with Marina and your son?

Mrs. Oswald. Well, that was a very happy month, Mr. Rankin. Marina was very happy. She had the best home, I believe, that she had ever had. And Lee—I was taking Lee out to work every morning, looking for work, through the unemployment commission, and ads in the paper. And I was taking care of the baby and doing the cooking, and Marina was helping clean up. And she would wash the dishes. And Lee and Marina would go for long walks every afternoon, and I would take care of the baby. Marina would sing around the house, and watch the television and comment on different programs, programs that she had seen in Russia.

She knew—there was a picture with Gregory Peck, and she said, "Mama, I know Gregory Peck."

And she was singing Santa Lucia.

And here again in my stupidity, I said to Lee, "Lee, she knows English, she is singing Santa Lucia."

He said, "Mother, that is an international song."

Marina was very happy, and I was very happy to have the children.

And Lee desperately looked for work.

He was offered several good jobs from the State Employment Office of Texas. One in particular, I remember he said that he regretted not getting the job, but they told him because his wife was not an American citizen, that they would not be able to hire him.

He met obstacles all the way.

This one particular woman at the Texas employment agency took an interest in Lee and went out all the way to give Lee clues for jobs. And I, myself, took Lee job-hunting every day.

And it is through the employment office that he became employed 3 weeks later, after he was in my home, by the Leslie Manufacturing Co. in Fort Worth, which is a sheetmetal place.

Mr. Rankin. Now, while Marina was living with you there, and your son, and the little baby——

134 Mrs. Oswald. June.

Mr. Rankin. Did you talk to Marina, and did she speak English to you?

Mrs. Oswald. Yes, she spoke English, Mr. Rankin. Like she would say—and we used the dictionary when she didn't understand.

She would say—I would say, "Marina, you now nurse your baby."

"Yes, Mama. The time."

Or "No time."

With motions—"no time. Mama."

She spoke English.

Mr. Rankin. What I would like to find out for the Commission, if we can, in regard to speaking English, did you think she was able to talk English fluently, or did you think she was in the process of learning it?

Mrs. Oswald. She was in the process of learning. But she understood more than she could talk.

And I have a letter from Lee stating that Marina also speaks and understands French, that she had learned at grammar school.

Mr. Rankin. Did you know French?

Mrs. Oswald. No, sir.

Mr. Rankin. So you could not tell?

Mrs. Oswald. I could not tell.

And I didn't think a thing of it.

And, of course, Marina and Lee spoke Russian all the time, even in front of me.

And you asked about this time—it was a very happy time. They would sit at the table. They were playing a game, and I said to Lee, "What is it you are doing?"

Because they were always talking in Russian.

"Mother, we are playing a game which is similar to American tic-tac-toe."

And they also taught each other. They had books. They are both children—very intelligent and studious. Lee was teaching Marina English, and Marina was teaching him some things that he wanted to know about Russia, in my home.

Mr. Rankin. Now, you were saying that he got this job at the Leslie Manufacturing Co.

Mrs. Oswald. Yes, sir.

And then his first pay—he kept his first pay. And then the second pay, he rented the home on Mercedes Street, which is the south side, and approximately 10 blocks from where I lived at the Rotary Apartment, and approximately 10 blocks from where he was to work.

Lee had no car, and Lee walked to and back from work, which helped to save money.

Now, you must understand that this couple had no money, and had nothing. I gave them some dishes, and some silverware, and just a few little things that I could help out with.

But Lee did have the first week's pay.

And then the second week's pay. And he rented this home which was $59.50 a month. It was a nice little one-bedroom furnished duplex, in a nice neighborhood, convenient to his work.

But then that leaves the boy broke.

I brought food into the house. I never like to talk about the other members of the family, because to me that is speculation. But I know that Robert brought food, also, in the house. And they were not in want. Marina nursed June.

Now, it has been stated in the paper that the Russian friends have gone into the home and they are talking about this home, and found that they were in desperate straits, that there was no food in the house, and no milk for the baby.

I say Marina nursed the baby.

They may have walked into this home, where maybe they didn't have at that particular time any milk in the box. Maybe Lee was going to bring groceries home. But I know they were not in destitute circumstances in that respect.

They had no money and didn't have anything. I brought groceries, and I brought a roll of scotch toweling. I had bought two packs and I gave them one.

135 And the next day when I went by, the scotch toweling was in the kitchen, on a coat hanger, with a nail.

And I think that is real nice, a young couple that doesn't have any money, that they can use their imagination, and put up the scotch toweling to use on a coat hanger. They are just starting married life in a new country. And they have no money. But here is the point. The Russian friends, who were established, and had cars and fine homes, could not see this Russian girl doing without. They are the ones that interfered. They are the ones that interfered, and were not happy the way this Russian girl—and within a short time, then, this Russian girl had a playpen, had a sewing machine, had a baby bed, and a Taylor Tot. And this all came out in the paper—that they supplied this to the girl, because she was in need of these things.

I say it is not necessary for a young couple to have a playpen for a baby. We have millions and millions of American couples in the United States that cannot afford playpens for the children. I, myself, have been in that position.

So I think those things were immaterial.

The point I am trying to bring out is that these Russian friends have interfered in their lives, and thought that the Russian girl should have more than necessary.

And my son could not supply these things at that particular time. He was just starting to work.

This, to me, is very strong in my mind, that there are a lot of Russian friends that were made immediately, that have interfered and have publicly stated—a circle of friends, approximately eight or nine, that would not give their names in the paper, they were interviewed by Mr. Tinsley of the Star Telegram—that has downed Lee for every way possible.

So these are the Russian friends who are established with cars, and didn't think that the Russian girl was getting a good break in America.

Mr. Rankin. Were there any differences between you and Lee Oswald or Marina while they were in your home? Did you have any quarrels?

Mrs. Oswald. No, sir, no, sir, none at all.

Now, there was one thing. And I will point out the character of my son, and what I am saying about the playpen and so on.

Now, this was all done within a few weeks time. They moved there—they left my home in July, and they moved there in August, and then they moved to Dallas in October. So it was in this period of time that all these things were accumulated from Russian friends.

And no man likes other people giving—interfering in his way of living, and giving all these things to his wife that he himself cannot supply. This is a human trait, I would say.

Now, I want to bring this story up.

I could not afford to buy a bed for my grandchild, because I have worked prior to this for nothing. The job that I had quit I was making $25 a week, gentlemen—a 24-hour live-in job. The jobs prior to this I worked for $10 a week, 7 days a week, a live-in job.

Because of Lee's so-called defection, and my accident, the way I was treated, left destitute, without any medical or compensation, I decided to devote my life to humanity, and I became a practical nurse. And I have worked for $5 a week, living in the place.

So I had no money, I had $200 saved, when I came to Fort Worth, and that is what I rented the house with, and brought the food with.

So then that leaves me broke.

So I gave up a job in order to help this girl.

So to get back now to the home, Mr. Rankin—we had no quarrels. This month was beautiful. Marina was very happy.

I had the car and the television, and we went around.

As I say, they were free to go and come like they want. They would take long walks.

If you are not familiar with Fort Worth, Tex., from the Rotary Apartment to Leonard Brothers is approximately 3 miles, and they used to walk there, and they came home—Marina came home with a Cancan petticoat and some136 hose that Lee bought here with a few dollars that Robert and I had given him—he spent on his wife.

So that was a very happy time.

Now, when they lived in the home on Mercedes Street that he rented, I was employed as an OB, a nurse, in Fort Worth, Tex., at an OB's salary. And that salary, gentlemen, will astonish you. I worked, lived in, for $9 a day, 24 hours duty.

On an OB case—I am very busy with the baby all day long because people are coming in and out, giving presents and so on. I have a 10 o'clock feeding for the baby. And it is approximately 11 o'clock before I am through and in bed. The baby is up again at 2 o'clock. It is approximately 3:30 before I am through again with the baby. The baby is up again at 5:30. And it is approximately—then my day starts. I am stressing the point that I worked for $9 a day during all that, a $9 a day job. So that is 7 days a week, $63.

Now, this is the first time I have had a nurse's salary, I want you to understand.

So with my first pay, I bought Marina clothes, I bought the baby clothes, and I brought food into this home. I went all out for Marina. I just love her, and was just thrilled to death with her. And I bought a highchair. I could not afford a bed, because I didn't have enough money to buy the bed. So that is why I bought the clothes and things of that sort. But I bought the baby a highchair.

Mr. Rankin. How did Marina treat you then?

Mrs. Oswald. Fine. But then Marina was not satisfied with the things that I bought her.

As you see, the way I am properly dressed—I don't say I mean to be the height of fashion, but I have—before becoming a nurse I was in the business world, and I have been a manager in the merchandise field. So I do know clothes.

And I bought her some shorts. And she wanted short shorts, like the Americans. She pictured America in her mind evidently.

And I bought her a little longer shorts.

And "I no like, Mama."

I said, "Marina, you are a married woman and it is proper for you to have a little longer shorts than the younger girls."

"No, Mama."

And I will stress this—that Marina was never too happy—"No, Mama, no nice, no, Mama, no this."

That was perfectly all right. I thought she didn't understand our ways. I didn't feel badly about it.

I am going to get back to the highchair, to give you a picture of my son.

I bought the highchair and brought it over there, and Lee was not at home. And Marina didn't know what a highchair was. And she told me in Russian. I said, "How do they feed babies in Russia?" By this time, June was 4 or 5 months old, just getting ready to sit up.

"We put baby on lap, Mama, and baby eat on lap."

And so a highchair to me, I think, was new to Marina.

So approximately 2 or 3 days later I go over there and Lee says to me, "Now, Mother, I want you to understand right here and now—I want you to stop giving all these gifts to me and my wife. I want to give Marina whatever is necessary, the best I can do. I want you to keep your money and take care of yourself, because today or tomorrow you take sick, and you spend all your money on us, I will have to take care of you." Which makes very good sense.

But he strongly put me in my place about buying things for his wife that he himself could not buy.

Mr. Rankin. What did you say to that?

Mrs. Oswald. I agreed with him. And I said—the shock of it—I realize what a mother-in-law I was in interfering. And, of course, that is part that we mothers-in-law do unconsciously. We try to help out our children, and 137 in a way we are interfering in their life. They would rather have their own way of doing things.

And I realize that I had interfered, and the boy wanted to take care of his wife. So no more was said about it.

I go into many homes, being a nurse, and I see this problem also, where the mothers and mothers-in-law bring things, and the men strongly object to it—they would rather do without, and have their wife do without, and they themselves be the master of the home.

So then I realized I was being a foolish mother-in-law, and that he was perfectly right.

I should save my money and take care of myself. He had a wife and baby to take care of. If I didn't have any money, he might have to take care of me. So I agreed with that.

Mr. Rankin. Did Marina say anything about that?

Mrs. Oswald. Well, no, Marina didn't know—unless she understood the English part. I have no way of knowing, you see.

Mr. Rankin. All right. Tell us what happened after that, then.

Mrs. Oswald. Now, let me think just a minute.

This, gentlemen, is very emotional to me, because it is a humanitarian side that I am trying to bring out. Material things are involved to me that are of no consequence. And I am trying to point out the fact that these Russian people seemed to think that the Russian girl should have material things.

And all through my story, I can prove things that have happened of this nature.

Yes—I will continue.

I was on the OB case for very wealthy people. I then became a nurse and by word of mouth I had worked in the finest homes in Fort Worth at this salary. I have worked for Ammon Carter, Jr., who is the owner of the Star Telegram. I have worked in his home. I have worked for Dr. Ross seven weeks in his home. I have worked for Mayor Vandergriff. I took care of his last baby in his home. And I can go on and on.

So I have been employed in over 200 homes at this salary. So I know the difference of working in very poor homes, people on welfare, that I worked in, and then working in the rich homes. So I have experience, gentlemen, is what I am trying to say.

So I mentioned to Mrs. Rosenthal that Lee and Marina didn't have a baby bed, and Lee didn't have work clothes. He had had his suits from the United States yet with him when he went to Russia. But he needed work clothes since he got this job.

She said, "Mrs. Oswald, what build is he?"

And I told her. And he was about the same build as her husband.

So she got out a lot of work clothes that her husband didn't want. However, she asked me $10 for 12 pairs of used pants. And I would not buy—give her $12. Here is a very wealthy woman, and she knows the story. And she knows that I have no money. And yet she expects me to pay for his used clothing. And so I have this principle about me. And I did not buy the used clothing, the clothing for Lee.

Now, Lee is having a birthday, which is October 18th. And this is approximately the 6th or 7th of October.

Now, this Sunday, October 12th, I went—this is very important, gentleman—I went to this home and I was there—I asked to get off an hour or two to see the children, from this OB case at the Rosenthals. I went to see my son and daughter-in-law, and they were nicely dressed. And while there, about 10 minutes, a young couple came into the home, approximately the same age as Marina and Lee, and they had a little boy who I would say was about 6 or 8 months older than June. The woman put the little boy in the playpen with June, and June went to touch him, and Marina got up and said, "Oh, no, hurt baby." She spoke in English. So I said, "Do you speak Russian?" to this couple. And they said, "No, we don't. We are Americans. But my father"—and I will have to say this—"or grandfather"—I do not know which—"is a Russian, from Siberia, and that is how we know Marina and Lee."

So the conversation was general. And in the general conversation—now,138 this couple was from Dallas, visiting my family in Fort Worth. The conversation was general.

And she said, "Lee, my father has this place of business in Dallas, and will offer you a job in Dallas."

I said, "Lee, I didn't know that you wanted to give up your job and work in Dallas, because the Rosenthals that I am working for, her father owns the meatpacking house in Dallas, and she has told me that he employs hundreds of people, and if ever any time that you are in need, to go see her father, that she would be sure that he would give you a job."

So, gentlemen, this was on a Sunday.

I made coffee, and the house was in order. There was nothing packed.

Lee got paid on a Friday, from the Leslie Sheetmetal Works.

Monday Lee and Marina packed their belongings and went to Dallas.

The point I am bringing, is that Lee had no idea of quitting his job in Fort Worth, because he was not packed. This was on a Sunday. And this couple offered a job in Dallas. And their father, her grandfather, was a Russian, and Lee went to Dallas on a Monday, and worked for the Arts Graphic. I do not know—but you probably have that information. His very first job there.

Mr. Rankin. Do you know whether he was discharged by the Leslie people?

Mrs. Oswald. No, sir, he was not discharged by the Leslie people. He just didn't show up. He was paid on a Friday, and that Monday he did not show up for work, because he came to Dallas.

The point I am bringing out is this job was also offered to Lee from a Russian father. He had no idea of moving. There was nothing packed.

Now, I understand that my son Robert helped him to move. And the way I know this—I went there on a Tuesday, and the children had gone, because they had left on a Monday. So then I went to Robert's home, and Robert was at work. So I was all upset. They didn't tell me they were leaving.

I said to Veda. "Marina and Lee are no longer there, the house is vacant."

Mr. Rankin. You spoke someone's name.

Mrs. Oswald. Veda, V-e-d-a. Robert's wife is Veda. I said they had to move yesterday.

She said "Robert helped them to move, and they gave us the food in the refrigerator."

I said it came up all of a sudden, and I told the story about the couple being there.

Mr. Rankin. Do you know the name of that couple?

Mrs. Oswald. No, sir. And I have not been able to find out.

I have asked Mrs. Paine recently, and she said she does not remember. And the night I was in Mrs. Paine's home, I asked Marina and Mrs. Paine, and they did say a name. Marina would know the name of the couple. But I do not have that information.

Mr. Rankin. And was he the owner of this business?

Mrs. Oswald. The father was the owner of the business. And this was an American couple. And they did not speak Russian, either one. The father was a Russian, or the grandfather—that owned this place of business.

Mr. Rankin. I think you said the grandfather before.

Mrs. Oswald. I said either the father or the grandfather. I cannot be sure.

It was the girl's father or grandfather, and not the boy.

So I told my daughter-in-law about this, and she knew about it.

So now here is something that I would like to have my daughter-in-law as a witness.

It has been stated in the paper that my son was giving Marina black eyes and possibly had beat her. And this is by the Russian people.

Now, living in this home in Fort Worth, I had gone by several times I had a day off, and Marina was not at home.

I said to her, "Marina, Mama come to see you yesterday. You no home." She didn't answer.

I said, "Marina, Mama come see you. You no home, Marina."

"No. I go to lady's house to take English lessons."

Mr. Rankin. Do you know who she was speaking of?

Mrs. Oswald. I do not know for a fact. But my son Robert will know.139 And that is why it is important to call him. That is what I am trying to say, Chief Justice Warren. These others will know this part of my story, give you the facts.

I am assuming it is Mr. Peter Gregory's wife that started these lessons. But Marina was taking English lessons.

Now, they lived at a corner house, and there is Carol Street, and opposite Carol Street is a parking lot for Montgomery Ward. They live approximately two blocks from Montgomery Ward. So I had gone by, as I am stating, several times. You have to understand—this is just 6 or 7 weeks that they are in this home.

Mr. Rankin. You say "they." I am sorry to interrupt.

Mrs. Oswald. Marina and Lee, in this home.

Then Marina was not home. I could not understand where so fast that they could have so many friends, that this Russian girl didn't speak English and know her way about, could be gone all day long. That worried me.

So I sat in the car on Montgomery Ward's parking lot, where I could see the house, because I wanted to see who Marina was going to come home with.

The door was open. I went in the house and no one was there.

By this time, I was wondering how she could be gone all the time, being a stranger in town.

I sat in the car all day long. She didn't show up.

Finally, I went home, had my supper, left my apartment, and on the way going back to the house Lee was leaving Montgomery Ward.

Now, they did not have a phone. I am just assuming—this is not a fact—that Lee went to a telephone trying to locate his wife, because I was coming from Montgomery Ward. He got in the car with me, and we had about a block to go. I entered the home with Lee, and I said, "Lee where is Marina?" Of course, I knew that she wasn't home, because I had stayed in the car all day.

He said, "Oh, I guess she is out with some friends."

"Would you like me to fix your supper?"

"No, she will probably be home in time to fix my supper?"

So I left. I am not going to interfere in their married life. But I did offer to fix him supper. And I went back to make sure Marina still wasn't home.

I walked in the home with my son.

So approximately 2 days later—not approximately, but 2 days later I went to the home and my son was reading, he read continuously—in the living room, and Marina was in the bedroom, I could not see Marina. And I said to Lee, "Tell Marina, I am here."

Marina made no appearance.

So I went into the bedroom, and she was nursing June with her head down. And I started to talk. And she still had her head down. And I came around to the front and I saw Marina with a black eye.

Now, gentlemen, I don't think any man should hit his wife, as is stated in the paper, or beat his wife. But I will say this. There may be times that a woman needs to have a black eye. I am not condoning the act. But I strongly am saying that this girl was not home. And this man was working. And I saw, myself, that this man came home and didn't have any food. This couple doesn't have a maid or anyone to give this working man food. And I think it was her duty to be home and have his supper ready.

That is a little thing, maybe. But to me it shows the character of what I am trying to bring out.

And so there may have been reasons that the children fought. And I also know that many, many couples fight, of our finest people, because I made it clear before that I have worked in these very fine homes, and have seen very fine people fight. I have seen a gentleman strike his wife in front of me. We know this happens. It is not a nice thing to do. But it happens in our finest homes. I am not condoning the act. But I am telling you that there probably was reasons, we will say. The woman has a black eye, and he is a louse—he gave her a black eye, but we must consider why did he give her a black eye. We always must consider the second aspect of the case.

Mr. Rankin. Did she take the baby with her when you looked——

Mrs. Oswald. Yes, sir, she took—always the baby was with her.

140 Mr. Rankin. Did you ask Marina how she got the black eye or anything about it?

Mrs. Oswald. Yes, in the bedroom. I was shocked.

"Mama—Lee." Just like that.

So I went in the living room and I said, "Lee, what do you mean by striking Marina?"

He said, "Mother, that is our affair."

And so that ended. I wasn't going to interfere any further.

Now, this has been publicly stated by the Russian friends, that he beat his wife. I don't know if he did beat his wife. I happened to see the black eye. I know that he hit her and gave her a black eye. Marina said so, and my son has said so. But how many times does this happen, I don't know.

149

But I am trying to point out that I don't approve of it. But I am trying to point out that everything is not according to Hoyle, as we say in our American way of life.

Mr. Rankin. Is there any other time that you recall that you saw that she had bruises or a black eye?

Mrs. Oswald. No, sir; that is the only time.

And then the children moved to Dallas.

Now, this will end that part of the story.

I have accepted and I have the public papers, in 1959, when Lee went to Russia—I made a statement that as an individual I thought he had a right to make up his own mind in the decision to do what he wanted. I am of that nature, because, gentlemen, today or tomorrow I may decide to go to Russia, I will go. We are taught that in America, that we have the right to do what we want as an individual. So I publicly stated in 1959 that Lee had a right, if he wanted to live in that country. And I think it was courage that he did so, instead of staying in America and talking about America, and living here and downing his country. It took courage to go and live where he wanted to live.

I was criticized highly for making that statement. And it is published in 1959—as far back as that.

So I will get back now to when the children left.

They did not tell me they had left.

So I accepted the fact that my son Lee did not want me to know that he was in Dallas.

Why I accepted the fact is because of Lee's so-called defection.

I have had it very hard, Mr. Rankin, and gentlemen—I have lost jobs, I was in a position, if I was in a home and television was on, and something political was on television, and the people commented, I felt it was necessary to keep quiet, because of it. Because of the defection I thought if I would express my views they might think I was a Communist like my son was supposed to be. And in many a home I have been in—after three or four days they would tell me my services were not needed.

I cannot say, sure it was because of Lee's defection. However, I feel sure that it is, because I am a respected person, and a very good nurse, as has been stated in the paper. And my jobs were gotten from word of mouth.

But you must understand that I deal with a lot of people. So naturally it is natural that some of them would feel resentful against me because of my son defecting to Russia and presumably being a Communist.

Mr. Rankin. Did you ever find out where Marina was that day that you tried to locate her?

Mrs. Oswald. No, sir, no sir, that ended that.

So I respected my son's wish, since he didn't want to tell me where he was in Dallas, that I would accept that fact.

Now, gentlemen, this may seem hard that I accept these things. But it is not. I am self-supporting. I have a life of my own. And if Lee decides that that is the way he wants it, I am not going to grieve and worry about it. I have to get my sleep in order to work. I have the ability of accepting things, the ability granted me by the grace of God, because of my difficulty in life. I have been a widow. I have had many, many obstacles, and I have had to face them. And my faith gets stronger. I do accept things.

141 As now, I accept the death of my son. I don't brood over that. I have that ability of doing that.

So I just accepted the fact—when Lee gets ready to let me know where he is, fine—up until that time, it is his privilege to do what he wants.

Now, that is the last contact I have had with Marina and Lee until the news broke in Dallas that Lee was picked up because of the assassination of President Kennedy.

Mr. Rankin. Tell us about this period you were talking about, when he went to Dallas. Was that before or after the time he went to New Orleans?

150

Mrs. Oswald. That was before the time, sir—he lived—from my apartment, the Rotary Apartments, when Lee got the job he lived on Mercedes Street from the end of July, I would say, or the beginning of September, until October, when he left to go to Dallas.

Mr. Rankin. What year was that?

Mrs. Oswald. That was in 1963.

Mr. Rankin. You mean '62?

Mrs. Oswald. I am sorry—1962. And that was the last I had seen of Marina and Lee.

Mr. Rankin. Did you ever find where they were in Dallas?

Mrs. Oswald. No, sir. I explained before that I made no attempt. I thought when they get ready to let me know, that is fine. Up until then, I had to do my own work and take care of myself. And I do respect other people's privileges. If that is the way they want it, fine.

When they get ready to let me know, I will welcome them. If not, I will go about my own business.

Mr. Rankin. Had you learned they had gone to New Orleans?

Mrs. Oswald. I had not learned of that until after the assassination. I knew nothing, I had no contact with them.

So, then, the next thing we should start then would be the Dallas—the assassination.

Mr. Rankin. Whatever you know.

Mrs. Oswald. Well, I was on a case in a rest home, and I had a 3 to 11 shift. I was dressed, ready to go to work. I was watching—I am a little ahead of my story.

I watched the television in the morning before I was dressed. And Richard Nixon was in Dallas, and he made a television appearance approximately 2 hours before President Kennedy was to arrive in Dallas. And, as a layman, I remember saying, "Well, the audacity of him, to make this statement against President Kennedy just an hour or two before his arrival in Dallas."

And then I had my lunch, and I dressed, with my nurse's uniform on, to go to work, for the 3 to 11 shift. And I have to leave home at 2:30. So I had a little time to watch the Presidential procession.

And while sitting on the sofa, the news came that the President was shot. And there was a witness on television, a man and a little girl on television. However, I could not continue to watch it. I had to report to work.

So I went in the car, and approximately seven blocks away I turned the radio on in the car. I heard that Lee Harvey Oswald was picked up as a suspect.

I immediately turned the car around and came back home, got on the telephone, called Acme Brick in Fort Worth, and asked where Robert was, because he had been traveling, and I must get in touch with Robert immediately, because his brother was picked up as a suspect in the assassination. So they had Robert call me.

Robert didn't know that Lee was picked up.

Mr. Rankin. Was this the day of the assassination?

Mrs. Oswald. Yes, sir, the day of the assassination, they picked Lee up.

Mr. Rankin. And 3 to 11—that is in the afternoon?

Mrs. Oswald. This was 2:30, because I was on my way to work, and I had to be at work at 3 o'clock.

Mr. Rankin. Three in the afternoon is when you had to be at work?

Mrs. Oswald. Yes, sir, and it was 2:30 I heard the news and went back home.

142 I had Acme Brick call Robert to give him the news, and Robert called me, and he had not heard his brother was picked up.

Now, Robert is in Denton. So I called the Star Telegram, and asked that—if they could possibly have someone escort me to Dallas, because I realized I could not drive to Dallas. And they did. They sent two men to escort me to Dallas.

The name of one is Bob Shieffer, the other name I will have for you gentlemen.

Mr. Rankin. Who are those? Are those reporters?

Mrs. Oswald. Star Telegram reporters, sent by the Star Telegram editor to escort me to Dallas.

Now, upon arriving in Dallas, I did not ask—I did not want to talk to the police. I asked specifically to talk to FBI agents. My wish was granted, I was sent into a room. I have to backtrack my story.

The policemen do not know I am here—"I want to talk to FBI agents."

Mr. Rankin. What time of the day is this?

Mrs. Oswald. This is approximately 3:30. So I am escorted into an office, and two Brown FBI agents, they are brothers, I understand, and there was another man that I do not know the name.

Mr. Rankin. By that you mean their names were Brown?

Mrs. Oswald. Their names were Brown. And I have the correct names, also. But we were in this room, and I told them who I was. And I said, "I want to talk with you gentlemen because I feel like my son is an agent of the government, and for the security of my country, I don't want this to get out."

But, first, I said to them, "I want to talk to FBI agents from Washington."

"Mrs. Oswald, we are from Washington, we work with Washington."

I said, "I understand you work with Washington. But I want officials from Washington," and I believed they would be in town because of protecting the President.

I said, "I do not want local FBI men. What I have to say I want to say to Washington men."

Of course they wanted the news. They said, "Well, we work through Washington."

I said, "I know you do. But I would like Washington men."

So I had no choice.

Mr. Rankin. Did you tell them why you thought he was an agent?

Mrs. Oswald. Yes, sir. I am coming to this.

So I said, "I have information that"—I told him who I was.

I said, "For the security of my country, I want this kept perfectly quiet until you investigate. I happen to know that the State Department furnished the money for my son to return back to the United States, and I don't know if that would be made public what that would involve, and so please will you investigate this and keep this quiet."

Of course that was news to them.

They left me sitting in the office.

And I also told them that Congressman Jim Wright knew about this.

"You can be sure we will question Jim Wright."

And I gave them the names of the four men I had talked with while in Washington.

Would you like those four names now?

Mr. Rankin. Yes.

Mrs. Oswald. One is Mr. Boster, who was special counsel in charge of Soviet affairs. One was Mr. Stanfield. I should know the names.

Well, gentlemen, Mr. Doyle will see that I give you the names of these men. I had it in a little card and carried it all these years from my Washington trip and gave it to the FBI men to investigate.

So they left me.

Mr. Rankin. When you say you understand that the State Department paid your son's way back from the Soviet Union——

Mrs. Oswald. Yes, sir.

Mr. Rankin. Did you ever learn that that was a loan?

143 Mrs. Oswald. I have the document to state that they loaned Lee the money to come back.

Mr. Rankin. But you didn't know that at the time?

Mrs. Oswald. Yes, sir. But I stated—you see, I was worried about the security of my country. I didn't know if the public would find out—how they would take the news that the State Department loaned him the money, since now he is a Marxist and an accused assassin.

I was worried about my country. And I didn't want the public to know. I wanted the FBI, not the police, to know.

Mr. Rankin. Did you know anything else that you told them about why you thought he was an agent?

Mrs. Oswald. No, I didn't tell them anything. But they questioned me, started to question me.

One of them said, "You know a lot about your son. When was the last time you were in touch with him?"

That wasn't the Browns. That was the other man.

I said, "I have not seen my son in a year."

He said sarcastically, "Now, Mrs. Oswald, are we to believe you have not been in touch with your son in a year? You are a mother."

I said, "Believe what you want. But I have not been in touch with my son in a year. My son did not want me involved. He has kept me out of his activities. That is the truth, God's truth, that I have not seen my son in a year."

And the gentleman left, and I did not see them after that.

They sent the stenographer that was in the outer office to sit with me, and she started to question me.

I said, "Young lady, I am not going to be questioned. You may just as well make up your mind that I am just going to sit here. What I want, if you will relay—have these two Star Telegram men come in here, please. I would like to ask them something."

So they came in. And I said, "Bob, I have rights and I want to see Lee."

Of course the men didn't answer.

But I sat in the office approximately 2 or 3 hours alone, gentlemen, with this woman who came in and out.

I said, "If you think you are going to question me or get information from me, you are not."

And I sat in the office 2 or 3 hours.

Every now and then I would walk up to the outer corridor and say to whoever was there, "Now, listen, I am getting tired of this. I want to see Lee."

Mr. Rankin. What office was this?

Mrs. Oswald. The courthouse in Dallas.

Mr. Rankin. Whose office was it in? Do you know?

Mrs. Oswald. No, I don't know. It was a private office that lead—for instance, it would be like in the corner, a glass-enclosed office. And then you could see the outer corridor where the stenographers and the police and everybody was.

Mr. Rankin. You don't know whose office it was?

Mrs. Oswald. No, sir, I do not. So I sat there approximately 3 hours. And I never did get to see Lee.

So at 5:30—then Robert came in. And he was questioned by the FBI.

Mr. Rankin. Were you there when he was questioned?

Mrs. Oswald. No, sir.

And I will state now emphatically that I have never been questioned by the FBI or the Secret Service—never, gentlemen. If they can produce my voice or anything, they can produce it.

So then I was escorted into the office where Marina and Mrs. Paine was. And, of course, I started crying right away, and hugged Marina. And Marina gave me Rachel, whom I had never seen. I did not know I had a second grandchild, until this very moment. So I started to cry. Marina started to cry. And Mrs. Paine said, "Oh, Mrs. Oswald, I am so glad to meet you. Marina has often expressed the desire to contact you, especially when the baby was being born. But Lee didn't want her to."

And I said, "Mrs. Paine, you spoke English. Why didn't you contact me?"

144 She said Marina didn't know how to get in touch with me.

She said, "Well, because of the way they lived, he lived in Dallas, and came home to my home on weekends. I didn't feel like I wanted to interfere."

And she acted as—excuse me, gentlemen, but this is very, very emotional.

The Chairman. That is all right.

Mrs. Oswald. She acted as interpreter for Marina. We are in the courthouse now, in the jailhouse.

So her testimony, gentlemen, the testimony that the Dallas police have, is the testimony of Mrs. Paine, that Marina assumed Lee had given her.

Could we state now maybe it is not the correct testimony that Marina gave—just one interpreter, and Marina's friend, is the testimony that the Dallas police has.

I have no way of knowing, and you have no way of knowing, gentlemen, whether it is the correct testimony.

So Mrs. Paine told me that she acted as interpreter.

And I said, "I don't know what I am going to do. I want to stay in Dallas and be near Lee, so that I can help with this situation as much as possible."

She said, "Mrs. Oswald, you are welcome in my home—if you care to sleep on the sofa."

I said, "Thank you very much, Mrs. Paine, I will accept your offer. I will sleep on the floor in order to be near Dallas."

So we left. We went to Mrs. Paine's home.

I am going to say again I did not see my son.

So—I had my nurse's uniform on for 3 days.

Mr. Rankin. What day was this at Mrs. Paine's?

Mrs. Oswald. This was the night of Friday, November 22d. We arrived there approximately 6 o'clock. Upon entering the home, about 5 minutes after I was in the home, there was a knock on the door.

Now, this is a little vague. On the way leaving the courthouse we may have been in the company of the two Life representatives. They may have taken us to Mrs. Paine's home. I did not ask who was taking us to Mrs. Paine's home, because I was holding my grandbaby and talking to Marina, and sitting in the back of the car. And it didn't interest me at the time how I was getting to Mrs. Paine's home.

Why I am bringing this up was because after I was in her home, about 5 minutes, there was a knock on the door, and these two Life representatives entered the home.

The name of the men, one is Allan Grant, and the other is Tommy Thompson.

And I was not introduced.

Mr. Rankin. Had you ever seen them before?

Mrs. Oswald. No, I had never seen them before. As I say, they could have been the men driving the car. But I want you to understand at the time I didn't notice that, because I was holding my new grandbaby, and comforting my daughter-in-law, and talking to Mrs. Paine in the back seat of the car.

So Mrs. Paine sat on the floor. And she said to the photographer—he had a camera in front of him—"Now, I hope you have good color film, because I want good pictures."

Mr. Rankin. What time of the day was this?

Mrs. Oswald. This was approximately 6:30. We had just arrived in Mrs. Paine's home—I would say 6 and 7 o'clock, approximately, between that time. We are home 5 minutes when they knocked on the door.

Mrs. Paine immediately says, "Gentlemen, I hope you have colored film so we will have some good pictures."

I didn't know who they were.

But then I knew they were newsmen, because of her statement and the camera.

So Tommy Thompson started to interview Mrs. Paine. He said, "Mrs. Paine, tell me, are Marina and Lee separated, since Lee lives in Dallas?"

She said, "No, they are a happy family. Lee lives in Dallas because of necessity. He works in Dallas, and this is Irving, and he has no transportation, and he comes every weekend to see his family."

"Well," he said, "What type family man is he?"

145 She said, "A normal family man. He plays with his children. Last night he fed June. He watches television and just normal things."

She went on.

So he said, "Mrs. Paine, can you tell me how Lee got, the money to"—I am sorry—"can you tell me how Lee was able to return back to the United States financially?"

She said, "Oh, yes, he saved the money to come back to the United States."

Now, while this little episode went on, I was fuming, gentlemen, because I didn't want this type of publicity. I thought it was uncalled for, immediately after the assassination, and the consequent arrest of my son.

But I was in Mrs. Paine's home.

Now I had an opportunity to be gracious. I spoke up and I said—I am ahead of myself.

She answered that he saved the money.

I spoke up and I said, "Now, Mrs. Paine, I am sorry. I am in your home. And I appreciate the fact that I am a guest in your home. But I will not have you making statements that are incorrect. Because I happen to know you have made an incorrect statement. To begin with, I do not approve of this publicity. And if we are going to have the life story with Life magazine"—by that time I knew what it was—"I would like to get paid. Here is my daughter-in-law with two small children, and I, myself, am penniless, and if we are going to give this information, I believe we should get paid for it."

Mr. Rankin. Did you think Mrs. Paine was trying to get paid for it?

Mrs. Oswald. Possibly. But I do know this. It was prearranged. That is the point that is important. That after a few hours time, the Life representatives were invited to her home, into her home, because she expected them, you see.

Mr. Rankin. You think she arranged it, then?

Mrs. Oswald. Yes, sir, possibly with Marina's help.

I do not know. It was arranged—I am positive—the way they entered the home. She invited them in, without even introducing me. And immediately said she hoped they had color film.

Mr. Rankin. Were they talking to each other, Marina, and Mrs. Paine, while you were there?

Mrs. Oswald. Yes, they talked in Russian. And that is a difficult part. I didn't know Russian.

Then, with that, the Life representative got up and said, "Mrs. Oswald, I will call my office and see what they think about an arrangement of your life story."

So he did call the office. He closed the door and called in private. And nothing was said—in the living room.

When I say nothing was said, it was between myself and the other representative. Mrs. Paine was talking to my daughter-in-law in Russian. I was talking to my daughter-in-law in English. It was a regular general conversation, as far as I knew.

He came out from the telephone conversation and said, no, that the company would not allow him to pay for the story. What they would do—they would pay our expenses while in Dallas, and our food and expenses, hotel accommodation.

So I told him that I would think about it.

Now, they continued to hang around. And they were taking pictures continuously, all the while this was going on—the photographer, Mr. Allen was continuously taking pictures. I was awfully tired and upset. I rolled my stockings down, and the picture is in Life Magazine. And he stopped that. So I got up and said, "I am not having this invasion of privacy. I realize that I am in Mrs. Paine's home. But you are taking my

155

picture without my consent, and a picture that I certainly don't want made public." It is the worst—with me rolling my hose. I wanted to get comfortable.

He followed Marina around in the bedroom. She was undressing June. He took pictures of everything. And Mrs. Paine was in her glory—I will say this. Mrs. Paine was very happy all these pictures were taken. And I had to go behind Marina to see that the photographers were not taking her, and they146 were taking me. And it was just a regular—the home was a living room and a hall and a bedroom and kitchen, and we were all going around in circles.

And the photographer was taking pictures, until finally I became indignant, and said, "I have had it. Now, find out what accommodations you can make for us, for my daughter-in-law and I so that we can be in Dallas to help Lee, and let me know in the morning."

So they left.

However, about an hour later there was a telephone call to Mrs. Paine from a Life representative. I know by her conversation who she was talking to.

Mr. Rankin. Who was that?

Mrs. Oswald. One of the men—either Allen Grant or Tommy Thompson.

And after the conversation, I said to her, "Was that one of the Life representatives?" And she said, "Oh, yes, he just was a little upset about what happened."

So I got no information there.

The Chairman. Would you like to take a short recess, Mrs. Oswald?

Mrs. Oswald. Yes, I am getting thirsty.

The Chairman. Suppose we do. We will take one for about 10 minutes.

(Brief recess.)

The Chairman. The Commission will be in order. Mrs. Oswald, you may continue with your statement.

Mrs. Oswald. Yes, sir. Now, we are in Mrs. Paine's home yet.

The Chairman. Yes. This is on the day of the assassination?

Mrs. Oswald. Yes, sir—the 22d, Friday, the 22d.

I am worried because Lee hasn't had an attorney. And I am talking about that, and Mrs. Paine said, "Oh, don't worry about that. I am a member of the Civil Liberties Union, and Lee will have an attorney, I can assure you."

I said to myself but when? Of course, I didn't want to push her, argue with her. But the point was if she was a member of the Union, why didn't she see Lee had an attorney then. So I wasn't too happy about that.

Now, gentlemen, this is some very important facts.

My daughter-in-law spoke to Mrs. Paine in Russian. "Mamma," she says. So she takes me into the bedroom and closes the door. She said, "Mamma, I show you." She opened the closet, and in the closet was a lot of books and papers. And she came out with a picture—a picture of Lee, with a gun.

It said, "To my daughter June"—written in English.

I said, "Oh, Marina, police." I didn't think anything of the picture.

Now, you must understand that I don't know what is going on on television—I came from the jailhouse and everything, so I don't know all the circumstances, what evidence they had against my son by this time. I had no way of knowing. But I say to my daughter, "To my daughter, June," anybody can own a rifle, to go hunting. You yourself probably have a rifle. So I am not connecting this with the assassination—"To my daughter, June." Because I would immediately say, and I remember—I think my son is an agent all the time—no one is going to be foolish enough if they mean to assassinate the President, or even murder someone to take a picture of themselves with that rifle, and leave that there for evidence.

So, I didn't think a thing about it. And it says "To my daughter, June." I said, "The police," meaning that if the police got that, they would use that against my son, which would be a natural way to think.

She says, "You take, Mamma."
I said, "No."
"Yes, Mamma, you take."
I said, "No, Marina. Put back in the book." So she put the picture back in the book. Which book it was, I do not know.

So the next day, when we are at the courthouse—this is on Saturday—she—we were sitting down, waiting to see Lee. She puts her shoe down, she says, "Mamma, picture." She had the picture folded up in her shoe.

Now, I did not see that it was the picture, but I know that it was, because she told me it was, and I could see it was folded up. It wasn't open for me to see. I said, "Marina." Just like that. So Robert came along and he says,147 "Robert" I said, "No, no Marina." I didn't want her to tell Robert about the picture. Right there, you know. That was about the picture.

Mr. Rankin. Did you ever tell her to destroy the picture?

Mrs. Oswald. No. Now, I have to go into this. I want to tell you about destroying the picture.

Now, that was in Mrs. Paine's home.

I want to start to remember—because when we leave Mrs. Paine's home, we go into another phase, where the picture comes in again. So I have to tell the—unless you want to ask me specific questions.

Mr. Rankin. No, you go right ahead.

Mrs. Oswald. Mrs. Paine, in front of me, gave Marina $10. Now, Mrs. Paine, when I said, after the representatives left—I said, "You know, I do want to get paid for the story, because I am destitute, and here is a girl with—her husband is going to be in jail, we will need money for attorneys, with two babies."

She said, "You don't have to worry about Marina. Marina will always have a home with me, because Marina helps."

Now, Mrs. Paine speaks Russian fluently. "She helps me with my Russian language. She babysits for me and helps me with the housework, and you never have to worry about Marina. She will always have a home with me."

Now, Mr. and Mrs. Paine are separated. Mr. Paine does not live here. So it is just the two women.

So, Mrs. Paine didn't graciously do anything for Marina, as the paper stated—that Lee never did pay Mrs. Paine for room or board. Mrs. Paine owes them money. That is almost the kind of work that I do, or the airline stewardesses do, serve food and everything. Marina was earning her keep, and really should have had a salary for it—what I am trying to say, gentlemen, Mrs. Paine had Marina there to help babysit with the children, with her children—if she wanted to go running around and everything.

So actually she wasn't doing my son or Marina the favor that she claims she was doing.

But the point I am trying to stress is that she did tell me Marina would never have to worry, because Marina would have a home with her.

At this particular moment, I cannot remember anything of importance in the house. Otherwise, about the picture I have stated. And Mrs. Paine with the Life representative, and her saying that Lee would have an attorney, and Mrs. Paine giving Marina a $10 bill.

Oh, Marina told me, "Mamma, I have this money." It was money in an envelope—in the bedroom, when she showed me the picture. I said, "How much money, Marina."

"About how much?" I asked her.

"About $100 and some."

Now, Mrs. Paine has stated to the Life representative that Lee and Marina were saving his pay in order to have a home for themselves for Christmas time, because they had never been in a home of their own at Christmas time—in order to celebrate Christmas. So, the hundred and some odd dollars isn't a big sum, considering that Lee paid $8 a week room in Dallas—and it has been stated by the landlady that Lee ate lunchmeat or fruit. And Lee was very, very thin when I saw him. And Lee gave his salary to his wife in order to save to have this home for Christmas.

So, that is not a lot of money to have in the house—I would not think so, because I believe Lee was earning about $50 a week. And let's say he could live for about $10 or $12. And he gave the rest of the money to his wife.

And so I reported this money to the Secret Service while we were in Six Flags—that Marina had the money. I wanted them to know. She showed me the money.

I cannot think now—I did think of the money after going back—but I cannot think of anything at this particular moment that would be of any benefit that happened in this house.

Mr. Rankin. In regard to the photograph, I will show you some photographs. Maybe you can tell me whether they are the ones that you are referring to. Here is Commission's Exhibit 134.

Mrs. Oswald. No, sir, that is not the picture.

Mr. Rankin. And 133, consists of two different pictures.

Mrs. Oswald.. No, sir, that is not the picture. He was holding the rifle up, and it said, "To my daughter, June, with love." He was holding the rifle up.

Mr. Rankin. By holding it up, you mean——

Mrs. Oswald.. Like this.

Mr. Rankin. Crosswise, with both hands on the rifle?

Mrs. Oswald.. With both hands on the rifle.

Mr. Rankin. Above his head?

Mrs. Oswald. That is right.

Mr. Rankin. Did you ever see these pictures, Exhibits 133 and 134?

Mrs. Oswald. No, sir, I have never seen those pictures.

Mr. Rankin. Now, you were going to tell us about some further discussion of the picture you did see?

Mrs. Oswald. Yes—all right.

Now, so the next morning the two representatives of the Life Magazine, Mr. Allen Grant and Mr. Tommy Thompson come by at 9 o'clock with a woman, Russian interpreter, a doctor somebody. I have not been able to find this woman. I have called the universities, thinking that she was a language teacher, and I—maybe you have her name. But she is very, very important to our story.

And I do want to locate her, if possible.

During the night, I had decided I was going to take up their offer, because I would be besieged by reporters and everything. So why not go with the Life representatives, and let them pay my room and board and my daughter-in-law's. They came by at 9 o'clock, without calling, with this Russian interpreter. So Marina was getting dressed and getting the children dressed. He was taking pictures all the time.

Mr. Rankin. They came by where?

Mrs. Oswald. Mrs. Paine's home. And there was no hurry, though, to leave the home, because Mrs. Paine was most anxious for the Life representatives to talk to her and get these pictures and everything—whether Marina has any part in this I don't know, because they spoke Russian, and she didn't tell me about it. But I know Mrs. Paine did.

We left with the two Life representatives. They brought us to the Hotel Adolphus in Dallas. I immediately upon entering the hotel picked up the phone and called Captain Will Fritz, to see if Marina and I could see Lee at the jailhouse.

Mr. Rankin. Who is he?

Mrs. Oswald. He is one of the big men in Dallas on this case.

Mr. Rankin. The Chief of Detectives, or something like that?

Mrs. Oswald. Yes. And I called him from the hotel, and the man that answered the phone said he would relay my message to him, that I wanted to see if Marina and I could see Lee. I waited on the phone. He came back and said, "Yes, Mrs. Oswald, Captain Fritz said you may see Lee at 12 o'clock today."

We arrived at the Adolphus Hotel between 9:30 and 10:00.

Mr. Rankin. This was what day?

Mrs. Oswald. This was Saturday, November 23, the morning of Saturday, November 23.

While we were there, an FBI agent, Mr. Hart Odum entered the room with another agent, and wanted Marina to accompany him to be questioned.

Mr. Rankin. Were these FBI agents?

Mrs. Oswald. Yes, sir; Mr. Hart Odum is an FBI agent. And I said, "No, we are going to see Lee." We were all eating breakfast when he came in. I said, "No, we have been promised to see Lee. She is not going with you."

So he said, "Well, will you tell Mrs. Oswald, please"—to the interpreter, "I would like to question her and I would like her to come with me to be questioned."

I said, "It is no good. You don't need to tell the interpreter that, because my daughter-in-law is not going with you. We have been promised to see Lee. And besides Marina has testified, made her statement at the courthouse yesterday, and any further statements that Marina will make will be through counsel."

Mr. Odum said to the interpreter, "Mrs. Oswald"—to the interpreter—"will you tell Mrs. Oswald to decide what she would like to do and not listen to her mother-in-law."

149 I said, "It is no good to tell my daughter-in-law, because my daughter-in-law is not leaving here with you, Mr. Odum, without counsel."

And I had been telling Marina, "No, no."

She said, "I do, Mamma," she kept saying.

Just then my son, Robert, entered the room, and Mr. Odum said, "Robert, we would like to take Marina and question her."

He said, "No, I am sorry, we are going to try to get lawyers for both she and Lee."

So he left.

We went to the courthouse and we sat and sat, and while at the courthouse my son, Robert, was being interviewed by—I don't know whether it was Secret Service or FBI agents—in a glass enclosure. We were sitting—an office, a glass enclosed office. We were sitting on the bench right there.

Mr. Rankin. Where was this?

Mrs. Oswald. In the Dallas courthouse, on Saturday.

So we waited quite a while. One of the men came by and said "I am sorry that we are going to be delayed in letting you see Lee, but we have picked up another suspect."

I said, to Marina, "Oh, Marina, good, another man they think maybe shoot Kennedy."

Mr. Rankin. Did you ask anything about who this suspect was?

Mrs. Oswald. No, sir; I did not. He just give the information why we would be delayed. We sat out there quite a while. The police were very nice. They helped us about the baby. We went into another room for privacy, for Marina to nurse Rachel. It was 2 or 3 hours before we got to see Lee. We went upstairs and were allowed to see Lee. This was in the jail—the same place I had been from the very beginning, and we were taken upstairs. And by the way, they only issued a pass for Marina and myself, and not for Robert. And Robert was very put out, because he thought he was also going to see his brother. Whether Robert saw his brother or not, I do not know, Mr. Rankin.

Mr. Rankin. About what time of day was this?

Mrs. Oswald. Just a minute now. We arrived there at 12 o'clock. This would be about 4 or 4:30 in the afternoon, before we got to see Lee.

Mr. Rankin. Was anyone else present when he saw you?

Mrs. Oswald. No. Marina and I were escorted back of the door where they had an enclosure and telephones. So Marina got on the telephone and talked to Lee in Russian. That is my handicap. I don't know what was said. And Lee seemed very severely composed and assured. He was well-beaten up. He had black eyes, and his face was all bruised and everything. But he was very calm. He smiled with his wife, and talked with her, and then I got on the phone and I said, "Honey, you are so bruised up, your face. What are they doing?"

He said, "Mother, don't worry. I got that in a scuffle."

Now, my son would not tell me they had abused him. That was a boy's way to his mother—if he was abused, and it was shown in the paper his black eyes—he wouldn't tell how he got that. He said that was done in the scuffle. So I talked and said, "Is there anything I can do to help you?"

He said, "No, Mother, everything is fine. I know my rights, and I will have an attorney. I have already requested to get in touch with Attorney Abt, I think is the name. Don't worry about a thing."

Mr. Rankin. Did you say anything to him about another suspect?

Mrs. Oswald. No, sir, I did not. That was my entire conversation to him.

Gentlemen, you must realize this. I had heard over the television my son say, "I did not do it. I did not do it."

And a million of the other people had heard him. I say this. As a mother—I heard my son say this. But also as a citizen, if I had heard another man say, I didn't do it, I will have to believe that man, because he hasn't been—hasn't had the opportunity to present his side of the case. So here is my son. When I saw him people had said, "Did you ask him if he did it?"

No, sir. I think by now you know my temperament, gentlemen. I would not insult my son and ask him if he shot at President Kennedy. Why? Because I myself heard him say, "I didn't do it, I didn't do it."

So, that was enough for me, I would not ask that question.

150 Mr. Rankin. Who told you that there was—they had found another suspect?

Mrs. Oswald. One of the officers. That, sir, I don't know. He just walked in real fast while we were sitting down and said they had picked up another suspect, and it was in the paper that they had picked up another suspect at that particular time, which would have been approximately 1 o'clock that day.

Mr. Rankin. But you don't remember the officer's name?

Mrs. Oswald. No, sir, that is all he said and he left. He was just relaying why we would be delayed. But it was also published. I do not have the paper or the information. But I do know from the reporters, when I told my story, that part to them—they said that substantiates the newspaper story that they did pick up a suspect at that time.

Mr. Rankin. About how long did you and Marina spend there with your son?

Mrs. Oswald. I would say I spent about 3 or 4 minutes on the telephone, and then Marina came back to the telephone and talked with Lee. So we left. So Marina started crying. Marina says, "Mamma, I tell Lee I love Lee and Lee says he love me very much. And Lee tell me to make sure I buy shoes for June."

Now, here is a man that is accused of the murder of a President. This is the next day, or let's say about 24 hours that he has been questioned. His composure is good. And he is thinking about his young daughter needing shoes.

Now, June was wearing shoes belonging to Mrs. Paine's little girl, Marina told me—they were little red tennis shoes, and the top was worn. They were clean, and the canvas was showing by the toe part, like children wear out their toes.

I ask you this, gentlemen. If Marina had a hundred and some odd dollars in the house, why is it necessary that my son has to tell her at the jailhouse, remind her to buy shoes for his baby, for their child? Just a few dollars out of that hundred and some odd dollars would have bought shoes for this particular child.

Another way to look at this, as I stated previously—that the boy is concerned about shoes for his baby, and he is in this awful predicament. So he must feel innocent, or sure that everything is going to be all right, as he told me.

Mr. Rankin. Now, in this telephone conversation, when you talked to your son, can you explain a little bit to the Commission how that is? Was your son on the other side of a wall or something?

Mrs. Oswald. Yes, sir. My son was on the other side of the wall, and then back of the wall was a door with a peephole, where an officer was.

Now, we are going to come from the door, with the peephole and the officer, to my son. Then a glass partition and then glass partitions like telephone booths. But not really inclosed—just a little separation.

Mr. Rankin. So you could not reach in there and take your son's hand?

Mrs. Oswald. No, sir. We talked by telephone.

Mr. Rankin. And he had a telephone on his side, and——

Mrs. Oswald. And he had a telephone.

Mr. Rankin. And you talked back and forth?

Mrs. Oswald. Back and forth, that is right. That is the way we talked. And the boy was badly beat up. I have proof in the papers—his face, black eyes, all scratched up, his neck was scratched. He was badly beat up. But he assured me they were not mistreating him, that he got some of the bruises in the scuffle. As I say, the boy, if he was being mistreated, would not tell his mother that.

Mr. Rankin. And whatever Marina said to him was in Russian, and you didn't understand it?

Mrs. Oswald. No, sir, I did not understand. But I would say this, it seemed to be just an ordinary pleasant conversation. He was smiling. And she told me he said he loved her very much, she said she loved him, and told about buying the shoes for the baby. That is all she said. She did not tell me any other part of the conversation. And they talked quite a while. She talked with him twice. She talked with him the first time. I got on the phone. Then she talked to him again.

Mr. Rankin. Did it sound like there was any dispute or argument?

151 Mrs. Oswald. No. It was a pleasant conversation. But she did not volunteer to tell me what was said, and I did not ask her what was said.

Mr. Rankin. What did you do after that?

Mrs. Oswald. So then after that we went back to the Adolphus Hotel. And upon arriving at the hotel—I am a little ahead of my story.

The police and the detectives at the Dallas jail were most courteous to Marina and I. There were hundreds of reporters out in the corridor. And we were getting ready to leave, so they said that they would take us down the back way—incidentally, the same place where my son was shot. And they had arranged for two to go down and to get a car and to bring into this basement, and take us down the back elevator, and try to avoid the reporters. And there were approximately six or seven in the elevator. When we got down there, there were just a few reporters, and they went way out of their way to elude any reporters. We were at the Adolphus Hotel as I explained to you. And instead of from the jail going straight to the Adolphus Hotel, they drove around 20 or 25 minutes time in circles in order to lose anybody who might be following Marina and I.

So, as we got to the floor of the Adolphus Hotel, we knocked on the door where we were, and no one answered. We were with two men. Immediately around the corner comes Mr. Tommy Thompson, the Life representative.

Mr. Rankin. What two men were you with?

Mrs. Oswald. Two men from the Dallas courthouse.

Mr. Rankin. From the police?

Mrs. Oswald. Yes, from the police.

So Mr. Tommy Thompson came and they asked for his credentials. I had never even—as thorough as I am trying to be—I am trying to tell you there are some things I don't know because of the confusion—I didn't ask for the credentials. I could have been with anybody. I just assumed they were Life representatives. I had not asked. But

161

these Dallas detectives or police, in plain clothes, asked Mr. Tommy Thompson for his credentials, and then left us in his care again.

Immediately Mr. Tommy Thompson said, "Mrs. Oswald, what do you plan to do now?"

The interpreter was gone, and so was the other representative, Mr. Allen Grant.

I said, "Well, the arrangement was that we were going to stay here in the hotel for a few days, and you were going to pay expenses."

He said, "But you have not given us any facts."

They were not interested—and to me it seems very strange that they were not interested in my conversation at the jail with my son. They did not even ask if we saw Lee. Yet they knew we left the Adolphus Hotel in order to go see Lee. But they did not even ask if we saw Lee. And I have often wondered about that.

So when I told him that we expected to stay there, he said, "Well, Mrs. Oswald, the reporters will be coming in flocks, they know where you are. Just a minute."

He got on the telephone. Mr. Allen Grant—they had a Life—the Life representatives had a room on the ninth floor where they had a lot of men working on this case, and we were on the 11th, I believe. So Mr. Allen Grant came down from the ninth floor with another man—I do not know his name—because the baby's diapers had to be changed and things of this sort. He said, "Mrs. Oswald"—they left. Tommy Thompson said, "Mrs. Oswald, what we are going to do is get you on the outskirts of town, so the reporters won't know where you are, and here is some money for your expenses in case you need anything."

Well, I took the bill, and I put it in my uniform pocket without looking at it. That may sound strange to you gentlemen, but this is confusion. I knew it was money, and I just put it in my uniform pocket.

So Mr. Allen Grant escorted my daughter-in-law and I out of the hotel, the Adolphus Hotel, and took us to the Executive Inn, which is on the outskirts of Dallas. We sat in the car. He went in and came out, then, and said, "Mrs. Oswald, I have arranged for you all to stay here for 2 or 3 days. I have to be152 back in San Francisco. Anything you want you have your cash that Mr. Tommy Thompson gave you. And he will be in touch with you."

Well, I didn't think too much of it. He escorted us with a porter up to our room.

We had two beautiful suites—two, not one—completed rooms and baths, adjoining, at the Executive Inn. And that was the last time I had seen either representative. I was stranded with a Russian girl and two babies. I didn't realize in the beginning. But then it was time for food, and I had to order food. I told Marina to stay aside and that I would let the man in. She stayed in her room. I let this man in with the food, and then I became uneasy, that he might know who we were is what I was uneasy about, because I didn't realize the danger actually Marina and I were in.

I sensed we were alone. And there I was with a Russian girl. And I didn't want anybody to know who we were, because I knew my son had been picked up.

So this is where the picture comes in.

While there, Marina—there is an ashtray on the dressing table. And Marina comes with bits of paper, and puts them in the ashtray and strikes a match to it. And this is the picture of the gun that Marina tore up into bits of paper, and struck a match to it.

Now, that didn't burn completely, because it was heavy—not cardboard—what is the name for it—a photographic picture. So the match didn't take it completely.

Mr. Rankin. Had you said anything to her about burning it before that?

Mrs. Oswald. No, sir. The last time I had seen the picture was in Marina's shoe when she was trying to tell me that the picture was in her shoe. I state here now that Marina meant for me to have that picture, from the very beginning, in Mrs. Paine's home. She said—I testified before—"Mamma, you keep picture."

And then she showed it to me in the courthouse. And when I refused it, then she decided to get rid of the picture.

She tore up the picture and struck a match to it. Then I took it and flushed it down the toilet.

Mr. Rankin. And what time was this?

Mrs. Oswald. This—now, just a minute, gentlemen, because this I know is very important to me and to you, too.

We had been in the jail. This was an evening. Well, this, then, would be approximately 5:30 or 6 in the evening.

Mr. Rankin. What day?

Mrs. Oswald. On Saturday, November 23. Now, I flushed the torn bits and the half-burned thing down the commode. And nothing was said. There was nothing said.

Mr. Rankin. That was at the Executive Inn?

Mrs. Oswald. At the Executive Inn.

Now, Mr. Hart Odum, the same FBI agent, that insisted upon my daughter-in-law going with him from the Adolphus Hotel, knocked on the door at the Executive Inn. I had had my robe and slippers on, and I pushed the curtain aside when he knocked. He said, "This is Mr. Odum."

So, I opened the door. This is very important. I would like to not talk about it. I would like to show you what I did. This is so important.

I opened the door just a little, because I had the robe off and I didn't want anybody to come in. The door is just ajar. I am going to take my shoes off, gentlemen, because I have this worked out. This is my height. He said, "Mrs. Oswald, we would like to see Marina."

I said, "Mr. Odum, I stated yesterday you are not going to see Marina. We are awful tired."

"Well, we just want to ask her one question."

"Mr. Odum, I am not calling my daughter. As a matter of fact, she is taking a bath."

She wasn't.

He said, "Mrs. Oswald, I would like to ask you a question."

I said, "Yes, sir." The door is ajar. This is my height. I wear bifocals, which enlarges things. And in his hand—his hand is bigger than mine—in the 153 cup of his hand, like this, is a picture. And the two corners are torn off the picture. This is a very glossy black and white picture of a man's face and shoulder.

Now, Mr. Odum wasn't too tall. I need somebody else. Mr. Odum's hand with the picture—what I am trying to say—he is facing this way—showing me. So my eyes are looking straight at the picture. And I have nothing else to see but this hand and the picture, because the door is ajar. And there is nothing on the picture but a face and shoulders. There is no background or anything. So I can identify this picture amongst millions of pictures, I am so sure of it. It was a glossy black and white picture. So I said, "No, sir, believe me. I have never seen this picture in my life."

With that, he went off.

There was another man with him.

About an hour later the telephone rang, and it was Mrs. Paine. She said, "Mrs. Oswald, Lee called and he was very upset because Marina was not with me, and he asked me to get a lawyer for him, a Mr. Abt. I would like to talk to Marina."

So I put Marina on the telephone, and Marina said about two or three words.

So when she got off the telephone, I said,—Now, Marina talks in Russian, gentlemen. I said, "Marina, Mrs. Paine told me that Lee called and you were not home at Mrs. Paine, and Lee tells Mrs. Paine to get a lawyer."

Marina didn't answer.

And I then sensed—well, now, why isn't she answering me? This is very peculiar. And there was no more said about that conversation.

Mr. Rankin. Did you ask her about this lawyer?

Mrs. Oswald. Ask Marina?

Mr. Rankin. Yes.

Mrs. Oswald. No, sir. There was no more said about this conversation.

Mr. Rankin. You didn't say anything about Mr. Abt to her then?

Mrs. Oswald. No, sir. But here is the point to this whole thing.

The FBI agent would have to know where we were, and Mrs. Paine would have to know where we were, because of these two Life representatives, who, I am assuming, probably went back to Mrs. Paine's home in order to get more information. And she—they would have told her where we were, because no one knew where we were. This girl and I had no protection or anything. We were sent out there with this Mr. Allen Grant, the representative. And no one knew who we were. And Mr. Hart Odum would have to know where we were through Mrs. Paine, which is a normal procedure, let's say. He might have gone to Mrs. Paine's home looking for Marina there, and Mrs. Paine might have told him we were at the Executive Inn. I will grant that.

But the point I am going to make is that the picture was tried to be shown to Marina before the telephone conversation.

Now, if there are any questions why I say that, I would be happy to answer.

Mr. Rankin. Yes—why do you say that?

Mrs. Oswald. Because they wanted Marina——

Mr. Dulles. Could we get what picture this is? Is that the picture held in the hand?

Mrs. Oswald. Yes, sir—the picture that is held in the hand, that the FBI agent, Mr. Hart Odum showed me.

Mr. Rankin. I understand you didn't recognize who the picture was at all.

Mrs. Oswald. No. I told Mr. Hart Odum I had never seen the man before, "Believe me, sir," and he left.

So the picture was shown—was tried—had tried to be shown to my daughter-in-law, but they were not successful.

So then they received—Marina receives a telephone call.

Now, I am under the impression, since I know it was Mr. Jack Ruby's picture I saw—at the time I didn't.

Mr. Rankin. How do you know that?

Mrs. Oswald. Because I have seen his picture in the paper. Now I know it is Mr. Jack Ruby.

I am under the impression that Marina was threatened——

Mr. Rankin. What was the date now?

Mrs. Oswald. This is Saturday, November 23d. This is approximately 6:30 in the evening, that the FBI agent came. And the telephone call was later.

Now, I have no way of knowing whether Lee had permission to use the telephone. Remember, Lee is in jail.

Mr. Rankin. About what time do you think the telephone call was?

Mrs. Oswald. I would say it was about 7:30, 8 o'clock in the night.

Mr. Rankin. That was still on Saturday night?

Mrs. Oswald. Yes, sir, still on Saturday night at the Executive Inn. And that was after the picture was shown to me—she received this telephone call, and became very silent.

And the next day my son was shot.

Now, it is now that I have done investigation of this case that I believe that the picture was meant for Marina to see, meant for Marina to see.

Mr. Rankin. Why do you think that?

Mrs. Oswald. Because now it has been proven that Jack Ruby killed my son. And I think there is a connection there. Because Marina did not tell me about her conversation. And you men hold the answer whether Lee used the telephone from the jailhouse. I don't know that.

Mr. Rankin. You base that on just your own conclusion that you arrive at now, do you?

Mrs. Oswald. Yes—because of the FBI agent, Mr. Hart Odum, insistence on taking my daughter-in-law—and he being the same agent that came and showed the picture. And Mr. Ruby being the man that shot Lee—yes, these are definite conclusions.

Mr. Rankin. That is what you base it on?

Mrs. Oswald. Yes, sir, that is what I base it on.

Mr. Dulles. Do I understand correctly that Marina did not see the picture at any time?

Mrs. Oswald. That is correct, sir. But they tried awfully hard for Marina to see the picture.

Mr. Rankin. And when they could not show it to her——

Mrs. Oswald. They showed it to me—yes, sir.

Mr. Rankin. Have you ever seen that picture since?

Mrs. Oswald. On a Wednesday—Lee was shot on a Sunday—neither Marina nor I knew how he was shot. They kept it from us. You have to visualize this.

We were at the Six Flags with approximately 18 to 20 FBI agents, Secret Service men running in and out, a woman with a Russian girl and two sick babies, and the girl and I do not know what is going on.

Mr. Rankin. When you had gotten over to the Six Flags, you must have skipped something there—you were in the Executive Inn before.

Mrs. Oswald. Yes. I was going to make a point about letting you know why I didn't know.

Mr. Rankin. All right.

Mrs. Oswald. All right—let's go back to the Executive Inn.

So that night I was very upset and very worried. I realized that we were there alone. And we were not going to go in town, into Dallas. I wasn't going to take this Russian girl and the two babies. And the babies were all chapped. We had no diapers. We were not prepared for this. And it was hectic, gentlemen.

So all night long I am wondering how can I get in touch with Robert, what can I do.

And I was a little suspicious of Mrs. Paine. I was suspicious of Mrs. Paine from the time I entered her home.

Mr. Rankin. Had you found out how much money the Life man gave you?

Mrs. Oswald. No, not even yet.

Mr. Rankin. All right.

Mrs. Oswald. So I signed for the food. I called the operator and I asked the operator what name the room was registered under. She said, "Well, this is an unusual request. Don't you know what room—what name?"

I said, "Frankly, I don't. We are three couples. I don't know which name they used."

So she told me that the room was registered under Mrs. Allen Grant, which is the name of the Life representative. So I charged and signed. And they would have that for proof—Mrs. Allen Grant, on the food.

Mr. Rankin. Why did you say three couples?

Mrs. Oswald. I just said that to the operator, because I had to give her a reason why I didn't know which name the room was registered under.

So I just wanted to elaborate a little bit—let her know. I didn't want to give my name. Because I was by this time a little concerned about the situation.

During the night I thought—"We are in a position here, I am in a position with a Russian girl and two babies, and I just don't know what to do."

I had no contact with Robert. Robert was trying to get an attorney. And I didn't know if Robert knew where we were. And I did not want to call Mrs. Paine. I wanted to stay clear of Mrs. Paine.

So this is a very unusual coincidence.

Now, I have to go back a little bit. But, believe me, gentlemen, the story will get together for you to understand.

About 1 month prior to this, there was an ad in a Fort Worth paper that the public library was going to have language lessons, and one was Russian classes.

Well, I then, as I told you—I was employed for the 3 to 11 shift. And I was getting a day off. And this would have been a steady job because this woman was not that sick, just an invalid.

So I decided on my day off I wanted to do something. So I decided I would call up about it, and on my day off—make Tuesday my day off and take up Russian in case—because I had always hoped in my heart that Marina and Lee would contact me some day. After all, I am a mother first.

So I went to the library. And Mr. Peter Gregory was the instructor.

Now, you must remember—I did not know that he knew Marina and Lee. This is public notice for the Russian language.

So Mr. Peter Gregory is the instructor.

I went to the second class. My car broke down just one block from the library, and I had to have it towed, and I went to the class. And Mr. Peter Gregory was there, and several of the women waiting for his classes to start. I said I don't imagine I will learn anything, because my car has broken down and I am pretty upset. And Mr. Gregory said, "Where do you live, Mrs. Oswald? Maybe I could help you and take you home." And the other couple said, "We would be happy."

And I said I live in Arlington Heights. And he happens to live about 10 blocks away. Now, I have to go back.

The point I am going to make is this: Mr. Peter Gregory is the engineer who knew my son Robert, who was friends with Lee and Marina. Yet when I registered for a class, and the librarian had come back down before the class, and read off the names of the people that were going to take the Spanish lesson, isn't it peculiar that Mr. Gregory did not remember me as the mother of Lee—didn't acknowledge me as the mother of Lee? I find that very peculiar.

Even the second lesson, there was no acknowledgment.

So I went home with Mr. Peter Gregory. And there was still no acknowledgment.

So we were talking about the Russian language, that is is very hard to learn. And I said, "I am sure I will never master it." And I thought I think I will tell him why I want to take lessons is because of my Russian daughter-in-law, and my son speaks Russian. But I didn't do it.

But I am going to point out again that Mr. Gregory did not acknowledge me.

I am going to give and take. Maybe he didn't connect me. But it would seem very odd—Mrs. Marguerite Oswald was the name—that he didn't connect as Marina's mother-in-law and Lee's mother, when he was such a friend with them.

Mr. Rankin. I am not clear as to what lessons you were taking.

156 Mrs. Oswald. Russian lessons at the public library in Fort Worth, Tex., and Mr. Gregory was the teacher.

Mr. Rankin. You said something about Spanish.

Mrs. Oswald. Oh, did I? I am sorry. No, sir, the Russian language.

The Chairman. What days were these?

Mr. Rankin. What days were these that you talked to Mr. Gregory?

Mrs. Oswald. You mean the Russian language?

Mr. Rankin. Yes.

Mrs. Oswald. I do not have this information. But I can get it for you from the public library, because there was a public notice in the paper.

Mr. Rankin. Can you tell us approximately?

Mrs. Oswald. Yes, it was just right before the assassination. I had taken two lessons. Yes, I had taken two lessons, and then I didn't go for the third lesson, because this was on a Friday—the lessons were on a Tuesday. So I had taken two lessons, the two Tuesdays prior to the assassination.

Mr. Rankin. I see.

So it would be around a little over 3 weeks before the assassination?

Mrs. Oswald. Yes, sir. Two Tuesdays before, and then my next lesson would have been the Tuesday after the Friday of the assassination.

Yes, sir, that is the time.

So then I thought of Mr. Gregory.

Now, believe me, gentlemen—and I will swear again, if you want me to—nothing was said about Mr. Gregory and Marina being friends. But I do have a guardian angel. And, as I go along, some of the things I know have been from this guardian angel.

This was just a coincidence.

I thought of calling Mr. Peter Gregory. I have no friends in Fort Worth. I never—I live a very lonely life. I am not lonely. But I live to myself. I am kept very busy. I had my work, 24 hour duty. So really I have no friends. And because of Lee's defection, I didn't make any new friends.

So I am racking my mind who can I call for help. And I think of Mr. Peter Gregory. So I call Mr. Peter Gregory at 6:30 in the morning, Sunday, the 24th—Sunday morning the 24th.

And I didn't want the hotel operator to know who I was. So I gave a fictitious name. He said, "I am sorry,"—I said, "I can't tell you who I am, Mr. Gregory."

I am ahead of my story.

Marina, when I said, "Marina, we need help, honey. I am going to call a Mr. Gregory."

And I told her about me taking Russian lessons.

"Oh, Mama, I know Mr. Gregory, Lee know Mr. Gregory, the man at the library that gives Russian lessons."

So I find that very much of a coincidence.

So I called Mr. Gregory. I said, "Mr. Gregory, I won't say who I am, but you know my son and you know my daughter-in-law, and I am in trouble, sir. I am over here."

He said, "I am sorry, but I won't talk to anybody I don't know."

Mr. Rankin. What name did you give him?

Mrs. Oswald. I didn't give him any name.

He said, "I am sorry, but I won't talk to anyone I don't know."

And I said again, "Well, you know my son real well."

He said, "Oh, you are Mrs. Oswald."

I said, "Yes sir, this is Mrs. Oswald. We are at the Executive Inn in Dallas, stranded. And do you know of anyone who would give my daughter-in-law and I a home, and put us up for the time that this is going on, so we can be near Lee at the courthouse? I need help. Mr. Gregory."

He said, "Mrs. Oswald, what is your room number? I will help you. Hold still. Help will be coming."

And so that was the end of my conversation with Mr. Gregory.

At 11:30 Sunday, November 23d, my son Robert and Mr. Gregory came to the Executive Inn, all excited. We had diapers strung all over the place. My uniform was washed. I had no clothes with me.

157 I went with the uniform.

"Hurry up, we have got to get you out of here."

I am not one to be told what to do, and you gentlemen know that by this time. I said, "What's your hurry? We have the diapers and all. I want to tell you what happened."

"Mother, Mother stop talking. We have to get you out of here."

Mr. Gregory said, "Mrs. Oswald, will you listen and get things together. We have to get you out of here."

I said, "That is all we have been doing since yesterday, running from one place to the other. Give us just a minute. We are coming, but we have to pack things."

"Hurry up."

I said, "I want you to know how we got here. I was shown a picture of a man last night. And Mrs. Paine called and said that Lee called."

I told him exactly.

So Mr. Gregory and Robert knew about the things I told you. I told him that while I am gathering up the things.

"Mrs. Oswald, we will talk later. We have to get you out of here."

I have found out since that my son was shot. But they did not tell us.

Mr. Rankin. Did you have a television in this room?

Mrs. Oswald. Yes, sir.

Now, here is another Godsend. We watched the television, Marina and I. She watched more than I did. We were very busy, Mr. Rankin. The babies had diarrhea and everything. I was very busy with the babies and the Russian girl. And just like at the end of the Six Flags, we were just getting snatches of it. But Marina wanted to know, "Mama, I want see Lee." She was hoping Lee would come on the picture, like he did. So this morning, Sunday morning, I said, "Oh, honey, let's turn the television off. The same thing over and over."

And I turned the television off. So Marina and I did not see what happened to my son.

We had the television off.

So we did not know.

But frantically Robert and Mr. Gregory kept insisting that we pack and run.

So when we get downstairs, here was Secret Service men all over.

Mr. Rankin. Now, before you leave that, what did Robert say about the story about the picture, when you told him that? Did he say anything?

Mrs. Oswald. No. He and Mr. Gregory both didn't want to listen to me. I told them, but they didn't want to hear my story. They wanted to get us out of here.

Mr. Rankin. They didn't say anything about it?

Mrs. Oswald. No, sir, not that I can recall. And I don't believe they did. They didn't want to hear what I had to say. They kept fussing at me and saying "Mother, stop talking. Hurry up, we have got to get you out of here."

I kept saying, "All we have been doing is run from one place to the other. The diapers are wet."

I was kind of having my way about this.

So when we get downstairs, there is Secret Service all around.

I am ahead of my story.

Robert went downstairs to pay the bill, and that is when I gave Robert the money, and it was a $50 bill that the Life representative had given to me. They gave me some money. I took it out——

Mr. Rankin. That is the first time you looked at it?

Mrs. Oswald. The first time I looked at it, sir. I charged the food, and I had no need for money. Wait a minute—I am wrong. Yes.

Representative Ford. Mrs. Oswald—didn't you say you had washed your uniform?

Mrs. Oswald. Yes.

Representative Ford. When you washed your uniform, didn't you——

Mrs. Oswald. Just a minute, if you let me explain. I just said I was wrong. The first time—it was Puerto Rican that brought the dinner in. We needed baby lotion for the baby. And then I took the bill out and I saw it was a $50 bill, because he went to the drug store—I gave him the $50 bill, this Puerto Rican, that brought the food in—the first food we had—to go to the drug store and pay for the necessities that Marina and I needed—really it was for the baby, the lotion and everything. And he came back and the drug store was closed—it was on a Sunday. And so I did know about the $50 bill before this time.

And then when Robert came, I gave Robert the $50 bill and he went downstairs to pay the bill.

Now, the representatives had not paid the bill. Robert used the $50 to pay the bill. The bill was not paid. So we were really stranded. Those men left two women stranded. Now, let me see if there is anything I have forgotten.

Mr. Rankin. Where did you put the $50 after the Puerto Rican brought it back?

Mrs. Oswald. In my uniform pocket, because that was all the clothes I had. I kept it in my pocket.

Mr. Rankin. When you washed your uniform——

Mrs. Oswald. I naturally took it out of my pocket to wash my uniform, because I stated I gave Robert the $50 bill to pay the hotel. But that was all the clothes I had. You have to visualize that all of this is really rush business. We are doing all this in a hurry.

So I didn't even put it in my pocketbook. And I would not be the type to put it in my pocketbook, because it is a $50 bill and all the money I have to get out of the hotel—I don't know if I am going to get help—so I want to keep it on my person, just like I keep my important papers right now on my person.

I took it out of my pocket to wash the uniform, I know. This can be proven by the bellhop who brought the food. And he went to the drug store, and the drug store was closed on Sunday. And we did not get the lotion. And I gave him the $50 bill to buy the things with.

Mr. Rankin. And then after you paid the bill there——

Mrs. Oswald. Robert paid the bill.

Mr. Rankin. What happened next?

Mrs. Oswald. Nothing was said about the bill. I didn't know then that the representatives had not paid the bill. Robert took the $50 and checked us out. Then the Secret Service——

Mr. Dulles. Could we have the time when you checked out?

Mrs. Oswald. Yes—approximately 11:30 to 12 o'clock, on Sunday.

Mr. Rankin. Can you tell us the amount of the bill?

Mrs. Oswald. Yes. Since then I have called Robert and Robert said the amount of the bill was 40-some-odd dollars—about $48, I believe. That is what Robert told me. I have no way of knowing, otherwise than what Robert told me.

And I would think so. If I remember correctly the rooms were $17.50. I told you before that they put us in exclusive suites, and two. And the rooms were $17.50. And we had some meals. So that would make it about 40-some-odd dollars.

Mr. Rankin. And then after Robert checked you out, what happened?

Mrs. Oswald. Then Robert got in a car with Secret Service, and then Marina and I and Mr. Gregory were in another car, with two Secret Service agents in the front.

Mr. Rankin. And did you go someplace?

Mrs. Oswald. Here comes me again. They wanted to take us—as soon as we got in the car Mr. Gregory says, "We are taking you to Robert's mother-in-law's house."

Now, they live out of Boyd, Tex., in the country. Boyd, Tex., is a little bit of country town. But they live in a little farm house. They are dairy people—Robert's in-laws. And they wanted to take us there, which would have been approximately 45 miles from Dallas.

And I said, "No, you are not taking me out in the sticks, in the country. I want to be in Dallas where I can help Lee."

"Well, for security reasons, this is the best place. Nobody would ever find it."

I said, "Security reasons? You can give security for me in a hotel room in town. I am not going out in this little country town. I want to be in Dallas where I can help Lee."

159 And so I am not being well liked, because all the arrangements was made, that we were going to go to this little farm house. But I would not go.

I could not survive if I was 40 or 50 miles away and my son was picked up as a murderer. I had to be right there in Dallas.

Mr. Rankin. Now, this was after——

Mrs. Oswald. When they left the Executive Inn, when we got in the car.

Mr. Rankin. And this was after your son was killed?
Mrs. Oswald. Well, yes, but they didn't know this.
Mr. Rankin. And Robert didn't know that?
Mrs. Oswald. They kept it from us—I guess being women. Marina and I did not even know he was shot.

I will go on to that story and tell you. No, sir, we did not know.
Mr. Rankin. The Secret Service people didn't tell you either?
Mrs. Oswald. No, sir; nothing was said. They wanted us for security reasons——
Mr. Dulles. If the time is 11:30——
Mr. Rankin. They left at 12 or 12:30, I thought.
Mr. Dulles. You said 11:30 to 12.
Mrs. Oswald. Approximately that time.
Mr. Dulles. It might not have taken place.
Mrs. Oswald. I know Lee was shot. But at this time I am telling you I don't know this.

This has to go in sequence, sir. Lee was shot, or else we wouldn't have had all these Secret Service men around. But I know then after that Lee was shot. Not now—I do not know this.

Are there any questions? I am willing to answer anything you want to ask.
If you will bear with me, I can go into——
Mr. Rankin. Did you later learn at what time of that Sunday he was shot?
Mrs. Oswald. No, sir; I did not.
Mr. Rankin. You never did?
Mrs. Oswald. Not until about 3 days later. That is what I was telling you about Six Flags. I am trying to explain to you why I don't know these things is because we did not sit down and watch television and read papers. Marina and I—I had two sick babies there. There was a doctor coming in twice a day. I was a very busy woman. And the men were not telling us anything. They were not interested in us.
Mr. Rankin. Now, after you told them that you wanted to stay in a hotel, you could be protected there, what happened?
Mrs. Oswald. Then, of course, nothing was said that they were going to give me my way. But we needed clothes—Marina and the baby needed clothes. So then they decided that they should go to Irving, through my suggestion and so on, and pick up clothes for Marina and the baby, because we were short on diapers. So they are going to Irving.

We got to Irving. There is police cars all around. So that is why I feel sure my son was shot.
Mr. Rankin. How far away is that from this Executive Inn?
Mrs. Oswald. I would think—now, this is just hearsay. But I would think it is about 12 to 15 or 18 miles.

When we reached there, they brought us to the chief of police's home. And there were cars all around.

As soon as the car stopped, the Secret Service agent said, "Lee has been shot."
And I said, "How badly?"
He said, "In the shoulder."
They brought Marina into the house.
Mr. Rankin. Did you ask him how he knew that?
Mrs. Oswald. It came over—I thought he had the radio in the car, Secret Serviceman, and he had talked to someone. This was all set up, sir, and I can prove to you. They didn't want us to know. They are now telling us this, Marina and I.

He talked, and then he turned around and said, "Lee has been shot."
I said, "How badly?"
He said, "In the shoulder."
160 I cried, and said, "Marina, Lee has been shot."

So Marina went into the chief of police's at Irving home, to call Mrs. Paine, to get the diapers and things ready. They decided and told us, with me in the car and Marina, that it would not be a good thing for us to go to Mrs. Paine's home and get these things, that Marina should go in the chief of police's home and call and tell Mrs. Paine what she wanted.

And one or two of the agents would go and get the things for Marina.

So I am sitting in the car with the agent. Marina is in the home now—remember.

So something comes over the mike, and the Secret Service agent says, "Do not repeat. Do not repeat."

I said, "My son is gone isn't he?"

And he didn't answer.

I said, "Answer me. I want to know. If my son is gone, I want to meditate."

He said, "Yes, Mrs. Oswald, your son has just expired."

Mr. Rankin. Now, which agent told you this?

Mrs. Oswald. This is the agent that was also now sent to me to protect me in Fort Worth, Tex.—Mr. Mike Howard, who was the agent that rode in the car with President Johnson, who was the agent that was at Six Flags, that was in charge, who was the agent that was assigned to protect Baine Johnson at the dormitory. He is also the same agent that was sent to protect me in Fort Worth, Tex.

Mr. Rankin. Now, who was the other agent that was with you that day? Was there another Secret Service agent with you?

Mrs. Oswald. He went into the home—he escorted Marina into the chief of police's home, and I do not know his name. And he is not the other agent that I want to know the name of.

Wait just a minute.

I don't know this man's name. But he is not the other agent that is involved.

Mr. Rankin. Now, about what time on that Sunday did you learn of your son's death?

Mrs. Oswald. Well, now, here is your time element. I said Robert and Mr. Gregory and the Secret Service were there approximately from 11:30. And I knew nothing about the shooting. And then we had to go to Irving and everything. Then they told us Lee was shot. So now we are bringing up to the time—it all fits in—which was 1 o'clock or 1:30.

As a matter of fact, then when I got the news, I went into the home, and I said, "Marina, our boy is gone."

We both cried. And they were all watching the sequence on television. The television was turned to the back, where Marina and I could not see it. They sat us on the sofa, and his wife gave us coffee. And the back of the television was to us. And the men and all, a lot of men were looking at the television. It probably just happened, because the man said, "Do not repeat." And I insisted.

They gave us coffee.

And then it later came out in the paper that—a story about the chief of police, how it was set up for the women, that we should not know.

We were to go to his house. There was a story about that from this chief of police of Irving.

Mr. Rankin. What paper is that?

Mrs. Oswald. The Star Telegram paper.

All of my papers were taken out of my home by Secret Service men. While at Six Flags, they saved the papers for me. We would not let the maids take the papers. And I brought all of those papers from the Six Flags, from the very beginning, to my home in Fort Worth, Tex. And every piece of paper out of my home was taken. So I did not—believe me, gentlemen, this seems strange, but it was 2 weeks later before I saw the picture of the way my son was shot.

Mr. Blair Justice of the Star Telegram gave me the back issues of papers. And it wasn't until then that I actually knew the tragedy, how my son was shot. Because they

171

took all the papers, all my clippings and everything. I was left stranded, without any papers. And until Mr. Blair Justice brought me these 161 back issues, some 2 weeks later, was the first time that I saw exactly the tragic way my son was shot.

Mr. Rankin. Was there any discussion between you and Marina about this?

Mrs. Oswald. About the shooting?

Mr. Rankin. Yes.

Mrs. Oswald. No. We didn't know. I was with Marina at the Executive Inn from the 22d until the shooting, the 24th—as I told you.

Then we left. And from the 24th to the 28th, at the Inn of the Six Flags, the agents and my son kept this from us. We did not know. We knew Lee was shot and dead. But we didn't know how. We didn't get to read a paper or watch television. We just had snatches of the television.

Mr. Rankin. Well, when you both learned that he was shot on that Sunday afternoon, did you and Marina say anything to each other?

Mrs. Oswald. Oh, yes. That is another story.

Immediately I said, "I want to see Lee." And Marina said, "I want see Lee, too."

And the chief of police and Mr. Gregory said, "Well, it would be better to wait until he was at the funeral home and fixed up."

I said, "No, I want to see Lee now."

Marina said, "Me, too, me want to see Lee."

They led us to believe that now they have taught her to do like this. But Marina has always spoken like that. I have acted as an interpreter for her, as I stated before, for an FBI agent. And she understood me. And he was satisfied that he didn't need an interpreter.

So she said, "I want to see Lee, too."

They didn't want us to see Lee, from the ugliness of it evidently. But I insisted, and so did Marina. So they could not do anything about it with the two women. So they decided to pacify us.

We got in the car. On the way in the car they are trying to get us to change our minds. And he said, Mr. Mike Howard—he was driving the car—"Mrs. Oswald for security reasons it would be much better if you would wait until later on to see Lee because this is a big thing."

I said, "For security reasons I want you to know that I am an American citizen, and even though I am poor I have as much right as any other human being, and Mrs. Kennedy was escorted to the hospital to see her husband. And I insist upon being escorted, and enough security to take me to the hospital to see my son."

Gentlemen, I require the same privilege.

So Mr. Mike Howard said, "All right, we will take you to the hospital.

"I want you to know when we get there we will not be able to protect you. Our security measures end right there. The police will then have you under protection. We cannot protect you."

I said, "That is fine. If I am to die, I will die that way. But I am going to see my son."

Mr. Gregory says—and in the most awful tone of voice, I will always remember this—remember, gentlemen, my son has been accused, I have just lost a son.

He said, "Mrs. Oswald, you are being so selfish. You are endangering this girl's life, and the life of these two children."

I want to elaborate on this. He is not thinking about me. He is thinking about the Russian girl. I am going to bring this over and over—that these Russian people are always considering this Russian girl. He snapped at me.

I said, "Mr. Gregory, I am not talking for my daughter-in-law. She can do what she wants. I am saying I want to see my son."

And so they brought us to the hospital. And Marina said, "I too want to see Lee."

After Mr. Gregory said that—"I, too, want to see Lee."

So then they did leave us at the entrance of the hospital, the Secret Service men, and then the police took over. We were escorted by the police in the hospital.

Mr. Rankin. About what time was that?

Mrs. Oswald. Well, I would not think it would be more than between 2 and 3 o'clock.

162 Mr. Rankin. Sunday afternoon?

Mrs. Oswald. Sunday, November 24th.

Mr. Rankin. And then what happened?

Mrs. Oswald. Then Mr. Perry, the doctor, came down. We were escorted into a room. And he came in. He said, "Now, you know the Texas law is that we have to have an autopsy on a body."

I said, "Yes, I understand."

And Marina understood.

Marina is a registered pharmacist.

So Marina understands these things. And Marina understood.

And he said, "Now, I will do whatever you ladies wish. I understand that you wish to see the body. However, I will say this. It will not be pleasant. All the blood has drained from him, and it would be much better if you would see him after he was fixed up."

I said, "I am a nurse. I have seen death before. I want to see my son now."

Marina—as I am trying to say, she understands English—she said, "I want to see Lee, too." So she knew what the doctor was saying.

We were escorted upstairs into a room. They said it was a morgue, but it wasn't. Lee's body was on a hospital bed, I would say, or a table—a table like you take into an operating room. And there were a lot of policemen standing around, guarding the body. And, of course, his face was showing. And Marina went first. She opened his eyelids. Now, to me—I am a nurse, and I don't think I could have done that. This is a very, very strong girl, that she can open a dead man's eyelids. And she says, "He cry. He eye wet." To the doctor. And the doctor said, "Yes."

Well, I know that the fluid leaves, and you do have moisture. So I didn't even touch Lee. I just wanted to see that it was my son.

So on the way, leaving the body in the room—I am in the room——

Mr. Rankin. You were satisfied it was your son?

Mrs. Oswald. Yes, sir. That is why I wanted to see the body. I wanted to make sure it was my son.

So while leaving the room, I said to the police—"I think some day you will hang your heads in shame."

I said, "I happen to know, and know some facts, that maybe this is the unsung hero of this episode. And I, as his mother, intend to provide this if I can."

And, with that, I left the room.

Then we were escorted into a room downstairs, and introduced to the chaplain. I have asked several reporters to give me the chaplain's name, because I wanted to have all this information for you. But you have to realize I just knew Thursday. And I have three times as many papers as I have here. So it has been a chore for me to do all of this. But that is easy to find out—the name of the chaplain at Parkland Hospital. So I asked to speak to the chaplain in private. So I spoke to the chaplain in private, and I told him that I thought my son was an agent, and that I wanted him to talk to Robert. Robert does not listen to me, never has, and I have had very, very little conversation with Robert, ever since Robert has joined the Marines, because of the way our life has intervened.

Mr. Rankin. Did you tell the chaplain why you thought your son was an agent?

Mrs. Oswald. No, sir, but this is what I told the chaplain. No—I am always thinking of my country, the security of my country before I would say anything like that.

And I told you why I told the FBI men, because of the money involved, and I didn't know how the public would take this, because they helped a Marxist.

So I didn't tell him. But I did say I wanted him to talk to Robert, because we financially were in very poor straits. And then I wanted my son buried in the Arlington Cemetery.

Now, gentlemen, I didn't know that President Kennedy was going to be buried in Arlington Cemetery. All I know is that my son is an agent, and that he deserves to be buried in Arlington Cemetery. So I talked to the chaplain about this. I went into quite detail about this. I asked him if he would talk to Robert, because when I talked to Robert about it, as soon as I started to say something he would say, "Oh, Mother, forget it."

163 So I asked the chaplain to talk to Robert about Lee being buried in the Arlington Cemetery.

Mr. Rankin. Did he report to you about it?

Mrs. Oswald. No, sir. But he did call Robert in. We were getting ready. The police were getting ready to escort us out of his office, and he said, "If you don't mind, I would like to talk to Robert Oswald just a minute."

So he brought Robert into the room he had taken me, and stayed in there a little while with Robert. So I feel sure that the chaplain relayed my message to him, because we were getting ready to leave, and he asked the police if he could talk to Robert.

Mr. Rankin. The chaplain never told you anything more about it?

Mrs. Oswald. No, sir, I have not seen the chaplain since.

Mr. Rankin. Did Robert say anything about it?

Mrs. Oswald. No, sir, Robert says nothing. I have tried to contact Robert for important matters, and Robert will not talk.

Lee was left handed. Lee wrote left handed and ate right handed. And I wanted to know if Lee shot left handed. Because on Lee's leaves, as I stated, they live out in the country, and Robert goes squirrel hunting, and all kinds of hunting. And on leaves from the Marines, Lee has gone out to this farmhouse, to Robert's family house, and he and his brother have gone squirrel hunting. And so Robert would know if Lee shot left handed, and he would not give me the information, gentlemen.

Mr. Rankin. Is Robert left handed?

Mrs. Oswald. Yes, Robert is left handed. I am left handed.

Mr. Rankin. Is John Pic left handed?

Mrs. Oswald. No, John is not.

Mr. Rankin. But you are?

Mrs. Oswald. Yes, sir.

Now, I write left handed, but I do everything else with my right hand.

But Lee was more left handed than I am.

I write left handed, but I do everything else with my right hand. But Lee was left handed.

Mr. Rankin. Was Lee Oswald's father left handed?

Mrs. Oswald. That I do not remember, Mr. Rankin. No—I am the left handed one. I would say no.

Now, there is another story. And we have stories galore, believe me—with documents and everything.

A gun will be involved in this story, that Lee had bought. But I don't want to confuse the committee. That is another part that we will have to go into, that I will have to lead up to. The only way I can do this and not forget things is to do the way I am doing it. And if you have any questions, if you feel the story I have told so far—I would like to know, myself, if I have forgotten anything.

It is awfully hard for me to remember everything. If you want to question me, I am more than happy, if I know the facts, to give them to you.

Mr. Rankin. Well, you go ahead and tell us in your own way.

Mrs. Oswald. May I have some fresh water, please?

Mr. Rankin. You have never told us about the Walker matter. Did you know something about that?

Mrs. Oswald. No, I didn't know about that.

The Chairman. You are going to let her finish this other, are you not?

Mr. Rankin. Yes.

Mrs. Oswald. I didn't know about that until it came out in the paper. But I have a story on that.

Mr. Rankin. You want to finish this incident about the gun you are talking about?

Mrs. Oswald. About Robert knowing about the gun—I have already said that. About Lee being left handed, and he and Robert going squirrel hunting.

Mr. Rankin. You said there was another gun matter.

Mrs. Oswald. That is a long, long story.

The Chairman. I think she has gotten to the point——

Mrs. Oswald. I got to the point. I finished this story, really, don't you think—about the gun?

The Chairman. I don't know.

Mrs. Oswald. I think about Robert knowing Lee was left handed.

The Chairman. Has anything happened since that, that you care to call to our attention, things that you know about?

Mrs. Oswald. On the particular story that I have said this morning—you mean of Lee?

This is where it gets confusing.

Representative Ford. Where did you go after the Parkland Hospital? What happened then?

Mrs. Oswald. Oh, yes. This is interesting.

After the Parkland Hospital, then this Mike Howard said, "Well, what we will do, we have a place, and this is where we will take them."

And they took us to the Inn of the Six Flags, which is on the outskirts of Arlington, Tex. They took us there.

And I am assuming that it is a Secret Service hideout or something, because they had made no arrangements or anything. We just were welcomed right in the Inn. They knew where to go.

Mr. Rankin. What happened there?

Mrs. Oswald. Well, now, Mr. Rankin, that is so important—if we are going to recess, I am going to ask not to start that story, because that is a very long, important story to this Commission.

Mr. Dulles. How far is that from Dallas—the Six Flags Inn?

Mrs. Oswald. Well, it is in between Dallas and Fort Worth, Tex. It is near Arlington, Tex.

The Chairman. We will recess now until 2 o'clock.

(Whereupon, at 12:55 p.m., the President's Commission recessed.)

Afternoon Session
TESTIMONY OF MRS. MARGUERITE OSWALD RESUMED

The President's Commission reconvened at 2 p.m.

The Chairman. The Commission will be in order. Mrs. Oswald, you may continue with your statement.

Mrs. Oswald. On the way leaving, I remarked to Mr. Doyle that I had forgotten one very important factor in the story.

I had in Mrs. Paine's home, when Marina closed the door, and I was in the room—before she showed me the picture—she told me at the police station that they had showed her Lee's gun and asked her if that was Lee's gun, and she said she didn't know, that Lee had a gun, but she could not say whether that was Lee's gun or not. But that she knew that Lee had a gun.

Mr. Rankin. When was this?

Mrs. Oswald. This was in Mrs. Paine's home the night of November 22, when we came from the jail. She told me that she told the police. I am going to explain, because I don't want to be put in why I didn't say it.

Mr. Mark Lane had hoped to come before the Commission, and he wanted to ask me two questions. He didn't say what the questions were. But I know the affidavit presented to the Warren Commission passed on that. And so that is why I had put that particular thing off my mind, thinking Mr. Lane would bring it up. But I immediately told Mr. Doyle when I left, that Mr. Lane not being here I should have made that statement.

Was there something else I told you?

Mr. Doyle. No. I think that was the matter you had mentioned to me, ma'am.

Mr. Rankin. You mean the gun or the picture of the gun?

Mrs. Oswald. No—the gun. The police showed Marina a gun—showed Marina a gun, and asked Marina if that was Lee's gun, because Marina had testified at the police station, she told me that Lee had a gun in Mrs. Paine's 165 garage, and this was the gun that was presumably used to assassinate the President, that the police had and showed it to Marina, and asked Marina if that was Lee's gun that was in the garage. She said she didn't know—that Lee had a gun in the garage, but she did not know whether that was the gun or not.

Mr. Rankin. Did you have any discussion with Marina about the gun after that?

Mrs. Oswald. No, sir—when she said that, that was it. Any comments—as I said before—that was it.

Now, where did I finish, please, so I can continue?

Mr. Rankin. Well, you had gotten to the Six Flags, and you had heard about your son being killed. And then you had gotten to the Parkland Hospital.

Mrs. Oswald. We were through at the Parkland Hospital.

Mr. Rankin. You had gotten through with the Parkland Hospital.

Mrs. Oswald. And then we got to the chief of police's home in Irving. And we finished that. So now we are at the Six Flags.

Mr. Rankin. Correct.

Mrs. Oswald. So the FBI agent took us to the Six Flags.

I was never questioned by the Secret Service or the FBI at Six Flags. My son, in my presence, was questioned and taped, and Marina was continuously questioned and taped. But I have never been questioned.

I had all the papers from the State Department, and all of my research from Lee's I say so-called defection. And I wanted them to have them. All the papers were at home.

I told them I thought I could save a lot of manpower, while they were getting the original papers, because I know that each department in the State Department had a reference on Lee, and I had the whole thing condensed, and by them having my papers, they could get the picture. They were not interested in any papers I had. They were not interested.

Mr. Rankin. Were you not questioned on November 22, 1963?

Mrs. Oswald. No, sir. Here is what you may have on tape.

I insisted so much that they talked to me, because I had all this—that Mr. Mike Howard finally agreed—not 22d, though.

Mr. Rankin. This is Mr. Harlan Brown and Mr. Charles T. Brown?

Mrs. Oswald. That is the two FBI agents, Mr. Brown, questioned me in the office. But all they wanted to know is how did I know my son was an agent, and how did I know that he had the money from the State Department. And I told them Congressman Wright knew, and that they would investigate Congressman Wright. That was a very short questioning. I mean I explained that before. I told them I wanted to talk to the FBI, and I did. And it was the two Mr. Browns, and there were two other men.

Mr. Rankin. Then Mr. Howard was what date?

Mrs. Oswald. Mike Howard? Mike Howard was toward the end, because I was so persistent in them talking to me, that finally he decided he would put me on tape. But I do not consider this questioning. It was the date of the funeral—I remember now.

Mr. Rankin. November 25th?

Mrs. Oswald. Was that the day of the funeral? If this was the day of the funeral—I can tell you why. He decided he would put me on tape. So I started to tell him about my having the papers, and Lee's defection. And then Robert came out of the room and was crying bitterly. I saw Robert crying.

Wait, I am ahead of my story.

You have to understand this. As a family, we separated—not maybe for any particular reason, it is just the way we live. I am not a mother that has a home that the children can come to and feed them and so on. I am a working mother. I do 24-hour duty. So I am not that type mother, where I am a housewife with money, that the children have a home to come to.

So I said to Mike Howard, "I would like Robert to hear this. Maybe he will learn something." Because Robert never did want to know about my trip to Washington. He doesn't know. Robert never was interested in anything. Lee did not want to know about my trip to Washington. So I thought well now this is an opportunity, since the tragedy has happened, for Mr. Robert166 Oswald to know some of these things that his mother has known all of these years.

So I started.

Then Robert had a phone call and he came out of the room, and he was crying bitterly. So I ended the tape—I would say I talked approximately 10 minutes. I ended the tape saying, "I'm sorry, but my thoughts have left me, because my son is crying."

I thought for a moment that Robert was crying because of what I was saying, and he was sorry that he had not listened to me before, because I tried to tell him about the defection and my trip to Washington. But Robert was crying because he received a telephone call that we could not get a minister at my son's grave.

They had three ministers that refused to come to the ceremony at my son's grave—for church. And that is why Robert was crying bitterly. So that ended the testimony. That little while I testified, that ended it.

Mr. Rankin. Now, that questioning was a question and answer. You were questioned by the FBI agent, Mr. Howard——

Mrs. Oswald. No, sir. I was just talking.

Mr. Rankin. The Secret Service man?

Mrs. Oswald. Mr. Mike Howard. I was talking on tape.

Mr. Rankin. Didn't he ask you questions?

Mrs. Oswald. I don't recall him asking any questions. It could be. But I frankly do not recall him asking any questions. But it was a very short session. And that is the way I ended the tape. I said, "My thoughts have left me because I see my son crying bitterly."

That is the way I ended the tape. And it was a very short tape. I do not remember him questioning me. I think I started to tell my story. And that is the only time.

It was from my persistence that I got on tape just that little while. They did not want to hear anything from me.

Mr. Rankin. You don't think, then, that at that time there were questions and answers for about 28 pages taken from you?

Mrs. Oswald. From me—no, sir. Definitely not. If they have that, what they have is my talking, like I said, when I saw on television. They said—they were showing Lee's gun. And I was not watching television—I am getting snatches of it, and I said, "Now, how can they say, even though it is Lee's gun, that Lee shot the President. Even being his gun doesn't mean that he shot the President. Someone could have framed him."

If they have 28 pages of that, they have me doing that kind of talking, and had the room bugged, or whatever you want to say. But no, sir, I did not sit and testify. I swear before God 10 times I never have. And that is the point that has bothered me.

Even before Lee's defection no one came along to the house. I called Mr. John Fain in the FBI myself to make friends with him. If they have 20 pages of testimony—that is when they got it, my talking. They got it with a tape recorder going. But I did not, no, sir.

Mr. Rankin. Well, then, what happened after that?

Mrs. Oswald. Now—we got off of that. About Robert crying?

Mr. Rankin. You said that that ended the interview with Mr. Howard.

Mrs. Oswald. Yes, that ended the interview with Mr. Howard, because Robert was crying. I was not consulted. I want you to know this, too. I was not consulted about the graveyard services or any part of my son's funeral.

What I know—when my son was going to be buried—it was approximately 1 hour before the time for my son to be buried. My son Robert knew.

Mr. Rankin. Do you know whether Marina was consulted?

Mrs. Oswald. I do not know. And I am assuming that she was. You see, Mr. Gregory taught Russian to Marina. And I believe Marina might have been consulted. But I do not know whether she was consulted or not. But I was not consulted. And since then—we will go on to the story. They have put a marker on the grave. I have not been consulted. I have found out my son is encased in cement, and I did not know anything about it until I investigated and asked the man at the cemetery.

167 They did not consult me about anything, never have. I want that made clear—because that is the part I cannot understand.

Mr. Rankin. You don't know whether the laws of Texas give the widow the right to say what shall be done?

Mrs. Oswald. Well, naturally, she is his wife, and I am just the mother. But from a moral standpoint, what are they doing to me? Law and right—but from a moral standpoint, I should go out to the graveyard and see a marker? I should find out from strangers that my son is now in a concrete vault?

Mr. Rankin. Well, then, did you go to the funeral?

Mrs. Oswald. Well, let me get—we will get to the story of the ministers.

Mr. Rankin. All right.

Mrs. Oswald. Now, I was not consulted. Had Robert asked me—they are Lutheran, we are raised Lutherans. I have no church affiliation. I have learned since my trouble that my heart is my church. I am not talking against the church. But I go to church all day long, I meditate. And my work requires that I don't go to church. I am working on Sunday most of the time, taking care of the sick, and the people that go to church, that I work for, the families, have never once said, "Well, I will stay home and take care of my mother and let you go to church, Mrs. Oswald, today."

You see, I am expected to work on Sunday.

So that is why—I have my own church. And sometimes I think it is better than a wooden structure. Because these same people that expect me to work on Sunday, while they go to church, and go to church on Wednesday night—I don't consider them as good a Christian as I am—I am sorry.

Well—I would not have let Robert be so upset trying to get a Lutheran minister. If he could not get a Lutheran minister, I would have called upon another minister, because there would have been many, many ministers of many denominations that would have been happy to come and help the sorrowing family.

Well, a Reverend French from Dallas came out to Six Flags and we sat on the sofa.

Reverend French was in the center, I and Robert on the side. And Robert was crying bitterly and talking to Reverend French and trying to get him to let Lee's body go to church. And he was quoting why he could not.

So then I intervened and said, "Well, if Lee is a lost sheep, and that is why you don't want him to go to church, he is the one that should go into church. The good people do not need to go to church. Let's say he is called a murderer. It is the murderers and all we should be concerned about".

And that agent—I am going ahead of my story a little bit—that man right here——
Mr. Rankin. You are pointing to——
Mrs. Oswald. This agent right here. You may pass the picture around.
Mr. Rankin. The figure on the left hand of the picture you have just produced?
Mrs. Oswald. Yes, sir. I do not know his name. The man had the decency to stay at the far end of the room, near the entrance door, while the minister and myself and Robert were sitting on the sofa. And when I said to the minister about the lost sheep, this agent, who I will have a much longer story to talk about, left the group and came and sat on the other sofa—there were two sofas and a cocktail table—and he said, "Mrs. Oswald, be quiet. You are making matters worse."

Now, the nerve of him—to leave the group and to come there and scold me.

This Mr. French, Reverend French, agreed that we would have chapel services, that he could not take the body into the church. And we compromised for chapel services.

However, when we arrived at the graveyard, we went to the chapel. There is the body being brought into the chapel. There is another picture. Here is another picture of the chapel.

Mr. Rankin. Before we go on——
Mrs. Oswald. And the chapel was empty. My son's body had been brought into the chapel, but Reverend French did not show up. And because there was a time for the funeral, the Star Telegram reporters and the police,168 as you see in the picture, escorted my son's body from the chapel and put it at the grave site. And when we went to the cemetery, we went directly to the chapel, because we were promised to have chapel services. And the chapel was empty. My son's body was not in it. Robert cried bitterly.

Mr. Rankin. Mrs. Oswald, can I interrupt a minute?

We will have the reporter identify this photograph that you just referred to, where the FBI agent is in the lefthand corner.

(The photograph referred to was marked Commission Exhibit No. 165 for identification.)

Mr. Rankin. The photograph I have just referred to is Exhibit 165, is it?
Mrs. Oswald. Exhibit 165.
Mr. Rankin. And the FBI agent you refer to is in the upper lefthand corner of that exhibit.
Mrs. Oswald. That's right. And this is the other FBI agent, Mr. Mike Howard, who is going to be involved quite a bit. He is the one that was taking care of Baine Johnson. He is the one that they have now sent to protect me in Fort Worth. He was the lead man at Six Flags.
Mr. Rankin. And he stands right behind you there in that picture?
Mrs. Oswald. Yes, that is Mr. Mike Howard.
Mr. Rankin. Isn't he a Secret Service man?
Mrs. Oswald. Secret Service man—they are both Secret Service.
Representative Ford. That was the point I wanted to make, because she had said he was an FBI agent.
Mrs. Oswald. Yes—please interrupt. It is awful hard for me to remember and say things. So I appreciate you doing that. It is a long story. And I have many stories, gentlemen. I have many stories that I am sure you do not have.

Mr. Rankin. Mrs. Oswald, I'll ask the reporter to mark the other picture with the chapel and the casket as Exhibit 166.

(The photograph referred to was marked Commission Exhibit No. 166 for identification.)

Mr. Rankin. Can you tell us if Exhibit 166 is a photograph showing the removing of the casket?

Mrs. Oswald. The way the men are coming this way, they are leaving the chapel. That is the way I would assume. They are leaving the chapel. But the body was not at the chapel. What an awful thing we went through, gentlemen.

Mr. Rankin. We offer in evidence Exhibits 165 and 166, and ask to substitute copies.

The Chairman. They may be admitted.

(The documents heretofore marked Commission Exhibits Nos. 165 and 166 were received in evidence.)

Mr. Rankin. Mr. Reporter, I will ask you to mark the picture of the chapel with the casket apparently going in as Exhibit 167.

(The photograph referred to was marked Commission Exhibit No. 167 for identification.)

Mr. Rankin. And the picture of the chapel and the casket being placed on a carrier in front of it, as Exhibit 168.

(The photograph referred to was marked Commission Exhibit No. 168 for identification.)

Mr. Rankin. Mrs. Oswald, do you recall that Exhibit 167 is the picture of them taking the casket into the chapel?

Mrs. Oswald. Yes.

Mr. Rankin. And Exhibit 168 is apparently a picture in front of the chapel where they are putting the casket on a carrier?

Mrs. Oswald. Yes, sir.

Mr. Rankin. We offer in evidence Exhibits 167 and 168 and ask leave to substitute copies.

The Chairman. They may be admitted.

(The photographs previously marked Commission Exhibits Nos. 167 and 168 for identification were received in evidence.)

Mrs. Oswald. Now, I don't remember if I stated while at Six Flags that169 this particular agent identified as being to the left of the picture, while the television was on continuously—I have stated before I never did sit down and watch it, because we were quite busy. And this was published in the Star Telegram by Mr. Blair Justice, and also on the radio.

He was very, very rude to me. Anything that I said, he snapped. And I took it for quite a while. At this particular time that they showed the gun on television, I said, "How can they say Lee shot the President? Even though they would prove it is his gun doesn't mean he used it—nobody saw him use it."

He snapped back and he said, "Mrs. Oswald, we know that he shot the President."

I then walked over to Mr. Mike Howard and I said, "What's wrong with that agent? That agent is about to crack. All he has done is taunt me ever since I have been here."

He said, "Mrs. Oswald, he was personal body guard to Mrs. Kennedy for 30 months and maybe he has a little opinion against you."

I said, "Let him keep his personal opinions to himself. He is on a job."

Now, there was another instance with this same agent. He followed Marina around continuously. I'm going to make this plain. He followed Marina around continuously. The pictures will always show him by Marina.

We were in the bedroom, and he was in the bedroom. And we were getting ready for the funeral.

Marina was very unhappy with the dress—they bought her two dresses. "Mama, too long." "Mama, no fit." And it looked lovely on her. You can see I know how to dress properly. I am in the business world as merchandise manager. And the dress looked lovely on Marina. But she was not happy with it.

I said, "Oh, honey, put your coat on, we are going to Lee's funeral. It will be all right."

And we had 1 hour in order to get ready for the funeral.

I said, "We will never make it. Marina is so slow."

She said, "I no slow. I have things to do."

I am trying to impress upon you that Marina understands English, and has always talked broken English.

Now, this agent was in the room and Robert was on the telephone. That is why he was allowed in the bedroom.

While Marina was complaining about her dress, my little grandbaby, 2 years old—and she is a very precious little baby, they are good children—was standing by her mother. And Marina was very nervous by this time. She was not happy with the dress. And Marina was combing her hair. She took the comb and she hit June on the head. I said, "Marina, don't do that." And this agent—I wish I knew his name—snapped at me and said, "Mrs. Oswald, you let her alone." I said, "Don't tell me what to say to my daughter-in-law when she was hitting my grandbaby on the head with a comb" in front of Robert Oswald.

Now, why did this man do these things?

Mr. Rankin. Are you saying that the agent did anything improper, as far as Marina was concerned?

Mrs. Oswald. Now, what do you mean when you say improper?

Mr. Rankin. Was there any improper relationship between them, as far as you know?

Mrs. Oswald. No. I am saying—and I am going to say it as strongly as I can—that I—and I have stated this from the beginning—that I think our trouble in this is in our own Government. And I suspect these two agents of conspiracy with my daughter-in-law in this plot.

The Chairman. With who?

Mrs. Oswald. With Marina and Mrs. Paine—the two women. Lee was set up, and it is quite possible these two Secret Service men are involved.

Mr. Rankin. Which ones are you referring to?

Mrs. Oswald. Mr. Mike Howard and the man that I did not—did not know the name, the man in the picture to the left. I have reason to think so because I was at Six Flags and these are just some instances that happened—I have much more stories to tell you of my conclusions. I am not a detective, and I170 don't say it is the answer to it. But I must tell you what I think, because I am the only one that has this information.

Now, here is another instance——

Mr. Rankin. What kind of a conspiracy are you describing that these men are engaged in?

Mrs. Oswald. The assassination of President Kennedy.

Mr. Rankin. You think that two Secret Service agents and Marina and Mrs. Paine were involved in that, in the conspiracy?

Mrs. Oswald. Yes, I do. Besides another high official. I will tell you the high official I have in mind when we go through that part of the story, if you please.

Mr. Rankin. Well, now, could you tell us what you base that on—because that is a very serious charge.

Mrs. Oswald. It is a very serious charge, and I realize that. I base that on what I told you, the attitude of this man, and Mike Howard's attitude also.

Now, I have to continue.

Mr. Rankin. Have you described that?

Mrs. Oswald. Yes. I have to continue.

While at Six Flags, Marina was given the red carpet treatment. Marina was Marina. And it was not that Marina is pretty and a young girl. Marina was under—what is the word—I won't say influence—these two men were to see that Marina was Marina. I don't know how to say it. Are you getting the point? Let me see if I can say it better.

Mr. Rankin. You mean they were taking care of her, or were they doing more than that?

Mrs. Oswald. More than taking care of Marina.

Mr. Rankin. Well, now, describe what more.

Mrs. Oswald. All right, I will describe it for you.

I am not quite satisfied with the way I said that. Let me get my thoughts together.

I noticed that—and of course as I have testified, the way the man treated me—and I was told he was a body guard for Mrs. Kennedy. We were at Six Flags on November 24th, at Lee's death, and on November 26th Marina and I—before November 26th—Marina and I were very, very friendly, very loving, everything was "Mama"—"Mama has a big heart." And we planned to live together.

I had an insurance policy that had expired on Lee. I was not able to keep up the premium. And I had $863. But however I had not looked at the policy for some years, and I was not quite sure that it was in force. But otherwise I had no money and no job. I had given up my job to come to the rescue. So I was very anxious to get home and get my papers and let them see the copies of everything I had, and to find out if I had my insurance policy, if it was in force, and also get some clothes.

From the 24th until the 26th I lived in my uniform, gentlemen. I did not have any clothes at the Six Flags. Yet Robert Oswald was taken to his home a couple of times to get clothes. And when I wanted to go home and get clothes, they put me off. One time I broke down crying. I said, "I don't understand it. You won't do anything for me, yet you drove Robert all the way to Denton to get clothes."

So the night of the 26th they took me home, and I got my papers. I found that my insurance policy was in force. So I said to Marina, "Marina, we all right. Mama has insurance policy, $800. You stay home with baby and mama work, or mama stay home with baby and you work, and at least we have a start."

"Okay, Mama. I not want big house, Mama. I want small place."

And this is the girl that has never had anything, and she only wanted small things. Fine.

On the date of the 22d, approximately 10 o'clock—this was in the morning—I want to say something to Marina, and Marina shrugged me off and walked away.

Mr. Dulles. What date was this?

Mrs. Oswald. The 27th. That morning I had acted as interpreter for an171 FBI agent, and Mr. Mike Howard said, "Would you like us to get a Russian interpreter?" And he said, "No, Mrs. Oswald is doing fine." And he took the testimony from me as an interpreter. So, you see my daughter-in-law did understand English and answered me in her Russian broken English, because the FBI man was satisfied.

So when Marina shrugged me off, I thought right away that she thought—because I had to use the name Lee so many times—that I was hurting her husband, and maybe that is why she felt this way. So I thought maybe I am just imagining things. So I waited quite a while, I would say half an hour. I went to Marina again. And she walked away and shrugged me off.

So I walked into the living room, where my son, Robert Oswald, and the Secret Service were and I said to Robert, "Robert, something is wrong with Marina. She won't have anything to do with me."

He said, "I know why. Marina has been offered a home by a very wealthy woman"—all of this was done without my knowledge—"by a very wealthy woman who will give her children education, and she didn't know how to tell you."

I said, "Well, Robert, why didn't you tell me?"

Of course when I said it. I was emotionally upset. I said, "Robert, why didn't you tell me?"

He said, "Because just the way you are acting now."

I said, "What do you mean the way I am acting now? I am acting in a normal fashion. You are telling me that you are taking my daughter-in-law and my grandchildren away from me, and I have lost my son, and my grandchildren and daughter are going to live with strangers. This is a normal reaction."

"Well, that is why we didn't tell you. We knew you would take it that way."

And that is the last time I have talked to my daughter-in-law, Marina. And that is the rift between Marina and I. There is no rift, sir? We were going to live together. But this home was offered Marina—and I will present this in evidence.

Now, Mr. Gregory is involved—Mr. Gregory did all the Russian talking. They all knew better but me. And I have more to the story.

Yes, here it is.

And there are other offers Marina had—other offers.

So I was not able to be around Marina. The Secret Service saw to it. And they gloated.

Gentlemen, I am not imagining these things. These two men gloated of the fact that now Marina is going to be fixed—you know, she is fixed financially and otherwise.

Mr. Rankin. Is this Mrs. Pultz?

Mrs. Oswald. I didn't even read this, sir, believe me. This was handed to me by a reporter before I left, saying, "Mrs. Oswald, maybe these things"—because he knows the story. This has all been published publicly in newspapers, what I am saying. The Star Telegram could give you all I am saying here. It has already been made public in the paper, all of this. And he handed that to me. I never did see that article until the other day.

Mr. Rankin. This article refers to Mrs. Oswald being offered a home, and apparently a newspaper account—a newspaper account of the offer, according to this newspaper account—the offer was by a Mrs. Pultz. That is the one that you refer to when you handed this paper to us.

Mrs. Oswald. Yes, sir, that is offering her a home.

Now, I have not read that. I know she was offered a home by a woman and I will tell you further what I do know about this.

Mr. Rankin. Mr. Reporter, I will ask you to identify this as the next exhibit.

(The document referred to was marked Commission Exhibit No. 169 for identification.)

Mr. Rankin. Mrs. Oswald, the reporter has marked that Exhibit 169, the newspaper article you have just given us, is that correct?

Mrs. Oswald. Yes, sir.

172 Mr. Rankin. I now offer in evidence Exhibit 169 and ask please to substitute a copy.

The Chairman. It may be admitted.

(The document heretofore marked Commission Exhibit No. 169 for identification was received in evidence.)

Mr. Rankin. Do you recall the date?

Mrs. Oswald. I left there on the 28th, so it would have to be the 27th. It would have to be the 27th.

Mr. Rankin. Now——

Mrs. Oswald. Now, there were other people that offered her homes.

Mr. Rankin. But you seemed to think there was something improper or bad about your son Robert wanting to get your daughter Marina taken care of in this manner. I don't understand that. Can you explain it?

Mrs. Oswald. Yes. Well—no—as I have explained before, Robert and I are not close, we are not close as a family. But Robert is a very easy-going person. He is not opinionated, particularly like I am. My older son and Lee are my disposition. But because you are a Secret Service man or somebody, if you tell him something, he will go along and yes you. So he was part of this arrangement. They probably had to have his consent. But he knew of the arrangement with Mr. Gregory and Marina. They all knew it but me. I was not consulted about this at all.

Mr. Rankin. Do you think Robert was trying to do something bad by it, or just trying to look out for——

Mrs. Oswald. He thought it was a good idea, that Marina should go and live in this home. But I took a different attitude. I am not interested in material things, gentlemen. I then went into my speech, that I thought, as a family, Marina and I should stick together and face our future together. I could see no reason—and I made this at the Six Flags, and have made it public in the newspapers, I could see no reason, no advantage of Marina living with strangers. I said that before. I thought it would be better, original idea, Marina and I had made, to live in my apartment and do the best we can. And I even said—we have $863 to start with, and then if we don't make it "What about you helping us?"

"But give us a chance as a family. Don't put the girl in a strange home, a Russian girl, a foreign girl, taken away from her Mama."

Marina has no mother and father—she has a stepfather. But I was her Mama up until this time. And I could not see Marina in a strange home.

Well, I am going to prove this story to you. It is a fantastic story. But as I go along—I have witnesses—and that is why I asked you, sir, I would like these people called to back up these fantastic stories I am telling you. It can be proven, sir.

So I had no further contact with my daughter-in-law—once they came out and said what they had planned. I had no inkling of it. That was the—they wanted to keep her and the children away from me.

That night, the night of November 27th—now, we were in a bedroom with twin beds that we shared. They opened the studio couch in the living room, and rolled June's bed, the baby bed in the living room, sir.

Mr. Rankin. What do you mean by "they"?

Mrs. Oswald. The Secret Service had the maid come in with sheets and everything and they got—opened the sofa into a bed. The Secret Service rolled the baby bed from the bedroom into the living room. And I knew that I was not wanted or involved. And I have a very dignified way about me. I didn't say a word. What I did—I sat up in a chair all night long in the living room, rather than to be so indignant as to sleep in the bedroom where they had taken my daughter-in-law from me. I sat up in a chair in the living room rather than be pushed aside like I was being pushed aside.

Mr. Rankin. Well, now, what Secret Servicemen were these—Mr. Howard?

Mrs. Oswald. Mr. Howard was involved, and this other man.

Mr. Rankin. The same man?

Mrs. Oswald. This same man. And my son is in this, too. Robert was part173 of this conspiracy that they were going to let her go to a home, and they didn't tell me—and Mr. Peter Gregory.

Mr. Rankin. And did they move your daughter-in-law out into the living room?

Mrs. Oswald. Yes, sir, she slept on the sofa. And they moved June's baby bed from the bedroom into the living room, by my daughter-in-law. And I sat in a chair. I can do that. I am a nurse, and I can do without sleep. And I had all the papers. I told you that the night before they took me home to get my papers. And that is why I knew I had the insurance money. So I started to work on the papers. And I sat up all night long.

Mr. Rankin. What did Marina say about that arrangement?

Mrs. Oswald. There was nothing said between Marina and I. The last time I had seen Marina was when she shrugged me off, and then this came out why she shrugged me off. I have had no contact with Marina since.

Mr. Rankin. Now, why do you think there is a conspiracy about this? Can you explain that to us?

Mrs. Oswald. About this particular instance?

Mr. Rankin. Yes.

Mrs. Oswald. Well, I don't say that is a particular instance. But it is certainly a very unusual way to do a thing, a very unusual way—not to consult me. Marina and I were friends. She was going to come and live with me. I was going to share my money with her. And then they went ahead and planned all this without my knowledge.

Maybe you know the answer to it, I don't know. But there was no hard feelings—even now I love Marina and I would take and help her any way I can.

So I don't understand these things. But I am telling you the way things happen, the way I was excluded. And your Secret Service agents had part of this.

Mr. Rankin. And you do not think Robert and the Secret Service agents could be acting in good faith to try to just help Marina and her children along?

Mrs. Oswald. Well, I cannot see from my point of view that it would be good that a foreign girl lives in a stranger's home, a perfect stranger who has come to the police department and offered her a home. We are talking about a perfect stranger. If she is a perfect stranger—maybe she wasn't. I have no way of knowing. But I am going to assume what I read. It would be much better for this girl to go live in this stranger's home than to be with her family? This girl and my grandchildren needed a family, which I was that family. I cannot see that.

Mr. Rankin. What I am asking you is: Do you think it is possible that Robert was just mistaken when he and the Secret Service man, if they are involved, thought this might be a good plan. Isn't it possible they were trying to do the right thing?

Mrs. Oswald. No, sir, I think it was deliberate. I am sure—I don't think. I am positive it was deliberate. And I will tell you why as we go along.

Mr. Rankin. Now, you said you thought it was deliberate.

Mrs. Oswald. I am trying to get everything in, so you can get a clear picture.

Mr. Rankin. Well, this plan to have your daughter-in-law go and live with another lady—this Mrs. Pultz—you said you did not think it could be innocent or in good faith?

Mrs. Oswald. Yes—because then this same Secret Service man, that I don't know the name—now, I may be wrong about this—just a moment. No—this is not the same man.

One of the other Secret Service men had gone to talk to Robert's boss, because Robert was worried about his job. So this happened in the afternoon. I had no contact with Marina. And he came in and in front of me he patted Robert on the shoulder and said, "Now, Robert, I have talked to your boss and you are all right. I assured him you are not involved in any way."

So, gentlemen, Marina is taken care of; Robert is taken care of—I am not feeling sorry for myself, believe me, because I can take care of myself. But here is a mother who has come to the rescue, lost her job, offered her good love174 and insurance money, and nobody has wondered what is going to become of me.

Mr. Rankin. Well, did you think it was improper that the Secret Service man would go to Robert's boss and tell him he was not involved, that there was nothing improper?

Mrs. Oswald. No, sir; I do not. I think it was a fine gesture. And that is the point I am trying to make out. Why are these fine gestures to see that Marina is going to have a home and be taken care of, and Robert's job is secure—but I am nothing. I was not included in the plans. And what is going to become of me? I have no income. I have no job. I lost my job. And nobody thought about me.

I don't mean to imply I'm sorry for myself. I am trying to bring out a point that through all of this, that I have not been considered, even as much as to testify. I want to know why. I don't understand why.

It is very strange.

I packed during the night, sat up in the chair, as I said.

So the next morning I am on my way home. I have no purpose to be there. I was helping my daughter-in-law, and helping the children. But now I am out of everything, so I insist on going home.

Before going home, I asked to tell Marina goodby, and my grandchildren, and what they have done this morning—they have taken her out of these quarters and brought her next door, to the other quarters of the Inn—it is just one door and a little courtyard to the other door.

Mr. Rankin. What day is this?

Mrs. Oswald. This is the 28th. So the agent that was taking me home—I'm sorry, but I'm very bad at names, and there were so many agents, it is awfully hard for me to remember it all. I told him that I wanted to tell Marina that I was going. He knocked on the door. The Russian interpreter from the State Department, Mr. Gopadze, came to the door, and the agent said, "Mrs. Oswald is going home and wants to tell Marina and the children goodby."

He said, "Well, we are interviewing her, and she is on tape. She will get in touch with you."

So I never saw Marina after that time.

Now, what worried me so was what did Marina think. What did Marina know of this, and what did she think? Did she think I deserted her? Did they think I left without telling her goodby? This worried me very much. I could picture the girl. What did she think? I didn't even get to tell her goodby.

So I tried in vain to see Marina. I have called Mr. F. V. Sorrels over and over and over, and he has never told me that Marina did not want to see me. And this, gentlemen, I have proof of. He always said, "Well, Mrs. Oswald, I am not able to divulge where she is" and the regular push-around. He is not telling me plainly I am not going to see Marina, he is being very courteous to me, but not letting me see Marina—if I am making this plain. And I have publicly blasted that. Over and over I have tried unsuccessfully.

Mr. Mark Lane, who is representing my son, talked with Mr. Jim Martin and Mr. Thorne—Jim Martin is Marina's business manager, and Mr. Thorne is her attorney. And Mr. Jim Martin and Thorne have stated to Mr. Mark Lane that Marina did not want to talk to me.

Now, this is approximately a month ago, I would say, when I first engaged Mr. Mark Lane. And Mr. Mark Lane said to me that he was not satisfied, when he gave me the information. I said, "No, I want Marina to tell me that." How did I know it was Marina's quote?

Mr. Sorrels never told me that Marina did not want to talk to me. But this was told to Mr. Mark Lane. But I would not take that as a quote. I wanted to hear it from Marina.

So we persistently tried to see Marina. When I say we, almost every reporter in the city of Fort Worth and Dallas has tried to see Marina. Mr. Mark Lane has tried to see Marina. Mr. Olds, who is head of the Civil Liberties Association—I don't know if that's the proper name—in Fort Worth has tried to see Marina. And there have been many prominent people trying to see Marina, because they could not understand how Marina could be under such strict surveillance that no one could be allowed to see Marina. There have been many, many175 people question this. It has been questioned, why Marina would be under strict seclusion for 6 weeks, with not a soul seeing Marina. I say not a soul. My son saw Marina at Christmas time, and probably had seen her before then.

His family went with him—I checked with my daughter-in-law, Vada, and she said she went with Robert for Christmas time. It came over the news in Fort Worth that Marina's brother-in-law, Lee's brother, would be with her at Christmas time, and Mrs. Marguerite Oswald was unavailable for news.

Gentlemen, I stayed home crying, hoping against hope that the Secret Service would come and let me be with my family for Christmas time, waiting there patiently. I was available for news. I had blasted this in the paper over and over. I waited for them to come get me. But there again, I am excluded.

Do you know the answers to all these exclusions? I do not.

The first time Marina ever made any statement or public appearance was approximately 2 weeks ago, or maybe not that long. She was on an exclusive television program. Channel 4 in Fort Worth, Tex., when she stated publicly that in her mind she thought that Lee shot President Kennedy. What an awful thing for this 22-year-old foreign girl to think. She thinks in her mind. She doesn't know. But she thinks, gentlemen. That tape can be sent back to you. That was her quote. I watched every television program, and I took it down in black and white. "In my mind, I think Lee shot President Kennedy."

She doesn't know our American way of life. Lee Harvey Oswald will be the accused assassin of President Kennedy when this information is over with, believe me.

She is a Russian girl, and maybe they do this in Russia. But what I am going to say is that Marina Oswald was brainwashed by the Secret Service, who have kept her in seclusion for 8 weeks—8 weeks, gentlemen, with no one talking to Marina.

Marina does not read English. Marina knows none of the facts from newspaper account. The only way Marina can get facts is through what the FBI and the Secret Service probably are telling her, or some of the facts that Marina has manufactured since.

I am sorry, gentlemen, but this is a true story.

Mr. Rankin. What do you base your claim on, that Marina was brainwashed?

Mrs. Oswald. Because for 8 weeks no one has been allowed to see Marina. I do not believe in my mind that that is an American way of life. I question the fact that it is even legal, that they can keep her in strict seclusion with no one seeing her for 8 weeks, gentlemen.

Now, there may be a reason for that. I don't know. But the American people want some answer to that. I have over 1,500 letters questioning that. The papers have blasted it continuously.

Mr. Rankin. If she didn't have somebody to look out for her, do you think the various people that wanted to see her would keep her so busy she could not even take care of the children?

Mrs. Oswald. Now, Mr. Rankin, I am not saying, even implying that the Secret Service should not protect my daughter-in-law. I am grateful for that, and I have expressed it. I am most grateful she has protection. But would there have been any harm for me to talk to Marina with the Secret Service around and let Marina tell me that she does not want to see me?

Mr. Rankin. Well, let's leave you out of it. What about all the rest of the people that would want—or did want to see Marina?

Mrs. Oswald. All right.

Mr. Rankin. And take her time, while she had to take care of the children.

Mrs. Oswald. I agree with that. Marina should not see every Tom, Dick, and Harry. I think they are doing a wonderful job in protecting her. But when Mr. Mark Lane, who is an attorney, requested it, so we can solve this, to just let Marina tell him that she doesn't want to see her mama, and Mr. Olds, who is head of Civil Liberties, was refused permission to see her, then we question it.

No, I don't think all the people should see Marina. But people are asking these questions, Mr. Rankin. They want to know why a high official cannot see Marina, to satisfy the public's demand.

176 Mr. Rankin. Well, Marina had her own counsel at that time, she said. Mr. Thorne was her attorney.

Mrs. Oswald. Yes. Now, we will get to Mr. Thorne.

When I first contacted Mr. Thorne I said, "Mr. Thorne, how is my daughter-in-law and grandchildren?"

And Mr. Thorne really apologized to me. He said, "Mrs. Oswald, they are fine. But I am unable to divulge their whereabouts."

He volunteered the information to me.

And I said, "Well, sir; I am not asking where they are"—because I had already—by the time she got this attorney—by the time I had contacted him, we had been fighting this thing to see Marina. But he volunteered the information. He said, "Your daughter-in-law and grandchildren are fine, but I am not able to divulge their whereabouts."

I said, "I am not asking about their whereabouts." I said that I had Lee's Marine book, which is a big, colorful book, the life of a Marine, that Lee had sent to me, and Lee's baby book; that I had had in my possession ever since he was a baby, that I gave to Marina and Lee when they returned to Russia, and my husband's gold pocket watch I had all those years I gave to Lee. So I asked Mr. Thorne about these things and he said he would inquire about it.

I said, "Mr. Thorne, while I am on the 'phone I do want to bring something up. While I was at Six Flags, the day I left, the morning I left, is the first time that sympathy cards started coming in, and money. And these envelopes were addressed to Mrs. Marina Oswald and Marguerite Oswald, or Mrs. Marguerite Oswald and Marina, to both."

The Secret Service started to open the envelopes, and there were checks and cash. Because of my prior story that they had pushed me aside, I said, "Now, my moneys that come in that says 'and mother' I definitely want my share."

Believe me, gentlemen, I have never received 1 penny.

Mr. Rankin. What did he say about that?

Mrs. Oswald. They said yes—and my son was there when I said that—they said they would divide it. If it was a $10 bill and it said the mother of Lee and the wife, that I would get 5 and Marina would get 5. So when I talked to Mr. Thorne I said, "I want to tell you, Mr. Thorne, while I was at Six Flags, I know of moneys coming in, but I have never received a penny. But I want you to know that the Secret Service in my home, because they were in my home from the 28th until the 3d"—I believe it was——

Representative Ford. Third of what?

Mrs. Oswald. This would be December. Because this was the 28th of November—approximately the 3d. The money that came into my home that way, 'Mrs. Marguerite Oswald and Marina Oswald' the Secret Service divided right then and there. If it was a $10 bill, I got 5 and they took 5 to give to Marina. Whether Marina ever got the money or not, I have no way of knowing. But the money in my home was divided and the share given to Marina. But I never did get the share from the Secret Service at this time.

So 2 weeks later——

Mr. Rankin. How much did that amount to, that was divided in your home?

Mrs. Oswald. Very little. My contributions up to now are just a little over $900—about $905. That is the money that has been given direct to me, the mother of Lee Harvey Oswald.

So about 3 weeks later—now, Mr. Lane comes in here. He has all of these documents and all of these dates and everything. I don't know about the dates.

Mr. Thorne—from Mr. Thorne's office and Mr. Martin I receive an envelope about this size with mail for me, Mrs. Marguerite Oswald—not "and Marina"—everyone open, gentlemen—opened, no cash, but checks, made out to Mrs. Marguerite Oswald, that nobody else of course could have any benefit from. This late date. And there were checks way in November, in the beginning of December, that were held all this time. But until I complained, then they decided to send them to me.

Mr. Lane has in his possession photostatic copies of my mail that has been opened by the Fort Worth Police. I had a tip from a reporter that my mail at the mayor's office and the Fort Worth Police and the chief of police was being 177 photostatic copied. So I sent a telegram—and I have these things—you will have everything I have—to each one, the same telegram, saying that any mail addressed to Mrs. Marguerite Oswald should be forwarded to her immediately—to me immediately at 2220 Thomas Place. I received no mail.

Three days later—I received no mail.

So I called Mr. Sorrels and told Mr. Sorrels about the tip that I had. And I knew it was a positive tip—I could feel sure this young man was giving me the right information. I had much information that the public knows, that they have helped me in this case, Mr. Rankin. So Mr. Sorrels sent Mr. Seals, I think his name was, a Secret Service man down and the chief of police gave Mr. Seals—we have this—my mail opened and photostatic copies. I can produce this evidence.

Now, what right—I am not an attorney—but we have a moral issue all through this that I am fighting for.

If the mail went to the chief of police, Mrs. Marguerite Oswald, in care of the chief of police—it well could be that they have the legal right to open such mail. But they do not have the moral right, because I was an international figure, and everybody knew my address. And the chief of police and everybody else knew my address. And that mail should have remained unopened. How much cash was taken out of those mails? I do not know. And I am not really saying there was. But there is quite a possibility that it was.

Then I received another package from Mr. Thorne, and my mail was opened. I called Mr. Sorrels about that. He said he knew nothing about it.

First I called Mr. Thorne and he said that is the way he got the mail. So then I called Mr. Sorrells and he said he knew nothing about it. I said, "Mr. Sorrels, I'm getting awfully tired of this. Mr. Thorne doesn't know how my mail is being opened. He says that he got the mail from the Secret Service. And now you are telling me that you do not give the mail to Mr. Thorne. Where does my mail come from opened?" So nobody knows anything, the things that have happened to me.

My rights have been invaded continuously—continuously. Every newspaper clipping was taken out of my home. Three letters from Lee, from Russia. I offered all my information, as I explained over and over, to the Secret Service. And while in my home, I was showing them things—because I was proud of the things I have, and I think, gentlemen, when you see everything I have you will see a different picture of this boy.

There were three letters taken from my letters from Lee. And how I came to know that—a New York reporter had offered—he was going to write a story and had offered to buy three of my letters. I told him he could have his choice. And so he looked through the letters, and I looked through them with him, and I missed these three letters. These three letters would have been of importance to the Secret Service and to our government.

But you must remember, I have offered over and over to give any information I have.

One letter stated that Marina's uncle was a colonel in the Russian Army—I may produce this now. Is that what we need to do next—the letters?

Representative Boggs. Was a colonel in what?

Mrs. Oswald. Pardon?

Representative Boggs. One letter said he was a colonel in what?

Mrs. Oswald. That Marina's uncle was a colonel in the Russian Army.

Would you like to look at these letters while I continue, Mr. Doyle?

Mr. Dulles. Are these the lost letters?

Mrs. Oswald. No, sir, these are letters from Lee to me from Russia.

Mr. Dulles. I thought you said three were lost.

Mrs. Oswald. Yes, three were lost. The one about the Russian colonel was lost—that the Secret Service men took—three letters—that would be of importance for them. But I offered to give it to them. But they were taken from my home.

Representative Boggs. How did you get them back?

Mrs. Oswald. I am going to tell the story, and I have witnesses.

So when I missed them, Mr. Jack Langueth, who we can call as a witness, who is a reporter for the New York Times, wanted to pay me for letters—he178 printed the story in the paper with the three letters that he bought from me, three different letters I am talking about now, and printed how many letters I had, including the three letters that the FBI man that Marina's uncle was a colonel. He printed the things in the paper.

So approximately 5 or 6 days later the Secret Service man—and I can find his picture probably—came to my home and returned the three letters and got a receipt from me for the three letters.

Mr. Rankin. How much did this reporter offer to pay you for the letters and other things?

Mrs. Oswald. I got $50 for each letter. And I have the receipt.

Mr. Rankin. I don't understand yet. You offered to sell the letters to him, or let him have use of them for $50 apiece?

Mrs. Oswald. Yes, sir.

Mr. Rankin. $150.

Mrs. Oswald. Yes, sir.

Mr. Rankin. And then he published them?

Mrs. Oswald. No. Yes—he published the letters. It was published in the New York Times, the three letters.

Mr. Rankin. Then they were returned to you.

Mrs. Oswald. No, he never did take the letters. Mr. Langueth never did take the letters he bought from me out of my hand. As I told you gentlemen, we went to a photostatic place and the letters were copied, and I kept the originals. He paid me $50. That was printed in the story. But the three letters that the Secret Service men had, he printed in the story about Marina's uncle being a colonel in the Russian Army. And that is the letter that the Secret Service man had.

Mr. Rankin. And you did not get paid for those at all?

Mrs. Oswald. No—these are different letters. So they returned those letters to me, the Secret Service, and I gave them a receipt for them. But they did not ask my permission to take them, or let me have a receipt when they took them. So I am trying to point out the fact that I got the three letters back, I would think, because the story in the paper said that the Secret Service had these three letters and parts of what they contained. So the three letters were returned to me, and I had to sign a receipt for those three letters.

Am I making that clear now?

May I have some water, please?

Representative Ford. Are we going to get these letters in the record?

Mrs. Oswald. Yes, sir. Let me get the letters in the record, then.

Mr. Doyle. Let me go off the record a minute.

(Discussion off the record.)

Mrs. Oswald. I am not able to go into the defection now, because I am not through with this part. The defection starts an entirely different story, if you want to know the true facts, and it will take quite a while.

What sticks in my mind is this one particular letter about Marina's uncle. The other two I am not quite sure.

Representative Boggs. What does it say about her uncle?

Mrs. Oswald. Well, I have to find the letter, sir.

I want to say this, gentleman. And maybe you are not in agreement with me. But all my life I have known and I have thought that a title does not make a man. It may be presumptuous of me that I am accusing the Secret Service—because they are the Secret Service. But there are men in our Government, and the Secret Service, who are undesirable, just like in any other organization—let's face it. We have such men as Bobby Baker, who was a citizen well thought of. Charles Van Doren who was well thought of. Mr. Fred Korth who was under investigation, he was a wonderful citizen. I can go on and on. Yet these men turned out not to be the right type.

I say this because my son was a self-styled Marxist, and a known defector, and that is why his guilt was proven by the Dallas Police. And my son—had he been a Senator or someone in the higher field, maybe they would not have picked him up so fast. Now, that is a fact of our way of life, of human nature. Having a title doesn't mean that you are the man back of the title.

Mr. Rankin. Could we take those letters now and have the reporter identify them? Here is the one about the uncle in the Army?

Mrs. Oswald. That is one I am sure of.

Now, I did not finish the story of the woman offering Marina a home. I have not finished that story, really. This affidavit that I showed you about the woman offering Marina the home the morning of the 28th—I picked up the newspaper and I read in the newspaper—I will be through with this story in 1 minute. I picked up the newspaper on the 28th of November and I read in the newspaper where this woman had offered Marina a home. So I said to the agent that was sitting up—everybody was sleeping, and as I told you I sat up all night——

Mr. Rankin. This was 1963, after the assassination?

Mrs. Oswald. 1963. November 28. It was on the 27th that I knew my daughter was offered a home. Nothing was said where. In fact, at the time I thought she was going to live in Mr. Gregory's home. I just thought that. I did not ask. I was so hurt, I did not ask.

But on the morning of the 28th I picked up the paper and read this story about the woman going to the Dallas Police offering Marina a home. So I said to this agent, "Evidently that is who Marina is going to live with." But I did not know. But on the 28th is when I saw the story of the woman offering Marina the home.

Mr. Rankin. Now, you have produced a number of letters that you described as being letters received from your son, Lee Oswald, while he was in the Soviet Union.

Mrs. Oswald. Yes, sir.

Mr. Rankin. And we have asked you if you could identify the three letters that the Secret Service brought back to you and asked you to give a receipt for. You said it is very difficult, if not impossible, for you to do that. Is that right?

Mrs. Oswald. No, sir, I did not say that. I said that one letter I was sure of, because it stated that her uncle was an officer in the Soviet Union. That letter I am sure of. The other two letters—I would have to go through the letters. I think I could spot them, because it would be of importance to our country and the Secret Service to know—in other words, it was important for them to know she had an uncle in the Soviet Union. And the other two letters would be on that order. And I believe maybe I could—I would not want to state a fact that these two letters—I think I would be pretty close to choosing the other two letters as the proper letters.

Mr. Rankin. Mrs. Oswald, I wonder if it would be agreeable to you if we would identify all of those letters that you received from your son while he was in the Soviet Union, and then possibly when we recess you could look them over and see——

Mrs. Oswald. Yes, sir, that's perfectly all right.

Mr. Rankin. See if you can pick out the ones you gave a receipt for.

Mrs. Oswald. That is perfectly all right. Any way you want to do it is all right with me.

Mr. Rankin. Mr. Reporter, I will ask you to mark them, and Mr. Liebeler, will you help in the marking, because the letters are covered with glassine, and it may be hard to mark them with ink. I think by putting those stickers on we can help you.

Mrs. Oswald. Not all of the letters have dates. I think by taking the date on the back of the envelope it would be all right. And we had them in order. I don't know if they are still in order. But we had them by the dates.

Mr. Rankin. Mr. Reporter, I offer in evidence Exhibits 170 to 179, both inclusive, being pictures of the funeral and the casket that Mrs. Oswald has produced here for the Commission, and ask leave to substitute copies.

The Chairman. They may be so introduced.

(The photographs referred to were marked Commission Exhibits Nos. 170 to 179 inclusive for identification, and received in evidence.)

Mr. Rankin. I then offer the various letters that Mrs. Oswald produced, that she said were sent to her by her son, Lee Harvey Oswald, from the Soviet Union.180 And I think it would be better for our record if I briefly state the date that the envelopes bear in each case, so it can be compared with the number.

The Chairman. Very well.

Mr. Rankin. Exhibit 180 bears the date of July 18, 1961, on the envelope.

Mr. Dulles. Mr. Rankin—is that the American or the Russian postmark?

Mr. Rankin. That is the American postmark.

Mr. Dulles. Time of receipt in this country?

Mr. Rankin. That's right.

Now, Mrs. Oswald, I understand from you there was one letter before the letter bearing the date July 18, 1961, on the American postmark on the envelope, and you do not have that here?

Mrs. Oswald. I may have it. I have many more papers and documents. I have a suitcase almost full that I have not yet opened. The suitcase was lost. We did not receive it until about 9 o'clock last night.

Mr. Rankin. You have not produced it today, though.

Mrs. Oswald. No. But there is one more letter. It is the very first letter I received from Lee.

Mr. Rankin. I call the attention of the Commission to the statement in Exhibit 180, "She was living at her aunt's place when I met her. They are real nice people. Her uncle is a major in the Soviet Army."

Exhibit 181, dated August 3, 1961, was the envelope postmarked United States, August 10, 1961. I also offer that.

Exhibit 182, dated October 2, 1961, with the American postmark October 10, 1961. I also offer that.

In each case, Mr. Chairman, I ask leave to substitute copies in accordance with our understanding.

The Chairman. Yes. We will make a blanket ruling on all of them when you finish.

Mr. Rankin. Yes, sir.

Exhibit 183, dated October 22, 1959, with the American postmark on the envelope October 30, 1961. I offer it.

Mr. Dulles. Did you say 1959 and then 1961?

Mr. Rankin. '61——

Mr. Dulles. It is all '61?

Mr. Rankin. You are correct—October 22, 1959, is the date on the letter.

Mrs. Oswald. That is incorrect.

Mr. Rankin. And on the envelope it is October 30, 1961, Vernon, Tex. Mrs. Oswald, can you explain that?

Mrs. Oswald. Yes. Evidently Lee put the date incorrect—because I had no contact with Lee from the time—I had one contact with Lee from the time that he defected to Russia. And the only contact was when he was at the Metropole Hotel in Moscow. Then the next contact was when the State Department wrote me his address, which was July, or June 1961. So where Lee put the 1959, I would say it was just an error, because the postmark proves the date.

As I have been saying FBI instead of Secret Service—I mean it is just——

Mr. Rankin. A slip of some kind?

Mrs. Oswald. Yes.

Mr. Dulles. Is the 1959 letter available, the Metropole Hotel letter?

Mrs. Oswald. When we go into the defection, I have letters from 1959 that I myself have sent to Lee and have been returned, and, gentlemen, they are unopened, and I will give you the privilege of opening my thoughts to my son. They were returned unopened, because he was not located.

Mr. Rankin. I might answer your question, Mr. Dulles. We have a copy of the Metropole letter of 1959.

Mr. Doyle. Mr. Rankin, could I check—your Exhibit 182, the one you called just before this—I gathered that you gave a date of the letter and also a date of the postmark. Am I correct—October 2, 1961, is the date of the letter, and October 10, 1961, is the postmark.

Mr. Rankin. That's correct.

Mr. Doyle. Thank you, sir.

Mr. Rankin. Now, with regard to Exhibit 183, which bears the date October 22,181 1959, in error, with October 30, 1961, as the postmark on the envelope, I wish to call the Commission's attention to this reference.

"Marina's maiden name was Prusakova. Her aunt and uncle's address in Minsk is"—and then the address is set out in Russian. And then continuing the same sentence—"they don't speak any English. However, her uncle is an Army colonel soon to retire."

Mrs. Oswald. And that I would think would be the letter that the Secret Service—was one of the letters that the Secret Service, as I previously stated, had.

Now, may I say something here?

Marina uses two names—Prusakova and Nikolaevna. Whether she was married before, or whether she uses two maiden names, I do not know. But I have a record of both names.

Mr. Rankin. I offer in evidence Exhibit 183.

Representative Ford. Mr. Rankin, don't we have a record of those two names? Isn't one her maiden name and the other by her mother—and the other by her stepfather?

Mr. Rankin. That is the record we have. That is what Mrs. Marina Oswald testified to. She testified in regard to Nikolaevna. And the other name appears on her papers as the father.

Mrs. Oswald. But now Lee has said in one of those letters that her name is Nikolaevna. But then when he asked me in one of the letters to get an affidavit of support that Marina could come to the United States, that name appeared—Nikolaevna. Yet there are a couple of letters where he refers to her name as Prusakova. And I have it in his handwriting—when he gave me the slip of paper for the baptism he used Prusakova—Marina Prusakova Oswald. He did not use the name in the letters. That is what I find peculiar.

Mr. Rankin. The explanation was that the Prusakova was the identification of the father, which is often done. And she explained that with regard to the child they did not want to name June Lee Oswald with your son's name, if you recall—that is your son did not want that. But the Russian Government insisted that the father's name had to be shown.

Mrs. Oswald. Yes, I am familiar with that. I have done research on that. In Russia the father's name is used even if it is a girl. Now, Mr. Peter Gregory—his name is Peter Gregory, and his father's name is Peter, so his name is Peter Peter Gregory. They always use the father's name as a second name, regardless of sex. So June is named June Lee Oswald, which is Lee's name. And if there were two Lees it would be Lee Lee Oswald. That I know of.

Mr. Rankin. Exhibit 184 is dated November 8, 1961, and bears a postmark on the envelope November 18, 1961. I offer it in evidence.

Exhibit 185 is dated November 23d, without any year on the letter itself, with the postmark December 4, 1961, as the American postmark on the envelope. I offer Exhibit 185.

Exhibit 186 is Christmas greetings and bears the date December 12, 1961, stamped on the envelope. I offer Exhibit 186.

Exhibit 187 bears the date December 13, 1961, on the letter, and bears the postmark date December 26, 1961, on the envelope. I offer Exhibit 187.

Exhibit 188 bears the date December 20th, without any year on the letter, and the date January 2, 1962, stamped on the envelope. I offer Exhibit 188.

Exhibit 189 bears the date January 2d, and the stamped postmark on the envelope January 11, 1962. I offer Exhibit 189.

Exhibit 190 bears the date January 23d, on the envelope, January 22, 1961, written on the back of the envelope. I offer in evidence Exhibit 190.

Exhibit 191 bears the date January 20th, and stamped on the envelope is January 29, 1962. I offer Exhibit 191.

Mr. Dulles. These are all airmail letters?

Mrs. Oswald. They are all registered return receipt mailed. Everything I had to sign for.

Mr. Dulles. Nine or 10 days apparently, it took.

Representative Boggs. That is right—about 10 days, each one of them.

Mr. Rankin. Apparently—it states "Par Avion". But this one bears a mark182 February 1, 1962, on Exhibit 192, and the letter itself is February 1, 1962. That is pretty fast.

Mr. Dulles. It must be 11. Isn't there a 1 left out on the other side?

Mr. Rankin. Well, it is in handwriting. So that would be pretty fast mail. I offer Exhibit 192.

Exhibit 193, dated February 9, 1962, on the letter, and it is stamped on the envelope as February 23, 1962. I offer Exhibit 193.

Exhibit 194 is dated February 15, 1962, on the letter, and stamped on the envelope March 1, 1962. I offer Exhibit 194.

Exhibit 195 is dated February 24th, without a year date, and the envelope is stamped March 7, 1962. I offer Exhibit 195.

Exhibit 196 is dated March 28th, stamped on the envelope is April 9, 1962. I offer Exhibit 196.

Exhibit 197 is dated April 22d, without a year date on the letter, and stamped on the envelope is April 28, 1962. I offer Exhibit 197.

Exhibit 198 is dated May 30, 1962, on the letter, and is stamped on the envelope June 6, 19—it doesn't show clearly what the year is, but there is a 196, and I take it is 1962. I offer Exhibit 198.

The Chairman. All of the documents that have just been offered in evidence may be admitted and take the numbers assigned to them.

(The documents heretofore marked Commission Exhibits Nos. 180 through 198 for identification, were received in evidence.)

Mrs. Oswald. I don't believe this letter belongs with the letters. May I see it, please? Is that a letter from Russia? I don't think so, from what I can see from here.

Mr. Rankin. It purports to be, Mrs. Oswald. I hand it to you. It is Exhibit 198 you are speaking of?

Mrs. Oswald. Yes. I'm sorry. There was another very important letter of this size that I thought maybe became confused with the Russian letters. You will have to forgive me, Chief Justice Warren, but this is quite a big undertaking.

The Chairman. Yes. I just wanted to keep the record straight. It is all right.

Mr. Rankin. I ask leave, Mr. Chairman, to substitute copies in each instance.

The Chairman. That may be done.

Mr. Rankin. Now, Mrs. Oswald, will you proceed with telling us how you determined or concluded that there was a conspiracy between the Secret Service people that you described and Marina Oswald?

Mrs. Oswald. Well, when I stopped—I have to remember where I stopped. Now, am I still at the Six Flags?

Mr. Rankin. The last I recall you were still there. You had also described, if you remember, the offer of Mrs. Pultz to take your daughter-in-law and provide her a home. You have said that you had not seen your daughter for quite some time, and you tried to communicate with her.

Mrs. Oswald. Oh, yes—I was trying to communicate with her.

Mr. Rankin. And you talked to Mr. Thorne?

Mrs. Oswald. Yes—that was where my mail had been opened. And Mr. Mark Lane has my mail and the photostatic copies of the mail.

Mr. Rankin. I think the Commission would be very much interested in how you conclude that there was a conspiracy—if you can help on that.

Mrs. Oswald. Yes, I can help you. But I have many, many stories. I have to start from the defection. I have a story of Lee's life at age 16 that maybe you know about, maybe you don't. And I have many stories, gentlemen. I cannot do all these stories in these 6 hours I have been here today. I have covered quite a bit. I have many stories.

Representative Boggs. Why did your son defect to Russia?

Mrs. Oswald. I cannot answer that yes or no, sir. I am going to go through the whole story, or it is no good. And that is what I have been doing for this Commission all day long—giving a story.

Representative Boggs. Suppose you just make it very brief.

Mrs. Oswald. I cannot make it brief. I will say I am unable to make it brief. This is my life and my son's life going down in history. And I want183 the opportunity to tell the story with documents, as I have been doing. I am not going to answer yes or no, because it is no good.

Representative Boggs. Well, you use the expression "defector." I did not use that expression.

Mrs. Oswald. I said "so-called defector." The papers have "defector" and blown it up.

The Chairman. Well, Mrs. Oswald, you have told us, though, that you believed that Mrs. Marina Oswald and Mrs. Paine and two Secret Service agents were in a conspiracy that resulted in the assassination of the President.

Mrs. Oswald. Yes, sir. And I also say——

The Chairman. What Mr. Rankin has asked you is what led you to the belief that there was such a conspiracy?

Mrs. Oswald. I can answer that, sir. But just to answer in one sentence——

The Chairman. No, you don't have to do it in one sentence. Take your own time, but stick to that one subject, please, until we get rid of that, and then we will go to the other things.

Mrs. Oswald. Well, it is now quarter to four. And this is a very long story.

The Chairman. Don't worry, we will give you the time.

Mrs. Oswald. Would you please consider I am very emotionally upset and tired, sir. I was up until 1 o'clock this morning fixing these papers for the Commission. When Mr. Rankin asked me to come on Thursday, they were not in the order they are now.

The Chairman. You mean you cannot go on this afternoon?

Mrs. Oswald. Not the whole story.

The Chairman. Well, give us as much as you can of it, and we will stop whenever——

Mrs. Oswald. Well, I have so far given you enough story to state this as a fact—that I believe—I am saying as I believe, sir, because if I knew who shot President Kennedy, I would be more than happy to tell you, and we would end it right then and there. But there is speculation among everyone. So naturally there is speculation by myself, and these stories I have told you are fact.

Marina became very unhappy with America. This I know for a fact. And then I will say this is part of another story.

Marina told me at Mrs. Paine's home that she wrote to the Russian counsel to go back to Russia because, "Lee not get work." Now, that is why Lee tried to get a visa in Mexico. But you see, sir, I was going to tell that whole story of that. But I will answer this—and that is what I based that on, too.

It was Marina who wrote to the Russian counsel for exit visas, and Lee followed it up. That is Marina having Lee do this. And she told me herself. Yet she states that Lee wanted to live in Russia and Cuba. But Marina wrote to the Russian counsel, "Mama,

Lee not get work." So she wanted to go back to Russia. She liked America. She wanted to stay here.

Mr. Rankin. About what date was this?

Mrs. Oswald. This was the night in Mrs. Paine's home. I didn't tell you that, because these other stories are important, and I was going to bring it in for the Mexican trip. That is why I think you are confusing me. I'm sorry. But these stories—the way I want to say it, I would not forget anything by going in sequence. This way, when you are bringing me questions from the Mexican story and from the defection, you are throwing my mind off.

The Chairman. What story do you want to get to now?

Mrs. Oswald. I have so many stories. And I have gone through about three or four today, complete stories.

The Chairman. Well, select one of them, please, and let's don't argue about the order. I want you to tell your story——

Mrs. Oswald. My energy is exhausted, sir.

The Chairman. I want you to tell your story in your own way. And if this one exhausts you, select another story, and tell that.

Mrs. Oswald. Well, can you tell me what short story I can tell, Mr. Doyle?

Mr. Doyle. Why don't you start with—start and tell the members of the Commission about your accident and Lee's going to Russia.

Mrs. Oswald. That is a very long story.

184 Mr. Doyle. I know. But start it, and if you get tired at all, you advise the Commission, and I am certain that——

Mrs. Oswald. I will have something very important to this Commission that I would like to say, that would take up some time.

Mr. Rankin, I spoke with you, I think it was Thursday, December 6th, and I told you that since it was publicly known I was going to appear before the Warren Commission, that I would like to have protection, as you recall. I did not get protection, sir. And so the next morning I called you, approximately 9 o'clock, in the morning and told you that I didn't have protection, and I was very concerned. And this would have been Friday, the second call, and that I was going to the bank, to my safety deposit vault, and get the necessary papers. And I definitely wanted complete surveillance, because the papers were going to be with me in my home, and the public knew I was going to testify, and I wanted that protection.

Now, you said, you would get in touch with Mr. Sorrels, sir, and have Mr. Sorrel's call me, which he did approximately an hour after my request to you that I did not have protection. Mr. Sorrels called me and said "Mrs. Oswald, I understand that you want to go to the bank and get your important papers out of the bank, and you have requested protection."

I said, "Yes. I thought I had protection last night. I woke up 4 o'clock in the morning with all the lights lit, getting papers together and cleaning the house." Because the telephone started to ring consistently.

I would have never done that if I would have known I didn't have protection. I was leaving myself wide open.

So he said, "Well, is your attorney in town?"

I said, "No, he is not."

He said, "May I suggest this, Mrs. Oswald"—first, he said, "What do you intend to do with the papers?"

I said, "The papers will stay with me."

He said, "Is your attorney in there?"

I said, "No, sir, he is an out of town attorney."

He said, "May I suggest this. May we get a large brown envelope and put sealing wax on it, and you put the papers in our safety deposit vault."

I said, "No, sir, those papers do not leave my hands. I have had an understanding with Mr. J. Lee Rankin that the papers were going to stay with me, and that I would have complete surveillance while the papers were in my home. Now, Mr. Sorrels, I want that surveillance. I am very uneasy."

He said, "Mrs. Oswald"—this was approximately 10 o'clock in the morning—"Mrs. Oswald, I will not be able to have anyone there before 1 o'clock."

I said, "That is just fine."

Mr. Mike Howard came out at 1 o'clock. We did some errands. I had to buy some luggage, and a few little things for the trip. Then we had supper. And at 5:30 we picked up the papers, because on Friday in Fort Worth, Tex., the bank opens from 4 to 6—on Friday evening. So we picked up the papers before 6 o'clock.

Now, I thought I had protection that night. I had protection that night until 12 o'clock. And then I understand that the Fort Worth police were circling the neighborhood.

Now, that is not complete protection.

I am a government witness, with important papers. And Mr. Rankin had—I requested protection—suppose someone had come to the door, or just shot through my home? The police circling three or four blocks away is not complete protection.

So Saturday morning I wanted to go out to breakfast. I kept opening the door and looking through the windows. And I never did see any men circling the neighborhood. There was nobody around. At 10:30 this morning I was still doing that. And by the way, a police car passed by and I hailed him and asked him if he could check in the neighborhood for the Secret Service, if they were circling the neighborhood—because I want to put my garbage out, and I needed to go out, didn't have breakfast. He said he didn't know what the Secret Service looked like, and he offered to come to the back and put the garbage out for me, which this Fort Worth policeman did.

185 So at 11 o'clock I called Mr. Mike Howard's home. His wife answered the phone.

I said, "I am very uneasy. I don't have protection. I have been looking for Secret Service men all morning."

I was going out on the porch—I was opening the screen door and going out on the porch. There is a school ground opposite my house. And nobody ever came. I was not under protection.

So she said, "Mrs. Oswald, they have their orders."

I said, "Well, where is Mr. Howard?"

She said, "He is on his way to your home."

This was Saturday, at approximately 11:45. Well, I have it written down. 11:45.

So Mr. Mike Howard when I told him that I was stranded, and could not go out to breakfast, and there was things I needed to do, he realized I was very upset, and I had a legitimate complaint, and he realized I was on my way to Washington.

So in my home he called Mr. Sorrels, who is a special agent in charge of the Secret Service and Mr. Sorrels was not at home. He talked to his daughter. And he said, "It is most important. Would you have him call me?"

So he sat in my home and waited for the call. About half an hour later Mr. Sorrels called.

He said, "Mr. Sorrels. I want to know what to do on this particular case?"

And there was some conversation back and forth. And it went on back and forth conversation.

So I said, "I am getting very upset about not knowing the entire conversation. I want to tell Mr. Sorrels that if he doesn't have the authority, to give me complete protection, I want to know the man over him, so I can get complete protection."

Mr. Mike Howard said, "He heard you, Mrs. Oswald."

So I don't know what went on on the other end of the line.

But Mr. Mike Howard was on the spot.

He said, "Well, Mr. Sorrels, it is this way. She is going to Washington, and Mrs. Oswald wants to go here and wants to go there. And if we are not around to take her, she will certainly complain when she gets to Washington."

So I am assuming now—I am speculating, like everybody else—that Mr. Sorrels probably could have said, "Well, let her think she has protection," because Mr. Mike Howard had to come back in front of me, to his superior, and say, "That is no good. She might want to go some place, so we have to be here. I want to know what to do."

And then I got protection.

Now, isn't that peculiar—that I am a witness, with important papers, and supposed to be under surveillance, and I am not getting protection?

I would like to know the answer to these things. And Mr. Rankin himself called Mr. Sorrels.

Mr. Rankin. I talked to Mr. Kelley.

Mrs. Oswald. I am sorry—but I knew you had placed a call, because Mr. Sorrels called me and said you had placed a call.

So why didn't I have complete protection?

There is a lot of "why's." There are a lot of "why's" that have to be answered.

Now, the man last night that met me at the airport—there were two Secret Service men. One of the NBC men, I think it is—I am not quite sure—was at the station. He asked me questions, and he knows about all of this, because he was in Fort Worth, Tex.

I would know his name if you would say it. Dave Benoski, I believe it is.

But he asked me a question. He said, "Mrs. Oswald, have you seen your daughter-in-law?"

I said, "No, I have not seen my daughter-in-law since Thanksgiving Day."

"Well, is it the Secret Service who have kept you from seeing your daughter-in-law?"

And I said, "Yes, it is the Secret Service who has kept me from seeing my daughter-in-law."

186 Which, to me, is a fact.

So in the car, with your two Secret Service agents, one was Mr. Brown and one was—I am very bad about names—he said, "Mrs. Oswald, what makes you want to blame the Secret Service? The time to have blamed the Secret Service was when it happened."

And I said, "I did blame the Secret Service when it happened. I made a report in Fort Worth, Tex., about that."

And I said, "The question was asked me." I answered him truthfully, "Yes, that the Secret Service have kept me from my daughter-in-law."

So he said, "Well, has it occurred to you that your daughter-in-law doesn't want to see you?"

And I said, "She made the statement in Washington, the first time I have known of that, from my daughter-in-law's lips, that she did not want to see me."

And Mr. Sorrels never told me.

Now, again, I don't believe this Secret Service man had the right to quiz me like he did. I was very upset. Mr. Doyle can verify the fact. When he came to the hotel I was on the verge of tears, because of this quizzing.

The point I want to make—he said, "Isn't it true that you have had complete protection by the Secret Service for the last 2 weeks, ever since the testifying began?"

I said, "No, sir; it is not true."

Now, where does he get the idea I have been under surveillance for 2 weeks? I don't understand these things.

Mr. Doyle. Tell them about the defection.

Mrs. Oswald. Would you please consider that I can't go any more today? It is 4 o'clock. The defection is a very long and important story that leads into a story where a recruiting officer at age 16 tried to get Lee to enlist into the Marines. And it is a very important story, gentlemen. And I think you would be quite interested in it for the record.

The Chairman. We will recess now until tomorrow. Mr. Doyle, I understand in the morning you have a court appearance that you must make. But you will be available at 2 o'clock.

Mr. Doyle. Two o'clock. Your Honor.

The Chairman. Very well, we will recess now until 2 o'clock tomorrow afternoon.

Mrs. Oswald. I appreciate it, because I was up until late last night trying to get the papers for you. It wouldn't do you any good if I break down.

The Chairman. Well, we don't want to overdo the situation in any way. So we will adjourn until 2 o'clock tomorrow.

(Whereupon, at 4 p.m., the President's Commission recessed.)

Tuesday, February 11, 1964

TESTIMONY OF MRS. MARGUERITE OSWALD RESUMED

The President's Commission met at 2 p.m. on February 11, 1964, at 200 Maryland Avenue NE., Washington, D.C.

Present were Chief Justice Earl Warren, Chairman; Representative Hale Boggs, Representative Gerald R. Ford, and Allen W. Dulles, members.

Also present were J. Lee Rankin, general counsel; Wesley J. Liebeler, assistant counsel; John Doyle, attorney for Mrs. Marguerite Oswald; and Leon Jaworski, special counsel to the attorney general of Texas.

The Chairman. The Commission will come to order. Are we ready to proceed?

Mr. Doyle. If it please Your Honor——

The Chairman. Mr. Doyle.

187 Mr. Doyle. Mr. Mark Lane is present as counsel, as I understand, for Mrs. Oswald. Although I have not talked to Mrs. Oswald about the matter, as I understand it Mr. Lane represented her from time to time, in one capacity or another in the past.

I do not know the particulars. Mrs. Oswald or Mr. Lane could better advise the Commission about the point.

Of course my designation was at the request of Mrs. Oswald to act in her behalf, since there was no counsel of her choice present at the time.

The Chairman. True.

Mr. Doyle. In view of the appearance—I wonder if it might be straightened out—if Mr. Lane wishes to enter his appearance in the matter.

Of course I would immediately respectfully move for leave to withdraw.

The Chairman. Mrs. Oswald, what is your wish?

Mrs. Oswald. Well, Mr. Lane is just here for a few hours, Chief Justice Warren. He flew in just for a few hours. He is catching a 4 o'clock plane out. And I thought—he had asked permission just to sit in for these few hours.

The Chairman. Either he represents you or he does not.

Mrs. Oswald. No, sir, he does not represent me.

The Chairman. Then we will excuse Mr. Lane.

Mr. Lane. Mr. Chief Justice——

The Chairman. Mr. Lane, now really—either you are here as the attorney for Mrs. Oswald or you are not entitled to be in this room—one of the two.

Mr. Lane. May I ask, Mr. Chief Justice, if it is permissible for me to function at Mrs. Oswald's request as her counsel together with Mr. Doyle, just for an hour or two, and then be excused.

The Chairman. Mr. Doyle has said that if you are her attorney he is not. And Mr. Doyle is doing this as a public service. We must respect his views in the matter.

Mr. Lane. I see. I did explain to Mr. Doyle before I came into the room exactly what the situation was. It was not until now that I understood his response.

Under those circumstances, I wonder if I might confer with Mrs. Oswald for just a minute or two.

The Chairman. If Mrs. Oswald wants to, she may.

Mrs. Oswald. Yes, thank you.

The Chairman. All right.

You may take another room, if you wish.

(Brief recess.)

The Chairman. All right.

Mr. Lane. Under the circumstances, since I do have to leave and I will not be able to be here for the rest of the afternoon's session and for subsequent sessions—under those circumstances, since Mr. Doyle will not remain on jointly with me, I will at this time withdraw.

The Chairman. Very well. Now, we will continue. Mr. Rankin, you may continue with the hearing.

Mr. Rankin. Mrs. Oswald, could you tell us first now, while you are fresh, about this conspiracy that you said that you knew about?

Mrs. Oswald. Yes—If you would like me to do it now. I was going to lead up to all the fundamentals, to my way of thinking. I have no proof, because naturally if I did I don't think we would be here.

But I feel like there is a lot of speculation about everything.

My way of thinking is because the involvement of myself at Six Flags and the way I was treated, as I have already put into the testimony, and as I stated yesterday, also, that I was supposed to be under protective custody, and I was not.

I wonder why I didn't have protective custody, why I am not important enough, with papers out of the vault, and appearing before the hearing, that Mr. Sorrels, head of the Secret Service, didn't give me protective custody, even though you, yourself, Mr. Rankin, required it.

These are the things I have to face that to me are very unusual.

Mr. Rankin. Well, it is such a serious charge to say that these two Secret Service men and your son and—I didn't understand for sure whether you included188 anyone else in your charge—were involved in a conspiracy to assassinate the President.

Mrs. Oswald. No, no——

Mr. Rankin. And your daughter-in-law.

Mrs. Oswald. That is not my statement. I said I thought that we have a plot in our own government, and that there is a high official involved. And I am thinking that probably these Secret Service men are part of it.

Now, I didn't say in a conspiracy—make it as strong as you did. I have made it strong. But I am under the impression that possibly there is a leak in our own government. And when I come to these papers—and I specifically yesterday morning asked about Senator Tower.

Now, I am not throwing any reflection on Senator Tower. But he made the statement in the paper that he had a letter from the State Department saying that Lee had renounced his citizenship.

Now, you see, I don't have that paper with me. I had it yesterday morning. But his whole quotes—the dates and everything of the letter that he was supposed to have had is not in correspondence with the dates that I have from the State Department papers which you gentlemen know that I have all these papers from the State Department. Nothing corresponds with what I have.

So I wanted to know and see this letter that Senator Tower claims he has. It could have been that it was an error in newspaper reporting, and I will say in slang he could have shot his mouth off, because he said he would not help the boy when the boy wrote him the letter.

Representative Ford. Mr. Chairman, I saw the letter that Lee Harvey Oswald wrote to Senator Tower the day after the assassination. And I believe I also saw the response that he received from one of the agencies of the Federal Government. Senator Tower had the original of the letter. If it is not in our Commission files, I am sure it is available for the Commission files—along with, whatever exchange of correspondence he had with the Department of State concerning the matter.

Mrs. Oswald. Well, now, what is of utmost interest to me in this particular case is if there is such a letter, and it does not correspond with anything that I have, I would like to know who in the State Department wrote this particular letter.

Representative Ford. I would not know who in the State Department wrote the letter. I would suspect it was the Assistant Secretary for Congressional Affairs, Fred Dutton, I believe.

Mrs. Oswald. I am not suspecting, because I have many, many letters from the State Department, and I also have something else that I will present that maybe would be another party involved. There is very conflicting testimony.

You must realize that I went to Washington in 1961 and was in conference with three officials. And this was another Administration.

Now, I don't know much about politics, gentlemen. But I do know a little from the news.

Lee's defection was in one Administration—right?

And now this is of another Administration, the Kennedy Administration. And there could be a leak in the State Department. That is not impossible.

So I have two instances that I, myself, am not satisfied.

Mr. Rankin. A leak is so much different from a conspiracy to assassinate the President, though.

Mrs. Oswald. Yes, but this leak this could be the party involved in the assassination of the President—the high officials I am speaking of. I cannot pin it down to one sentence, gentlemen.

Mr. Rankin. Well, you named the Secret Service men, two of them.

Mrs. Oswald. That is right.

Mr. Rankin. Now, do you have anything that shows you that either of those men were involved in the conspiracy to assassinate President Kennedy?

Mrs. Oswald. I will answer that emphatically no. What I have stated is the way they treated me, sir. I elaborated the way these two men treated me—correct? I did that testimony yesterday.

So I have to consider these two men. I will put it that way.

Mr. Rankin. Let's consider Marina Oswald. Do you have anything that will189 show that she was involved in any conspiracy to assassinate President Kennedy?

Mrs. Oswald. I feel like Marina is involved and also Mrs. Paine, yes.

Mr. Rankin. Now, what do you have in that regard?

Mrs. Oswald. All right—because Marina—now this I have said to Mr. Jack Lengett, who is a New York Times newspaperman a long time ago. And I was ashamed to say it to anyone else. And I didn't tell it to him for a long time.

The story yesterday at the Six Flags, when I said to you Marina shrugged me off, and the second time she shrugged me off. The second time she said—and I would not say it now unless I had told Mr. Jack Lengett—she said, "You no have job."

In other words, since Marina was being offered a home, then you go to—"You don't have job."

Before she was satisfied to take $863 and live with me. I was giving her my money and giving her my love. And then, "You no have job."

I am trying to show you the disposition of my daughter-in-law. I love her. But I am trying to show you that there is two sides. I told you how she hit the little girl with the comb. "Mama, I no need you, Mama. You don't have job."

Mr. Rankin. Why does that show she was involved in any conspiracy?

Mrs. Oswald. Because I am going to try to show there is discrepancies all along. She was not supposed to speak English.

I testified that I, myself, questioned her for an FBI agent. I acted as interpreter. So Marina did know English and understand English. So that is a question.

Mr. Rankin. I thought you said she spoke broken English.

Mrs. Oswald. Broken English. But she is not supposed to speak English at all, until now that she has learned English. That has been publicized over and over.

Mr. Rankin. And you think she could understand English fluently?

Mrs. Oswald. Yes, sir. I also told you when she lived with me that month in my home, how we conversed and talked. And yet the impression is that Marina came here and didn't speak English at all.

Mr. Rankin. How does that show she conspired to assassinate the President?

Mrs. Oswald. Because Marina now is not happy. Marina was very happy, I explained to you, the month she was with me in the beginning that they had rented this house. And then Marina made friends, very, very many friends. And Marina became discontented with Lee. Lee could not give her the things she wanted, what he told her about America. And Marina now has become discontented with me. I don't mean now—I mean at the Six Flags.

Mama always had a big heart. I quit a job to help these children, and that is perfectly all right. That is my nature.

But then, when she has somebody else, you are pushed aside.

I am trying to show this. And, as I go along—I cannot help but face this, gentlemen, it is a fact. I cannot help but face these things.

So I am under the impression—and this is speculation, like anything else—circumstantial evidence, let's say.

I am just a layman. That is what you have against my son. Nobody saw him with a rifle shoot the President. So you have mostly circumstantial evidence.

I have to think of all these things, who might be involved in this.

The Secret Service men, surely you will admit, did not guard our President properly.

Now, that was also stated in the newspaper by, I think it is, Secret Service Judge Baughman—am I saying that right? He is the one that—how Lee got out of the building, and why the President—there are many, many people that wonder. So I, too, am wondering.

So I say that President Kennedy was improperly guarded. And I am not the only one that says that, sir. So I have to consider that. I have to consider the way I, myself, was treated at Six Flags for the three days.

When I came here today—I have these notes, something very important about that particular incident at Six Flags, to back up my story with a witness. You don't have to take my word for it.

190 Mr. Rankin. What else is there now in regard to Marina that caused you to think she conspired to kill President Kennedy?

Mrs. Oswald. Yes—because everything is laid out in Mrs. Paine's home and Marina's home. The gun was in the garage.

Mr. Rankin. Well, that doesn't make Marina do it, does it?

Mrs. Oswald. No, but Marina told the police that the gun was there the night before. She saw the gun in the garage the night before. She didn't see Lee take it that morning. But she made a statement that she saw the gun the night before.

The pictures of Lee with the rifle came from that home. If Lee is going to assassinate the President or anybody else, is he going to have photographs laying all around with the gun? No, sir.

And there is too much evidence pointing to the assassination and my son being the guilty one in this particular house.

All through the testimony, sir, everything has come from this particular house. And so I am a thinking person, I have to think.

Mr. Rankin. Why does that show that Marina had anything to do with the conspiracy?

Mrs. Oswald. Well, we are speculating, let's say. Marina is not happy. Lee can't give her any money and things. And she has made friends with these Russian folks that have cars and homes. And they are not happy because this Russian girl doesn't have anything. They are not happy about that.

And I am trying to show the disposition of the girl.

I love my daughter-in-law even now. Believe me, it is a sore spot to have to say this. But I have to face these facts of what I know.

Mr. Rankin. You realize it is a very serious charge.

Mrs. Oswald. Yes, sir. And it is also a serious charge that my son is the assassin of President Kennedy.

You see, we have two sides here. It is a very serious charge, because no one saw him shoot the President. And yet this is an international affair. And the conclusion has come to the conclusion that Lee Harvey Oswald has shot President Kennedy, and he alone. Lee Harvey Oswald, or Mr. J. Lee Rankin, or anyone in this room could not have been in that many places in 29 minutes time. It is utterly impossible.

And this has been gone over by hundreds of people. There are investigations. I have 1,500 letters, sir—not just letters of sympathy—people that are investigating this. And I don't read all thoroughly, and I am a layman. But he step by step has been taken, from what the reports said—that he was on the sixth floor, and then they saw him in the cafeteria drinking a Coca Cola, and the President came. Then he had to leave the building. He had so many blocks to walk before he caught a bus. He had to board the bus, he had to pay his fare, he had to get out of the bus, then he walked a few blocks, then he caught a taxicab, paid the taxi man, then he walked a few blocks, went to his home and got a coat. Then he walked a few more blocks and shot the policeman. Then he walked a few more blocks and he was in the theater.

In 29 minutes time it cannot be done.

So I am convinced my son, and my son alone, if he is involved—I am a human being, and I say my son could have shot the President, and he could have been involved. I am not the type mother to think that he is perfect and he could not do it. But I say he did not do it alone—if he did it. Because it is utterly impossible.

And I do not believe my son did it.

I think my son was framed because, gentlemen—would his rifle be in the sixth floor window of the depository—unless you want to say my son was completely out of his mind. And yet there has been no statement to that effect. Wade has publicly said on the television when it happened that he is sane, he is well reasoned, he knows what he did. And Lee never did break, with his black eyes. He kept saying he was innocent. And yet in 12 hours time he was proven guilty. That doesn't make sense to me, an ordinary layman. So I have to consider who is involved.

Now, I am telling you that this girl was not happy with her situation. She had turned against me twice.

191 You, yourself, yesterday said that she testified that I told her to tear up the picture. God give me the grace—I did no such thing. My testimony is true.

So now she has lied there, I have found out.

And every evidence of any importance has come from this house. I have to face that.

Mr. Rankin. What else do you have that shows that she had any part in the conspiracy to assassinate the President?

Mrs. Oswald. Yes. I am under the impression that probably she—I think Lee is an agent. I have always thought that, and I have as much circumstantial evidence that Lee is an agent, that the Dallas police has that he is a murderer, sir.

Mr. Rankin. What do you base that on?

Mrs. Oswald. Well. I am going to tell my story. I have it all there. That is what I base it on.

Mr. Rankin. Can you tell us in summary?

Mrs. Oswald. No, sir, I don't think I want to tell it to you that way, because I cannot, almost.

Mr. Rankin. That is a very serious charge, that he was an agent, too.

Mrs. Oswald. Well, fine. So all right.

If I feel that way, sir, don't I have the right, the American way, to speak up and to tell you what I feel? Isn't that my privilege?

Mr. Rankin. Yes. But can't you tell us what you base it on?

Mrs. Oswald. Yes, sir, I will, as I go along, sir.

Mr. Rankin. Is that the only way you can tell it?

Mrs. Oswald. I don't see how I can say to you I know he is an agent, and I have papers. I want to tell the whole story. I still have more papers. I have documents that I know you do not have, sir.

Mr. Rankin. Have you told us all that you know that would bear on your claim that Marina Oswald was——

Mrs. Oswald. Had a part in it.

Mr. Rankin. Had a part in it or conspired to assassinate the President?

Mrs. Oswald. Yes, sir—I cannot prove it. And I cannot prove Lee is an agent. I cannot prove these things.

But I have facts that may lead up to them. I cannot prove it, because if I did we would not be having this Commission, sir. I could say who shot President Kennedy.

Mr. Rankin. So in both cases of the agent—Lee being an agent, your son, and Marina Oswald and the Secret Service agents or anybody else conspiring with him for the assassination of President Kennedy, that is just suspicions. You cannot prove it—is that right?

Mrs. Oswald. I would not use the word suspicion, because I am not the type person to be suspicious and imagine things.

You may think so, because I am a woman. And this is my son. But my children were never tied to my apron strings.

And I can prove to you, in his defection in 1959, I made the statement that Lee, as an individual, had the right to think and do what he wanted to. They even said he was a Communist. If that is what he studied, and that is what he wanted to do, I accepted that, because that was his privilege as an individual. And that is public in 1959, my statement, which shows that I am not the sobbing mother kind because he has gone to Russia, and cry about it. I acknowledge that.

I have acknowledged that if the children, like Lee, went to Dallas, as I testified that yesterday, and didn't tell me he was going to Dallas—I don't grieve and lose my sleep over that. I have accepted that fact, because when Lee and Marina got ready to come to me that would be fine. In the meantime, I still have to live.

Mr. Rankin. Are you telling the Commission that your son was part of a conspiracy to assassinate the President?

Mrs. Oswald. I am saying that I realize that my son could possibly be part—yes—I realize he is a human being and he could possibly be in this, yes, sir.

Mr. Rankin. Are you saying he was?

Mrs. Oswald. No, I do not know. I am saying possibly he is involved.

192 Mr. Rankin. And you are saying possibly Marina was involved?

Mrs. Oswald. Well, exactly what I am trying to say. If I had proof, sir, I would give the proof in an affidavit and this case would be closed, like Mr. Wade said.

But I have as much right to my way of thinking as Mr. Wade has.

Mr. Rankin. You are saying that possibly the Secret Service agents were involved, too? You don't have any proof of that?

Mrs. Oswald. That is exactly what I have been trying to say. I have told you how I was treated, which has given me cause for this particular way of thinking—because I believe that my son is innocent. And I think that is the purpose of this Commission, is to hear all witnesses and arrive at a conclusion. Am I not right, gentlemen?

So this is my way of thinking. So grant me my way of thinking. If I am wrong, fine. But you may learn something.

Mr. Rankin. What about the high official now. Can you tell us who that was?

Mrs. Oswald. No, sir. I wish I did know. I have my own idea about that. I would rather not—because it is a high official—I would rather not give a name.

But I have my own very strong suspicions as to the official who he might be.

Mr. Rankin. We would appreciate your telling us within this group what you think.

Mrs. Oswald. Fine—and I expect to, Mr. Rankin. I am a person that is very outspoken, as you know by now, and I will certainly do that.

But will you grant me the privilege first of finding out the name of the man in the State Department that wrote the letter to Senator Tower, because it is an incorrect—it is incorrect—the whole testimony is incorrect.

Mr. Rankin. We will get that correspondence for you.

Mrs. Oswald. All right. I was going to go into something else, but while we are here, I will continue this.

And this, to me, will be in this line. And I think very important to you gentlemen. And you do not have a copy of what I am going to show you. I am the only person that has this copy.

I am sorry to take time, but these were not copied, sir. We sealed them up, and we were going to have them copied this afternoon. But I can get to this particular one. This is the defection. I have much more testimony than this. I have testimony, sir.

Mr. Rankin. Do you think that you can tell us the name of the high official you spoke about?

Mrs. Oswald. Yes, I think so. And I am going to tell you. But please do not ask me at this particular moment. I do not think this is the proper time for me to—it is just—I have no proof. Understand? As I said, it is my right to think and my analysis of the papers I have. I have papers where I can come to a conclusion, just like you gentlemen are going to have papers and witnesses and come to a conclusion.

Now, this particular instance——

Mr. Dulles. I wonder if we could not possibly explore that agent matter. I am very much interested in that. I cannot be here tomorrow. We laid all the groundwork for that.

The Chairman. Mr. Dulles would like to know her reasons for believing that he was an agent.

Mrs. Oswald. Yes, sir, I have two very long stories.

Mr. Dulles. I have to be absent, unfortunately, tomorrow, so I would like very much to have it.

Mr. Rankin. If you could go into that question, Mrs. Oswald, because Mr. Dulles is not going to be here tomorrow.

Mrs. Oswald. We have everything just so, and yet when we come here we don't have it. The International Rescue Committee is what I am looking for.

I have also the original application from the Albert Schweitzer coming that you gentlemen do not have.

The Chairman. Let's stay on one thing, please.

Mrs. Oswald. All right. I am a little excited now, because I meant to go story by story.

193 Gentlemen, I have at least four more stories to tell—two I don't think there are some parts you possibly can know about.

Mr. Rankin. Well, if you could tell about why you think your son was an agent, it will help to get that taken care of this afternoon while Mr. Dulles can be with us. That is why I asked you that.

Mrs. Oswald. Yes, sir. We have a special file. You see, gentlemen, all morning long I was in the backroom and we were copying things. We had everything just so. So now I don't know what condition they are in. Mr. Doyle and I worked on the papers again last night and we had them just so. And then when they were copied, evidently they were mixed up again.

Mr. Rankin. We tried to have you present so that would not happen. Mrs. Oswald. I guess you didn't accomplish that.

Mrs. Oswald. Well, they did take it into the other room, and we saw that they took it. Well, I can be telling the story about it.

It is the International Rescue Committee, and a telegram.

I received a letter from Lee—this is going to be real short, Chief Justice Warren. It is going to continue this one story. And then I will go into the defection—is that right—because this will continue that.

A letter from Lee asking me to go to the Red Cross in Vernon—I was on a case there—and asking me to show the letter to the lady at the Red Cross. And this is from Moscow. This is the letter from Moscow. And telling her that all exit visas and everything had been documented and he is ready to come home, but he needs help financially to come home.

Evidently you have that information. That I know, sir.

Mr. Rankin. Yes.

Mrs. Oswald. So when I entered the Vernon Red Cross—now, this came with Lee's letter, Chief Justice Warren—the letter you have there direct from Moscow. That is why I have it, sir—because it was in Lee's letter asking me to go to the Red Cross in Vernon. So I have the original from Moscow.

I told the young lady, showed her the letter and showed her the paper. And I said, "Would you find out, please, the address of the International Rescue Committee? My son is in Russia and asked me to contact you."

She said, "What is your son doing in Russia?"

I said, "I don't know."

"You are his mother and you don't know what he is doing in Russia?"

I said, "Young lady, I said I do not know what he is doing in Russia."

"Well, I think anybody goes to Russia doesn't need any help to get back, they should stay over there."

So I said, "I am not interested in your personal opinion. I need help. Would you please contact, give me the address of the International Rescue Committee so I can continue to try to get money for my son to come home?"

She did not know of any address for the International Rescue Committee.

I asked her if she had a private line to Wichita Falls, which was approximately 40 miles away, which would be the next big city. She called Wichita Falls, and they did not know the address of the international committee.

So I called Robert and told Robert what I had and asked him to try to find out the address of the International Rescue Committee. However, he gave me no satisfaction.

Now, I sent a telegram—and you know this part of it—to the State Department, asking—I told them I was in a small town, Vernon, Tex., and I had received a letter from Lee asking me to get the address and help from the International Rescue Committee. But being a small town I had no success—could they help me out?

So they sent a telegram back with the address of the International Rescue Committee. That you have.

And this is Lee's letter—that goes with the other part.

Now, this young lady was very, very regalish. She didn't want to help anybody going to Russia. So when I received the telegram from the State Department, it was on a Saturday. I called her that morning. I was delayed 4 or 5 days. And to me it was very important, since my son and daughter-in-law194 had all documents finished with to get the money to come home, because I wanted that baby to be born here.

So I called her at her home and told her that I had the address from the State Department of the International Rescue Committee, and would she be so kind enough as to come to the office and write the letter for me.

She said, "Well, Mrs. Oswald, I don't have a key."

This is on a Saturday morning and she is in the courthouse.

I said, "Do you mean to tell me you are in charge of the Red Cross and you don't have a key?"

"No, I don't."

"Well, young lady, you have delayed me 4 days, and I don't like your attitude. I am going to ask you especially to make a point to come to the office and get this in the mail for me. It is very important."

So, reluctantly, after much persuasion, she came.

So she wrote the letter to the International Rescue Committee, and handed it to me, and I mailed that letter—I mailed the letter.

This is dated January 22, 1962.

So she called me—her name—Mrs. Harwell. She is the only woman in the Red Cross office in Vernon, Tex.

She called me and told me she had received word from the International Rescue Committee. She read me this letter. So I said to Mrs. Harwell, "Do you mind if I take the letter, because I am very forgetful?"

So she took a scissors, gentlemen, and she cut this part out, which was her title and her address—it was addressed to her. This lady wanted no part of anybody in Russia—understand? So she cut this out.

But on the back page was the name. But that is why this space is here—she cut it out.

Now, the letter reads: "Since we had a call from the State Department on Mr. Oswald's case, your communication of January 14th did not come as a surprise."

So this young lady has followed up with a letter of her own to the International Rescue Committee.

"Since we have had a call from the State Department, your letter does not come as a surprise."

I mailed the first letter, and it was just—so she followed up her feelings about a boy in Russia.

Now, why does the State Department dicker with me—that is not the word—and then see fit to put in a personal call to the International Rescue Committee?

I would like to know who from the State Department called the International Rescue Committee.

There is my information there that I requested. Why is a call necessary?

Mr. Rankin. You think that shows there was a conspiracy?

Mrs. Oswald. I am wondering and questioning why a call is necessary, a call, when they had contacted—and I am showing you what I have here. I don't see any necessity of the State Department to call the International Rescue Committee.

And, gentlemen, you have a copy of this—Lee will not be helped.

I would like to know who called the International Rescue Committee from the State Department—yes, sir, I would.

Mr. Rankin. Yes, but you don't think that shows there is a conspiracy?

Mrs. Oswald. Well, no—now. Mr. Rankin, don't pin me down everything I say to the word conspiracy. I am trying to analyze a whole condensed program of things that are not correct. I am telling you about this. It could be just a simple thing, that he called. But I would like to know who called when it wasn't necessary to make a call, and Lee was not going to get the money. Read the letter.

Mr. Rankin. The reason I ask you about the conspiracy is because that is such a serious charge. And, as you say, if you could prove that, that would decide everything around here.

Mrs. Oswald. That is right. And I am going to see if I cannot show you these things.

195 Mr. Rankin. If you are speculating, which you have a right to do, that is something different.

Mrs. Oswald. Well, I have explained that I am speculating, that I have all these documents, that some of them don't make sense. That is what I am trying to tell you. I mentioned that before.

Mr. Rankin. You are not trying to say to the Commission that you have the proof that there was a conspiracy?

Mrs. Oswald. I have emphatically stated that I do not have the proof, because if I had the proof I would have an affidavit and give you gentlemen the proof. I made that clear two or three times. I wish I did have the proof, sir.

I think I said yesterday—it doesn't surprise me that there may be someone in our State Department or some official who would have part in this. He is a human being just like we are. He may have a title, but that doesn't make him a man back of the title.

Mr. Dulles. What is this conspiracy now, Mr. Rankin? Is this the conspiracy to do away with the President, or is this a different conspiracy?

Mr. Rankin. The conspiracy I was asking about was the conspiracy, she said, about the assassination of President Kennedy.

And she said that it involved the two Secret Service agents and her daughter-in-law and her son. That is the one I was asking about.

The Chairman. And Mrs. Paine.

Mrs. Oswald. And Mrs. Paine. I feel like the facts have come from this particular source.

Mr. Rankin. Now, as I understand she says now that she is speculating as to that being a possibility.

Mrs. Oswald. Well, now, Mr. Rankin. I have not changed my testimony, if you are implying that. I may not have put it in a position you understood. Because as I say, I certainly did not mean to imply that I had proof, because if I had proof I would not be sitting here taking all my energy and trying to show you this little by little. I would have had an affidavit and show you the proof. So if you want to call it speculation, call it speculation. I don't care what you call it. But I am not satisfied in my mind that things are according to Hoyle. And I believe that my son is innocent. And I also realize that my son could be involved. But I have no way of knowing these things unless I analyze the papers that I have, sir.

Mr. Rankin. The Commission would like to know what you base your assumption that your son was an agent on. Could you help us?

Mrs. Oswald. Would you like me to go into this story—I will start with my son's life from the very beginning.

Mr. Rankin. Can't we get down to——

Mrs. Oswald. No, sir, we cannot. I am sorry. This is my life. I cannot survive in this world unless I know I have my American way of life and can start from the very beginning. I have to work into this. I cannot answer these questions like in a court, yes or no. And I will not answer yes or no. I want to tell you the story. And that is the only way you can get a true picture. I am the accused mother of this man, and I have family and grandchildren, and Marina, my daughter-in-law. And I am going to do everything I can to try and prove he is innocent.

Mr. Rankin. Well, now, Mrs. Oswald, you are not claiming before this Commission that there was anything back at the beginning, at the early childhood of your son, in which you thought he was an agent?

Mrs. Oswald. Yes, sir—at age 16.

Mr. Rankin. Well, why don't you start with age 16, then.

Mrs. Oswald. Well, aren't you gentlemen—I have a letter from you, Mr. Rankin. Aren't you gentlemen interested in my son's life from the very beginning? I think you should, because it has been exploited in all the magazines and papers. And this is not my son is what I am trying to say. He is not a perfect boy, and I am not a perfect woman. But I can show a different side of Lee Harvey Oswald, which I hope to do to this Commission.

Mr. Rankin. Well, I plan to ask you about his early life and these other parts. But I thought it would be helpful if you would be willing to do it to196 tell the Commission, while Mr. Dulles is here, what you base this claim upon that your son was an agent of the Government.

Mrs. Oswald. Yes, and I would be happy to do it.

Mr. Rankin. If you have to go to when he was 16 years old as the first point, that will be fine.

But if you could cover that—then we will go on to the other things.

Mrs. Oswald. All right. I have your word that you will let me have my life story from early childhood and Lee's life story from early childhood.

Now, I will start from age 16. Is that satisfactory?

Mr. Rankin. Would you do that?

Mrs. Oswald. Thank you very much. We were in New Orleans, La., at this particular time. On or about October 5th or 7th—and you have this, gentlemen, as my proof, that I am telling a true story, and I will have witnesses that will be called—is a letter——

Mr. Dulles. What year, Mrs. Oswald?

Mrs. Oswald. I said 1959—I am sorry. 1955. No, wait now. 1956—when we left New Orleans is 1956. Am I not correct? I am a little excited now, because of what happened before. The note——

Mr. Rankin. He joined the Marines in 1956. Does that help you?

Mrs. Oswald. No, sir. Wait. We have a note from the Beauregard School by me that I was going to San Diego. Do you have the note?

Mr. Rankin. We do.

Mrs. Oswald. May I see that note, please? And that is approximately October 5th or the 7th, I think it is, 1955.

Mr. Dulles. I think you moved to Fort Worth with Lee in September 1956.

Mrs. Oswald. Yes, sir. So it was in '55. I think that is correct. Let me see.

Mr. Rankin. We are handing you this book that we received from the State of Louisiana that is Commission's Exhibit No. 365, and turn to page 11 and you will find the note you referred to.

Mrs. Oswald. To the school. All right, gentlemen, this is a surprise. This is my note, isn't, to the school, that I am moving to San Diego. And it has been blasted in all the papers how I moved around, and I was going to San Diego.

Gentlemen, I had nothing to do with this note, nothing whatsoever.

Lee, my son, wrote the note—on or about October 5th or the 7th—October 7th. And now comes the story why he wrote the note.

If you will see here, this is Lee's handwriting, to the letters.

Mr. Rankin. We offer in evidence that note on page 11.

(The document referred to was marked Commission Exhibit No. 199, and received in evidence.)

Mrs. Oswald. I had nothing to do with this note.

Now, I am working at Kreeger's Specialty Shop, 800 and something Canal Street in New Orleans, La. I received a telephone call from the principal of the Beauregard School saying. "Mrs. Oswald, I understand you are going to leave town, and we are awfully sorry to lose Lee."

Of course now, gentlemen, I am working and this is news to me.

So I said—I kind of went along with it a little bit.

Lee came into this shop later on that day. Miss Lillian New, I think her name was, who is manager of Kreeger's Shop, and has been for years—she will witness this.

He said, "Mother, I have quit school."

Mr. Rankin. You say when the school authorities asked you, you sort of went along with it. What do you mean by that?

Mrs. Oswald. When the lady called me and said that, "I understand you are leaving town, Mrs. Oswald."

Mr. Rankin. What did you say?

Mrs. Oswald. Well, because there was a switchboard, and my job was in jeopardy, I don't know the exact words, but I said—I had to be kind of vague about it and not discuss it. I knew I wasn't leaving town, sir.

Mr. Rankin. Did you tell her you were not?

Mrs. Oswald. No, I don't think I told her. But I had to be very—I would lose my job if they thought I was leaving town. It was news to me.

So Lee that afternoon, from school, came into Kreeger's Specialty Shop197 where I was working and said, "Mother. I want to join the Marines, and I have quit school."

Now, Mr. Kreeger—and he may be leaving—Mr. Frank Kreeger who is owner of Kreeger's Specialty Shop, and all of the personnel there—this is a very small shop, and Miss Lillian, who was manager, knows of this. I became very excited and I started to cry. And they let me go home with Lee.

So Lee was determined at age 16—his birthday was going to be October 18th, right—and this was October 7th—was going to join the Marines. So what Lee wanted me to do was falsify his birth certificate, which I would not do. And he kept after me, like a boy.

Now, this is a normal boy, wanting to join the Marines.

"I don't see why you don't just put that I am 17 years old."

I said, "Lee. We cannot do that."

He said, "Everybody else"—

I said, "No, I am not going to do it."

For 2 or 3 days Lee and I bickered back and forth about me falsifying his age.

So I have a very good friend, Mr. Clem Sehrt, who is an attorney in New Orleans, La. I called him and told him I had a personal problem. I had not seen Mr. Sehrt since early childhood. I knew the family. That Lee was not of age and he wanted to join the Marines. And he quit the school and told them we were going out of town.

He said, "Marguerite, I cannot advise you. It would be unethical. But a lot of boys join the service at age 16."

So he could not advise me.

My sister, Mrs. Charles Murret, 757 French Street, knows of the complete story. And so does my brother-in-law, Mr. Charles Murret, who also said, "Let him join, let him go. If he wants to go so badly, let him join the Marines."

I, at that time, was living at 126 Exchange Place, which is the Vieux Carre section of the French Quarter of New Orleans.

And, by the way, the papers said we lived over a saloon at that particular address.

Gentlemen, if you have this information, that is just the French part of town. It looks like the devil. Of course I didn't have a fabulous apartment. But very wealthy people and very fine citizens live in that part of town, and there are hotels and saloons, and courtyards where the homes are.

So I was very upset.

There was a colonel on the street that I stopped—I didn't know him—I said, "Sir, I would like to talk with you." I told him about the boy wanting to join the Marines and I didn't know what to do. I was frantic. And he was insistent that I let him join the Marines at age 16.

So he advised me, "Well, if he doesn't want to go to school, let him join the Marines. It is done all the time."

Now, I was not too happy about this situation.

Now, a recruiting officer from the Marine Reserve in New Orleans, La., was in my home the next day when I arrived from work, with Lee, in uniform, in the home when I got into the home. He introduced me to him and he said, "Mrs. Oswald"—he didn't tell me what to do. He was very vague about the thing.

I said, "No, Lee is too young, age 16, to join the Marines. They are liable to send him overseas."

He said, "There is less delinquency in Japan and those places than we have here." He saw nothing wrong with it.

What he was doing was telling me to falsify his birth certificate, but not in plain words. He was telling me it would be all right for the boy to join the Marines. He came to my home personally.

So I went to an attorney with Lee, because—here is the thing.

Lee's birth record is in New Orleans. And I knew that the Marine Corps could easily check on this child, age 16—his birth record. So in order to have a happy situation, so I could work, and to see Lee, I went to an attorney and paid $5 and said that I lost Lee's birth certificate, and kind of motioned to the 198 attorney. I knew it would not stand up. I bought Lee a duffle bag and everything, and Lee went—we told him goodby, and Lee was going to join the Marines.

I had to accept that, gentlemen. There was no other way I could do, but accept the fact to let him go.

Mr. Rankin. Who was that attorney?
Mrs. Oswald. Mr. Clem Sehrt.
Mr. Boggs. What did Mr. Sehrt allegedly tell you?
Mrs. Oswald. Pardon?
Mr. Boggs. What did Mr. Sehrt tell you?
Mrs. Oswald. Mr. Sehrt is a family friend.
Mr. Boggs. I know Mr. Sehrt very well.
Mrs. Oswald. He said according to attorney ethics that he would not be able to advise me. Before you came in, sir, I had stated that.

Now, when I get interrupted, I lose—this is a big thing for me. I am not making excuses. But, gentlemen, it is awfully hard to do this.

So Lee came home. And he said the captain said that he was too young.

Now, I don't question much. I don't know whether Lee changed his mind, or they sent Lee home. I do not know. I do not question that.

All right.

Lee, at age 16, read Robert's Marine manual back and forth. He knew it by heart. Robert had just gotten out of the Marines, and his manual was home. And Lee started to read communistic material along with that.

Mr. Rankin. What communistic material did he read?
Mrs. Oswald. It was a small book that he had gotten out of the library. And I knew he was reading it, Mr. Rankin.
Mr. Rankin. Was it in Marxism, or what was it about?
Mrs. Oswald. No—if you are saying the title is Marxism—no, sir, the title was not.
Mr. Rankin. Was it about communism?
Mrs. Oswald. It was more about communism. I knew he was reading it. But if we have this material in the public libraries, then certainly it is all right for us to read. And I think we should know about these things, and all of our scholars and educators and high school boys read subversive material, which we call subversive material. So I, as a mother, would not take the book away from him. That is fine. Lee is a reader. I have said from early childhood he liked histories and maps.

So that is fine.

What I am saying now—we are getting to this agent part.

He is with this recruiting officer and he is studying the Marine manual—he knew it back and forth. In fact, he would take the book and have me question some of the things. And he was reading communism.

Lee lived for the time that he would become 17 years old to join the Marines—that whole year.

Mr. Rankin. What did he do during that time?
Mrs. Oswald. Pardon?
Mr. Rankin. What did he do during that year?

Mrs. Oswald. What did he do during that year? He was working for—as a messenger for Tujaque and Son.

Mr. Rankin. He had quite a few jobs, did he not?

Mrs. Oswald. Yes. I can explain that to you.

His first job was Tujaque and Son, who was steamship people, and he was a messenger. And then he had a lot of friends.

Now, they say Lee didn't have friends. There were boys of his age—while he was working he had an opportunity to make friends, coming to my home. And one of the young men knew of a better paying job, where they had coffee breaks and everything, so Lee took that job, which was with a dental laboratory—if you have that information, sir.

And I think that is the only two jobs—no, Lee worked after school for Dolly Shoe Co. I was working there, in charge of the hosiery department, and Lee worked on Friday afternoon and Saturday as a shoe salesman.

That was his first job—while he went to school he worked there.

And then when he left school, as I told you, at age 16—the first job was199 Tujaque and Company, steamship, and then the dental laboratory. And that is the only jobs he had in New Orleans.

Mr. Rankin. Were there not times he didn't have any job during that year?

Mrs. Oswald. No, sir—because when we left New Orleans, Lee left this dental laboratory job—that is correct.

So I moved back to Fort Worth, Tex., because Robert did not want to live in New Orleans. Robert was raised in Texas, and has his girl friends and all his friends in Texas. So when Robert got out of the Marines, he wanted to live in Texas. So I know that Lee wants to join the Marines at age 17, so in the month of July 1956—and, gentlemen, I have always been broke, and I mean broke. About a week before rent time, we had it pretty hard in order to have that rent. Yet I take my furniture and ship it to New Orleans so Lee could be with his brother and we could be with the family—thinking maybe with Robert he would not join the Marines at age 17 and finish his schooling.

When Lee became age 17, October 18th, he joined the Marines.

The reason why he didn't go into the Marines until October 24th was the recruiting officer at the Marines could not understand his birth certificate, because his father had died 2 months before. So I had to send for an affidavit, even though I had the death notice from the paper and everything, and they could have—they could not understand that about that two months. I had to send to New Orleans for an affidavit of his father's death.

And so then Lee joined the Marines on October 24th.

From the 18th to the 24th every day Lee was leaving. We even laughed about it. Because he would leave in the morning and come home in the evening. And it was because he was born 2 months before his father—so he did join the Marines at age 18.

Now—that, Mr. Dulles, is the part you wanted to know. But, before, that has something to do with it. Lee——

Mr. Rankin. Mr. Dulles wanted to know what you based this idea that he was an agent on?

Mrs. Oswald. That is one part. That is the beginning of it, Mr. Dulles. I have much more. That is the beginning of it, sir.

Mr. Dulles. Did he join at 18 or 17?

Mrs. Oswald. He joined at age 17. I signed the paper. You will please forgive me when I make mistakes, and if you will correct me.

Now, at age 15½ Lee was a member of the Civil Air Patrol.

Do you have that information, gentlemen?

I don't think you have.

Now, just a minute. I am sorry—this morning, when they were copying my papers. I put this in my bag.

I have a picture right here—this is Lee at age 15½ in the uniform of the Civil Air Patrol. This is before the recruiting officer. We are going back.

And this is what helped Lee to make up his mind to join the service.

The Chairman. Go right ahead, Mrs. Oswald.

Mrs. Oswald. At age 15½ or so, Lee joined the Civil Air Patrol. He went on an airplane, on flights and everything. I got him the uniform, with Robert's help. This young man—now, I do not know his name. He is from New Orleans. And I am checking on these things. I have to do research on all of this, and do it alone.

This young man and Lee were very friendly. The young man that gave Lee the idea of—went to Beauregard School with him, and he and Lee joined the Civil Air Patrol together. That is the way I wish to state this. And he often came to the house. So there is a close friend of Lee. Lee is not supposed to have any friends.

Mr. Rankin. Did he have any girl friends, too?

Mrs. Oswald. No. Now, neither did Robert or John Edward. No, sir. Neither of my boys had girl friends until after about age 17.

Mr. Rankin. Did he have other close friends, boy friends, besides these that you recall?

Mrs. Oswald. No, sir, I would not say he had—unless during working—he was working at this time, and I was working during the day. But I mean at the 200 house this young man came to the house, and several of the other young men, as I told you before.

Now, we are at the Civil Air Patrol.

And that is why Lee went to the Marine Corps, is because of the Civil Air Patrol. He wasn't in the Civil Air Patrol long.

Mr. Rankin. Now, up to this point, you haven't told us anything that caused you to think he was an agent, have you?

Mrs. Oswald. Well, maybe, sir, I am not doing a very good job of what I am saying.

Mr. Rankin. What do you think you have said that caused you to think——

Mrs. Oswald. I have said that a Marine recruiting officer came to my home, and that Lee then continued reading Robert's manual by heart, and started reading communist literature. He is preparing himself to go into the Marine service—at age 17—this year before he actually joined the service. I am saying he is already preparing himself.

Mr. Rankin. To become an agent?

Mrs. Oswald. Yes, I think with the influence of this recruiting officer.

Mr. Rankin. You think the recruiting officer inspired him——

Mrs. Oswald. Yes, sir, influenced this boy.

Mr. Rankin. ——to read the communist literature?

Mrs. Oswald. Yes, sir—and Robert's Marine book.

Mr. Rankin. Is there anything else you base that on, except what you have told us?

Mrs. Oswald. About him being an agent?

Mr. Rankin. Yes.

Mrs. Oswald. Yes, sir, when I get through the whole story.

Mr. Rankin. I mean as far as the recruiting officer.

Mrs. Oswald. No. Otherwise than Lee's attitude. Lee read this manual. He knew it by heart. I even said, "Boy, you are going to be a general, if you ever get in the Marines."

Mr. Rankin. And you base the idea——

Mrs. Oswald. He had the idea.

Mr. Rankin. He was being prepared to become an agent, and inspired by this recruiting officer?

Mrs. Oswald. Yes, sir.

Mr. Rankin. By what you have told us about his reading the communist literature and this one pamphlet, and also the manual of the Marine Corps?

Mrs. Oswald. Yes, sir. And then living to when he is age 17 to join the Marines, which I knew, and which he did at age 17 on his birthday.

Mr. Rankin. Now, what else do you base your idea that he was—ever became an agent or was going to become an agent on?

Mrs. Oswald. Many, many things. We always watched—it is "I Led Three Lives"—the program—Philbrick. We always watched that. And when Lee returned from the service and the Marines, the three days—that program was on, and he turned it off. He said, "Mother, don't watch that, that is a lot of propaganda."

It has been stated publicly that the FBI did not know—didn't have Lee on the subversive list—I am probably not saying this right, gentlemen—but the rightwing in Dallas. I don't know anything politically. The FBI and Secret Service had a list of names in Dallas of people that had to be watched, and Lee Harvey Oswald was not on that list. That would lead to believe there was some reason he was not on the list.

Mr. Rankin. Who did you get that from?

Mrs. Oswald. From the newspapers and all over. And there has been a lot of comment about this all through.

Now, I don't say it is correct. But what I have explained to you before—my way of thinking has to go with this, because I know the boy and the whole life, and you do not, sir.

Mr. Rankin. Well, I want to try to find out all you know about it.

Mrs. Oswald. Fine. And I want you to.

Also, Lee's letters—and I have them in the hotel—I didn't bring them, because 201 I thought we were through, and you have the copies—most every letter from Lee tells me something.

When Lee is coming back from Russia he says, "I plan to stop over in Washington a while."

Lee says in the letter, "Marina's uncle is a major in the Soviet Union."

"I am an American citizen and I will never take Soviet citizenship."

If you will read every letter—if you think he is an agent—every letter is telling his mother—"If something happens to me, Mother, these are facts."

I might be elaborating. But I think my son is an agent. And these things piece by piece are going together, as far as I am concerned.

Representative Ford. When did you first think he was an agent?

Mrs. Oswald. When Lee defected. And I have always said a so-called defection, for this reason.

Now, we come to another letter. I am going to have to take some time now, because we are not going in sequence. The letter Lee wrote to me from New Orleans is what I need.

Mr. Rankin. Do you have the letter in which he says he was going to Washington?

Mrs. Oswald. Yes, sir, I gave you that copy yesterday. I don't have the letter with me. They are at the hotel.

Mr. Rankin. You gave it to us yesterday?

Mrs. Oswald. Yes, sir—that he would stop over in Washington.

Mr. Rankin. Do you recall the date of that one?

Mrs. Oswald. Well, now, he was supposed to arrive in New York on the 13th of June, 1962. And that is the letter. When he arrived, I do not know. And I do not know if he went to Washington.

As I stated yesterday, he went to Robert's house, and I was on a case. So I don't know when he arrived in New York.

Now, this is the letter. Lee is out of the Marines, and he stays home with me 3 days. And I have publicly stated—and this came out of my book this morning—Lee came home September 14, 1959. He stayed 3 days with me. Said he would like to travel on a ship working his way. Possibly export and import. He remarked he could make more money that way.

The next page is the letter he sent me, and then came the news of his being in Russia. This is the letter.

"Dear Mother"———-

Mr. Dulles. Is that dated?

Mrs. Oswald. Yes, sir. This is just dated September. He was released from the Marine Corps on September 14th—I believe I am correct, Mr. Rankin.

And he stayed with me 3 days.

And then this is—well, the date on the envelope is September 19th. He stayed with me 3 days.

"Dear Mother, well, I have booked passage on a ship to Europe. I would have had to sooner or later, and I think it is best to go now."

"I would have had to sooner or later, so I think it is best that I go now. Just remember above all else that my values are very different from Robert or us, and it is difficult to tell you how I feel. Just remember this is what I must do. I did not tell you about my plans because you could hardly be expected to understand. I did not see Lillian while I was here. I will write you again as soon as I land. Lee."

Mr. Rankin. What do you think he meant by that?

Mrs. Oswald. That is what I want to tell you. All of this speculation, gentlemen. And that is why I say the Warren Commission—unless they hear my story and the witnesses involved, cannot arrive at a true conclusion.

Now, what would you think about this?

A few days later you get headlines. "Fort Worth Boy Has Defected to Russia." And I made the letter public. This letter says to his mother he is defecting to Russia—right? That is the way you would read the letter.

It is easily read this way when you think a boy has defected to Russia. So you would read the letter that way.

202 Mr. Dulles. Mr. Rankin, do we have correspondence while he was in the Marines?

Mr. Rankin. Mrs. Oswald, do you recall any letters you received from your son during the time he was in the Marines?

Mrs. Oswald. Yes, sir. I have a special delivery letter. You see, gentlemen, that is why I have tried to explain to you before—if I could have gone from the story we would not all be so mixed up. This is a letter from the Marines saying he is going to contact the Red Cross—when I told him about my illness.

Mr. Rankin. Well, that is the correspondence in regard to his getting out of the Marines because of your need of his help and support.

Mrs. Oswald. Yes, that is right.

Mr. Rankin. Now, except for that correspondence, you don't have any other correspondence from him while he was in the Marines?

Mrs. Oswald. Yes, sir, I did have several letters.

What has happened, Mr. Rankin—when Lee stayed with me the 3 days, he left his seabag with me. And that is why I have his discharge papers and things. And then, as you know, when the defection broke, I had no place to go. So the lady I was working for even threatened to call the police, because of the defection. I was working for $5 a week, gentlemen, taking care of her son. But I was happy to have a home and food, because I had had this accident, and I could rest. But my salary was $5 for the whole week. But when the news broke, she didn't want to be involved with anyone who had a son as a defector, so she asked me to leave. It was a very cold winter night. And I said I would.

But I didn't want to leave—didn't have any place to go.

She said, "You will leave now or I will call the police."

So I called Robert and he told me to come out to his home.

When I went out to his home, I brought Lee's seabag, Mr. Rankin, with me. And I stayed there just a short time. And Robert Oswald would not let me have Lee's seabag. And there were a few letters in there from Lee in the seabag.

And so I don't have the seabag.

You can read this letter, then, this way. That he is telling me he is defecting to Russia.

We all agree there.

Then this same letter could be read the way I read it, as a mother.

After three days he is leaving his mother. But we had a talk. When Lee arrived home—and I will go into this thoroughly. I was ashamed when he arrived home. I was in a one bedroom and bath and a small kitchen. And my son came in about 2 o'clock in the morning. I have never lived lavishly, but we have always had a nice clean little moderate house. And, remember, I was destitute. I had no money. You have the affidavits evidently from the Red Cross. If you don't, I have copies.

The first thing I said to him, "Honey, the first thing we will have to do is to move and find a decent place."

I had a studio couch, which has two parts. The top part I put on the floor for my son to sleep on that particular night, in the one room.

So he said, "We will talk about it in the morning, Mother."

So morning came.

I brought the subject up immediately. I said, "The first thing we will have to do is find a place. I am well enough that I can babysit or pick up a few dollars. And until I settle my claim, I think we will be able to manage, and you will get a job."

He said, "No, Mother, my mind is made up. I have thought this out thoroughly. I have no background. If I stay here, I will get a job for about $35 a week, and we will both be in a position that you are in. I want to board a ship and work in the import and export business, where there is some real money."

Mr. Rankin. He had quite a little money saved, didn't he, from the Marines?

Mrs. Oswald. I will tell you about this—please, gentlemen, I will have to break if you don't. This is a very, very serious life that I have gone through.

I didn't answer Lee.

This is the way I do the children.

203 The Chairman. We will take a 10 minute recess now.

(Brief recess.)

The Chairman. The Commission will be in order. Mr. Rankin, you may continue.

Mrs. Oswald. Mr. Rankin, you mentioned about the $1,600. Now, I don't know if you know for a fact that Lee had $1,600. It was publicized in the paper that he had $1,600, which is right here in 1959.

Mr. Rankin. Did he tell you anything about that at the time?

Mrs. Oswald. No, sir, he gave me $100. And he and his brother Robert had arrived. And I am assuming it was over me because Robert did not help me. And I have made that public in the Red Cross papers, that he had a family of their own, that they probably thought their duty was to their family. I had no help from the other two boys. And he gave me $100, and I stayed in this little place a few weeks, and then I got the job for $5 a week. And that is Lee's defection.

So here is my only contact with Lee in Russia, at the Metropole Hotel—this is dated December 18, 1959.

Now, I have settled with the insurance company, and I have a little money. So I sent a check to Lee for $20. And this is his little note. The only contact I had with Lee from the time of his immediate defection until the State Department 2 years later informed me of my son's address. And this is his little note that he needs money.

So I would say that Lee didn't have $1,600, according to this proof.

Now, we are speculating, as you will admit, because you thought the letter to the school was from me. And you will have to admit that I have given you new evidence.

And so maybe Lee didn't have $1,600, because he is asking for money there. That is when he is right in Moscow.

Mr. Rankin. Of course, that is quite a while later.

Mrs. Oswald. No, sir. He defected the end of November. This is December 1959.

Mr. Rankin. But he——

Mrs. Oswald. He had to make passage, and have some money. I don't know if it took $1,600. I do not know, sir. But I am saying 5 weeks later he needs money. We haven't gotten to this file yet.

I will quote from a newspaper, the Star Telegram, 1959, his defection, by Mrs. Aline Mosby, who interviewed Lee in Moscow. It says here, "I saw my mother always as a worker, always with less than we could use, he said. He insisted his childhood was happy despite his poverty."

We had a very happy family. He insisted—this is the story in 1959. Lee had a normal childhood.

And now he is criticizing the United States. He says, "Many things bothered him in the United States. Race discrimination, harsh treatment of underdog, Communists and hate." Then on the other letter he is going to Russia to write a book. And there is another story and another story. And all kind of stories. So what are we to believe, gentlemen. Is he throwing us off the track because he is an agent. We are talking about speculation and newspaper papers, and so on. And we know when he came back that he did go to Mrs. Bates, a Fort Worth stenographer, and talked about the Soviet Union. She made it public. And he only had $10. And he did not finish that story. And she said he was very nervous. And he did not say he was an agent. But she got the impression that he was an agent. This has been made public in the Star Telegram—if you do not have that, I do.

Mr. Rankin. Mrs. Oswald, is this the photostatic copy of the letter about his booking passage?

Mrs. Oswald. Yes, sir.

Mr. Rankin. You read the original?

Mrs. Oswald. Yes, sir.

Mr. Rankin. And this material on the bottom is just your own writing?

Mrs. Oswald. Yes. This was in this book. That is my writing at the bottom.

Mr. Rankin. The letter I was referring to is Exhibit 200.

Mrs. Oswald. Yes, sir, it is this letter.

Mr. Rankin. We offer in evidence Exhibit 200.

204 The Chairman. Admitted.

(The document referred to was marked Commission Exhibit No. 200 and received in evidence.)

Mr. Rankin. Now, this one starting, "Dear Mother, received your letter, and so forth"—that is the one about the Marines, when he was asking you about getting out of the service and your need, and so forth?

Mrs. Oswald. This is the letter which shows the different character of the boy that the newspapers are making of him—when I wrote and told him I had sold my furniture, and that my compensation and medical was stopped, immediately my son sends a special delivery letter, and that is the letter "received your letter, was very unhappy. I have contacted the Red Cross, and they will contact you." This is a nice boy to do this immediately, when he finds his mother is in trouble. He is not a louse, like the papers have been making him out. He might have some bad points, but so do all of us.

Mr. Rankin. We will ask the reporter to mark this.

(The document referred to was marked Commission Exhibit No. 201 for identification.)

Mr. Rankin. Exhibit 201 is the letter you are just referring to?

Mrs. Oswald. Yes, sir.

Mr. Rankin. We offer in evidence Exhibit 201.

The Chairman. Admitted.

(The document referred to was marked Commission Exhibit No. 201 and received in evidence.)

Mr. Rankin. Then, Mrs. Oswald, the other one that you received from Russia, with the check and the little note from your son Lee is the one I am showing you?

Mrs. Oswald. Yes, sir.

Mr. Rankin. Will you mark that as Exhibit 202?

(The document referred to was marked Commission Exhibit No. 202 for identification.)

Mr. Rankin. We offer in evidence Exhibit 202 and ask leave to substitute a copy.

The Chairman. Admitted.

(The document referred to was marked Commission Exhibit No. 202 and received in evidence.)

Mrs. Oswald. I have followed up that request and sent the $20 bill in an envelope. And I have all of this. But I am not going to go through all this paper. You will have all of this.

Mr. Dulles. Did that get through—just as a matter of curiosity.

Mrs. Oswald. Yes, that is what I am going to tell you. So I put a $20 bill immediately in an envelope and sent it to Lee. And then after I thought about it, I thought of a foreign money order. And gentlemen I have all this in black and white for you, and this gentleman will copy and have it—everything I am saying. So then I went to the bank and I got a foreign money order for $25, and I sent it to Lee. It all went air mail. But it came back about 2 months later, Mr. Dulles—the $20 bill I got back in cash and the Chase National Bank foreign money order, that check came back in cash. I will have that proof for you. I understand it comes back by boat, and that is why it took so long.

So I had no way of knowing that my contact with my son was successful. I didn't know until about 2 months later he had not received my money. And by that time—well, I didn't know where he was, because I came to Washington in January of 1961, had a conference with Mr. Boster—Mr. Stanfield——

Mr. Rankin. Did you think he was a Russian agent at this time?

Mrs. Oswald. No, sir; I did not think he was a Russian agent.

Representative Ford. I thought you answered in response to a question I asked, when you thought he was an agent, you said when he defected.

Mrs. Oswald. I might have said defected to Russia. No, sir; I never thought Lee was a Russian agent.

Representative Ford. I meant an agent of the United States. It is my recollection that you said when he defected to the Soviet Union, you then thought he was an American agent.

Mrs. Oswald. Yes, that is right. That is correct.

Mr. Rankin. What else caused you to think he was an American agent?

Mrs. Oswald. All right. I might be letting things out the way I am going. And I am very unhappy about this. Had I started with his childhood I could have worked up to age 15 very peacefully, and you would have gotten everything. I hope I am not forgetting anything important. But now we have letters from the State Department.

Well, my trip to Washington has to come before the letters to the State Department, sir. So I am in conference with the three men. I showed them the letter from the—the application from the Albert Schweitzer College, and Lee's mail had been coming to my home. I didn't know whether he was living or dead. I did not want to mail these papers. So I made a personal trip to Washington.

I arrived at Washington 8 o'clock in the morning. I took a train, and borrowed money on an insurance policy I have, which I have proof. I had a bank account of $36, which I drew out and bought a pair of shoes. I have all that in proof, sir, the date that I left for the train. I was 3 nights and 2 days on the train, or 2 days and 3 nights. Anyhow, I took a coach and sat up.

I arrived at the station 8 o'clock in the morning and I called the White House. A Negro man was on the switchboard, and he said the offices were not open yet, they did not open until 9 o'clock. He asked if I would leave my number. I asked to speak to the President. And he said the offices were not open yet. I said, "Well, I have just arrived here from Fort Worth, Tex., and I will call back at 9 o'clock."

So I called back at 9 o'clock. Everybody was just gracious to me over the phone. Said that President Kennedy was in a conference, and they would be happy to take any message. I asked to speak to Secretary Rusk, and they connected me with that office. And his young lady said he was in a conference, but anything she could do for me. I said, "Yes. I have come to town about a son of mine who is lost in Russia. I do want to speak—I would like personally to speak to Secretary Rusk." So she got off the line a few minutes. Whether she gave him the message or what I do not know. She came back and said, "Mrs. Oswald, Mr. Rusk"—so evidently she handed him a note—and Mr. Boster was on the line—"that you talk to Mr. Boster, who is special officer in charge of Soviet Union affairs"—if I am correct. And Mr. Boster was on the line. I told him who I was. He said, "Yes, I am familiar with the case, Mrs. Oswald." He said, "Will an 11 o'clock appointment be all right with you?" This is 9 o'clock in the morning. So I said—this is quite an interesting story—I said, "Mr. Boster that would be fine. But I would rather not talk with you." I didn't know who Mr. Boster was. I said, "I would rather talk with Secretary of State Rusk. However, if I am unsuccessful in talking with him, then I will keep my appointment with you."

So I asked Mr. Boster—I said, "Mr. Boster, would you please recommend a hotel that would be reasonable?" He said, "I don't know how reasonable, Mrs. Oswald, but I recommend the Washington Hotel. It will be near the State Department and convenient to you."

So I went to the Washington Hotel. And as we know, gentlemen, there were nothing but men. They asked me if I had reservation. I said, "No, I didn't, but Mr. Boster of the State Department recommended that I come here." So they fixed me up with a room. I took a bath and dressed. I went to the appointment—because this is 9:30, I am on the phone, and I had to take a cab to the hotel. I arrived at Mr. Boster's office at 10:30.

But before arriving at Mr. Boster's office. I stopped at a telephone in the corridor, and I called Dean Rusk's office again, because I didn't want to see Mr. Boster, and I asked to speak to Dean Rusk. And the young lady said, "Mrs. Oswald, talk to Mr. Boster. At least it is a start."

So then I entered around the corridor into Mr. Boster's office. I have all the pictures of the State Department and everything to prove this story is true. I told the young lady. "I am Mrs. Oswald. I have an 11 o'clock appointment."206 Mr. Boster came out and said, "Mrs. Oswald, I am awfully glad you came early, because we are going to have a terrible snow storm, and we have orders to leave early in order to get home."

So he called Mr. Stanfield—the arrangements had been made—now, the other man—I don't have that name here for you, Mr. Rankin.

Mr. Rankin. Is it Mr. Hickey?

Mrs. Oswald. Yes, Mr. Hickey. You are correct.

So then we were in conference. So I showed the papers, like I am showing here. And I said, "Now, I know you are not going to answer me, gentlemen, but I am under the impression that my son is an agent." "Do you mean a Russian agent?" I said, "No, working for our Government, a U.S. agent. And I want to say this: That if he is, I don't appreciate it too much, because I am destitute, and just getting over a sickness," on that order.

I had the audacity to say that. I had gone through all of this without medical, without money, without compensation. I am a desperate woman. So I said that.

Mr. Rankin. What did they say to you?

Mrs. Oswald. They did not answer that. I even said to them, "No, you won't tell me." So I didn't expect them to answer that.

The Chairman. Did you mean you were seeking money from them?

Mrs. Oswald. No, sir. I didn't think that my son should have gone—in a foreign country, and me being alone. What I was saying was that I think my son should be home with me, is really what I implied.

The Chairman. Did you tell them that?

Mrs. Oswald. In the words that I said before—I didn't come out and say I want my son home. But I implied that if he was an agent, that I thought that he needed to be home.

Mr. Rankin. Did you say anything about believing that your son might know full well what he was doing in trying to defect to the Soviet Union, he might like it better there than he did here?

Mrs. Oswald. I do not remember saying this. I know what I did say, and they agreed with me. I said—because I remember this distinctly. I said, "Now, he has been exploited all through the paper as a defector. If he is a defector"—because as we stated before, I don't know he is an agent, sir—and if he is a defector, that is his privilege, as an individual.

And they said, "Mrs. Oswald, we want you to know that we feel the same way about it." That was their answer.

Mr. Rankin. Did you say anything about possibly he liked the Soviet way of life better than ours?

Mrs. Oswald. I may have. I do not remember, sir. Honestly. I may have said that. I recall that they agreed with me, and they said, "We want him also to do what he wants to do."

So now this is January 2, 1961, is my trip to Washington. Approximately 8 weeks later, on March 22, 1961—which is 8 weeks—I received a letter from the State Department informing me of my son's address.

Mr. Rankin. Do you recall that they assured you there was no evidence he was an agent?

Mrs. Oswald. No, sir, there was no comment to that effect.

Mr. Rankin. And they told you to dismiss any such ideas from your mind?

Mrs. Oswald. No, sir.

Mr. Rankin. You are sure they didn't tell you that?

Mrs. Oswald. I am positive. I said to them, "Of course, I don't expect you to answer me." No, sir, there was nothing mentioned about the agent at all. And in fact, I would think, just as a layman, that the State Department would not even consider discussing that with me. But I mean it was not discussed. I am positive of that.

Mr. Rankin. If they recorded in a memorandum as of that date that they did say that to you, that would be incorrect?

Mrs. Oswald. That is incorrect, emphatically incorrect. That is incorrect. Because I said, "I don't expect you to tell me. But if he is an agent," I didn't think it was the thing to do.

Well, on January 21 was my trip to Washington, 1961. Approximately 8207 weeks later, on March 22, 1961, I received a letter from the State Department informing me of my son's address, which you probably have, if you don't, sir, I have the copies. And also stating that my son wishes to return back to the United States—just 8 weeks after my trip to Washington.

Now, you want to know why I think my son is an agent. And I have been telling you all along.

Here is a very important thing why my son was an agent. On March 22 I receive a letter of his address and stating that my son wishes to return back to the United States. You have that, sir?

Mr. Rankin. Yes.

Mrs. Oswald. On April 30, 1961, he marries a Russian girl—approximately 5 weeks later.

Now, why does a man who wants to come back to the United States, 5 weeks later—here is the proof—April 30, 1961, is the wedding date—marry a Russian girl? Because I say—and I may be wrong—the U.S. Embassy has ordered him to marry this Russian girl. And a few weeks later, May 16, 1961, he is coming home with the Russian girl. And as we know, he does get out of the Soviet Union with the Russian girl, with money loaned to him by the U.S. Embassy. I may be wrong, gentlemen, but two on two in my books makes four.

I have many more things that can go to this, and that has been published. I will probably never know whether my son was an agent, because I do not expect to be told these facts. But isn't it peculiar that a boy is coming home, and the Embassy informs me of that—I have all this, Mr. Rankin, and you know I do. You will have the copies. And then 5 weeks later he marries a Russian girl. And the proof of it is that he does come home with the Russian girl in a short length of time. And Lee would have been home 1 year earlier. But because of the lack of money to come home.

Mr. Rankin. Did you ever ask him whether he married the Russian girl because they ordered him to?

Mrs. Oswald. No, sir. I have never asked Lee any questions of that kind. The only question I asked Lee was when they were living with me that 1 month, I said, "Lee, I want to know one thing. Why is it you came back to the United States when you had a job and you were married to a Russian girl," and they sent me lovely gifts and photographs and everything. So they seemed to be well off.

I have a beautiful scarf—they sent tea, boxes of candy, which the postage is terrific. He says, "not even Marina knows that." And that is the only question I have ever asked my son. This may be hard to believe. But I have explained to you over and over that I think we, as individuals, have a right to our own life.

Mr. Rankin. You saw your daughter-in-law and your son living together with you, didn't you, for some time?

Mrs. Oswald. Yes. They lived with me 1 month.

Mr. Rankin. Did you think they were in love with each other?

Mrs. Oswald. Yes, they were definitely in love with each other. Yes, I think they were in love with each other.

Mr. Rankin. Did you think at that time it was just because he was an agent and ordered to marry her that he married her?

Mrs. Oswald. No. I would say this. This is purely speculation. He knew Marina, and he loved Marina. They met at a dance. So that was—he had a girl friend. We are saying if he is an agent—I have to say "if." Then he tells the Embassy that he is in love with a Russian girl. And so it is a good idea to bring the Russian girl to the United States. He will have contacts.

Now, when I was in Mrs. Paine's home, on the table was a lot of papers from Lee. The Daily Worker I happen to know about. And many, many subversive—now, I say if Lee is going to assassinate a President, or Lee is anything that he is otherwise than an agent, Lee would not have all these things, he would not have his finger in everything.

He would not be reading only communism and Marxism, that he would be a fanatic about that one thing and have a cause to assassinate the President.

But that is not the picture of Lee Harvey Oswald. Lee has his hand in everything.

208 Mr. Rankin. What do you mean by everything?

Mrs. Oswald. Well, Cuba—because we know in New Orleans he was arrested for Fair Play for Cuba. He read the Daily Worker. And the other ones I don't know. But it was in the paper. There is plenty of subversive material.

Mr. Rankin. What about books? Did he read books much while he was living with you?

Mrs. Oswald. Yes, he read continuously. He went immediately to the library upon coming to the United States. He read continuously. All kinds of books. I tried, when he defected—I went to the library to find out the kind of literature that Lee read. But they could not give me that information. They said the only way they could give that information was when a book was overdue, and was out. But otherwise they have no record.

Now, it has been stated in the paper—maybe New Orleans is different, I don't know, but I know in Fort Worth I could not get the information. Stated he had books—the assassination of Huey Long and things of that sort. They must have a different system. Because in Fort Worth, Tex., they do not have that system. The only way they can tell is if a book is out. But I know Lee read. And I have stated in 1959 all of this.

Anyway, from Vincent Peale on down to anything you want to mention. Lee read continuously.

Mr. Rankin. Now, was there any time that Marina said anything to you to lead you to believe that she thought your son, Lee, married her because he was an agent?

Mrs. Oswald. No, sir, no, sir. Not at any time at all.

Mr. Rankin. You think she loved him?

Mrs. Oswald. I believe that Marina loved him in a way. But I believe that Marina wanted to come to America. I believe that Lee had talked America to her, and she wanted to come to America. I say this for a lot of little things that happened—that Marina wanted to come to America. Maybe she loved him. I am sure she did, anyway. She said that she did.

Mr. Rankin. I am not clear about this being ordered to marry her. You don't mean that your son didn't love her.

Mrs. Oswald. Well, I could mean that—if he is an agent, and he has a girl friend, and it is to the benefit of the country that he marry this girl friend, and the Embassy helped him get this Russian girl out of Russia—let's face it, well, whether he loved her or not, he would take her to America, if that would give him contact with Russians, yes, sir.

Mr. Rankin. Is that what you mean?

Mrs. Oswald. I would say that.

Mr. Rankin. And you don't think it was because your son loved her, then?

Mrs. Oswald. I do not know whether my son loved her or not. But I am telling you why he would do this—in 5-weeks time. Now, you have a 5-week period in here.

Mr. Rankin. I understand that. But I think it is a very serious thing to say about your son, that he would do a thing like that to a girl.

Mrs. Oswald. No, sir, it is not a serious thing. I know a little about the CIA, and so on, the U-2, Powers, and things that have been made public. They go through any extreme for their country. I do not think that would be serious for him to marry a Russian girl and bring her here, so he would have contact. I think that is all part of an agent's duty.

Mr. Rankin. You think your son was capable of doing that?

Mrs. Oswald. Yes, sir, I think my son was an agent. I certainly do.

Mr. Rankin. Have you got anything more that caused you to think he was an agent?

Mrs. Oswald. Yes, I have things that have been coming out in the paper. And I am not the only one that thinks my son is an agent. There has been many, many publications questioning whether Lee was an agent or not because of circumstances, and so on, and so forth, through the newspapers.

Mr. Rankin. That is newspaper accounts you are talking about now?

Mrs. Oswald. Yes. And as I said about the FBI.

Mr. Rankin. What about your own knowledge?

209 Mrs. Oswald. Well, that is why I wanted to go into the story. I wouldn't have become emotionally upset had I started in sequence.

I told you about him not wanting me to see that program. And then the letters. There is so much. About him being an agent—all of his correspondence with the Embassy in Moscow. I have the letters in the hotel. One of the letters states that the Russians cannot hold you—"the Russians cannot hold you. You are an American citizen. You are not a bona fide Russian resident." We have the letters. You have a copy of the letter, Mr. Rankin.

And "if you will show this letter to the Russians, they cannot hold you in Minsk."

Mr. Rankin. They would say that about you if you were over there, or anyone.

Mrs. Oswald. The point I am trying to bring there is Lee has always been an American citizen—according to all of my papers from the State Department.

Mr. Rankin. Yes.

Mrs. Oswald. And they would say that about anyone—all right, I will grant you that. You are probably right.

Mr. Rankin. So that doesn't prove he is an agent, that I can see.

Now, how do you feel it shows he was an agent?

Mrs. Oswald. Because he has the sanction of the American Embassy all through this affair.

Mr. Rankin. They would give that to any of us.

Mrs. Oswald. All right—so you are telling me that. But this man is married to a Russian girl, and does come back within a short time, and could have come back sooner. It was the lack of money. And that is another thing.

The State Department repeatedly kept writing me, and I have the letters, for the money. I have copies of my letters also. I could not raise the money. I said I had a '54 Buick car, and all I could get a loan on was $250. They wrote back and said could you ask some friends, or do you have any relatives—800 and some odd dollars they needed. And I went to 12 very prominent people in Vernon, Tex.—one who is a very respected citizen that they recommended me to go, who has a citizen award. And I felt very confident maybe he would help me. I told him that my son, who was a very young man, who was an American citizen, is trying to get back to the United States, but there is lack of money, and if he knew of any way possible he could help me.

He said "You mean he is a defector?" I said, "Possibly so. The paper has said he was a defector." And he said, "Well, I am sorry, Mrs. Oswald, but these boys that are in the service and defect, I don't have any use for."

And I said, "Do you go to church, sir?" He said, "Yes, I do." And I said, "Probably you go to church to put your hat on. Because here is a boy. Let's say he has made a mistake. He has gone to Russia. But let's say he realizes now he has made a mistake, and he wants to come back. Are you telling me you won't help him?"

"That is what I am telling you, Mrs. Oswald. I don't have any use for anybody." Which Senator Tower said that he would not help Lee—made it public. These are nice people saying this. I say the ones who are down and out are the ones that need the help. This boy was a young boy. Let's say he is not an agent. Let's say he defected to Russia. Yet he wants to come back. He deserved a helping hand. I went to 12 people. I did not beg. But I presented my case. And not a one offered to help.

Mr. Rankin. Didn't you understand that the State Department had to try to find out if they could—or you or your son could get the money from other sources before they could advance the money?

Mrs. Oswald. Yes, sir, I understand that. I am trying to tell you that I tried awfully hard, but with no success.

Mr. Rankin. So they were just trying to do their duty in that regard, were they not?

Mrs. Oswald. It could be, yes. It could be.

Mr. Rankin. You don't think that makes him an agent, just because they asked you——

Mrs. Oswald. I think—well, as you say, they would probably help anyone. And then again, because he is married to a Russian girl, and because all these 210 documents and everything are handled through the U.S. Embassy. And because of my trip to Washington—which was red carpet treatment. Let's say, gentlemen, if a woman gets on the phone at 9 o'clock and has an appointment at 11 o'clock with three big men, that is wonderful treatment.

223

Now, they probably would do that to anybody. I don't know.

Mr. Rankin. They might have done that——

Mrs. Oswald. I haven't been that fortunate before.

Mr. Rankin. Well, that shouldn't be held against them that they treated you nicely.

Mrs. Oswald. No, I have told you, Mr. Rankin, they were most gracious to me. The Administration was most gracious to me.

Mr. Rankin. I don't see why you should think that because they treated you nicely, that was any sign he was an agent.

Mrs. Oswald. Well, maybe you don't see why. But this is my son. And this is the way I think, because I happen to know all of the other things that you don't know—the life and everything. I happen to think this. And this is my privilege to think this way. And I can almost back it up with these things.

This is a stranger to you folks. But this is a boy I have known from a child.

Mr. Rankin. How much money do you think, he received for being an agent?

Mrs. Oswald. That I do not know.

Mr. Rankin. You have no idea?

Mrs. Oswald. But I do know this, and I have stated this. I have approximately 900 and some odd dollars. And I lost my job. That can be proven. I was a nurse on the 3 to 11 shift, working in a rest home, for a very wealthy woman. And it would have been at least a year, a year and a half case. She is not that bad off. She is just an invalid. She is going to live quite a while.

When I returned home from the Six Flags on Thanksgiving Day, the Deputy Sheriff at Fort Worth, Tex. went to get my pay. And the nurse, the 7 to 3:30 o'clock nurse—I went 3 to 11—and my patient cried and said that they were awfully sorry, but they could not have me back on the case. That the woman at the rest home refused to have me.

Now, I was not working for the rest home. I was doing private duty. But I understand that this is her place of business, and my presence there might have been—hurt her money part. But this is our Christian way of life. The boy was accused of killing the President, with no proof. And then the mother loses her job.

Now, that is my position. You asked me the question. But Marina has $35,000 publicly. What she has, I do not know.

Now, gentlemen, $35,000 is a lot of money in donation dribs and drabs—is a very large sum of money. I question where does that money come from. Yes, some of it could be coming from Lee's back pay. And she might have more than that. That was the amount made public—$35,000. And here is a mother without a job. And everybody knows I have no money. And my contributions are 900 and some odd dollars.

Mr. Rankin. Now, when you say that money that Marina has might come from your son's back pay, what do you base that on? Just speculation?

Mrs. Oswald. I am basing all of this on speculation. Sir, if I had proof, I would not be taking my energy and my emotional capacity to bring all this out—if I had proof he was an agent.

Mr. Rankin. When they asked you to contribute some money to help bring him home from Russia, did it occur to you that if he is an agent the government could just pay his way?

Mrs. Oswald. Yes. But they don't want the public to know he is an agent. They want me to have all of this. They don't want the public to know. I am going around to people—you brought up a very good point. I am going around trying to get money for this boy to come home, so the public knows. Sure, they could have given him the money to come home.

Mr. Rankin. Are you trying to get money now? I don't understand what you mean by that?

Mrs. Oswald. I think, Mr. Rankin, you asked me the question that if he was211 an agent, that the Government would have given him the money to come home without any trouble. I say just the opposite. That it was a very good point. If he was an agent, it would make it hard for him to get the money to come home.

Remember, I am under the impression he is coming home with this Russian girl in order to continue his work. So he cannot be given the money immediately to come home, because his mother might tell the story to someone. Lee was almost a year coming home for lack of money. So then they have an excuse to loan him the money.

Mr. Rankin. Did you ever learn that he was getting money from the Red Cross in addition to his pay—that is the Russian or Soviet Red Cross, when he was over there?

Mrs. Oswald. No, sir.

Mr. Rankin. You don't know what he did with that?

Mrs. Oswald. I don't know anything about that. The Red Cross from here?

Mr. Rankin. The Soviet Red Cross.

Mrs. Oswald. No, sir, I know nothing about that.

Mr. Rankin. You didn't know he was supposed to have gotten an amount equal to the pay he received from his job. He got that from the Red Cross.

Mrs. Oswald. I don't follow you. I do not know. I don't understand.

Mr. Rankin. He got so much a month from his job in the electronics factory. You understood that.

Mrs. Oswald. In Russia?

Mr. Rankin. Yes.

Mrs. Oswald. He was not in an electronics factory. I thought he was working in a radio factory. All right, fine.

Mr. Rankin. And then he got an equal amount, we understand, from the Red Cross of the Soviet Union. Did you know that?

Mrs. Oswald. No, sir. Now, explain to me—when you say the Red Cross of the Soviet Union. Is that our American Red Cross in the Soviet Union, or this is part of the Russian Red Cross?

Mr. Rankin. This is part of the Russian Red Cross.

Mrs. Oswald. I do not know that.

Mr. Rankin. It is not any part of the American Red Cross.

Mrs. Oswald. No, I do not know that.

Mr. Rankin. Their Red Cross is somewhat different than ours, I understand, because the Government has so much to do with activity there that the Red Cross is closely associated with the Government itself, while in this country, as you know, it is generally supported by the public.

Mrs. Oswald. No, I did not know that.

Now, one other thing pertaining to this. When Marina and Lee returned from Russia, and they were at my daughter-in-law's home, Robert's home, and I came in from the job in the country to see them, I said—up until this time, gentlemen, I thought Russians were peasant-looking people, like the public. And I said, "Lee, she doesn't look Russian at all. She looks American." He said, "Of course, mother, that is why I married her, is because she looks American." In front of my daughter-in-law and Robert. He bragged that she looked like an American girl. And there is all little things of that sort.

As I say, I cannot remember everything in my life, because I am going—this is way back—in a few hours time, Mr. Rankin. But there is many, many things that come up.

Mr. Rankin. How does that show that he was an agent at that time. I don't understand that.

Mrs. Oswald. I don't either. But I am telling you the expressions. He is making a point. And what I was going to make a point—Lee loved his work, and Lee loved the Marines. Lee loved the Marines, Mr. Rankin. Even coming back—he was a military man. And that has also been stated in the paper, that he had a military manner about him. I think District Attorney Wade remarked something of that order. People have noticed that.

Mr. Rankin. What made you think he loved the Marines? Was there something he did when he came back?

Mrs. Oswald. Yes. He loved the Marines because his brother was a Marine,212 for one thing. And John Edward—that is his career—14 years. My brother was in the Navy. His father was a veteran. We are a servicemen family. And I know Lee loved the Marines. I told you how he read the manual before he left. And on leaves, coming home, Lee would brag. He even said when he came home from Japan, "mother, my stay in Japan, just the trip alone would have cost about $2,000."

Now, Lee, I know also, was in the Air Force of the Marines, and he went to Biloxi, Miss., for schooling. Lee has had quite a bit of schooling. And Lee spoke Russian equivalent to 1 year when he defected to Russia. I have that on his application from the Albert Schweitzer College. And Lee spoke and wrote Russian fluently when he went to Russia. So Lee learns Russian in the Marines.

Mr. Rankin. Did he ever talk about reenlisting into the Marines after he returned?

Mrs. Oswald. Well, when Lee returned he was with me 3 days, and then, of course, he went over to visit Robert's house. So actually we didn't talk. I was trying to find a home. And I didn't think he would go. I was hoping that Lee would not go on the ship and work. I was hoping he would stay home. We were interrupted before. When he said to me about, that he wanted to work on a ship in the import and export business, I started to tell you I agreed with him. And this is how you have to do—particularly when you are a woman. A father could tell the man, "You are not going to do this." But I went along with that. And then the next day I said, "Lee, why don't you stay," and I went into that—"until I settle my claim, and I can babysit and we can get along." He said, "No, my mind is made up. If I stay, we will both be in these circumstances." So on the third day—I knew he wanted to do this, but I didn't think he was going to do it for a month or two. But on the third day he came with his suitcase in the room and he said, "Mother, I am off." So since his mind was made up, I told him goodby.

Mr. Rankin. He said nothing about reenlisting in the Marines?

Mrs. Oswald. No, the three days he was home. That was the conversation, about him going on a ship. I saw his passport. And his passport was stamped "import and export" on his passport.

Mr. Rankin. Did it say anything about Soviet Russia on it?

Mrs. Oswald. No. What I am saying is that I saw the passport with big writing "export and import." I think it was blue. I did not read the passport, because Lee was there, but I happened to see the passport, "export and import" stamped.

Whether he had another passport, I do not know. I didn't ask. I am saying this—and God knows I am telling you the truth. I am just this type person. It is because of my life.

Mr. Rankin. Did you know that he spoke Russian at that time, when he had this passport?

Mrs. Oswald. No, sir; I did not know. The only time I knew that he spoke Russian is what came out in the news. But when I really knew was Lee's application for the Albert Schweitzer College. Shall we go into that—the application?

Mr. Rankin. Yes.

Mrs. Oswald. Now, the first that I knew—no, I am wrong. It is not the first I knew. I had received a letter from Lee while in the Marines before he knew of my trouble, stating that he was accepted by the Albert Schweitzer College. And that letter was in the sea bag that I told you about, that I do not have.

Mr. Dulles. Would you give us the date of that letter?

Mrs. Oswald. The other letter would have been—let's see. Lee was told in July about my trouble. And the other letter I would say would be about May or June. This is March 22. I received this in care of Lee. And you see, sir, I have a lot of addresses, because I am now living in these homes.

Mr. Dulles. '57 or '58?

Mrs. Oswald. 1960.

Let's see now. Then I heard from the State Department in 1961.

"Due to a number of circumstances, we found ourselves forced to make a slight change in the arrival and departure dates of the third term. The first213 lecture will be held on Tuesday afternoon 16.00 o'clock, April 19, instead of taking place on the 21st with the arrival day on the 20th. It will mean that the students arrive either on the evening of Monday, the 18th, or before noon on April 19th. This change, however, makes it possible to end the term on the weekend of July 2. We hope that you will still be able to fit this change of dates into your travel plan. Should it not be possible for you to arrive on the earlier date we, of course, understand the difficulty. In the latter case, please drop us a line."

So that is how I knew that Lee—I opened his mail. I didn't know whether my son was living or dead, sir. And that is how I knew—I won't go into all this. He made a deposit. I have all of this for you.

He made a deposit. And this is my copies to them.

Now, one thing I have forgotten.

While at the State Department, the State Department told me that Lee had gone to Finland before Russia. And I did not know that.

Now, Lee had applied at a college in Finland, evidently, because on the application it states such a fact. I did not know, because the paper just said he arrived in Russia—until I went to the State Department.

So what I am trying to say—I may be forgetting a lot of important things, because I am just now remembering what the State Department told me.

I don't think I am forgetting too much.

But, after all, I am going through a whole life, and it is very hard.

This is Lee's original application, that you cannot possibly have had. This is the only application there is. So this is something new for you gentlemen. I am not going to go through it all, because you have a copy. But I am going to show you the thinking of this young man.

"Special interests: Religious, vocational, literary, sports, and hobbies. Philosophy, psychology, ideology, football, baseball, tennis, stamp collecting"—Lee had a stamp collecting book. "Nature of private reading: Jack London, Darwin, Norman Vincent Peale, scientific books, philosophy, and so on."

Representative Ford. That is an application to where?

Mrs. Oswald. This is an original application for the Albert Schweitzer School.

"Active part taken in organizations. Student body movement in school for control of juvenile delinquency, member YMCA, and AYA association."

I don't know what that is.

Mr. Rankin. Where did you get this copy?

Mrs. Oswald. I had contacted Congressman Jim Wright, that has helped me—helped me to locate Lee through the State Department. But Mr. Jim Wright was not successful.

I was successful because of my trip to Washington, as you know.

And from the trip to Washington, I went to the building where Mr. Jim Wright worked, and I went in to tell the secretary about the trip to Washington. And that I had heard from Lee.

Well, I had information here that Lee had paid a deposit. So I had written the school and asked if we were entitled to the return of the deposit, since he didn't show up. But I did not get an answer.

So Mr. Wright's secretary said that, "Mrs. Oswald, I will write and see what we can do."

So she wrote, and then they sent the application and everything back to Jim Wright's office. And that is how I got the application.

Mr. Doyle. They may be interested in knowing where the college is.

Mrs. Oswald. It is in Switzerland. Albert Schweitzer College, Chur Walden, Graubuenen, Switzerland. "Application Form. High School. Completed high school by correspondence."

I have that. His original correspondence in the service—completed high school.

Mr. Rankin. Is that part of his Marine work—he finished high school that way?

Mrs. Oswald. Yes, sir.

"January '58, Passing 65 on scale of 100 B plus. College: None."

And then I read his books.

Now, we go down to here.

214 "Vocational Interests if decided upon: To be a short story writer on contemporary American life."

Now, "General statement regarding reasons for wishing to attend the Albert Schweitzer College: In order to acquire a fuller understanding of that subject which interests me most, philosophy, to meet with Europeans who can broaden my scope of understanding, to receive formal education by institutes of high standing and character, to broaden my knowledge of German, and to live in a healthy climate and good moral atmosphere."

This is very good thinking, gentlemen. We are getting a picture now of the boy which has been not told in the paper.

I have read this one particular statement at three press conferences. The first press conference was about 80 members there, from foreign lands and everything. Nothing was printed. Then I had a second press conference with 16 men and I said, "Now, I am tired of the things that are being said about my family, myself, and Lee. We are not perfect. But I know there is some good things. And I have read a particular statement that has not been printed. Let's see if one of you has the courage to print it."

There was 16 there. That did not come out. I had a third conference, and I said the same thing and quoted this. That was not made public in the paper.

I hold a lot of these answers, gentlemen, as you know by now.

Mr. Rankin. You notice the next paragraph, about his plans?

Mrs. Oswald. Yes, "Plans to be pursued after the period at Albert Schweitzer College: To attend the short summer course of the University of Turku, Turku, Finland."

Now, I have a brochure. This I cannot understand—from this college, dated 1960. I have this for you, Mr. Rankin—dated 1960.

Lee is in Russia.

And the men in the State Department told me he went to Finland before Russia. But this is dated 1960. I have it for you.

But I don't understand that.

"Then to return to America and pursue my chosen vocation."

Mr. Rankin. I want to ask you about that. Do you think he meant this at the time?

Mrs. Oswald. I do not know. I am saying—and I am going to stick to my story—that Lee is an agent, then a lot of this is a lot of baloney. I cannot make it any stronger. I don't know, sir. The boy is gone, and I didn't hear from his own lips.

Mr. Rankin. You think that he decided to defect after this application, then?

Mrs. Oswald. I do not know, sir, because I have not had this from the boy. I am speculating. But I have a lot of documents to sustain my speculation.

Mr. Rankin. Now, this, you cannot tell one way or another about whether he is an agent by this.

Mrs. Oswald. I cannot tell by anything he is an agent, if you want proof. I am becoming a little discouraged about this, because I keep telling you—I did not have proof, sir. But I am giving you documents leading to it.

Mr. Rankin. All I am trying to find out is what you have. You are giving us that. I am also trying to find out whatever proof you have about these various things that we can rely on.

Mrs. Oswald. Well, I am going to state once and for all, because it upsets me very much emotionally. And I have stated before, I do not have proof, sir. I do not have proof of an agent. I do not have proof my son is innocent. I do not have proof.

Mr. Rankin. You don't have any proof of a conspiracy?

Mrs. Oswald. Of anything. It is just as I feel, like the Dallas police do not have proof my son shot President Kennedy. If they have anything, it is circumstantial evidence. I have as much circumstantial evidence here that Lee was an agent as the Dallas police have that he shot President Kennedy.

"Familiarity with foreign languages, if any. Russian equal in fluency to about 1 year's education or schooling. I also speak a very little German. General condition of health: Good. Have you ever had any serious illness or nervous disturbances: No."

Mr. Rankin. Is that correct?

215 Mrs. Oswald. That is correct.

I want to get to that psychiatric. There will be a story there.

"Does such a condition still exist: No."

I don't understand this—do you?

"General condition of health: Good. Have you had a serious illness or nervous disturbance, no. If so, explain."

Then he has a dash.

"Are you at present receiving medical or psychiatric care? No."

And then he gives as references—you have this, so I won't go into it.

A chaplain—would you like me to go into all these names for the record?

Mr. Rankin. No, we can offer this.

Did you know any of those people that he showed as references?

Mrs. Oswald. No, sir. I do not. And that is dated the 3d, 4th, '59. And this is another application form from the Albert Schweitzer College.

"I hereby apply to attend the student course from April 12, 1960 to June 27, 1960. Surname: Oswald. Christian name: Lee Harvey. Mr. Age, 20. Mother tongue: English. Other language you know: Russian. Equal in fluency to 1 year of schooling. Occupation: Student. Nationality: American. Exact address: MCAF, MACS-9, Santa Ana, California, USA. Remarks: Please inform me of the amount of the deposit if required so I can forward it and confirm my reservation and show my sincerity of purpose. Thank you. Lee Harvey Oswald."

Well, he did, and I have this here, make a deposit of $25, which the school informed me that they would not be able to refund, because it would take care of any incidentals that had occurred for him not appearing.

Gentlemen, it is 10 minutes to five, I believe I had a full day. I worked last night on the papers. I came early to have copies made.

This was a complete story, I believe, and I have at least three other complete stories. And I have a story of my life that I believe from newspaper accounts that you will be very surprised also to know the type person I am. But according to the newspaper—of course, really nothing bad has been said about me, otherwise than one particular instance. That I can prove and have witnesses that it is not the case.

The Chairman. Mrs. Oswald, you said you had three more stories. Just name them. Name what stories they are, so we will know what they are.

Mrs. Oswald. Yes, sir.

It would be Lee's life, sir, from early childhood, and the psychiatric treatment in New York, that I want to tell you about.

The Chairman. Up to 16?

Mrs. Oswald. Yes, sir, because we have finished that, because we went into that.

And then my life, from early childhood, which you have asked, Mr. Rankin, in a letter.

The third was Lee as an agent, which I have gone into.

The Chairman. Lee what?

Mrs. Oswald. Lee being an agent.
But I have really gone into that.
The Chairman. So really, there are only two more?
Mrs. Oswald. Yes, sir, my life and Lee's life.
Now, I would like you to have this picture—if you have not seen it. And I will not comment on it. I want you to study it thoroughly, use a magnifying glass, if possible, and if you care to, we will discuss it.
Now, this is out of the Post Magazine.
There is another picture that I would like the Commission to get which, is in the Memorial Issue of President Kennedy—I think it is the Post. I will get that information for you.
Mr. Doyle. Would you like to advise the Commission generally what you believe they will find out from this?
Mrs. Oswald. I would rather not comment on that at this particular moment. I submit it to them for them to look over all the people, to study it. I have two. You may have that one for the record.
216 Mr. Dulles. What does this purport to be of?
Mrs. Oswald. That is a picture of the book depository the day of the assassination of President Kennedy. And there are people in the picture.
The Chairman. Well, is there anything you want us to see in the picture?
Mrs. Oswald. Well, I would rather you see it yourself. I see what I see.
The Chairman. What do you see?
Mrs. Oswald. Well, all right.
I see Marina and the child—the girl and the baby, it could be Marina.
The Chairman. Will you show us, please?
Mrs. Oswald. And, again, I am saying—I cannot be sure this is the picture. But this right here. This girl with this baby could possibly be Marina and June.
Mr. Rankin. And that is the girl——
Mrs. Oswald. This girl holding the baby.
Mr. Rankin. Right next to the door?
Mrs. Oswald. Yes, sir, right next to the door. In back of her is the hat of a man. I have started this. I will continue.
(The document referred to was marked Commission Exhibit No. 203, for identification.)
Mr. Rankin. Mr. Chairman, may I offer this?
The Chairman. Yes.
Mr. Rankin. I offer in evidence Exhibit 203.
And that is the photograph that you were just referring to, Mrs. Oswald?
Mrs. Oswald. Yes, sir, that is the photograph the day of the assassination.
Mr. Rankin. And you pointed out the girl on the left column——
Mrs. Oswald. Of the entrance to the book depository, holding a child.
(The document heretofore marked for identification as Commission Exhibit No. 203 was received in evidence.)
Mr. Dulles. Do we know the time this was taken?
Mr. Rankin. Can you tell about the time this was taken?
Mrs. Oswald. Yes. This, I understand, was when President Kennedy was shot. He is supposed to be holding his throat here. And this is the car. This is right after he passed the book depository, when he is supposed to have been shot.
The Chairman. Very well. We will adjourn until tomorrow at 10 o'clock.
(Whereupon, at 4:55 p.m., the President's Commission recessed.)

Wednesday, February 12, 1964

TESTIMONY OF MRS. MARGUERITE OSWALD RESUMED

The President's Commission met at 10 a.m. on February 12, 1964, at 200 Maryland Avenue NE., Washington, D.C.

Present were Chief Justice Earl Warren, Chairman; Representative Hale Boggs and Representative Gerald R. Ford, members.

Also present were J. Lee Rankin, general counsel; Wesley J. Liebeler, assistant counsel; and John F. Doyle, attorney for Mrs. Marguerite Oswald.

The Chairman. The Commission will be in order.

We will proceed to the hearing.

The Chairman. Mrs. Oswald, did you have anything you wanted to say to us this morning before we start the questioning?

Mrs. Oswald. Yes, I meant to yesterday morning. I have two or three things that are worrying me.

Mr. Rankin, on Monday, when I testified that I had not been questioned officially, you told me that I had. And if I remember correctly, sir, you said that there was 28 pages of testimony, or was it 8 pages?

Mr. Rankin. Twenty-eight, I think.

217 Mrs. Oswald. Well, Mr. Doyle, as my attorney—I am very concerned about that, because I want to know—if it is my testimony—because the little while—the testimony that I gave to the FBI when I entered the courthouse was approximately about 10 minutes. They immediately left to investigate. They did not talk to me again, sir.

And then the only other testimony that I gave on tape was the starting of Lee's defection at the Six Flags Inn, which I would say ran approximately 10 or 15 minutes. And that is the only time I have testified.

Now, if you have all this other testimony from me, I don't think it is fair, because I should know what I am supposed to have said. I need to know what I am supposed to have said.

The Chairman. Mrs. Oswald, whatever we have that we are told you have said, you and your attorney are entitled to see, and I will see that you can. We won't delay the proceeding this morning. But you may see it before you leave the building.

Mrs. Oswald. Yes—it is very important to know that.

Thank you, Justice Warren.

The Chairman. All right.

Mr. Rankin. Mr. Chairman, on that point, will it be satisfactory if we furnish a clean photostatic copy to Mr. Doyle?

The Chairman. Yes, that will be satisfactory. You may do that, yes.

Mrs. Oswald. I certainly need to know what I am supposed to have said.

There is an FBI agent by the name of Mr. John Fain. I will ask you, Mr. Rankin, if you have his address, or do you know about Mr. John Fain?

Mr. Rankin. I know of Mr. John Fain as one of the agents that had some interviews with your son.

Mrs. Oswald. Now, Mr. John Fain is the agent that I called upon myself after Lee's defection. I read where the Secret Service were investigating the family background, and I mistook it for the FBI. So I called the FBI and he came to my home. And he is the agent who recommended me to talk to Jim Wright and Sam Rayburn as a friend, and to write the letters.

Now, the one point I am going to bring out is this. When Lee returned from Russia and was at Robert's home, Mr. Fain—in the meantime he had come over to Robert and talked to him several times, and to me, supposedly as a friend—he said he was not on the case. I do not know this. But he came to Robert's home and said to Lee—my daughter-in-law is a witness there—"Lee, I am not on the case, but I would like you voluntarily to come to the office at your convenience and tell me your story, because I am interested in your case. Your mother was the one who contacted me. And I have been to see Robert. And I am quite interested in a young boy going to Russia. And you must have a story."

So Lee voluntarily went with Mr. Fain to the FBI office.

Then when Lee returned, his remark was "Well, he didn't believe me. He wanted me to take a lie detector test, which I refused."

Now, Mr. John Fain may have the story we are looking for, you see—because Lee went and gave the story.

And I want to make sure you know where he is now.

I have information from Senator Mike Monroney that in March—I am ahead of my story.

The FBI agents now in Fort Worth have told me they do not know Mr. John Fain. I said I happen to know that is his name.

"Well, Mrs. Oswald, I worked in this office 9 years, and there has never been such a person as Mr. John Fain."

So I have investigated. And Senator Mike Monroney gave this information. He did work in the Fort Worth office from March 1949 to October 1962, and then he retired in January 15, 1963. He is not a man to retire as far as age, as far as I am concerned. I don't think Mr. John Fain is that old.

The Chairman. We will check that out.

Mrs. Oswald. I have his last address in Houston, if you don't have it.

All right. Fine.

Now, one thing about Lee being an agent I read.

The neighbors that were interviewed in Fort Worth, Tex., by the FBI—this is from newspaper accounts—said that Lee always walked a few feet in218 front of his wife when they went walking, and they wondered about that, because it was very strange that he should walk ahead. I am speculating maybe, but maybe there is a reason that Lee would walk ahead to protect his wife.

That is my reasoning—as an agent.

The letter that is missing—and Mr. Doyle can verify this—the first letter to Lee is missing, that Lee wrote to me, rather, from Russia. And this letter stated—and it seemed to me, Mr. Rankin, I have seen it in one of the magazines—as I have stated I have sold several of Lee's letters. And maybe in the rush the letter got lost or stolen, I don't know.

But his first letter, he told me not to send him any money.

"I repeat, do not send any money as it is not necessary for you to pay me back. You could send reading matter. I am lonesome to read. Also, send a can of Rise Shaving Cream, a Gillette Razor," and there was a book he wanted to read, I believe it was 1984.

Mr. Rankin. What date was this you sent that?

Mrs. Oswald. This is a letter Lee sent to me that is missing—the first letter that Lee sent to me. And why I sent the money—because I had used his income tax return, which was $33, because Lee was lost—and I was destitute, and I knew Lee would never prosecute his mother for using his money, because Lee would help me.

Mr. Rankin. You mean that was a refund.

Mrs. Oswald. A refund. And I got the refund and used it, sir. And I also used Lee's first check that came from the Marines. And I had no way of knowing where Lee was. And I used it. And so I offered to pay Lee back. And this letter has been printed. I have seen it. But I do not have it. So that is very important.

Mr. Doyle. As you had mentioned, you and I went through the papers that you had brought with you from your home in Texas to Washington, and we did not find such a letter among those papers.

Mrs. Oswald. That is right. I have those letters laminated, and I didn't give a list, and if it was taken I don't know what became of the letter.

Mr. Rankin. Mr. Liebeler said he had seen references to the letter.

Mrs. Oswald. References. And I am sure it was probably one of the letters I had sold, as I told you.

Yes, sir, you are correct there.

Now, there is another thing that we have skipped.

While in Dallas 2 weeks ago I had a press conference, and I called Jaggars-Chiles-Stovall Inc., 522 Browder, in Dallas.

Now, this is a printing shop, where Lee worked.

Now, this is another thing.

Mr. Rankin. That was the photoengraving place that you talked about, wasn't it, in your testimony?

Mrs. Oswald. Photoengraving place. I talked to Mr. Stovall. Now, Lee was employed there, he informs me, from October 12th to April 6th, and I asked him about the young couple coming to the house, if he was the father of the girl, or if he knew of a couple who had a Russian—the girl had a Russian father, the grandfather, as I testified.

Mr. Rankin. What did he say about that?

Mrs. Oswald. No, sir, he said, no. And he didn't know about that. He said—this is the part—that Lee had worked at a place prior to his place. That is not so, and I can prove it. I was on an OB case for Mrs. Rosenthal. We will have to get a 1962 calendar. October 12th, or thereabouts, is when I was released from this OB case. And this was the Sunday that I asked to get off an hour or two, and went to Lee's house, and saw this couple.

Mr. Rankin. October 12th was a Friday.

Mrs. Oswald. Was a Friday. All right.

Now, so, let's see where I am.

This woman would not give me the information, of her last check to me. I tried and tried, and told her how important it was. It was a Friday. So then it would have to be, then, Mr. Rankin, the week before—the Sunday of the week before then.

219 Mr. Rankin. That would be October 7, 1962.

Mrs. Oswald. I am still going to try to investigate this thoroughly, because it is very important.

He claimed that Lee worked another place first.

Now, do you know if Lee——

The Chairman. Let's don't—we will go into those things.

Mrs. Oswald. But if you don't know, Chief Justice Warren, how will you go into it?

The Chairman. Please don't turn this into examining the Commission. We will go into those things very thoroughly.

Just go ahead with your story.

Mrs. Oswald. Well, this is a lie, and I want to know about this lie.

The Chairman. All right, you have told us.

Mrs. Oswald. I have not finished, sir.

The Chairman. Well, you may go ahead and tell what you want. But don't question the Commission. That is the only thing I am asking you.

Mrs. Oswald. Well, I don't know about questioning.

Mr. Doyle. I think if you compose yourself, if you would, and just go ahead and give the Commission all the information you have.

Mrs. Oswald.. Well, that is what I think I am doing. If I am doing it a wrong way, you will have to understand. I am a layman. I am the mother of this accused boy. I understand that is what the Commission is for, to get all information possible to come to a conclusion.

And if I have found out that my date of employment is the date that Lee was employed in Dallas, and this man said he worked some place before, I think that is very important information.

The Chairman. We will check on that.

Go right ahead with your own story.

Mrs. Oswald. Maybe I should apologize for taking up so much of the Commission's time, sir.

Mr. Doyle. Go right ahead with the business, and when you give the Commission the facts, then the Commission will take on from there in their own judgment.

Mr. Rankin.. Mr. Doyle, while she is taking a moment, I will hand you a photostatic copy of this tape recording of an interview with Mrs. Marguerite Oswald—it purports to be that—recorded on November 25, 1963, an interview by J. M. Howard.

Mr. Doyle.. Thank you.

Mrs. Oswald. Now, one thing we have not covered was Lee's discharge.

The Chairman. May I interrupt just a minute?

Is that the document we were talking about just a little while ago, a copy of which was to be given to Mrs. Oswald?

Mr. Rankin. That is right, that is the one requested.

The Chairman. And the one you were speaking of——

Mr. Rankin. As a 28-page document.

The Chairman. Yes—all right.

Now, you may continue, Mrs. Oswald.

Mrs. Oswald. Thank you very much.

This is Lee's questionable, dishonorable discharge, where I come in.

The first envelope was addressed to Lee Harvey Oswald, airmail. And Lee was in Russia, as we know. We have the proof. And you have all of the copies of this, I am sure.

The Chairman. Yes.

Mrs. Oswald. And this you do not have. You have a copy now, but you do not have the story, Mr. Rankin.

It states that the discharge by reason of unfitness, recommendation for discharge, reason of unfitness.

Well. I wrote to the U.S. Marine Corps—now, where is the copy of my letter?

I talked to a commandant at the Marine Corps and read this to him. And he advised me how to write to the Marine Corps, the official of the Marine Corps. And that is a copy of the letter.

I asked—well, he will get me the letter, I am sure.

220 So then I will read the answer to my letter.

Is that satisfactory?

Mr. Rankin. Yes. Mr. Liebeler is going to get the copy that he has.

Now, can you tell the Commission when you first learned about this matter?

Mrs. Oswald. It would be on the envelope, sir. The envelope is mailed, Glenview, April 29, Illinois. But, as you see, it had gone to a lot of addresses, because I had moved around quite a bit. So we would have to say I got it some time later than the original.

Mr. Rankin. Now, does this involve the question of the undesirable discharge?

Mrs. Oswald. Yes, sir; it does.

Mr. Rankin. And did you ever write to Secretary Connally about that, later Governor Connally?

Mrs. Oswald. No, sir, I never did write to him.

Mr. Rankin. All right. Will you tell us what happened?

Mrs. Oswald. I wrote a letter, and was told how to write the letter.

And this is the answer to the letter.

I won't read it all, because you have a copy. But I have a few points to make here.

Mr. Rankin. Do you recall who told you that—the name of the man?

Mrs. Oswald. It was the Marine Base in Fort Worth, Tex., one of the captains there.

Mr. Rankin. Thank you.

Mrs. Oswald. Told me who to write to.

Mr. Rankin. You don't remember the name?

Mrs. Oswald. No, sir; I do not.

Mr. Rankin. All right.

Mrs. Oswald. The letter to Commandant, Marine Air Reserve, 50 JTMGR, 26 April 1962, "to your son was prompted by his request for Soviet citizenship. An investigation concerning this matter has been conducted by military authorities and the case will be placed before a board of officers which will recommend that your son be retained in or separated from the U.S. Marine Corps Reserve. Your son, of course, has the right to appear in person or to present any facts or evidence which would assist the board in reaching its decision. The letter of 26 April 1960 informed him of his rights. In view of the fact that he has not been informed—that he has not informed this headquarters of his current address, and that he has left the United States without permission, it is considered that a letter sent to the last address on file at this headquarters is sufficient notification. A letter will be sent by certified mail informing your son of a convening date of the board. Should you be aware of any facts or information which would assist the board in evaluating your son's case, it is suggested that you forward them to this headquarters. It is regretted that action of this nature must be taken in your son's case. M. G. Letscher, First Lieutenant, United States Marine Corps, Administrative Office, Aviation Class 3, Reserve Section."

Now, my letter is important.

Now, this was addressed to me. This is what I want the Commission to know. This was addressed to Lee, the original. Then I wrote in behalf of my son, and this was addressed to me.

Then I received a letter addressed to Mr. Lee Harvey Oswald.

By now, I am corresponding with these people, and I ask for—I need my letter. And I ask for the reason for the dishonorable discharge, and said that I would act in behalf of my son, because I have pertinent information to that fact.

Mr. Rankin. Mrs. Oswald, I will ask the reporter to mark this as the next number.

(The document referred to was marked Commission Exhibit No. 204, for identification.)

Mr. Rankin. This is correspondence with regard to the dishonorable discharge.

Mrs. Oswald, will you look at a photostatic copy of that correspondence?

Mrs. Oswald. Yes, that is the letter I just read. That is the back of the envelope. And this letter.

Mr. Rankin. That is a very poor copy.

Mrs. Oswald. Is this the letter we taped?

Mr. Liebeler. I don't believe so, no.

221 Mrs. Oswald. I know we taped one, because we could not copy it.

Mr. Rankin. Can you read it?

Mrs. Oswald. Yes. "I desire to inform"——

Mr. Rankin. That is your letter of April 10, 1960?

Mrs. Oswald. Yes.

Mr. Rankin. And who did you send it to?

Mr. Liebeler. May I say this, Mr. Rankin: We did tape that, and I do have a transcription of it here.

Mrs. Oswald. "I ask for a stay of action, and I will be willing to act in his behalf."

Mr. Rankin. Mrs. Oswald. I will hand you what I am asking the reporter to mark as Exhibit 205.

I ask you if Exhibit 205 is a correct transcription of your letter.

MRS. Oswald. Yes.

(The document referred to was marked Commission Exhibit No. 205, for identification.)

Mrs. Oswald. "I am writing you on behalf of my son. He is out of the country at present, and since I have no contact with him I wish to request a stay of action concerning his discharge. Also, I desire to be informed of the charges against him.

Please state reasons for such discharge. After hearing from you, I will be willing to act in his behalf."

So then comes a registered return receipt, addressed only to Mr. Lee Harvey Oswald.

Mr. Rankin. Now, will you examine the rest of Exhibit 204 and state whether that is the rest of the correspondence in regard to the matter that you know about?

Mrs. Oswald. This is addressed to me—this envelope is addressed to me, that is right, sir.

Mr. Rankin. And those photostatic copies in Exhibit 204 are all copies of your papers that you furnished to us, so we could make them, is that right?

Mrs. Oswald. Yes, sir, that is correct.

Mr. Rankin. I offer in evidence Exhibits 204 and 205.

The Chairman. They may be admitted, with those numbers.

(The documents heretofore marked for identification as Commission Exhibits Nos. 204 and 205 were received in evidence.)

Mrs. Oswald. I believe, Chief Justice Warren, I am giving information that this Commission did not have before. I do not think they had this return addressee, which is important, because after corresponding with me, as Mrs. Marguerite Oswald, they sent the dishonorable discharge in Lee's name, addressee only, when they knew he was out of the country.

I would like to know why.

That is another reason why I think that Lee was probably an agent.

Mr. Rankin. What do you mean by that, Mrs. Oswald? Could you explain that a little more?

Mrs. Oswald. Yes. I do not think they wanted me to have the dishonorable discharge.

Again, they wanted me to be upset and tell people about it, but not have the proof of the dishonorable discharge.

Mr. Rankin. Don't you think it is possible that they felt he was the one involved, and, therefore, they had to get the word directly to him for legal reasons?

Mrs. Oswald. No, sir, because, legally—I am glad you brought up the point, Mr. Rankin.

Your copies state that anyone can act in your behalf. And I wrote, as I read the copy, that I would be willing to act in my son's behalf, and I was making arrangements to get money and go there and act in his behalf because I had pertinent information. And they ignored my letter and sent this—yes, sir.

Mr. Rankin. They may have felt you had not been given authority to act.

Mrs. Oswald. Well, what they may feel and what they should do—I am saying I am an American citizen, and I have some rights. And when I want to act in behalf of my son, we don't know whether he is living or dead, then I should act in behalf, I should not get a return.

222 I am glad you are bringing these points up. My rights have been invaded and my son's.

I make that statement for the record.

Now, we shall go to Lee's childhood.

The Chairman. Yes.

Mrs. Oswald. Now, Chief Justice Warren, I have pictures of my son that Mr. Jenner would like this Commission to have, because it shows Lee at age 15 and 16, and myself, which was supposed to be a life of psychiatric treatment. And I am more than happy—I volunteered to help my country in every way possible—to let the Commission have everything that I have. But you must understand that these are very valuable pictures, sir. I am having people wanting rights to a book, and these pictures are very, very valuable to me. And I would not want any of these pictures lost. Financially they are valuable, and to my story, sir. And they are the only pictures in existence.

I have sold a few pictures in order to live.

But the way I have done it—the photographer had this picture in particular—have come to my home and copied the pictures and gave it to me back in my hand. I cannot afford to have any of these pictures lost, sir. It is my story that some day I hope to write.

So I was told that if I continue with the life history of Lee as a child and show the pictures, then they would have to be admitted for the record.

Am I correct, sir?

The Chairman. That is our way of proceeding, yes.

Mrs. Oswald. So now when I show the pictures, will you personally give me assurance that these pictures will in no way be used?

The Chairman. No, I cannot do that. The Commission cannot do it. If you have something that you consider your personal property, that you do not want to give to the Commission, you may withhold it.

Mrs. Oswald. I did not say, sir, I did not want to give it to the Commission.

The Chairman. Just a minute. I do not believe they bear directly on the matter we are investigating. They might be helpful. They might not be helpful. But you may have the choice of determining whether you want to introduce them or not.

But if you do introduce them, the Commission cannot put any limitation upon the use that it might make of them.

Now, I don't mean by that that we are going to necessarily distribute them or anything of that kind. But the Commission cannot limit itself in the reception of its evidence. It must have the power to do with it whatever is necessary to develop the facts.

Mrs. Oswald. Well, I give you that power. And I voluntarily would like for you to have everything I have, including pictures. But I just wanted assurance that these pictures would not be exploited in any way. For some reason or other—I am not putting it into words—but these are my personal pictures. And I want the Commission to have them. And it is pertinent to the story, I understand, Mr. Doyle, is that correct—because it shows Lee smiling, and his life and my life in New Orleans, which, I understand that the Commission is very interested in.

Am I not correct, Mr. Doyle?

Mr. Doyle. Mrs. Oswald, as the situation has developed here, the introduction of the pictures into evidence, of course, must necessarily involve their physical copying, and the retention of the copies in the file. The Commission itself has stated that it can give you no assurance whatsoever concerning the use of these papers.

I would, myself, be of the view that the pictures introduced into the record here would be certainly used for the purposes of the investigation and the purposes of the Commission as established by the Executive order.

But they can give you no blanket—or have not chosen to give you any blanket assurance of the use of the pictures, and have given you completely the choice that if you have any concern about it whatsoever, that you retain the pictures yourself.

The choice they have given you is if you wish to have—to present the pictures to the Commission in the course of your testimony, they will be glad to receive223 them, they will—there will be copies made of them, the originals, of course, will remain in your custody. Their purposes will be—their use will be the uses of the Commission. But the Commission gives you no assurance whatsoever of the use, and gives you the complete choice of either submitting them or not under those circumstances.

Mrs. Oswald. Well, being a layman, I understand, I think, what you are telling me, in a way. But, on the other hand, being a layman, I feel actually I have no choice.

You have to understand I am not an attorney.

Mr. Doyle. But you do have a choice, because you are not here under subpena. Your materials have not been subpenaed. The Commission has advised you openly here that you may submit them or not as you see fit to do. So there is no force, no legal force at all. This is absolutely up to you.

The only thing that has been expressed to you is that they can give you no assurance or guarantee as to what use the Commission will make of them, that they will make what use they believe in their judgment is required by the Executive order and the purposes of their investigation.

Mrs. Oswald. I understand. And that is why I wanted the Commission to have all pictures that I have.

Now, may I request something? I don't think it is presumptuous of me. Maybe it is. Could I sign for my rights for these pictures, and then let you have the pictures? I am afraid that they may get lost.

The Chairman. I think, Mrs. Oswald, if you have any doubt us to whether a misuse will be made of your papers, or if they are as valuable, moneywise, to you as you think they are, then I would suggest to you that you retain them yourself. We, of course, would be interested to see them, and they might be helpful—I don't know, because I don't know what you have there, or what context the pictures will be in.

But as your lawyer has told you, you are not under subpena here, you appeared voluntarily because you requested to testify before us. Those documents are not under subpena. They belong to you. They are in your possession. I have not seen them. You are at liberty to use them in your testimony or not, as you please.

But if you do, the Commission cannot put any limitations on the use that it will make of them.

Mrs. Oswald. Even though you have stated, Chief Justice Warren, just now, that you do not know if they are valuable to the Commission—and yet I have information from Mr. Jenner that they are valuable to the Commission, because they pertain to Lee's life at age 13 to age 16.

The Chairman. Yes, I say they might be. I don't know. I have never seen them.

But the choice is with you, Mrs. Oswald. You may do just as you please. If you wish to testify concerning them, and put them in the hands of the Commission, you may do so.

But the Commission cannot limit itself in the use of its testimony.

Mrs. Oswald. I want the Commission to have this.

Moneywise, it is more important for the Commission to know this boy's life and my life—but also I need to protect myself financially, because I am a widow, and do not have the money. And this will mean—these are valuable pictures.

I am not questioning the integrity of this Commission or the loyalty. What I am questioning is that possibly they may get lost or someone may somehow or other get ahold of these pictures and exploit them, and get money for them, which has happened to some other pictures already, sir, and then——

The Chairman. Not those that you have given to the Commission?

Mrs. Oswald. No, sir—but with another——

The Chairman. Well, I think, Mrs. Oswald, it would serve no purpose for us to debate the matter. I have tried to tell you very frankly, and your lawyer has told you very frankly and correctly, that you have a free choice224 to do just as you please. And we will abide by that choice that you may make.

Mrs. Oswald. May I confer with my lawyer for about 10 minutes?

The Chairman. Yes. We will take a recess, and you may talk to him.

(Brief recess.)

The Chairman. Come to order, please.

Mrs. Oswald. Last night, Mr. Rankin, I read Lee working at one place after Tujaque. I do not know the name, sir. I think he worked there just a few days. He had the keys to the office. And, as I returned home from work one day, another young man was at the apartment, the door of the apartment, and said that Lee was discharged, and that Lee had the keys to the office, and just then Lee walked up and gave this young man the keys.

Now, I do not know the name of the place. And I believe he just worked there, sir, a few days.

I read that afterwards.

If you will refresh me, I will give you any information I have. But it is hard for me to think of everything.

I believe we have cleared up the business today that we have missed.

I have decided—and maybe I am wrong, because to me money is only good as to its use. However, there have been so many things since the assassination that has not been in my favor, I believe that I am going to keep my personal pictures.

The Chairman. You may do so.

Mrs. Oswald. If at any time in the future that you would like to have these pictures, I will be more than happy to have copies made and give them to the Commission.

There is another matter, Mr. Rankin, that is very important, that you asked me—Governor Connally's letter.

Mr. Rankin. Yes.

Mrs. Oswald. I had read this at the press conference. A letter from Lee Harvey Oswald to John Connally, Secretary of the Navy. This is just written from the newspaper article.

"I have been in the Soviet Union with the full sanction of the U.S. Embassy in Moscow." He asked the Navy Department to take the necessary steps to repair the damage to me and my family. "I shall employ all means to right the gross mistakes or injustices to a bona fide U.S. citizen, an ex-serviceman."

Now, I do not consider this a threat, because I, myself, if I had a dishonorable discharge, and I was a good marine for 3 years, and I felt like it hurt my mother and my children, and my wife, I would make such a statement, because I am a very definite person, as you know by now. I have been testifying for 3 days. And my son is of the same nature. He loved the Marines, and as far as he was concerned, he served his country 3 years. And it was a stigma to me and his children, and he wanted to right the wrong.

So I do not consider this a threat.

He went to Austin. There was an article in the paper—trying to get this rectified, and the young lady gave a very nice report of Lee, said he was very polite.

This is not a threat.

This is just how Lee was tried immediately in a few hours time, newspaper talk, and so on and so forth.

I would state this emphatically more maybe than Lee did, if I had a dishonorable discharge, sir.

Mr. Rankin. Did you ever hear your son say anything against Governor Connally?

Mrs. Oswald. No, sir.

But here is what I have written down. The day at Robert's house, when I came in from the country, I, myself, gave Lee the copy—we had many copies—you showed me the copy—I gave him the copy and told him—I had written him and told him about the dishonorable discharge, but I did not send any papers, because I didn't want the Russians to know.

But when I came, I had a scrapbook, and I gave him a copy, Mr. Rankin, of225 the reason for dishonorable discharge. He says "Don't worry about it, mother. I can fix that. It is no problem."

So then the boy tried to fix it. And this is not a threat. My son is of this disposition, and he felt like he was a good marine. That I know. I would do the same. And I will read it now to Governor Connally: "I shall employ all means to right the gross mistake done to my family and my now dead son."

I expect to write to anybody officially to rectify this mistake.

I have shown this publicly at press conferences, and so I will employ all means to rectify this mistake—the mother of Lee Harvey Oswald. I intended to do that. That is my life's work.

I have the name of the man I talked to.

Chief Justice Warren—I will start from Lee as baby, before I get to this.

Lee was born October 18, 1939, in New Orleans, La. His mother, Marguerite Claverie Oswald, his father's name was Robert Edward Lee, he was named after General Lee. The family's name is Harvey—his grandmother's name was Harvey. And so he was named Lee Harvey Oswald.

Lee was born 2 months after the death of his father, who died from a heart attack, coronary thrombosis.

Lee was a very happy baby.

I stayed home with the children as long as I could, because I believe that a mother should be home with her children.

I don't want to get into my story, though.

Lee had a normal life as far as I, his mother, is concerned. He had a bicycle, he had everything that other children had.

Lee has wisdom without education. From a very small child—I have said this before, sir, and I have publicly stated this in 1959—Lee seemed to know the answers to things without schooling. That type child, in a way, is bored with schooling, because he is a little advanced.

Lee used to climb on top of the roof with binoculars, looking at the stars. He was reading astrology. Lee knew about any and every animal there was. He studied animals. All of their feeding habits, sleeping habits. He could converse—and that is why he was at the Bronx Zoo when he was picked up for truancy—he loved animals.

Lee played Monopoly. Lee played chess. Lee had a stamp collection, and even wrote to other young men and exchanged stamps, sir.

And Lee read history books, books too deep for a child his age. At age 9 he was always instructed not to contact me at work unless it was an emergency, because my work came first—he called me at work and said, "Mother, Queen Elizabeth's baby has been born."

He broke the rule to let me know that Queen Elizabeth's baby had been born. Nine years old. That was important to him. He liked things of that sort.

He loved comics, read comic books. He loved television programs. But most of all he loved the news on radio and television. If he was in the midst of a story, a film—he would turn it off for news. That was important.

And I have stated in 1959, which is in print, that Lee loved maps. Lee would study maps, sir. And he could tell you the distance from here and there. And when he was home on leave, I was amazed. Something was said about an airplane trip. Immediately he knew how many miles in the air that that plane took.

Lee read very, very important things. And any and everything he could do.

Yet he played Monopoly, played baseball.

He belonged to the "Y." He used to go swimming. He would come by work with his head wet, and I would say, "Hurry home, honey, you are going to catch cold."

And I considered that, sir, a very normal life.

I am probably forgetting some things.

So then Robert joined the Marines in 1956—am I correct—that Robert joined the Marines?

No, Robert joined the Marines in 1952. We are now in Fort Worth, Tex., until 1952.

So then I decided, since I was working, I did not want Lee to be alone. Up until this time, sir, he had a brother. So I sold my home at 7400 Ewing226 Street, and went to New York City, not as a venture, but because my older son, John Edward Pic, lived in New York, and had lived in New York for years. He was in the Coast Guard, as a military man. He has now been in the service 14 years, and at that time it would have been approximately 8 or 9 years—I may be off because that is approximately. So he was stationed in New York. So I had no problem of selling my home and going there, thinking that John Edward would leave New York.

But the main thing was to be where I had family. And I moved to New York for that reason.

Mr. Rankin. About what date was that?

Mrs. Oswald. This was exactly August 1952, because I wanted to get there in time for Lee's schooling. And if I am not mistaken, Robert joined the Marines in July of 1952. And that was my reason for going.

I immediately enrolled Lee in a Lutheran school, because Lee was not confirmed—he was baptized in the Lutheran faith, but because of moving around—I had married Mr. Ekdahl in this period and so on, Lee was not confirmed.

I enrolled him in the Lutheran school which took him approximately an hour or longer by subway to get there. It was quite a distance. That is when we first arrived in New York.

I believe that Lee was in that school a very short time, 2 or 3 weeks, because at this time I was living in my daughter-in-law's home and son. And we were not welcome, sir. We were welcome for a few days. But then we were to get a place of our own—because her mother lived with her, and her mother had left to go visit a sister. So Lee and I could come to visit. But we were not going to live with John and his wife.

So we just stayed there a short time.

Mr. Rankin. Was there any time that you recall that there was a threat of Lee Oswald against Mrs. Pic with a knife or anything like that?

Do you remember that?

Mrs. Oswald. Yes, I do. I am glad you said that.

My daughter-in-law was very upset. The very first time we went there—I stated before, and I am glad I said that—that we were not welcome. And immediately it was asked what did we plan to do, as soon as we put our foot in the house. And I had made it plain to John Edward that I was going to have a place of my own, that we were just coming there to get located.

My daughter-in-law resented the fact that her mother—this went on before I got there—that her mother had to leave the house and go visit a sister so I could come, John Edward's mother. I had never met my daughter-in-law. She didn't like me, and she didn't like Lee.

So she—what is the word to say—not picked on the child, but she showed her displeasure.

And she is a very—not, I would say so much an emotional person—but this girl is a New Yorker who was brought up in this particular neighborhood, which I believe is a poor section of New York.

The mother had lived in this home all her life. And this girl cursed like a trooper. She is—you cannot express it, Mr. Rankin—but not of a character of a high caliber.

At this particular time she had never been out of this neighborhood, or out of New York. And Lee loved the little baby. And he played with the baby and wanted to hold the baby and everything, which she objected.

We were not wanted, sir, from the very beginning. So there was, I think now—it was not a kitchen knife—it was a little pocket knife, a child's knife, that Lee had. So she hit Lee. So Lee had the knife—now, I remember this distinctly, because I remember how awful I thought Marjorie was about this. Lee had the knife in his hand. He was whittling, because John Edward whittled ships and taught Lee to whittle ships. He puts them in the glass, you know. And he was whittling when this incident occurred. And that is what it occurred about, because there was scraps of the wood on the floor.

227 So when she attacked the child, he had the knife in hand. So she made the statement to my son that we had to leave, that Lee tried to use a knife on her.

Now, I say that is not true, gentlemen. You can be provoked into something. And because of the fact that he was whittling, and had the knife in his hand, they struggled.

He did not use the knife—he had an opportunity to use the knife.

But it wasn't a kitchen knife or a big knife. It was a little knife.

So I will explain it that way, sir.

So immediately then I started to look for a place.

I did find a place, I think, off the Concourse. I do not remember the street.

Mr. Rankin. Was that in the Bronx?

Mrs. Oswald. Off the Concourse, in the Bronx. And it was a basement apartment.

I had shipped some of my furniture. It was in a storehouse at this time. So I got it out and put it in this basement.

Lee had his own single bed. It was a one—one great big, big room. But we had the kitchen—regular New York type style—the kitchen and the bedroom and everything together, but large enough—a big one-room apartment. And there was a single bed that Lee slept on, and I slept on the studio couch.

Then Lee went to school.

Mr. Rankin. Was that Public School 117?

Mrs. Oswald. I have that information here.

Went to school in the neighborhood, Public School 117, which is a junior high school in the Bronx. It states here he attended 15 of 47 days. This is the place we were living that Lee was picked up by the truant officer in the Bronx Zoo.

I was informed of this at work, and I had to appear before a board, which I did.

Lee went back to school.

Then he was picked up again in the Bronx Zoo. And I had to appear before a board committee again.

Then the third time that Lee was picked up, we were—I never did get a subpena, but we were told that he had to appear at Children's Court. But I never—how I got the notice to appear at Children's Court—I am at a loss, sir.

But I did not contact at this time a lawyer or anything. I did not know. I did not think it was anything serious, because the Texas laws are not like the New York laws. In New York, if you are out of school one day you go to Children's Court. In Texas the children stay out of school for months at a time.

Lee had never done this. So I appeared with my son in court. There was a judge asked me if I want to be represented by court counsel. And I believe I said, yes, I believe I was represented by the court counsel at this particular time. And within a few minutes time—because there were hundreds of people sitting, waiting with their truant children, and it was just like this—you didn't take the time we are taking here, a half hour, to discuss the case. It was done immediately.

My child was taken from me in the courtroom.

Mr. Rankin. Had he been out of school quite a bit?

Mrs. Oswald. No, sir. At this time, he had not been out of school quite a bit.

So then I was given a slip of paper—no, I am sorry. I was told where to go, where Lee was, which was another office.

They took Lee from me in the courtroom, two men, officers, presumably. Then I went into another office and here was Lee. Lee was wearing his brother's Marine ring, just an ornament ring. They gave me Lee's ring and the things he had in his pocket, and told me that Lee was going to be at this home, which I think the name was the Warwick Home for Boys. And gave me a slip of paper and told me when I could visit Lee.

And that was all I knew at this particular time.

The child was immediately taken, and I was told to visit the child.

Now, I believe it was—this home was in Brooklyn. I may have the name wrong. It was an old, old home in Brooklyn.

So I went to visit my son.

242

228 And I hope some day to rectify this, because I think conditions of this kind in our United States of America are deplorable. And I want that to go down in the record.

Mr. Rankin. Did they tell you why he was taken to this home, your son?

Mrs. Oswald. For truancy, yes, sir.

So I had to stand single file approximately a block and a half, sir, with Puerto Ricans and Negroes and everything, and people of my class, single file, until we got to the main part of this building, which had a wire, a very heavy wire, partition wire, a man sitting back of the desk, but a man in the front of the gate that let me in. I had packages of gum and some candy for my son. And I sat down there. And the gum wrappers were taken off the gum, and the candy wrappers were taken off.

And my pocketbook was emptied. Yes, sir, and I asked why. It was because the children in this home were such criminals, dope fiends, and had been in criminal offenses, that anybody entering this home had to be searched in case the parents were bringing cigarettes or narcotics or anything.

So that is why I was searched.

So I was escorted into a large room, where there were parents talking with their children.

And Lee came out. He started to cry. He said, "Mother, I want to get out of here. There are children in here who have killed people, and smoke. I want to get out."

So then I realized—I had not realized until I went there what kind of place we had my child in.

We don't have these kinds of places in Texas or New Orleans, sir.

Then I realized what a serious thing this was. And this is when I decided I needed an attorney.

But Lee, I think, was approximately in that home—I am not sure—5 or 6 weeks, which accounts for his truancy that the papers say that Lee was a truant, that he was out of school so long.

It is because he was in this home, sir. That accounts for a lot of the truancy.

Mr. Rankin. Did you talk to him about his truancy, say anything to him about it, or ask him about it, how he happened to stay out of school?

Mrs. Oswald. Yes, sir, I asked Lee.

Well, this comes in another part.

Mr. Rankin. All right.

Mrs. Oswald. So I left my son that day, and I think I visited him a couple of times after that. I am not quite sure.

But in the meantime, I engaged an attorney. I do not know the name of the attorney, and I wish I did.

When I told the attorney about Lee—and I have stated this at a press conference—he raised the roof, so as to say. He was indignant. I cannot quote his exact words. But what he said was that New York State picked up these boys and put them on a farm, and they pay these boys to work on this farm for the State of New York.

Now, I may not be saying this exactly. You may have the picture of the home.

But these boys work on the farm and are paid for it, I understand. That is all I can remember, sir, about this unpleasant thing, because I did not think it would ever come in my life, and after the time it happened I tried to put it out of my mind.

But now I am refreshed a little on that.

So Lee was in this home 5 or 6 weeks, I believe. You probably have the record.

So then we were asked to appear to court. I went into court with this attorney. And there, again, real fast we were in the courtroom and Lee was brought in, and Lee sat down by me. And I remember this distinctly, because Lee had ear trouble quite often. And I saw his ear running, and I said, "Lee, you are having an earache." And the judge heard me saying something to Lee.

He said, "What did you tell your boy, Mrs. Oswald?"

I said, "Judge, I asked him if he had an earache."

I didn't know they were going to give me the child then.

So the judge talked to Lee and asked Lee if he was going to be good, and229 go back to school. Lee answered, "Yes, sir." And he said to me, "Mrs. Oswald, I understand that you and your daughter-in-law do not get along." I said, "That is correct." And he suggested that Lee would be much better off back in the open wide spaces that he was used to instead of in New York, where we had no family then, because the daughter-in-law and son were not friendly with us. And this judge suggested that. And the judge gave me my son, right then and there, gentlemen.

I left the courtroom with my boy. He was given to me in my custody.

Now, that is all I know of the case. The particular case.

From there, we went into an office where there was a probation officer, Mr. John Carro. Mr. Carro talked with Lee and asked Lee if he was going to go back to school.

"Yes, sir."

He reprimanded him a little bit—maybe not that, but gave him a little talk. And he said, "Lee, you are to report to me once a week for probation."

I am going to stress this.

I have been in this Commission 3 days. And you know I am very definite. So I was very definite with Mr. Carro. I did not mince my words. I said, "Mr. Carro, my son is not reporting to you once a week. This is not a criminal offense. He was picked up for truancy, he has assured the judge, promised the judge that he would be back to school. He has promised you he would be back to school. Let's give this boy a chance, and let's see if he will go to school."

"And then, Mr. Carro, if he doesn't go to school, then you can have him report to you."

Mr. Carro didn't take that graciously, which is true. When you don't agree with anyone over you, then you are in the minority, and you just as well make up your mind right then and there, that is it.

So from that time on Mr. Carro pestered me and Lee. Mr. Carro would call me at work, sir, and say that he had gone by the school, and that they were having trouble with Lee. And I went to the school and talked to the principal and she said, "Mrs. Oswald, what happened while the probation officer was here—Lee moved the chair back, and it made a little noise."

And that is what Mr. Carro reported.

In plain words, gentlemen, Mr. Carro was indignant at my attitude, because he was an official.

Mr. Rankin. What school was that?

Mrs. Oswald. This was the first school, sir.

Then I moved. I am a little confused. Just a minute.

I took Lee out of the first school because the children knew that he had been in the home, and I thought he didn't stand a chance.

So I moved to help my child again.

And I personally went with Lee to the principal and told the principal—not in front of Lee—had a talk with her—that Lee had been in this home, and that if she could help him in any way, and knew of any friends, children his age that lived in the neighborhood where we lived, I would appreciate it. And she did help. There was a young lady in this building that we lived, in the Bronx—now we are living near the Bronx Zoo.

Mr. Rankin. Is this the new school?

Mrs. Oswald. This is the new school. And we are living near the Bronx Zoo, which is 100 and something street.

Mr. Rankin. And this is Public School 44?

Mrs. Oswald. Yes, sir—Public School 44. So I talked to the principal and told her about the trouble and asked if she could not help us.

Mr. Rankin. Now, the place that he was committed to was—do you recall that was Berkshire Farms?

Mrs. Oswald. No, because he was not committed to a farm, as far as I knew, sir. All I knew was that he was in this home in Brooklyn. He was never committed to a farm, as far as I know, sir. He was in this home all this time. And this is where I am assuming, because I knew nothing about this—the psychiatric treatment took place, and naturally that is why they would have him in this home to observe him.

And, by the way, I was called one day to go to the home and a young lady230 talked with me. And I sensed that she was questioning me for a reason, because I had been on my own all these years, and I am a business woman. So I remembered one distinct incident. She said, "Mrs. Oswald, how strong do you believe in education?"

And I said, "I believe strongly in education, but not to an extent that a mother should go out and work and deprive her children of a mother's home and love in order to make the extra money to give her children a college education," because I happen to know that a college education sometimes is not as important as wisdom. There are college graduates that do not know how to apply their ability. And so to me—I could never be home with my children. I had to work and leave my children—which was a very sore spot, let's say. I would have given the world if I could have been home and raised my children. And here are women, because of material things, and because they want to give their children a college education, deprive their children of this motherly love, that I myself was deprived of because of an unfortunate affair.

So to get education to that extent, no, sir, I do not approve of it. I think it is more important for children to come home and have someone in that home when they come home from school, and do without a college education. I am strongly for that, because of my experience.

Mr. Rankin. Was Lee Oswald a good student?

Mrs. Oswald. I have his records from all the schools in New Orleans, sir. But we are not through with New York—that will show he passed satisfactory grades.

Mr. Rankin. How about New York? Was he a good student there?

Mrs. Oswald. I think he was an average student. Yes.

Now, I personally brought Lee to the school and talked to some of the teachers. And they told me that Lee was a bright boy, but that he was bored with school—there was just something there. Lee was in a sense bored with school in this sense—that Lee was an overly bright boy, studious boy, and he should have been placed in a school that we have now, I understand, for special children of this sort.

Mr. Rankin. But his grades were not too good during this period?

Mrs. Oswald. They were passing grades, I would say. Now, that is what I know about the New York situation.

Now, it has come out, gentlemen, that he had had psychiatric treatment there. I did not know of any psychiatric treatment there. But now I am assuming naturally he did have it then. There is a report on it.

I wish to say this. I am just a practical nurse. I became a nurse because of my experiences, and I wanted to devote my life to humanity, which I have stated before. But I do know this. I work in hospitals, rest homes, private homes, and all of our hospitals, and all of our rest homes, and all of our institutions are understaffed.

Now, I think you will agree there. We are all understaffed. Every one I have ever been in. So I will say if Lee had psychiatric treatment in this home, there are hundreds and hundreds of children, he could not have had a complete psychiatric examination. We do not know. I do not know if he had a complete. But I will say that according to other institutions, that this institution was also understaffed.

I am going to make one remark to Mr. Jack Ruby. He has to have five psychiatrists. Now, here is one little psychiatric examination on a 13-year-old boy.

So, then we will go to Lee's schooling in New Orleans.

Mr. Rankin. Before you leave New York, did you ever tell anybody that you took Lee Oswald to New York so he could have mental tests at the Jacobi Hospital?

Mrs. Oswald. No, sir, never. My child was a normal child—and while in New York, I explained to you he had a dog with puppies. The school teachers talked well about him. He had a bicycle. There was nothing abnormal about Lee Oswald.

It has been stated also I was offered psychiatric treatment which is incorrect. This Mr. Carro I understand is a very big man. He may be supplying the files with all of this. But, sir, it is untrue.

231 Mr. Rankin. Then you went to New Orleans after that?

Mrs. Oswald. No. Then they assigned a big brother to Lee. This is important to the story.

So this man came out to the apartment on several occasions and saw the type person I was and my son was. And he did not see anything wrong with the child. Evidently not. Because he suggested that it might be a good idea—I had told him the way Mr. Carro was doing. Mr. Carro was pestering me, sir, at work, with just little insignificant reports that I would call the school and the principal would assure me everything was all right.

So he thought that it would be better if I would take the child away. And I didn't know I could do that. I didn't know exactly the charge.

So, I said, "Is it all right? They won't arrest us and bring us back?"

He said, "No, there is no extraditing"—that was his words.

So, I wrote Mr. Carro a letter explaining that I was taking—Lee and I were going to New Orleans, and Lee had cousins his age in New Orleans, and I thought the child would be better off amongst his own family. And the judge had recommended that if we could possibly leave New York that it would be better for Lee. And I wrote Mr. Carro the letter, sir. I did not flee New York. I had the decency to write him a letter. And the Big Brother is the one that recommended this.

Now, that is what I know of the New York.

Mr. Rankin. Do you remember the name of the Big Brother?

Mrs. Oswald. No, sir; I do not know the name of the Big Brother. But from the newspaper accounts, they know the name. The Big Brother stated how clean the apartment was, and how nice we were.

Mr. Rankin. And then you went to New Orleans, did you?

Mrs. Oswald. Yes, sir. Then we went to New Orleans. And we stayed at my sister's house, 757 French Street, and immediately Lee enrolled in—let's get back to this. This is in Fort Worth, Tex. Lee attended the Ridglea West School and graduated—was promoted to junior high in 1952. In 1952 is when we went to New York. Now, we are in New Orleans.

Lee was immediately enrolled in Beauregard School in New Orleans, La., upon arriving in New Orleans. And here is his certificate of promotion to high school. And they have stated that his attendance was very good. He just missed 9 days, I think, out of the whole term, which is considered very good.

Mr. Rankin. How was he as a student in New Orleans?

Mrs. Oswald. C grades. He was promoted, or he wouldn't have C grades. So that is two certificates there.

Then I have another certificate. He went to—no, I would not have the certain, and then from the promotion he was promoted to the Warren Easton High School. And that is the school that Lee wrote the note—am I correct?

Mr. Rankin. Yes. It is already in evidence. He wrote and said you were going to San Diego, and it was not your note at all. He signed your name.

Mrs. Oswald. That is right. And then, as you know, Robert was discharged from the Marines, and Robert did not want to live in New Orleans. So there again—so we could be a family—and this young boy, who was the youngest, could be with a brother. I moved back to Fort Worth, sir, because Robert was in Fort Worth so we could be a family again. However, I moved in July, and Lee joined the Marines in October. So we were just there a few months.

Lee attended Arlington High School there. And when we came back to Fort Worth, Tex., the school did not know what to do with Lee. Lee, I think, was approximately 2 weeks entering the school. He was too far advanced from the New Orleans and New York schools, and not advanced enough—let's see if I can explain this right—according to his age. He was too old to be in the junior, or vice versa. But I do know, and I have witnesses to this, that Lee could not immediately enter school. They had to have a conference, a board conference, because of Lee's curriculum from school. They didn't know which school to place him in.

Mr. Rankin. How did he get along with you? Did you get along well together?

Mrs. Oswald. Yes. Lee was a very quiet and studious boy. None of my children gave me any trouble, thank God. We have no police record, sir, or232 anything like that. And the children were always more or less home. And particularly Lee. Lee would go to the movies, and things like that. He was a normal boy. But when he was home, he was most happy. And I am of this disposition.

He could keep himself occupied—reading and when he watched a football game on television, he would have the score pad, and things of that sort. And so he was quite happy in his own way.

Now, here is something very important.

While in New Orleans, in order to go to Arlington Heights school, which is one of the ritziest schools in New Orleans, all the wealthy people go there, and we happened to live in the vicinity—Lee wanted a two-wheel bicycle, sir, and I bought him one. So when school opened, Lee went to school on a two-wheel bicycle. Can you picture this. A 16½-year-old boy going to school on a bicycle, when all the other children had their own cars? Just picture this. My children never did want anything, and particularly Lee.

Mr. Rankin. How did he get along with his brothers?

Mrs. Oswald. Well, now, at this time he didn't know too much about his brothers. John Edward had been in the service since age 17, so it has been a number of years, other than leaves. And Robert had just finished his 3-year hitch. So you see the brothers have had nothing to do with Lee since age 13 actually—otherwise than visits. Because when Robert came back, then Lee joined the Marines.

Now, this is the U.S. Marine Corps acceptance. And it says "I am very pleased to notify you that your son, Lee Harvey Oswald, has successfully passed the mental, moral, and physical examinations," and so forth. My son was a marine. And I understand a very important marine.

He was in electronics. I have read—one of the marines that was with him said when he defected to Russia they had to change the system. He must have had a real responsible position, if Lee defected to Russia, and all the systems had to be changed. I don't know if this is correct. But this man made the statement, sir.

Mr. Rankin. Did he have any courts-martial that you knew about while he was in the Marines?

Mrs. Oswald. I did not know until what came out in the paper. And I have discussed that with several high officials, marines, and so on and so forth. A lot of men, they tell me, carry a gun. And if you did curse an officer, that is done sometimes, too—that is not anything criminal. I mean we all get provoked at some particular time. I am not taking up for the boy. I don't know what happened. But I know I myself would be guilty of that, if someone pushed me, that I may curse him. And I am sure it is done quite often. And I understand that Lee slashed his wrist. I find that from the paper.

Mr. Rankin. Did you know anything about that? How that happened?

Mrs. Oswald. No, sir—otherwise than what I know in the paper. I do not know, sir.

Mr. Rankin. What about a man that was killed, that was one of his buddies in the Marines?

Did you ever know anything about that?

Mrs. Oswald. No. This is the first time I have heard about that. I haven't even read that in the paper. I did not know about that. If I can help you in any way—his picture in the Marines—there are names of the men on the back. I do not know what they mean. But the names of the men are on the back of picture, sir.

The Chairman. When was it that he slashed his wrist—in the Marine Corps?

Mrs. Oswald. I understand when he was in Moscow—is that correct? I do not know otherwise from what I read in the paper. These things, how could I know.

Representative Ford. May I see that picture?

Mr. Rankin. In the Soviet Union?

Mrs. Oswald. Yes. And that is why, too, it has been stated that he was possibly an agent, to show, when the Russians would not give him citizenship, he slashed his wrist, to show that he did not want to return back to the United States, and forced the Russians to keep him there. That has been stated.

233 Mr. Rankin. Did you ever know that he shot himself while he was in the Marines?

Mrs. Oswald. I read that in the paper.

Mr. Rankin. He never told you that?

Mrs. Oswald. No, sir. And I read in the paper that it could have been an accident.

Mr. Rankin. Did you know anything about how good a shot he was? Did he ever tell you that?

Mrs. Oswald. Lee came home with a trophy, but it is a Marine trophy—may I have that please, I need a number. It is not on this. We have another picture. But it had Lee Harvey Oswald. But it was given not to him, but to the platoon. And he was very, very proud of it. Lee was very proud of his Marine hitch, because every time he came on leave, that is all he talked about. That I know. And I am the only one that knows this.

Mr. Rankin. Was that trophy with regard to marksmanship?

Mrs. Oswald. Yes. Now, Marina would have that. I gave that to Lee and Marina when they returned from Russia, and the Marine book that Lee was so proud of, and the baby book that I had all these years. And I think it was in regard to marksmanship.

Now, I have Lee's—they are copying all of this, Mr. Doyle—Lee's shooting record. I have that, sir. I have anything you want. It was left in his sea bag. And all of this was left in Lee's sea bag.

This is a picture of Lee with his marines, and, it is a special, I think he was doing special work there. I am not familiar—I wasn't told that. But it is different than the other picture. Lee went to many, many a school, gentlemen. He went to the Marine Air Force Base in Biloxi, Mississippi, to schooling. He went to Jacksonville and some others. I remarked, "Your brothers were not sent from here to there like you were." Lee was in Japan, Lee was in Corregidor, Lee was in the Philippines, and Lee was in Formosa. That has not been publicly stated.

Mr. Rankin. Do you know what schooling he had at these various places?

Mrs. Oswald. No, sir. I would think that it was special schooling.

Mr. Rankin. He never told you?

Mrs. Oswald. No, sir. But the other brothers didn't have that type schooling. And I even remarked about it.

Mr. Rankin. Did you ever hear your son say anything for or against President Kennedy?

Mrs. Oswald. While Marina and Lee were in my home that month, and I had a television——

Mr. Rankin. About what time was that?

Mrs. Oswald. This was July, 1962—when they stayed the month with me. Yes, they were delighted with President Kennedy, both.

Mr. Rankin. What did they say about him?

Mrs. Oswald. Nothing political—just "Like President Kennedy." He was telling Marina about President Kennedy. "I like President Kennedy"—"I like, too."

My son has never said anything to me politically about anyone. My son loved the Marines, and loved his work and has never, never said anything against—the only time I questioned my son was ask him why he decided to come home, and he said, "Not even Marina knows that."

That was the one question I wanted to know, because of the many things that they sent me from Russia, as I have previously stated. That was the only thing. So that satisfied me.

Mr. Rankin. Did you know anything about his guns—what guns he had?

Mrs. Oswald. Oh, this is very important, and I am glad you brought this up. This is the part in New Orleans that I forgot about.

While Lee was working for Tujague & Co. he started to have a bank account, and it was in a Homestead. I do not know the name, but it was on Canal Street, 900 or 100 block of Canal Street, because it was even with Exchange Place. And he started to save his money. The purpose of saving his money was to go on a tour with a young group. He was working for a steamship place as a mess engineer so he was going around to all of these seagoing trips.234 And I saw the brochure. It was sponsored by very prominent people. There was nothing wrong with it. If he wanted to go, that was all right—could go on this. So he started to save his money to go. However, this was in January—you want the date?

Mr. Rankin. Yes.

Mrs. Oswald. Are we in 1955 in New Orleans? Yes. No, 1956 this would be. January, 1956—Lee took his money out of the Homestead, which was approximately $150, or something like that. And Lee Harvey Oswald bought an electric football machine—cost approximately $10. He bought a bow and arrow set—maybe about $6 or $7. And he bought a gun. Now, I don't know about guns. I was going to say BB gun, but I will not say it was a BB gun—but Robert Oswald will know—or a rifle. But it was not an expensive gun. He was just 16½ years old. And I am of the opinion if he bought a real gun, I would have had to sign or something. I may be wrong. But anyhow it was a gun to go squirrel hunting or rabbit hunting. I will identify it like that. And then we can go into it further.

And he paid $35 on a coat for me. And the very first job that—the very first pay that Lee got from this job from Tujague sir, he came home with a bird cage on a stand that had a planter. It had the ivy in the planter, it had the parakeet, and it had a complete set of food for the parakeet. His very first pay. And then he paid his room and board. I kept this bird cage—the stand was collapsible—all these years, in the back of my car, and put it up, no matter where I was on a case, and had the bird up until about 2 years ago—no, I had the bird, and gave it to Lee when they came back from Russia. What has become of it I do not know. I gave the bird and bird cage to Lee and Marina when they came back from Russia. I am trying to give you the picture of this boy. Would you ask me some more questions, please? It is awful hard for me to remember everything.

Mr. Rankin. Do you remember any other guns he had?

Mrs. Oswald. No, sir. This is the only gun that I have known Lee to have.

Mr. Rankin. Now, about Officer Tippit.

Mrs. Oswald. Let me finish about Robert and his gun. This is important to you.

When we came to New Orleans, I worked at Washer Bros., in New Orleans—transferred from—Goldrings in New Orleans is Washer Bros. in Fort Worth, Tex. So I worked at Washer Bros. Lee came into the place I worked one day with the gun and wanted me to sign a paper so he could sell the gun. Well, I was indignant that he came where I was working with a gun. I said, "Lee, we will talk about it later." And several of the salesladies thought that I brushed him off real fast. Well, now, Robert bought that gun from Lee, and gave Lee $10 for the gun. It was 3 months we were living in New Orleans. So Robert gave Lee $10 for the gun. And Robert used to go hunting with it at his mother-in-law's house. I have stated they live in the country and they go rabbit and squirrel hunting. Robert would know about the gun, the type gun and everything. I do not know.

Mr. Rankin. You have told us all you know about the gun?

Mrs. Oswald. That is all I know about the gun. And Robert bought the gun from Lee, gave him $10.

Mr. Rankin. You haven't told us whether you thought your son killed Officer Tippit.

Mrs. Oswald. I strictly do not believe that Lee killed Officer Tippit.

Mr. Rankin. Can you tell us why?

Mrs. Oswald. Yes. I am sorry to have to elaborate so, but this, as you know, is very important.

Mr. Lane and myself are investigating, with hundreds of investigators. I have over 1,500 letters. We have reporters and people investigating for us, that are not satisfied with the whole case. And Mr. Lane has a lot of affidavits. I cannot say what Mr. Lane has. But he is doing a very good job about this. And we have come to the conclusion that Lee is not guilty of Officer Tippit.

Now, I gave you a picture yesterday—you might have it there, I don't know, Mr. Rankin—that could possibly be Marina and the child. We have found235 out that the Book Depository Building—Mr. Lane has this information—it is owned by the city of Dallas—I should not go into that, I don't know. He has all of this information. Or it is a lease. It is government-owned some way or other. I should not say. Mr. Lane has all of this. We have been investigating night and day.

The Chairman. Well, we have the picture, Mrs. Oswald.

Mrs. Oswald. All right. On the picture, then—and I have talked to Mr. Doyle about this—you might think I am crazy to say so. The first thing I saw in this picture—this picture was sent to me by a woman with a letter telling me to look at the picture carefully. I did not read the letter. I did not want her opinion, or other people's opinion about this picture. We have a lot of comments about this picture. I immediately looked at the picture when I opened it. The first thing I saw was my son Lee and Marina and the child. Then when I called this woman long distance. I said, "You want to know what I saw in the picture?" and I told her. She says, "No, that is not what I see."

Representative Ford. Did you say your first reaction was that you saw Lee, Marina and the child?

Mrs. Oswald. That was my first reaction. And, if I am correct—I don't say I am correct—but if I am correct, this would be the solution. Lee was escorted out of the building. Kennedy is shot now—I will have to show you the picture. He has passed the window where Lee's rifle is supposed to be. And he is shot in the neck. He has passed this particular part. He is shot in the neck. And then this man that I think is Lee—and I wish I could swear to it, but I am fully convinced—is being escorted out of the building and could be escorted—I am speculating, sir—I have no proof of this. I wish I did. Could be escorted out of the building by a policeman.

Mr. Rankin. Is the picture you are looking at the one you referred to?

Mrs. Oswald. Yes, sir, it is—Exhibit 203.

Mr. Rankin. That is Exhibit 203?

Mrs. Oswald. Now, this is who I think Lee is.

Mr. Rankin. That is——

Mrs. Oswald. There is no face.

Mr. Rankin. That is the man right in the doorway?

Mrs. Oswald. Yes, sir. This is Lee's build and everything. The first thing I saw. Now, they think this is Lee.

No, sir, I do not.

Everybody thinks this is Lee.

Mr. Rankin. When you say they think—it is the man leaning against the side of the doorway, is that right?

Mrs. Oswald. Yes. That is the picture that everybody is convinced is Lee.

Mr. Rankin. And you think it is the one next to him that doesn't show any face? It shows the arms over the head?

Mrs. Oswald. He has his arms up in the air.

Now, that is what I saw immediately—against everybody else seeing it. And this woman and child could possibly be Marina.

Now, to explain this—whether I thought Lee shot Officer Tippit or not—Lee could be escorted out of this building with a gun in his back possibly. I am just speculating, sir. But there is a lot of speculation in this case all over the world. From foreign countries I have letters. And that is how he got out of the building. And this same officer could have been killed, because he was involved in this, and then he could have been killed, to be kept quiet. There is a possibility of this, gentlemen.

Mr. Rankin. Mrs. Oswald, will you take this blue pencil and carefully mark on Exhibit 203?

Mrs. Oswald. I don't mean to be telling this Commission what to do. And I cannot do it. But I would like to have this picture printed. And I am willing—I have some few dollars—I have been selling some pictures. I am willing to give a reward of $1,000 if this picture can be printed and these people come—it would have to be Secret Service, FBI, and state their names.

I would like to have the people here—let us find out who those people are.

236 Mr. Rankin. Will you mark the letter "A" above the part that you have circled on Exhibit 203, that you say are Marina and the little girl?

Mrs. Oswald. All right.

Mr. Rankin. And "B" over what you circled as being your idea of Lee Oswald being there.

Mrs. Oswald. Now, that is what I saw, and nobody else has seen this. They see the man next to him.

Would you want me to put the man next to it that they see as Lee? He has the same clothes on as Lee.

Mr. Rankin. Well—you can testify the man that other people said was Lee Oswald, that you pointed to before on Exhibit 203, would be the one in between, would that be right?

Mrs. Oswald. Yes. He has the same clothes as Lee.

Mr. Rankin. Mr. Chairman, we offer in evidence Exhibit 203 as now marked with the identification.

(The document referred to was received, as indicated, as Commission Exhibit No. 203.)

Mr. Rankin. Do you have any other reasons why you think that Officer Tippit was not killed by your son Lee Oswald?

Mrs. Oswald. I do not.

But, gentlemen, Mr. Mark Lane has affidavits. And we are investigating this—if you will have his testimony. He has pertinent information to this. I intend, when I finish here—I am going to be very quiet about what happened here, with no comments. But when I finish here, I am going on speaking tours. I am going to continue the investigation of the shooting. This is for you. But I intend to continue as long as this Commission is in session, to investigate, like we have been doing, we have come up with some very——

The Chairman. Some very what?

Mrs. Oswald. Very important factors in this case.

The Chairman. Well, I thought that is what you were here to tell us about.

Mrs. Oswald. I am not the investigator. Mr. Lane is the investigator. Mr. Lane is my son's attorney, representing my son. And he is investigating the death of President Kennedy and the consequent murder of my son.

And he is making tours. And we have these reporters. And we have people giving us their opinions. We have many, many letters from expert riflemen. And I have in my possession—they also write to me—that have gone through this particular instance, and say it cannot possibly be done in that length of time and so on and so forth. We have a lot of expert opinions.

Mr. Rankin. Are you willing to give those to the Commission?

Mrs. Oswald. Yes, sir, we want to. This is what I say is our American way of life. This boy was shot down handcuffed, within a few hours time, without trial or jury or counsel, even. He did not have a right to defend himself. So Mr. Lane immediately started to defend this boy. And people have come to our rescue.

When I read Mr. Lane's brief, and I realized the truth of some of the statements he said, I contacted Mr. Lane, as you know, and we tried to come before the Commission.

So from now on, when I am through with this Commission, I am going to work with Mr. Lane in my own way—I am booked in New York on a tour next week. And I am going to talk only about the investigation.

We have help, sir. We have Mr. Laurence Ross, who is in New Zealand, who writes articles—very good. And Captain Wooster, is an expert rifleman of New Zealand. He does this all the time. He goes all over.

I am not saying it correctly.

But he is an expert. And he said that he himself could hardly do it. And he practices all the time. That is his—that is what he does for a living. He is an expert.

And we have many, many such letters. I have 1,500 letters, sir. Mr. Doyle has seen my letters and read a few.

We have attorneys writing us. We have ministers. We have all types of people that are not satisfied with this boy being charged with the assassination of President Kennedy. And, of course, not satisfied with the way he was shot237 down without trial. And we are going to continue to investigate and fight this in our own way, when I leave the Commission, sir.

The Chairman. Do you have an agent for this tour, lecture tour you are making?

Mrs. Oswald. No, sir; I do not. Mr. Lane has—well, I don't say booked me, because that would not be the word. But I am supposed to appear Monday at Town Hall in New York—no, Tuesday, the 18th. It is going to be a forum. There are three very prominent men going to be on the panel. And we are going to ask questions and talk. We will have our public support by bringing these matters before the public, because we are convinced—and there are millions of other people convinced, also—that this is not as plain as it seems to be, that there is more to it. And they are not satisfied.

We are going to continue to investigate, with the help of the public.

The Chairman. Are you to be compensated for these lectures?

Mrs. Oswald. No. My trip is being paid to New York. And I am to live in a home with a family.

As far as that, I know nothing else about this.

The Chairman. Who does know the details of it?

Mrs. Oswald. Well, now, Mr. Lane would know the details. And maybe you think I am being a very foolish woman. But here. When I read—because I have been very cautious so let's say now I am not being cautious. But here is why. When I read Mr. Lane's brief—and I don't know, gentlemen, if you have read it—but I believe it would be pertinent to this Commission to get a copy. It is written in the Guardian—two or three briefs. And I was convinced this man had some pertinent ideas about it. And when I engaged Mr. Lane, he said, "Mrs. Oswald, I will tell you about myself."

I said, "I do not want to hear. As far as I am concerned, you could be a Communist. But to me a Communist is a human being. That is just his way of life."

We are Americans. We have Japanese people. That is their way of life. A Communist, as long as he is not hurting our Government, that is his right to be a Communist. That is his way of life.

I did not want to know anything about Mr. Lane, because I knew Mr. Lane wrote sensible things, that Mr. Lane was interested. And what he wrote made sense. And that is all I am interested in, sir.

If Mr. Lane is getting money, and I am appearing, that is just fine. I am not interested. If I can get before the public and through Mr. Lane doing it, I want to get before that public and state my American way of life and try to prove my son is innocent.

The main part of this is to try to prove Lee Harvey Oswald innocent.

The Chairman. Very well.

Mr. Rankin. You said during your testimony that an agent showed you a picture at the Six Flags Inn. Do you remember that?

Mrs. Oswald. Yes, and I am glad you brought that up, because I have notes on this, too. I have something important to say about that.

Mr. Rankin. I will ask the reporter to mark this.

(The document referred to was marked Commission Exhibit No. 237 for identification.)

Mrs. Oswald. Before I see a picture, see—if it was in a square, cupped in a hand, I believe it would be better for me for identification. That is the way I saw it. It was cupped in his hand.

Mr. Rankin. Mrs. Oswald, all I have is Exhibit 237, in the shape it is in. And I will hand it to you and ask you if you recall that as being the picture that was shown to you.

Mrs. Oswald. No, sir. This is not the picture shown me. The picture that was shown me was a full face and just shoulders. This is not the picture.

This picture was about this size, very glossy black and white, with a big face and shoulders. I have background here, a lot of white. But this took the whole picture—the face and shoulders. And this door was just ajar. And this man had this picture—and the two corners were cut.

Mr. Rankin. About what size is the picture you are looking at?

Mrs. Oswald. That is about three by four—approximately three by four, cupped in this man's hand, and the two corners were cut. The two top corners. And a238 very glossy picture, black and white, with a big face and shoulders. This is the picture shown me, sir.

Now, at Six Flags Inn, about 3 days later, when I entered the room, on the table were a lot of newspapers. I walked into the room in the presence of my son, and all of the agents. As I stated before, Marina and I knew nothing of what went on. We did not know how Lee was shot or anything, because we did not sit down and watch television.

Mr. Rankin. What son are you talking about?

Mrs. Oswald. Robert. So this is approximately the Wednesday, the 25th—no—Sunday was the 24th. About the 26th—it was a few days after Lee was shot, a couple of days. So I walked into the room, and I picked this paper up and turned it over, and I exclaimed, "This is the picture of the man that the FBI agent showed me."

And one of the agents said, "Mrs. Oswald, that is the man that shot your son."

Believe me, gentlemen, I didn't even ask his name. And nothing more was said.

Now, that is very unusual.

Mr. Rankin. Now, the picture that you are talking about that you picked up, was a picture in the newspaper?

Mrs. Oswald. In the newspaper. The bottom part of the newspaper. I can see that like I can see the picture. I had never seen the picture before.

Mr. Rankin. Did you later learn whose picture that was?

Mrs. Oswald. Yes, when I returned to my home in Fort Worth, Tex., about a week later, Mr. Blair Justice, of the Star Telegram, brought me all the papers, that was the next time I saw the pictures and knew it was Mr. Ruby. And it was a bottom page, and it was this picture shown me.

Now, this is what I want to know.

Mr. Rankin. Tell us who was there when you said that, about the picture in the paper?

Mrs. Oswald. Mr. Mike Howard, Mr. Garry Seals—well, all of the agents there. The room was full. And Robert Oswald was there. The room was full.

Mr. Rankin. Was Marina there?

Mrs. Oswald. Marina was in the bedroom. Marina and I stayed in the bedroom with the children. We could get snatches of the television and so on. The children had diarrhea and so on. We were busy.

As I picked the paper up and turned it over, it was on the back. This picture I saw, the same picture.

Mr. Rankin. Do you know whether your son Lee Oswald knew Jack Ruby?

Mrs. Oswald. No, sir, I have no way of knowing that. I just hope that he did, if I am right. If Lee is an agent, I hope he knew Jack Ruby.

Representative Ford. When you made that statement, after looking at the newspaper, did you say it loudly enough for people in the room to hear it?

Mrs. Oswald. Yes, sir, because they answered me. They said, "That is the picture of the man that shot your son."

But nothing has been said since that. That is the part that I question all about this.

And then I am not asked to be subpenaed at Jack Ruby's trial or anything.

The FBI says yes, they showed me a picture, but that wasn't a picture of Jack Ruby, not even giving me a chance.

I don't understand. Something is not according to Hoyle. I keep telling you gentlemen.

Now, I can identify this picture, I believe, out of a hundred pictures.

It was a black and white glossy picture of a big face and shoulders. And why I express it—he had it cupped in his hand, and he poked his arm and his hand with my bifocals, and all I could see was the picture and the hand. I didn't even see Mr. Odum so much. That was that hand poked in front of me. I am positive of this. Yet I am not asked any more about the picture. They state, yes, they showed me a picture, but not this picture. I am positive, gentlemen.

Mr. Rankin. I will ask you about a list of names and see if you know any of them, or if your son, Lee Oswald, knew any of them, to your knowledge.

Mrs. Oswald. I will be happy to answer.

Mr. Rankin. Karen Bennett, do you know that?

239 Mrs. Oswald. Yes. I have inquired about this Karen Bennett.

Mr. Rankin. Did you know her?

Mrs. Oswald. I do not know whether I knew her or not. I have asked several people to investigate this for me.

Upon returning from the country on an OB case. I went to work for Royal Clothiers, in Fort Worth, Tex., as an outside sales lady. In OB you have to wait for the babies— and I needed to live. There was a young lady there by the name of Carol, I called her. It could be Karen. Looked very much like the young lady I saw on the television. That is the first time I connected the two. Her father was one of the biggest gangsters in Fort Worth, Tex. And he himself was killed by the gangland of Fort Worth, Tex.

Why I know that—the manager of this Royal Clothiers had remarked who Karen's father was, and I said to him, "I don't appreciate your broadcasting that. I think what her father did has nothing to do with the girl. She is working. Give her a chance to her own life."

I am always standing up and getting myself in trouble. I want you to know that. Maybe I am not liked. But if that makes not being liked, I will continue not being liked, sir.

So this is when I first started to work. However, I found out that the young lady also had another job at night, which is all right. She was working as a barmaid in a tavern on Hemphill Street, in Fort Worth, Tex., and she had two small children, and so if she worked at the Royal Clothiers during the day, it was necessary that she work at this saloon, or whatever you want to call it at night.

Mr. Rankin. Was she married?

Mrs. Oswald. No, she was not married. That maybe is what she had to do to support her children. And I understand, because I was left alone.

But—she and I became involved in this way. In the front of the store was a showcase with cheap jewelry. This is a credit place, rings, diamond rings, and bracelets. And Carol had the key to this case, and so did I. And there was some talk about a ring or something missing. I realized right then and there I could not put myself in a position of things being stolen, because here was a girl who they said her father was a gangster, and she was working in a bar. And my son was a known defector. So I quit that job.

Now, on television for the Ruby trial here comes the girl. I thought I recognized this girl. The name is Karen Bennett. And I called her Carol, it could be Karen Bennett. I didn't have much to do with the girl. So I immediately told this story to Mr. Jack Langueth of the New York Times, and I told also to another Star Telegram reporter, Mr. John McConnoch, because I wanted them to investigate.

But I have not heard anything about it.

Mr. Rankin. How about Bruce Carlin?

Mrs. Oswald. No, sir.

Mr. Rankin. You don't know whether your son knew him?

Mrs. Oswald. No, sir. I would not know anybody that my son knew. That I am positive—because he never did tell me any of this. But continue.

Mr. Rankin. Robert Kermit Patterson, also known as Bobby Patterson?

Mrs. Oswald. No, sir.

Mr. Rankin. Donald C. Stuart?

Mrs. Oswald. No, sir.

Mr. Rankin. Charles Arndt?

Mrs. Oswald. No, sir.

Mr. Rankin. James A. Jackson?

Mrs. Oswald. No, you know, a few of those names sound to me like they might be on the back of both of these pictures. I am not sure.

Mr. Rankin. They are supposed to be associates or friends or people that Mr. Ruby knew and associated with closely.

Stanley or Katya Skotnicki?

Mrs. Oswald. No, sir.

Mr. Rankin. Larry Crafard, or Crawford?

Mrs. Oswald. No, sir.

Mr. Rankin. Do you remember that name?

Mrs. Oswald. No, sir. I was trying to connect the name with a couple.

240 Mr. Rankin. Do you know whether he ever spent any time in the Silver Spur?

Mrs. Oswald. If Lee ever did?

Mr. Rankin. Yes.

Mrs. Oswald. I have had no knowledge of Lee for 1 year. None whatsoever.

Mr. Rankin. And before that do you know whether he spent any time in the Silver Spur in Dallas?

Mrs. Oswald. No, sir.

And before that, as to what I do know, that Lee did not drink and Lee did not smoke, and Lee wasn't the type—not that he did not maybe go into saloons—but from what I know of him, he did not go into places like that of his own. If he was working he might have gone into these places.

Mr. Rankin. These are the nightclubs Jack Ruby was associated with. You recognize that?

Mrs. Oswald. No, I don't.

Mr. Rankin. And the Vegas Club was another one. Do you know whether he spent time there?

Mrs. Oswald. I would have no way of knowing.

Mr. Rankin. And the Sovereign Club?

Mrs. Oswald. I have no way of knowing. I am going to say, again, Mr. Lane would have ways of knowing about all these clubs and everything, because that is his part of our investigation. I would like to get back to Patrolman Tippit.

Mr. Rankin. All right. I just want to try to cover this book about Lee Oswald's marksmanship. That has been marked Exhibit 238.

(The document referred to was marked Commission Exhibit No. 238, for identification.)

Mr. Rankin. It is a book that you brought here.

Mrs. Oswald. Yes, it was left in his sea bag, when he came home from the Marine Corps.

Mr. Rankin. And that reads, "U.S. Marine Corps Score Book, Oswald, L. H."

Mrs. Oswald. That is correct.

Mr. Rankin. That is your son's?

Mrs. Oswald. That is correct. That is his platoon, 2060, that is the one he got the trophy with.

Mr. Rankin. Were the various marks in that book in pencil that you see there in the book when you first found it?

Mrs. Oswald. Yes, sir, I have not touched the book.

Mr. Rankin. Is it in the same condition?

Mrs. Oswald. That is the same condition that it was in his sea bag.

Mr. Rankin. We offer in evidence Exhibit 238, and ask leave to substitute a copy.

The Chairman. It may be introduced.

(The document heretofore marked as Commission Exhibit No. 238 was received in evidence.)

Mr. Rankin. Mr. Reporter, will you mark this 239?

(The document referred to was marked Commission Exhibit No. 239 for identification and received in evidence.)

Mr. Rankin. Mrs. Oswald. I will ask you to glance through Exhibit 239 and state whether or not that appears to be photostatic copy of——

Mrs. Oswald. Yes, that is the photostatic copy——

Mr. Rankin. Of Exhibit 238?

Mrs. Oswald. That is correct.

Mr. Rankin. And you will see it has the same markings.

Mrs. Oswald. Yes, sir, that is correct.

Mr. Rankin. This is a copy we will substitute.

Now, do you want to tell about the shooting of Officer Tippit?

Mrs. Oswald. Yes. I have many, many clippings—as I say, we have all these people working. And we have come to the conclusion, and have never seen where they had an autopsy on Patrolman Tippit or even his gun or anything. In other words, Patrolman Tippit's life has been quiet from the very beginning after the shooting. I have never seen anything about him in print. And we question241 where all the money that has been given to Mrs. Tippit has come from. That is a tremendous amount of money—tremendous for donations.

The Chairman. You say you question the money?

Mrs. Oswald. Yes, sir; the donations to Mrs. Tippit.

The Chairman. You mean you question whether she received them or not?

Mrs. Oswald. No—where is the money coming from? As far as she knows, sir, they are donations. But where is the actual money coming from, because it is such a large amount? Like I question Marina's money. She has now $38,000. That is just what they have stated she has. What she has may be more. But that is a lot of money for donations, a tremendous lot of money.

And Mrs. Tippit has, I think, almost half a million dollars. Is that correct? I am not quite sure. But, anyhow, it is a large amount of money. And with our investigation and things that are not according to Hoyle, we do question where the money is coming from.

The Chairman. Do you have any idea where it comes from, after your investigation?

Mrs. Oswald. Well, Mr. Lane has. I do not have all the information. He has this information. And we are still investigating it, sir. And we will investigate if it takes another year or two. We are going to continue to arrive at the truth.

Mr. Rankin. You referred to an article in the Time Magazine of February 14, 1964, volume 83, No. 7, when you said there were some things that were wrong in it—do you remember that?

Mrs. Oswald. Yes, sir.

Mr. Rankin. Did you write a letter about this assassination of President Kennedy to President Johnson at some time?

Mrs. Oswald. No, sir; I never have.

Mr. Rankin. Did you send a telegram?

Mrs. Oswald. No, sir. The only telegram I sent to President Johnson was stating that I had sent a telegram to you and Chief Justice Warren, if you remember.

Mr. Rankin. Did you get any response from the White House?

Mrs. Oswald. No, sir; I did not get a response from the White House. And I am indignant at the response that I did get. What it did was to inform me, I was so graciously treated by Mr. Kennedy and his Administration, as I have stated and testified, that I am shocked that I am now to be told that I am not to worry the President. "In response to your telegram to the President, I wish to inform you that any requests or any information dealing with the inquiry conducted by Chief Justice Warren should properly be directed to the Commission. I note in your telegram that you have directed your request to the Chief Justice and to Mr. Rankin, the Commission's General Counsel. Sincerely, Lee C. White, Assistant Special Counsel to the President."

Mr. Rankin. That is the response that you received from the White House?

Mrs. Oswald. From the telegram that I sent, when I sent a telegram to you and Chief Justice Warren—I sent him a telegram. I have it right here, sir. You don't know about the telegram.

Here is a copy of the telegram.

"President Lyndon B. Johnson. I have sent night letters to Chief Justice Earl Warren and J. Lee Rankin imploring both in the name of justice and our American way of life to let my son Lee Harvey Oswald be represented by counsel so that all witnesses including my son's widow will be cross-examined. Respectfully yours, Mrs. Marguerite Oswald."

And this is the response to that. And I don't think that is a gracious response at all. If I want to write the President or send him a telegram, I think I have as much right as anyone else to do so.

Mr. Rankin. Did you comment on the fact of this response from the White House when you received it to anybody?

Mrs. Oswald. Yes, sir. There was a reporter from Time Magazine that I commented to, because I was indignant, as I said. And he said, "Well, if you or your next door neighbor or anybody walking in the street wanted to write the President, that is our American way of life." And I agreed with him.

242 Mr. Rankin. Now, you are quoted in this article as saying "Why, I have got as much right as any citizen to write the President of the United States, to petition him, and let me tell you this, Mr. Johnson should also remember that I am not just anyone, and that he is only President of the United States by the grace of my son's action." Is that a correct quote?

Mrs. Oswald. No, that is not a correct quote. And that is why I was indignant yesterday when I read that. And there is more discrepancies.

I did tell him about receiving the letter, and I had just received it—that I was indignant they should write and as much intimate that I should not write the President.

I made a special appeal to the President.

Mr. Rankin. Do you recall what you did say? Did you say anything like this?

Mrs. Oswald. No, sir. There was nothing said to this reporter about President Johnson—because I believe my son is innocent. So if I say that, then I would be saying that my son is guilty. And that is why the President is now the President. No, sir. I did not say that.

Mr. Rankin. What reporter for Time Magazine was that that you were talking to?

Mrs. Oswald. I can find out the name for you, or I can think about it. Let's see. I think the name is Sullivan. I did not want to think—but I think it is Sullivan. Do you have that information?

Mr. Rankin. No.

Mrs. Oswald. Well, I will get it for you, or maybe it will come to me.

Mr. Rankin. All right.

Mrs. Oswald. But I do know, because I was paid for the picture—one of the pictures in that magazine.

Mr. Rankin. We would appreciate your telling us as accurately as you can.

Mrs. Oswald. I want to give you any and every information I can.

The Chairman. Did the man who interviewed you in this matter also pay for the picture—the same man?

Mrs. Oswald. Yes sir—for the Time Magazine.

Mr. Rankin. Did he pay you for any part of the story?

Mrs. Oswald. No sir. No, I am wrong there, he did. He paid me for part of the story. That is not the story.

This isn't the story that was supposed to have come out. It was a much nicer and softer story. But we have found out that when we give these press notices, that they don't come out the way you give them. And they explain—like if I was to tell Mr. Sullivan, "I am disappointed in your story"—"Well, Mrs. Oswald, our editor edits to make room," and so on. That is what you get. I was disappointed in the story, because the story was that I felt so sorry for Marina, to think that she had to go through the rest of her life thinking in her mind that her husband was the killer of President Kennedy, and that she would have to tell her children that she had gone down in history, that their father was the killer of President Kennedy. And I went on with a long story. I said—they said "Marina had stringy hair, and she didn't have this or that." Let me tell you, I would rather have Marina with the stringy hair and less clothes, but thinking that her husband was innocent, like she thought the 3 days I was there—rather than the picture now, where she smokes, she no longer nurses her baby, she left her baby in Texas to come to the Warren Commission, which is not the Marina I know.

"Marina, Mama, no, no, she never left her children." And well groomed. But she thinks now her husband shot President Kennedy. What an awful thing. I would much rather have no money and stringy hair and be the girl I was before, and believe my husband was innocent.

The Chairman. How much did Life pay you for your story?

Mrs. Oswald. Is that pertinent?

The Chairman. Or Time, rather.

Mrs. Oswald. Is that pertinent to the Commission, or is that my personal?

Mr. Doyle. I don't think the Chief Justice—he has simply asked you a question. If you wish to answer the question that is fine. If you don't, if you tell the Chief Justice you don't wish to answer the question——

243 Mrs. Oswald. Well, it doesn't have any bearing. I think the amount I got would be immaterial to the Commission. I don't know.

The Chairman. Well. I think it might be material under some circumstances. But if she doesn't wish to tell us, that is all right.

Mrs. Oswald. It is not—just like the pictures. I want you to have the pictures. And you didn't seem to think they were important enough.

I am asking if this is important to the Commission, because that is my personal life. It is no crime to sell the pictures. I have no job or income. If I want to sell a picture to a magazine or a newspaper, and protect myself financially, I am going to continue to do that.

Mr. Doyle. The Commission has stated to you that it would be interested in knowing, that it feels it might be of some value to them. But if you do not wish to say anything about it, they would not press you.

So again, it would be completely up to you.

Mrs. Oswald. I think that would probably, like these pictures, be my personal——

Mr. Rankin. Did you learn about the attempt of your son to shoot General Walker?

Mrs. Oswald. I am delighted you asked me that question. I have these notes here, and didn't go through that.

The first time I knew about General Walker was through the paper.

Now, I became indignant. I do not remember the quotes. But why I became indignant, was that I had Lee's handwriting in Russian. But no one came to me to find out about this note. That is the part, gentlemen, that is so peculiar about this whole thing.

I understand through reporters that the note was shown to Mrs. Ruth Paine, and wanted to know if the handwriting was Lee's handwriting. But no one has come to find out if I had any handwriting of Lee in Russian, which I have.

Mr. Rankin. Did you think this was in Russian?

Mrs. Oswald. Yes. I am under the impression that the note was in Russian. It stated in the paper.

Mr. Rankin. When did you learn about the Walker incident?

Mrs. Oswald. Through the newspaper. And it has been changed, the story, now. If I can remember. Now, I will get this for you. I have a friend that has one of the most complete scrapbooks in the United States, that helps in this investigation. And I can get all these articles, sir. And I will help in every way possible.

If I remember correctly, it was stated that Marina found this note in the room that says "I may be arrested, and if so get in touch with the Russian consul" and told her where to go to the jailhouse. I wish I knew the exact quote. So we are getting back to an agent now.

From what I remember in the beginning, he did not say in the note that he was going to kill General Walker—that he would be involved in something that might cause him to be arrested and so on. I remember this. That was in the very beginning, sir. It came out in Fort Worth, Tex.

So he is going to be involved in something. That doesn't mean he is going to shoot General Walker.

Mr. Rankin. When did you learn that he did try to shoot General Walker?

Mrs. Oswald. As the story started to leak out from the paper, what we call leaks. I have to say this, because we are investigating this. I am not the main investigator. But I talk to people. They call, and I get letters from them. Every now and then Mr. Jim Martin, who is the business manager for Marina, would quote Marina—not Marina, but he would quote Marina about General Walker, quoted her about thinking in her mind that her husband had killed the President.

And I was firing back through the newspapers and saying Mr. Jim Martin was an American citizen, and I didn't appreciate him quoting my daughter-in-law about these things, because they are of no advantage. How can they prove that Lee had killed General Walker, because now maybe they would not have the bullets—and so on. It happened before.

Mr. Rankin. You knew that he was not killed.

Mrs. Oswald. What good would it be for Mr. Martin to make a statement like244 this that Marina said, and publicize it, when they possibly could not now prove that Lee had anything to do with it, gun or bullets or anything. I could not see his purpose in doing this—which has hurt my daughter-in-law very much. I have many letters from people expressing their opinion that they did not appreciate her coming out with these remarks. But it is Mr. Jim Martin.

Marina is a foreign girl, and doesn't know what these people are doing to her, Mr. Rankin. I have publicly fought this over and over—if you have my quotes from the Fort Worth Star Telegram and so on, and probably the New York papers. I deeply feel sorry for Marina. Marina is a Russian girl. Maybe if her husband was picked up to be a murderer, maybe they would shoot him in Russia. I don't know.

But here we have an American way of life that Marina is not familiar with.

Mr. Rankin. Don't you want her to tell the truth about it?

Mrs. Oswald. I want Marina to tell the truth just like I want to tell the truth. But from my testimony here, I have found out that Marina has lied.

Mr. Rankin. What have you found out about the Walker incident? Have you found anything about that was untrue that Marina said?

Mrs. Oswald. That Marina said it?

Mr. Rankin. Yes.

Mrs. Oswald. I have not heard Marina say it. I have not heard Marina say it. I can answer this way. This comes from Mr. Jim Martin. There is many, many things about Mr. Jim Martin and Mr. Thorne that I don't think maybe it is right that I should say these things in front of the Commission, because they are rumors.

But a rumor, you will have to, in a case as big as this, and where there are so many people involved, you have to analyze these rumors. I will say this: I understand from many, many a source that the Dallas Bar Association is going to have Mr. Jim Thorne before them. Now that is my understanding there.

Mr. Rankin. So all you know about the Walker incident is what you have read in the papers.

Mrs. Oswald. What I have read in the paper. And I certainly did not appreciate that. Mr. Jim Martin is a citizen, if Marina is not.

Mr. Rankin. Now, did you ever ask your son, Lee Oswald, whether he was an agent of anybody?

Mrs. Oswald. No sir, I have never asked Lee Oswald if he was an agent because I felt like he would not tell me.

Mr. Rankin. But you have not asked him.

Mrs. Oswald. No, I have not asked him.

Oh, one very important thing that I must tell you. On November 26—that was the night of November 26, and the day of November 26 was when I found out that Marina was going to live with someone else, and we had no contact. So I knew I wasn't wanted or involved. I was in the bedroom. And I left the Inn of the Six Flags, gentlemen, under strict security protection. I opened the door and had my coat and pocketbook, and I went out doors. And I was about 15 feet when they realized that I had left the Inn. Now, there was a man on the outside, stationed there night and day. But there was a little arbor. And this was in the bedroom. We had two entrances—one to the living room and one to the bedroom. I opened the bedroom door. I had my coat and bag and I was going to go home. I was going to take a bus and go home because I didn't get to talk to my daughter-in-law—they had taken over.

And I was 15 or 20 feet when two agents came and took me by the arm and I went back in. I didn't make a stink or anything about it. And that night I sat up all night, and the next morning I insisted upon going home. But the point that has to be made is was I under arrest or not—since these men came and took me by the arm and brought me back to the Inn of the Six Flags.

The Chairman. Were you all dressed to go home when they took hold of you that way?

Mrs. Oswald. Yes, sir, when they took hold of me this way. And I didn't say anything. I just went back in. So then the doctor—I do not know his name, you have his name—the doctor came in to see the children, they had diarrhea. And the man whispered something to the doctor. And we closed the door. The doctor asked me for Lee's social security number. And I have245 testified that I had gone home the night before to get all my papers, after much persuasion. I started to look through the papers for Lee's number. And I started to cry. He and I were in the room alone. I think this was purposely, because they said something to the doctor.

I said I am very upset and told the doctor what happened. And I said "You know, my heart is breaking. I cannot understand how they would do something like that, and not tell me about it."

So he talked with me, and he gave me two pills. When we opened the door he said to the agents "She is all right, she has a right to her feelings." So they must have thought that I was—something was wrong with me. They thought—because I took the attitude immediately—well, Robert said it—I said "Why didn't you let me know." "Well, just because the way you are acting now." I said "How am I acting. I am acting in a normal way. I have lost my son. Now you have made arrangements without consulting me to take my daughter and two grandchildren to live with strangers. This is a normal reaction. Am I going to say yes, take my daughter-in-law and grandchildren, I don't need my part of them."

This is a normal reaction.

Reverend Saunders, Louis Saunders, who is a minister at the grave, accidentally came at the very last minute. He had not preached a sermon in 8 years. He is head of the Council of Churches.

He heard we could not get a minister so he was able to come at the very last minute. And Rev. Granville Walker was sent to my home in Fort Worth, Tex., the next day after I arrived home, to help, to console me about this case. So he said "Mrs. Oswald, I understand that Marina has been offered a very fine home, and how do you feel about that. Are you not glad that your daughter-in-law is going to be taken care of and the children have an education."

I said "No, Reverend Saunders, I do not feel that way about it. Those are material things. How do we know if these children will live to derive any benefit from this education. I think that we should stick together as a family. Her Mama, like she wanted. The girl said she has no Mama. Everything was arranged for the Mama. She is talking about money and material things. I expressed my opinion at the Six Flags, that we start with $863—no contributions were coming in. And then if we cannot make it, then let the ones that are so concerned help us. And I remarked—I am working for a very wealthy woman.

Who knows, maybe she will give us $5,000. Let us stick together as a family. Reverend Saunders says "Mrs. Oswald, your philosophy of life is beautiful, and it is a Biblical way. But you know you have to be practical."

So the very next day, sir—and this is in "Christianity Today," to prove my point—Mr. Jim Cox, who writes for "Christianity Today" and is a Star Telegram reporter called me and said "Mrs. Oswald, Reverend Saunders called me and wanted me to get a story from you, because he thought you had such a wonderful philosophy of life."

I sat down, and Mr. Jimmy Cox stayed home from Church—I gave Mr. Jimmy Cox a story that is in Christianity Today, that only goes to ministers, and it is because of Reverend Saunders. So I do have people to testify about this particular thing. And I did act in a normal way. That is a normal reaction, to not want to give up my family.

Mr. Rankin. Mrs. Oswald. I will give you Exhibits 206 through 227, both inclusive, and ask you if that is—if those are photostatic copies of your correspondence—would you look at each one of them—with the State Department that you have referred to in your testimony?

Mrs. Oswald. Yes, sir. Do you want the numbers as I go along?

Mr. Rankin. No. You just look at them.

Mrs. Oswald. That is correct.

Representative Ford. These are copies, Mr. Rankin, of her letters to the State Department and the responses?

Mrs. Oswald. That is correct.

Mr. Rankin. Yes, that is correct, is it not, Mrs. Oswald?

Mrs. Oswald. Yes, that is correct.

246 Mr. Rankin. And these copies were made under your supervision were they not.

Mrs. Oswald. That is correct. And I voluntarily gave you every copy I have. That is correct. That is correct. That is correct.

Some of this seems to be scratched out here.

Mr. Doyle. On Exhibit No. 221, there seems to be some X markings around. Will you put that aside, and we can compare that with the original.

Mrs. Oswald. This is correct. That is correct. That is correct. I don't remember writing to Mrs. James. I remember calling her on the telephone. This is my handwriting. I guess I did.

Yes, that is my handwriting. That is correct.

That is correct. That is correct. And this is correct, but should have a card with it.

Mr. Doyle. You are referring to 227?

Mrs. Oswald. Yes. And it should have with it a card, a postcard, from Lee.

Mr. Doyle. Set 227 aside with 221.

Mr. Rankin. Do you have a copy of 221?

Mrs. Oswald. Yes.

Mr. Rankin. Will you please check to see that is a correct copy.

Mr. Chairman, I think that we might gain time now if we would check these exhibits out with Mrs. Oswald, and be able to offer them at whatever time we reconvene. That is all we propose to do now.

The Chairman. All right.

Mrs. Oswald. This is the card that should have gone with that.

Mr. Rankin. Mrs. Oswald, were you able to find your copy of Exhibit 221, and compare it and see whether that which is marked on is on your copy?

Mrs. Oswald. No sir, we have not found that yet.

"Yours 11th" is scratched out.

Mr. Rankin. So that 221 is correct, but apparently there are some errors——

Mrs. Oswald. There are more errors, too. Because it doesn't say "Services Department of State."

Mr. Doyle. 221 does not appear to be a photostat of the exhibit.

Mr. Rankin. But it does have exactly the same material on it, doesn't it?

Mrs. Oswald. It doesn't have this—"collect." I would not say it was an exact copy.

Mr. Doyle. It appears to have substantially the information on it. It is not a photostat of it.

Mr. Rankin. I might advise you, Mrs. Oswald, this is from the State Department's file, from which the telegram was made up that was sent to you.

Mr. Doyle. It is not a photostat, but it does have substantially the information that is set forth in the telegram itself.

Mr. Rankin. Now, you have examined all of the exhibits, 206 through 227, both inclusive, and found them, except for what you and your counsel said about exhibit 221, and the card that was with 227, to be correct.

Mrs. Oswald. That is correct.

Mr. Rankin. We offer in evidence Exhibits 206 through 227, both inclusive.

The Chairman. They may be admitted.

(Commission Exhibit Nos. 206 through 227, heretofore marked for identification, were received in evidence.)

Mrs. Oswald. This is the card that goes with this letter, as an explanation.

(The card referred to was marked Exhibit No. 240 for identification.)

Mr. Rankin. Exhibit 240 is the card you have just referred to that goes with Exhibit 227, is that right?

Mrs. Oswald. Yes, sir.

Mr. Rankin. We offer in evidence Exhibit 240, and ask that a copy be substituted.

The Chairman. That may be admitted.

(The card referred to was received in evidence as Commission Exhibit No. 240.)

Mr. Rankin. Mrs. Oswald, would you examine exhibits 228 through 236, both inclusive? And tell us whether or not those appear to be photostatic copies of correspondence about the Albert Schweitzer College and application?

247 Mrs. Oswald. Yes, that is right. That is right. This is correct. That is right. That is right. That is right. That is right. That is right. That is right. That is right. That is right. That is right.

Those are all right, sir.

Mr. Rankin. You have just finished comparing Exhibits 228 through 236 both inclusive, and found them to be correct photostatic copies of your files concerning the Albert Schweitzer matter?

Mrs. Oswald. That is right.

Mr. Rankin. We offer in evidence, Exhibits 228 through 236 both inclusive.

The Chairman. They may be admitted.

(The photostatic copies referred to were received in evidence as Commission Exhibit Nos. 228 through 236, inclusive.)

The Chairman. Have you introduced all the records you have now?

Mr. Rankin. Just a few more, Mr. Chairman.

(The document referred to was marked 241 for identification.)

Mr. Rankin. Mrs. Oswald, I hand you Exhibit 241 and ask you if that is one of the letters that you referred to in your testimony?

Mrs. Oswald. That is right.

Mr. Rankin. And it is one that you received?

Mrs. Oswald. It is one that I received in a letter from Russia, from Lee. And you have the letter, telling me to go to the International Rescue Committee, and to show the papers to the Red Cross in Vernon. This is the letter inclosed in that letter.

Mr. Rankin. We offer in evidence Exhibit 241, and ask leave to substitute a copy.

The Chairman. It may be admitted.

(The letter referred to was received in evidence as Commission Exhibit No. 241.)

(Documents marked 242 and 243 for identification.)

Mr. Rankin. Exhibits 242 and 243 are the telegram and the letter you received back from your transmission to the White House that you have testified about this morning, is that right?

Mrs. Oswald. That is right.

Mr. Rankin. And you say you would like to have the originals back?

Mrs. Oswald. Yes, sir.

Mr. Rankin. We offer in evidence Exhibits 242 and 243 and ask leave to substitute copies.

The Chairman. It may be admitted on that condition.

(Commission Exhibits Nos. 242 and 243 were admitted in evidence.)

The Chairman. Are all the records identified now and admitted, Mr. Rankin?

Mr. Rankin. Mr. Chairman, we have one further matter, and that is some correspondence that involves her son's communications with the Embassy, which correspondence was examined in the presence of Mr. Mark Lane when we were taking photostatic copies. And during that examination, Mrs. Oswald was able to identify the handwriting on part of them, and not able to identify it on another part. Is that right, Mrs. Oswald?

Mrs. Oswald. That is right; yes, sir.

Mr. Rankin. And we think we should probably, to cover that matter, ask her briefly to point those out.

The Chairman. Very well. Let's get that done before we adjourn, and then we will adjourn for lunch.

Mr. Rankin. Mr. Reporter, I will ask you to mark these exhibits, which are the ones that I understand Mrs. Oswald was able to identify the handwriting on.

(Documents were marked Commission Exhibits Nos. 244 through 250 for identification.)

Mr. Rankin. Mrs. Oswald, will you examine Exhibits 244 through 250, both inclusive, and tell us whether or not those are photostatic copies of communications of your son that you recognize the handwriting on of the originals?

Mrs. Oswald. Yes, sir.

248 Mr. Doyle. If you do not on any one of them, announce the number.

Mrs. Oswald. This is one I would believe that I have stated—if he wrote it, he wrote it very careful. It is not scribbled like he usually does.

Mr. Doyle. That is 246.

Mr. Rankin. Can you tell whether or not that is his signature on the second page of Exhibit 246?

Mrs. Oswald. It is just a little different. That could be forged. Just a little difference. We write left handed, and we have a trend.

Mr. Rankin. Is that one that you said before that you thought you could recognize?

Mrs. Oswald. I don't know, sir. I have no way of knowing. How would I know?

Mr. Rankin. Do you recognize the handwriting now?

Mrs. Oswald. As I have stated before, when I am looking at it, it doesn't appear to be immediately as Lee's handwriting. But it could be something that he has recopied over and over to get such a perfect lettering. It is not scribbled like we usually scribble. Now, this was one also that I would say——

Mr. Rankin. That is Exhibit 247.

Mrs. Oswald. That is scribbled.

Mr. Rankin. That is more scribbled, you say?

Mrs. Oswald. It is not quite as his ordinary writing. It is a little more thoughtfully written.

Mr. Rankin. You think it is his, though?

Mrs. Oswald. I would say this is his.

Mr. Rankin. Yes.

Mrs. Oswald. Now, this is thoughtfully written, too, yet it is his.

Mr. Rankin. Exhibit 248.

Mrs. Oswald. I am looking at this handwriting, because the rest of it is printed. I do not know too much about Lee's printing.

Mr. Rankin. Can you tell about the handwriting?

Mrs. Oswald. The signature looks like Lee's signature.

Mr. Rankin. Yes.

Mrs. Oswald. I will state again this looks like Lee's handwriting, but very thoughtfully written.

Mr. Rankin. That is Exhibit 249. Is that right?

Mrs. Oswald. That is right. And this is Lee's signature.

Mr. Rankin. That is Exhibit 250 that you just referred to?

Mrs. Oswald. Yes, sir. Now, I would say it is all Lee's handwriting, but very thoughtfully written.

Mr. Rankin. Thank you. We offer in evidence Exhibits 244 through 250, both inclusive.

The Chairman. They may be admitted.

(The documents referred to were received in evidence as Commission Exhibits Nos. 244 through 250, inclusive.)

(A group of documents was then marked 251 through 258 for identification.)

Mr. Rankin. Mrs. Oswald, I will hand you Exhibits 251 through 257, both inclusive, and ask you to examine those, and state whether you recognize the handwriting.

Mrs. Oswald. That doesn't look too much like Lee's handwriting. It could be a finer pen and more thoughtfully written. But I cannot identify this as Lee's handwriting.

Mr. Rankin. Can you tell about the signature?

Mrs. Oswald. The signature looks a little like Lee's signature.

Mr. Doyle. You refer to 251, when you are discussing this?

Mrs. Oswald. Yes, 251.

Now, this one I would say was not Lee's handwriting.

Mr. Rankin. That is 252?

Mrs. Oswald. 252.

I have never known Lee to sign Lee Harvey Oswald. He always signed Lee H. There again, that could be Lee's handwriting with a fine pen. But249 very thoughtfully written. But I will say it is not Lee's. I don't think it is. I cannot be positive. But I do not think it is Lee's handwriting.

Mr. Rankin. That is Exhibit 252 that you have been referring to?

Mrs. Oswald. Exhibit 252.

Here is another of the same caliber. It is too perfect. The writing is too perfect.

Mr. Rankin. What about the signature?

Mrs. Oswald. The signature looks like Lee's signature.

Mr. Doyle. That is 253.

Mrs. Oswald. 253. Yes, sir. This is a little different signature, I would say, than his normal signature.

Mr. Rankin. 254?

Mrs. Oswald. 254, yes, sir.

Mr. Rankin. You think that Exhibit 254 is your son's handwriting or not?

Mrs. Oswald. I would have to say with reservations again. It would have to be rewritten very thoroughly. It is not scribbled enough.

Mr. Rankin. You think that those letters, 251 through 254, are too carefully done for your son Lee?

Mrs. Oswald. Yes, sir. And if he did do them, he would have to have four or five copies to do it so perfect.

This is a little more scribbled. This signature looks more like Lee's than the other did.

Mr. Rankin. That is 255?

Mrs. Oswald. Yes, sir. 255.

This looks like Lee's handwriting—a lot of misspelling, and his signature. 256.

Now his Russian handwriting I know only from return addresses. However, I do have two brown papers with Russian writing on, from gifts that were sent to me. But I don't know if Lee addressed them or not.

And this is Lee's handwriting with a very fine pen. Isn't this handwriting backwards for a left hand? It seems when I looked at "my," it should be going this way—because I write like Lee, left handed.

Mr. Rankin. When you refer to this—or asked whether it was backwards, you were referring to Exhibit 257, were you?

Mrs. Oswald. Yes. This "m" should be going this way—which it is really. But it is kind of hard to testify to. I would say this is Lee's handwriting with a very fine pen, with reservations.

Mr. Rankin. Exhibit 257.

We offer in evidence Exhibits 251 through 257, both inclusive.

The Chairman. They may be admitted.

(The documents referred to were received in evidence as Commission Exhibits Nos. 251 through 257, inclusive.)

The Chairman. Mrs. Oswald, are you now ready—we are not going to ask you to do it right now, but we are going to recess at 2 o'clock. But are we now at the point where we can hear whatever you want to tell us about your life?

Mrs. Oswald. I am sorry, but I would like to have lunch.

The Chairman. I said that we were going to have lunch. But when we return—you have things up to that point of your story?

Mrs. Oswald. Yes, sir.

The Chairman. Very well.

You have another question you want to ask before we recess for lunch?

Mr. Rankin. I should like to offer for the limited purpose, Mr. Chairman, of the fact that we presented this picture to Mrs. Oswald and she said it was not the picture that was presented to her—for that limited purpose I should like to offer Exhibit 237.

The Chairman. It may be so admitted.

(The picture referred to was received in evidence as Commission Exhibit No. 237.)

Mr. Doyle. Mr. Chief Justice, during the noon hour may I have the custody of this transcript of a tape recording of an interview with Mrs. Oswald,250 the 28 pages which was tendered to us by Mr. Rankin this morning—and I will return it.

Mr. Rankin. That is for them to have.

The Chairman. That is to become your own.

Mr. Doyle. To become the property of Mrs. Oswald.

The Chairman. The property of Mrs. Oswald, yes. That is what we gave it to you for. She requested that.

Mr. Doyle. Thank you very much.

The Chairman. Very well, we will recess now until 2 o'clock.

(Whereupon, at 12:55 p.m., the President's Commission recessed.)

Afternoon Session
TESTIMONY OF MRS. MARGUERITE OSWALD RESUMED

The President's Commission reconvened at 2:05 p.m.

The Chairman. All right, Mr. Rankin, will you proceed with the hearing?

Mr. Rankin. Mrs. Oswald, you said that you would like to turn now to telling us about your life. We would appreciate that if you would do that.

Mrs. Oswald. Yes.

The Chairman. Mrs. Oswald, if you would prefer not to tell the story of your life, that is perfectly all right.

Mrs. Oswald. I want to tell the story but there is something else that upsets me.

The Chairman. It is perfectly all right if you don't wish to. You may take your time now and go right ahead.

Mrs. Oswald. I am sorry, you will have to excuse me about the story of my life, and Mr. Doyle knows why, but there is one part of the story of my life that will have a great connection with this, I believe.

I married Mr. Edwin Ekdahl who was an electrical engineer and a $10,000 a year man with an expense account. Mr. Ekdahl had a woman before he married me. Of course, I didn't know about it, sir. I made him wait a year before I married him, but the way I found this out, I received a telephone call, a telegram rather, he traveled—lots of times Lee and I traveled with him—stating he wouldn't return home when he was supposed to and for me not to meet him.

So, I called his office, I was familiar with, knew his secretary, and I was going to tell her that Mr. Ekdahl would be delayed 3 or 4 days. But immediately she said, "Mrs. Ekdahl, Mr. Ekdahl is not in, he has gone out to lunch."

So, I said, the general conversation went "When will he be back" and so on, and so that evening I took the car and I went to the Texas Electric Co., works for the Texaco, the main office in New York, but he was working in Fort Worth at the time, went to the building and saw him leave the building and I followed him and to an apartment house, saw him go into this apartment house.

Then I went back home, and my oldest son, John Edward Pic, who is in the service, had a friend at the house who was about 2 years older. I told them about what happened. So it was night by this time. The kids went with me.

I called Mr. John McClain, who is an attorney, and we live next door to Mr. McClain, and told him that I had seen Mr. Ekdahl go into a home when he was supposed to be out of town and what should I do.

He said, "Mrs. Oswald, just ring the phone. Do you know the woman?"

And I said, "Yes."

"Just ring the phone and let him know that you know he is there, that you saw him."

After I thought about it I thought that is not a good idea because he could leave and say he was just there on business and I wanted to catch him there.

So the kids and I planned that we would say she had a telegram, so we went up the stairs, I believe it was the second or the third floor, and the young man knocked on the door and said, "Telegram for Mrs. Clary"—was her name.

She said, "Please push it under the door" and I told him no; he said, "No, you have to sign for it."

251 So with that she opened the door to sign for it and with that I, my son, and with the other young man walked into the room and Mrs. Clary had on a negligee, and my husband had his sleeves rolled up and his tie off sitting on a sofa, and he said, "Marguerite, Marguerite, you have everything wrong, you have everything wrong."

He says, "Listen to me."

I said, "I don't want to hear one thing. I have seen everything I want to see, this is it."

My two boys, in military school, the two older boys, I am paying for the two older boys because I have sold a piece of property. I wanted to take care as long as I had money of my own children and when I married Mr. Ekdahl if he would support me and Lee I would be able to take care of John Edward, and Robert in military school, we couldn't have them with us because Mr. Ekdahl traveled.

This man never let me share with his insurance policies, beneficiary, in other words, I was another woman to him. I received $100 a month and that was it. That was all the money I had from Mr. Ekdahl, and when we traveled, for instance, we were in Santa Fe, N. Mex., and he was with all the businessmen, we would have to wait until Mr. Ekdahl got through, the baby and I, in order to eat, whether it was 2 or 3 o'clock in the evening because here I was, registered under Mrs. Ekdahl and I had a checking account, but under the name of Oswald, which was the money I was using for the children so it was kind of inconvenient for me to write a check under the name of Oswald.

I am trying to point out the kind of man he was.

I had a nice living in this sense. We lived in the finest hotels and we had the finest food because all of this was charged to his expense account but he gave me nothing but this $100. That was a standard thing and he expected me to account for every cent of the hundred dollars that I spent, which I refused to do.

So, we argued naturally, because this is not a marriage. Any man who marries a woman naturally shares, she shares in his bank account and in his insurance and so on and so forth.

I wanted to divorce Mr. Ekdahl naturally but my two boys as I have stated before were in the military school, and I wanted to wait until the end of the season, the school season.

So, Lee and I went to Covington, La., and I picked the boys up at military school because this was summer time—rather I wasn't back to him.

I left him and went back to him. But this particular time I picked the boys up at military school and we spent the summer in Covington, La., and by the way, I forgot to say that Lee had a beautiful voice and sang beautifully at age 6 in Covington, La., he sang a solo in the church, Silent Night, and that can be verified. This is a very small town and the only Lutheran Church there.

So, Mr. Ekdahl came to Covington, La., and I went back again to Mr. Ekdahl. But this time I went back to him I hadn't found out about the woman. I got excited. Then I found out about the woman, he rented a place on 8th Avenue, a home.

And after I was there about a day I was in the yard hanging out some things and it was in the apartment house downstairs and a woman came along and I said, "How are you? I am Mrs. Ekdahl."

She looked astonished, and after I had made friends with her she informed me Mr. Ekdahl had a woman in this particular house while I was in Covington and she thought she was his wife but now I am the wife come.

Then I found out about the woman and we went to her apartment and caught her there. This is the end of the season by this time.

In the meantime Mr. Ekdahl filed suit for divorce from me. I thought I was sitting pretty. He didn't have anything on me. I had him for adultery with witnesses and everything and I didn't have an idea that he could sue me for a divorce, but Mr. Ekdahl did sue me for a divorce, and Mr. Ekdahl got the divorce. It was a jury case, and Mr. John McClain, was my attorney, the man I told you that I called to find out what to do.

Now, Mr. Fred Korth represented Mr. Ekdahl and when I walked into the courtroom, gentlemen, there were witnesses there that I had never seen before.

252 A Mr. George Levine, who is a very big businessman and who Mr. Ekdahl was representing in Fort Worth for the electrical part of his plant. I knew him this way.

One time we went to the circus with his wife, my husband, myself and Lee, before going to the circus we had dinner. Now, understand we are having dinner in a public place. From the dinner we go to the circus, we are in a public place and I want you to know that it is the only time I had seen Mr. George Levine, when Mr. George Levine rushed from work in his khaki pants and got on the witness stand swore how I nagged Mr. Ekdahl and how I threw bottles at him and so on and so forth.

There were other witnesses that I had never seen, sir, who swore how I nagged Mr. Ekdahl, and Mr. Ekdahl got his divorce from me.

Now, 2 days after the assassination, after Lee's death, while I am at Six Flags it comes over the radio that Mr. Korth knew the family, this happened in 1948, sir, then Mr. Korth knew the family, and that he had represented Mr. Ekdahl in divorce proceedings and, of course, talked to the reporters where they got the information that I hit him with a bottle and so on and so forth.

Now, that is my story there. I am not even guilty of that divorce, as you see. This can be proved by my son John Edward Pic because he was a witness, sir.

I do not think I am going—I am not going to speculate but give my thoughts to anyone who would immediately make a statement that he had represented the mother of the accused assassin as an attorney years ago, and that I nagged Mr. Ekdahl and so on and so forth.

That was publicly announced about 2 days after my son was shot, sir.

Now, the name then, of course, he probably knew the name Oswald, but the name then was Ekdahl that I would say would stick in his mind more.

I will try to get to the very beginning of my life, Chief Justice.

The Chairman. Any time. Just take your time.

Mrs. Oswald. My mother died when I was quite young and my father raised us with housekeepers. My aunt lived in the neighborhood and I had a lot of cousins and a lot of aunts. My father was French, his name was Claverie, and my mother was German, the name is Stucke. All of my father's folks spoke French and my father spoke French to his sisters. I was a child of one parent, and yet I have had a normal life, a very hard normal life that I had been able to combat all by myself, sir, without much help from anyone.

I am saying that in reference to Lee being alone; there have been so many psychiatrists saying he was by himself and he had a father image and that is why he did the shooting. There are many, many children with one parent who are perfectly normal children and I happen to be one myself.

I had a very happy childhood. I sang. I sang from the kindergarten at grammar school, and all through grammar school I was the lead singer. I was one of the most popular young ladies in the school. I also play piano by ear. I don't know a note. I used to play the marching school song for the school children.

At my grammar school graduation I had the honor of wearing a pink dress instead of a white dress and sang the song "Little Pink Roses." So I had a very happy childhood and a very full childhood. I played the piano. We had house parties in those days and a lot of gatherings and it was everything Marguerite—and I also played a ukulele, so I have a very full happy childhood.

At the age of 17, I am ahead of my story—I have had 1 year high school education. I know that on my applications I had that I had completed high school but that is almost necessary to get a job.

But I had 1 year of high school education is all that I had, sir.

I then went to work at age 17, not quite 17, for one of the biggest corporation lawyers in New Orleans, La. The name then was DuFour, Rosen, Wolff, and Kammer. Mr. DuFour died while I was there and Mr. Kammer, I believe, is still living but they were corporation attorneys for that firm plus 4 or 5 other attorneys that handled divorce cases and similar cases and I was receptionist in the outer office.

So, everybody who came into the office had to state their business to me, because the attorneys were very busy, and if it was a particular case I had to know who to refer the party to this particular man.

253 So, naturally, I got a very large education, let's say, by doing this, and the mayor and everybody in the town, these are the largest attorneys, corporation attorneys in New Orleans, sir, and they were attorneys representing the New Orleans Public Service and big things of that sort, and the mayor and all used to call me the boss. When the mayor came in he had an appointment but I still had to ring the phone to see if the men were ready to see him. So they called me the boss.

I was also a maid in one of the carnival balls. I am a very poor young lady but a very, let's say, popular young lady.

My early childhood. We lived on the Phillips Street in New Orleans which was a very poor neighborhood. My father was one of the very first streetcar conductors and stayed on the very same line all these years until he retired and they gave him a citation because he was on the same line all those years from retirement, and we lived in a mixed neighborhood of Negroes and white, and my childhood I played with Negroes, sir, right next door to me was a lovely family that I grew up with this Negro family.

I married Mr. Edward John Pic, Jr., while working at the law firm. I was married to Mr. Pic two and a half years when I became with child, and he did not want any children. His family and my family tried to talk to him, and, well, his family almost beat him up to say, but nobody could do anything with him.

So, at 3 months I left Mr. Pic. Mr. Pic did not divorce me, and you have the records there of me divorcing Mr. Pic, contrary to all other stories, sir.

This child, John Edward Pic then I bore alone, without a husband. I was 3 months pregnant. I had 6 more months to go, and I had this child without a husband.

So, I have had two children without a husband present, Lee and the first child.

Mr. Oswald was an insurance agent, and he used to collect insurance at my sister's house, and the day that I left Mr. Pic he helped move my furniture, the things that I was going to take.

I didn't see Mr. Ekdahl for some time and——

The Chairman. Ekdahl or Oswald.

Mrs. Oswald. Mr. Oswald, sir, I am sorry.

John Edward and I were coming from the park one day, and Mr. Ekdahl picked—Mr. Oswald picked me up, and he was separated from his wife, however, not divorced but had been separated for a number of years, and I started dating Mr. Ekdahl and we decided to marry and he divorced his wife.

Mr. Rankin. You said Ekdahl again.

Mrs. Oswald. Oswald, I am sorry, and then he got the divorce proceeding. He was separated for a long time but never had been divorced from his wife but when we knew he was going to marry, and I also then got the divorce from Mr. Pic. I was not divorced there from Mr. Pic, either. We were legally separated but I was not divorced from him.

So, Mr. Oswald and I married and of that marriage Robert was born 9 months later, and as you know consequently Lee, 2 months after his father had died.

Now, Mr. Oswald was a very good man. There was the only happy part of my life. When he died hardly anybody knew that John Edward Pic was not his son. He wanted to adopt John Edward, but because his father was supporting him which I think was only $18 a month, I explained to Lee that I thought we should save this money for the boys' education and let his own father support him and naturally we would educate and do all we could do but that was no more than right. So that is why he did not adopt John Edward.

Now, that is the story of my three marriages. I have been married approximately 9 years in the three times that I have been married, sir, and I would say, I am probably guilty of a lot of things but the initial guilt has never been mine in any of these marriages, the first marriage I had explained, the second marriage was death, and the third marriage was Mr. Ekdahl.

I think then you know the rest of the story, how I lived with my children and tried to support my children.

I have often held two jobs trying to support my children. I have a whole file that the Commission has copies of jobs that I have worked, and I have also worked for these places twice, and have gone back. I have wonderful recommendations.254 I think I have been fired about five times in my life, and I have had much, much employment, and the reason for that is finances, in other words, I have always had a very low salary, and I am a very aggressive sales person, as these papers say, and I always produce for my people and I was in demand actually.

They would come to me and offer me 20, 25 dollars more, believe me, gentlemen. I would quit the job where I was and quit the new job because 25 dollars paid my light and heat bill and gave my children some clothes and that is mostly the reason for all of this employment, and also I used to quit my job as much as possible in the summer time when the children were little in order to be home with them.

Now, I skipped a part in the beginning about the children being placed in the Lutheran Home. I am Lutheran and I was a church member, a church worker, I should say. I helped, I sewed, natural gifted, I never did take a lesson, I never did use a pattern, my sister can verify this.

I used to come home from the attorneys with material, cut out the material, sew it, press it and go out on a date. I just had the knack of doing things that way, sir, and she can verify this because my niece, I taught her to sew and my sister said, "You are so slow, Aunt Marguerite used to sew on the material and go out on a date," and my niece would say, "Is it true, my mother said you would sew on material and go out on a date," and I said, "I wish I had a nickel for every time I did."

So those are gifted things I can't explain.

Lee had certain gifted ways about him also.

In the early part of my life that I had skipped when the war broke out and my finances were gone, I talked with the church. It was on Alva Street in New Orleans, not too far where my home was and they investigated the money I had, and I had a little money left at this time and they let me place the two older boys in the Lutheran Home which is a home only for the Lutheran Church.

This is not an institution. They have their own private school on the ground, and it is primarily based for children of one parent. However, they do take orphans. It was really not designed to be an orphan home. It was for children of one parent and you pay according to your circumstances, and they investigated my salary and after I went to work, I paid according to my circumstances for my two boys.

I took my two boys home with me every weekend, sir, and brought them back in time for Sunday so they can go to church with the children in the home. They got a wonderful education because the school on the school grounds had very few children in them.

There would be maybe two or three children to a particular grade so they had wonderful school. Lee was too young. They would not take Lee into the home until he was 3 years old.

So, I have hired maids and I have quit many a job for this. You have a background on my job, this accounts for it. Many a position and I have always had title and no money, assistant manager or manager in charge of a department, and I have had to quit that, because the maid wouldn't show up, and you couldn't get a maid for love or money.

War had broken out and the Negroes in New Orleans were going into factories and so on and so forth so there is many a job I had to leave in order to stay home and mind Lee until I could get help.

Then my sister helped with Lee. There is one particular instance, I let a couple have my home, plus $15 a month in order to care for Lee while I worked, and this couple after about 2 month's time had neglected Lee and so I had to put them out of the house and there again I had to quit a job, and take care of Lee until I could make arrangements and my sister could help me with it.

So when Lee was 3 years old I was having it very difficult with Lee, because of the different people to take care of Lee, and the different jobs that I had to give up.

However, I was never in want of work. It was during the war and I was always able to get work, but I realized if I continued to quit jobs because I couldn't hold the jobs that some day I wouldn't have enough jobs in New Orleans for me to hold one.

255 So, then at age 3 Lee was placed in the home. I waited patiently for age 3 because I wanted naturally for the brothers to be together. It was hard on Lee also because Lee was at a different place and his brothers were at a different place. So at age 3 I placed Lee in a Lutheran home. Of course, you have to be under strict investigation financially and otherwise to do this because this is a church placement, sir.

Then, I became manager of Princess hosiery shop on Canal Street. I opened that shop and I was left by myself and in 6 days' time I hired four girls. There was the first shop this man has had. He now has, I think, 54 stores and he always remembers me as on the road of starting him to success, because this young man didn't have much money at the time. And this is where I met Mr. Ekdahl and there is why I didn't want to marry right away because the children were being taken care of and I was manager of the hosiery shop.

So, now, I was sitting pretty in our American slang and I did not want to marry. But he persisted. He decided he wanted to marry me and I decided to marry him. I went to the Lutheran home and talked to the, well, you don't call him a manager, the head of the home, and I was going to marry Mr. Ekdahl, and I asked if I should have, if I could have Lee, that I didn't want the children, John Edward, and Robert to miss their schooling and I told them that I would wait until the children got out of school to marry Mr. Ekdahl but Mr. Ekdahl traveled, and, yet, he had a stroke and Mr. Ekdahl had offered, if I would come to Dallas, he was being transferred to Dallas, that he would pay my room, my living quarters and everything if I would cook and take care of him and I told the home, the Lutheran home about this arrangement, so there was nothing going to be immoral about it, sir, or I wouldn't have explained to the Lutheran home and they let me have Lee under those circumstances because they knew that I was a good woman and doing the best I could.

So, I got Lee, and when we went to Dallas, I then realized I did not want to marry Mr. Ekdahl, but I had already given up my position as manager of the hosiery shop, and had taken Lee out of school so with the money, I told you I had some money, and I had sold a piece of property, I bought another piece of property for a very small down payment on Victor Street in Dallas, Tex., and Mr. Ekdahl traveled.

Now, Mr. Ekdahl used to come on weekends and stay at my home. Of course, in his bedroom with my children, just maybe not even every weekend because he traveled, and then I decided I would marry Mr. Ekdahl. I mean I decided not to, I mean, he was a persistent one.

Then I married Mr. Ekdahl and the home was sold and I traveled with Mr. Ekdahl and the children were put into military school with the money I sold the home with.

I believe I have covered everything. I am not quite sure.

Are there any questions, Mr. Rankin, that I haven't gotten?

Mr. Rankin. I think that is very helpful.

I would like to ask you about those pictures that you offered and then decided you didn't want to give us. If you would get those out, I would like to identify them so that there cannot be any misunderstanding about just what they are about.

Could you do that?

Mrs. Oswald. By the way, one of the reporters when I came downstairs said "What is all the commotion about those pictures, you have, Mrs. Oswald?" Where do those leaks come from? That is the example. They wanted to know about the pictures.

Mr. Chief Justice, this is Lee at 6 months.

The Chairman. He was a good looking baby.

Mrs. Oswald. This is Lee there at 2 years. Would—if you would like a copy of the Marina pictures, sir, I would be more than happy to do that.

I think they are in an envelope. This is important, Mr. Rankin. This has something to do with Time Magazine is what I think he did. This is where he got that from. These were copied for this session. These are from my other boys to mother, and John Edward and which I wanted to show we were a family but as soon as the boys married—here is another thing, which is true to human nature.

256 I am a widow woman with no money and I happened not to have the type daughter-in-laws who wanted a widow woman in case they have to support me. My children make very low salaries and so I am not alone, we have thousands and thousands of women like me. It is hard to say the children don't want you. But there are many, many mothers whose sons have married because it is different with a girl.

Now a girl will take care of the mother but the boy's mother is usually nothing and I am not going to be helped or supported.

I am going to take care of myself because that is the attitude and that was the attitude when I was sick.

Lee Harvey Oswald was the only one who has helped his mother at any time but I wanted to show mothers today cared and everything until they married. That was the type family we were, sir.

And this was the picture, Mr. Rankin, of the three children which is a happy life and he wanted to be in New Orleans.

Mr. Rankin. Mrs. Oswald, I am going to call your attention to Exhibit 258 which you just referred to and said maybe that is what you meant.

Mrs. Oswald. Yes, because I gave him this when he entered the home.

Mr. Rankin. This Exhibit 258 refers to the letter you received from me as general counsel for the Commission, and then a letter to the President, and your appeal to the President, is that right?

Mrs. Oswald. That is correct.

Mr. Rankin. And this is a copy you released for the press conference in Dallas. That is Exhibit 258. I offer Exhibit 258.

The Chairman. It may be admitted.

Mr. Rankin. If you will permit me, I will ask the court reporter to identify these pictures and I don't intend to offer them but then I will ask you each one by number so we can make it clear, and then return them to you, so you can tell us what they are about, is that all right with you?

Mrs. Oswald. Yes, that is just fine, thank you.

Mr. Rankin. Now, Mrs. Oswald, I will hand you Exhibits 259 through 269, both inclusive, and ask you to take them starting with Exhibit 259 and referring to the exhibit in each case, tell the Commission what the picture is about.

Mrs. Oswald. 259 is of the three children, John Edward, Robert, and Lee and the three are smiling. In fact this picture was in a magazine because of the three good poses. It is hard to get three pictures alike.

Mr. Rankin. About how old are the children in that picture?

Mrs. Oswald. I know Lee was approximately going on 6 years old. There is 5 years difference in Robert so Robert would be 11, that is correct and John Edward would be 13. That is when they went to military school.

This is a picture of Lee at age 6 months.

Mr. Rankin. You are talking about Exhibit 260?

Mrs. Oswald. 260, yes, sir.

This is a picture of Lee at the Bronx Zoo, Exhibit 261 at age 13.

Mr. Rankin. That is the Bronx Zoo in New York?

Mrs. Oswald. Yes, sir.

Mr. Rankin. That is the Bronx Zoo in New York that you told us about.

Mrs. Oswald. Yes, sir.

262 is a picture of Lee in Atsugi, Japan in 1958 showing his strength.

Mr. Rankin. That shows him in Marine uniform also, does it?

Mrs. Oswald. In his Marine uniform showing his muscles to his mother.

And this is a picture, Exhibit 263 taken in Corregidor 1957 in the wilderness.

Mr. Rankin. He is still in the Marines there?

Mrs. Oswald. Oh, yes, he is in fatigues, there. This is a picture taken August 19, 264 taken in California coming home on leave from Japan.

Mr. Rankin. 264 he is still in the Marines?

Mrs. Oswald. Yes, he is still in the Marines August 19. This is a picture of Lee taken in Minsk, Russia June 1st, 1961, Minsk, USSR, Exhibit 267.

There is a picture of Marguerite Oswald, the mother taken in New Orleans.

Mr. Rankin. What is the number?

Mrs. Oswald. 265.

Mr. Rankin. Thank you. That is your own picture?

257 Mrs. Oswald. Yes, sir.

This is a Mother's Day card sent to me from Santa Ana, California on May 7, 1959 from Lee.

Mr. Rankin. That is Exhibit 266?

Mrs. Oswald. And this is Exhibit 268 which is a Christmas card I had sent Lee on his first Christmas away from home—he joined in October—that Lee had kept all these years in his sea bag, this was found in his sea bag he left with me.

This is a book of Christmas carols Exhibit 269 that was also found in Lee's sea bag.

Mr. Rankin. Now, Exhibits 259 to 269 both inclusive, are those all of the pictures that you were offering the Commission this morning?

Mrs. Oswald. I have many more pictures, I would be happy to show you but these are the pictures that your Mr. Jenner said he would like to have for the Commission.

Mr. Rankin. And that you were referring to when you offered them to the Commission?

Mrs. Oswald. Yes.

Mr. Rankin. Thank you very much and we would like to return them to you at this time.

The Chairman. We will return them to you, Mrs. Oswald.

Mr. Rankin. That is all I have, Mr. Chairman.

The Chairman. Well I think that will be all then. Thank you Mrs. Oswald and if you become too tired with your testimony, we know it has been a long and arduous task for you, but we appreciate your presence.

Now, Mr. Doyle.

Mr. Doyle. Sorry for the interruption, sir. Mrs. Oswald, do you care to make any comment to the Commission about the tape recording, the transcript of the tape recording of Mrs. Marguerite Oswald furnished to you by the Commission this morning? Do you care to make any comment about that?

Mrs. Oswald. Should I go all the way and make the comment?

Mr. Doyle. You make any comment you desire on that paper. I ask you whether or not you have any comment to make concerning that paper that you sent, that you were given?

Mrs. Oswald. I am concerned about one thing, Mr. Doyle, if I may just step over there and ask you a question.

The Chairman. You may step out in the hall and talk to Mr. Doyle.

Mrs. Oswald. Chief Justice Warren and Mr. Rankin, I have read this and it has upset me very, very much, that is what I was upset about. I have stated before in my testimony that at the end of the Six Flags I insisted upon going home and getting my important papers and I was ignored.

I wanted to testify. They put Robert on tape many a time and Marina continuously and I didn't have an interview. I have stated this previously, if you remember, and then finally a Mr. Howard put me on tape for about 5 or 10 minutes only, sir, and I had started with the defection because I was under the impression that we missed a bet when we didn't find out how Lee got to Russia and as far as I know, no reporter has been able to find out what ship he left on, and then Robert left the bedroom because he had the news that we could not get a minister, if you recall, and cried, and I said to Mr. Howard "Now all that I have left me because I see my son crying bitterly." I have stated these facts before, a very short interview.

This interview is supposed to have been by Mr. Howard, sir. The same Mr. Mike Howard that I have previously identified before on many occasions, and I swear before this Committee that now my life is more in danger which I have said before, because I did not give this testimony. This is the testimony that has been gathered by known facts because I have been a public figure.

I have had three press conferences, I have written for magazines and newspapers. I have not kept quiet, sir, as you know, so these things have been accumulated. I was not questioned and answered, sir. I have stated it before and I state it now. This is the same man who was sent to me in Fort Worth, Tex. that I have complained that I did not get protection, if you will recall. This is the very same man, sir. This is the same man that I have told you that gave my daughter-in-law a red-carpet treatment if you will recall along258 with the other one I identified in the picture. This is the man I have been sitting here complaining about. Here is my evidence. I am ready to have a heart attack. I was sick, sir, when I read it because I realize now how my life is in danger and I want to say this: Many people know about this, many people, sir, Mr. Jack Langdon of the Morning Times, Mr. Blair Justice of the Star Telegram and I immediately called Mr. Blair Justice of the Star Telegram when this man knocked on my door last week to protect me, and told Blair Justice that this was the man, there was an article written in the Star Telegram, not printed but about pointed every lie at the Six Flags I made it plain that the other one if he had a gun would have shot me in my prior testimony, Mr. Rankin you remember that, so I told Mr. Justice, I said "Justice I am scared to death. This is the same man that I am suspicious of that they have now sent to guard me," and as you know, sir, I was not protected.

I was not protected while in Fort Worth. I have testified to that, if you will recall. This is the man, and I did not give this testimony, sir.

I have repeatedly stated to newspapermen and to everybody publicly that I have never been questioned. The only thing I could figure why I was never questioned is because Lee was an agent, and I have stated that fact. Why they left me alone, because I have never been questioned.

Mr. Tom Whalen who is an announcer for one of the television stations in Fort Worth he kept calling Lee the assassin of President Kennedy, and I called Mr. Whalen and I said to Mr. Whalen "You don't know that Lee assassinated President Kennedy. I object to that."

I said "I can't tell you what to do, sir, but I would like to you to say the accused assassin because this is what he is" and he apologized and we talked a little while and I said no sir, I told him I was not—I had never been interviewed. He says "I can't believe that, Mrs. Oswald." I said "Believe it or not I have never been interviewed," which I made a statement upon arriving in Washington that I have never had a complete tape recording or question and answer.

I went to the courthouse, and gave my information to the FBI men as I stated previously, which took a few minutes.

I never did see those men after that. They weren't investigated and at the Six Flags I repeatedly wanted to go home and get my papers and give the documents that I have here, as I stated, and I was not questioned, sir at Six Flags.

I was questioned for about 5 or 10 minutes and I stopped this way. All of my thoughts have gone from me because I see my son crying. I have previously stated that.

Mr. Rankin. Mrs. Oswald, in light of your saying that you didn't give this interview evidenced by this document, a copy of which we gave to you which purports to have been recorded on November 25, 1963, by Mr. Howard, I would like to have that identified by the reporter and then give you another copy that you can compare, and I would like to ask you just a few questions about it.

Mrs. Oswald. Fine.

Mr. Rankin. Mrs. Oswald, I hand you back the 28-page reported interview that I just referred to that has just been marked Exhibit 270 and ask you if that is the document that you were referring to in your testimony?

Mrs. Oswald. Yes, sir; this is the document I am referring to.

Mr. Rankin. That you just said you did not give that interview?

Mrs. Oswald. That is correct. And I will finish something, too, Mr. Mark R. Lane called and I told Mr. Mark Lane about the Secret Service man. He knows about this, many know about this, I have witnesses by this.

Mr. Rankin. What do you mean by this?

Mrs. Oswald. About this man, Mr. Howard.

Mr. Rankin. I see. But not that you said that you did not give this interview.

Mrs. Oswald. Pardon?

Mr. Rankin. When you say this, you didn't mean that they know that you did not give this interview?

Mrs. Oswald. No. They knew that I didn't testify, I am sorry. But Mr. Mark Lane called me the morning that I was to—the day I was supposed to259 leave Fort Worth to come to Washington, sir, and I said to Mr. Mark Lane, "I am not going in the car with Mr. Mike Howard." and there was another Mr. Howard by the way who came there that day. I don't know whether he was his brother or not, we will have to find out, sir, the day I was going to leave for Washington, and I said, "Lane, I am scared to death." He says "Don't worry. I will call Mr. Walden, who is the Star Telegram reporter and ask him to accompany you." and Mr. Mark Lane called Mr. Walden of the Star Telegram and asked him to accompany me and Mr. Walden did accompany me with these two Secret Service men to the airport and when Mr. Walden entered my home I told him I am so glad you are here because I didn't want to go with this agent by myself.

And this is the same agent now—Chief Justice are you interested enough for me to tell you a little more?

The Chairman. About this?

Mrs. Oswald. Yes.

The Chairman. Tell what you wish about it.

Mrs. Oswald. We are going to go back now a little bit and then you will see the pattern. At the end of the Six Flags; I will make it as short as possible and when everything was Mama and we were going to live together and I told you they took her from me and I didn't see her, then Marina's testimony started to change, sir. Marina's testimony was not this testimony the first 3 days.

I have testified, and she has testified differently than me. I don't know of all of her testimony but the first 3 days, this was not her husband's rifle, at the police station and she admitted but it wasn't her husband's rifle. She was going to live with her Mama and everything was fine and then when I told you the way they did, then Marina turned against her Mama, you no have work, and from that time Marina has been changed to a different personality, let's admit it, sir, Marina has been changing to a different personality.

Her statements, her way of life, she smokes, as I said today. I am not saying it now, she stopped nursing her baby. This is a Russian girl, I know she lived with me 1 month, how untouched of worldly things she was, and I mentioned before there was a lot of rumors that I didn't feel like I wanted to go into but that I couldn't overlook.

Sir, if you would know the rumors, then you would put two and two together what I have been trying to say. This man, along with the other one that I have identified, are definitely in this pattern, and Marina Oswald, yes, Marina Oswald has changed completely.

She made a statement on television now she is happy that she has ever been and people have written, her husband is only gone 2 months.

Mr. Rankin. Mrs. Oswald, this Exhibit 270, you understand, is a transcription, that is the writing out of what was on the tape, you understand that?

Mrs. Oswald. But I was never taped, sir.

Mr. Rankin. We have asked, Mr. Chairman, that the tape be sent over so that it can be heard, if you wish.

The Chairman. Now, you mean.

Mr. Rankin. Yes. It is on its way over.

The Chairman. Oh, yes.

Mrs. Oswald. I have stated previously, if I was taped it was during a conversation going on that they taped me. I have never sat down and been taped, sir. I don't think I am out of my mind, I wonder why.

The Chairman. May I see this.

Mrs. Oswald. Mr. Max Phillips, who is a Secret Service agent brought a dictaphone into my home, on Thomas Place, when I left Six Flags, and I saw it connected and Mr. Jim Cox of the Star Telegram can prove that I disconnected it. When I was telling Mr. Jim Cox my story about putting my children into a Lutheran home and I thought it was a personal story that had nothing to do with this particular case I disconnected the tape recorder.

Mr. Max Phillips brought a tape recorder into my home and as you know I do a lot of talking. And I never did sit down.

Mr. Rankin. This was a tape recording at the Six Flags.

Mrs. Oswald. No, sir.

Mr. Rankin. It purports to be. You understand that?

260 Mrs. Oswald. Yes, I understand that thoroughly.

I would like to produce some other evidence that I have also to this Commission. I have, as Mr. Doyle knows, a tape recorder with a few recordings on it, and there are several, two, I believe. Mr. Sorrels' recordings on that. I found it necessary, because my mail was being opened, my mail, I have reported to the Postal Inspections, I have stated in the beginning that all of my rights were taken away from me, and, sir, believe me they were, and when I was a lone woman I would say something I was supposed to be out of my mind and didn't know what I was talking about I started to decide I needed some evidence too and Mr. Sorrels kept pushing me off about seeing my daughter-in-law, I have him on tape, and I have Mr. Thorne on tape about my mail being opened. I have some other evidence.

Mr. Rankin. Have you ever transcribed that?

Mrs. Oswald. No sir.

Mr. Rankin. Would you transcribe that and send us copies of it?

Mrs. Oswald. Yes, sir. That is a very long document. I was never questioned and answered.

The Chairman. It would hardly seem possible, Mrs. Oswald, that unless this is a complete fabrication that anyone could have given these answers but you, it is—so many of these questions and answers are exactly what you have told us.

Mrs. Oswald. Exactly what I have told you, sir, I have been in the news continuously, I have made the same statements over and over in magazines and newspapers and press conferences, yes, sir, that is not news to anybody.

And as a matter of fact, I was taped, oh, this might be a point, I was taped at my first press conference which was at the Fort Worth Press Club which I talked approximately 2 hours, and there was a tape recorder there. I talked over 2 hours at that press conference.

Mr. Rankin. This is question and answer?

For instance, and I am looking at page 18, there are different questions and answers.

Mrs. Oswald. That is a condensed version of my whole testimony, as I say, because I have been in the public eye and I have all of these things public.

These things have been made public.

Mr. Rankin. This purports to be following the tape recording as to your son Robert, you remember his giving a tape recording interview?

Mrs. Oswald. Yes, Robert gave a tape recording, I told you, and so did Marina and I was not asked to be tape recorded.

I myself asked to give testimony and I did give about 5- or 10-minutes testimony that I say again that I ended up with now all my thoughts are gone, I see my son crying, a very short, and if I remember correctly, I started with the defection. I do know because I said "Robert doesn't know anything about my trip to Washington. He wasn't interested and maybe he should listen to my testimony." And I got not far from it when Robert cried and that ended that testimony.

The Chairman. Mrs. Oswald, while we are waiting, you may relax. We will take a little recess, if you want to refresh yourself, you may step out. That is perfectly all right.

Mrs. Oswald. One thing, of course I am not supposed to tell you what to do, I know and I don't mean to, Chief Justice, but since this man was reassigned to guard me in Fort Worth I would like to know if he was free or if he was taken off another assignment to come to Fort Worth to guard me for this trip? Because it is the same man, understand?

Mr. Rankin. Mrs. Oswald, I think in regard to that I had better state on the record we had nothing to do, that is the Commission or myself, about the selection of any of the personnel. We just asked the Secret Service to handle it and so we don't at this time know what the answer is to your question.

Mrs. Oswald. Thank you.

(Short recess.)

The Chairman. All right, Mr. Rankin, you may continue.

Mr. Rankin. Mr. Chairman, we have this transcript at this time that we are ready to play now and it starts out with Robert Oswald's testimony or answers and questions like the transcription, written transcription states at 261 the head of it, and I think it might be helpful if we just start with that and we can move on if you wish to with the other.

The Chairman. All right.

(Playing of tape recording.)

Mr. Rankin. Mrs. Oswald, this is about 3 pages out of around between 13 and 14 of your son's transcription. Do you recognize your son's voice?

Mrs. Oswald. Yes, I have to listen really, it is a recorder, I am sure, but I have to, you know, listen, that story is right. There are two discrepancies so far as dates.

Mr. Rankin. But you do recognize it? It sounds like him?

Mrs. Oswald. Yes, it sounds like him. It is the recorder.

Mr. Rankin. Is it all right for us to pass down to yours at this time?

Mrs. Oswald. Yes, and I want the time on it.

Mr. Rankin. Yes.

Mrs. Oswald. That would be how many pages? About the 2 months he made an error, it is June 13 and they were in my home with me by July 14.

(Transcription played.)

Mr. Rankin. Mrs. Oswald, do you have any problem about that being your voice on the tape?

Mrs. Oswald. No, sir, but I think probably the rest of it is my voice. I had a news conference at the Fort Worth Press Club at Fort Worth, Tex., that I was on tape for 2 hours.

Now, here is what—this is probably a little over 10 minutes to hear "Pardon me, you will have to excuse me." And there was a lot of break there. That is exactly 10 minutes. I have testified that at the Inn of Six Flags I talked for about 10 minutes and then I stopped because my son was crying, and I still say I testified for 10 minutes approximately at the Inn of Six Flags.

I had a press conference at the Fort Worth Press Club, that can be verified that I talked for over 2 hours that I was on tape. I was sitting on a desk with many, many reporters because this was when it just happened, and we had a lot of reporters, and in the back of me was a man, and everything I said was on this tape, and it was over 2 hours that I talked at this press club.

Mr. Rankin. Did you say the things that you say here?

Mrs. Oswald. Yes.

Mr. Rankin. In answer to these questions?

Mrs. Oswald. Yes, and all through here is my story, yes, sir.

Mr. Rankin. At the press club?

Mrs. Oswald. Yes, sir. I talked for 2 hours.

Mr. Rankin. And you didn't say it to this agent?

Mrs. Oswald. I said, and I am going to continue to say this, that I had approximately 10 minutes interview at the Inn of Six Flags, and then the telephone rang and Robert came out and started crying, and I said I see my son crying so now all my thoughts have left me and I was not interviewed any further at the Inn of Six Flags, sir.

Mr. Rankin. On this tape you heard a little child talking, didn't you?

Mrs. Oswald. Yes, that is right.

Mr. Rankin. Now, was there a little child like that at this——

Mrs. Oswald. Yes, June was at the Inn of the Six Flags and if I am as smart as they are and if they are as smart as I am, there could be a little child crying all during the rest of the testimony.

Mr. Rankin. I see, but there wasn't a little child at the place where you gave your press conference?

Mrs. Oswald. No, but I am not familiar with—but couldn't a tape be added and spliced and couldn't a child voice be put in? I am just saying, because I have said before and I am saying now I was taped for about 10 minutes, just where this business came in was exactly 10 minutes, "Pardon me," now I spoke for over two and a half hours at the Fort Worth Press Club and was taped there.

What they can do with that tape, I don't know.

Mr. Rankin. Who asked you the questions when you were answering them at the Fort Worth Press Club?

Mrs. Oswald. Now, it was not in this sequence, answer and questions. So, I am saying, I do not know how they can get my voice and do the tape and answering questions for the rest, but gentlemen, I am not out of my mind and I have said this over and over publicly, that I have never been interviewed, answer and question, but for about 10 minutes at the Inn of the Six Flags.

Mr. Rankin. Mr. Chairman, then I would like to go down about 5 or 6 minutes more maybe and see what it sounds like and the background if we play for just a few minutes.

The Chairman. All right.

Mr. Rankin. Would you drop down for another 5 minutes? Skip about 5 minutes, please.

Mrs. Oswald. After you start may I say something else?

Mr. Rankin. Yes.

Mrs. Oswald. All of this here I have said and also said in my home and I have testified that there was a tape recorder in my home brought in by Mr. Max Phillips, Mr. Rankin. Why can't—I don't know anything about tape but it can be spliced and edited and so forth, that much I know because when I have talked for reporters, they don't use everything I say. They splice.

Mr. Rankin. But you recognize, Mrs. Oswald, it would be quite a job to splice in each one of those questions.

Mrs. Oswald. Well, the assassination of the President of the United States and a scapegoat for it would be quite a job, it would be worth while, yes, sir, I realize that.

Mr. Rankin. Let's try a little more.

(Transcription played.)

Mr. Rankin. Do you want to say anything more about this?

Mrs. Oswald. Yes, I do. I haven't gone through all of this. I have made the statement over and over that my conversation was stopped. It was approximately a 10-minute conversation and it was stopped with the remark "I see my son crying. All my thoughts have left me."

Is that remark in this any place?

Mr. Rankin. I don't recall that it is.

Mrs. Oswald. Well, we will have to recall, because this, I have stated and was said and that is when I stopped the conversation at the Inn of the Six Flags. Robert came out crying because he couldn't get a minister and I said, "I see my son crying, now all my thoughts have left me," and the interview stopped at the Inn of Six Flags which I have testified was approximately 10 minutes.

Now, sir, there was a microphone in my home. This is not news to anybody. I have said this over and over and over. The ordinary layman by now knows my whole story, Chief Justice Warren. There was Mr. Max Phillips who had a microphone in my home. I testified on tape for over 2 hours at—talked at the Fort Worth Club, which would be, it is the same story over and over, I have told you all the same story that you already have here.

The Chairman. Yes, but it wasn't the same man interrogating you at this place as it was at this hotel, was it?

Mrs. Oswald. About now—I don't know if this is the same man on the whole tape because I haven't listened to it. No, no one interrogated me at the Fort Worth Press Club, sir. I talked, there was an open press.

The Chairman. But it is the same voice we are hearing now asking you questions as at the beginning of this tape, isn't it?

Mrs. Oswald. That is correct. I have just stated, since this is a very big operation, that this could be edited and this man's voice put on there. This I know, because the radio stations called me and they edited what I do. Isn't this possible, that this could be edited, and that this man asked the questions and then my voice be put in. It would be a big job but I am asking isn't that possible? I swear that I have never had answers and questions of this sort, gentlemen.

The Chairman. Shall we turn over about 10 minutes more and see if the same voices are in it there?

(Transcription played.)

Mrs. Oswald. I am not sure but I think it was possible it was an editor that he put me on there.

(Transcription played.)

The Chairman. Well, Mrs. Oswald, those are the same voices.

263 Mrs. Oswald. That is Mr. Mike Howard's voice, yes, sir, I recognize his voice, yes, sir.

The Chairman. And that is your voice?

Mrs. Oswald. That is my voice.

The Chairman. Yes.

Mrs. Oswald. But I am not going to vary from my story.

The Chairman. Yes, all right.

Mrs. Oswald. That is an interview just 10 minutes at the Inn of Six Flags and that was the only time when going to the courthouse and asked for the FBI of Lee getting the money to come home from the State Department and Congressman Wright knew about it and they left and they didn't even come back and talk to me, sir, yes, sir.

Mr. Rankin. Play just the last part.

Mrs. Oswald. The last 25 minutes.

Mr. Rankin. These last remarks that we listened to were on page 13.

(Transcription played.)

The Chairman. Those are the same two voices, Howard's voice and your voice.

Mrs. Oswald. Yes, I say those are the two same voices, Mr. Mike Howard's voice, yes, sir.

Mr. Rankin. That is on page 21 of the transcript. Mr. Chairman, do you think there is any need for any more?

The Chairman. I don't see any need for going any further with it.

Mrs. Oswald says she didn't have this interview, these questions were not asked of her and these answers given but she does identify the voices as being hers and all we have is her word, and this tape, and the transcription at the present time. So for the moment, I suppose we will just have to leave it where it is.

I don't see any other answer to it.

Mrs. Oswald. All right.

Mr. Rankin. Mrs. Oswald, I have shown you during a recess what has been marked as Exhibit 271, and you have examined the handwriting of that exhibit.

Mrs. Oswald. Yes.

Mr. Rankin. And the various letters there. Can you tell us whether or not those handwritings on those various letters are those of your son, Lee Harvey Oswald?

Mrs. Oswald. It looks like his handwriting, I would say so. I am not handwriting expert. It looks very much like his writing.

Mr. Rankin. Thank you. We offer in evidence Exhibit 271.

The Chairman. It will be admitted.

(The document was received in evidence as Commission Exhibit No. 271.)

Mr. Rankin. We understand, Mr. Doyle, that you have examined the original documents of Exhibits 244 through 257, and compared them with the photostatic copies that have been marked.

Mr. Doyle. I have.

Mr. Rankin. And stipulate for the record that the photostats are correct, of the originals, is that agreeable?

Mr. Doyle. I do.

Mr. Rankin. Thank you.

Mr. Chairman, I have nothing further unless Mrs. Oswald has something or Mr. Doyle cares to interrogate Mrs. Oswald about anything.

The Chairman. Mrs. Oswald, do you have anything more you want to say?

Mrs. Oswald. No, I don't have anything more. Do you have any questions, Mr. Doyle?

The Chairman. Mr. Doyle, do you have anything to say?

Mr. Doyle. I have no further questions, no.

The Chairman. Well, thank you very much, Mrs. Oswald, for appearing voluntarily before the Commission and giving your testimony, and Mr. Doyle, I want to express the appreciation of the Commission for the help you have been to Mrs. Oswald and to the Commission in representing her on this occasion. We know that it disrupted your week very badly. We know that you responded to264 this call for public service on a moment's notice, and we appreciate it all the more because of that.

My own personal thanks to you in addition to those of the Commission.

Mr. Doyle. Thank you, Your Honor. I assume that my designation was for the purpose of the hearing and with the conclusion that will have finished my job.

The Chairman. Thank you. Unless Mrs. Oswald should like to ask you some questions about the matter at the conclusion of the testimony, I think that will be all.

Mr. Doyle. Very well.

The Chairman. Thank you both.

Mrs. Oswald. You and I are through as attorney and client?

Mr. Doyle. Yes.

Mrs. Oswald. This will not be pursued any further?

Mr. Doyle. Unless you have some questions, thank you.

Mrs. Oswald. Gentlemen, you are making a very big mistake. I thank you very much for inviting me here.

The Chairman. I don't understand you.

Mrs. Oswald. I think you are making a very big mistake not pursuing this further because I have told important people about this particular incident and I say it is correct and I hope you will continue while I am gone not just to ignore what I have said.

The Chairman. Mrs. Oswald, you misjudge the Commission when you say we will not pursue it further.

Mrs. Oswald. Fine, I don't know, I am asking.

The Chairman. You may be sure we will pursue it further.

Mrs. Oswald. Thank you, and I have more people that I could call. I have told Mr. Doyle the people.

Would you like me to name the people on the record for you? Mr. Lane, I called Mr. Lane——

The Chairman. To what purpose are you naming these people?

Mrs. Oswald. To the purpose that Mr. Mike Howard who came to Fort Worth last week to protect me, I called these people and told them how concerned I was that he was the one.

The Chairman. I think you have told us what you told them, so that we have it here in the record now.

We are adjourned.

(Whereupon, at 5:15 p.m., the President's Commission recessed.)

Thursday, February 20, 1964

Testimony of Robert Edward Lee Oswald

The President's Commission met at 9:30 a.m., on February 20, 1964, at 200 Maryland Avenue NE., Washington, D.C.

Present were Chief Justice Earl Warren, Chairman; Senator John Cooper, Representative Hale Boggs, Representative Gerald R. Ford, and Allen W. Dulles, members.

Also present were J. Lee Rankin, general counsel; Albert E. Jenner, Jr., assistant counsel; Wesley J. Liebeler, assistant counsel; William McKenzie, attorney for Robert Edward Lee Oswald and Leon Jaworski, special counsel to the attorney general of Texas.

The Chairman. Gentlemen, the Commission will be in order.

I will make a brief statement for the benefit of Mr. McKenzie and Mr. Oswald, so you will know just what this is about.

265 On November 29, 1963, President Lyndon B. Johnson issued Executive Order No. 11130, appointing a Commission "to ascertain, evaluate and report upon the facts relating to the assassination of the late President John F. Kennedy and the subsequent violent death of the man charged with the assassination."

On December 13, 1963, Congress adopted Joint Resolution S.J. 137, which authorizes the Commission or any member of the Commission or any agent or agency designated by the Commission for such purpose to administer oaths and affirmations, examine witnesses, and receive evidence.

On January 21, 1964, the Commission adopted a resolution authorizing each member of the Commission, and its General Counsel, J. Lee Rankin, to administer oaths and affirmations, examine witnesses, and receive evidence concerning any matters under investigation by the Commission.

The purpose of this hearing is to take the testimony of Mr. Robert Oswald, the brother of Lee Harvey Oswald, who prior to his death was charged with the assassination of President Kennedy.

Since the Commission is inquiring fully into the background of Lee Harvey Oswald and those associated with him, it is the intention of the Commission to ask Mr. Robert Oswald questions concerning Lee Harvey Oswald on any and all matters relating to the assassination.

The Commission also intends to ask Mr. Robert Oswald questions relating to the assassination of President Kennedy and the subsequent violent death of Lee Harvey Oswald. Mr. Robert Oswald has also been furnished with a copy of this statement and a copy of the rules adopted by the Commission for the taking of testimony and the production of evidence. Mr. Robert Oswald has also been furnished with a copy of Executive Order No. 11130, and Congressional Resolution S.J. No. 137, which set forth the general scope of the Commission's inquiry and its authority for examining witnesses and receiving evidence.

That is just for your general information, Mr. Oswald.

You are here with your attorney, Mr. McKenzie.

Would you state your name for the Commission?

Mr. McKenzie. Mr. Chief Justice and members of the Commission, my name is William A. McKenzie. Our office is 631 Fidelity Union Life Building, Dallas, Tex. I am a member of the State Bar of Texas and licensed to practice before the Supreme Court of that State.

The Chairman. And you are here to advise and represent Mr. Robert Oswald?

Mr. McKenzie. I am here to advise and represent Mr. Oswald. And I might state, further, that Mr. Oswald will freely give answers to any questions that the Commission might desire to ask of him.

The Chairman. Thank you very much.

There are present at the Commission this morning Mr. Allen Dulles, Commissioner, and myself. I will be leaving fairly shortly to attend a session of the Supreme Court, but in my absence Mr. Allen Dulles will conduct the hearing.

Mr. Oswald, would you please rise and be sworn?

Do you solemnly swear that you will tell the truth, the whole truth, and nothing but the truth, so help you God, in all of these proceedings at which you are to testify?

Mr. Oswald. I do.

Mr. McKenzie. Mr. Chief Justice, if you may pardon me for just a second. In coming down to the Commission's hearing room, I left part of my file in Mr. Jenner's office, and I have asked Mr. Liebeler if he will step out and get the file.

The Chairman. You would like to wait for that?

Mr. McKenzie. If you don't mind.

The Chairman. I might add, while we are waiting for that to come back, that Mr. Albert Jenner, one of the associate counsel for the Commission, will conduct the examination this morning.

Mr. McKenzie. Yes, sir.

I would like to state for the record that I have furnished to Mr. Jenner and Mr. Liebeler this morning a letter dated February 17, 1964, dictated by myself, but signed by Robert L. Oswald and witnessed by Pete White, Joan Connelly,266 and Henry Baer, which I would like for the Commission to have a copy of, and which I furnished to the Commission.

And, further, that I have furnished to Mr. Jenner and Mr. Liebeler, counsel for the Commission, a letter dated February 18, 1964, signed by Mrs. Marina N. Oswald and witnessed by Declan P. Ford, Katherine N. Ford, and Joan Connelly.

The reason that I furnish these letters to the Commission I think will be obvious from a reading of the letters, and, secondly, will likewise explain my position to some extent.

And, further, I have furnished to Mr. Jenner and Mr. Liebeler letters dated February 18, 1964, addressed to Mr. James H. Martin, 11611 Farrar, Dallas, Tex., signed by myself, and likewise signed by Marina N. Oswald, and witnessed by Katherine Ford, a copy of which I furnished to Mr. Lee Rankin, counsel for the Commission; and a letter of like date, February 18, 1964, addressed to Mr. John M. Thorne, Thorne and Leach, Attorneys and Counselors-at-Law, of Grand Prairie, Tex., signed by Mrs. Marina N. Oswald, and witnessed by Mrs. Katherine Ford.

I furnish these to the Commission for the Commission's information.

The Chairman. Thank you. Thank you very much, Mr. McKenzie.

Is there anything, Mr. McKenzie, you would like to know about our procedure that you are not acquainted with? It is very informal.

Mr. McKenzie. Mr. Chief Justice, I will say this. This is the first time I have had the privilege of appearing before such a distinguished group of citizens of this country, headed by yourself, and that we are ready to proceed.

The Chairman. Mr. Jenner?

Mr. Jenner. Thank you, Mr. Chief Justice.

May I suggest the wisdom of identifying each of these series of four letters with an exhibit number, and may the reporter supply me with the next number.

The first letter mentioned by Mr. McKenzie is the letter dated February 17, 1964, addressed to Mr. McKenzie, and signed by Mr. Robert L. Oswald, witnessed by Mr. Henry Baer, Joan Connelly, and Peter White. That will be marked Commission Exhibit No. 272.

(The document referred to was marked Commission Exhibit No. 272, for identification.)

Mr. Jenner. The second letter mentioned by Mr. McKenzie is dated February 18, 1964, also addressed to Mr. McKenzie, signed by Mrs. Marina N. Oswald, and witnessed by Declan P. Ford, Katherine N. Ford, and Joan Connelly. That will be marked Commission Exhibit 273.

(The document referred to was marked Commission Exhibit No. 273, for identification.)

Mr. Jenner. The next letter is dated February 18, 1964, and addressed to Mr. James H. Martin, identified by Mr. McKenzie, and signed by Mrs. Marina N. Oswald, witnessed by Mrs. Katherine Ford. Two pages.

(The document referred to was marked Commission Exhibit No. 274 for identification.)

Mr. Jenner. The next and last of the series is a letter of the same date, February 18, 1964, addressed to Mr. Thorne, John M. Thorne, signed by Mrs. Marina N. Oswald, and witnessed by Mrs. Katherine Ford, two pages.

(The document referred to was marked Commission Exhibit No. 275 for identification.)

Mr. McKenzie. Mr. Jenner, if I may at this time, I would like to make one other statement to the Commission.

The Chairman. Before you do that, may I ask if you want those introduced into evidence?

Mr. Jenner. Yes. Thank you, Mr. Chief Justice.

I offer in evidence as Commission Exhibits 272 through 275, inclusive, the documents that have been so identified and marked.

The Chairman. They may be admitted.

(The documents heretofore marked Commission Exhibits Nos. 272 through 275, inclusive, for identification, were received in evidence.)

The Chairman. Now, Mr. McKenzie?

Mr. McKenzie. Thank you, Mr. Chief Justice.

267 We have brought with us the original copies of various letters received from— dating from 1959 through 1962, from Lee Harvey Oswald to Robert L. Oswald, together with some copies of a contract between Mr. Oswald—Robert Oswald, Marina Oswald, John Thorne, and James Martin. We bring those voluntarily and gladly. I would like to give them to the Commission with the understanding and stipulation that they will not be released to the press or to any news media, with the exception and understanding of your final report.

The Chairman. That is the only purpose we would have in having them, and we will not release them to the press or to any other person.

Mr. McKenzie. I understand that, sir. And the only reason I make that stipulation is for the record.

The Chairman. Yes. With the understanding that the Commission will use it for any purpose that is within the scope of the Executive order.

Mr. McKenzie. Absolutely.

The Chairman. And for no other purpose.

Mr. McKenzie. Absolutely.

The Chairman. Do you want to keep the originals and have copies made for us, or do you want to leave the originals with us?

Mr. McKenzie. Well, sir, we have already started making the copies this morning.

The Chairman. That is all right. Either way you want to do it.

Mr. McKenzie. Whichever way the Commission would prefer.

But we have started making copies this morning.

The Chairman. That is all right, then. You may do it that way.

Mr. Jenner, I guess you may proceed.

Mr. Jenner. Thank you, Mr. Chief Justice.

We have made copies of a number of the originals, additional ones of which are also being made. And as I identify the documents, I will be asking leave to introduce photostatic or xerox copies of the originals, and I will so indicate at the appropriate moment.

The Chairman. Very well.

Mr. Jenner. Mr. Chief Justice, Mr. Dulles—we have had a very short session with Mr. McKenzie and Mr. Oswald, which has been pleasant and of the character indicated here, with full cooperation by both gentlemen. And we have explained to Mr. Oswald that this particular phase of the matter covers Lee Harvey Oswald's entire life, and I added it also covered Mr. Oswald's life.

At times the particular thrust of the examination might not be particularly apparent to Mr. McKenzie, but he is at liberty to inquire as the case might be. But we are covering the entire lives.

Mr. Jenner. Mr. Oswald, would you be good enough to state your full name?

Mr. Oswald. Robert Edward Lee Oswald.

Mr. Jenner. And you reside now where?

Mr. Oswald. At 1009 Sierra Drive, Denton, Tex.

Mr. Jenner. What is your present business or occupation?

Mr. Oswald. I am employed by the Acme Brick Co. in the capacity of sales coordinator.

Mr. Jenner. What city or town?

Mr. Oswald. Denton, Tex.

Mr. Jenner. What is the nature of your employment by that company?

Mr. Oswald. I am in the market department of the Acme Brick Co., coordinating between the marketing and plant department, scheduling the plant's production, processing and handling all orders, correspondence relating to the orders, and generally following through in the line of customers service, from prior to placing the orders by various customers, architects, home builders and so forth, to the completion of the invoices.

Mr. Jenner. And how long have you been so employed by the Acme Brick Co.?

Mr. Oswald. April of this year, 1964, will be 4 years.

Mr. Jenner. And I think it might be helpful at this point—what is the date of your birth?

Mr. Oswald. April 7, 1934, sir.

Mr. Jenner. Can you tell me how many years old you are?

268 Mr. Oswald. I will be 30 years old April 7, 1964.

The Chairman. Mr. Jenner, if you excuse me now, I am going to attend a session of the Supreme Court. And if you are here this afternoon, I will be back to be with you.

Mr. Dulles (presiding). You may proceed, Mr. Jenner.

Mr. Jenner. Thank you. Mr. Dulles.

Would you identify your family—Mrs. Oswald, and your two fine children?

Mr. Oswald. Thank you. My wife's name is Vada Marie Oswald. My daughter's name is Cathy Marie Oswald, and my son's name is Robert Lee Edward Oswald, Jr.

Mr. Jenner. The ages?

Mr. Oswald. Cathy is 6 years old, and Robert Lee will be 3 years old this April.

Mr. Jenner. Would you give us Mrs. Oswald's maiden name?

Mr. Oswald. Vada Marie Mercer.

Mr. Jenner. She is a native of your present town?

Mr. Oswald. No, sir. She is from Keeter, Tex. My wife was raised on a farm. This community is located close to Boyd, Tex., which is approximately 35 miles northwest of Fort Worth.

Mr. Jenner. All right.

Your father's full name?

Mr. Oswald. Robert Edward Lee Oswald.

Mr. Jenner. Edward?

Mr. Oswald. Yes, sir.

Mr. Jenner. And he is now deceased?

Mr. Oswald. That is correct, sir.

Mr. Jenner. And as I recall, he died in August of 1939.

Mr. Oswald. That is correct.

Mr. Jenner. You were then about what—5 years old?

Mr. Oswald. Five years old, sir.

Mr. Jenner. Now, your mother is Marguerite Oswald?

Mr. Oswald. That is correct, sir.

Mr. Jenner. Do you recall her middle name?

Mr. Oswald. Claverie.

Mr. Jenner. And what was her maiden name?

Mr. Oswald. I don't remember.

Mr. Jenner. I think it was Claverie. You have a brother, John Pic?

Mr. Oswald. That is correct. John Edward Pic.

Mr. Jenner. And he is a stepbrother?

Mr. Oswald. Yes, sir; that is correct.

Mr. Jenner. And born of a marriage of your mother with whom?

Mr. Oswald. Pardon me. He is a half brother.

Mr. McKenzie. He is a half brother, Mr. Jenner.

Mr. Jenner. I am sorry to say that meant the same thing to me. But I am probably in error. A half brother.

Mr. Oswald. I am sorry. I didn't hear the next question.

Mr. Jenner. That is all right. You correct me when I am wrong. Don't hesitate to do that.

Your half brother's father was whom?

Mr. Oswald. This I do not know. I don't know his full name.

Mr. Jenner. Was it John, to the best of your recollection?

Mr. Oswald. I would be of the opinion it was John.

Mr. Jenner. Have you ever met him?

Mr. Oswald. No, sir; I have not.

Mr. Jenner. You never had any acquaintance with him?

Mr. Oswald. No, sir. I might further say I don't believe I have ever seen a picture identified as being John's father.

Mr. Dulles. You are speaking of the father now?

Mr. Jenner. That is correct, sir.

And your half brother, John Pic, is older than you, is he not?

Mr. Oswald. That is correct.

Mr. Jenner. Do you happen to recall his age?

269 Mr. Oswald. Yes, sir; he is now 33 years old. His birthday is January 17, 1932.

Mr. Jenner. During your lifetime, you have had contact with him, have you not?

Mr. Oswald. Yes, sir.

Mr. Jenner. And as boys, the family lived together?

Mr. Oswald. Yes, sir.

Mr. Jenner. Now, your mother, Mrs. Marguerite Claverie Oswald, was married a third time, was she not?

Mr. Oswald. Yes, sir; that is correct.

Mr. Jenner. To whom?

Mr. Oswald. Mr. Edwin, I believe his middle initial was M. Ekdahl.

Mr. Jenner. When did that marriage take place, to the best of your recollection?

Mr. Oswald. 1944 or early '45.

Mr. Jenner. Were you present on that occasion?

Mr. Oswald. No, sir; I was not.

Mr. Jenner. Had you become acquainted with him prior to the time of the marriage of your mother to Mr. Ekdahl?

Mr. Oswald. Yes, sir; I certainly did.

Mr. Jenner. Would you indicate the general circumstances?

Mr. Oswald. Well, we was residing at Dallas, Tex. I don't recall the address. It was Victor Street.

Mr. Jenner. When you say "we"——

Mr. Oswald. It was my mother, John Edward Pic, myself, and Lee Harvey Oswald. Residing at the Victor Street address, in Dallas, Tex. I recall that perhaps more numerous occasions he was there—now I can say three or four times he was around the house prior to the marriage.

Mr. Jenner. And what was the nature of your mother's employment, if she was employed, in the period immediately preceding the marriage of your mother to Mr. Ekdahl?

Mr. Oswald. I am sorry, sir, I don't remember.

Mr. Jenner. But she was employed?

Mr. Oswald. Yes, sir. I do recall that this was quite a large house. It was a two-story house. And she was renting apartments.

Mr. Jenner. Serving as a rental agent?

Mr. Oswald. No. She owned the house, to my knowledge—she owned this house. I believe there were two upstairs apartments.

Mr. Jenner. In addition to that, was your mother separately or independently employed—that is independently from——

Mr. Oswald. I believe so, sir. Where, I do not recall.

Mr. Jenner. And at that time all three of you boys were attending—would that be elementary school at that time?

Mr. Oswald. Elementary school, that is correct.

Mr. Jenner. In Dallas?

Mr. Oswald. Lee was not.

Mr. Jenner. I beg your pardon?

Mr. Oswald. This would have been prior to Lee's sixth birthday, I believe, and he would not be attending at that particular time.

Mr. Jenner. But you and your brother John were?

Mr. Oswald. That is correct.

Mr. Jenner. Would you be good enough to tell the Commission as much as you can recall, especially of your early life—elementary school days. We are not going to probe into this in any great length. But we would like the background and flavor in which the family lived.

Start as early as you have any reasonable recollection.

Mr. Oswald. All right, sir.

I believe after my father's death in 1939, John was attending elementary school. We lived at the corner of Alvar and Galvez, in New Orleans, La. And the school was right across the street from us, elementary school.

John, of course, started——

270 Mr. Jenner. Excuse me, sir.

Did I ask you where you were born?

Mr. Oswald. No, you did not.

Mr. Jenner. Would you state that?

Mr. Oswald. I was born in New Orleans, La.

Mr. Jenner. All right.

Excuse the interruption.

Mr. Oswald. John attended the school approximately 2 years before I started elementary school. And during this time, the way I remember it, it was a frame building. But by the time I attended first grade it was a brick school building.

I do not recall attending for a very long period, because I believe——

Mr. Jenner. Do you recall the name of the elementary school?

Mr. Oswald. No, sir; I do not.

Mr. McKenzie. Mr. Jenner, if I may interrupt at this time—Robert, in giving this narrative, tie it down as closely as you possibly can to date, to names, to street addresses—just give us as complete detail as you possibly can.

Mr. Oswald. All right, sir.

Mr. McKenzie. The names of the school, the names of your teachers, and so forth, if you recall.

Mr. Oswald. I believe I was at the point that I don't recall attending this school very much. I perhaps was there the first full year. However, approximately around this time—this would be in 1941—mother placed John Edward and myself in a Catholic school, which I do not recall the name of, but it was located in Algiers, La.

Mr. Jenner. Is that a suburb of New Orleans?

Mr. Oswald. Yes, sir.

Mr. McKenzie. Just across the Mississippi River from New Orleans proper.

Mr. Dulles. Could I ask a question, Mr. Jenner?

In this school, did you live there, and spend the night there—you were living there all the time?

Mr. Oswald. Yes, sir.

Mr. Dulles. Or were you going home?

Mr. Oswald. No, sir; we were living there.

Lee, of course, at this time, was still very young, and he stayed with mother. I don't recall any address particularly at that time. We were at the Catholic school for approximately 1 year.

Mr. Jenner. That would take you to 1942.

Mr. Oswald. Yes, sir.

And, at that time we were moved by mother from the Catholic school and placed into the Bethlehem Orphan Home, in New Orleans, La.

We used to refer to it as the BOH.

Mr. Jenner. Excuse me, sir, if I interrupt you at that point.

That would be 1942?

Mr. Oswald. The best I can remember.

Mr. Jenner. Lee was only 3 years old. So the "we" did not include Lee, is that correct, sir?

Mr. Oswald. That is correct. It included John Edward and myself.

Mr. Jenner. As Mr. Dulles inquired of you at the Catholic school—was this an orphan home in which both you and John lived at the home?

Mr. Oswald. That is correct, sir.

Mr. Jenner. Twenty-four hours a day?

Mr. Oswald. Yes, sir.

Mr. Jenner. Where did Lee reside during this period of your life?

Mr. Oswald. I do not recall the address at that particular time.

I might state that I know mother had sold the house on Alvar and Galvez Streets in New Orleans, and they were living elsewhere, I remember the house, but I cannot remember the address.

Mr. Jenner. I was particularly interested in whether Lee was living with your mother.

Mr. Oswald. Yes, sir. He was at this time living with mother. And it is my understanding from her, during later years, discussing with her, that she had various maids or housekeepers come in to keep Lee at this early age.

271 Mr. Jenner. So, I take it, she was employed.

Mr. Oswald. Yes, sir.

Mr. Jenner. Was she also employed during the 1 year when you boys were at the Catholic school?

Mr. Oswald. I am sure—I feel sure she was, sir.

Mr. Jenner. Could we say, except as I might return to the subject specifically, that from the time of the death of your father, in August of 1939, at least until the time of her marriage with Mr. Ekdahl, she was always employed, either continuously or with short breaks?

Mr. Oswald. Yes, sir; we certainly can.

Mr. Jenner. She was the sole support, as far as you know, of your family?

Mr. Oswald. That is correct, sir.

Mr. Jenner. All right.

I interrupted you—pardon me.

You and John entered the Bethlehem Orphan Home. Would you describe to us the nature of that school?

Mr. Oswald. Well——

Mr. Jenner. Was it a public or private institution?

Mr. Oswald. I would say it was a private home. The atmosphere generally—of course all the boys and girls were separated—I recall just one large dormitory building, sleeping area and so forth. The cafeteria was located——

Mr. Dulles. Could you tell us about how many there were in this orphanage, roughly? Was it 50, 100, 200?

Mr. Oswald. I would say around 75 to 100, sir.

Mr. Jenner. So you are now about 8 years old, am I correct?

Mr. Oswald. 1942—that would be correct, sir.

The cafeteria was located in a separate, or perhaps a wing of this large dormitory building. The school area was located in a separate building towards the entrance of the home. There was quite a large playground there, and quite a large playroom within that large dormitory.

Mr. McKenzie. The home itself was located in New Orleans, is that correct?

Mr. Oswald. That is correct.

Mr. Jenner. In the city proper, rather than a suburb?

Mr. Oswald. I would say that was so, sir. I still recall that it was pretty close to the end of the St. Charles Street carline at that particular time.

My recollection of the atmosphere and the general conditions there—it was nice, I had a lot of friends there at the home. It was a Christian atmosphere.

Going back to the Catholic school—we had to go to church every morning and so forth like that.

But here at the tables and so forth we had our grace and such as that. It was generally a Christian atmosphere there. He treated us well, I might add—better than the Catholic school did. They were not as strict as far as discipline was concerned, but they certainly kept us in line.

Mr. Dulles. Could I ask a question there?

Was this a denominational school, or a publicly maintained school?

Mr. Oswald. I don't believe it was a denominational school. I believe it was a public—I feel it was a private school or home. But that the religious background did not have anything to do with it. It might have been just a Protestant home.

Mr. Jenner. I am curious, if I may, Mr. Dulles—the name of this school or home is the Bethlehem Orphan Home. But neither of you boys was an orphan.

Mr. Oswald. No, sir.

Mr. Jenner. I take it, then, that apart from the name of the school, there were orphans and young people, children such as you, whose mothers, or perhaps fathers, were unable to take care of them during the daytime completely, and the school accepted children under those circumstances.

Mr. Oswald. Yes, sir; that is my understanding.

Mr. Jenner. Therefore, it was not exclusively for orphans?

Mr. Oswald. No, sir.

Mr. Dulles. I think I have read somewhere—I would like to ask, if I may—I understand there had to be only one parent, though. I don't think if you had272 two parents you were eligible for this school. I don't know where I read that, but I recollect that.

Is that the case, do you remember?

Mr. Oswald. My recollection on that, sir, was that I do recall mother saying something that there was a little difficulty in placing us in there, because we were not orphans. But that they had from time to time made exceptions to this, where one parent was living and unable to attend the children fully during the day and so forth, and even at night.

Mr. Jenner. Now, you entered in 1942. Did you and John continue in this school—for what period of time?

Mr. Oswald. Until we moved to Dallas, in 1944, sir.

Mr. Jenner. Before we get to that, has Mr. Oswald responded to the questions you had in mind, to describe the nature of the school?

Mr. Dulles. Yes.

Mr. Jenner. Were you visited by your mother and Lee to the extent that she brought him along, when you and John were in the Bethlehem Orphan Home?

Mr. Oswald. Yes, sir; we were. I do recall quite vividly that on Wednesdays—this perhaps might have been during the summer months only—that John and I would go to downtown New Orleans and meet mother at her place of employment, and either spend the afternoon with her, or she would give us money to go to a movie or something. And at this time mother was employed as a manager or assistant manager of a hosiery shop located on Canal Street. I don't recall the name of it, or the exact address of it.

Mr. Jenner. Would you be good enough to inform the Commission to the best of your recollection about weekends? Did your mother visit you on weekends? Were you free to return home and spend the weekend? Describe that, please.

Mr. Oswald. I do not recall on the weekends—a weekend, I should say, that we visited mother. Normally, we just saw her once a week at that particular time. I do not recall—I have been thinking about this—seeing Lee too often at that time.

Mr. Jenner. You and John would be naturally curious to see him once in awhile?

Mr. Oswald. Yes, sir; I know we did. I cannot remember it too clearly. But I would say that it wasn't too frequently that we did see Lee.

Mr. Jenner. Now, you moved to Dallas in 1944?

Mr. Oswald. That is correct.

Mr. Jenner. Was there anything unusual prior to the time you moved to Dallas about your life and your relationships with your mother and with Lee, if any? Was there an event that is now etched on your mind?

Mr. Oswald. I would like to back up there just a little bit. Lee was placed at the Bethlehem Orphan Home for approximately the last year that we were there.

Mr. Jenner. That would be, then, 1943?

Mr. Oswald. Yes, sir.

Mr. Jenner. I see.

Mr. Dulles. He would have been 4 to 5 years old then?

Mr. Jenner. Yes. He was born in October 1939. So he would then be approximately 4—well, when he was placed in Bethlehem Home it was some time during the year 1943, to the best of your recollection?

Mr. Oswald. Yes, sir.

Mr. Jenner. Would you be good enough to relate to the Commission the circumstances that brought that about? What do you recall as to why?

Mr. Oswald. My opinion on that, sir, was this. That mother had wanted to bring Lee to the home at an earlier date, but that they had a minimum age required before he could be placed in there, because they did not have any real small children there. I mean there was no nursery there that I recall. And there was no very young children. When I say very young—say under 3 years old.

I remember some children there that perhaps were four or three and a half years old.

Mr. Jenner. I take it, Mr. Oswald, your mother put Lee in the orphan home at the first opportunity open to her under the rules or policy of the Bethlehem Orphan Home in that respect.

Mr. Oswald. That is correct.

Mr. Jenner. Now, did she come to visit the home when Lee was placed in the home?

If I may, you recall you said you were free on Wednesdays, it may have been limited to the summer time, and you and John would go into the New Orleans town district and visit your mother.

Did she come to see Lee? Does that stimulate your recollection that she did come to visit?

Mr. Oswald. Yes, sir; she did come to visit us. I recall after Lee was placed in the home, that all three of us would go down and visit mother, and we always took Lee with us.

Mr. Jenner. I see. What contact did you have with Lee in that 1-year period, in 1943, when he was with you boys in the home?

Mr. Oswald. John and I both looked on Lee as our kid brother, and we stayed pretty close to him, and defended him whenever we had to.

Mr. Jenner. How did Lee get along during those days?

Let's confine it to up to 1944, when you moved to Dallas.

Mr. Oswald. I don't recall any instance where it would stand out in my mind that he did not get along with anybody.

Mr. Jenner. He had the normal life of a 4-year-old at that particular time—got into his fights to the extent everyone else did?

Mr. Oswald. Yes, sir.

Mr. McKenzie. You mean at the time he was 4 years old?

Mr. Oswald. Yes, sir.

Mr. Jenner. There may be others who would be interested in his course of conduct and his reactions even at age 4. You will forgive me for going into that.

Mr. Oswald. Certainly.

Mr. Jenner. But your present recollection, as far as Lee's relationship with other 4-year-olds or 5's or 3's, his general course of conduct, with regard to the interplay between himself and others at or near his age, is what you would describe as normal?

Mr. Oswald. Yes, sir; that is correct.

Mr. Jenner. All right.

Now we are moving to Dallas in 1944. You brought out the fact that Lee became enrolled in Bethlehem Orphan Home, because I asked you questions whether there was anything unusual etched on your mind at that time that had occurred up to the point of your moving to Dallas. Was there anything else that this discussion, that is now stimulated that you would like to report?

Mr. Oswald. No, sir, I cannot think of anything else.

Mr. Jenner. Now, what was the reason you moved to Dallas?

Mr. Oswald. I don't really know, sir. Of course we were quite happy to leave the Bethlehem Orphan Home. By that, I don't mean to imply that they didn't treat us well there. But, of course, we were quite happy to be with mother again, all of us together.

As to the reason why mother moved us to Dallas, I do not know.

Mr. Jenner. Now, when you moved to Dallas, you resided—can you recall the address or at least approximately where you lived in Dallas?

Mr. Oswald. As I recall, it was Victor Street. It was a corner house, a large two-story white—I feel sure it was a frame white house. The garage was to the back side of the house. Victor Street ran in front of the house, and another street down the side where you entered the garage.

Mr. Jenner. I don't think I asked you this. It is a little bit out of order.

Do you happen to recall your brother John's date of birth?

Mr. Oswald. Yes, sir; you did ask me that. It was January 17, 1932. Yes, sir.

Mr. Jenner. All right. Thank you.

274 Your mother, did she become immediately employed in Dallas, or had she already arranged for employment in Dallas?

Mr. Oswald. This I do not recall, sir. I feel more like that she perhaps had arranged for employment in Dallas before we moved there. I would think this would be the natural thing to do. We had never been to Texas before. And, to my knowledge, she didn't know anybody in Texas.

And why we moved to Dallas, I certainly don't recall any reason at all.

Mr. Jenner. Did you have any relatives in Dallas?

Mr. Oswald. No, sir.

Mr. Jenner. Where did Mr. Ekdahl reside? Was he living in or a native of Dallas?

Mr. Oswald. I understand Mr. Ekdahl was from Boston, Mass., and he was at that time—I believe that is correct, sir—at least the way I remember it—employed by the Texas Electric Co.

Mr. Jenner. At what office?

Mr. Oswald. At Dallas. It might not have been Texas Electric. Texas Power and Light, perhaps—something like that.

Mr. Jenner. But Mr. Ekdahl was then living in Dallas when you, your mother, your brother John, and your brother Lee moved to Dallas?

Mr. Oswald. That is correct.

Mr. Jenner. And had you become—you boys become acquainted with Mr. Ekdahl prior to the time you moved to Dallas?

Mr. Oswald. No, sir.

Mr. Jenner. And do you recall any discussion of Mr. Ekdahl prior to the time of your moving to Dallas?

Mr. Oswald. No, sir.

Mr. Jenner. Now, your education was, of course, continued when you moved to Dallas.

Would you tell us about that—all three of you? You and your brother John first, because Lee was not yet of school age.

Mr. Oswald. All right, sir.

I recall the elementary school there in Dallas. It was the Davy Crockett Elementary School, which was approximately three or four blocks from the house.

Mr. Dulles. What was that name?

Mr. Oswald. Davy Crockett.

Mr. Jenner. Both you and your brother John were enrolled?

Mr. Oswald. Yes, sir. And there was—I believe it was a city park right across the street from this elementary school that I recall playing ping pong and croquet and swimming over there, and such as that.

Mr. Jenner. This period of your life, as you recall it, was a pleasant one?

Mr. Oswald. Yes, sir.

Mr. Jenner. And except for the restrictions that you and John encountered in the Catholic school and in the Bethlehem Orphan Home, what is your recollection of that early period of your life—subject to those limitations—normal and pleasant?

Mr. Oswald. The only thing I can remember—I did have a little difficulty because I had something of a southern drawl.

Mr. Jenner. When you reached Texas?

Mr. Oswald. Yes, sir. And I do recall having a little difficulty in school myself, to make myself clearly understood.

Mr. Dulles. May I ask a question there?

When you went to the Davy Crockett School, was that a school where you lived, or did you live at home and just attend the school during the school hours?

Mr. Oswald. That was a public school in Dallas, and we did not live there. We lived at home.
Mr. Dulles. And your mother then was employed, as I understand it.
Mr. Oswald. To the best of my knowledge—I feel certain she was employed.
Mr. Jenner. Do you recall the nature of her employment there?
Mr. Oswald. No, sir; I do not.
275 Mr. Jenner. She was employed full-time during the daytime, home on weekends?
Mr. Oswald. Yes, sir.
Mr. Jenner. Now, what was happening to Lee when you were living in Dallas—in the sense of who took care of him during the daytime, if anyone? What was done for his comfort?
Mr. Oswald. This I don't remember, sir. I don't remember any housekeeper or any maid that mother had at this time. Something is coming into my mind about a day nursery. I think perhaps——
Mr. Jenner. A day nursery?
Mr. Oswald. Yes, sir—that Lee was taken to during the day when Mother was working, and brought home with her at night. I believe that is correct.
Mr. Jenner. Would you boys take him to the day nursery and bring him home?
Mr. Oswald. No, sir.
Mr. Jenner. Did you play any part in that at all?
Mr. Oswald. No, sir, I do not have any recollection of taking Lee to the day nursery or bringing him back.
Mr. Jenner. Now, would you please indicate how long you remained in the Davy Crockett Elementary School, you and John?
Mr. Oswald. Say for 1 year, sir, 1 school year.
Mr. Jenner. All right.
Now, during this year, did you become acquainted with Mr. Ekdahl?
Mr. Oswald. Yes, sir; I would say towards the latter part of that school year.
Mr. Jenner. He could come—he did on occasion come to visit your mother's home?
Mr. Oswald. Yes, sir.
Mr. Jenner. Would you please indicate whether the contact that you boys had with Mr. Ekdahl about that—that is, he would visit the home occasionally?
Mr. Oswald. Yes.
Mr. Jenner. Did he take you boys out?
Mr. Oswald. I don't recall. I think perhaps on maybe two occasions we did go to the zoo. I don't recall any other occasions.
Mr. Jenner. We now have you towards the latter part of the year—you were now 9 years old. Am I correct about that?
Mr. Oswald. 1944, I would be 10 years old.
Mr. Jenner. Your brother John was 12?
Mr. Oswald. That is correct.
Mr. Jenner. And your brother Lee was then 5?
Mr. Oswald. Yes, sir.
Mr. Jenner. Did you continue—when did you change—you said you stayed at Davy Crockett Elementary School a year. And then you entered what school?
Mr. Oswald. In the fall of that year we entered Chamberlain-Hunt Military Academy, at Port Gibson, Miss. That was the fall of 1945.
Mr. Jenner. You and John?
Mr. Oswald. That is correct.
Mr. Jenner. Now, what was the date that you gave me as to the marriage of your mother and Mr. Ekdahl?
Mr. Oswald. Approximately the early part of 1944. That is what I stated before. And I think now that it would be more correct—after we completed the year at Davy Crockett, I believe they were married shortly after the end of the school year.

Mr. Jenner. That is in June, probably?
Mr. Oswald. Yes, sir; somewhere along that time.
Mr. Jenner. And that would be—June of '44?
Mr. McKenzie. June of '45.
Mr. Jenner. So that following the marriage of your mother and Mr. Ekdahl—what was his full name?
Mr. Oswald. Edwin A. Ekdahl. I believe his middle initial was "A."
Mr. Jenner. And he was employed, as you stated, by a utility company in Dallas at that time?
Mr. Oswald. Yes, sir.
276 Mr. Jenner. Now, do you have a recollection or did you come to learn the arrangements, if any, between Mr. Ekdahl and your mother as to the financing of the attendance of yourself and your brother John at Chamberlain-Hunt Military Academy?
Mr. Oswald. My mother told us that she was taking care of all the expenses at the Academy.
Mr. Jenner. She told you at this time?
Mr. Oswald. Yes, sir. This is my recollection.
Mr. Jenner. And that was your understanding of both you and John at that particular time?
Mr. Oswald. Yes, sir.
Mr. Jenner. That she was financing your attendance at the military academy?
Mr. Oswald. Yes, sir.
Mr. Dulles. Was she working at that time, or during the period that she was married to Mr. Ekdahl was she a housewife?
Mr. Oswald. I believe after the marriage to Mr. Ekdahl, she was not working.
Mr. Jenner. Did you have a conversation with her, and did you then come to learn, or have you subsequently come to learn as to how she did finance your attendance at the military academy?
Mr. Oswald. No, sir; I do not. I assume at that particular time that—I did not know the quantity of life insurance that my father had when he passed away. I thought it was perhaps substantial. Perhaps to me at that time, a young age, $4,000 or $5,000 was a lot of money. From the insurance money, from my father's death, she was able to place us in this military school in Mississippi.
Mr. Jenner. Do I recall correctly that you also testified earlier that your mother sold—there was a home in New Orleans which was sold?
Mr. Oswald. Yes, sir; that is correct.
Mr. Jenner. And possibly some of the proceeds of the sale of that home were still intact?
Mr. Oswald. This would be my opinion, that it was. I do not know if the home was paid for or anything.
Mr. Jenner. This is all speculation?
Mr. Oswald. Yes, sir.
Mr. McKenzie. Mr. Jenner, if I may interrupt.
Robert, don't speculate, and don't give any conjecture. Tell what you know, and give them the facts as fully as possible. But I am confident that the Commission is not interested in any speculation.
Mr. Jenner. And if you do speculate, tell us so.
Mr. McKenzie. Yes—indicate that you are speculating.
Mr. Dulles. Do we know the amount of insurance on Mr. Oswald's life?
Mr. Jenner. I cannot give you the figure, but it is small.
Mr. Dulles. It is known in the record?
Mr. Jenner. Yes, sir.
Representative Ford. May I ask a question?

Following your mother's marriage to Mr. Ekdahl, did he move in to the residence where you were living, or vice versa, or what were the circumstances?
Mr. Oswald. No, sir. He did move into the home on Victor Street, following the marriage.
Mr. Dulles. You were living, though, in the military academy. Was that a school where you lived?
Mr. Oswald. Yes, sir.
Mr. Dulles. You lived there?
Mr. Oswald. Yes, sir.
Mr. Dulles. Day and night?
Mr. Oswald. During the period that we went to the military school, we stayed there day and night, through the 9 months of the school year.
Mr. Jenner. What was the distance from Dallas—in general—to the military school?
Mr. McKenzie. It is approximately 600 or 700 miles.
Mr. Oswald. It was 30 miles south of Vicksburg, Miss.
Mr. Jenner. Quite a distance?
277 Mr. Oswald. Yes, sir.
Mr. Dulles. So you could not go home weekends?
Mr. Oswald. No, sir; we did not go home weekends.
Mr. Jenner. From the time of the marriage of your mother to Mr. Ekdahl, to the time you boys left for military school, you all lived in the home on Victor Street?
Mr. Oswald. That is correct, sir.
Mr. Jenner. He moved into the home immediately upon the marriage?
Mr. Oswald. Yes, sir.
Mr. Dulles. Could I ask one question?
Was there a summer holiday, then, when you went home from the military academy?
Mr. Oswald. Yes, sir.
Mr. Dulles. You were home for 3 months, roughly?
Mr. Oswald. Yes, sir; that is correct.
Mr. Dulles. That would be in the summer of '45?
Mr. Oswald. The summer of '46.
Mr. Jenner. It might help if you tell us how long you and John remained at the military school.
Mr. Oswald. Three school years.
Mr. Jenner. That would be in 1945, 1946, and 1947.
So that you left the military school approximately in June of 1947, is that correct?
Mr. Oswald. That would be correct.
Mr. Jenner. '48 or '47?
Mr. Oswald. Well, the school year would be 1945 through '46 would be 1 year, '46 through '47 would be 2 years, '47 through '48 would be the third year.
Mr. Jenner. All right. June of '48?
Mr. Oswald. Yes, sir. And I might say there, when school—the last year that we were there, when school was completed, mother had indicated to us that she wanted us to go to summer school and stay up there that summer. And we did, John and I, stay there at the school after practically all the other ones had left, because I recall helping pack away some old Springfield rifles at that time in Cosmolene.
Mr. Jenner. The marriage of your mother and Mr. Ekdahl terminated in divorce, as I recall it.
Mr. Oswald. That is correct.
Mr. Jenner. Do you recall approximately when that was?
Mr. Oswald. No, sir. I believe that this would be some time in '47. I believe she had divorced Mr. Ekdahl before our final year at the academy.
Mr. Jenner. Mr. Liebeler will get the date. I don't recall it myself at the moment.

Did your mother and Mr. Ekdahl have occasion during this 3-year period, plus the summer school, to visit you and John in the military academy?

Mr. Oswald. Yes, sir; they did. I recall Mr. Ekdahl coming there with mother and Lee in a 1939 Buick at that time, that I recall. I don't recall many occasions that Mr. Ekdahl was there. I might state that at Christmas time I believe on each year that we were up at the military school that we returned home. By home, I mean Fort Worth, or wherever they were living. One year I believe it was Benbrook, Tex., outside of Fort Worth.

Mr. Jenner. Now, would you be good enough, having mentioned that, to state for the record where your mother and Mr. Ekdahl resided during the period of time you were at the military school?

Mr. Oswald. I believe the first year——

Mr. Jenner. Chronologically.

Mr. Oswald. The first year that we attended there, Mr. Ekdahl was on the road quite a bit. And they had during the winter of 1945 gone to Boston, where they stayed, I would say, for approximately 6 months. I understand Mr. Ekdahl had been married and had a son by a prior marriage, and they had lived together, all of them—Lee, my mother, Mr. Ekdahl, and his son—in Boston. But that he was on the road quite a bit. And I recall a picture of mother and Lee in Arizona.

278 Mr. Jenner. Living in Arizona?

Mr. Oswald. No, sir; not living. On one of the trips.

Mr. Jenner. I see.

Representative Ford. One of the trips with Mr. Ekdahl?

Mr. Oswald. Ekdahl, and mother and Lee had gone along with him. Whether this was a business trip or a vacation trip, I don't recall.

Mr. Jenner. I see.

Following their living for 6 months in Boston, where did they live thereafter, during that period of time, until the divorce?

Mr. Oswald. I believe after they left Massachusetts, they moved to Benbrook, Tex., and resided at Benbrook, Tex.

Mr. Jenner. And where is Benbrook with respect to Dallas?

Mr. Oswald. It is—well, with respect to Fort Worth, that to me would be easier to say, it is just a little ways northwest of Fort Worth, on the edge of the city limits of Fort Worth now. At this particular time it was just more or less a wide spot in the road. The house—I recall going there, perhaps this was during Christmas leave from the academy—the house was a good sized stone home that had some acreage with it. There was a creek that was perhaps 400 or 500 yards behind the house. I remember, I believe, right before we arrived on this first occasion, Lee had found a skunk out there. He didn't know what a skunk was, but he found out.

Mr. McKenzie. Benbrook is a suburb of Fort Worth.

Mr. Oswald. Yes, Benbrook is a suburb of Fort Worth.

As I indicated, at that time——

Mr. Jenner. Could you fix the year?

Mr. Oswald. This would be—I feel certain that this was the first year that we were in military school, and the first Christmas.

Mr. Jenner. The first Christmas. That would be Christmas 1945.

Mr. Oswald. Pardon me. Let me back up earlier.

They were in Massachusetts at that time.

This would be the second year.

Mr. Jenner. I take it, then, the first Christmas, 1945, included the period when your mother, Mr. Ekdahl, and Lee resided in Boston with Mr. Ekdahl's son by a former marriage.

Mr. Oswald. That is correct.

Mr. Jenner. And that the living in Benbrook, Tex., followed the termination of the stay in Boston?

Mr. Oswald. That is correct.

But I do recall now the first Christmas that I was at the military school, because they were so far away, and it was impractical to travel that distance in that length of time—that John went with some friends of his that he made at the academy and stayed at their home—I don't recall where.

I remember I went with one of my friends and stayed at his home during Christmas.

Mr. Jenner. These were friends of yours in the academy?

Mr. Oswald. That is correct. And their parents agreed to that—because they didn't want us to stay up in the academy at Christmas time more or less by ourselves. They wanted to have us with them.

Mr. Jenner. You seem to have a rather vivid recollection of the Benbrook, Tex., home. I take it that during a summer vacation you lived in Benbrook, Tex., with your mother and Mr. Ekdahl and Lee.

Mr. Oswald. This particular house I refer to, a native stone home—I believe that is correct.

Mr. Jenner. So that you did have at least two summers at home while you were at the military academy, and the third summer your mother asked you to stay during summer school, and you did not come home?

Mr. Oswald. She asked us, and it was the intent that we stay. But at the last moment we did not go to summer school that year at the academy. We did come to Fort Worth.

Mr. Jenner. I see.

Mr. McKenzie. Mr. Jenner, may I interrupt you please?

279 Robert, when did you leave, or when did your mother sell the house on Victor Street in Dallas, Tex., if you recall?

Mr. Oswald. I believe she sold it at the time that they moved to Boston, Mass.

Mr. McKenzie. That was some time prior to Christmas of 1945, is that correct?

Mr. Oswald. That is correct.

If I may ask this, sir: If someone would furnish me the date of the divorce. I believe this would help tie down some other dates.

Mr. McKenzie. Off the record.

(Discussion off the record.)

Mr. McKenzie. I want to assure the Commission and counsel that the copy of the transcript of Robert Oswald's testimony will not be given to the press until such time as the Commission makes its final report—if at that time.

Representative Ford. I think that is most important, that we don't indicate that they will never be given to the press.

Mr. Dulles. No. That was made clear before you came in—that this would be available for use in connection with the report in any way that the Commission saw fit.

Mr. Jenner. Is it all right to proceed, sir?

Mr. Dulles. Yes, please, Mr. Jenner.

Mr. Jenner. The second residence, then, was—I mean the second one during this particular period we were talking about, was in Benbrook, Tex.

How long, or over what period of time did your family reside in Benbrook, Tex.?

Mr. Oswald. I would say at least approximately a year or a year and a half at that particular house.

Mr. Jenner. You say in that particular house. Did they occupy another home in Benbrook, Tex.?

Mr. Oswald. This was—on our return from military school, the last year we attended, when we returned, mother had purchased a small home there in Benbrook, a little bit closer in to Fort Worth.

Mr. Dulles. This was after the divorce?

Mr. Oswald. Yes, sir; this was after the divorce.

Representative Ford. She owned the original house in Benbrook?

Mr. Oswald. No, sir; not the stone house. I believe Mr. Ekdahl had rented that house, or leased it.

Representative Ford. Then she purchased this second house?

Mr. Oswald. That is right. After the divorce, she purchased this smaller home.

Mr. Jenner. Until you boys returned from military academy, or at least until the time of the divorce of your mother and Mr. Ekdahl, she was not employed? She was home?

Mr. Oswald. To my knowledge, that is correct. She was not employed at that time, or during the marriage to Mr. Ekdahl—she was not employed at any time I am aware of.

Mr. Jenner. And able to give the normal and full time and attention of a mother to her son, Lee?

Mr. Oswald. That is correct, to the best of my knowledge.

Mr. Jenner. Well, during the summertime, when you did spend summer vacations back in Benbrook, Tex., you had an opportunity to observe personally on this subject, did you not?

Mr. Oswald. Yes, sir.

Mr. Jenner. That your mother was not employed, and she was caring for Lee during that period?

Mr. Oswald. Yes, sir.

Mr. Jenner. Did she have any assistance?

Mr. Oswald. No, sir, she did not. None that I recall.

Mr. Jenner. No household help?

Mr. Oswald. No, sir; none that I recall.

Mr. Dulles. Could I ask a question there? Maybe you are going to cover280 that. I would like to ask as to—was Lee Harvey going to kindergarten at this time, or where was he from an educational point of view?

He was 7 or 8 years old now.

Mr. Jenner. Yes. He was 8 years old—he was 6 years old when they moved to—the commencement of the military school period, your brother, Lee, was 6 years old?

Mr. Oswald. Six years old.

Mr. Jenner. And that is about the time when you enter elementary school, is it not?

Mr. Oswald. That I entered elementary school?

Mr. Jenner. No—children generally.

Mr. Oswald. Yes, sir.

I don't believe, however, though, that Lee at the age of 6 went to elementary school.

Mr. Jenner. Would you tell us what the circumstances were in that connection, to the best of your recollection, and now.

Mr. Oswald. All right, sir. To the best of my recollection, it was that Mr. Ekdahl was traveling quite a bit, and that mother was traveling with him, and Lee did not attend a school during that year.

Mr. Jenner. Did Lee travel with them?

Mr. Oswald. I believe that he did during that time.

Mr. Jenner. That is your best recollection?

Mr. Oswald. Yes, sir; that is my best recollection.

Mr. Jenner. You are trying not to speculate.

Mr. Oswald. That is correct, sir.

Mr. McKenzie. Off the record.

(Discussion off the record.)

Mr. Jenner. Back on the record.

Mr. McKenzie. I believe, to my best recollection, that the school age—commencement age was 7 years old.

Mr. Dulles. I think what we are trying to get at is what was Lee doing—was he with the mother, was he in some kind of kindergarten?

Do you recall during those 3 years you were in the military academy—where was Lee?

Representative Ford. When you say the school age, in Texas, you mean the mandatory attendance age?

Mr. Jaworski. That is correct.

Mr. McKenzie. Yes, that is what I have reference to.

Mr. Jaworski. I recall, if I may add, at the age of 6, children were normally sent to kindergarten in those days.

Mr. Jenner. As you have now related it to us, Mr. Oswald, in this period, let's call it the military school period because we have identified the time question—at the commencement Lee was then 6 years old. And as we now learn, normally that would be a kindergarten period.

He was traveling or accompanied his mother, your mother, and Mr. Ekdahl in their travels in connection with Mr. Ekdahl's business, and he was not either in kindergarten or otherwise in school.

Mr. Oswald. Yes, sir; I am of this opinion—he was not.

Mr. Jenner. And that was your information at the time that you and John were attending military school?

Mr. Oswald. That would be correct, sir.

Mr. Dulles. Do you know where he was, and who was taking care of him during that period—if your mother was traveling with Mr. Ekdahl?

Mr. Oswald. I believe Lee was going with them, sir, during these travels. I don't recall—other than this one photograph—at one time they were out in Arizona. I don't recall any other places that they traveled to. I am sure mother, she was writing us quite frequently, John and I, usually just one letter to both of us—any other names or areas that they had traveled during this period.

Mr. Jenner. Now, may we proceed to the succeeding school period, which would be the year '46-'47. He is now at that time 7 years of age. Your mother and Mr. Ekdahl and Lee were then residing in Benbrook, Tex.

281 Mr. Oswald. Benbrook; yes, sir.

Mr. Jenner. Did Lee enter elementary school at that time?

Mr. Oswald. Yes, sir; he did. I don't know if the school name was Benbrook School.

Mr. Jenner. It was an elementary school?

Mr. Oswald. Yes, sir; I know where it is located there and everything. I believe it is closed down now.

Mr. Jenner. You learned of this during the summer vacation, or from letters from your mother?

Mr. Oswald. Yes, sir—perhaps both—one way or the other during that period we were aware that Lee was attending school in Benbrook.

Mr. Jenner. Up to this point what were the relationships between yourself and your brother John? Cordial and normal brother relationships?

Mr. Oswald. I might say then as now they were cordial. We always got along. He was a little bit older than I was, of course. He had his group of friends, I had mine. We got along just fine.

Mr. Jenner. And the relationship of your brother John and yourself on the one hand, and Lee on the other—let us take the 6- to 7- to 8-year-old period.

Mr. Oswald. John and I both, I feel, especially from my side, that we were his big brothers, and when we were around Lee we took care of him. We played together, to some extent, anyway. Perhaps our interests were a little bit different than Lee's at that early age of his life—a spread of 5 years between Lee and I and 7 years between Lee and John.

Mr. Jenner. Yes. That is quite a gap.

A boy 6 years old who has a brother 11 years old—that would be you—and a brother 13 years old, that would be John—at that age, that is quite a gap.

Did you spend much time with him, for example, when you were home during the summer vacations?

Mr. Oswald. Yes, sir; I would say we did spend quite a bit of time—both John and I—with Lee.

I recall going fishing, things like that. But mostly I recall staying at the house at Benbrook, the native stone home, out there, and staying within the confines out there, and playing, and staying out there most of the time.

I do recall on a number of occasions that Mr. Ekdahl, my mother, and all three of us would drive into Fort Worth and go to the movie theater, which at that time was the closest one coming in from Benbrook into Fort Worth. I recall going there quite a few times.

Mr. Jenner. Would you relate for us as you recall now the relationships between you and John—between you boys and your mother? Was that a pleasant one? Were there any difficulties that you now recall? Personality-wise, for example.

Mr. Oswald. None that I recall. At that time, I do recall one instance out there at the house, stone house there in Benbrook—my mother was a little upset with Mr. Ekdahl over the fact that—this was, I am sure, the second Christmas we were there from military school.

Mr. Jenner. That would be 1947?

Mr. Oswald. That would be 1947, Christmas 1946. He was showering us with candies, cokes, and so forth. And mother thought that he was overdoing it. And we argued the other way. We was on Mr. Ekdahl's side.

Mr. Jenner. But your relations with your mother, as you recall them now, during this period were pleasant, normal, and you were having no difficulties with her?

Mr. Oswald. No, sir; pleasant memories to me.

Mr. Jenner. Anything other than the difficulties two lively boys have when they are naughty?

Mr. Oswald. Yes, sir.

Mr. Dulles. Were you conscious at that time of the growing difficulty between your mother and Mr. Ekdahl? Was that apparent at that time? Or did that only come later?

Mr. Oswald. No, sir. At that time, it was not apparent to me.

Mr. Dulles. At no time was that a factor in your life, particularly?

Mr. Oswald. No, sir. I would say at no time it was. In moving up perhaps282 there to the time of the divorce and everything, I don't remember when Mr. Ekdahl moved out of the house. At that time we were living on Eighth Avenue in Fort Worth. This was during a summer period there. And I think this was the summer after the second year that we attended there—this would be the summer of 1947.

Mr. Dulles. If it is agreeable, I think we will adjourn for just a minute. It is now 11 o'clock.

Representative Ford. Mr. Dulles, may I suggest that we get what the law was in Texas at the time, as to when children mandatorily had to attend school? I think that can be checked out very simply and put in the record.

Mr. Dulles. Yes. I think that should be in the record.

(Brief recess.)

Mr. Dulles. The Commission will come to order. We will resume, Mr. Jenner, with your questions.

Mr. Jenner. Thank you.

It may well be, Mr. Chairman, that the Exhibits 272 through 275, which although already admitted in evidence, may play some part in these proceedings at some future date. And may I further qualify the exhibits.

Mr. Dulles. Certainly.

Mr. Jenner. Mr. McKenzie, would you be good enough to hand them to the witness?

Would you turn to the second page of Exhibit No. 272, Mr. Oswald? Are you familiar with the signatures on the second page of that exhibit?

Mr. Oswald. Yes, I am.

Mr. Jenner. And would you identify them, please, in the order in which they appear, and state whether or not they are the signatures of the persons who purported to have signed?

Mr. Oswald. My signature, Robert L. Oswald, I signed it. Witnessed by Henry Baer, Joan Connelly, and Pete White. And they are known to me.

Mr. Jenner. Did they affix those signatures in your presence?

Mr. Oswald. Yes, sir; they did.

Mr. Jenner. And they are persons known to you?

Mr. Oswald. Yes, sir.

Mr. Jenner. Would you identify them for the record?

Mr. Oswald. Mr. Henry Baer is a partner in William A. McKenzie's law firm, in Dallas, Tex.

Mr. Jenner. He is Mr. McKenzie's partner?

Mr. Oswald. Yes.

Miss Joan Connelly is the secretary in that firm.

And Mr. Pete White is an associate partner in the law firm of Mr. McKenzie.

Mr. Jenner. I take it, then, that that document was executed in Mr. McKenzie's office.

Mr. Oswald. That is correct.

Mr. McKenzie. Now, Mr. Jenner, may I interrupt at this point? I would like to add for the record that I was not present at the time that this letter was executed or witnessed. However, I did dictate it in the presence of Mr. Oswald and, of course, to my secretary, and, of course, to my partner, Henry Baer.

Mr. Jenner. Is Miss Connelly your secretary?

Mr. McKenzie. Yes, sir.

Mr. Jenner. Now, would you take the second letter in that group, and give me the exhibit number—turn to the exhibit page and identify the situation similarly, if you are acquainted with them, and state whether it was signed in your presence and where.

Mr. Oswald. Commission Exhibit No. 273—I was not present when this letter was signed.

Mr. Jenner. Does the letter bear your signature?

Mr. Oswald. No, sir; it does not.

Mr. Jenner. Are you familiar with the signatures of those who purported to have signed it?

Mr. Oswald. I am not familiar with the signature—I am familiar with the 283 signature of Mrs. Marina N. Oswald. I am not familiar with the signature of Mr. Declan P. Ford or his wife, Katherine N. Ford.

I am familiar with the signature of Joan Connelly, Mr. McKenzie's secretary.

Mr. Jenner. Would you please identify who Mr. and Mrs. Ford are?

Mr. Oswald. The best way I could do that, I believe, is that they are friends of Marina N. Oswald. I became acquainted with Mrs. Ford on Wednesday 2 weeks ago, whatever date that is, and Mr. Ford the following day.

Mr. Jenner. What were the circumstances under which you became acquainted with Mrs. Ford?

Mr. Oswald. Pardon me just a minute.

I would like to correct that.

It was Tuesday rather than Wednesday 2 weeks ago that I first became acquainted with Mrs. Ford.

At that time, Mrs. Ford acted as an interpreter between Mr. Thorne and myself to relate to Mrs. Marina Oswald what we were talking about.

Mr. Jenner. Excuse me, sir. You mentioned a Mr. Thorne?

Mr. Oswald. Yes, sir.

Mr. Jenner. That is Mr. John Thorne who at that time was the attorney for Mrs. Marina Oswald?

Mr. Oswald. That is correct.

Mr. Jenner. And where did this take place?

Mr. Oswald. At my residence, at 1009 Sierra Drive, Denton, Tex.

Mr. Jenner. Who was present at that time in addition to yourself, Mr. Thorne, and Mrs. Ford?

Mr. Oswald. My wife, Vada Marie Oswald, was present.

Mr. Jenner. And your acquaintance with Mr. Ford, you say, was the following day?

Mr. Oswald. Yes, sir; that is correct.

Mr. Jenner. Where did that take place, and in whose presence?

Mr. Oswald. At my residence, again, in Denton, Tex., in the presence of my wife, Vada, Mrs. Marina Oswald, and Mrs. Kathy Ford.

Mr. Jenner. As to Mrs. Ford, it is 2 weeks ago last Tuesday, or 2 weeks ago today?

Mr. Oswald. Pardon me just a minute.

Mr. McKenzie. Two weeks ago this past Tuesday.

Mr. Oswald. Pardon me.

Mr. Jenner. I wish you would hesitate and make reasonably certain of this.

Mr. Oswald. Yes, sir; I believe I have erred here.

Instead of being 2 weeks ago this past Tuesday, it was a week ago Tuesday that I first met Kathy Ford. And it was the following day, on that Wednesday, that I met Mr. Ford. In other words, I wish to correct it was not 2 weeks ago, but 1 week ago.

Mr. Jenner. Now that you have a calendar before you, would you give us the date so we will have it in the record now?

Mr. Oswald. On Tuesday, February 11, 1964, was the day I first met Mrs. Kathy Ford in the presence of Mr. John Thorne and my wife, Vada, in my home in Denton, Tex.

On February 12th I met Mr. Ford in the presence of my wife in my residence at Denton, Tex.

Mr. Jenner. Returning to the exhibit to which you have been directing your attention, which is No. 273, you were able to identify Mrs. Marina Oswald's signature, and Miss Connelly's?

Mr. Oswald. Yes.

Mr. Jenner. The others you were unable to identify?

Mr. Oswald. That is correct.

Mr. Jenner. All right.

Would you turn, then, to the next exhibit, give us the number?

Mr. Oswald. Commission Exhibit No. 274.

Mr. Jenner. Is it signed on its face?

Mr. Oswald. Yes, sir.

Mr. Jenner. Well, then, directing your attention to the first page of the exhibit, does it bear a signature?

284 Mr. Oswald. Yes, sir; it does.

Mr. Jenner. Are you familiar with that signature?

Mr. Oswald. Yes, sir; I am.

Mr. Jenner. Whose signature is it?

Mr. Oswald. Mr. William A. McKenzie.

Mr. Jenner. This is the Mr. McKenzie present here representing you?

Mr. Oswald. Yes, sir.

Mr. Jenner. And does that exhibit consist of more than 1 page?

Mr. Oswald. Yes, sir; it does.

Mr. Jenner. Turn to the second page. Does it bear a signature?

Mr. Oswald. Yes, sir; it does.

Mr. Jenner. Are you familiar with those signatures?

Mr. Oswald. The two signatures appear on the second page. One I am familiar with—Mrs. Marina Oswald.

Mr. Jenner. Excuse me, sir. Is that the first of those that are in a series?

Mr. Oswald. Yes, sir; that is correct.

Mr. Jenner. And you are familiar with that, and that is her signature?
Mr. Oswald. Yes, sir.
Mr. Jenner. The next signature purports to be that of whom?
Mr. Oswald. Mrs. Katherine Ford.
Mr. Jenner. And your testimony, if I repeated the questions that I did as to the previous exhibit, regarding Mrs. Ford, would be the same? You are not familiar with her signature?
Mr. Oswald. That is correct.
Mr. Jenner. And the next signature, please?
Mr. Oswald. Sir?
Mr. Jenner. The next signature?
Mr. Oswald. That is the only two signatures that appear on that second page.
Mr. Jenner. Would you proceed to the next exhibit?
Mr. Oswald. 275.
Mr. Jenner. That consists of how many pages?
Mr. Oswald. Two pages.
Mr. Jenner. Does it bear a signature on the first page?
Mr. Oswald. There is a signature on the first page. The signature is Mr. William A. McKenzie.
Mr. Jenner. You are familiar with that signature, and that is his signature?
Mr. Oswald. Yes, sir.
Mr. Jenner. The same gentleman we have identified?
Mr. Oswald. Yes, sir.
Mr. Jenner. All right. Are there any signatures on the second page of that exhibit?
Mr. Oswald. Yes, sir. There are two signatures on the second page, and in order as they appear——
Mr. Jenner. Excuse me. Are you familiar with either of them?
Mr. Oswald. I am familiar with one of them.
Mr. Jenner. All right. Let's take the first one, which is what?
Mr. Oswald. Mrs. Marina N. Oswald.
Mr. Jenner. You are familiar with her signature?
Mr. Oswald. Yes, sir; I am.
Mr. Jenner. Is that her signature?
Mr. Oswald. Yes, sir. I would say that was her signature.
Mr. Jenner. And the second name appears to be that of whom?
Mr. Oswald. Mrs. Katherine Ford.
Mr. Jenner. And your testimony with respect to her, were I to pursue it, would be the same as you testified to a previous exhibit, insofar as your familiarity with her signature is concerned?
Mr. Oswald. That is correct.
Mr. Jenner. Thank you, sir.
Forgive the interruption, Mr. Chairman.
Mr. Dulles. That is all right.
Mr. Jenner. Mr. Chairman, Mr. McKenzie has produced for us and tendered to us four documents, during the recess, which I would wish to identify. They285 have a relationship to the exhibits, the signatures of which I have just finished having identified.
Would you mark those, please, Mr. Liebeler?
Mr. Dulles. Do you wish these admitted as exhibits?
Mr. Jenner. If you please, sir. I would like to identify the exhibits and indicate their content first.
I would call on you, Mr. McKenzie, to identify the series of exhibits. They are numbered, Mr. Chairman, Commission Exhibits 276, 277, 278, and 279.
If you will identify them, I may have some questions of the witness.

Mr. McKenzie. Mr. Chairman, Exhibit No. 276 is a contract dated December 6, 1963, addressed to Mr. James H. Martin, Dallas, Tex., and signed by Mrs. Marina N. Oswald, consisting of four pages.

Mr. Dulles. I wish that admitted at this time with that description.

Mr. Jenner. If I may put one question to the witness: Mr. Oswald, would you look at the last page of that exhibit? Does it purport to bear a signature?

Mr. Oswald. Yes, sir.

Mr. Jenner. Are you familiar with that signature?

Mr. Oswald. There are three signatures.

Mr. Jenner. Are you familiar with all of them?

Mr. Oswald. May I ask my attorney something here?

Mr. Jenner. Surely.

Mr. McKenzie. Mr. Jenner, if I may interrupt you, and pardon me for doing so—on page 3 there is likewise a signature. And I think perhaps he should start at that page.

Mr. Jenner. That is a fine suggestion.

Will you now refer to page 3. Does it bear a signature?

Mr. Oswald. Yes, sir; it does.

Mr. Jenner. Are you familiar with that signature?

Mr. Oswald. Yes, sir; I am.

Mr. Jenner. Whose signature is it?

Mr. Oswald. Mrs. Marina N. Oswald.

Mr. Jenner. Turn to page 4. There are several signatures on that page, is that correct?

Mr. Oswald. That is correct. There are three.

Mr. Jenner. Are you familiar with any of them?

Mr. Oswald. Yes, sir; I am.

Mr. Jenner. Would you take them in order, taking the uppermost one first. Indicate whether you are familiar with that signature, and whose signature it is.

Mr. Oswald. It is my own signature, Robert Oswald.

Mr. Jenner. The next under that?

Mr. Oswald. Mr. James H. Martin.

Mr. Jenner. Are you familiar with that signature?

Mr. Oswald. Yes, sir.

Mr. Jenner. And it is his signature?

Mr. Oswald. Yes, sir.

Mr. Jenner. Who is Mr. James H. Martin?

Mr. Oswald. He was, at that time, when this contract was signed, appointed as Marina's business agent. But employed at the Inn of the Six Flags at Arlington, Tex.

Mr. Jenner. He has been identified in previous sessions before the Commission. And there is a third signature?

Mr. Oswald. Yes, sir; there is.

Mr. Jenner. And are you familiar with that signature?

Mr. Oswald. Yes, sir; I am.

Mr. Jenner. Whose is it, please?

Mr. Oswald. Mr. John M. Thorne, Attorney.

Mr. Jenner. And he is the Mr. Thorne that we have identified a few moments ago?

Mr. Oswald. Yes, sir.

Mr. Jenner. He was at that time the attorney for Mrs. Marina Oswald?

Mr. Oswald. That is correct.

286 Mr. Jenner. Is there a fourth signature?

Mr. Oswald. No, sir; there is not.

Mr. Jenner. Were those signatures affixed in your presence?

Mr. Oswald. Yes, sir; they were.

Mr. Dulles. Mr. Jenner, I believe these are photostatic copies, are they not, that are being identified?

Mr. Jenner. Yes, sir.
Mr. McKenzie, would you please make a statement with respect to that?
Mr. McKenzie. Yes, sir. I was going to at this time, Mr. Jenner, state for the record that Exhibit 276 is a photostatic copy. And this photostatic copy was furnished to me by Mrs. Marina N. Oswald.
Mr. Dulles. Where is the original of that?
Mr. McKenzie. Marina N. Oswald has the original.
Mr. Dulles. Has that been so compared, that we know this is a true copy?
Mr. McKenzie. Mr. Chairman. Pardon me.
I retract that statement.
Marina N. Oswald furnished to me a copy of this exhibit, but it was a signed copy, and it was an original copy.
Mr. Jenner. A duplicate original?
Mr. McKenzie. Yes. And I presume Mr. James Martin had the original, since it is addressed to him.
Mr. Dulles. And both the original and this duplicate bear these signatures, do they?
Mr. McKenzie. I have never seen the original, sir, but I presume that they do. And I think Robert Oswald here can clarify that, because he was present at the time that the original was signed, and also the duplicate copies.
Mr. Oswald. That is correct.
Mr. Dulles. And the duplicates were signed by the same parties as the original?
Mr. Oswald. Yes, sir.
Representative Ford. May I ask—did you get a copy of the original at the time?
Mr. Oswald. No, sir. I received a copy in the mail the second day after the signatures were signed. My copies were unsigned.
Mr. Jenner. Mr. Oswald, were you present when all of the copies were contemporaneously signed, if they were contemporaneously signed?
Mr. Oswald. Yes, sir; I was.
Mr. Jenner. So you know of your own knowledge that what has been termed here the original, which may be in the possession of Mr. Martin, was signed, and was signed in your presence?
Mr. Oswald. Yes, sir.
Mr. Jenner. And the document which we are now discussing is a photostatic copy of a carbon copy of the original?
Mr. Oswald. That is correct.
Mr. Jenner. Executed contemporaneously with the original?
Mr. Oswald. Yes, sir.
Mr. Jenner. Would you have any further questions?
Mr. Dulles. No, I have no further questions.
Shall we admit this at this time, or do you want to wait until you have gone through them all, and then admit them all?
Mr. Jenner. It might be more convenient to identify them all, because they are of a series, if I have your permission.
Mr. Dulles. Certainly.
Mr. McKenzie. The next document is Commission Exhibit 277, and purports to be a photocopy, or is a photocopy of a purported contract between Marina N. Oswald and Robert Oswald, bearing the date of December 9, 1963, and purportedly signed by Marina N. Oswald, Robert L. Oswald, John M. Thorne, attorney, and James H. Martin, approved as to form, and consisting of two pages.
Mr. Jenner. Now, if you would turn to the second page, please, sir—I notice a recital, "Executed by the undersigned parties this Ninth day of December A.D., 1963," and what purports to be your signature.
287 Was this document, or that of which this is a Xerox copy, executed on that date?

Mr. Oswald. I do not have a calendar before me. If the ninth day of December was a Monday, it was signed on that date.

Mr. Jenner. Mr. Dulles is checking the calendar.

Mr. Dulles. I am afraid I don't have a 1963 calendar here.

Mr. Jenner. I am observing a calendar, and the ninth was a Monday.

Mr. McKenzie, does the previous document also bear a date?

Mr. McKenzie. It bears the date of December 6, Mr. Jenner.

Mr. Jenner. December 6, then, was a Saturday.

Mr. McKenzie. If Monday was the ninth, Friday was the sixth.

Mr. Jenner. Was the previous exhibit, which is numbered 276, executed on December 6th?

Mr. Oswald. No, sir; it was not.

Mr. Jenner. On what date was it executed?

Mr. Oswald. It was executed on Monday, December 9th.

Mr. Jenner. Despite its bearing a date of December 6th, it was actually executed on the ninth, when Commission Exhibit 277 was executed?

Mr. Oswald. Yes, sir; that is correct.

Mr. Jenner. Now, directing your attention to the second page of Exhibit No. 277, that likewise bears a series of signatures. I ask you first whether those signatures were affixed in your presence?

Mr. Oswald. Yes, sir; they were.

Mr. Jenner. Now, was the document now identified as 277, which is a Xerox copy—was the original of Exhibit 277 executed at the same time as the copy which you have produced for us executed?

Mr. Oswald. May I have that again, please, sir?

Yes, sir; that is correct.

Mr. Jenner. That is, there were a series of papers, original and carbon copies, signed, at one and the same time?

Mr. Oswald. Yes, sir.

Mr. Jenner. And all of them were signed in your presence?

Mr. Oswald. Yes, sir.

Mr. Jenner. All right.

Now, there are four signatures on that page. Would you proceed to state your familiarity with those signatures and identify them?

Mr. Oswald. All right.

Left to right, as the signatures appear—my signature, Robert L. Oswald.

Mr. Jenner. And to the right of that?

Mr. Oswald. And to the right of that, the signature of Mrs. Marina N. Oswald, which I am familiar with.

The next signature is Mr. John M. Thorne, attorney, and I am familiar with his signature.

And the last signature that appears on this second page, Mr. James H. Martin. I am also familiar with his signature.

Mr. Jenner. And these persons are the same persons you have heretofore identified?

Mr. Oswald. Yes, sir.

Mr. Jenner. And is the document of which this 277 is a Xerox copy in the same condition now as it was the time those signatures were affixed to it?

Mr. Oswald. May I have a moment, sir?

Mr. Jenner. Yes.

Mr. Oswald. Yes, sir; that is correct.

Mr. Jenner. Is that likewise true of Exhibit No. 276?

Would you take a look at it, please?

Mr. Oswald. Yes, sir; that is correct. And if I may say this about this—on page 3 of Exhibit 276, you will note that towards the upper right-hand part of this page there was—on this copy, there is a dark mark, following the word "royalties."

Representative Ford. What page is that?

Mr. Oswald. Page 3, the sixth line, the word that was crossed off or out of the contract was the word "gifts."

288 Mr. Jenner. And was that done in the course of the discussion and preceding the execution of the document?

Mr. Oswald. Yes, sir; that is correct.

Mr. Jenner. So the document is in the same condition it was when executed?

Mr. Oswald. Yes, sir.

Mr. Jenner. Would you identify the next exhibit, Mr. McKenzie?

Mr. McKenzie. The next exhibit is a photocopy of an investment agency agreement. It is Commission Exhibit No. 278. This exhibit bears the date of December 30, 1963, and is an agreement by and between John M. Thorne and James H. Martin, co-trustees, of Dallas County, Tex., referred to in the exhibit as principal, and the First National Bank of Fort Worth, Tex., referred to in the exhibit as agent.

The exhibit consists of 3 pages, together with a schedule A and a letter addressed to the Trust Department of the First National Bank of Fort Worth, Tex.

This exhibit is a photocopy of a photocopy of a duplicate original.

I have seen the duplicate original upon which it had the names, handwritten names of John M. Thorne, co-trustee, and James H. Martin, co-trustee, as principal, on page 3, and Preston A. Utterbach, Vice President and Trust Officer of the First National Bank of Fort Worth, Tex.

However, these Xerox copies of a copy, being a photocopy, do not have the signatures on, because the second photocopy did not reproduce the signatures.

I have seen those.

Mr. Jenner. The Xerox machine was unable to pick up the signatures?

Mr. McKenzie. No. The prior photocopy was unable to pick up the signatures.

Mr. Dulles. Because they had not been put on, or because they didn't pick them up?

Mr. McKenzie. It would not pick them up, Mr. Dulles. The signatures were on the instrument itself, but the photo machine would not reproduce the signatures.

Mr. Jenner. You actually saw the signatures?

Mr. McKenzie. Yes, sir.

Mr. Jenner. Where did you see that document, Mr. McKenzie?

Mr. McKenzie. Marina N. Oswald gave it to me in my office.

Mr. Jenner. Would you state the thrust or substance of those agreements?

Mr. McKenzie. The substance of it is that Mr. Thorne and Mr. Martin, as principals, constituted the First National Bank of Fort Worth as the agent to hold certain trust funds, consisting, as shown by the exhibit, attached to this exhibit, of $25,000.

Mr. Jenner. It was deposited with the First National Bank of Fort Worth under this trust and deposit agreement, agency agreement?

Mr. McKenzie. Yes, sir.

I presume that to be true. I know Preston Utterbach. And if his signature was on it, I know that the funds were deposited there at the bank, or else he would not have executed it.

Mr. Dulles. Could I ask the source of these funds, if you know?

Mr. McKenzie. I do not know them, sir. But Marina Oswald has told me that she felt that the funds came from contributions made to herself and her children, from various sources, of which I know nothing.

Mr. Jenner. Excuse me, Mr. McKenzie.

Did you use the word "felt." She told you she felt?

Mr. McKenzie. Yes, I did.

Mr. Jenner. That is the extent of your personal knowledge?

Mr. McKenzie. Yes, sir.

Mr. Jenner. Mr. Oswald, do you have any personal knowledge, apart from or in addition to that of Mr. McKenzie, with respect to the source of the funds?

Mr. Oswald. I would say this was monies received through the mails, and delivered in person to Mr. Thorne or perhaps Mr. Martin by various people who wanted to contribute to Marina's welfare and her children's welfare.

Mr. Jenner. Upon what is your statement based? Conversations?

Mr. Oswald. Conversations, and also being——

Mr. Jenner. With whom, sir?

Mr. Oswald. Marina N. Oswald.

289 Mr. Jenner. She related this to you?

Mr. Oswald. Yes.

Mr. Jenner. All right.

Anybody else? What about Mr. Thorne and Mr. Martin? Had you had conversations with them as to the source of these funds?

Mr. Oswald. Yes, sir. I would say that would be correct, too.

Mr. Jenner. Did these conversations take place in the presence of Mrs. Marina Oswald? Your conversations with Mr. Thorne and Mr. Martin?

Mr. Oswald. Not that I recall, sir. I am thinking perhaps, when I was aware at first that the $25,000 was to be placed in the trust fund at the First National Bank of Fort Worth, I learned this through a conversation on the telephone.

Mr. Jenner. With whom?

Mr. Oswald. With Mr. Jim Martin.

Mr. Jenner. Are you familiar with Mr. Martin's voice?

Mr. Oswald. Yes.

Mr. Jenner. Did you call him or did he call you?

Mr. Oswald. I do not recall, sir.

Mr. Jenner. When did this take place?

Mr. Oswald. Approximately a week prior to the actual deposit and setting up of the trust fund at the First National Bank in Fort Worth.

Representative Ford. Mr. Jenner, I suggest we get a copy of the deposit slip or some other validation of the actual amount.

Mr. Jenner. Thank you, sir. We will undertake to do that. These documents, as I have indicated, were produced for us during the recess. We don't have the full information.

Perhaps, Mr. McKenzie—you have been quite helpful. You might be further helpful to us—you might have the deposit—evidence of the deposit.

Mr. McKenzie. Mr. Jenner, I wish I did have it. However, I know that the First National Bank of Fort Worth would gladly duplicate that for you. And I contemplate that I will be in the process of obtaining a copy from either Mr. Thorne or Mr. Martin in the very near future, because I have asked both of those gentlemen, on behalf of Marina Oswald and her children, for a full and complete accounting as of February 18, 1964, and I will likewise say that she has informed me up until February 18, 1964, she has had no accounting from either of those gentlemen.

Mr. Jenner. Is there another exhibit?

Mr. McKenzie. Yes, sir.

The next exhibit, Mr. Jenner, is Commission Exhibit No. 279, which is a Xerox copy of a power of attorney granted to the firm of Thorne and Leach, attorneys and counselors at law, bearing the date of December 5, 1963, in which it has three—I presume these are omissions from the exhibit—commencing on line 4, following the words "trust funds", there is an omission, and then the word "bequests", and then there is another omission, and on line 5, at the beginning of that line, there is an omission.

Mr. Dulles. What is the nature of the omissions?

Mr. McKenzie. Mr. Dulles, I have been told that the word "gifts" was omitted. The word "gift" was originally in it. But I have been told the word "gift" was omitted, or struck out.

Mr. Jenner. Mr. Dulles, I had intended to question the witness about that.

Mr. McKenzie. This contract provides that Marina N. Oswald, "bargain, transfer, sell and assign an undivided 10 percent of all such sums when collected or paid to my account," referring to the fund in the preceding paragraph. The agreement is signed by Marina N. Oswald, witnessed by James H. Martin, and accepted by John M. Thorne.

I am familiar with Marina N. Oswald's signature, and this is a copy of her signature, or is her signature. I am not familiar with Mr. Martin's signature or Mr. Thorne's signature.

Mr. Jenner. Directing your attention to that document, Mr. Oswald, are you familiar with any of the signatures it bears?

Mr. Oswald. Yes, sir; I am.

290 Mr. Jenner. Would you identify each signature and indicate those with which you are familiar?

Mr. Oswald. As they appear in order, the first signature is Mrs. Marina N. Oswald. I am familiar with this signature.

The second signature is Mr. James H. Martin. I am familiar with his signature.

Mr. Jenner. It is his signature?

Mr. Oswald. I would say yes, it is.

Mr. Jenner. All right.

Mr. Dulles. Is that under "Accepted"—is that first word there "John"?

Mr. Oswald. Yes, sir. And the last signature as appears on this Exhibit 279 is the signature of John M. Thorne.

Mr. Jenner. Do you know the day upon which that document was executed? It bears a date of December 5, which is a Thursday.

Mr. Oswald. No, sir; I do not.

Pardon me—the 5th day of December is the date purported—that this document was executed at. I am not familiar that it was executed on that date.

Mr. Jenner. Are you familiar with the date when it was in fact executed?

Mr. Oswald. No, sir; I am not. I might further state I was not present when this document was signed, and I was not aware of this document until Thursday, February 13th.

Mr. Jenner. 19——

Mr. Oswald. 1964.

Mr. Jenner. May I inquire of you, Mr. McKenzie, whether you have seen the original of the document of which this purports to be a Xerox copy?

Mr. McKenzie. I have not, sir. But I have seen a duplicate copy, an original copy.

Mr. Jenner. A duplicate executed copy?

Mr. McKenzie. Yes, sir.

Mr. Jenner. That was furnished to you by whom?

Mr. McKenzie. By Marina N. Oswald.

Mr. Jenner. And this is a photostatic copy of what, with respect to an original, carbon copy or otherwise?

Mr. McKenzie. It is a photocopy of a carbon copy.

Mr. Jenner. And have you personally seen the carbon copy of which this is a photo?

Mr. McKenzie. Yes, sir; I have.

Mr. Jenner. And is the document now identified as Commission Exhibit No. 279 in the same condition now as it was when you first saw it?

Mr. McKenzie. Exactly.

Mr. Jenner. And to the best of your recollection, is it a duplicate of the original?

Mr. McKenzie. Yes, sir.

The next exhibit is Commission Exhibit No. 280 entitled "The Oswald Trust," and bearing a heading, "The State of Texas, County of Dallas, Know all men by these presents," and it is a trust agreement dated December 30, 1963, by and between Marina Nikolaevna Oswald "a widow, hereinafter called grantor, and John M. Thorne and James H. Martin of Dallas County, Texas, co-trustees, hereinafter called the trustee" in which it describes certain funds described on Schedule A attached to this exhibit, which consists of some six pages, plus the Schedule A, Schedule A describing the trust funds as cash, $25,000. And I might add, in my opinion, Mr. Jenner, for whatever it may be worth, that this trust grants to John Thorne and James Martin purportedly grants unto those two men as co-trustees absolute discretion as to the distribution of the trust funds.

In fact, on page 2 it says, "as the trustee shall in either case in its uncontrolled discretion deem advisable."

Mr. Dulles. Who is the beneficiary of this trust?

Mr. McKenzie. Marina Oswald and her children, in the discretion of John Thorne and James Martin.

Representative Ford. Is that $25,000 the same $25,000 referred to in a previous exhibit?

291 Mr. McKenzie. Mr. Ford, I presume so. But that is only a presumption on my part. I do not know.

I might further add, for the benefit of counsel and the Commission, that Marina Oswald has informed me, and I think Robert Oswald can testify as to this, which I leave to your discretion, that at no time have these, up until February 14—have these—

Mr. Jenner. 1964?

Mr. McKenzie. 1964—have these exhibits, numbered consecutively from 276 through 280, been read to her in Russian. And at the time of execution, they were not interpreted, nor did they show of the contents—what the contents were, except as explained to her in English.

Mr. Jenner. Mr. McKenzie, the document is identified as Commission Exhibit No. 280, directing your attention to page 5, has blanks for signatures, and names of grantor and co-trustees under those lines.

Could I ask you whether you have seen the original of this document?

Mr. McKenzie. I have not, sir. I have seen a copy.

Mr. Jenner. An executed copy?

Mr. McKenzie. To the best of my recollection, it was an executed copy, yes, sir.

Mr. Jenner. And from what source did you obtain or was the document exhibited to you?

Mr. McKenzie. The document was given to me by Marina Oswald.

Mr. Jenner. And you observed that it was executed?

Mr. McKenzie. Yes, sir.

Mr. Jenner. By the persons whose names appear on page 5 of the Exhibit 280?

Mr. McKenzie. Yes, sir.

I have made these exhibits available to the Commission for whatever purpose they may serve the Commission, and for no other purpose.

Mr. Dulles. Yes. I think we might want to reserve on that until the whole Commission can get together. We want to examine everything within the mandate we have been given by the President. We don't want to go afield, quite naturally. And we cannot tell at this stage what bearing these particular papers might have. So I think I would like to reserve judgment on these.

Mr. McKenzie. Well, Mr. Dulles, I made that statement in view of that fact. I felt that that would be true.

Mr. Jenner. Mr. McKenzie, for the purpose of our record, would you be offended if we had you sworn, so you could then state that the statements you have made to the Commission are true and correct?

Mr. McKenzie. I would not be offended in any way.

Mr. Dulles. Do you, Mr. McKenzie, swear that what you have stated, is the full truth, and nothing but the truth, so help you God?

Mr. McKenzie. I do, Mr. Dulles.

Mr. Jenner. Mr. Chairman, I offer in evidence as Commission Exhibits 276 through 280, inclusive, the documents that have been so identified.

Mr. Dulles. They may be accepted.

(The documents referred to were marked Commission Exhibits Nos. 276 through 280, inclusive, for identification, and received in evidence.)

Mr. Dulles. I wish to state, in accepting these documents, the Commission does not want to pass on or assume any responsibility with respect to the financial or other arrangements described in these documents.

Mr. Jenner. I sought to identify them, Mr. Chairman, and gentlemen, and to tender them in evidence because of events of the past few days, and to confirm Mr. McKenzie's authority to speak on behalf of Mr. Oswald.

Mr. Dulles. Very well.

Mr. Jenner. At the recess, Mr. Oswald, we were dealing with—excuse me.

We were dealing with the period of time that you and your mother and your two brothers lived in Benbrook, Tex. This brought us through the summer of 1948, I believe.

Am I correct?

Mr. Oswald. That is correct, sir.

Mr. Jenner. Mr. Liebeler has determined that the divorce of Mr. Ekdahl and292 your mother took place in 1948. We cannot give you the month and the day in 1948, but it was during the year 1948.

We had reached the point in which you related to us that, I believe, following the divorce of Mr. Ekdahl and your mother, she purchased a small home.

Mr. Oswald. That is correct.

Mr. Jenner. And refresh my recollection, please—was that in Benbrook, Tex.?

Mr. Oswald. That was in Benbrook, Tex.

Mr. Jenner. Have we reached a point now at which your brother, Lee, had entered elementary school?

Mr. Oswald. Yes, sir; we have.

Mr. Jenner. And you boys have now terminated your attendance at the military academy?

Mr. Oswald. Yes, that is correct.

Mr. Jenner. And would you please relate what elementary school you and your brother, John, attended, and Lee, if he attended the same school?

Mr. Oswald. Prior to the school year of 1948–49, we moved to Ewing Street, 7408 Ewing Street, within the limits of the city of Fort Worth.

Mr. Jenner. Was the home that had been purchased in Benbrook, Tex., sold?

Mr. Oswald. I would say yes, sir.

Mr. Jenner. Well, you state that you would say. Is that your best information?

Mr. Oswald. Yes, sir.

I am not aware of any transactions in regards to the selling of that home or anything. Since we did move, and she did purchase this home on 7408 Ewing Street, in Fort Worth, I would assume that she did sell the house at Benbrook, because she didn't rent it, and we no longer went out there. I feel sure she did sell it.

Mr. Jenner. Did I understand you to say that your mother purchased a home at 7408 Ewing?

Mr. Oswald. Yes, sir; that is correct.

Mr. Jenner. Would you, in very short compass, tell us the physical characteristics of that home?

Mr. Oswald. It was a two bedroom, asbestos siding, with an attached garage, red roof, small porch on the front, and an average sized lot.

Mr. Jenner. These homes you have been describing all have, as I recall it—have either attached garage or separate garages.

Mr. Oswald. Yes, sir—with the exception of the home there in Benbrook that my mother purchased after the divorce from Mr. Ekdahl—it did not have a garage, and I did not recall a garage at the native stone house in Benbrook.

Mr. Jenner. The purpose of my inquiry was, did the family have an automobile?

Mr. Oswald. Yes, sir.

Mr. Jenner. Was that true when you lived in Louisiana?

Mr. Oswald. To my best recollection on that—my father did have, at the time of his death, either a 1937 or 1938 Chevrolet. I believe my mother sold it after his death. I believe she did not own an automobile in New Orleans, when we were at the Bethlehem Orphan Home.

Mr. Jenner. Were you boys interested in automobiles, as most young teenagers are?

Mr. Oswald. I think so, sir.

Mr. Jenner. Tinker around with them, drive them?

Mr. Oswald. Yes, sir.

Mr. Jenner. Both you and your brother John?

Mr. Oswald. Yes, sir.

Mr. Jenner. Later on, in later years, did your brother Lee—was he likewise interested in automobiles, did he tinker with them?

Mr. Oswald. Not to my knowledge, sir, did he tinker with them. Even though I can recall a couple of occasions with automobiles that I owned that he would assist me in any repairs I might be making on the automobile at that time.

Mr. Jenner. Well, I have in mind his interest now. Was he a good driver?

Mr. Oswald. To my knowledge, he did not drive.

Mr. Jenner. He did not drive at all?

293 Mr. Oswald. No, sir; he did not.

Mr. Jenner. Did you ever see him drive an automobile?

Mr. Oswald. No, sir; I did not. On two or three occasions in later years, I offered to teach him to drive.

Mr. Jenner. You recall this specifically now, do you? Would you relate to the Commission this course of events in his life—a young man who never did learn, at least to your knowledge, to drive an automobile?

Mr. Oswald. Yes, sir; that is correct.

The first occasion that I recall that I offered to Lee to teach him how to drive—at that time, I owned a '56 Chevrolet. I had married, and I was residing at 7313 Davenport, Fort Worth, Tex., a home which I had purchased. And Lee was home on leave.

Mr. Jenner. Give us the time, please, as closely as you can.

Mr. Oswald. This would be some time in 1958.

Mr. Jenner. He was then in the Marine Corps?

Mr. Oswald. Yes, sir; that is correct.

Mr. Jenner. And he was home on leave?

Mr. Oswald. Yes, sir; that is correct.

Mr. Jenner. State the circumstances, will you please?

Mr. Oswald. With relation to my offer to teach him how to drive?

Mr. Jenner. Yes. How did that come about?

Mr. Oswald. Well, he was spending a day, or part of a day over at our house. We were going to the grocery store or something—Lee and I. As I backed out of the driveway, I recall saying something to him, or he brought it up, or something—about wanting to learn how to drive.

And I said, "Well, we can start right now."

It was an automatic transmission.

"It is the easiest thing in the world to do. There is nothing to worry about. And I would be right here with you."

Well, he didn't think that was the time to try to start. He did want to learn how to drive, though. And he did not take the wheel.

Mr. Jenner. He did not?

Mr. Oswald. No, sir.

At no time was I present when he took the wheel of a car and drove it.

Mr. Jenner. And on any occasion in your lifetime, did you ever see him, whether you were in the vehicle—whether or not you were in the vehicle—behind the wheel and actually operating in motion an automobile?

Mr. Oswald. No, sir; I have never known him to operate an automobile, to drive it.

Mr. Jenner. What about Mrs. Marina Oswald in that respect?

Mr. Oswald. No, sir; to my knowledge she does not drive and she does not know how to drive, and I have never seen her operate an automobile.

Mr. Jenner. I notice when you are smoking that you hold the cigarette in your left hand. Are you left handed?

Mr. Oswald. Yes, sir. I am left handed when I write and eat.

Mr. Jenner. And you are right handed otherwise?

Mr. Oswald. Yes, sir.

Mr. Jenner. Throwing a baseball?

Mr. Oswald. Throwing a baseball.

At one time I could handle it with both hands—especially a football better than a baseball. But I have returned to my right hand on that. I was more accurate with my right hand than with my left hand, in throwing things. I kick footballs right footed and so forth.

Mr. Jenner. What about your father? Was he right handed or left handed?

Mr. Oswald. This I do not know, sir.

Mr. Jenner. Your mother?

Mr. Oswald. My mother is left handed.

Mr. Jenner. And your brother Lee?

Mr. Oswald. He was right handed.

Representative Ford. Was there ever a time that he appeared to be left handed, as far as you recollect?

294 Mr. Oswald. No, sir. I have never known him to handle anything—throw a baseball, football, et cetera, fire a rifle, or do anything, left handed.

Mr. Jenner. In order to be certain of the details in this respect, when he wrote, did be write with his right or his left hand?

Mr. Oswald. Right handed.

Mr. Jenner. Right handed?

Mr. Oswald. Yes, sir.

Mr. Jenner. And you in fact have seen him write with his right hand?

Mr. Oswald. Yes, sir, I have.

Mr. Jenner. During your youth?

Mr. Oswald. Yes, sir.

Mr. Jenner. Did you ever—was there ever an occasion when you saw him write or attempt to write with his left hand?

Mr. Oswald. No, sir, I have never seen him at any time, on any occasion, ever attempt to write or do anything left handed.

Mr. Jenner. You really covered my next question, but I would like to ask it anyhow.

There are men in athletics who are either right handed or left handed, but who throw or bat or do something from the other side.

Did he ever throw left handed or in any athletic endeavor employ his left hand predominantly as against his right hand?

Mr. Oswald. No, sir; not to my knowledge, he never did.

313

Mr. Jenner. From your many years of experience with him, being associated with him, as his brother, was he a predominantly right-handed person?

Mr. Oswald. Yes, sir; he most certainly was.

Representative Ford. And you personally saw him throw, kick, or do anything athletic over the years, and saw him use his right hand exclusively?

Mr. Oswald. Yes, sir. I would say without qualification—I might be repeating myself here—at no time did I ever know him to do anything left handed, to the extent that it would be predominant. Of course his hands worked together, and so forth. But I have never known him to do anything left handed.

Mr. Jenner. From your long acquaintance with him, and your intimate knowledge of his physical characteristics in that respect, do you have an opinion as to whether he was instinctively right-handed or instinctively a left-handed person?

Mr. Oswald. I would say he was instinctively a right-handed person.

Mr. Jenner. In all the years you were with him, you had opportunity to see him react instantaneously without having time to think about using his right hand or left hand?

Mr. Oswald. Yes, sir.

Mr. Jenner. Did you observe him on many occasions?

Mr. Oswald. Yes. I have never known him to use his left hand in any manner when an occasion would require that he use either hand—instinctively went to his right hand.

Mr. Jenner. Was he a coordinated person in the use of his right hand? Some are not coordinated athletically.

Mr. Oswald. My opinion of this, sir, would be that he was coordinated to the extent that looking at myself and many, I would compare us as two peas in a pod. Quite fast, well coordinated.

Mr. Jenner. He was dextrous?

Mr. Oswald. Yes, sir.

Mr. Jenner. And well coordinated?

Mr. Oswald. Yes, sir.

Mr. Jenner. And you had an opportunity over the years to see him engage in athletics, did you?

Mr. Oswald. Yes, sir.

Mr. Jenner. During your youth, as a young man, in any event, did you and your brother John and Lee have an interest in guns, rifles, pistols, cap guns, firearms generally?

Mr. Oswald. Yes, sir; we certainly did. I would say this.

Mr. Jenner. Now, this includes all three of you?

Mr. Oswald. Yes, sir; I understand that.

Of course John and I, when we attended military school, we had more of an opportunity to become acquainted with firearms. We certainly played with cap pistols, rubber guns, et cetera, when we were young. Lee did the same thing.

However, I would say this. Mother did not like firearms.

Mr. Dulles. We will recess now until 2 o'clock this afternoon.

(Whereupon, at 12:30 p.m., the President's Commission recessed.)

Afternoon Session
TESTIMONY OF ROBERT EDWARD LEE OSWALD RESUMED

The President's Commission reconvened at 2 p.m.

Mr. Dulles. The Commission will come to order.

Mr. Dulles. Mr. Jenner, will you please continue?

Mr. Jenner. Thank you, sir.

Mr. Reporter, would you read the last question and answer we have so we can orient ourselves.

To refresh your recollection, Mr. Oswald, I had commenced to examine you with respect to the interests of yourself, your brother John, and your brother Lee in firearms, even at the children's stage. And you had indicated developments in that area as you became older.

I think you reached the point where, as an example, you said of course your brother John and yourself had attended military school.

Mr. Oswald. And, also, I believe, sir, the question referred to all three of us.

Mr. Jenner. Yes.

Mr. Oswald. To what extent we were familiar with firearms.

To elaborate, at military school John was by far the better shot of the two of us. He was on the school rifle team. And, at this time, I was 10 years old—when I first attended there. My hunting instinct came alive.

Mr. Jenner. Hunting?

Mr. Oswald. Hunting instinct came alive, and at the first opportunity I started hunting squirrels and so forth there in Mississippi. I did this on practically every occasion I had. John was on the rifle team. And up to that time, a number of years after that, we never had a firearm in the house. My mother didn't like them. She was scared of them. And after we moved to 7408 Ewing Street, none of us owned a rifle, even a .22, or a shotgun, or any type of firearm. And when I wanted to go hunting from there, I had various friends that had rifles that I would borrow, and I would go to the west side of Fort Worth, and Benbrook, and do my squirrel hunting.

I don't recall at anytime during that period that Lee went with me. I don't know that John did—because approximately this time he had reached the age of 17, at which time he joined the U.S. Coast Guard.

Mr. Jenner. This is when you moved over to Ewing Street in Fort Worth?

Mr. Oswald. Yes, sir.

Mr. Jenner. Up to that time, had you and Lee at any time gone hunting?

Mr. Oswald. No, sir; I do not recall any time that we went hunting at that time.

Mr. Jenner. This was 1948–49. So he was 9 to 10 years old?

Mr. Oswald. Yes, sir.

Mr. Jenner. Had, to your knowledge, Lee gone hunting or used firearms or played or been interested in firearms with you or with your brother?

Mr. Oswald. No, sir. To my knowledge I don't remember any time he went hunting with myself or my older brother John. As I stated, there was no firearms in the house.

He liked cap pistols, like any other kid. And to the extent that we didn't even own a BB gun.

Mr. Jenner. Had you ever had BB guns around your home?

Mr. Oswald. No, sir.

296 Mr. Jenner. Had you boys ever owned one?

Mr. Oswald. No, sir.

Mr. Jenner. By this time, I assume you had shot one.

Mr. Oswald. Yes, sir.

Mr. Jenner. Owned by one of your pals or somebody around the neighborhood?

Mr. Oswald. Yes, sir.

Mr. Jenner. And Lee had what you would describe as a normal interest in firearms?

Mr. Oswald. Yes, sir.

Mr. Jenner. That every boy has?

Mr. Oswald. Yes, sir.

Mr. Jenner. But not beyond that?

Mr. Oswald. No, sir.

Mr. Jenner. Were there any pistol or rifle ranges around that you boys attended?

Mr. Oswald. No, sir; there was not.

Mr. Jenner. Now, your brother John at this point entered the Coast Guard?

Mr. Oswald. Yes, sir.

Mr. Jenner. You were attending—you were then 15. You were now attending high school, I assume.
Mr. Oswald. Junior high school.
Mr. Jenner. In Fort Worth?
Mr. Oswald. Fort Worth, W. C. Stripling Junior High School.
Mr. Dulles. What was the name of that?
Mr. Oswald. W. C. Stripling Junior High School.
Mr. Jenner. Did your brother John attend high school?
Mr. Oswald. Yes, sir.
Mr. Jenner. What high school did he attend?
Mr. Oswald. We went for awhile—to get this thing in sequence, before he went into the Coast Guard he attended Arlington Heights High School in Fort Worth, I believe, for one-half year, and then he transferred to Paschal High School in Fort Worth.
Mr. Jenner. Had you attended either of those high schools?
Mr. Oswald. Yes, sir; Arlington Heights High School.
Mr. Jenner. I think I might go back a little bit. I will return to the firearms.
But to maintain the sequence, when you and your brother John came to Benbrook, Tex., after you completed your schooling at the military school, I assume you attended school in Benbrook, Tex.
Mr. Oswald. No, sir; we did not, because we were just there during the summer months. And we moved prior to the school year of 19——
Mr. Jenner. '48?
Mr. Oswald. '48—we moved to the address on Ewing Street.
Mr. Jenner. All right. And each of you then enrolled in Arlington?
Mr. Oswald. I was in the ninth grade, which was junior high school in Texas. I enrolled in W. C. Stripling.
Mr. Jenner. First?
Mr. Oswald. Yes, sir. And John Edward enrolled in Arlington Heights High School.
Mr. Jenner. W. C. Stripling High School was a junior high school?
Mr. Oswald. Yes.
Mr. Jenner. And Arlington Heights High School was senior high school?
Mr. Oswald. Yes, sir; the last 3 years.
Mr. Jenner. And, at this time, your brother Lee was enrolled in——
Mr. Oswald. West Ridglea Elementary School.
Mr. Jenner. So at this point each of you was attending a different school?
Mr. Oswald. Yes, sir; that is correct.
Mr. Jenner. And Lee was 9 years old.
You continued at Arlington Heights Junior High School for how long?
Mr. Oswald. No, sir—W. C. Stripling Junior High School. For 1 year, the ninth grade.
If I may, sir, perhaps correct something—I don't know for sure which way it297 was. When I said Lee attended West Ridglea Elementary School, I think perhaps the first year he attended Arlington Heights Elementary School, because I don't believe the West Ridglea Elementary School was completed at that time.
Mr. Jenner. We might take you in sequence so that at least I don't get confused.
You spent a year at W.C. Stripling High School?
Mr. Oswald. Yes, sir.
Mr. Jenner. So we now have—we are now into '49-'50, is that correct?
Mr. Oswald. That is correct, sir.
Mr. Jenner. And after a year at W.C. Stripling High School, you enrolled where?
Mr. Oswald. At Arlington Heights High School.
Mr. Jenner. And that would be in the fall of 1949?
Mr. Oswald. Yes, sir.
Mr. Jenner. And you attended Arlington Heights High School how long?

Mr. Oswald. I attended my sophomore year. In my sophomore year I started——
Mr. Jenner. Would that be 1951, the end of your sophomore year?
Mr. Oswald. No, sir; 1950 would be the end of the school year. That summer there I started a job with an A&P Supermarket there in Fort Worth.

I might say along this period mother seemed to be having difficulty keeping a job or making enough money and so forth to raise us. I stayed out of school that next year and worked for A&P.
Mr. Jenner. Out of school 1950–51?
Mr. Oswald. Yes, sir.
Mr. Jenner. Did your brother remain in school—John?
Mr. Oswald. John at this time was in the Coast Guard.
Mr. Jenner. Already in the Coast Guard?
Mr. Oswald. Yes, sir.
Mr. Jenner. All right. And you worked at the A&P during this period?
Mr. Oswald. Yes, sir.
Mr. Jenner. Did you contribute your earnings to your mother?
Mr. Oswald. Yes, sir.
Mr. Jenner. They were probably not a great amount at this age. Do you recall what they were, per week?
Mr. Oswald. Perhaps my starting salary was somewhere around $48 a week, or something like that. I believe by the end of the year I had become a checker, and perhaps it was $65 or $70 a week.
Mr. Jenner. What proportion of that did you contribute to the sustaining of the family?
Mr. Oswald. I would say practically all of it, but what I needed for expenses, a little spending money.
Mr. Jenner. Do you know whether your brother John made an allotment of any kind to your mother or sent her any money?
Mr. Oswald. To my knowledge, he did not.
Mr. Jenner. Was there any illness or disability of any kind that contributed to your mother's difficulty in obtaining positions during this period?
Mr. Oswald. No, sir; she was not disabled. I don't recall any particular length of illness that she had at this time that would not allow her to work.
Mr. Jenner. What was the reason, if you recall, she was having difficulty in obtaining work, or was there any particular reason?
Mr. Oswald. None that I recall, sir. No particular reason I can recall.
Mr. Jenner. Your brother Lee was living at home during this time?
Mr. Oswald. Yes, sir.
Mr. Jenner. Was he working after school, or making any effort to earn some money?
Mr. Oswald. No, sir; he was not. He might have on occasion mowed somebody's lawn or something like that, where he would have a little spending money, or something. But nothing frequently, consistently.
Mr. Jenner. I see.

Proceeding with you, at the end of the school year '50-'51—I assume you continued working there the summer of '51?
298 Mr. Oswald. Yes, sir.
Mr. Jenner. And did you reenter school that fall?
Mr. Oswald. Yes, sir; I did.
Mr. Jenner. Where?
Mr. Oswald. Arlington Heights High School.
Representative Ford. May I ask a question?

During this 1-year period that you worked for the A&P, Mr. Oswald, were you the principal source of income for your mother, Lee, and yourself?

Mr. Oswald. Mother was working. Whether or not I was making more than she was at that time, I do not know.

Representative Ford. She was working spasmodically or regularly during this period?

Mr. Oswald. I believe almost regularly, very little off. I cannot recall right now what she was doing. I think perhaps during this period she was selling insurance.

Representative Ford. While she was in this occupation, who took care of Lee?

Mr. Oswald. Well, no one did. Lee was, of course, at school. When he returned home from school in the afternoon, he managed for himself, until I or my mother returned home from work.

Representative Ford. He was 9 or 10?

Mr. McKenzie. Eleven years old.

Representative Ford. Thank you.

Mr. Jenner. I think Representative Ford's question may have been induced by the fact you said that at about this time of which we are speaking your mother was having trouble retaining her position or obtaining positions. I assumed from that, perhaps incorrectly, that there were gaps, there were times when she was not employed, and, therefore, did need you to remain out of school to help. Is that a fair statement?

Mr. Oswald. I would say that is a fair statement and generally so. A little more comes to mind there.

I believe, perhaps, that she might have been selling insurance. I think she was acting at that time as what you would call a hostess or a welcoming party for the city of Fort Worth. In other words, she went out and met new people coming into Fort Worth—something along that line. And apparently it wasn't very much money, very little. And I think during this period also she was trying to locate other types of work that would perhaps earn her more. I believe that would be more accurate to what I really had in mind, there.

Mr. Jenner. But during all of the period, from the divorce of your mother and Mr. Ekdahl, proceeding from that time forward, she again returned to what she had been doing prior to the marriage—that is, working to sustain the family?

Mr. Oswald. Yes, sir; that is correct.

Mr. Jenner. And if I may use the expression you did, Lee was left to shift for himself during the daytime, get to school, get back to school, and be around until either you boys returned to the home or your mother returned to the home?

Mr. Oswald. Yes, sir; that is correct.

Mr. Jenner. Because he didn't have anybody particularly assigned or who undertook to care for him?

Mr. Oswald. No, sir.

I might say you mentioned "you boys." Of course at this time John was in the Coast Guard, so it was either myself or my mother.

Mr. Jenner. And particularly during the year you were employed at the A&P, and your mother was also employed, then certainly during that period there was no one even available to take care of him, is that correct?

Mr. Oswald. That is correct.

Mr. Jenner. What were your hours?

Mr. Oswald. My hours varied somewhat. We had different types of shifts for different days. Normally perhaps from 7 to 4 or 5 o'clock, and on the weekends—stock day was Wednesday, when all shipments came in, to restock the store. That was Wednesday and Saturday. Usually they were long days. I worked from 7 o'clock to 8 o'clock or 9 o'clock at night. And on Saturdays practically always after the store was closed, we did the cleanup, and rewaxing299 the floors and sometimes it was anywhere from 10 to 10:30 at night, and perhaps even 11 o'clock before I was home.

Mr. Dulles. Did Lee's school at that time keep him until about 4 o'clock, do you know?

Mr. Oswald. I believe, sir, that would be—he was, of course, at that time, attending West Ridglea Elementary School. I believe it would be about 3 o'clock, because I believe high school at that time—we were getting out at 3:40. And I believe the elementary school was either 40 minutes or an hour earlier.

Mr. Jenner. You attended Arlington Heights High School for the school year '51-'52?

Mr. Oswald. Yes, sir; that is correct.

Mr. Jenner. And what about the year '52-'53?

Mr. Oswald. July 1952 I joined the Marine Corps.

Mr. Jenner. And in July 1952, when you joined the Marine Corps, what do you recall was your status as far as your schooling was concerned?

Mr. Oswald. I completed my junior year in high school.

Mr. Dulles. Did you enlist for 3 years?

Mr. Oswald. Yes, sir.

Mr. Jenner. And your brother was still in the Coast Guard?

Mr. Oswald. Yes, sir; he was still in the Coast Guard at that time.

Mr. Jenner. And, at that time, I take it your brother Lee was attending Arlington Heights High School? That would be 1952?

Mr. Oswald. Just a minute, please.

In 1952 Lee was 13 years old. He would be attending W. C. Stripling Junior High School then.

Mr. Jenner. I see. For the school year 1951–52?

Mr. Oswald. Yes, sir. Junior high school there was from the seventh to the ninth grades. And as soon as he was through with his sixth year, he started attending W. C. Stripling Junior High School.

Mr. Jenner. As soon as he finished the sixth year at Ridglea Elementary School, he entered W. C. Stripling High School, as a seventh grader?

Mr. Oswald. Yes, sir—junior high school.

Mr. Jenner. Now, the condition that you described as to Lee shifting for himself during the daytime, when your mother was away working and you were away working, and your brother John was in the Coast Guard, continued, I take it, when he began attendance and while he was attending W. C. Stripling Junior High School?

Mr. Oswald. Yes, sir.

Mr. Jenner. Was there a discussion, a family discussion when you enlisted in the Marines, or prior to your enlisting in the Marines, as to your doing so, and quitting high school?

Mr. Oswald. No, sir; there was not.

Mr. Jenner. That was of your own volition?

Mr. Oswald. Yes, sir.

Mr. Jenner. Did you talk to your mother in advance about it?

Mr. Oswald. No, sir.

Mr. Jenner. Not at all?

Mr. Oswald. No, sir.

Mr. Jenner. Had anything preceded in the way of family discussion of your brother John's entry into the Coast Guard?

Mr. Oswald. I feel like it was, sir. He had previously——

Mr. Jenner. This is your best recollection?

Mr. Oswald. Yes, sir.

He had previously, before going into the Coast Guard, joined the Marine Corps Reserve, the base of which was, at that time, at Grand Prairie, Tex. I believe it was 105 Howitzer, something like that. And he was perhaps in that 4 or 5 months before he joined the Coast Guard. When it came up about the Coast Guard, I believe we all talked about it, or at least he talked to Lee about it in front of me.

Mr. Jenner. You used an expression, "I believe we talked about it." Is it your recollection that you did?

Mr. Oswald. Yes, sir. Nothing that I remember particular about that.

300 Mr. Jenner. What was the character of the discussion, Mr. Oswald? You had a family in which your mother was having some difficulty supporting you boys? You had a brother who needed to be supported. Was there any discussion—or was there a discussion of what would happen in the event that first John and then you joined the service?

Mr. Oswald. I believe reflecting on what mother said to me when I made my decision to join the Marine Corps was that perhaps it was the best thing, where I would not be a burden to her to that extent, and also perhaps be able to help her when she needed help. And I think this would be in line with what was said when John left for the Coast Guard, that this would be, of course, one less for her to take care of at the house, to feed and to clothe, and so forth. And it would relieve her of her responsibility along that line—it would help her, because of the limited amount of funds that she had coming in.

Mr. Jenner. Did you ever make an allotment of any portion of your service pay to your mother?

Mr. Oswald. No, sir; I did not.

Mr. Jenner. To your knowledge, did John?

Mr. Oswald. No, sir; he did not.

Mr. Jenner. You were single at this time?

Mr. Oswald. Yes, sir.

Mr. Jenner. Your brother John was?

Mr. Oswald. 1952?

Mr. Jenner. When he entered the Coast Guard.

Mr. Oswald. When he entered the Coast Guard he was single.

Mr. Jenner. Did he marry while he was in the service?

Mr. Oswald. Yes, sir; he did.

Mr. Jenner. Now, was he in the Coast Guard when he married?

Mr. Oswald. Yes, sir; he was.

Mr. Jenner. I take it he did leave the Coast Guard.

Mr. Oswald. Yes, sir; he has.

Mr. Jenner. And did he enter into military service when he left the Coast Guard?

Mr. Oswald. Yes, sir; he did. He transferred from the Coast Guard into the U.S. Air Force.

Mr. Jenner. And when was that?

Mr. Oswald. I believe this to be around 1955. I believe it would be accurate to say in 1954. I do recall a letter from John to the extent that he lost a stripe when he transferred from one service to the other, and I believe this letter came to me when I was in Korea, which was 1954 and early '55. I believe it was 1954.

Mr. Jenner. When you were in Korea, did you say?

Mr. Oswald. Yes, sir.

Mr. Jenner. When did you say, if you did, that your brother John married? Do you recall the year?

Mr. Oswald. I believe this would be late 1950 or '51.

Mr. Jenner. That was during the period you were working at the A&P?

Mr. Oswald. Yes, sir.

Mr. Jenner. And where was he stationed at that time?

Mr. Oswald. New York City.

Mr. Jenner. Staten Island, I guess.

I would like to ask some questions about that later on, but I prefer now to return to this.

You enlisted in the Marines, then, in the summer of 1952.

Mr. Oswald. July 11, 1952.

Mr. Jenner. Would you give us in very short compass your military career?

Mr. Oswald. I went to boot camp at San Diego, Calif., and from San Diego I went to combat training at Camp Pendleton, Calif. When I left Camp Pendleton, I was transferred from the infantry into the Marine Air Wing.

I went to Jacksonville, Fla. to a preparatory school down there in Marine aviation—more or less to determine your ability and what your strong points301 were, and what field you would be best qualified in the aviation division.

From Jacksonville, Fla., I went into Millington, Tenn., right outside of Memphis, Tenn., a Navy school, where for approximately 6 months I attended metalsmith school.

From Memphis, Tenn., or Millington, Tenn., I went to Miami, Fla. for approximately 9 months. I was not in school any longer. I was on the job. And from Miami, I was sent overseas to Korea.

Mr. Jenner. And how long were you overseas?

Mr. Oswald. Approximately 18 months, sir.

Mr. Jenner. From when to when?

Mr. Oswald. I reported to Santa Ana, Calif. in January or February of 1954.

Mr. Jenner. And you were discharged from the Marines——

Mr. Oswald. July of 1955.

Mr. Jenner. So you had a full 3 years in the Marines.

Mr. Oswald. Yes, sir; that is correct.

Mr. Jenner. During that 3-year period, what contact did you have with the members of your family, and with particular reference, if you can give that first, with your brother Lee—his writing you, you writing him?

Mr. Oswald. Yes, sir; we were corresponding infrequently, I would say—not very many letters between I and Lee direct when I was in the service, especially the first part of my tour in the service.

In 1952, after traveling from Camp Pendleton, Calif., to Jacksonville, Fla., I did have a 10-day leave. They were in New York City at that time.

Mr. Jenner. This was then some time in 1953, I take it?

Mr. Oswald. No, sir—1952.

Mr. Jenner. 1952?

Mr. Oswald. Yes, sir. This was——

Mr. Jenner. You mean your mother and Lee—that is the period of time they were in New York City?

Mr. Oswald. That's correct.

Mr. Jenner. Living there.

Mr. Oswald. Yes, sir.

Mr. Jenner. Did you see them?

Mr. Oswald. No, sir; not at that time. I spent my leave in Fort Worth, because I did not feel I had enough time to travel to New York and down to Jacksonville, Fla. After completing metalsmith school at Millington, Tenn., I took a 10-day leave.

Mr. Jenner. Fix the time.

Mr. Oswald. This was July or August of 1953. I had my orders to go to Miami, Fla. I took a 10-day leave and left Millington, Tenn., by car and came to New York City and spent 10 days in New York with Lee, mother, John, and his family.

Mr. Jenner. Where did you stay?

Mr. Oswald. At mother's apartment, with Lee, in the Bronx some place—I do not recall the address.

Mr. Jenner. What, if anything, did you learn at that time regarding Lee's attendance or nonattendance in school?

Mr. Oswald. Nothing on that, sir. This was in the summer time. Lee, of course, was home and not supposed to be in school. And I do not think anything was brought up that I recall about whether or not Lee had been attending school regularly or not.

Mr. McKenzie. Can we go off the record?

Mr. Jenner. Yes.

(Discussion off the record.)

Mr. Dulles. Back on the record.

Mr. Jenner. Referring to the 10-day leave in New York City, did you spend time with your brother Lee?

Mr. Oswald. Yes, sir.

Mr. Jenner. Your mother was working during that period of time, was she not?

302 Mr. Oswald. Yes, sir.

Mr. Jenner. In spending time with him, did you take him around, or accompany him, visiting various places in New York City?

Mr. Oswald. He took me around, sir.

Mr. Jenner. Did you have occasion during that period to take any photographs, snapshots, of Lee?

Mr. Oswald. I certainly can identify the one appearing in Life—yes, sir; I did.

Mr. Jenner. Just hold your answers right in this area exactly to my questions.

Mr. Oswald. I'm sorry.

Mr. Jenner. Were these taken with your camera, or was it a camera that your mother or brother owned or had?

Mr. Oswald. This was my camera.

Mr. Dulles. What do these questions refer to? Do they refer to the pictures in Life?

Mr. Jenner. Well, I really did not want to refer to that at the moment.

Do you remember any of the places at which you took snapshots of Lee during this 10-day leave?

Mr. Oswald. The Bronx Zoo I believe was about the only time I can recall taking any pictures of him.

Mr. Jenner. I am at liberty to advise you, Mr. Oswald, that when your mother testified before the Commission she did produce a number of photographs, snapshots, and otherwise, among which was a snapshot of your brother, Lee, taken at the New York Zoo—that she testified was taken at the New York Zoo.

Is that the incident in which you took the photograph of your brother Lee, as far as you know?

Mr. Oswald. You say the New York Zoo, sir. As far as I know there is just one zoo up there referred to as the Bronx Zoo. I do recall, and I still have the picture that I took of Lee at the Bronx Zoo. I certainly feel that perhaps either I sent copies of it to mother, or to Lee after I had the film developed.

Mr. Jenner. Mr. Chairman, may I go off the record a moment?

(Discussion off the record.)

Mr. Dulles. Back on the record.

Mr. Jenner. For the purpose of the record, I have before me the February 21, 1964, issue of Life magazine, on pp. 68-A, 68-B, and 70 of which there appear a number of photographs. I think it would be well if we gave this spread page an exhibit number. And since it really consists of two separate pages—the next exhibit numbers are what?

Mr. Liebeler. 281 and 282.

Mr. Jenner. We will mark 68-B as 281 and page 69 as 282.

(The material referred to was marked Commission Exhibits Nos. 281 and 282, respectively, for identification.)

Mr. McKenzie. Mr. Jenner—the only thing you are offering to the Commission at this time as I understand it are the pictures that appear on those two pages and not the text.

Mr. Jenner. That's correct, sir.

Directing your attention to page 69, identified as Commission Exhibit 282, there is a picture of a young boy and the background looks like it might be taken in a zoo. You mentioned that you had taken a snapshot of your brother on this 10-day leave.

Could you examine that and see if you can identify that as being the snapshot you took?

Mr. Oswald. Yes, sir, I do so identify that picture. That was taken at the Bronx Zoo—a picture of Lee Harvey Oswald, taken during my 10-day leave in New York City in 1953, approximately July or August of 1953.

Mr. Jenner. Was school in session at that time?

Mr. Oswald. No, sir, school was not in session at that time. This was during the summer months.

Mr. Jenner. So there was no obligation on the part of your brother to have been in school at this particular time?

Mr. Oswald. That's correct, sir.

303 Mr. Jenner. Now, appearing immediately above that snapshot is a snapshot or a photograph, a picture of two boys. Do you recognize either or both of those children?

Mr. Oswald. Yes, sir; I do. I recognize the young boy standing, and I recognize him to be Lee Harvey Oswald.

Mr. Jenner. And who is the boy appearing lower in that photograph?

Mr. Oswald. I do not recognize him, sir.

Mr. Jenner. This is in the upper right hand corner of Commission Exhibit 282. Appearing immediately to the left—but before I proceed to that, are you able to identify that sufficiently to indicate to us the age of your brother at the time that picture was taken?

Mr. Oswald. I would say he was approximately 11 or 12 years old at that time.

Mr. Jenner. And at this time he was residing where?

Mr. Oswald. If he was 11 years old at the time the photograph was taken, he was residing in Fort Worth, Tex. If he was 12 years old, he would be residing in New York City.

Mr. Jenner. To the left appears another photograph of a young man in a striped shirt, a striped T-shirt. Do you observe that?

Mr. Oswald. Yes, sir; I do.

Mr. Jenner. It is apparently a blowup from a group picture. Who is that?

Mr. Oswald. I recognize him to be my brother, Lee Harvey Oswald.

Mr. Jenner. And do you recognize the clothing, have you seen him in that clothing before?

Mr. Oswald. Not that I recall. The tennis shoes look familiar.

Mr. Jenner. And are you able to make out the age of your brother at the time this picture was taken?

Mr. Oswald. I would say approximately 10 or 11 years old.

Mr. Jenner. So if it were at age 10, he would have been residing where?

Mr. Oswald. In Fort Worth, Tex.

Mr. Jenner. And you have already given the age.

To the left of that picture is another photograph or apparently a snapshot. I notice that there are part of some persons behind the central figure. Do you recognize the figure in that photograph?

Mr. Oswald. Yes; I do.

Mr. Jenner. Who is it?

Mr. Oswald. I recognize it to be Lee Harvey Oswald.

Mr. Jenner. At what age?

Mr. Oswald. Seven or eight years old.

Mr. Jenner. And assuming age 7, where was he residing at that time?

Mr. Oswald. This would be—the year when he was 7 would be 1946 or 1947. He would be residing in Fort Worth, Tex.

Mr. Jenner. And if he were 8, he still would be residing in Fort Worth, Tex.

Mr. Oswald. That's correct, sir.

Mr. Jenner. To the left of that picture is a picture of—I don't know whether that is one snapshot or two.

Mr. Oswald. It is one, sir.

Mr. Jenner. Showing three persons, three children. Are you able to identify all three?
Mr. Oswald. Yes, sir; I am.
Mr. Jenner. Would you please identify and give the ages?
Mr. Oswald. Left to right, I identify myself at the age of 10.
Mr. Jenner. With the sailor hat on?
Mr. Oswald. With the sailor hat on, right. In the center I identify it to be Lee Harvey Oswald at the age of 5. On the far right I identify John Edward Pic at the age of 12.
Mr. Jenner. And you boys were residing where at that time?
Mr. Oswald. At Dallas, Tex., on Victor Street. That was taken right outside, at the side of the house.
Mr. Jenner. Do you recall the circumstances under which the picture was taken?
Mr. Oswald. No, sir; other than we wanted to take some pictures.
Mr. Jenner. Your present recollection is who took the picture?
Mr. Oswald. My mother.
Mr. Jenner. In the background is what?
Mr. Oswald. The house that we lived in on Victor Street.
Mr. Jenner. There is a spread picture at the bottom of the double page. Are you familiar with the area which is shown in that picture?
Mr. Oswald. Yes, sir; I am.
Mr. Jenner. What is that area?
Mr. Oswald. That is on the playground of Ridglea West Elementary School.
Mr. Jenner. And do you recognize any of the persons shown in that reproduction?
Mr. Oswald. Yes, sir; I do.
Mr. Jenner. Would you identify those, if any, you so recognize?
Mr. Oswald. The only person I recognize in this photograph is this young man right here—I do not recall his name—I believe his name was Donald. He lived right around the corner from us.
Mr. Jenner. Mr. Oswald, I hand you a brush pen. Would you indicate by an arrow the person to whom you made reference? Thank you.
Would you do the same on the picture identified in the extreme upper right hand corner on Exhibit 282.
Now, I notice on the spread picture at the bottom of the page, which was identified as a schoolmate, that there is to the left of that picture a picture with an imprinted arrow. Do you recognize the person to whom the arrow is pointing?
Mr. Oswald. No, sir; I do not.
Mr. Jenner. Are you able to say whether that is or is not your brother Lee?
Mr. Oswald. No, sir; from this picture, I cannot determine if it is Lee or not.
Mr. Jenner. Are you able to see it clearly enough to say that it is not?
Mr. Oswald. No, sir; I am not able to see it clearly enough to make a positive statement one way or the other. It appears to be a little fuzzy.
Mr. Jenner. Do you have an opinion as to whether it is or not?
Mr. Oswald. No, sir; I do not.
Mr. Jenner. You just do not recognize it?
Mr. Oswald. I just do not recognize it.
Mr. Jenner. All right.
Now on page 68-A, which we will mark as Commission Exhibit No. 283—do you recognize that photograph depicted on that page?
(The material referred to was marked Commission Exhibit No. 283 for identification.)
Mr. Oswald. Yes, sir; I do.
Mr. Jenner. Who is it?
Mr. Oswald. I recognize Lee Harvey Oswald.
Mr. Jenner. Have you seen the original of that reproduction?

Mr. Oswald. Yes, sir; I most certainly have. I might add that I wore that same baby suit.
Mr. Jenner. That is shown in that picture?
Mr. Oswald. Yes, sir. And John Edward did, too.
Mr. Jenner. Now, turning to pages 70 and 71, which we will have marked as Commission Exhibit 284, so far as page 70 is concerned, and page 71 marked as 285.
(The material referred to was marked respectively Commission Exhibits Nos. 284 and 285 for identification.)
Mr. Jenner. Spread across page 70 and partially on page 71 is a photograph, or a reproduction of a photograph.
Do you recognize any of the persons depicted on that spread page?
Mr. Oswald. Yes, sir.
Mr. Jenner. And do you recognize more than one person?
Mr. Oswald. No, sir; I do not.
Mr. Jenner. And which one do you recognize?
Mr. Oswald. In the foreground on the left-hand side, on page 70, I recognize that to be Lee Harvey Oswald.
305 Mr. Jenner. Is that the boy with the V-shaped design on his sweater or T-shirt, with his hand on his chest?
Mr. Oswald. Yes sir; that is correct.
Mr. Jenner. Would you identify that by an arrow.
Are you able to, in looking at that—to tell at what age that was taken, and where?
Mr. Oswald. I would say approximately 14 years old. I cannot recognize the classroom there. At 14 Lee would have been——
Mr. Jenner. He was in New York City, was he not?
Mr. Oswald. 1953, yes, sir.
Mr. Jenner. On page 72, which we will mark as Commission Exhibit 286, there is a photograph or reproduction of a photograph in the lower right-hand corner.
(The material referred to was marked Commission Exhibit No. 286 for identification.)
Mr. Jenner. Do you recognize anyone in that reproduction?
Mr. Oswald. Yes, sir; I do.
Mr. Jenner. Do you recognize both people?
Mr. Oswald. No, sir; I do not.
Mr. Jenner. Would you indicate the person you recognize?
Mr. Oswald. I recognize the person on the left-hand side of this photograph.
Mr. Jenner. That is the man?
Mr. Oswald. Yes, sir. I recognize him to be Lee Harvey Oswald.
Mr. Jenner. At about what age?
Mr. Oswald. Since I am aware of where this picture was taken, at the age of 17.
Mr. Jenner. Would you elaborate——
Mr. Oswald. I am aware where this picture was taken. This is in Arlington Heights High School. I believe this exhibit right behind him in the background was on the third floor of Arlington Heights High School.
Mr. Jenner. And that was taken at the high school?
Mr. Oswald. Yes, sir.
Mr. Jenner. And he was of what age at that time?
Mr. Oswald. 17.
Mr. Jenner. Well, it is pretty clear, since there is a gentleman and a lady in this picture, the only two persons indicated, and you have identified your brother—would you still, however, put a arrow pointing to your brother. Thank you.
Turning to page 74-A, which is Commission Exhibit 287, there are two pictures reproduced in the lower right-hand corner.

(The material referred to was marked Commission Exhibit No. 287 for identification.)

Mr. Jenner. Do you recognize those?

Mr. Oswald. Yes, sir; I do.

Mr. Jenner. And would you state what they are?

Mr. Oswald. Both pictures are pictures of Lee Harvey Oswald.

Mr. Jenner. And he appears to be in military garb. Were those taken when he was in the Marines?

Mr. Oswald. Yes, sir.

Mr. Jenner. By the way, did you see him in his service uniform at any time?

Mr. Oswald. No, sir; I did not.

Mr. Jenner. But you do recognize these pictures as depicting your brother?

Mr. Oswald. Yes, sir.

Mr. Jenner. On pages 74 and 75 of Life Magazine, which will be Commission Exhibits 288 and 289, there is a spread picture.

(The material referred to was marked Commission Exhibit Nos. 288 and 289, respectively, for identification.)

Mr. Jenner. Do you recognize any of the persons depicted in that spread picture?

Mr. Oswald. Yes, sir; I do, but only one.

306 Mr. Jenner. Identify the one you recognize, and locate it in the picture.

Mr. Oswald. I recognize Lee Harvey Oswald being in the foreground of the picture, approximately in the center of the picture.

Mr. Jenner. Would you identify him with this brush pencil?

Then on Exhibit 288, which is page 74-B of this issue of Life Magazine, there appears at the bottom a reproduction of identity cards. I direct your attention to the left-hand identity card upon which appears a photograph, a reproduction of a photograph. Do you recognize that?

Mr. Oswald. I would have to say that he appears heavier, his face is fuller, he has more hair on his head, but the eyes and the nose and the mouth are Lee Harvey Oswald's. I had not studied that picture before. But he does seem to be quite fullfaced, if that is the terminology to use there, and much more hair on his head—there again in relation to the hair I am assuming here this photograph of Lee was taken after he returned from Russia.

Mr. Jenner. I would rather not have you assume anything at the moment.

Do you identify that as a reproduction of a picture of your brother?

Mr. Oswald. Yes, sir; I do.

Mr. Jenner. Are you acquainted with—were you at the time acquainted with the circumstances under which there was issued or purported to be issued a Selective Service System classification card in the name of Alek James Hidell?

Mr. Oswald. No, sir; I was not.

Mr. Jenner. And did you ever have a discussion with your brother with respect to his use, if he did, of the name Alek James Hidell, A. J. Hidell, or any combination of that, in which the surname Hidell was employed?

Mr. Oswald. No, sir; I did not. And if I may say, at no time have I ever known him to use any other name than Lee Harvey Oswald.

Mr. Jenner. I take it, then, you are unacquainted with any circumstances under which he employed, if he did employ at any time, the surname Hidell?

Mr. Oswald. That is correct, sir.

Mr. Jenner. Or any other alias?

Mr. Oswald. That's correct, sir.

Mr. Jenner. Did you ever know him to employ an alias?

Mr. Oswald. No, I had not.

Mr. Jenner. Have you ever employed one?

Mr. Oswald. Off the record, please.

Mr. Jenner. I will withdraw that question.
Mr. Oswald. This is what it amounts to.
Mr. McKenzie. Let me state this for the purposes of the record. In order to avoid publicity or avoid newsmen, we did travel to Friendship Airport from Dallas, Texas, yesterday evening, February 19th, and Robert Oswald traveled under the name of F. M. Johnson.
Mr. Dulles. Off the record.
(Discussion off the record.)
Mr. Dulles. Back on the record.
Mr. Jenner. On the following page, which is page 76, Commission Exhibit 290, is a photograph, reproduction of a photograph in the lower right-hand corner.
(The material referred to was marked Commission Exhibit No. 290 for identification.)
Mr. Jenner. You recognize the person depicted in that photograph?
Mr. Oswald. Yes, sir; I do.
Mr. Jenner. Would you identify them?
Mr. Oswald. I recognize the two people in the photograph—the woman being Mrs. Marina Oswald, and the man being Lee Harvey Oswald.
Mr. Jenner. Have you ever seen that picture before?
Mr. Oswald. Yes, sir; I believe I have.
Mr. Jenner. Did you see it prior to November 22, 1963?
Mr. Oswald. Yes, sir; I believe I did, and the reason why I say I believe—I believe I either have a copy of this photograph myself, or one very, very similar to it.
Mr. Jenner. How did you come into the possession of the photograph?
Mr. Oswald. Lee had sent it to me from Russia, showed me pictures of him307 and his wife on their wedding day in April, 1961. I received the photographs, though, in approximately May, 1961.
Mr. Jenner. Do you still have those photographs in your possession?
Mr. Oswald. Yes, sir; I do. If I may say, I did turn over I believe four photographs that Lee had sent me from Russia, and I believe in all four photographs Lee and Marina were in them. And I turned these over to Mr. Jim H. Martin.
Mr. Jenner. But they are your personal property.
Mr. Oswald. Yes, sir; they are.
Mr. Jenner. I want to get into that period of time when you were in correspondence with your brother at a later moment.
Turning now to page 78, which is Commission Exhibit 291, in the lower left-hand corner of that is a reproduction, or what purports to be a reproduction of a photograph.
(The material referred to was marked Commission Exhibit No. 291 for identification.)
Mr. Jenner. Do you recognize either of the two persons depicted in that photograph?
Mr. Oswald. Yes, sir; I recognize the man on the right with the piece of paper in his hand, and a notebook I believe under his left arm, to be Lee Harvey Oswald.
Mr. Jenner. Do you recognize the other man who is partially shown in that photograph?
Mr. Oswald. No, sir; I do not.
Mr. Jenner. Did you see that photograph at any time prior to November 22, 1963?
Mr. Oswald. No, sir; I had not.
Mr. Jenner. And on page 80, which is Commission Exhibit No. 292, there are two photographs, one showing a lady and a child, in the upper right-hand corner.
(The material referred to was marked Commission Exhibit No. 292 for identification.)
Mr. Jenner. Directing your attention to that picture first, do you recognize either of the persons shown in that photograph?
Mr. Oswald. Yes, sir; I do. I recognize both persons.

Mr. Jenner. Would you identify them, please?

Mr. Oswald. The child is June Lee Oswald, and the woman is Mrs. Marina Oswald.

Mr. Jenner. And June Oswald is your brother's child?

Mr. Oswald. That's correct, sir.

Mr. Jenner. Had you seen that photograph at any time prior to November 22, 1963?

Mr. Oswald. No, sir; I had not.

Mr. Jenner. In the lower right-hand corner is a photograph of a man holding a firearm or rifle with a pistol on his right hip and some papers of some kind in—he is holding the rifle in his left hand, the papers in his right hand. Do you recognize the person depicted in that photograph?

Mr. Oswald. Yes, sir; I do. I recognize him to be my brother, Lee Harvey Oswald.

Mr. Jenner. Had you seen that photograph at any time prior to November 22, 1963?

Mr. Oswald. No, sir; I had not.

Mr. Jenner. Have you seen the photograph of which that is a reproduction since November 22, 1963?

Mr. Oswald. Yes, sir; I have.

Mr. Jenner. Under what circumstances?

Mr. Oswald. At the Inn of the Six Flags at Arlington. Tex., approximately November 27, 1963, in the presence of U.S. Secret Service and Marina Oswald and myself.

Mr. Dulles. Your mother was not there then?

Mr. Oswald. She was there at the time, but I do not believe she was in the room when this photograph was shown.

308 Mr. Jenner. Mr. Chairman, I offer in evidence as Commission Exhibits 281 through 292 the pages of the issue of Life Magazine I have identified that bear those exhibit numbers.

Mr. Dulles. Yes. I understand counsel for Mr. Oswald has pointed out that I believe you are offering only the photographs and not the text?

Mr. Jenner. Thank you, sir. May I amend my offer. I offer in evidence the reproduction of photographs which the witness has identified that appear on Commission Exhibits 281 through 292.

Mr. Dulles. They may be accepted.

(The portion of the documents heretofore marked Commission Exhibits Nos. 281 through 292 for identification were received in evidence.)

Mr. Jenner. I do not offer any of the text or any other portions of those pages.

Mr. Dulles. That is so noted.

Mr. Jenner. Are there any other events or happenings or circumstances during this 10-day period in New York City that come to your mind? You have told of the incident of taking the photograph which was identified. You told of visiting various places in New York City and being with your brother Lee. Was it a good deal during this 10-day period?

Mr. Oswald. Yes, sir; practically every day, and practically every night, with two exceptions at night, where my brother John fixed me up with a blind date for one night only—no, I take that back. It would be just one night Lee was not with me, and that would be on the night I had a blind date with a girl from New York City, with my brother John and his wife.

Mr. Jenner. Did you and your brother Lee visit your brother John's home during this 10-day stay?

Mr. Oswald. No, sir, we did not.

Mr. Jenner. Did you have any discussion with your brother Lee—put it this way—did you become aware during this 10-day period as to whether your mother and brother had stayed with your brother John at any time during their New York visit?

Mr. Oswald. Yes, sir. It was my understanding that when they first arrived in New York for a brief period they stayed together.

Mr. Jenner. Was there any discussion with you as to why they left the home of your brother John?

Mr. Oswald. No, sir; not to any extent—no, sir, no discussion.

Mr. Jenner. No discussion of any difficulties or any incidents that had arisen while they were living with your brother John's family?

Mr. Oswald. No, sir.

Mr. Jenner. That induced or had a bearing upon leaving and taking an apartment in the Bronx?

Mr. Oswald. I do not know of any discussion or any difficulty that was mentioned to me, but I understand there was some difficulty.

Mr. Jenner. Please, Mr. Oswald—the subject was not discussed with you during the 10-day period you were on leave?

Mr. Oswald. That's correct, sir.

Mr. Jenner. Was it discussed with you at any time prior to November 22, 1963?

Mr. Oswald. No, sir; it was not.

Mr. Jenner. Was there any discussion on the subject of your brother's progress in schooling in New York City?

Mr. Oswald. No, sir; there was not.

Mr. Jenner. Was the subject of his attendance at school, whether the attendance was good or bad—was school discussed at all, as you recall?

Mr. Oswald. No, sir; not to my recollection.

Mr. Jenner. And as a layman, and acquainted with your brother, what was your impression? Give us your present impression of your brother's state of mind during that 10-day period. Was he normal and happy and friendly?

Mr. Oswald. He was very normal. He did not appear to be unhappy. He was quite happy to see me. We spent a good deal of time together during that 10-day visit. At no time did he act abnormally.

Mr. Jenner. Did he complain to you about school?

Mr. Oswald. No, sir; he did not.

309 Mr. Jenner. In general did he complain about anything—any special gripes?

Mr. Oswald. None that I recall, sir.

Mr. Jenner. Do you recall that as being a happy 10-day visit on your 10-day leave in New York City?

Mr. Oswald. Yes, sir.

Mr. Jenner. Both you and your brother?

Mr. Oswald. Yes, sir; that's correct.

Mr. Jenner. Did you spend time with your mother as well as your brother Lee during the 10-day period?

Mr. Oswald. Yes, sir; I did.

Mr. Jenner. That would be when—the evenings and on Sunday?

Mr. Oswald. Generally in the evenings. That is the way I recall it.

Mr. Jenner. You and your brother Lee and your mother—did you do any visiting during the evening, movies, any entertainment, go out?

Mr. Oswald. Yes, sir; Lee and I did. Mother did not join us.

Mr. Jenner. What was your impression of your mother's state of mind and well-being and her general feeling while you were there during that 10-day period?

Mr. Oswald. May I have that again, please?

(The reporter read the pending question.)

Mr. Oswald. My impression of my mother at that time was that she was still having a little difficulty making enough money to have the things that she wanted to have, I should say. But generally her health was good, and nothing that I recall comes to mind that would indicate that there was any difficulty between her and Lee. They seemed to be getting along quite well.

Mr. Jenner. Your impression during the 10-day period, I take it then, was that the relationship between your mother and Lee was friendly, was it?

Mr. Oswald. Yes, sir; that's correct.

Mr. Jenner. Were there any arguments during the time you were there between them?

Mr. Oswald. Yes, sir; there were.

Mr. Jenner. Did he at any time during that period—was he discourteous to his mother?

Mr. Oswald. If I may in my own words here, sir——

Mr. Jenner. Yes, sir.

Mr. Oswald. The word "discourteous"—my mother did not wish us to go to certain places—I say certain places—I do not recall the places. She just did not want us going, inasmuch as we were going during the day. I wanted to see as much of New York as I could while I was there. And I recall that Lee and mother and I had something of an argument in reference to staying away from the house during the day so long, and so forth. And it was not her wish that we do that. And if this was being discourteous—that is why I qualify that.

Mr. Jenner. Nothing extraordinary.

Mr. Oswald. No, sir.

Mr. Jenner. Now, your leave terminated. You went back to Florida, and you eventually wound up in Korea.

Mr. Oswald. That's correct, sir.

Mr. Dulles. Could I ask a question before we leave the New York period?

While you were there, was there any discussion about these absences from school which I think took place just the months before you were there—although I am not absolutely clear on that. It seems to me as I understand it your mother and Lee arrived in the Bronx area around September of '52, I think it was, and this was in the summer of '53 that you visited them there, is that correct?

Mr. Oswald. That's correct, sir.

Mr. Dulles. So that according to what I recall—and this may not be accurate—what is referred to as the truancy, the 46 days absence from school, had occurred some time prior to your visit. Maybe you do not recall that. That did not come up at all?

Mr. Oswald. No; it did not come up at all.

Mr. Dulles. Did anything come up about a psychiatric examination?

Mr. Oswald. No, sir; it did not.

310 Representative Ford. There was no mention of the farm?

Mr. Oswald. No, sir.

Mr. Dulles. So the psychiatric examination was not mentioned in your presence?

Mr. Oswald. No, sir.

Mr. Jenner. It had taken place I think in May of 1953.

Mr. Oswald. If I may, sir—mother did mention that Lee had appeared before a judge, and she said it was a Negro judge. I asked why, and she said because he had been absent from school too long, no specific dates or length of time was mentioned, and that they were stricter in New York about that than in Texas.

Representative Ford. Did this bother her, disturb her? Did she indicate the reaction to that?

Mr. Oswald. No, sir—at that time I do not recall any reaction that she had, or any comment she made about it. She just very briefly stated that he had appeared before this Negro judge in New York City, and just what I previously related about it. That was the only thing she said about it.

Representative Ford. She did not mention a man named Carro?

Mr. Oswald. No, sir; nobody's name was mentioned, not even the judge's name.

Mr. Jenner. To the best of your present recollection, that is about all that occurred in the way of conversation respecting some possible truancy?

Mr. Oswald. Yes, sir.

Mr. Jenner. That is all you now can recall.
Mr. Oswald. Yes, sir; that's correct.
Mr. Jenner. You were mustered out of the Marines in July of 1955.
Mr. Oswald. That's correct, sir.
Mr. Jenner. Did you return—well, when you were mustered out, where did you go?
Mr. Oswald. Fort Worth, Tex.
Mr. Jenner. And where were your mother and brother living at that time?
Mr. Oswald. In New Orleans, La.
Mr. Jenner. Were you still single?
Mr. Oswald. Yes, sir.
Mr. Jenner. Would you explain why you went to Fort Worth, Tex., rather than to New Orleans?
Mr. Oswald. I considered Fort Worth, Tex., my home. I wanted to go there. I had quite a few friends. I wanted to find a job in Fort Worth, Tex. And that is where I wanted to live.
Mr. Jenner. And you did undertake residence there?
Mr. Oswald. I did, sir.
Mr. Jenner. Have you continued to be a resident of Fort Worth, Tex., ever since?
Mr. Oswald. No, sir, I have not.
Mr. Jenner. Indicate in short compass where you have resided since you got out of the service?
Mr. Oswald. From 1955 I resided in Fort Worth, Tex., until March of 1963. From March of 1963 until September 1963, I resided in Malvern, Ark. And from September until present date I have resided in Denton, Tex.
Mr. Jenner. Did you visit your mother and your brother in New Orleans when you returned from the service in July of 1955?
Mr. Oswald. Yes, sir; I did. I did not—yes, sir, it was in July 1955 when I made my first trip from Fort Worth, Tex., to New Orleans, La. I had purchased a car the second day I was home from the service, a 1951 Chevrolet, and I drove it on the third day or the second night to New Orleans, La.
Mr. Jenner. Were your quarters in a hotel, or did you join your brother and mother?
Mr. Oswald. I joined my mother and brother.
Mr. Jenner. How long did you stay in New Orleans on that trip?
Mr. Oswald. Approximately 1 week.
Mr. Jenner. And you lived with your mother and brother?
Mr. Oswald. That's correct.
Mr. Jenner. That was in July of 1955?
Mr. Oswald. Yes, sir; that's correct.
Mr. Jenner. He was not in school at that time.
Mr. Oswald. No, sir; he was not.
Mr. Jenner. Now, how did you find your brother, as to the state of health and state of mind?
Mr. Oswald. He seemed to be the same to me. He had joined at that time—no, sir—he had not at that time been in the Civil Air Patrol. At that time Lee was working I believe for an export firm there in New Orleans. I do not know the name of it. I do not believe I ever heard the name of it. I might have. Mother was also working at that time.
Mr. Jenner. Had you seen your brother in the interim—that is the interim between the 10-day leave in New York City and your return from Korea in July of 1955?
Mr. Oswald. There was one leave, or perhaps it was this time in 1955 that Lee was in the Civil Air Patrol there in New Orleans, because I remember his uniform that he had. And we went out to lunch on a Sunday afternoon. And he had his uniform on—mother, he, and I.
Mr. McKenzie. Robert, he asked you this—if between the time you went to New York City and left there, and the time you went to Korea and came back, and you were

mustered out of the Marine Corps, did you see your brother at any time during that period of time?

Mr. Oswald. Yes, sir; I recall now. Leaving Miami, Fla., in 1954—January or February—I took another 10-day leave, I believe it was, and I traveled to New Orleans first, where mother and Lee was, and at this time he was in the Civil Air Patrol. And I spent 3 or 4 days there in New Orleans.

Mr. Jenner. You stayed with your mother and brother?

Mr. Oswald. Yes; I did.

Mr. Dulles. When you come to a good place, Mr. Jenner, we will stop for 5 minutes.

Mr. Jenner. The Commission's convenience is my convenience.

Representative Boggs. May I ask one or two questions.

Your brother John—is he alive?

Mr. Oswald. Yes, sir.

Representative Boggs. Where is he?

Mr. Oswald. San Antonio, Tex., in the U.S. Air Force.

Mr. Dulles. He is a half brother.

Representative Boggs. He is your older brother?

Mr. Oswald. Yes, sir.

Representative Boggs. How old is he?

Mr. Oswald. He is 32 now.

Representative Boggs. You never had any problems in school or in the Marine Corps, did you—I mean serious problems?

Mr. Oswald. No, sir; no serious problems.

Representative Boggs. You always had problems. But you never were in any trouble?

Mr. Oswald. I have never been in any serious trouble in my life.

Representative Boggs. Ever been arrested?

Mr. Oswald. No, sir. The only time I was on the inside of a jail was one time in Hazel, Tex., when I refused to sign a traffic ticket on the spot and I requested to be taken to the courthouse.

Representative Boggs. Did you ever have any psychiatric mental troubles?

Mr. Oswald. No, sir.

Representative Boggs. Did you consider your brother a normal human being?

Mr. Oswald. Yes, sir; I most certainly did.

Representative Boggs. In every way?

Mr. Oswald. In every way.

Representative Boggs. Did he ever give you any indications of being—did he ever discuss with you such things as shooting at General Walker?

Mr. Oswald. No, sir.

Mr. McKenzie. In order to clear something up, Mr. Boggs, let me ask one question, if I may, for the record.

Mr. Dulles. Please. Do you want this on the record or off?

312 Mr. McKenzie. Robert, from the time that your brother, Lee Harvey Oswald came back from Russia, when was this?

Mr. Oswald. This was in June 1962.

Mr. McKenzie. And then when was the next time that you saw him after he came to your home in Fort Worth, Tex., in June of 1962?

Mr. Dulles. Just after he returned from Russia?

Mr. McKenzie. Yes.

Mr. Oswald. I saw him on a number of occasions there in Fort Worth, Tex., after he moved out of my residence to mother's, from mother's apartment to his apartment with Marina, and the children, and when they moved to Dallas, Tex., that was the last time I saw him.

Mr. McKenzie. When did he move to Dallas, Tex.

Mr. Oswald. This was approximately October 1962.

Mr. McKenzie. All right, from the time of October 1962, when was—from then when was the next time you saw him?

Mr. Oswald. On November 23, 1963.

Mr. McKenzie. Where was that?

Mr. Oswald. At the Dallas County Jail or Dallas City Jail.

Mr. McKenzie. It was the Dallas City Jail.

Mr. Oswald. Dallas City Jail.

Mr. McKenzie. What were those circumstances? Were you in a room with him or were you talking to him through a partition or over a telephone or what, explain that to the Commission, if you will?

Mr. Oswald. I was talking to him over a telephone through a glass window, and he was on the locked side.

Mr. McKenzie. So for a period of over a year from the time he left Fort Worth and moved to Dallas, Tex., you did not see him, is that correct?

Mr. Oswald. That is correct, sir.

Mr. McKenzie. All right

Representative Boggs. When you last saw him was October 1962, is that what you said?

Mr. Oswald. Yes, sir.

Mr. McKenzie. And you had previously seen him when he resided in your home for how long a period of time?

Mr. Oswald. Approximately 6 to 8 weeks.

Mr. Dulles. I imagine this would be covered later but it fits in. I think you are quite right. I have a question or two.

Representative Boggs. I have to go back to the House in a few minutes.

Mr. Dulles. Go right ahead. Ask him any questions you wish to.

Representative Boggs. At the time he resided in your home these 6 or 8 weeks were your relations with him cordial or friendly?

Mr. Oswald. It was cordial, yes, more or less like he had not been to Russia. We were just together again.

Representative Boggs. Did you have any political discussions with him at any time?

Mr. Oswald. No, sir; I did not.

Representative Boggs. He never discussed political matters with you?

Mr. Oswald. No, sir; he did not. I would say we had a tacit agreement it was never brought up.

Representative Boggs. By tacit, do you mean that——

Mr. Oswald. An unspoken agreement that we never would discuss it.

Representative Boggs. I understand. Had you arrived at this agreement because on previous occasions you had disagreed about political matters?

Mr. Oswald. No, sir; that was not the reason. We just never discussed politics.

Representative Boggs. Did you have any interest in political affairs, I mean——

Mr. Oswald. A little bit, sir.

Representative Boggs. I mean from a philosophical point of view?

Mr. Oswald. My own interest in politics from a philosophical point of view would be that I considered myself a conservative, a born conservative. Certainly agreed 100 percent with the U.S. Constitution and the laws that are set313 forth, and it is my upbringing, it is what I always believed in and I will always believe in it.

Representative Ford. Did you say that was your mother's philosophy, too?

Mr. McKenzie. No, sir; he did not say.

Mr. Oswald. Would I say that?

Representative Ford. Yes.

Mr. Oswald. I would say—I will tell you, at this present time I feel like perhaps she has been hurt a great deal and perhaps her thinking is being changed at this very moment and at the present time since November 22d.

333

But prior to that time my opinion would be that she would be of the same opinion that I was.

Representative Ford. That is why you said your attitude was based on your upbringing.

Mr. Oswald. Yes, sir. Of course, to qualify that my mother didn't actually bring me up too much. The orphan home and the military academy, and I believe there my basic philosophy was formulated. It was a very good school.

Representative Boggs. What military academy was that?

Mr. Oswald. Chamberlain Hunt Military Academy at Port Gibson, Miss.

Representative Ford. During the 6 or 8 weeks that Lee resided in your home, did he ever indicate why he went to Russia? You must have talked about it some.

Mr. Oswald. There again I believe we did more talking through the mails about why he went to Russia than we did when he returned from Russia. I, of course, wanted to talk to him about this.

Mr. Dulles. You have those letters, I believe.

Mr. Oswald. Yes, sir; we have those letters.

Mr. McKenzie. Those letters have already been given to the Commission.

Mr. Jenner. We will present them in evidence, I think probably this afternoon.

Representative Boggs. Did he ever tell you?

Mr. Oswald. No, sir; not point blank did he ever tell me why he went to Russia.

Representative Boggs. Did he tell you why he came back?

Mr. Oswald. Yes, sir; that he was in—the letters that I have from him while he was in Russia would indicate the same thing, that he was very unhappy living in Russia and he wanted to return to the United States, which, of course, made me very happy, and I felt like, and tried to look at it from the standpoint that maybe he just sowed some wild oats. He kind of went off to the far end of it, but I believe everyone of us at one time, especially around that age, might have done something or reached out far afield, so to speak, before we came to our senses and returned to a normal life.

Mr. Dulles. Did he seem different when he came back from Russia, was there a change in the man before and after?

Mr. Oswald. Physically?

Mr. Dulles. No, I mean at all—changes, outlook, attitude and general——

Mr. Oswald. The mental attitude he had from his letters that he wrote me when he first arrived in Russia were quite disturbing to me. Statements, various statements, I can't quote them word for word, but in the line of—well, he wanted to denounce his citizenship. He was a Marxist and he was a Communist and he wanted to stay in Russia, and so forth.

But when he started writing again in 1961—yes, 1961, his letters certainly indicated that he had changed his mind, and that he wanted to return to the United States and start his life as a U.S. citizen.

Representative Boggs. You got to know Mrs. Oswald when she returned with him?

Mr. Oswald. Yes, sir.

Representative Boggs. Was the relationship between your family and your wife and Mrs. Oswald, of course, I realize you had a language barrier, but was it pleasant?

Mr. Oswald. Yes, sir. I would describe it as very pleasant. We immediately, my wife and I both, took to Marina and June, the baby, at that time, and my wife and I both were just tickled to death, so to speak, for an opportunity to be314 with somebody like Marina and to show her things that she had never seen before in her life.

Representative Boggs. In the time, of course, you had known her ever since she came here, and you have seen her since the assassination of President Kennedy, have you had any feeling that she was anything other than a normal housewife? You know there has been speculation that in light of the fact she was born in Russia and that she got an exit visa without too much difficulty that maybe she had connections that were not entirely just that of a normal housewife. Did you ever have any feeling——

Mr. Oswald. The only time I had any reservations about Marina Oswald was on Friday, November 22, until approximately 2 days later. I say during this 2-day period I was not sure whether or not she had been involved in any of the happenings of that date. I wanted not to believe that she did, but I wanted to be cautious about it. I believe on Sunday night, November 24, in my presence she gave a complete—and freely stated everything up to that time that she was aware of to the U.S. Secret Service on a tape recorder. And I formulated my opinion then that apparently, and I feel this way now, that she did not have anything to do with that, and she is nothing other than just what she appears to be, just a housewife, having a very difficult time at this time.

Representative Boggs. Have you in your own mind reached any conclusions on whether or not your brother killed President Kennedy?

Mr. Oswald. Based on the circumstantial evidence that has been reported in newspapers and over the radio and television, I would have to say that it appears that he did kill President Kennedy.

Representative Boggs. Would you, having reached that conclusion under the circumstances that you outlined a moment ago, and having known him all of his life, although not too intimately the last year of his life, would you give us any reason for why he may have done this?

Mr. Oswald. No, sir; I could not.

Representative Boggs. It came as, I would think, a great shock to you?

Mr. Oswald. Yes, sir; it certainly did, and I might add that the Lee Harvey Oswald that I knew would not have killed anybody.

Representative Boggs. Have you discussed this matter with your stepbrother since it happened?

Mr. Oswald. Yes, sir.

Representative Boggs. This, as I understand, Mr. Counsel, is hearsay but we are just trying to establish——

Mr. McKenzie. Mr. Boggs, in order that the record be absolutely clear, you were not here when we commenced this morning due to your duties at the House, let me state this for the purpose of the record and yourself and the entire Commission, you ask Robert Oswald any question that you want to ask him.

Representative Boggs. Thank you very much.

Mr. McKenzie. And furthermore, any information we have or any information we can get from any source will likewise be turned over to the Federal Bureau of Investigation or to this Commission or to any other investigative agency, because——

Representative Boggs. The mandate that we are operating under is that we discover the truth.

Mr. McKenzie. I can assure you, sir, that the main reason that we are here, and I speak for Robert Oswald, is to see that the truth is given fully, and developed as fully as possible, to give any light to this tragic event.

Representative Boggs. I just have one or two other questions.

Mr. Oswald. I believe your last question was whether or not——

Representative Boggs. I am frankly reluctant to ask you the question, but you and your brother John must have speculated about how this event could have happened, did you not?

Mr. Oswald. Yes, and no, sir. To this extent: On Sunday night November 24, with the help of the Secret Service, I was able to reach my older brother John by telephone. He did not have a telephone in his house. We had to go through the Air Force base where he was located.

Mr. Dulles. Where was he living then?

Mr. Oswald. In San Antonio with the Air Force.

315 I talked to him that night and, of course, at that time he was aware that Lee had been killed. I talked briefly to him, I say briefly, perhaps 4 or 5 minutes, and discussed with him whether or not he thought it was best that he attended the funeral or not, and it

was my opinion that it would not be best for him or his family since he was, his name was Pic, and to a great extent he would be out of the picture and there was no sense in exposing him to the publicity of the funeral. Not to mention the travel time involved in coming up from San Antonio and the like.

Mr. Dulles. You were not in touch with him between the time of the assassination and the arrest of your brother and the time of his death, the 36 hours?

Mr. Oswald. No, sir.

Mr. Dulles. You were not in touch with your brother Pic at that time?

Mr. Oswald. No, sir; I was not.

Mr. McKenzie. But you attempted to reach him?

Mr. Oswald. No.

Mr. McKenzie. You did afterwards.

Representative Boggs. Have you seen much of your mother since the assassination?

Mr. Oswald. No, sir; I have not.

Representative Boggs. Is this because you had some emotional problems or difficulties, or what?

Mr. Oswald. Sir, I would say, of course, mother was out at the Inn of Six Flags with Marina and myself and the children during the week following up to Friday which would be, I believe, the 29th of November, when she went to her home and I left her to go after my wife and the children out at the farm, and Marina went over to Mr. Martin's house, this was the last time I have seen her since then. She has called quite a few times. I talked to her a number of times on the telephone. She is rather persistent to the extent that, and this is not new to me, we have never really gotten along, she tries to dominate me and my wife, and I might say that applies to John and his family, and also to the extent that it applied to Lee and his wife, and there is just generally the picture as far as I and my mother are concerned.

Representative Boggs. That is all, Mr. Chairman.

Mr. Dulles. The testimony we had here from Mrs. Oswald indicated that it was approximately a year prior to the assassination of the President that he had not been in touch with his mother, and your testimony is to the general effect that about the same period, you had not been in touch.

Is that just a coincidence, or did something happen about that time so that both of you, both brothers more or less separated from the mother?

Mr. Oswald. No, sir——

Mr. Dulles. Maybe it is geographic, maybe there is some other reason for it.

Representative Boggs. I had understood him to say he had not been in contact with his brother Lee, I didn't hear him say anything about his mother.

Mr. McKenzie. That is correct. For the year prior to November 22d had you been in touch with your mother or had your mother been in touch with you, Robert?

Mr. Oswald. No, sir; we had not been in touch.

Representative Boggs. Your mother in her testimony before the Commission, gave the impression and later in press stories that she thought that maybe your brother was an agent of the CIA. Did you ever have any reason to think that?

Mr. Oswald. No, sir; and the only time the thought ever entered my mind as to him being an agent of the CIA or any other U.S. Government bureau was on his return from Russia while residing at my residence in Fort Worth, the FBI had called and requested that he come down for an interview there in Fort Worth. On the completion of his interview when I came home from work that night, he discussed it briefly and I asked him how did they treat him, and so forth. He said just fine, and he says, "They asked me was I a secret agent," or some type of agent for the U.S. Government and he laughed and he said, "Well, don't you know?" I remember that. That was just crossed out of my mind.

Representative Ford. Between November 22 and the last time you saw your mother did she ever mention to you that she thought Lee was an agent of the Federal Government?

316 Mr. Oswald. This was prior to November 22?

Representative Ford. No, from November 22 until the last time you saw your mother, did she ever mention to you that she thought Lee was an agent of the Federal Government?

Mr. Oswald. Yes, sir; she did.

Representative Ford. Can you tell us when?

Mr. Oswald. During the middle to the latter part of the week that we were at the Inn of the Six Flags, and at least one conversation since we left the Inn of the Six Flags, I think it took place during December 1963.

Mr. Jenner. By telephone or personal?

Mr. Oswald. By telephone, sir.

Mr. Jenner. Would you be good enough to relate—for Representative Ford—who was present, what the circumstances were, what was said, and in the presence of whom by your mother at the Six Flags?

Mr. Oswald. I believe it was just mother and I, and I might say on numerous occasions she pulled me to one side or to one room to say something to me. It was on one of these occasions that she was talking to me about this.

Mr. Jenner. Relate as closely as you can recall it now what did she say?

Mr. Oswald. She said she had knowledge of facts in writing that almost conclusively proved to her that Lee was an agent of the CIA.

Mr. Jenner. Did she identify the facts in writing?

Mr. Oswald. No, sir; she did not.

Mr. Jenner. Did you inquire of her on that subject?

Mr. Oswald. No, sir; I did not.

Mr. Jenner. Did you ask her to state to you the basis, any specific basis of hers on which she predicated her statement?

Mr. Oswald. No, sir; I did ask her if she had such facts to please give it to the U.S. Secret Service.

Representative Ford. What did she say to that?

Mr. Oswald. I think she more or less shrugged her shoulders and walked off.

Mr. Dulles. Had she been in touch with the man who has appeared as her counsel at that time, Mr. Lane?

Mr. Oswald. No, sir; she had not.

Mr. Dulles. She had not.

Representative Boggs. You at various times have tried to help your mother, I gather, while you were growing up.

Mr. Oswald. Yes, sir.

Representative Boggs. I gather you found it rather difficult even when you were younger to get along with your mother?

Mr. Oswald. Yes, sir; that is correct.

Mr. Jenner. Excuse me, sir, is that also true of your brother, Lee, and your brother, John?

Representative Boggs. Those were the questions I was about to ask.

Mr. Oswald. I would say this would also apply to my older brother John, and also to Lee. It appears as though Lee was able to put up with her more than I or my older brother John could.

Representative Boggs. Your father died when you were what, about 5?

Mr. Oswald. Five years old, sir.

Representative Boggs. You were living in New Orleans when he died?

Mr. Oswald. That is correct, sir.

Representative Boggs. What did he do?

Mr. Oswald. He worked for the Metropolitan Life Insurance Company of New Orleans, in the office in New Orleans.

Representative Ford. Were your mother and father living a happy normal life at the time of his death?

Mr. Oswald. Well, sir, I was 5 years old and I would say that they were. Certainly I do not recall any instance that would indicate that they were not, and I think we had a very fine family atmosphere.

Mr. Jenner. Would you state for us, please, on the same subject, the life and relationship between your mother and Mr. Ekdahl, give us the same thing with respect to that period, did they get along well normally?

Mr. Oswald. Well, I was, of course, older and perhaps remember more, to317 this extent that on perhaps two or three occasions, I recall some very loud arguments where they were in one room with the door closed, and perhaps I by myself or perhaps in the presence of John was in another room. Nothing that I can recall that was said during this arguing other than it was just loud.

Mr. Jenner. During this period, Representative Boggs, the two boys John and Robert were at the military school. They were home during the summer vacation period but otherwise they were in military school.

Mr. Dulles. I think maybe we ought to give the witness a little rest. He has been on for 2 hours.

Hale, have you got anything more you want to ask now?

Representative Boggs. No, I would just like to thank the witness for his cooperation.

Mr. Oswald. Thank you, sir.

Mr. Dulles. Do you have anything? Do you have to go back?

Representative Ford. I am going to stay until we get some notice from the House if we have any call or a vote.

Mr. Dulles. Shall we take just 5 minutes off then and it might be agreeable.

(Short recess.)

Mr. Dulles. Proceed, Mr. Jenner.

Representative Ford. It would be helpful because we are likely to get a call almost any time to go back to the House, if I could ask a few questions.

Mr. Jenner. Go right ahead.

Mr. Dulles. Okay.

Representative Ford. Mr. Oswald, what was your reaction to Lee's discharge from the Marine Corps?

Mr. Oswald. He had an honorable discharge he told me. I had no adverse reaction to it.

Mr. Jenner. Did you have in mind, Representative Ford, the change in the status of that discharge?

Representative Ford. No, I was referring to the circumstances under which he was discharged prematurely. He did get an honorable discharge at the outset but he was released prematurely on a hardship basis.

Mr. Oswald. Yes.

Representative Ford. Were you familiar with that?

Mr. Oswald. I was not familiar with that at the time it was going on. Of course, I was familiar after he was released on that basis. I remember Lee telling me, he said, "Well, I only lack a month," or a few days anyway before his regular release was up and I believe that was all that was said between Lee and I about it.

Representative Ford. When did you learn about the change in his discharge?

Mr. Oswald. Sometime during the year of 1960, through my mother. She had advised me at that time she had received mail for Lee from the Marine Corps or from the Navy Department, stating that generally the reasons he had not notified them of changes of address, and perhaps even to the extent that he had left the country in the manner that he did, that it was going to go before a review board, and that he was to appear before this board to state his case, otherwise it would proceed without him. Then I became aware that the board's decision was an undesirable or a dishonorable discharge, I don't recollect which.

Representative Ford. Did you take any action when you learned of these circumstances to help your mother or to contact Lee about this situation?

Mr. Oswald. No, sir; because at this time in reference to Lee there he had already stopped writing to both I and mother and there was no way that we knew of to contact Lee, and mother said she was going to take care of it and try to have it postponed or something or other, and the board reached a final decision.

Representative Ford. When your mother went to Washington, did she tell you in advance or give you any indication she was going to do that?

Mr. Oswald. No, sir; she did not. I was aware of it after she came back from Washington.

Representative Ford. Did she fill you in in some detail about her return from Washington?

318 Mr. Oswald. No, sir; she did not. She did not go into any particular detail other than she tried to impress on me she had seen some, as she put it, some very important and influential people in Washington. And that was about the text of the conversation in reference to that.

Representative Ford. Did she volunteer this or did you ask her about it?

Mr. Oswald. She volunteered this because I did not know of the trip to Washington until after she returned from the trip to Washington. She volunteered information to me that she had been in Washington and saw numbers of people, different people.

Representative Ford. The principal information you have about Lee's return from the Soviet Union is included in the letters that you have from Lee?

Mr. Oswald. Yes, sir; that is correct.

Representative Ford. Those will be submitted subsequently.

Mr. McKenzie. They have been submitted already, Mr. Ford.

Mr. Jenner. Excuse me, did you address me?

Mr. McKenzie. The Commission has copies of the letters.

Representative Ford. The Commission has copies and they will be submitted for the record.

Would you care to comment in addition on what you found out from Lee subsequently of his experiences in the Soviet Union. Why he wanted to come back?

Mr. Oswald. No, sir; I never questioned him about that because we covered it, I believe quite fully in our letters. I was, of course, thoroughly convinced and quite happy that he did want to return to the United States and I felt there was no need to go into the reason why he changed his mind because I believe we had covered that in the letters.

Representative Ford. At the time he indicated a desire to come back to the United States, did he ever contact you about funds for that purpose?

Mr. Oswald. No, sir; I volunteered to help him any way I could on that. He turned down the offer. He turned it down one time I believe in letters offering him to come stay at our house when he returned with his wife and the baby.

Representative Ford. When he did return, after having borrowed money from the Federal Government, did he ever ask you for any help and assistance in repaying the loan?

Mr. Oswald. On his arrival in New York City, I believe the date to be June 13, back in 1962, my wife received a telephone call from Special Services Welfare Center located at New York City stating that Lee and his family were present and that they needed funds to reach their destination, Fort Worth, Tex., and the lady that talked to my wife put it to the extent they were unable to help them and if some member of the family was going to help them, they had better do so then. My wife didn't know anything else to say but of course that we would, and this is what I wanted her to say.

She called me at my office that day. The banks had closed but I do have a friend in Fort Worth who was employed at a bank, cashier, I believe his title, and I called him and asked him if it would be possible to withdraw $200. This was not at my bank, I would give him a check on my checking account, and at which time I wired the money to the welfare bureau in New York, care of Lee Harvey Oswald.

Representative Ford. And that was the money that they, Marina and Lee, used to get to Fort Worth.

Mr. Oswald. That is correct, sir.

Representative Ford. Did Lee ever repay you for that?

Mr. Oswald. Yes, sir; he did. He had actually spent a little over $100 for the plane tickets and, of course, we met him at Dallas, Love Field, on their arrival there. The next day even though I insisted that he keep it, he returned what he had left from the $200 and he said he would pay me back as soon as he was able to and I told him not to worry about that, but just to take his time.

Representative Ford. How long did it take him to repay the remainder?

Mr. Oswald. I say approximately $110 to $115 during the period he first started to work there in Fort Worth and prior to their departure to Dallas he repaid this $10-$20 a week from his pay check.

319 Representative Ford. Did you have any knowledge that Lee had become fluent in Russian, in the Russian language, at the time he came out of the Marine Corps?

Mr. Oswald. No, sir; I had not. There is also one of his first letters from the hotel in Russia that he pointed out to me that I didn't even know that he could write or speak Russian. He was being rather sarcastic in his first letters, and he pointed this out. I would answer it that I was not aware that he could speak or could write any foreign language when he was in the Marine Corps and after he got out of it.

Representative Ford. You had no prior knowledge that he was studying Russian or had become articulate in Russian?

Mr. Oswald. No, sir; I did not.

Representative Ford. In your experiences with Lee during your lifetime, did he ever show a skill at language, for languages?

Mr. Oswald. No, sir; I know of no time nor can I recall of any time that he studied any foreign language or in my presence that he even read a book in a foreign language or attempted to teach himself any type of foreign language.

Mr. Jenner. Representative Ford, if you have reached a break, I would like to identify the exhibit the witness provided and also identify the letter to which you now have reference.

Would you obtain that telegram and also identify the date of the letter to which you have lastly made reference so that I may identify our copies?

Mr. McKenzie. November 8, 1959, is the letter, Mr. Jenner, and the telegram is June 14, 1962.

Mr. Jenner. Mr. Chairman, we have marked photostatic copies of the telegram to which the witness referred as having been received from the Special Welfare Services as Commission Exhibit No. 293, and the letter of November 18, 1959, as Commission Exhibit 294.

(The telegram and letter referred to were marked Commission Exhibit Nos. 293 and 294, respectively, for identification.)

Mr. Jenner. Would you obtain the original of those or hand the witness the originals?

Mr. McKenzie. I have just handed them to him.

Mr. Jenner. Would you hand him the original of the letter, please?

Directing your attention to the telegram first, Mr. Oswald, which is now marked Commission Exhibit 293, is that the original of the telegram to which you made reference as having been received first by telephone call through your wife on June 14, 19——

Mr. Oswald. Pardon me, June 13.

Mr. Jenner. 13?
Mr. Oswald. Yes, sir. This reply that we are referring to here now is June 14.
Mr. Jenner. I see.
Mr. Oswald. We were first contacted on the evening of June 13.
Mr. Jenner. I take it then, sir, that you received a telephone call on June 13, is that correct?
Mr. Oswald. That is correct.
Mr. Jenner. Or your wife did. And Exhibit 293 which is dated the 14th, is what?
Mr. Oswald. I am sorry, sir.
Mr. Jenner. Following the receipt of the telephone call on June 13, did you receive or did you send any communication from or to the New York Welfare Center?
Mr. Oswald. Yes, sir. I sent a telegram on the afternoon of June 13, 1962, wiring a total of $200 to the Special Service Welfare Center at New York, and also enclosing a message to Lee to contact me or to the extent that someone there perhaps would notify me when to expect them in Fort Worth.
Mr. Jenner. Did you receive word from New York as to when Lee and Marina might expect to be in Dallas?
Mr. Oswald. Yes, sir; I did.
Mr. Jenner. And was that by telegram or telephone?
Mr. Oswald. This was by telephone I first received the word.
320 Mr. Jenner. Did you receive something in writing that confirmed that?
Mr. Oswald. Yes, sir; I did.
Mr. Jenner. Is that document before you?
Mr. Oswald. Yes, sir; it is.
Mr. Jenner. It is marked Commission Exhibit 293, and you actually received that document which is now before you?
Mr. Oswald. Yes, sir; that is correct.
Mr. Jenner. June 14.
Mr. Chairman, I offer in evidence as Commission Exhibit 293, the document so marked and identified.
Mr. Dulles. It may be accepted.
(The document heretofore marked Commission Exhibit No. 293 was received in evidence.)
Mr. Jenner. The letter of November 8, 19—do you have a better copy, is that 1959?
Mr. Oswald. It is 1959.
Mr. Dulles. May I just ask a question, are we putting in the original of that or is a photographic copy being substituted for it?
Mr. Jenner. We are employing as a substitute for the original a photostatic copy which has been marked Commission Exhibit 293.
Mr. Dulles. All right.
Mr. McKenzie. Mr. Chairman, could I be excused for just a moment, please?
(Short recess.)
Mr. Jenner. In view of the witness' testimony, may I suggest to the Commission the feasibility of identifying this particular exhibit since the witness referred to it in response to the questions put by Representative Ford.
Mr. Dulles. All right.
Mr. Jenner. Would you identify the date of Commission Exhibit 294, the original?
Mr. Oswald. The date of the letter is November 8, 1959.
Mr. Jenner. Whose handwriting is it?
Mr. Oswald. It is in Lee Harvey Oswald's handwriting.
Mr. Jenner. It is addressed, the second page of the exhibit, is an envelope, which is addressed to R. Oswald, 7313 Davenport Street, Fort Worth, Tex., U.S.A., is that you?
Mr. Oswald. Yes, sir; that is correct.

Mr. Jenner. Are you able to identify that which appears in the upper lefthand corner of the original.

Mr. Oswald. No, sir; I am not.

Mr. Jenner. Is that in Russian?

Mr. Oswald. I would assume that it would be.

Mr. Jenner. Did you receive the letter, Commission Exhibit 294, in due course?

Mr. Oswald. I did. I received it on the 13th day of November 1959.

Mr. Jenner. Is this the letter to which you made reference in responding to Representative Ford's questions?

Mr. Oswald. Yes, sir; that is correct.

Mr. Jenner. Is the letter in the same condition now and is the envelope now in the same condition now that it was when you received it except that the envelope has been opened to remove the contents?

Mr. Oswald. Yes, sir; they are.

Mr. Jenner. Does that include the scratching out that appears at the bottom of the second page?

Mr. Oswald. Yes, sir; it does.

Mr. Jenner. Is that which appears under the attempted obliteration, can you see what was obliterated on the second page, when you examine the original?

Mr. Oswald. I might refer to the first cross out there, it looks like he had signed his name there "Lee." The second cross out, one word or three words or four words out of the five are legible "this written in Russian" the balance of the words that were crossed out, I cannot make out.

Mr. Jenner. Mr. Chairman, I would suggest, if I may, that the witness might read this short letter aloud to the Commission which will, indicate to the Commission321 the mental state of Lee Harvey Oswald at the time he went to Russia in the very early days, and bring it to your attention immediately.

Mr. Dulles. What is the date of this?

Mr. McKenzie. November 8, 1959, sir.

Mr. Dulles. Proceed, if you will.

Mr. McKenzie. Do you mind if I read it, Mr. Jenner, and saving his voice a little bit?

Mr. Jenner. No.

Mr. McKenzie. This I believe is the second letter that Robert received from Russia after he had sent a telegram to Lee telling him what a mistake he had made, and this is the contents of the letter.

"November 8, 1959. Dear Robert:

"Well, what shall we talk about? The weather perhaps? Certainly you do not wish me to speak of my decision to remain in the Soviet Union and apply for citizenship here since I am afraid you would not be able to comprehend my reasons.

"You really don't know anything about me. Do you know, for instance, that I have waited to do this for well over a year? Do you know that I" then there is a parenthesis and some Russian printing which I presume to be Russian and the parenthesis is closed, "speak a fair amount of Russian which I have been studying for many months? I have been told that I will not have to leave the Soviet Union if I did not care to. This then is my decision. I will not leave this country, the Soviet Union under any conditions. I will never return to the United States which is a country I hate. Some day perhaps soon and then again perhaps in a few years I will become a citizen of the Soviet Union, but it is a very legal process in any event. I will not have to leave the Soviet Union and I will never leave.

"I received your telegram and I was glad to hear from you. Only one word bothered me. The word 'mistake' I assume you mean that I have made a 'mistake.' It is not for you to tell me this. You cannot understand my reasons for this very serious action. I will not speak to anyone from the United States over the telephone since it might be tapped by the Americans. If you wish to correspond with me you can write to the below address, but I really don't see what we could talk about. If you want to send me some money that I can use but I do not expect to be able to pay it back."

Then it is signed "Lee", and then over to the left-hand side on the bottom of the page it says, "Lee Harvey Oswald, Metropole Hotel, Room 233, Moscow, USSR," and then underneath some writing in Russian, which I take to be Russian, which is scratched out.

Mr. Jenner. Thank you.

Mr. McKenzie, you have stated that this was the second letter that had been received by Mr. Robert Oswald following Lee Harvey Oswald's taking up residence in Russia. Is that correct, Mr. Oswald?

Mr. McKenzie. I said it is the second or third letter. I don't know exactly.

Mr. Oswald. I believe, sir, it is the first letter, if I may have a moment here.

Mr. Jenner. I thought it was the first.

Mr. McKenzie. There is one other letter here from Santa Ana, Calif.

Mr. Jenner. That was earlier.

Mr. Oswald. This was the first letter Lee had written to me from Russia.

Mr. Dulles. Could you refresh my memory as to the date of his arrival in Russia?

Mr. Oswald. October 13.

Mr. Dulles. October 13.

Mr. Oswald. 1959.

Mr. Dulles. And this was——

Mr. Jenner. November 8.

Mr. Dulles. November 8. He had been there about 3 weeks.

Mr. Oswald. The first time I was aware he was in Russia was on Halloween Day 1959, October 31.

Mr. Dulles. Thank you.

Mr. Jenner. My attention is arrested to that portion of the letter in which322 there appears to be a reference to a telegram which you had previously sent him.

Mr. Oswald. Yes, sir.

Mr. Jenner. Had you sent him such a telegram?

Mr. Oswald. Yes, sir; I had.

Mr. Jenner. What impelled you or induced you to do that? What event, stimulation?

Mr. Oswald. After we were notified that Lee was in Russia.

Mr. Jenner. Who notified you?

Mr. Oswald. Star Telegram reporter in Fort Worth, Tex. Later on that same day there was quite a few newspaper reporters out to my house. I first objected to speaking to them until they stated that perhaps if we cooperated with them they would perhaps be the only source of information—that they could relay to us when they received anything about what Lee was doing, and so forth, and I agreed to talk to them.

After this interview with three or four newspaper reporters they had left the house, and another man, I do not recall his name, from the Star Telegram in Fort Worth, came to the house, and I spoke with him, and I believe at this time he suggested that it would not be wise because I was asking what did he think as to how I might contact Lee, and he suggested a letter—pardon me, a telegram, to Secretary of State Christian Herter, and a telegram to Lee.

I called the Western Union and sent telegrams, and at this time——

Mr. Jenner. Excuse me, sir, telegrams, you sent one to Mr. Herter and one to your brother?

Mr. Oswald. Yes, sir; sent two. At this time I advised the reporter of the contents of the telegram. I did not receive confirmation of these telegrams from Western Union.

Mr. Jenner. I take it from that you do not have copies?

Mr. Oswald. No, sir.

However, they are printed in their entirety in the next edition of the Star Telegram, which I believe would be November 1st edition.

Mr. Jenner. November 1, 1959?

Mr. Oswald. Yes, sir.

Mr. Jenner. Would you please state to the best of your present recollection what your instruction by way of message was to the Western Union?

Mr. Oswald. In the telegram to Secretary of State Christian Herter, I requested his assistance in contacting Lee Oswald through any means available.

Mr. Jenner. Did you indicate for what purpose, sir?

Mr. Oswald. I don't believe I did, sir.

And the telegram to Lee Harvey Oswald, I asked him to contact me through any means available. I did use the word "mistake."

Mr. Jenner. Would you please give me your best recollection of the message, as you recall it, that you dispatched or ordered dispatched?

Mr. Oswald. My best recollection of that is I sent the telegram to Lee Harvey Oswald care of the U.S. Embassy in Moscow, Russia, requesting Lee to contact me through any means available, and the one word "mistake. Keep your nose clean," signed "Robert L. Oswald, 7313 Davenport."

Mr. Jenner. The word "mistake" was by itself?

Mr. Oswald. Yes, sir; that is correct. The phrase of "keep your nose clean," is something we have said to each other since knee high, so he would know that I did send the telegram.

Mr. Jenner. Did you receive a response to that telegram?

Mr. Oswald. No, sir; I did not receive a response to either one of the telegrams.

Mr. Jenner. Neither from the State Department, Mr. Herter, nor an assistant on that telegram, nor from your brother Lee on his telegram?

Mr. Oswald. That is correct, sir.

Mr. Jenner. Other than the letter of November 8, 1959, now identified as Commission Exhibit No. 294?

Mr. Oswald. That is correct, sir.

Mr. Jenner. It is the first word you had from him in which he acknowledges or made plain that he had received the telegram?

Mr. Oswald. Yes, sir; that is correct.

323 Mr. Dulles. Excuse me, has 294 been submitted?

Mr. Jenner. I think it has not. May I offer in evidence as Commission Exhibit 294 the document that has been so identified.

Mr. Dulles. Accepted.

(The document heretofore marked Commission Exhibit No. 294 was received in evidence.)

Mr. Jenner. It being understood with Mr. McKenzie that we may introduce in evidence the photostatic copy in lieu of the original, the original having been produced before the Commission.

Mr. McKenzie. Yes, sir.

Mr. Jenner. Did you speak, did you have any conversation with your brother upon his return from Russia respecting your dispatch of the telegram and his reaction to it?

Mr. Oswald. No, sir; I did not. I had more or less forgotten it myself.

Mr. Jenner. There is a reference in your brother's letter of November 8 to his reluctance to engage in a telephone conversation. Had you attempted to reach him by telephone?

Mr. Oswald. I had decided to try to reach him by telephone on Sunday, November 1, 1959. I did not.

Mr. Jenner. You were unable to, you mean?

Mr. Oswald. No, sir; I did not. I placed the call and I received the New York operator, overseas operator, and there was some discussion as to what time it was in Moscow, and so forth, and I changed my mind and did not. However, I am aware that my mother tried and did for a moment have Lee on the telephone in Moscow.

Mr. Jenner. At that time?

Mr. Oswald. At approximately that same date.

Mr. Jenner. Did you ever make any effort to reach him by telephone thereafter?

Mr. Oswald. No, sir; I did not.

Mr. Jenner. Did he reach you by telephone or attempt to do so as far as you know?

Mr. Oswald. No, sir; not to my knowledge did he.

Mr. Jenner. There is a reference in the letter of November 8 to his willingness to accept money from you if you would send any. Did you send him any money?

Mr. Oswald. No, sir; I did not. My reply to that was if he used it to come back I would gladly send it.

Mr. Jenner. Your reply—did you write him a letter?

Mr. Oswald. Yes, sir.

Mr. Jenner. Do you have a copy of that letter?

Mr. Oswald. No, sir; I do not have a copy of any letter that I wrote to him.

Mr. Jenner. You do not know the whereabouts of that letter?

Mr. Oswald. No, sir; I do not, other than to say that I asked Mrs. Marina Oswald if Lee kept any of my letters and her reply was that "No, he always threw them away."

Mr. Jenner. In view of that, Mr. Oswald, would you please recite to the best of your recollection the contents of your letter in response to your brother's letter of November 8, 1959?

Mr. Oswald. Sir, I do not remember anything other than that statement referring to the money request. I do not recall anything else in the letter.

Mr. Jenner. You have heard Mr. McKenzie read that letter through. Did it refresh your recollection, or does it as to whether you made any comment upon his political statements in his letter to you of November 8?

Mr. Oswald. I do not believe I did at any time make any statement in reference to his political statements that he made in the letter of November 8. Generally, my statements to the members of the press at the time was that I felt Lee was not aware of what he was doing. I believe I referred to him as a kid. And that he just generally didn't know what he was doing, and that was just about the general text of anything I had to say to the members of the press at that time.

Mr. Jenner. There is an entry in your brother's diary of November 1,324 1959, somewhat cryptic, referring to three telephone calls from mother and brother. Now you say you didn't call. Do you know whether your brother John ever called him?

Mr. Oswald. No, sir, not to my knowledge. However, that was November 1, sir, 1959.

Mr. Jenner. That is when the entry was made.

Mr. Oswald. I would say that he did not at that time try to contact Lee by telephone, because I do not believe at that early date—he was in Japan and was not aware that Lee had gone to Russia, because we were just aware of it on October 31, and recalling a letter from John over there, that he was not aware of it for a number of days after he actually went over there.

Mr. Jenner. I see. But efforts were made on the part of your mother to reach him or she did reach him by telephone?

Mr. Oswald. Yes, sir, I understand he spoke to her briefly, and then he hung up.

Mr. Jenner. For the purpose of refreshing your recollection, would you be good enough to read your brother's letter to you or what purports to be your brother's letter to you of November 26, 1959, and in reading through it—the reason I have asked you to look at it is that the letter is framed as a response to what apparently were questions that you put to him in your letter which was in response to his letter of November 8, and seeking to refresh your recollection as to the contents of your letter.

Mr. Chairman, this is a fairly long letter, and if Chief Justice Warren has a little time perhaps we might have Mr. Oswald read the letter over this evening since we are quite late in the day and I can pursue it tomorrow.

Mr. Dulles. I think we had better adjourn fairly soon.

Mr. Jenner. This would be a convenient time if it is convenient with you gentlemen.
The Chairman. What does Mr. McKenzie think, I see him smiling.
Mr. McKenzie. I am not going to place myself in a position, Mr. Chief Justice, of overruling either you or Mr. Dulles.
Mr. Jenner. I can question the witness with respect to some unrelated matters. That matter is not related to this, if I might.
Mr. McKenzie. Mr. Jenner, one thing I would appreciate if you could bring out in response to some of Mr. Bogg's questions which I don't believe he was quite clear on, I would like for the sake of the record to show what Robert's career in the Marine Corps was from the standpoint of whether he was a noncommissioned officer, and so forth, and so on, if you could bring that out.
Mr. Jenner. All right.
I had asked him to state his military career and maybe out of modesty he just left left that out.
Would you—you did give us in detail in your various stages and your specialty.
Mr. Oswald. I might say going through boot camp at San Diego, Calif., during the second week of boot training I was selected as the right guide of the platoon which actually was a go-between the drill instructors and the rest of the platoon, and I retained that position all the way through the remainder of the boot camp. On completion of boot camp I was a Pfc. I retained that—excuse me, I retained that rank until I went to Miami, Fla., at which time on my departure from Miami, Fla., I received my corporal's stripe, and prior to leaving Korea in April of 1955 I received my sergeant's stripe which was my last stripe that I received in the Marine Corps.
I did receive, of course, an honorable discharge, a Good Conduct Medal, and the various citations of the unit in Korea, Presidential Unit Citations, and such.
Mr. Jenner. All right. Thank you.
I can't recall whether it was Representative Boggs or Representative Ford who was questioning you about conversations between yourself and your mother regarding her claim that your brother may have been a representative of the CIA or some other government agency, and you mentioned325 there were two occasions. I did ask you to state the detail of one of the occasions which was in the Six Flags Motel in Dallas.
Would you please state where the second conversation took place and who was present and what was said?
Mr. Oswald. The second conversation took place over the telephone in a call that originated from my mother's house in Fort Worth, Tex., to my home in Denton, Tex.
I do not know if my wife was present at my end or who was present on the other end, at my mother's home.
Mr. Jenner. You recognized her voice?
Mr. Oswald. Yes, sir; I did.
Mr. Jenner. It was your mother?
Mr. Oswald. It was my mother.
Mr. Jenner. What did she say on the subject?
Mr. Oswald. She was still pursuing this question or this speculation as far as I am concerned that Lee was an agent of the CIA, and that she was going to be able to, I believe use used the word "concrete", to be able to concretely establish that with the officials.
Mr. Jenner. You fixed that as having occurred subsequent to the occasion in the Six Flags Motel?
Mr. Oswald. That is correct, sir.
Mr. Jenner. Can you fix the time of the second occasion more definitely than that it followed the other?
Mr. Oswald. I would say this was approximately during the week of December 9, 1963.

Mr. Jenner. Was it before or after her trip to Washington which you have testified about when Mr. Ford questioned you?

Mr. Oswald. This was before her trip to Washington.

Mr. Jenner. Now, when your mother returned from Washington, when she made her trip here about which you testified in response to questions from Representative Ford, did she say anything about her claim or speculation, as you put it, that your brother was or might have been an agent of the CIA or some other agency of the United States?

Mr. Oswald. I have not talked to my mother since she has been to Washington.

Mr. Jenner. I see. So there has been no claim by her to you since the occasion of the second conversation which was a telephone call?

Mr. Oswald. That is correct, sir.

Mr. Jenner. During the time of your youth and your association with your brother Lee you testified this morning of the normal interest of boys in firearms. You have also testified that your brother Lee was right handed. Did you ever see him handle even a toy pistol or a cap gun other than with his right hand?

Mr. Oswald. No, sir, not that I can remember. You, of course, recall sometimes when maybe he was Two-Gun Pete, so to speak.

Mr. Jenner. He was what?

Mr. Oswald. He was Two-Gun Pete, so to speak, when we were playing cops and robbers or cowboys and Indians, where he would have two guns.

Mr. Jenner. With the exception of having two guns when he had one he had it in his right hand?

Mr. Oswald. That is correct.

Mr. Jenner. What ever type of playing, shooting, sitting, or otherwise, he always had the pistol, rifle or cap gun in his right hand?

Mr. Oswald. That is correct, sir.

Mr. Jenner. You said you were using B-B guns. Were there occasions when Lee also occasionally shot a B-B gun rifle?

Mr. Oswald. Not to my knowledge, sir.

Mr. Jenner. I have a recollection that when he was mustered out of the service in September of 1959 he spent two or three days at home in Fort Worth.

Mr. Oswald. That is correct, sir.

Mr. Jenner. And there was an occasion when you and he and some friends of yours went on a hunting trip.

Mr. Oswald. My brother-in-law.

326 Mr. Jenner. Or you went squirrel shooting or rabbit shooting.

Mr. Oswald. That is correct.

Mr. Jenner. Just the two of you, or did anybody accompany you?

Mr. Oswald. Three of us.

Mr. Jenner. Did you have a rifle?

Mr. Oswald. Yes, sir; I did.

Mr. Jenner. Those I take it were .22's.

Mr. Oswald. All three were .22 caliber, that is correct.

Mr. Jenner. Where did you obtain them?

Mr. Oswald. Two of them belonged to me and one of them belonged to my brother-in-law.

Mr. Jenner. Your brother-in-law?

Mr. Oswald. My brother-in-law.

Mr. Jenner. What is his name?

Mr. Oswald. S. R. Mercer, Jr.

Mr. Jenner. What was the occasion of this trip? How did it come about? Did you suggest it, your brother-in-law, Lee or how?

Mr. Oswald. The day that I recall that Lee stayed with us in—between the time he was discharged and the time he was supposed to be leaving for New Orleans was a period of 2 to 3 days. One of those days, I feel sure was a Saturday, either we spent all day out at my in-laws' farm or the afternoon at the farm at which time Lee and I, and my brother-in-law went hunting.

Mr. Dulles. Was this a couple of days before he left for Russia?

Mr. Oswald. This was a couple of days before he left for New Orleans or about 1 day or 2 days before he left for New Orleans.

Mr. Dulles. And then he shipped out?

Mr. Oswald. To locate a job.

Mr. Jenner. On that occasion, that incident, did he have occasion to discharge the .22 caliber rifle he was carrying?

Mr. Oswald. Yes, sir; he did.

Mr. Jenner. Did you see him do so?

Mr. Oswald. Yes, sir.

Mr. Jenner. From what shoulder did he, against which shoulder did he place the butt of the gun?

Mr. Oswald. The right shoulder.

Mr. Jenner. And with which hand or fingers of which hand did he pull the trigger and discharge the gun?

Mr. Oswald. The right hand, sir.

Mr. Jenner. Did he exhibit any proficiency in the use of that .22 caliber gun on that occasion?

Mr. Oswald. I would say an average amount.

Mr. Jenner. Hunting rabbits or squirrels with a rifle takes pretty good marksmanship. Did any of you boys bring down a rabbit or squirrel, on the fly, I mean?

Mr. Oswald. As I recall, one small, very small cottontail as he ran across the peanut field, all three of us were shooting at him, and my weapon that I had, one of the weapons that belonged to me, was a semiautomatic 22 and I perhaps had a burst of four or five rounds that I said I got him. But all three of us were shooting at him.

Mr. McKenzie. Did all three of you claim him?

Mr. Oswald. No, sir; I did.

Mr. Jenner. Was that your only victory on that hunting trip or did someone else shoot down a squirrel or a rabbit?

Mr. Oswald. No squirrels were killed that day and perhaps I believe this was the occasion that we went into what we called a briar patch located off to the left of the farmhouse; at that particular time it was very thick with cottontails, and I believe we exterminated about eight of them at that time between the three of us because it was the type of brush and thorns that didn't grow very high but we were able to see over them, so getting three of us out there it wasn't very hard to kill eight of them.

Mr. Jenner. Now, had you and your brother engaged in this very light form of hunting at any other time during your lifetime?

327 Mr. Oswald. Yes, sir.

Mr. Jenner. Would you indicate the frequency of that?

Mr. Oswald. If I recall, only one other occasion that we had been hunting together. This was during a leave that Lee had from the Marine Corps.

Mr. Jenner. During a leave that he had?

Mr. Oswald. Yes, sir. And at which time, if I may correct myself there, another time comes to mind, I recall two times that we had this type of light hunting out there at that farm, at the same place. One time was during a leave that he had from the Marine Corps. I don't recall of any game at that particular time that we shot. I know we did handle the rifle and fired maybe target practice, something along that line. I don't recall of anything.

The second time that I now remember is during his stay after he returned from Russia, during his stay at my home in Fort Worth, that my wife and I and our children took him and his wife and child out to the farm to meet our in-laws, my in-laws, and also to do a little hunting while we was out there, and which we did just a very little bit. I believe this was on a Sunday afternoon and we didn't stay out very long.

Mr. Jenner. What weapons did you use on that occasion?

Mr. Oswald. On that occasion, I believe the same weapons we used before.

Mr. Jenner. Would that be true of all three occasions?

Mr. Oswald. I believe on the first occasion, which was the occasion that Lee came home on leave, that at that time I only owned one .22 rifle.

Mr. Jenner. Was that the semiautomatic?

Mr. Oswald. No, sir; it was not the semiautomatic, it was a bolt action rifle, with a clip on it. However, I believe Lee either used my brother-in-law's rifle——

Mr. Jenner. Was that a bolt-action rifle?

Mr. Oswald. Yes, sir; it is a bolt-action rifle. He either used that rifle or a single-shot, bolt-action rifle, another .22 that was out at the farm.

Mr. Jenner. On the occasion during which you went hunting during that 3-day period, interregnum his return and his discharge and his departure for New Orleans, was the weapon he employed a bolt-action weapon?

Mr. Oswald. Yes, sir; it was.

Mr. Jenner. Is it a fair statement on my part that on all the occasions that you recall hunting with Lee he employed a bolt-action rifle?

Mr. Oswald. That is correct, sir.

Mr. Jenner. During your youth and prior to these occasions about which you testified, do you know of the fact or know by rumor or otherwise that your brother engaged in this light hunting or other kind of hunting where he used a firearm even though he was not with you or you did not accompany him?

Mr. Oswald. I feel surely that he did, without recalling any particular time that he told me, but his interest along that line was generally like mine, that is hunting and fishing, and I am sure when he had an opportunity to hunt that he did do so.

Mr. Dulles. Did he ever tell you about hunting in Russia?

Mr. Oswald. Yes, sir; he did.

Mr. Jenner. Would you relate that, please, tell us when the conversation took place and the circumstances, if it was a conversation?

Mr. Oswald. The circumstances was it was in a letter I received from him.

Mr. Jenner. Is that one of the letters you produced?

Mr. Oswald. Yes, sir; it is.

Mr. Jenner. Did you have any conversation with him in addition to the letter, apart from the letter?

Mr. Oswald. I believe I did along that line because as I stated our interests in hunting and fishing was mutual and he did state that he was able to——

Mr. Jenner. In response to Mr. Dulles' question, would you give the conversation? We will take care of the letter in the morning.

Mr. Oswald. No, sir; I am trying to give the conversation.

Mr. Jenner. Thank you. Proceed.

Mr. Oswald. That we talked about hunting over there, and he said that328 he had only been hunting a half dozen times, and so forth, and that he had only used a shotgun, and a couple of times he did shoot a duck.

Mr. Jenner. It was all shotgun shooting, no rifle shooting?

Mr. Oswald. No rifle shooting, no sir. That is all they were allowed to have, the shotgun.

Mr. Jenner. This conversation took place, as I understand it, on his return from Russia when he was living with you for that month, that would be June-July of 1962?

Mr. Oswald. Yes, sir; that is correct.

Mr. Jenner. And that is the extent of the conversation?

Mr. Oswald. Yes, sir; that is.

Mr. Jenner. As you now recall it—there have been some reports, and they are only reports as far as we of the staff are concerned, of speculation about a television set, whether your brother purchased or owned a television set and whether he purchased it outright or on time with a guarantee from you.

What information or knowledge do you have in that connection?

Mr. Oswald. I am not aware that he purchased a television set, sir. I did at his request, when he and Marina and the baby were living in Fort Worth.

Mr. Jenner. Where in Fort Worth?

Mr. Oswald. Mercedes Street in Fort Worth, in a small duplex which was——

Mr. Jenner. Can you fix even more definitely the time of this event?

Mr. Oswald. This was approximately the latter part of September, 1962. And at his request——

Mr. Jenner. He came to you, excuse me.

Mr. Oswald. He called me, sir.

Mr. Jenner. He called you by telephone?

Mr. Oswald. Yes, sir; he called me at my office from his place of employment in Fort Worth at that time.

Mr. Jenner. Give us the substance of what he said.

Mr. Oswald. We talked briefly about how each family was doing, and so forth, and he said that he would like to establish credit and he had tried to charge something at Montgomery Ward's at Fort Worth, the West 7th Street store, and they had stated that he needed to have somebody cosign or vouch for him, and this was his request to me, and I said gladly I would do so, and late that afternoon after work, this was approximately 5:30 by the time I arrived at Montgomery Ward, I did sign for Lee's charge account. However, I was not aware of what he was charging.

Mr. Jenner. There was no discussion, I take it, at that time of what—the use to which he intended to put his credit?

Mr. Oswald. No, sir; I believe perhaps he did mention something about a baby chair and a baby bed.

Mr. Jenner. Was there ever any discussion between you about his purchase or acquisition of a television set?

Mr. Oswald. No, sir; there was not.

Mr. Jenner. Were you ever in his home or apartment?

Mr. Oswald. Yes, sir; I was.

Mr. Jenner. Did you see a television set there?

Mr. Oswald. Pardon me, you are referring to the apartment on Mercedes Street, is that correct?

Mr. Jenner. Yes.

Mr. Oswald. Yes, I was in his home quite a few times and there was not a television set that I remember.

Mr. Jenner. On any occasion that you were there?

Mr. Oswald. No, sir.

Mr. Jenner. On any occasion when you were in any place of residence of your brother after his return to the United States, did you see in those premises a television set?

Mr. Oswald. Yes, sir.

Mr. Jenner. Where was that?

Mr. Oswald. At my house and at my mother's house.

Mr. Jenner. I should have been more specific and identified a residence as one of his own rather than living with you or living with your mother.

329 Mr. Oswald. At no residence that he lived in that I was aware of at any time did I see him with a television set that I would take to be his own.

Mr. Jenner. Did you ever have any discussions—did any discussion ever occur between the two of you with respect to his acquisition of a television set?

Mr. Oswald. None that I recall, sir.

Mr. Jenner. This is, as far as you are concerned, a total blank, this television set matter?
Mr. Oswald. That is correct, sir.
Mr. Dulles. I think we had better adjourn pretty soon. This man has had quite an ordeal for the day.
Mr. Jenner. It is acceptable.
Mr. Dulles. Is it acceptable to you?
The Chairman. Yes.
Mr. Oswald. I have no objection to continuing.
Mr. McKenzie. If you would prefer to reconvene tomorrow morning we can reconvene then.
Mr. Rankin. I think 9 o'clock is better. I think we can finish up in the morning.
Mr. Dulles. Thank you. At 9 o'clock in the morning.
(Whereupon, at 5:15 p.m., the President's Commission recessed.)

Friday, February 21, 1964

TESTIMONY OF ROBERT EDWARD LEE OSWALD RESUMED

The President's Commission met at 9 a.m. on February 21, 1964, at 200 Maryland Avenue NE., Washington, D.C.
Present were Chief Justice Earl Warren, Chairman; and Allen W. Dulles, member.
Also present were J. Lee Rankin, general counsel; Albert E. Jenner, Jr., assistant counsel; Wesley J. Liebeler, assistant counsel; and William McKenzie, attorney for Robert Edward Lee Oswald.

The Chairman. Gentlemen, the Commission will be in order.
As yesterday, I will only be able to be here for a comparatively short time, because we have our weekly conference of the Supreme Court today. And when I leave, Mr. Allen Dulles will conduct the hearing. We will now proceed with the testimony.
Mr. Jenner. Thank you, Mr. Chief Justice.
I would like to return, Mr. Oswald, to the time that your brother Lee was discharged from military service and spent approximately 3 days at home. You recall that period?
Mr. Oswald. Yes, sir; I do.
Mr. Jenner. Now, would you please describe his physical appearance the last time you saw him during that 3-day period?
Mr. Oswald. His hair was brown and curly, a full set of hair. His physical appearance—he was trim, weighed approximately 140 pounds, he was approximately 5 foot 9½, he seemed to be in fine physical shape at that time.
Mr. Jenner. I mentioned 3 days. Was I wrong about the 3 days, or was it a little longer period?
Mr. Oswald. No, sir; my recollection on that period was 2 or 3 days, and only during one of these day do I remember seeing him. He spent the day at our house.
Mr. Jenner. It was your impression, sir, that he was in good health, bright and alert mentally at that time?
Mr. Oswald. Yes, sir; he most certainly was.
Mr. Jenner. Did you describe his physical appearance as far as his head of hair was concerned?
Mr. Oswald. Yes, sir.
Mr. Jenner. A full head of hair?
Mr. Oswald. Yes, sir.
Mr. Jenner. Did he appear strained in any respect?
Mr. Oswald. No, sir; he did not.

Mr. Jenner. His mental condition, as far as you can tell, is what you would regard or had regarded as normal during your acquaintance with him as his brother?

Mr. Oswald. That is correct.

Mr. Jenner. Now, will you then jump to the first time you saw him subsequently thereto, which I understand was in June 1962. State the date, please, as closely as you can.

Mr. Oswald. This was June 14, 1962.

Mr. Jenner. And where did you see him?

Mr. Oswald. At Dallas, Love Field.

Mr. Jenner. Now, on that occasion—and take in also the period of time that he lived with you in your home during June and part of July 1962—what did you observe, and if in contrast by way of contrast, in his physical appearance and demeanor as against the last time you had seen him, in 1959.

Mr. Oswald. His appearance had changed to the extent that he had lost a considerable amount of hair; his hair had become very kinky in comparison with his naturally curly hair prior to his departure to Russia.

Mr. Jenner. Had his hair been in any respect kinky, as you put it, in November of 1959 immediately prior to his leaving for Russia?

Mr. Oswald. That would have been in September.

Mr. Jenner. September—I am sorry.

Mr. Oswald. No, sir; it was not. It was curly.

Mr. Jenner. Did that arrest your attention, the difference in the texture of his head of hair?

Mr. Oswald. Yes, sir; it certainly did.

Mr. Jenner. You, though 5 years old at the time of your father's death—do you recall his physical appearance insofar as his head of hair?

Mr. Oswald. My father's head of hair?

Mr. Jenner. Yes.

Mr. Oswald. He had a full set of hair.

Mr. Jenner. Do you have any baldness or tendency towards baldness in your family?

Mr. Oswald. None that I am aware of.

Mr. Jenner. Now, I include both your mother and father and relatives on either side, to the extent that you have met those people.

Mr. Oswald. No, sir; no one that I recall that I met, relatives on either my father's or mother's side, had any tendency towards baldness.

Mr. Jenner. And you have none?

Mr. Oswald. No, sir; I do not.

Mr. Jenner. And your brother John?

Mr. Oswald. No, sir.

Mr. Jenner. He still has a full head of hair?

Mr. Oswald. Yes, sir.

Mr. Jenner. Even now?

Mr. Oswald. Yes, sir.

Mr. Jenner. What else did you observe by way of his facial appearance—whether he was drawn, or bouncy and healthy, as he had been when you had seen him in September of 1959?

Mr. Oswald. He appeared the first couple of days upon his return, June 14, 1962, to be rather tense and anxious. I also noted that his complexion had changed somewhat to the extent that he had always been very fair complected—his complexion was rather ruddy at this time—you might say it appeared like an artificial suntan that you get out of a bottle, but very slight—in other words, a tint of brown to a tint of yellow.

331 Mr. Jenner. What else did you notice by contrast, so far as his physical appearance is concerned? And then, next, I want to go to his demeanor.

Mr. Oswald. I believe his weight perhaps was a little bit less at that time. I would say probably 5 pounds—approximately 5 pounds less than what he was in 1959, before he went to Russia.

Mr. Jenner. Did you say he appeared drawn as compared with his appearance in 1959—facially?

Mr. Oswald. I would say to some extent; yes, sir.

Mr. Jenner. Now, would you please relate to the Commission any other differences, if there were any, in demeanor?

Mr. Oswald. To me, he acted the same as he did in 1959 prior to going to Russia. Our conversations at the time he returned from Russia in June of 1962—he appeared to be the same boy I had known before, with the exception of what I noted on his physical appearance.

As far as his conversations were concerned at this particular time, June of 1962, I noticed no difference.

He appeared to have picked up something of an accent. But I took this to mean that because he had been speaking the Russian language and living in Russia during a period of approximately two and a half years, that this was the reason for the accent.

Mr. Jenner. Did these differences in physical appearance, especially his hair, his skin tone, his overall facial and physical appearance, lead you at that moment, in the light of what had occurred in the meantime, your exchange of correspondence, lead you to form an opinion, at least tentative, as to what might have occurred or happened to your brother while he was in Russia?

Mr. Oswald. In reference to that, sir; his hair—I did, either on the first or second night, when he was there at the house—I pointed it out to him and actually had him bend his head down to where I could look at the top of it, and it was very thin on the top—you could see just right down to his scalp.

And his comment on that was that he thought the weather had affected his hair, the cold weather.

Mr. Jenner. Did he make any comments when you met him at Love Field, and did you ride in with him from Love Field to your home?

Mr. Oswald. Yes, sir. We were in my personal car, and my wife and my children were with me. We met him and his wife and his baby. He seemed, perhaps the word is disappointed, when there were no newspaper reporters around. He did comment on this.

Mr. Jenner. Tell us what he said.

Mr. Oswald. I believe his comment was something, "What, no photographers or anything?"

I said, "No, I have been able to keep it quiet."

Mr. Jenner. And where was that remark made?

Mr. Oswald. At Love Field, as they came through the gate.

Mr. Jenner. Did he make any remarks on that subject as you drove into town?

Mr. Oswald. No, sir; he did not.

Mr. Jenner. Did he make any other comments that arrested your attention when he arrived at Love Field or while you were driving into town?

Mr. Oswald. Yes, sir; he did. In reference to newspaper reporters again, or photographers, he asked me if I had been receiving calls and so forth, and I told him I had received two or three calls, but I said nothing, and they were not aware of his schedule of arrival in the United States, and they were not aware at that time, to my knowledge, that he had arrived at Love Field, and that he was going to be at my home.

Mr. Jenner. Having in mind the changes in physical appearance, and also the course of events since the day of his arrival at Love Field to the present time, have you formed an opinion, Mr. Oswald, as to whether your brother may have undergone some treatment of some kind in Russia that affected his mind?

332 Mr. Oswald. Yes, sir. Since Lee's death on November 24th, I have formed an opinion in that respect.

Mr. Jenner. What is that opinion?

Mr. Oswald. That, perhaps in sheer speculation on my part—that due to the nature of the change in his hair, in the baldness that appeared, I reached the opinion that perhaps something in the nature of shock treatments or something along that line had been given him in Russia.

Mr. Jenner. You base this opinion on any factors other than or in addition to this change of physical appearance that you noted on his return from Russia?

Mr. Oswald. No, sir; I do not.

Mr. Jenner. Has the course of events affected the opinion you have now expressed?

Mr. Oswald. Yes, sir; since the course of events, since Friday, November 22, 1963, his death following on the 24th of November 1963, I have searched my own mind for possible reasons of why or how this all came about. That has been one of my opinions—in reference to his hair structure and so forth, and his baldness—pardon me just a minute, please.

Mr. Jenner. Have you concluded your answer?

Mr. Oswald. Yes, thank you.

Mr. Jenner. Has this course of events and your brother's physical appearance and any other factors you had in mind led you to form an opinion as to whether he was or had been an agent of the government of the USSR?

Mr. McKenzie. You are asking him, Mr. Jenner, to speculate.

Mr. Jenner. I am.

Mr. Oswald. May I have that again, please?

Mr. McKenzie. His question was—this is off the record.

(Discussion off the record.)

Mr. Oswald. No, sir.

Mr. McKenzie. Mr. Jenner, may I ask a question at this time?

Robert, at any time after your brother returned from Russia, or at any time after he went to Russia, did he ever remark to you as to whether or not he had been ill while in Russia?

Mr. Oswald. No, sir; he did not.

Mr. McKenzie. Has his wife, Marina Oswald, ever said anything to you about whether or not he was ill while he resided in Russia?

Mr. Oswald. Yes, sir; she has.

Mr. McKenzie. And what did she say?

Mr. Jenner. Could you fix the time, please?

Mr. Oswald. My conversation with Marina Oswald?

Mr. Jenner. Yes.

Mr. Oswald. Approximately 4 weeks ago, in one of our conversations.

Mr. Jenner. And where did that take place?

Mr. Oswald. I believe in my car on the way to the cemetery, or returning from the cemetery, to Mr. Martin's house, in Dallas, Tex.

Mr. Jenner. Anyone other than Marina and yourself present?

Mr. Oswald. No, sir.

Mr. Jenner. All right. State the conversation.

Mr. Oswald. If I may fix the date more accurately here, sir; if I could possibly refer to my diary.

I recall this conversation on January 13, 1964, between Marina Oswald and myself in my car, at which time she stated to me——

Mr. Jenner. Excuse me, sir, to what are you now referring to refresh your recollection?

Mr. Oswald. This would be to a followup of the conversation we had in reference to——

Mr. Jenner. Excuse me—the document.

Mr. Oswald. I am referring to my notebook that I have been keeping in various events that have occurred since November 22, 1963.

Mr. Jenner. For the purpose of the record, would you read the first three words and the last three words of the page to which you are making reference?

Mr. Oswald. "Sunday, January 13, 1964. Jim advised that"——

Mr. Jenner. That is on the first line?

Mr. Oswald. Yes, sir. The last line is "told her this story."

Mr. Jenner. All right. Proceed, sir.

Mr. Oswald. We had a discussion——

Mr. McKenzie. Pardon me just a second.

For the sake of the record, let me state this. A copy of this diary has been furnished to the Commission, photostated by the Commission, and Mr. Jenner has it in front of him.

Mr. Jenner. I will qualify it, Mr. Chief Justice. But I didn't want to take Your Honor's time at the moment, because I do want to cover another subject while you are still here.

Proceed, sir.

Mr. Oswald. What prompted my question as to whether or not Lee was ill while he was in Russia was the followup of a conversation that we had in relation to an incident that occurred some time in the year of 1963. I am not able to place the date of that purported incident. I was advised at that time in reference to this incident that on one day, that Lee was going to shoot at or shoot Mr. Richard M. Nixon, that Marina N. Oswald locked Lee Harvey Oswald in the bathroom for the entire day.

At the end of this brief remark in relation to Mr. Nixon, I asked her at that time had Lee been ill or been in the hospital while he was in Russia. And, at this time, she told me yes, that he had, on two occasions, been in the hospital in Russia.

I asked her what was the nature of the illness. My best recollection of that, sir, was that he was having difficulty with his sinus, and that the cold was bothering him somewhat. And I do not recall anything more specific than that in relation to the illness.

Mr. Dulles. Could I ask one question there?

Did Marina say whether this was while they were in Minsk, or she didn't indicate where he was at the time?

Mr. Oswald. No, sir, she did not.

Mr. Dulles. She did not?

Mr. Oswald. No, sir; she did not.

Mr. Jenner. Have you now stated and exhausted your recollection of everything she said on that subject of his illness on that particular occasion?

Mr. Oswald. Yes, sir; I have.

Mr. Jenner. And you did not pursue the matter any further than you have indicated with her?

Mr. Oswald. Sir, I believe I attempted to, and with her limited knowledge of the English language, we were encountering some difficulties. And I told her perhaps at a later date, or something of that nature, that we could discuss it more fully.

Mr. Jenner. Did you ever pursue it with her on any subsequent occasion?

Mr. Oswald. No, sir; I have not.

Mr. Jenner. If I may, Mr. Chief Justice, I will return to that illness feature at a later point.

You have an entry in your diary under the date of January 13, 1964——

Mr. Oswald. Yes, sir, in reference to Mr. Nixon?

Mr. Jenner. Yes.

Now, you have alluded to Mr. Nixon in testifying with respect to your conversation on the subject of illness with Marina.

Mr. Chief Justice, if I may, I will read the entry on that particular date, and will wish to question the witness about it.

"Sunday, January 13, 1964. Jim advised that Marina told him that Lee wanted to"—and there are a series of five dashes, followed by the letters, "NMR, also, but Marina locked Lee in the bathroom all day. This was confirmed later this day by Marina. On the way to the cemetery."

Is that in your handwriting?

Mr. Oswald. Yes, sir; it is.

Mr. Jenner. Would you please supply, if suppliable, what is indicated by the three dashes preceding the letters "NMR" and identify what the letters "NMR" refer to?

Mr. Oswald. If I may, sir, correct you there.334 There are five dashes there. And the word "shoot" was my intention to leave blank there. And the initials "NMR" stands for Richard M. Nixon in reverse.

Mr. Jenner. I take it, then, that the five dashes were inserted there as a substitute for the word "shoot"?

Mr. Oswald. That is correct, sir.

Mr. Jenner. And the initials are those of Richard M. Nixon reversed?

Mr. Oswald. That is correct, sir.

Mr. Jenner. Now, would you please state fully when this matter or this incident first came to your attention where and through and by whom?

Mr. Oswald. The first time I was aware of this incident was at Mr. Jim H. Martin's home in Dallas, Tex.

Mr. Jenner. On what day?

Mr. Oswald. On Sunday, January 13, 1964.

Mr. Jenner. What was the occasion for your being there?

Mr. Oswald. To visit with Marina, and to take her to the cemetery.

Mr. Jenner. You entered the home?

Mr. Oswald. Yes, sir.

Mr. Jenner. Was your wife, Mrs. Oswald, with you?

Mr. Oswald. Yes, sir; she was.

Mr. Jenner. Your children?

Mr. Oswald. Yes, sir; they were.

Mr. Jenner. You entered the home, and who was there?

Mr. Oswald. Mr. and Mrs. James H. Martin, I believe their children were also present, and in the living room of their home there was two Secret Service agents, or one Secret Service agent, and two Dallas police officers.

Mr. Jenner. Are you able to identify any of those four men?

Do you recall any of them at the moment?

Mr. Oswald. I believe, sir, that one of the Secret Service agents, if he was either the only one there, or two of them were there, the one that I do recall, Mr. Bob Jameson or Jimson, of the Dallas office—the U.S. Secret Service office in Dallas.

Mr. Jenner. Now, to what Richard M. Nixon did the initials "NMR" as you have placed them in this note refer?

Mr. Oswald. To the past Vice President of the United States.

Mr. Jenner. Now, proceed to tell us about how the circumstance arose, your first conversation of it, your first notice of it.

Mr. Oswald. I was talking with Mr. Jim Martin about various other matters.

Mr. Jenner. Excuse me, sir. Where were you in talking to Mr. Jim Martin?

Mr. Oswald. I was in the den of his home, sitting on a sofa.

Mr. Jenner. And who was present?

Mr. Oswald. Jim Martin and I were sitting on the sofa, and I believe my wife and his wife were at the end of the den in the kitchen part of it, standing by the sink.

Mr. Jenner. What is the distance between yourselves sitting on the sofa and the others?

Mr. Oswald. I would say approximately 12 or 15 feet, sir.

Mr. Jenner. And was there a doorway, was it open?

Mr. Oswald. No, sir; it is an open room.
Mr. Jenner. So you were all in the same room—one section of it you describe as a den?
Mr. Oswald. Yes, sir.
Mr. Jenner. And the other section consists of what?
Mr. Oswald. The kitchen, the sink, refrigerator, a washing machine, built-in oven and range.
Mr. Jenner. All right. Proceed.
Mr. Oswald. We discussed other matters. I do not recall what they were. Just talking to him about how Marina was doing and so forth, and any other thing that we might be talking about in general, small talk. And we finally—he finally brought up this question.
Mr. Jenner. What did he say and how did he approach it? Reproduce it as best you can, sir.
Mr. Oswald. I believe he moved very close to me. I was turned towards him.335 He was to my left. I might say at this time that the women at the sink would be on my far right, behind me generally. And he related to me——
Mr. Jenner. What did he say?
Mr. Oswald. This incident, that Marina had told him that on a day still not identified to me, that he, Lee Harvey Oswald, had the intention to shoot Mr. Richard M. Nixon, and that Marina N. Oswald had locked Lee in the bathroom for the entire day. And that was the text to my best remembrance—that was everything that was said from him.
Mr. Jenner. Have you now exhausted your recollection?
Mr. Oswald. Of Mr. Martin's conversation to me?
Mr. Jenner. Yes.
Mr. Oswald. Yes, sir; I have.
Mr. Jenner. Did he say how he had come about this information?
Mr. Oswald. No, other than he had a conversation with Marina N. Oswald.
Mr. Jenner. And he was relating to you a conversation he had had with her?
Mr. Oswald. Yes, sir.
Mr. Jenner. Did he say that she had reported this to him?
Mr. Oswald. Yes, sir; he did.
Mr. Jenner. Did you inquire of him as to why this had not been disclosed to you before?
Mr. Oswald. No, sir; I did not.
Mr. Jenner. Did you ask any questions of him in that connection?
Mr. Oswald. No, sir; I did not.
I might add that my reaction at that time was that I was rather speechless. I believe I just shook my head in utter disbelief to what I was hearing.
Mr. Jenner. Did Mr. Martin relate to you when Marina had told him this story?
Mr. Oswald. No, sir; not to my recollection.
Mr. Jenner. Did you question him with respect to that?
Mr. Oswald. No, sir; I did not.
Mr. Jenner. Did you make any effort to fix the time when the event in question had taken place?
Mr. Oswald. Yes, sir; in my own mind I did.
Mr. Jenner. You didn't question Mr. Martin about it, however?
Mr. Oswald. No, sir; I did not.
Mr. Dulles. At this time, did you know of the rumors with regard to the attack on General Walker or not?
Mr. Oswald. Yes, sir; I did. And I refer, again, to the entry on January 13, 1964, and the statement that Jim advised that Marina told him that Lee wanted to "blank NMR, also." And by that "also" I was aware of the attempt on General Walker's life.

Mr. Jenner. Was anything said during the course of your conversation with Mr. Martin in the den with respect to the information you had that an attempt had been made by your brother on the life of General Walker?
Mr. Oswald. No, sir, not at this conversation, it was not.
Mr. Jenner. Did you ever talk to Mr. Martin at any time subsequent to this, with respect to this event?
Mr. Oswald. Yes, sir—preceding this day of January 13, 1964, approximately 3 or 4 weeks prior to that——
Mr. Jenner. This particular event, I mean—Mr. Martin's relating to you that Marina had advised him that your brother wanted to shoot Richard M. Nixon, the Vice President of the United States. Did you have a further conversation with Mr. Martin at any time subsequent to that—that is, after January 13, 1964?
Mr. Oswald. No, sir; I did not.
Mr. Jenner. You have not up to this moment?
Mr. Oswald. No, sir; I have not.
Mr. Jenner. You did not at any time later that day? You had only this one conversation with Mr. Martin, and none other?
Mr. Oswald. On this subject, yes, sir, that is correct.
Mr. Jenner. On this particular subject, you made no effort to question him further about it?
336 Mr. Oswald. No, sir.
Mr. Jenner. And you have now exhausted your recollection as to all of your conversation on this occasion with Mr. Martin?
Mr. Oswald. Yes, sir; I have.
Mr. Jenner. And you at no time ever pursued it further with him?
Mr. Oswald. No, sir; I did not.
Mr. Jenner. Did you report or relate this to the Secret Service or the FBI or any other agency of the U.S. Government?
Mr. Oswald. No, sir; I did not.
Mr. McKenzie. Pardon me just a minute, Mr. Jenner. May I ask a question?
You have, have you not, furnished the FBI a copy of this diary that you have kept since November 22d?
Mr. Oswald. That is correct.
Mr. McKenzie. And likewise you furnished it to this Commission?
Mr. Oswald. That is correct.
Mr. Jenner. When was your diary furnished to the Commission for the first time?
Mr. McKenzie. Yesterday morning.
Mr. Oswald. February 20, 1964.
Mr. Jenner. Yesterday morning when you and your counsel tendered it to me?
Mr. Oswald. That is correct, sir.
Mr. Jenner. But between the 13th of January 1964 and yesterday morning, when you tendered the diary to me, you made no tender of any written materials nor did you relate orally to any agent or agency of the U.S. Government this particular incident?
Mr. Oswald. Yes, sir; I had.
Mr. Jenner. You had?
Mr. Oswald. Yes, sir.
Mr. Jenner. Please state to whom and when?
Mr. Oswald. This was two FBI agents on the night of—may I have a calendar, please?
On February 18, 1964, I turned over my notebook to two FBI agents at my home in Denton, Tex., at which time they asked me about this particular incident. I referred them to my diary, and turned over the diary, with the advice of my counsel.
Mr. Jenner. Was that incident related by you to them at your instance, or did they come to you with specific reference to it?

Mr. Oswald. They did have a specific reference to it on the night of February 18, 1964.
Mr. Jenner. Who raised it—you or the agents?
Mr. Oswald. The agents did, sir.
Mr. Jenner. Did they state to you as to how they had come to have that information?
Mr. Oswald. No, sir; they did not.
Mr. McKenzie. For the sake of the record, Mr. Jenner, I would like to state what I told the agents.
Mr. Jenner. Now, returning to—when did you tell them, Mr. McKenzie?
Mr. McKenzie. Mr. Jenner, the best I recall it was either Monday—it was Monday, February 17th.
Mr. Jenner. Monday of this week?
Mr. McKenzie. Yes, this past Monday.
And I might add that I received the diary myself sometime around 5:15 or 5 o'clock on Saturday, February 15th, and I read the diary Sunday evening, February 16th, and gave the information to the FBI agents on February 17th, at which time I suggested that if they would like to talk to Robert about it they could be free to do so.
Mr. Oswald. May I say something here, Bill?
Mr. McKenzie did not know the exact meaning of this statement on January 13, 1964. He asked me in his office on Monday afternoon, February 17, 1964, to fill in the blanks, and to give the man's name to the initials and what it meant, at which time I did.
Mr. Jenner. But from the 13th of January 1964 to Saturday February 15,337 1964, you had not drawn this matter to the attention of any agency of the United States or any agent of the United States, or any other person, is that correct?
Mr. Oswald. No, sir; that is not correct. I did not speak to any agent of the U.S. Government.
My wife read my diary, and she asked me what that entry was.
Mr. Jenner. When did you prepare this diary?
Mr. Oswald. I prepared it on the dates noted in the diary. In this particular instance, Sunday, January 13, 1964.
Mr. Jenner. That particular entry, I take it, then, from your testimony, was made contemporaneously with the event itself—that is, on January 13, 1964?
Mr. Oswald. That is correct, sir.
Mr. Jenner. This news from Mr. Martin startled and upset you, did it not?
Mr. Oswald. Yes, sir; it did.
Mr. Jenner. You mentioned that you had gone to the Martin home, one of the purposes being to take Marina to the cemetery.
Mr. Oswald. That is correct, sir.
Mr. Jenner. Did you do so?
Mr. Oswald. Yes, sir; I did.
Mr. Jenner. As soon as you were in her presence in the automobile, or while you were driving there, did you raise this subject with her?
Mr. Oswald. No, sir; I did not.
Mr. Jenner. You made no mention of what Mr. Martin had said to you?
Mr. Oswald. No, sir; I did not.
Mr. Jenner. Did you ever speak to Marina about it?
Mr. Oswald. Yes, sir; she raised the question to me, or told me of the incident.
Mr. Jenner. I see.
Was it on your way to the cemetery, while you were there, or returning from the cemetery?
Mr. Oswald. On the way to the cemetery, sir.

Mr. Jenner. Please try to reconstruct the circumstances, and state as clearly as you can how she raised the subject with you, and what she said—first stating, however, who was in the automobile as you were driving to the cemetery.

Mr. Oswald. It was Marina N. Oswald and myself, only.

Mr. Jenner. All right.

Now, try to—give us the scene just as it occurred—how she brought it out.

Mr. Oswald. We had been talking about the children, her children and my children, family affairs, and so forth, attempting to carry on a reasonable facsimile of a complete conversation within her limited knowledge of English. And at a pause in this conversation, she started relating to me this incident.

Mr. Jenner. Please, Mr. Oswald—when you say she started relating this incident, it doesn't help us any, it is not evidentiary. How did she do it? What did she say, as best you are able to recall? How did she bring it up?

Mr. McKenzie. In her own words, Robert, try to reconstruct exactly what was said to you from the time you left Jim Martin's house until you went—in Dallas, Tex., until you arrived in Fort Worth, Tex., at the cemetery.

Mr. Oswald. On this subject, to the best of my knowledge, Marina said to me, "Robert, Lee also wanted to shoot Mr. Nixon." And, at that time, I believe I gave her the statement that "Yes, Jim told me about this when we were sitting in the den that afternoon."

Mr. Jenner. You say you gave her the statement—you mean that is what you said to her?

Mr. Oswald. Yes, sir.

And she made her statement, referring to this incident of Mr. Nixon.

And then she related——

Mr. Jenner. What did she say?

Mr. Oswald. I might say this, sir. In practically the same words that Mr. Martin had told me, because he had reportedly received the conversation from Marina, within her limited English—it rang a bell to the extent that the words were close to being the same to the way Mr. Martin had related it to me.

It was a very brief statement on her behalf that Lee was going to shoot Mr. Richard M. Nixon, and that she, Marina N. Oswald, locked Lee in the bathroom all day.

338 I did ask her was he very angry. Her reply was at first he certainly was, or was, but later——

Mr. Jenner. When you say at first, you mean her first response to your question was, "He certainly was."

Mr. Oswald. Yes, sir; or that he was. I don't believe she knows the word "certainly." That he was angry, and that he calmed down during the period that he was locked in the bathroom.

And I asked her at the end of that statement, "Did he beat you or hurt you?"

She said, "No, he did not spank me."

That is, to the best of my recollection, the entire conversation on the incident of Mr. Richard M. Nixon.

Mr. Jenner. Did you inquire—you have now exhausted your recollection?

Mr. Oswald. That is correct, sir.

Mr. Jenner. Did you inquire of her as to when this incident took place?

Mr. Oswald. No, sir; I did not.

Mr. Jenner. Did she volunteer it?

Mr. Oswald. No, sir; she did not.

Mr. Jenner. Did you inquire of Mr. Martin as to when the incident took place?

Mr. Oswald. I do not recall that I did, sir.

Mr. Jenner. Did you make any inquiry as to where they were residing at the time the incident was alleged to have taken place, or might have taken place?

Mr. Oswald. No, sir; I did not.

Mr. Jenner. Did you assume any particular residence?

Mr. Oswald. I assumed that this took place in one of two apartments that they lived in in Dallas, Tex. The addresses I am not familiar with. They are the only two houses or apartments that I did see for myself from the outside on the night of Thanksgiving, 1963, whatever the date was, at which time we had dinner at the Martin's home for the first time that Mrs. Martin had met Marina N. Oswald.

And, at the conclusion of the dinner, the Secret Service agents, with us, wanted Marina to point out to them the two apartments that they had lived in in Dallas.

Mr. Jenner. And you accompanied them, did you?

Mr. Oswald. Yes, sir; I was in the car.

Mr. Jenner. Did you thereafter pursue this occurrence, or alleged occurrence, and obtain any additional information about it, with anybody—the Secret Service, the FBI, Mr. Thorne, Mr. Martin, Marina—anybody at all?

Mr. Oswald. No, sir; I have not.

Mr. Jenner. Did you inquire of Marina as to how she locked him in the bathroom?

Mr. Oswald. No, sir; I did not.

Mr. Jenner. Did it occur to you that it might be quite difficult for a 98-pound woman to lock your brother in a bathroom?

Mr. Oswald. Yes, sir; it has occurred to me exactly how this was possible, to the extent that a bathroom usually has a lock on the inside and not on the outside.

Mr. Jenner. Well, if he didn't want to be locked in the bathroom, she would have quite a difficulty—she could not force him into the bathroom.

Mr. McKenzie. Mr. Jenner, that is a question for rank speculation.

Mr. Jenner. I appreciate that, sir. I am trying to jog his recollection.

Mr. McKenzie. May I ask him a question at this time to maybe perhaps assist you?

The Chairman. You may ask, yes.

Mr. McKenzie. Robert, has Marina told you at anytime or do you now know where they were residing when this occurrence happened?

Mr. Oswald. No, sir; she has not. And I am not aware from any source where this event took place.

Mr. McKenzie. Were you ever in their apartments in Dallas, Tex., at anytime?

Mr. Oswald. No, sir; I was not.

339 Mr. McKenzie. Prior to going to—with the Secret Service and Marina on Thanksgiving evening, was that the first time that you had ever seen the apartments where they lived?

Mr. Oswald. That is correct, sir.

The Chairman. I think we will take a break now.

I must be going to my conference. So we will recess for just a moment.

(Brief recess.)

Mr. Dulles. The Commission will come to order.

Mr. Jenner, if you will proceed.

Mr. Jenner. Thank you, sir.

Mr. Oswald, we have some data that indicates or confirms the fact that Mr. Nixon was invited to Dallas in April of 1963, by the Southeast Dallas Chamber of Commerce to receive the Good American Award, but that at the last minute it was necessary for him to cancel his attendance—he was unable to attend, and did not come to Dallas on that occasion. There was some publicity in connection with the giving of the award prior to the event. But I take it from your testimony that at least you did not pursue with Marina or with Mr. Martin their fixing the time of the event in which Marina, according to the information given you, locked your brother Lee in the bathroom to prevent him from any violence on Mr. Nixon.

Mr. Oswald. That is correct.

Mr. McKenzie. Mr. Jenner, if I may, with Mr. Dulles' approval, interrupt you one more time for another statement.

I recall when Mr. Nixon was coming to Dallas at the invitation of Mr. Carlson and others to receive this award.

However, Mr. Nixon did come to Dallas some time within 6 weeks prior to November 22, 1963. The exact date I cannot fix, because I don't recall the exact date. But it is my best recollection that he was there in that period of time.

Mr. Jenner. Mr. McKenzie, that may well be so.

Our information indicates to the contrary—that he was in Dallas on the 21st of November 1963.

Mr. McKenzie. That is what I say, sir.

Mr. Jenner. You said several weeks prior.

Mr. McKenzie. I said some time within 6 weeks prior to November 22d.

Mr. Jenner. Well, our information is that he was in Dallas on the 21st of November 1963, and not prior to that time.

But we will——

Mr. Dulles. I think there is a misunderstanding there. You are technically correct. It was the day before.

Mr. McKenzie. I couldn't remember the exact date, Mr. Dulles, and I wasn't going to be tied down to any exact date.

Mr. Dulles. You are technically correct.

Mr. McKenzie. November 21 was before November 22.

Mr. Jenner. Well, the inference of the 6 weeks——

Mr. McKenzie. Mr. Jenner, the reason I say 6 weeks—as I explained to Mr. Dulles, I don't know exactly when it was, but I know it was prior to November 22d, Dick Nixon was in Dallas.

Mr. Jenner. Well, Mr. Chairman, we will obtain that information and make it part of the record.

Now, Mr. Oswald, in view of what you have related with regard to this particular event, I ask you this question: Would you please state why you did not report this circumstance to any agency or agent of the U.S. Government up to the time that you gave your diary to Mr. McKenzie and he turned it over to the FBI?

Mr. Oswald. An assumption on my part at the time this was told to me was that some Federal agents were aware of this. Nobody told me that they were aware of it. I repeat, again, it was an assumption on my part that somebody was perhaps aware of this, as they were, before I was—aware of the alleged shot at General Walker of the same year.

Mr. Jenner. I see.

Did you discuss this event with Mrs. Oswald, that is, your wife, Vada?

340 Mr. Oswald. Briefly I did, sir.

Mr. Jenner. Now, when did you do that?

Mr. Oswald. Some time around the latter part of January 1964, at which time——

Mr. Jenner. Excuse me. That is several weeks after you made this entry in your diary, and after the event occurred?

Mr. Oswald. Two or three weeks after I made this entry in my diary January 13, yes, sir, that is correct.

Mr. Jenner. What were the circumstances that led you to discuss the matter with her?

Mr. Oswald. My wife had read my diary, and she had come to this entry on January 13, 1964, and she asked me to fill in the blanks and state who it was, at which time I did.

Mr. Dulles. Did I understand you to say earlier that your wife also prepared a diary?

Mr. Oswald. No, sir, she did not. She had read my diary, sir.

Mr. Jenner. Until you retained Mr. McKenzie, had you retained counsel?

Mr. Oswald. I had consulted counsel.

Mr. Jenner. And what counsel?

Mr. Oswald. Mr. Weldon Knight, of Denton, Tex.

Mr. Jenner. Had you exhibited to Mr. Knight the diary we have been discussing?

Mr. Oswald. No, sir; he was not aware of the diary we are discussing.
Mr. Jenner. I take it from your testimony you did not discuss this particular event with Mr. Knight.
Mr. Oswald. That is correct.
Mr. Jenner. Did you ever exhibit your diary to Mr. Thorne?
Mr. Oswald. No, sir; I did not.
Mr. Jenner. Did you ever discuss the existence of the diary with Mr. Thorne?
Mr. Oswald. No, sir; I did not.
Mr. Jenner. Prior to the time you delivered the diary to Mr. McKenzie, had you disclosed to anybody other than Mrs. Oswald, your wife Vada, the existence of the diary?
Mr. Oswald. Yes, sir; I did.
Mr. McKenzie. To whom?
Mr. Oswald. Mrs. Marina Oswald, approximately the first week of February 1964, or January 1964—I advised her that I——
Mr. McKenzie. You say approximately the first week of January or February. You mean approximately the first week of February or the last week of January?
Mr. Oswald. Yes, sir—thank you—that I was writing down various happenings that had occurred since November 22, 1964.
Mr. Jenner. And you were in the process of preparing a memorandum, really, rather than a diary, of past events?
Mr. Oswald. That is correct.
Mr. Jenner. All right.
Did you do any more than just tell her that you were preparing such a statement or memorandum?
Mr. Oswald. No, sir; I did not.
Mr. Jenner. You did not have occasion, then, at that time to discuss further with her the Richard M. Nixon matter?
Mr. Oswald. No, sir; I did not.
Mr. Jenner. Since we have referred to this document, Mr. Chairman, could I pursue it, at least as to how it came into existence?
Mr. Dulles. Do you propose to introduce it in evidence?
Mr. Jenner. Yes, I do.
I propose now to qualify the diary which you so kindly produced yesterday, Mr. McKenzie.
Mr. McKenzie. Certainly.
Mr. Jenner. Mr. Oswald, yesterday morning your counsel, Mr. McKenzie, delivered to me as an agent of the Commission a ringed notebook, which you have before you, do you not?
Mr. Oswald. That is correct.
341 Mr. Jenner. And is that notebook still intact as it was when you delivered it to me yesterday?
Mr. Oswald. Yes, sir; it is.
Mr. Jenner. Does any part of that notebook contain any entries relating to anything involving your brother?
Mr. Oswald. Yes, sir; it does.
Mr. Jenner. Would you note the particular pages and put a paper clip on them, please?
Would you read the first paragraph of the first page which has been clipped?
Mr. Oswald. "Dated December 6, 1963, for the history of the past 2 weeks as seen through my eyes, and heard with my ears, and felt with my body, I write for future reference for myself and for the future members of the family."
Mr. Jenner. Would you read the last sentence of the last page you have clipped?
Mr. Oswald. "Marina said she was shocked when the FBI told her this story."

Mr. Jenner. May I approach the witness, Mr. Chairman?
Mr. Dulles. Please.
What was "this story"?
Mr. Jenner. May we consider that a question to the witness, please?
Mr. Dulles. Yes.
Mr. Oswald. If I may read the entire entry dated January 19, 1964.
Mr. Jenner. Is this entry in your handwriting?
Mr. Oswald. That is correct, sir.
Mr. Jenner. Was it made contemporaneously with the event recorded?
Mr. Oswald. Yes, sir; it was.
Mr. Jenner. This event took place on Sunday, January 19, 1964?
Mr. Oswald. Yes, sir.
Mr. Jenner. And you made an entry contemporaneously or shortly thereafter?
Mr. Oswald. Yes, sir.
Mr. Jenner. For what purpose?
Mr. Oswald. For the purpose of writing down a reference for myself and for my family on all events that I could learn about in relation to Lee's life.
Mr. Jenner. Mr. Chairman, before the paragraph is read, if I may—is there another entry in your handwriting on that page?
Mr. Oswald. Yes, sir; there is.
Mr. Jenner. Is it the only other entry on that page?
Mr. Oswald. Yes, sir; it is.
Mr. Jenner. Is it the entry of January—Sunday, January 13, 1964, relative to Mr. Nixon about which you have already testified?
Mr. Oswald. Yes, sir; that is correct.
Mr. Jenner. And which you have read in full into the record?
Mr. Oswald. Yes, sir; I have.
Mr. Jenner. Now, you are going to read for the purpose of the record the balance of that page, are you not?
Mr. Oswald. Yes, sir; that is correct.
Mr. Jenner. All right.
Mr. Oswald. "Sunday, January 19, 1964. Marina and the Martins had gone to Kathy Ford's house in Richardson, when we arrived at the Martin's house around 2 p.m. They returned approximately about 4:45 p.m. On the way to the grocery, Jim said the FBI had asked Marina during the week if she knew"——
Mr. Jenner. Is there a blank there?
Mr. Oswald. No, sir. I had omitted a word.
Mr. Jenner. What was the word?
Mr. Oswald. "that Lee".
Mr. Jenner. Was it an inadvertent omission?
Mr. Oswald. Yes, it was.
Mr. Jenner. And the omission was what word?
Mr. Oswald. "If she knew Lee had"——
Mr. Jenner. You now have a specific recollection you intended to write the word "Lee"?
342 Mr. Oswald. Yes, sir; that is correct.
"If she knew Lee had tried to commit suicide while in Russia prior to their marriage. She did not, and it was the first I knew about it. Marina later confirmed this, and said that she had asked Lee two or three times what was the cut on his wrist, pointing to the cut on his left wrist. Lee would become very mad and tell her nothing. The FBI read this in Marina's book."
Mr. McKenzie. "Read this in Marina's book." You misread there. "The FBI read this in Lee's book."
Mr. Jenner. That is correct?

Mr. Oswald. That is correct.

"Understand he had a date with another girl around 8 p.m. (This is in Moscow.)"

Mr. Jenner. Is that in parentheses?

Mr. Oswald. Yes, sir; it is.

Mr. Jenner. The words "this is in Moscow" are in parentheses?

Mr. Oswald. Yes, sir.

"And right before she was due to arrive, he cut his wrist. Marina said she was 'shocked' when the FBI told her this story."

Mr. Jenner. I will not question the witness further about that entry—unless you wish to pursue it at the moment.

Mr. Dulles. No, follow your own order.

There is one question I would ask that relates to the past. That is what you testified to just a moment before. This is with regard to locking in the bathroom for a day.

Did Marina indicate that that was for the purpose of keeping Lee away from possibly Nixon, if he was to be there that day, or was it to cool him down? Did you get any impression as to what the purpose was of the locking in the bathroom?

Mr. Oswald. Yes, sir; I most certainly did. Her intentions as related to me was to keep him from shooting at Mr. Nixon.

Mr. Jenner. On that particular day, or on some future occasion?

Mr. Oswald. I would say on the particular day—pardon me. I misunderstood the question.

Mr. McKenzie. I think he misunderstood the question.

Mr. Jenner. All right.

Was it your impression that Mr. Nixon was to be in Dallas on that particular day, and that that is the day that Marina locked him in the bathroom?

Mr. Oswald. Yes, sir.

Mr. Jenner. Was she locking him in the bathroom to cool him off so he would not attempt it when Mr. Nixon might be in town some later date?

Mr. Oswald. No, sir, it was her intention, or my impression of her intentions, that she locked him in the bathroom on that date, to keep him on that date from shooting at Mr. Richard M. Nixon.

Mr. Jenner. So your impression was this was an imminent event?

Mr. Oswald. Yes, sir.

Mr. Dulles. Or that she thought it was an imminent event?

Mr. Oswald. Yes, that, thank you.

Mr. Dulles. That is all I have now.

Mr. Jenner. I take it from your testimony that this ringed notebook, and in part a diary, is a record first of past events—that you prepared it subsequently to the events recorded therein.

Mr. Oswald. Yes, sir; that is correct.

Mr. Jenner. Now, start from the beginning, that is the first page, the first paragraph of which you have read, in order to identify it. I notice a date—December 6, 1963. Do you find it, sir?

Mr. Oswald. Yes, sir.

Mr. Jenner. Is that the date on which you prepared at least the first page or started this memorandum?

Mr. Oswald. Yes, sir; that is correct.

Mr. Jenner. Now, would you please take that memorandum or notebook and identify each page that you wrote at the first sitting—that is, what you first recorded in the book on the first occasion you wrote in it.

343 Mr. Oswald. On the eighth page, approximately midway down, in the left-hand margin I have a date of 12–7.

Mr. Jenner. All right.

Now, I take it, therefore, that your first entries were made—that you made, covered the pages commencing with the page dated at the top December 6, 1963, and proceeding consecutively to the eighth page, and in the center of that page approximately, at the margin, there appears the figures 12–7.

Mr. Oswald. That is correct.

Mr. Jenner. You wrote all the intervening material at one sitting?

Mr. Oswald. That is correct.

Mr. Jenner. And the 12–7 refers, I take it, to December 7, 1963?

Mr. Oswald. That is correct.

Mr. Jenner. And that is the day following your having made the first entries?

Mr. Oswald. That is correct.

Mr. Jenner. Which is December 6, 1963.

Are all the pages that intervene in your handwriting?

Mr. Oswald. Yes, sir; they are.

Mr. McKenzie. Mr. Jenner, if I may, and for the purpose of the record, to help speed up the proceedings, I will state on behalf of Mr. Oswald that all the pages of the diary which you have there in front of you, and which should be and will be marked an exhibit to the Commission's record, are in Mr. Oswald's handwriting, they were written simultaneously on the date as shown in the diary, and were his recollections of the event as it occurred on that date. Is that correct Robert?

Mr. Jenner. I appreciate your suggestion, Mr. McKenzie, but there are some breaks that I would like to identify.

Mr. McKenzie. Pardon me, sir.

Mr. Jenner. I have marked the document now as Commission Exhibit 323.

(The document referred to was marked Commission Exhibit No. 323 for identification.)

Mr. Dulles. And you wish to ask that it be admitted in evidence?

Mr. Jenner. If I may defer that for a moment.

Are all of the pages of the diary which you have separated and clipped together at my request in your handwriting?

Mr. Oswald. Yes, sir; they are.

Mr. Jenner. Now, proceeding from the eighth page, which contains the date entry December 7, 1963, would you please identify what you wrote on the particular occasion—that is, December 7, 1963?

I take it the balance of that page?

Mr. Oswald. The balance of that page, the following entire page, and the first part of the next page.

Mr. Jenner. Down to what?

Mr. Oswald. "for me to come to his office" and a date——

Mr. Jenner. Is the date 12-11-63?

Mr. Oswald. Yes, sir; that is correct.

Mr. Dulles. Are these pages numbered?

Mr. Jenner. They are not.

Mr. McKenzie. I think we should have them numbered at this time, if the Commission would so desire, sir. We can number them—Robert can number them at the bottom of the page consecutively all the way through, and likewise number the exhibit.

Mr. Jenner. I would like to number the photostat that we have rather than to place any markings on the original.

Mr. McKenzie. That is fine.

Mr. Jenner. Would it help you, Mr. Chairman, if I examined from the seat beside you, so you can see the exhibit?

The occasion next after December 7, 1963, when you made an entry in your notebook, I take it, was on December 11, 1963.

Mr. Oswald. That is correct.

Mr. Jenner. And would you please indicate commencing with that entry in the upper portion of the page how much—what portions of the notebook you wrote on that occasion?

344 Mr. Oswald. On the page referred to, from the date of 12-11-63, on the 11th page following that, I have an asterisk in the left-hand column.

Mr. Jenner. Would you read the first line of that page?

Mr. Oswald. "Complete with Marina."

Mr. Jenner. And the last line?

Mr. Oswald. "around 11 a.m., the first great shock of the day"——

Mr. Jenner. Just the last line.

Mr. Oswald. "also they were having a hard time locating".

Mr. Jenner. Now, there is an asterisk in the left-hand margin?

Mr. Oswald. Yes, sir.

Mr. Jenner. Approximately the center of the page?

Mr. Oswald. Yes, sir.

Mr. Jenner. I gather from your testimony that the entry you made then on 11th of December 1963, commenced at the point that you have that date in the margin, and runs to, throughout the pages consecutively—down to the asterisk of the page you have now identified.

Mr. Oswald. That is correct.

Mr. Jenner. When did you make the entry that is opposite the asterisk, and that follows the asterisk?

Mr. Oswald. I do not recall the exact date, sir. I do recall stopping at that period and making the balance of the entries at a later date after December 11, 1963, and prior to January 13, 1964.

Mr. Dulles. Were they all made at one time?

Mr. Oswald. Yes, sir.

Mr. Dulles. The post asterisk entries?

Mr. Oswald. Yes, sir. From the asterisk until the completion of the diary to the date of January 13, 1964, was made at one time.

Mr. Jenner. And it recorded past events. It was not made contemporaneously with the events recorded?

Mr. Oswald. That is correct.

Mr. Jenner. So that the first entries in this notebook that are diary entries in the sense that they are made contemporaneously with the event, to immediately record the event, are those appearing on the last page, consisting of two entries, one dated Sunday, January 13, 1964, and one dated Sunday, January 19, 1964?

Mr. Oswald. Yes, sir; that is correct.

I have noted an error in those dates to the extent that there is only 6 days in between those two Sundays. One date is wrong.

Mr. Jenner. You mean either January 13, 1964, is incorrect or Sunday, January 19, 1964, is incorrect?

Mr. Oswald. Yes, sir. It was an error on my part. And if I may refer to a calendar, I will correct the dates.

Mr. Jenner. Is that a '63 calendar you have there?

Mr. Oswald. No, sir; this is a '64.

I would correct the first date as appeared in my diary of Sunday, January 13, 1964, to be corrected to January 12, 1964, and the second date of January would be correct, sir.

Mr. Jenner. So wherever in your testimony this morning you have referred to the Sunday, January 13 date, that is to be corrected to January 12, 1964?

Mr. Oswald. That is correct.

367

Mr. Jenner. For the purpose of further identification of the exhibit, and in the context of Mr. McKenzie's and my agreement to substitute a photostatic copy for the original. I will undertake to number the pages of the exhibit on the photostatic copy.

Mr. McKenzie. Would you like Robert to do that?

Mr. Jenner. Well, I would like to have him follow, so that the numbers on the photostat correspond with the pages consecutively in the original.

As I number the pages, Mr. Oswald, would you follow me, so that the page numbers I place on the exhibit are correct in that they are in sequence with the original?

Mr. Oswald. Yes, sir.

345 Mr. Jenner. The first page I am marking No. 1. The next page, No. 2. The next, No. 3.

Would you observe each time that the photostat is a photostat of the original?

Mr. Oswald. Yes, sir; I am observing it.

Mr. Jenner. Page 4 is next.

Five is next. Six is next. Seven is next. Eight is next. Nine is next. Ten is next. Eleven is next. Twelve is next. Thirteen is next. Fourteen. Fifteen. Sixteen. Seventeen. Eighteen. Nineteen. Twenty. Now, page 20 is the reverse side of the page numbered on its face 19, is it not?

Mr. Oswald. No, sir; that is not correct. It is an insertion to the page that has not been numbered yet, page 21.

Mr. Jenner. But isn't it a fact that the entry on the page now numbered 20 is on the reverse side of the page numbered on its face 19?

Mr. Oswald. Yes, sir; I am sorry. You are correct, sir.

Mr. Jenner. But the point you are making is that the entry on page now numbered 20 relates to page 21?

Mr. Oswald. Yes, sir; that is correct.

Mr. Jenner. All right.

We will now mark page 21. Twenty-two.

Mr. Dulles. What are you marking that insert as far as our copy is concerned?

Mr. Jenner. As page 20.

Mr. Dulles. Wouldn't it be better to make it 20-A?

Mr. Jenner. I thought from the record that I had made clear that page number 20 was the reverse side of page numbered on its face 19.

Mr. Dulles. All right. Just so you are clear.

Mr. Jenner. Have we covered page 22?

Mr. Oswald. Yes, sir.

Mr. Jenner. Twenty-three. Twenty-four. Twenty-five. Twenty-six. Twenty-seven.

As I proceeded in numbering the photostat, you placed, did you not, in your own handwriting—followed me and placed the same page numbers in your own handwriting on the pages in question as you wrote the numbers on them—the same pages—on the photostat?

Mr. Oswald. Yes, sir; that is correct.

Mr. Dulles. Off the record.

(Discussion off the record.)

Mr. Dulles. Back on the record.

Mr. Jenner. Mr. Oswald, do the entries that you have made in the notebook on pages 1 through 27 now identified represent your recollection of the events recorded at the time that you recorded the events?

Mr. Oswald. Yes, sir; they do.

Mr. Jenner. Have you had an opportunity to review those entries since they were made?

Mr. Oswald. No, sir; I have not.

Mr. Jenner. Have you reread any portions of any of these entries, other than or in addition to those you read to the Commission this morning?

Mr. Oswald. No, sir; I have not.

Mr. Dulles. Mr. Chairman, I now offer in evidence as Commission Exhibit No. 323 the pages of the notebook which have been identified by the witness, and which have been numbered 1 through 27.

Mr. Dulles. Exhibit No. 323 will be accepted.

(The document heretofore marked for identification as Commission Exhibit No. 323 was received in evidence.)

Mr. Jenner. Now, I would like to direct your attention to page 5 of your notebook.

Mr. Oswald. Yes, sir.

Mr. Jenner. At that point you were recording the course of events on what day?

Mr. Oswald. Friday, November 22, 1963.

Mr. Jenner. To orient you and the Commission, the entry to which I refer, that is the paragraph, reads as follows. Follow me, please.

"Mother and I talked briefly and after about 30 minutes we were taken across the hall to where Marina and the two children were. (This was the first I knew of the new baby.) A Mrs. Paine was also present. We talked a little and shortly Mr. Paine—who the police had been talking to, came out of the office and Mrs. Paine introduced us. I did not like the appearance of Mr. Paine, nothing really to put my finger on, but I just had a feeling.

"I still do not know why or how"—what is that next word?

Mr. Oswald. "but".

Mr. Jenner. "But Mr. and Mrs. Paine are somehow involved in this affair. Shortly thereafter Mother, Marina, and the children and the Paines left to go to the Paines' house in Irving, and I advised them I would stay there and see them tomorrow."

When you recorded "I would stay there" you mean remain in Dallas? What did you mean?

Mr. Oswald. My full meaning there, sir, was that I would remain at the Dallas police station, and take a hotel room in Dallas, and spend the night.

Mr. Jenner. Now——

Mr. Dulles. May I ask just one question there for clarity? It refers to an office. Is that the office of the Dallas police?

Mr. Oswald. Yes, sir; that is correct.

Mr. Dulles. The Dallas police station?

Mr. Oswald. Yes, sir.

Mr. Jenner. I take it from this entry you had not heretofore ever met either Mr. or Mrs. Paine?

Mr. Oswald. That is correct.

Mr. Jenner. And would you elaborate upon, please, your statement recorded on December 6, 1963, that you did not like the appearance of Mr. Paine "nothing really to put my finger on, but I just had a feeling. I still do not know why or how, but Mr. and Mrs. Paine are somehow involved in this affair."

Mr. Oswald. Well, I was introduced to Mr. Paine at the Dallas police office on the night of November 22, 1963. His wife introduced us. His handshake was very weak and what I might term a live fish handshake.

Mr. Jenner. Live or dead?

Mr. Oswald. And his general appearance, his face, and most particularly his eyes to me had what I would term a distant look to them, and that he wasn't really looking at you when he was.

Mr. McKenzie. Mr. Jenner, if you will, please, would you ask the witness whether he meant a live fish or a cold dead fish.

Mr. Oswald. Sir, I believe I mean a live fish. A cold, dead fish would be stiff.

Mr. McKenzie. All right.

Mr. Jenner. We are seeking to obtain the basis upon which you made this entry.

Mr. Oswald. It was Mr. Paine's general appearance and the manner in which he held himself, and by this I mean the way he stood and the way he looked at you, and you had that feeling, as I stated before, that he was not really looking at you.

Mr. Dulles. You say there that Mrs. Paine introduced Mr. Paine to you. When had you previously made the acquaintance of Mrs. Paine—just before this?

Mr. Oswald. Yes, sir; that is correct.

Mr. Dulles. On that same day?

Mr. Oswald. Yes, sir; that is correct.

Mr. Jenner. And you record that in your memorandum, do you not, on a previous page?

Mr. Oswald. Yes, sir; I do.

Mr. Jenner. The fact of the introduction?

Mr. Oswald. Yes, sir; I do so.

Mr. Jenner. I think the Commission would be interested further in explaining your remark "I still do not know why or how, but Mr. and Mrs. Paine are somehow involved in this affair." What did you mean by that? That is on page 6.

347 Mr. Oswald. Yes, sir; I just wanted to verify that this was still under my date, original entry of December 6, 1963.

At the time I wrote the statement, "I still do not know why or how, but Mr. and Mrs. Paine are somehow involved in this affair." I meant by this statement that I had gathered that after our meeting of November 22, 1963, at the Dallas police station, to the date of December 6, 1963, that Mr. Paine and Mrs. Paine were separated, and that I had read approximately at this time—and I am not sure that I had read this particular thing in the newspaper prior to December 6, 1963—but I feel like I did—that in a Dallas paper it referred to an incident at a Grand Prairie Rifle Range where some people had identified Lee as being at this rifle range, and that on one occasion a man, and the description was given in the newspaper, had handed Lee Harvey Oswald a rifle over this fence where he was standing inside the rifle range. As I read this description in the newspaper, I reached the conclusion from that description that it was Mr. Paine.

Mr. Jenner. Any other basis that you now recall upon which you predicated the statement that, "Somehow Mr. and Mrs. Paine are involved in this affair."

Mr. Oswald. Yes, sir; if the newspaper I read at that particular time is dated after December 6, 1963, the statement that I just read a few minutes ago, "I still do not know why or how, but Mr. and Mrs. Paine are somehow involved in this affair"—I made that statement then based on my meeting Mr. and Mrs. Paine at the Dallas police station on Friday night, November 22, 1963.

Mr. Jenner. Now, would you please describe Mr. Paine as he appeared on that particular occasion—first, his physical appearance, and then follow with how he was dressed. Give his height, weight, color of eyes and hair, as you recall them.

Mr. Oswald. I recall Mr. Paine to be approximately 6 feet in height. I do not recall the color of his hair. He is of slender build. Perhaps I would establish his weight around 160 or 165 pounds. His facial appearance was quite drawn—and this is a conclusion on my part, because I had not met him before—he appeared to be quite drawn in the face.

His eyes, I would say, would have to me a hollow look.

Mr. Jenner. What color were his eyes?

Mr. Oswald. I do not know, sir.

Mr. Jenner. You don't presently recall?

Mr. Oswald. No, sir; I do not.

Mr. Jenner. You made no note of it at the time?

Mr. Oswald. No, sir; I did not.

Mr. Jenner. What was his complexion—ruddy, pale?

Mr. Oswald. I would say his complexion would be ruddy complected.

Mr. Jenner. Was he clean shaven?

Mr. Oswald. To the best of my recollection, he was, sir.

Mr. Jenner. No mustache, no beard?
Mr. Oswald. No, sir.
Mr. Jenner. What else did you notice about his appearance? How did he part his hair? Do you recall?
Mr. Oswald. No, sir; I do not.
Mr. Jenner. Do you recall whether he did part it?
Mr. Oswald. No, sir; I do not. I believe this to be correct—that I never did get any higher than looking at Mr. Paine's eyes, and I do not believe I looked at his hair or above his eyes at any time.
Mr. Jenner. How long were you with Mr. Paine on that occasion?
Mr. Oswald. Approximately five minutes.
Mr. Jenner. Had you ever seen Mr. Paine subsequently thereto?
Mr. Oswald. Yes, sir, I have.
Mr. Jenner. On how many occasions?
Mr. Oswald. On one other occasion, sir.
Mr. Jenner. When?
Mr. Oswald. This would be approximately a Sunday afternoon in the middle of December 1963.
Mr. Jenner. That would be approximately a week after you made this entry?
Mr. Oswald. Yes, sir. In the presence of Mr. Jim H. Martin, and Mr. John 348 Thorne. We traveled from Mr. Martin's home to the Paines' house in Irving to pick up Marina's and Lee's clothes that were still there.
Mr. Jenner. Still at the Paines' home?
Mr. Oswald. Still at the Paines' home. I saw Mr. and Mrs. Paine again on that day—I mean at that time. That was my second and only time I have ever seen them. Mr. and Mrs. Paine helped gather up the belongings of Marina and the children and Lee's personal belongings that were still there.
Mr. Jenner. To make it clear, Mr. Oswald, did Mr. Paine accompany you with Mr. Martin and Mr. Thorne to the Paine home, or did you meet Mr. Paine when you arrived there?
Mr. Oswald. We met Mr. Paine and Mrs. Paine on our arrival at their home in Irving, Texas.
Mr. Jenner. How long were you there?
Mr. Oswald. Approximately 45 minutes to an hour.
Mr. Jenner. How was he clothed on that occasion?
Mr. Oswald. In a sport shirt and a pair of slacks, sir.
Mr. Jenner. And how was he clothed on the occasion that you record here on page 6?
Mr. Oswald. I believe also at that time, sir, that he had a sport shirt on and a pair of slacks, and perhaps a sport jacket or jacket of some type.
Mr. Jenner. Was his head covered on either occasion?
Mr. Oswald. No. sir, it was not.
Mr. Jenner. What did you notice, if anything, as to whether he had straight hair or a full head of hair on him? Was he bald?
You have already said you don't recall the color of his hair, am I correct on that?
Mr. Oswald. That is correct, sir.
In referring to the second meeting of Mr. Paine and myself, in reference to his hair, I would say his hair was practically a full set of hair, dark and short.
Mr. Jenner. When you say short, you mean cut short, or a crew cut?
Mr. Oswald. No, sir, just cut short.
Mr. Jenner. How do you describe your own head of hair, as to its cut? Is it cut short?
Mr. Oswald. Presently, I would describe wearing mine at a medium length, for myself.
Mr. McKenzie. How about Mr. Jenner's?
Mr. Oswald. I would describe his as being in medium length.

Mr. Jenner. I think you are right.

Mr. Dulles. May I ask one question there?

Had you known prior to November 22d that Marina was living with Mrs. Paine?

Mr. Oswald. No, sir; I did not.

Mr. Dulles. You had not known that before November 22d?

Mr. Oswald. That is correct, I did not.

Mr. Jenner. Did you know at the time you were introduced to Mr. Paine?

Mr. Oswald. Yes, sir; I did.

Mr. Jenner. And you had become advised in that respect by whom?

Mr. Oswald. By Mrs. Paine.

Mr. Jenner. Are those the only two occasions you have had any contact with Mr. Paine?

Mr. Oswald. Yes, sir; that is correct.

Mr. Jenner. Would you describe her, please?

Mr. Oswald. A tall woman, approximately 110 pounds—and by tall I mean approximately 5 foot 11, or 6 feet in height.

Mr. Jenner. Weighing only 110 pounds?

Mr. Oswald. Yes, sir, very slender. A slender face, also—not a full face.

Mr. Jenner. When you say also, are you now referring to Mr. Paine?

Mr. Oswald. No, sir; I was referring to my statement that Mrs. Paine was slender, and also that she was slender in the face.

Mr. Jenner. All right. Thank you.

Mr. Oswald. Long hair, I believe to be brown in color.

349 Mr. Jenner. How did she do her hair, was it in braids?

Mr. Oswald. No, sir. I believe it was just hanging down long.

Mr. Jenner. When you say long, how long?

Mr. Oswald. Shoulder height.

Mr. Jenner. Mr. Oswald, would you accommodate us—not to do it now, but at noontime, if you have the time, to read through, your diary to the court reporter, because some of the writing I have difficulty interpreting. The Commission would appreciate it if you would interpret your own writing on the exhibit.

Mr. Oswald. All right, sir. I understand that you want me to read the entire diary, is that correct?

Mr. Jenner. Yes, to the court reporter—as part of the record, Mr. Chairman.

Mr. Dulles. You may proceed.

Mr. Jenner. What kind of a student were you, Mr. Oswald?

Mr. Oswald. I believe my average in school was—if I may, sir, ask you—are you talking about my over-all average?

Mr. Jenner. Yes, sir, I seek only the over-all.

Mr. Oswald. I would say a C or C-plus, sir.

Mr. Jenner. Are you acquainted with the scholarship in that respect of your brother John?

Mr. Oswald. No, sir; I am not. I could, if you wish me to, make an opinion on what I think it would be.

Mr. Jenner. This opinion being based upon your attending school with him, as you testified yesterday?

Mr. Oswald. Yes, sir; that is correct.

Mr. Jenner. And discussions with him back and forth between the both of you as to how you were getting along?

Mr. Oswald. Yes, sir.

Mr. Jenner. Common interest in your progress scholarshipwise?

Mr. Oswald. Yes, sir.

Mr. Jenner. What is your present recollection as to his scholarship?

Mr. Oswald. That would be a C-plus or a B.

Mr. Jenner. A touch higher than yours?

Mr. Oswald. Yes, sir.

Mr. Jenner. Did you have an opportunity during your lifetime to form a like opinion as to the scholarship of your brother Lee?

Mr. Oswald. Yes, sir; I have.

Mr. Jenner. And what was his scholarship?

Mr. Oswald. I would say a C to a C-plus, in the same category that I place myself.

Mr. Jenner. Mr. Oswald and Mr. McKenzie, Mr. Chairman, have furnished us with the originals of a series of letters and postcards which Mr. Oswald, the witness, received from his brother Lee Harvey Oswald. We have prepared photostatic copies on a Xerox machine of each of those letters, and each envelope relating to that letter. And in the case of postcards the front and reverse side of postcards.

We were further accommodated, by—yesterday afternoon following the close of the session—by sitting down with Mr. Oswald and in his presence comparing the photostatic copy of each document with the original, the original being in the possession of Mr. Oswald. And I am marking each of those documents with an exhibit number.

Mr. Dulles. Could you give us, Mr. Jenner, the first and last dates, so we have an idea of the period covered?

I have a general idea, of course.

Mr. Jenner. Yes. Two of these items are not in exact sequence, but——

Mr. Dulles. Two have been introduced already, have they not?

Mr. McKenzie. Yes, I think you are right, Mr. Dulles.

Mr. Jenner. That is correct. A letter of November 8, 1959, introduced in evidence yesterday. I don't recall what the second one was, but at least——

Mr. Dulles. Were they marked at that time as exhibits?

350 Mr. Jenner. That was marked as an exhibit. And Mr. Liebeler has it.

The November 8 letter, Mr. Chairman, is marked Commission Exhibit No. 294, and it is in evidence.

Mr. Dulles. There was only one letter, or were there two?

Mr. Jenner. There was just one letter. I think, if you please, you have reference to a telegram, which is Exhibit No. 293.

Mr. Dulles. That is it—the telegram.

Mr. Jenner. Being a telegram dated 14 June 1962.

Mr. Dulles. And these other exhibits cover what period?

Mr. Jenner. They commence—the first, Commission Exhibit No. 295, is a letter of eight pages dated November 26, 1959, and concluding with Exhibit No. 322, a letter of two pages dated March 16, 1963.

Mr. Dulles. Were those all from Russia?

Mr. Jenner. They were all from Russia, save the letter dated March 17, 1963, being Exhibit No. 322, a letter of two pages. All the others are from Russia.

Mr. Dulles. Where was that letter from—do you recall?

Mr. Jenner. It is postmarked—the envelope "Lee H. Oswald, P.O. Box 2915, Dallas, Texas."

And the cancellation stamp likewise says Dallas, Texas.

The date is that which I have already recited.

Mr. Dulles. That was after Lee Harvey's return from the Soviet Union?

Mr. Jenner. Yes, he returned in June of 1962.

Mr. Dulles. And that letter is dated what?

Mr. Jenner. March 17, 1963.

Would you follow me, Mr. Oswald? In each instance, when we compared the letters and the envelopes, it is a fact, is it not, Mr. Oswald, that the letter in question was contained in the envelope of which we have a photostatic copy—and was received by you intact? That is, the envelope was sealed, and the letter content was in the envelope, that you personally opened the envelope and removed the letter content? That in each instance, the letter content is in the handwriting of your brother, Lee Harvey Oswald, entirely, with the exception of Commission Exhibit 299, which is a letter of three pages dated May 31, 1961, upon the last page of which there is a paragraph in the handwriting of Marina Oswald, written in the Russian language?

Mr. Oswald. Yes, sir; I take that to be Mrs. Marina Oswald's writing at that time.

Mr. Jenner. And there appears on that page following that paragraph written in Russian what purports to be an English interpretation of it?

Mr. Oswald. That is correct.

Mr. Jenner. Furthermore, that in each instance the envelope and the letter content is—are in the same condition now as they were when you received them?

Mr. McKenzie. Except for opening.

Mr. Jenner. Except for the opening of the envelope which was necessary for you to do in order to remove the content. Is my statement correct?

Mr. Oswald. With this exception, sir. That a number of the letters were not opened by me personally. By that, I mean my wife opened them when she received the mail at the house.

I have marked the chronological date on the front of them in the last few days.

Mr. Jenner. So that there appears on these exhibits in your handwriting a date on the envelope and in some instances on the letter content?

Mr. Oswald. That is correct.

Mr. Jenner. Which you wrote thereon, and which was not on either the envelope or the letter at the time it was received by you?

Mr. Oswald. That is correct.

Mr. Jenner. Those exhibit numbers—excuse me. There are three postcards—Commission Exhibit No. 310, dated December 11, 1961, which is a Christmas card, Commission Exhibit 319, which is a postcard dated October 10, 1962, and Commission Exhibit 321, a postcard dated April 10, 1962. Each of those was received by you in due course, Mr. Oswald, as you related to me yesterday.

I want you to confirm this. And is in the handwriting of your brother, Lee Harvey Oswald.

And except for notations of dates which appear thereon or may appear thereon351 in your handwriting, they are in the same condition now as when you received them?

Mr. Oswald. That is correct.

Mr. Jenner. Now, I wish you would—I want to exhibit to you the postcard dated April 10, 1962, which is Commission Exhibit No. 321.

Mr. Dulles. As I understand it, these letters have not yet been formally introduced in evidence.

Mr. Jenner. They have not, sir.

Mr. Dulles. Very well.

I might add, Mr. McKenzie, that, of course, one does not know whether those letters were opened by the authorities in the Soviet Union before being forwarded. I think that ought to be on the record.

Mr. McKenzie. Yes, sir.

Mr. Jenner. Commission Exhibit No. 321 I now hand you, Mr. Oswald. There is a date appearing thereon which reads, according to my interpretation 10—and then I cannot quite decipher it.

Would you look at the original, please?

Mr. Dulles. The European system of marking is different from the American system.

Mr. Jenner. That is what I seek to bring out, sir.

Do you now have the original before you?

Mr. Oswald. Yes, sir.

Mr. Jenner. Would you read the figures to which I point? The first is 10?

Mr. Oswald. 10/4/62.

Mr. Jenner. Indicating what date?

Mr. Oswald. April 10, 1962, in accordance with the European system of dating.

Mr. Jenner. Of putting the day first, the month second, and the year last?

Mr. Oswald. That is correct.

Mr. Dulles. Do you recall whether these letters were opened by cutting or opened by unsealing?

Mr. Oswald. I believe without exception, sir, looking at the originals, that they were opened by unsealing, rather than cutting.

Mr. Dulles. I was asking because it is sometimes possible, by modern methods, to determine whether a letter has been opened and resealed, and if the letter is cut, that can be done.

If the letter has been torn open where the seal is, you cannot do anything with it. You cannot always do this, but there are certain techniques.

Mr. McKenzie. Mr. Chairman, did you have reference to when Robert opened the letters?

Mr. Dulles. Well, what I had reference to is to whether if the letters were cut and not resealed, then there is a certain possibility of ascertaining whether the letter has been previously opened by a censor, and then resealed. I was just getting at that.

Mr. Jenner. Mr. Dulles is interested, I see, in whether the letters had been censored in Russia before they arrived in the United States.

Mr. Dulles. That was my point.

Mr. Jenner. May I inquire of the witness on that subject further?

Mr. McKenzie. Let me state this for the record. When Robert Oswald or his wife opened the letters, as you can plainly see from the letters here in front of you, they were either opened by letter opener—a knife or a letter opener, or just torn open.

Mr. Jenner. Mr. Chairman, it is entirely possible and might even be probable that the Commission would be interested in examining the originals on this subject—that is, to determine through experts as to whether the envelopes had been opened and censored, and the contents censored, before being resealed, if they had been so opened, and dispatched to the United States. And I take it that your inquiry was directed towards that.

Mr. Dulles. That is correct.

Mr. Jenner. May I inquire of Mr. McKenzie, in the light of that fact, as to whether these originals of these letters would be available to us so that we may have expert examination of them for that purpose?

352 Mr. McKenzie. Yes, sir; I will make them available at any time that the Commission so desires.

And I would like further to say, Mr. Chairman, that it is my opinion, based on a reading of these letters—and I feel that Robert Oswald concurs in my opinion here—that many of the letters were censored, because the letters actually have reference to the censor in many instances. And I speak of that—the censor in the Soviet Union.

Mr. Dulles. Yes. I have not yet read the letters.

Mr. Jenner. The photostats that we have of the letters will reveal that to which Mr. McKenzie is now referring. We took the face of each envelope and in most instances of the reverse side of the envelope. And in each instance the front and reverse side of each postcard.

Mr. Dulles. And in each case I believe we will have in our records, will we not, the date when it was mailed and the date of receipt?

Mr. Jenner. To the extent that is revealed by the face and reverse side of the envelope; yes, sir.

Mr. Dulles. Because if you have a case where a letter takes four or five days, longer than another letter, that may mean nothing, or it may mean quite a good deal.

Mr. McKenzie. In some instances, Mr. Chairman, it took five days to receive a letter from the Soviet Union to Fort Worth, Texas.

Mr. Dulles. That is par for the course, I guess.
Mr. McKenzie. Yes, sir.
But I might also add sometimes it takes five days for a letter to get from downtown Dallas to the suburbs in Dallas, Texas.
Mr. Jenner. Now, Mr.——
Mr. Oswald. Pardon me, sir, if I may, I would like to say something to my attorney.
Mr. Jenner. Surely.
Mr. Dulles. Off the record.
(Discussion off the record.)
Mr. Dulles. Back on the record.
Proceed, Mr. Jenner.
Mr. Jenner. Would you turn to the letter of September 10, 1961, please? That is Commission Exhibit 305.
Mr. Oswald. All right, sir.
Mr. Jenner. Do you have it?
Mr. Oswald. Yes, sir.
Mr. Jenner. In addition—did anything accompany that letter in the way of photographs?
Mr. Oswald. Yes, sir, there was.
Mr. Jenner. Is a reference made to those photographs in the letter?
Mr. Oswald. Yes, sir; there is.
Mr. Jenner. And do you still have the photographs?
Mr. Oswald. Yes, sir; I do.
Mr. Jenner. And you have them there before you?
Mr. Oswald. Yes, sir; I do.
Mr. Jenner. And how many are there, and what do they depict?
Mr. Oswald. There is a total of three photographs depicting purportedly pictures in Minsk, Russia.
Mr. Jenner. Is there any handwriting on the reverse side of any of these exhibits?
Mr. Oswald. Yes, sir; on two of the three photographs there is.
Mr. Jenner. I will mark this Exhibit as Commission Exhibit 304, the next as 304-A and the next as 304-B.
(The documents referred to were marked Commission Exhibits 304 and 304-A and 304-B for identification.)
Mr. Jenner. The witness now has before him a photograph marked Commission Exhibit 304, on the reverse side of which appears some handwriting.
Do you recognize that handwriting?
Mr. Oswald. Yes, sir; I do.
Mr. Jenner. Whose is it?
353 Mr. Oswald. I recognize it to be Lee Harvey Oswald's.
Mr. Jenner. Would you read it?
Mr. Oswald. "Trade Union Hall on the Main Street."
Mr. Jenner. And on the opposite side on which this handwriting appears is a picture of a public building?
Mr. Oswald. Yes, sir; that is correct.
Mr. Jenner. I turn your attention to the document marked Commission Exhibit No. 304-A. On the reverse side of that does there appear some handwriting?
Mr. Oswald. Yes, sir.
Mr. Jenner. Whose handwriting is it?
Mr. Oswald. I recognize that to be Lee Harvey Oswald's.
Mr. Jenner. Would you read it, please?
Mr. Oswald. "A square in Minsk."
Mr. Jenner. And on the opposite side is also depicted a public building?
Mr. Oswald. Yes, sir, that is correct.

Mr. Jenner. Exhibit No. 304-B, does the reverse side of that exhibit contain any handwriting?
Mr. Oswald. No, sir, it does not.
Mr. Jenner. The face of the exhibit, however, depicts a plaza with some public buildings?
Mr. Oswald. Yes, sir.
Mr. Jenner. Would you replace those photographs, please, in the envelope with the original?
Mr. Oswald. Yes, sir.
Mr. Jenner. Now, would you turn to the letter dated January 30, 1962, being Commission Exhibit No. 314?
Mr. Oswald. All right, sir.
Mr. Jenner. Were there any contents accompanying this letter in addition to the letter itself?
Mr. Oswald. I believe it did contain, sir—since there is no reference within the letter itself——
Mr. Jenner. It is your recollection?
Mr. Oswald. Yes, sir; it is my recollection that it did contain two photographs.
Mr. Jenner. Is it not a fact, sir, that when you exhibited the original of the letter, the original of the envelope, and removed the contents yesterday afternoon in my presence, that the two photographs to which you now refer were contained in the envelope?
Mr. Oswald. Yes, sir, that is correct.
Mr. Jenner. Now, Mr. Liebeler, would you give us those A and B numbers, please?
Mr. Liebeler. 314-A and B.
(The documents referred to were marked Commission Exhibits 314-A and 314-B, for identification.)
Mr. Jenner. Directing your attention to Commission Exhibit 314-A, that is a photograph, is it not?
Mr. Oswald. Yes, sir.
Mr. Jenner. Is there handwriting on the reverse side of that photograph?
Mr. Oswald. Yes, sir; there is.
Mr. Jenner. Do you recognize the handwriting?
Mr. Oswald. Yes, sir; I do.
Mr. Jenner. Whose is it?
Mr. Oswald. Lee Harvey Oswald's.
Mr. Jenner. What does it say?
Mr. Oswald. "April 30, 1961. Marina—Lee."
Mr. Jenner. Now, turn to the face of the exhibit, do you recognize the persons depicted in that photograph?
Mr. Oswald. Yes, sir; I do.
Mr. Jenner. Who are they?
Mr. Oswald. Left to right, Lee Harvey Oswald and Marina N. Oswald.
Mr. Jenner. And is the exhibit in the same condition it was when you354 removed the exhibit from the envelope upon receipt of the envelope, except for the exhibit number?
Mr. Oswald. Yes, sir; that is correct.
Mr. Jenner. Would you turn to the other exhibit, Commission Exhibit No. 314-B? And does the reverse side of that exhibit contain some handwriting?
Mr. Oswald. Yes, sir; it does.
Mr. Jenner. Do you recognize the handwriting?
Mr. Oswald. Yes, sir; I do.
Mr. Jenner. Whose is it?
Mr. Oswald. Lee Harvey Oswald's.
Mr. Jenner. What does it say?
Mr. Oswald. "Marina, wedding day, April 30, 1961."

Mr. Jenner. Would you turn to the face of the exhibit. Do you recognize the person depicted on it?

Mr. Oswald. Yes, sir; I do.

Mr. Jenner. Who is it?

Mr. Oswald. Marina N. Oswald.

Mr. Jenner. Is that exhibit in the same condition now as it was when you received it and removed it from the envelope in which it was contained, being the letter dated January 30, 1962?

Mr. Oswald. Yes, sir; it is.

Mr. Jenner. Mr. Chairman, I offer in evidence the series of letters which I have identified, and which the witness has confirmed, and the contents, being the now five photographs which have been identified, as Commission Exhibits Nos. 295, being a letter of eight pages, dated November 26, 1959; 296, a letter of one page—we don't have a more accurate date than the summer of 1959; 297, a letter of one page, dated December 17, 1959; 298, a letter of two pages, May 5, 1961; 299, a letter of three pages, dated May 31, 1961.

Mr. McKenzie. Pardon me, Mr. Jenner, just a second.

The letter that you have referred to as being dated December 17, 1959, does not have a date on it. It's received December 17, 1959?

Mr. Jenner. That is in the witness' handwriting.

Mr. McKenzie. Yes; in the witness' handwriting.

Mr. Jenner. The letter itself is undated.

Mr. McKenzie. That is correct.

Mr. Jenner. The words "received" and the figures December 17, 1959, are written by you on the letter?

Mr. Oswald. That is correct.

Mr. Jenner. And is that in fact the date it was received here in America by you?

Mr. Oswald. It was, sir.

Mr. Jenner. Thank you for following me, Mr. McKenzie.

Mr. McKenzie. Yes, sir.

Mr. Jenner. Mr. Chairman, Exhibit 299 is the letter which contains in part the paragraph written in Russian which on its face purports to have been a notation by Marina, which we have already identified.

Exhibit 300 is a letter of two pages, dated June 26, 1961.

Exhibit 301 is a letter of two pages dated July 14, 1961.

Exhibit 302 is a letter of one page dated July 28, 1961.

Exhibit 303 is a letter of two pages dated August 21, 1961.

Exhibit 305 we have already identified. That is September 10, 1961, the letter of three pages which contain the pictures of the public buildings and plaza in Minsk, Russia.

Exhibit 306 is a letter of two pages dated October 22, 1961.

Exhibit 307 is a letter of three pages dated November 20, 1961.

Mr. McKenzie. Pardon me just a second, Mr. Jenner. Don't you have one dated November 1, 1961?

Mr. Jenner. Yes, it is out of order. I will reach it in due course. I am correct that there is a letter of three pages dated November 20, 1961?

Mr. McKenzie. Yes, sir.

Mr. Jenner. Exhibit 308 is a letter of two pages dated November 30, 1961.

355 Mr. McKenzie. Yes, sir.

Mr. Jenner. Exhibit 309 is a letter of two pages dated November 1, 1961. That is the one to which you have reference.

Mr. McKenzie. Yes, sir.

Mr. Jenner. Exhibit 310 is a Christmas card dated December 11, 1961. It is contained in an envelope, I believe.

Mr. McKenzie. Yes, sir, it is.
Mr. Jenner. Is my statement correct?
Mr. McKenzie. That is correct.
Mr. Jenner. Exhibit 311 is a letter of two pages dated December 14, 1961.
Mr. McKenzie. Yes, sir.
Mr. Jenner. Exhibit 312 is a letter of one page dated December 20, 1961.
Mr. McKenzie. December 20, 1961?
Mr. Jenner. Yes, sir.
Mr. McKenzie. Three pages?
Mr. Jenner. One page.
Mr. McKenzie. That is correct.
Mr. Jenner. Exhibit 313 is a letter of two pages dated January 5, 1962.
Mr. McKenzie. That is correct.
Mr. Jenner. January 5, 1962.
Mr. McKenzie. That is correct.
Mr. Jenner. Exhibit 314 is a letter of three pages which we have identified, dated January 30, 1962, and contains the two photographs, one of Marina on the wedding day and then one of both of them on their wedding day.
Exhibit 315 is a letter of three pages dated February 15, 1962.
Mr. McKenzie. Yes, sir.
Mr. Jenner. Exhibit 316 is a letter of two pages dated March 9, 1962.
Mr. McKenzie. Yes, sir.
Mr. Jenner. Exhibit 317 is a letter of two pages, dated April 12, 1962.
Mr. McKenzie. Again, on the letter of March 9, 1962, the date on that letter is the date written by Robert Oswald the day he received that letter. The letter itself is actually undated. But the envelope is dated by Robert Oswald.
Mr. Jenner. That is correct, Mr. Oswald?
Mr. Oswald. That is correct.
Mr. Jenner. And is the envelope postmarked?
Mr. Oswald. Yes, sir; it is.
Mr. Jenner. And the postmark is——
Mr. Oswald. March 9, 1962, sir.
Mr. Jenner. Thank you.
Mr. Dulles. That is date of receipt?
Mr. McKenzie. Yes, sir.
Mr. Jenner. Exhibit 317 is a letter of two pages dated April 12, 1962.
Mr. McKenzie. Yes, sir.
Mr. Jenner. Exhibit 318 is a letter of two pages dated May 22, 1962.
Mr. McKenzie. Yes, sir.
Mr. Jenner. Exhibit 319 is the front and reverse side of a postcard dated October 10, 1962.
Mr. McKenzie. No, sir. April 10, 1962.
Mr. Jenner. That is the postcard the witness——
Mr. McKenzie. Has previously identified as being in the European tradition of dating.
Mr. Jenner. Exhibit 320 is a letter of one page dated November 11, 1962. Or is that '61? Would you check me on that, please?
Mr. McKenzie. I don't find that. Is it a letter or a postcard?
That is November 11. That should be November 17, 1962. The photocopy did not pick up all of it. And if you would like for us, we will change that to November 17. It should be November 17th.
Mr. Jenner. Would you make that change, please, in ink.
Mr. McKenzie. That is Exhibit No. 320.
Mr. Jenner. Commission Exhibit No. 320, a letter of one page, the original dated November 17th. What year?

Mr. McKenzie. Just November 17th. But the postmark shows it was dated November 18, 1962.

Mr. Jenner. Exhibit No. 321 is a postcard dated April 10, 1962.

Mr. Oswald. To which you have previously referred.

Mr. Jenner. Have we got a duplication?

Mr. McKenzie. Yes, sir.

Mr. Jenner. Are Exhibits 319 and 321 duplicates?

Mr. McKenzie. I would have to look at the exhibit. I have the original here in front of me.

Mr. Jenner. They are different exhibits.

Mr. McKenzie. This is Exhibit 321.

The other one is this one you have here, and it is dated October 10, 1962.

Mr. Jenner. All right. To make sure the record is clear, Mr. Chairman—Exhibit No. 319, which is a postcard, is cancelled on its face at Dallas on the 10th day of October 1962, and it reads on the other side, "Dear Robert, for the new address you can write to Box 2915, Dallas, Texas. Also please stop by the house and collect any mail which may have come in before the post office had a chance to change my address to Dallas." And then in the center of the card "Lee", with two X marks. Is that correct?

Mr. McKenzie. That is correct.

Mr. Jenner. Now, that is Exhibit 319.

Now, Exhibit 321——

Mr. Dulles. Let me see. I would like to straighten that out.

Off the record.

(Discussion off the record.)

Mr. Dulles. Back on the record.

Mr. Jenner. Exhibit No. 321 is the postcard dated April 10, 1962.

Mr. McKenzie. That is correct.

Mr. Jenner. I might say, Mr. Chairman, I had marked the exhibits correctly.

Mr. McKenzie. And I concur in that remark.

Mr. Jenner. Exhibit No. 322 is a letter of two pages dated March 17, 1963.

Mr. McKenzie. Dated March 16, 1963. It is postmarked the 17th, but dated March 16, 1963.

Mr. Jenner. Mr. Chairman, I offer in evidence as Commission Exhibits, Exhibits 295 through 322, both inclusive, the documents that have been marked with the exhibit numbers so indicated, including the sub-exhibit numbers on the photographs which have been heretofore identified.

Mr. Dulles. They may be received.

(The documents referred to were marked Commission Exhibits 295 through 322, inclusive, and received in evidence.)

Mr. McKenzie. Mr. Jenner, if I may, I would like to say something for the purpose of the record.

Robert Oswald has brought these exhibits voluntarily. They are at the Commission's convenience at any time. We do not know whether or not they have been censored in Russia, but we are confident that they were, because some of the letters refer to the censor in Russia.

Mr. Jenner. That will appear, Mr. Chairman, from the photostats of the exhibits as offered in evidence.

Mr. Dulles. Thank you very much, Mr. McKenzie.

Mr. McKenzie. Yes, sir.

Mr. Jenner. Now, Mr. McKenzie, among the original postcards and letters which you produced for us is a postcard dated January 13——

Mr. McKenzie. January 10th.

Mr. Jenner. January 10, 1963. And may I have that, please?

Mr. McKenzie. Yes, sir; you may.

Mr. Jenner. That will be marked as Commission Exhibit No. 324.

(The document referred to was marked Commission Exhibit No. 324 for identification.)

Mr. Jenner. Does the witness have the original before him?

Mr. Oswald. Yes, sir.

Mr. Jenner. Examining Commission Exhibit No. 324, which purports to be a postcard, it is in fact a postcard, is it not?

357 Mr. Oswald. That is correct.

Mr. Jenner. And do you recognize the handwriting on the face and reverse side of that postcard?

Mr. Oswald. Yes, sir, I do.

Mr. Jenner. Whose handwriting is it?

Mr. Oswald. Lee Harvey Oswald's.

Mr. Jenner. Did you receive that postcard in due course or about the cancellation date appearing on the face of the card?

Mr. Oswald. Yes, sir; I did.

Mr. Jenner. And that cancellation date is January 13, 1963, is it not?

Mr. Oswald. No, sir; that is not correct. It is January 10, 1963.

Mr. Jenner. This photostat makes a 10 look like a 13.

This postcard was written to you, sent to you by your brother, Lee Harvey Oswald, thanking you for a Christmas gift, was it not?

Mr. Oswald. That is correct.

Mr. Jenner. And is the postcard in the same condition now as it was when you received it?

Mr. Oswald. Exactly, sir.

Mr. Jenner. Mr. Chairman, I offer in evidence as Commission Exhibit No. 324 the document which we have so marked.

Mr. Dulles. It may be received.

(The document heretofore marked for identification as Commission Exhibit No. 324 was received in evidence.)

Mr. Jenner. We will return, Mr. Oswald, to the period about which inquiries were made of you by Representative Ford and Representative Boggs yesterday. That is, you had testified, as you will recall, of efforts on the part of your mother to reach your brother by telephone in Russia when news reached America of his alleged defection. I am merely seeking to orient you at the moment.

Mr. Oswald. Yes, sir. Thank you.

Mr. Jenner. In due course, you received a letter communication from him, did you not?

Mr. Oswald. Yes, sir; I did.

Mr. Jenner. Including the letter of November 8, 1959, about which I questioned you yesterday.

Now, I wish to proceed to the next letter, which is the letter of November 26, 1959, a rather long letter.

As a matter of fact, it consists of eight pages.

Would you get that letter before you, please?

Mr. Oswald. All right, sir.

I have the letter before me now, sir.

Mr. Jenner. Now, you will note from the letter that it purports to be, and from its contents it is indicated that your brother Lee is responding to correspondence that he had in turn received from you.

I ask you this question first.

As to all of these letters which you have now identified this morning, or substantially all of them, had you been in correspondence with your brother in the sense that you also wrote him?

Mr. Oswald. Yes, sir, that is correct.

Mr. Jenner. Did you by any chance happen to retain a copy of, or copies of any of the letters you sent him?

Mr. Oswald. No, sir, I did not.

Mr. Jenner. So that at the moment we would have to call solely on your recollection as to what you might have written during this period of time while he was in Russia?

Mr. Oswald. That is correct.

Mr. Dulles. You made no copies of the letters yourself when you sent them—you just sent an original? There was no copy?

Mr. Oswald. That is correct, no copies were made.

Mr. Jenner. I suggested that you might, during the evening, read the letter of November 26th so as to refresh your recollection as to whether you had written him posing questions to which he responded. Have you had that opportunity?

Mr. Oswald. No, sir; I have not had that opportunity to read this letter.

358 Mr. Jenner. I would prefer to pass this letter, then, Mr. Chairman, until the witness does have an opportunity to read it. Would you try and do so at your first opportunity?

Mr. Oswald. All right, sir.

Mr. McKenzie. It won't take but a minute here to do it.

Mr. Jenner. All right.

(Discussion off the record.)

Mr. Dulles. We will recess for lunch at this time.

(Whereupon, at 12:15 p.m., the President's Commission recessed.)

Afternoon Session
TESTIMONY OF ROBERT EDWARD LEE OSWALD RESUMED

The President's Commission reconvened at 1:15 p.m.

Mr. Dulles. You may proceed, Mr. Jenner.

Mr. Jenner. Mr. Oswald, I have asked you—may I inquire of you whether during the noon hour recess you have read Commission Exhibit 295, which is a letter of November 26, 1959, from your brother to you?

Mr. Oswald. Yes, sir; I have.

Mr. Jenner. And have you also read the letter that preceded that one, to wit, the letter of November 8, 1959, which is to you from your brother, which is Commission Exhibit No. 294?

Mr. Oswald. Yes, sir; I have.

Mr. Jenner. Now, Mr. Chairman, the letter of November 8, which is the earlier of these two letters—this was written by Lee Harvey Oswald shortly after he arrived in Moscow in 1959. In substance, he said in the letter that he supposed his brother Robert, the witness here, did not wish to speak of his decision, that is, of Lee Harvey Oswald's decision to remain in the Soviet Union and apply for citizenship there, since Robert would not be able—and now I quote—"to comprehend my reasons"—that is Lee Harvey Oswald's reasons. "You really don't know anything about me. Do you know for instance, that I have wanted to do this for well over a year? Do you know that I speak a fair amount of Russian, which I have been studying for months?"

The letter also said that he would not leave the Soviet Union under any conditions, and would never return to the United States, "which is a country I hate." He made reference to the fact that he received a telegram from Robert in which Robert had apparently said that he thought Lee "was making a mistake."

Now, directing your attention to the November 8 letter first, would you please state your reaction when you read that letter?

(At this point the letters of November 8, 1959 and November 26, 1959 were physically set forth in the transcript of testimony. In order to achieve consistency in the handling of the exhibits upon the printing of the testimony, those letters are not reproduced in the printed transcript. They are reproduced in the exhibit section as Commission Exhibits Nos. 294 and 295.)

Mr. Oswald. I recall my reactions to this letter, sir. It was something I more or less expected in general, since this was, more or less in general what the newspapers had been publishing.

Mr. Jenner. Is that the only reason you make that remark—that you had expected it in general solely because of what you read in the newspapers, or had there been any other factor that led you to have that expectation?

Mr. Oswald. No, sir; there was no other factor that led be to believe that anything like this was going to happen prior to the happening. My reaction to the letter, as I have stated, was solely in general expecting from what I read in the newspaper that the letter would be something of this nature when I did hear from him.

Mr. Jenner. Had you had any conversation prior thereto during your lifetime359 and that of your brother Lee in which he expressed his views of the character that he wrote in this letter of November 8, 1959?

Mr. Oswald. No, sir; I most certainly did not.

Mr. Jenner. Had you ever discussed with him, in any conversation between you and your brother Lee, with or without your brother John present or your mother, in which his feeling toward or reaction to the government of the United States had been discussed?

Mr. Oswald. No, sir; at no time, as I stated yesterday, have we ever discussed politics, and most assuredly I did not have any inclination in any degree that anything of this nature was in his mind.

Mr. Jenner. So the views expressed by your brother in the letter of November 8 came to you as a complete surprise?

Mr. Oswald. Yes, sir; with the qualification that this is what I expected after reading the newspapers.

Mr. Dulles. May I ask one question there.

When your brother left, after that short stay following his service in the Marine Corps, did you know that he was going to Russia—did he say anything to you about going to Russia at that time?

Mr. Oswald. No, sir; he did not.

Mr. Jenner. What did he say to you as to his plans?

Mr. Oswald. That he was going to New Orleans, Louisiana, to visit my Aunt Lillian.

Mr. Jenner. Your Aunt Lillian whom?

Mr. Oswald. Murret.

Mr. Jenner. The family you identified yesterday—the Murret branch of your family?

Mr. Oswald. I don't recall identifying them.

Mr. Jenner. There was one occasion yesterday.

Mr. Oswald. All right. Yes, sir; that is correct. And that he was——

Mr. Jenner. That is an Aunt on which side—your father's or mother's?

Mr. Oswald. My mother's side. And that he was going to visit with them, and at the same time find a job in New Orleans, and make his home in New Orleans, Louisiana.

Mr. Jenner. Did he give you any indication at any time during his stay—this was in Fort Worth?

Mr. Oswald. Yes, sir.

Mr. Jenner. During his stay in Fort Worth, upon his return and discharge from the service, and while he was there, that gave you any indication whatsoever of any intention on his part to leave the country?

Mr. Oswald. No, sir; none whatsoever.

Mr. Jenner. Whether he was going to go to Europe, Russia, or anywhere else?

Mr. Oswald. No, sir. The only information he gave me was that he was going only to New Orleans, Louisiana, from Fort Worth, Texas.

Mr. Jenner. Did you spend a good deal of time with him while he was in Fort Worth, Texas, in this interim period?

Mr. Oswald. Approximately one day out of the two or three days he was there.

Mr. Jenner. Are you suggesting that most of your contact with him during this period was on one of those days, or that the total amount of time that you spent with him during that period aggregated one day?

Mr. Oswald. I believe, sir, that I at least talked to him on the telephone on one day, and then the next day he spent the day at our home.

Mr. Jenner. And that is the day that you went off hunting, which you testified about yesterday?

Mr. Oswald. Yes, sir; that is correct.

Mr. Jenner. And never during any of the contact that you had with him did he imply or state directly that he had any contemplation of a trip which would take him out of the United States?

Mr. Oswald. That is correct.

Mr. Dulles. You didn't know about his having applied for a new passport?

Mr. Oswald. No, sir, I did not know he applied for any passport.

360 Mr. Jenner. During the day that he visited you, did your mother visit at your home on that day?

Mr. Oswald. No, sir; she did not.

Mr. Jenner. At any time during the period between his discharge from the Marines and his arrival in Fort Worth, and his departure, was there any occasion on which both you, your mother, and your brother Lee were together?

Mr. Oswald. None that I recall, sir.

Mr. Jenner. Was there any discussion between you at any time during that period of the reason, if any special reason, for his discharge from the Marine Corps, earlier than he might have been discharged in normal course, which as I understand would have been in December of that year?

Mr. Oswald. I believe, sir, we had a brief discussion on that.

Mr. Jenner. Who initiated it?

Mr. Oswald. I feel certain like I did.

Mr. Jenner. And what did you do? Ask him—just tell us what you asked him. And why you were curious, if you were.

Mr. Oswald. To the best of my memory, I asked him—because I was aware of his approximate date of discharge, his regular date of discharge, or release from the service, and I asked him why he was discharged or released earlier than that date. And his reply was that mother had written the Red Cross and requested that he be released earlier.

Mr. Jenner. Written the Red Cross?

Mr. Oswald. Yes, sir. I also——

Mr. Jenner. Did he say why she had written requesting that he be released earlier?

Mr. Oswald. No, sir, not to my recollection.

Mr. Jenner. He just said mother had written the Red Cross asking that he be released earlier.

Mr. Oswald. Yes, sir.

Mr. Jenner. That is all he said?

Mr. Oswald. Yes, sir.

Mr. Jenner. He didn't elaborate on that?

Mr. Oswald. No, sir.

Mr. Jenner. And you didn't inquire of him beyond that?

Mr. Oswald. No, sir, I did not.

Mr. Jenner. When had you last seen your mother prior to this occasion?

Mr. Oswald. May I have his release date, please?

Mr. Liebeler. September 11, 1959.

Mr. Oswald. I would say approximately three or four months earlier.
Mr. Jenner. Three or four months. That would be sometime in May?
Mr. Oswald. Approximately, yes, sir.
Mr. Jenner. 1959?
Mr. Oswald. Yes, sir.
Mr. Jenner. Had you talked with her in the interim period?
Mr. Oswald. Yes, sir; I had.
Mr. Jenner. How long prior to his return to Fort Worth on September 11 or 12, 1959, had you talked to her?
Mr. Oswald. I do not remember, sir.
Mr. Jenner. Well, could you give us an estimate, that is in terms of whether it was weeks or several months?
Mr. Oswald. I can give an estimate of several months.
Mr. Jenner. Several months?
Mr. Oswald. Yes, sir.
Mr. Jenner. Your mother was then residing in Fort Worth, was she not?
Mr. Oswald. That is correct.
Mr. Dulles. Was she hospitalized at this period?
Mr. Oswald. No, sir, she was not. Not to my knowledge.
Mr. Jenner. Were you aware of her state of well being?
Mr. Oswald. Yes, sir.
Mr. Jenner. During the four month period?
Mr. Oswald. Sir? During the four month period?
Mr. Jenner. You say for three to four months prior to September 11, you361 had not seen your mother, that for several months prior to that, you had not talked with her.

I take it from that that you were not aware of her well being, whether she was in good health, poor health, or otherwise?
Mr. Oswald. During the approximate date of three or four months prior to Lee's release from the service, I was aware that she did have an accident at her place of employment there in Fort Worth, at which time, if memory serves me correct, something fell on her, on her face, and injured her nose.

I was aware from conversations with her at that time that she was consulting or going to various doctors. And she told me at that time——
Mr. Jenner. Excuse me. Having reached that point—is that how you first discovered that your mother had suffered an accident? You say she told you.
Mr. Oswald. Yes, sir; that is correct.
Mr. Jenner. And I take it, then, that you had not talked with her for several months prior to September 11 nor seen her before sometime, or later than sometime in April of 1959, that this telephone conversation must have taken place several months prior to September 11. Am I correct about that?
Mr. Oswald. It was not a telephone conversation, sir.
Mr. Jenner. You saw her?
Mr. Oswald. Yes.
Mr. Jenner. In the month of April '59?
Mr. Oswald. Approximately that date.
Mr. Jenner. And did you visit her, or did she visit you?
Mr. Oswald. I saw her at her place of employment.
Mr. Jenner. And how did that come about?
Mr. Oswald. I do not remember, sir.
Mr. Jenner. Would it refresh your recollection if I recited some possibilities—that she called you and asked you to come to see her, that you desired to inquire of her, see if she was all right, or was it that you just happened to be in the downtown Fort Worth area, and you stopped by to see her, knowing where she was employed?
Mr. Oswald. I believe the latter would possibly be more accurate.

Mr. Jenner. Is that your best recollection at the moment?

Mr. Oswald. Yes, sir. She was not employed at that time at the downtown area of Fort Worth, but rather at a suburb store, Cox's Department Store.

Mr. Jenner. This is a shoe store?

Mr. Oswald. No, sir, this is just a large department store, from wearing apparel to toys, a full line store.

Mr. Jenner. How did you become aware she was employed there?

Mr. Oswald. I do not remember, sir.

Mr. Jenner. How long—did you know then how long she had been employed at Cox's Department Store?

Mr. Oswald. No, sir, I did not.

Mr. Jenner. How did you become aware of the fact she was so employed?

Mr. Oswald. I do not remember, sir.

Mr. Jenner. You have no recollection?

Mr. Oswald. No, sir, I do not.

Mr. Dulles. About how long was this after the accident, or was it after the accident?

Mr. Oswald. My recollection of that, sir—this was shortly after the accident. She was still employed there, even though I understand from our conversation that day that she had been off for a while—I don't know how long a period—and that she was still employed there. Because this is where I did see her, at her counter in this department store.

Mr. Jenner. On this occasion, when you stopped by to see her, she related to you an accident she had suffered—that was the first news you had of it?

Mr. Oswald. That is correct. Yes, sir.

Mr. Jenner. You had not known she was ill or what her state of well being was prior to that time?

Mr. Oswald. None that I remember, sir.

Mr. Jenner. Where is the Cox's Department Store located with respect to your place of business? I am seeking now distance, and the convenience of getting there.

Mr. Oswald. From my place of business at that time in Fort Worth this was approximately four or five miles west. I might further state, sir, it was approximately two miles from my home.

Mr. Jenner. Did you come from your home to her place of business or from work to her place of business?

Mr. Oswald. I believe I went from home to her place of business.

Mr. Jenner. Was this a week day, a working day?

Mr. Oswald. No, sir, I don't believe it was.

Mr. Jenner. That is not for you. Was it for her?

Mr. Oswald. It was for her, sir, not for me.

Mr. Jenner. I take it, then, it was a Saturday.

Mr. Oswald. I would believe that would be correct, sir.

Mr. Jenner. And has this discussion served to refresh your recollection or stimulate your recollection now as to why you went by to see her?

Mr. Oswald. No, sir; it has not.

Mr. Jenner. May I ask you this, sir?

When had you last seen your mother prior to this occasion that you visited her?

Mr. Oswald. I do not remember, sir. I would say, as we said before, several months.

Mr. Jenner. All right. That would be several more months, back into the winter time of 1959?

Mr. Oswald. '58, sir.

Mr. Jenner. Yes—'58.

Well, would it be back in the winter of '58, say January? Or could it have been?

Mr. Oswald. No, sir, not that long. We are talking, if I am correct, sir, approximately April of 1959. January of 1958 would be well over a year. It had not been that long.

Mr. Jenner. Well, then—I had said January '59, and you said several months.

Now, several months prior to April of 1959, would be or might be as far back as January of 1959, am I not correct?

Mr. Oswald. Yes, sir, it could be that far.

Mr. Jenner. And your present recollection is that it might have been that much of a period of time—sometime in January, 1959, to this occasion in April of 1959 when you had—you visited her at Cox's Department Store?

Mr. Oswald. Yes, sir; or possibly even longer.

Mr. Jenner. Possibly even longer than that. Back into 1958.

Mr. Oswald. Yes, sir.

Mr. Jenner. Could you give me your best recollection at the moment as to the last time you saw your mother in the year 1958?

Mr. Oswald. I cannot recall any specific time during the year of 1958 that I did see her.

Mr. Jenner. Would it be if at all quite infrequent?

Mr. Oswald. Yes, sir, quite infrequent.

Mr. Jenner. This leads me to put this general question to you, Mr. Oswald.

I take it that for some period of time in that area of time—that is '58, '59, and perhaps even back of that—your contact with your mother was quite limited?

Mr. Oswald. Yes, sir; that is correct.

Mr. Jenner. Over what period of time did that persist? Give us the broad picture first.

Mr. Oswald. I would say, sir, quite frankly that the original occurred prior to my joining the Marine Corps in 1952.

Mr. Jenner. And persisted thereafter?

Mr. Oswald. Persisted thereafter that I saw her only very infrequently.

Mr. Jenner. Did your joining the Marine Corps—was that stimulated in any respect by your relations with your mother, or your mother's with you?

363 Mr. Oswald. Partly, sir; it was.

Mr. Jenner. Would you state that, please?

Mr. Oswald. At the end of the school year of 1952, which was approximately May 29, 1952——

Mr. Jenner. You were then 17 years old, is that correct?

Mr. Oswald. 18 years old. I, of course, was still living at home. In approximately the middle part of June 1962 a friend of mine in Fort Worth and I decided to take a hitchhiking trip to Florida. We left Fort Worth in the middle of June, 1962, and we——

Mr. Dulles. '52?

Mr. Oswald. Yes, sir. In June of 1952 we left Fort Worth and traveled I believed as far as Gulfport, Mississippi. And this friend I was with—he did have a defect from birth on one foot that was starting to bother him. And we decided it was best to return to Fort Worth, by a different route than we originally left Fort Worth. We went from Fort Worth to Shreveport, New Orleans, and Gulfport, Mississippi.

Our return was Gulfport, Mississippi, New Orleans, Houston, Big Springs, Tex., and Fort Worth, Tex.

At that time I stayed at his home, with his mother and himself.

Mr. Jenner. Why?

Mr. Oswald. Because mother and I was having a disagreement.

Mr. Jenner. About what?

Mr. Oswald. About whether or not I was old enough to start my own life generally.

Mr. Jenner. That is whether you would depart the family home and live on your own?

Mr. Oswald. Yes, sir, and generally whether or not I had the right to start my own life in the manner that I wanted to.

Mr. Jenner. Were you unhappy with the manner and fashion of life that you had led up to that moment?

Mr. Oswald. Not in the manner or fashion, sir. I objected quite strongly to the apparent efforts of our mother to control me completely in all respects.

Mr. Jenner. Did that condition or relationship exist with respect to your brother, John Pic?

Mr. Oswald. I would say generally it would, sir.

Mr. Jenner. It did rather than it would?

Mr. Oswald. That it did, yes, sir—thank you.

Mr. Jenner. And was that a factor in his enlisting in the Coast Guard?

Mr. Oswald. It is not to my knowledge that it was.

Mr. Jenner. I take it you and John, then, had had, if I may use my own expression, difficulties in your relationships with your mother, particularly with reference to what you gentlemen thought as you reached age 18, as the right to be independent and lead your own lives?

Mr. Oswald. That is correct.

Mr. Dulles. Do you think that your brother, Lee Oswald, had the same feeling, that may have affected his joining the Marines?

Mr. Oswald. Based on my own personal experience, sir, I would reach that conclusion.

Mr. Dulles. You would?

Mr. Oswald. Yes, sir, I would.

Mr. Dulles. Thank you.

Did your mother know about this hitch-hiking trip, or did you just go off on the trip?

Mr. Oswald. I just went off on the trip, sir.

Mr. Jenner. Without advising her?

Mr. Oswald. Yes, sir, that is correct.

Mr. Jenner. Did you get in touch with her upon your return to Fort Worth?

Mr. Oswald. No, sir; I did not. I would say this. I did attempt to call her before I left Fort Worth on this trip, and there was no answer at home.

Mr. Jenner. All right. Now what led us back along this trail was the conversation you had with your brother Lee when he was discharged from the Marines364 on September 11, 1959, and his statement to you that he had an early discharge because your mother had written a letter to the Red Cross.

Mr. Oswald. That is correct.

Mr. Jenner. And then you saw her in April, and that was the last time you saw her prior to seeing your brother on his discharge from the Marines?

Mr. Oswald. That is correct.

Mr. Jenner. Now——

Mr. Dulles. Could I ask one question there.

Do you know whether your brother stimulated this letter from your mother with regard to early discharge, or do you think she did this on her own, or don't you know?

Mr. Oswald. It is my understanding, sir, that she had originated the request to the Red Cross.

Mr. Jenner. And that understanding is based on what?

Mr. Oswald. Just a general feeling that I had at that time.

Mr. Jenner. Was it induced also by discovering from your brother that your mother had written a letter to the Red Cross?

Mr. Oswald. I am sure it was, sir. And I might add I pointed out to Lee why did you accept this early discharge, since he only had a few months more, I believe it was, to go. Because it had been my experience in the service that when I ran across somebody who, for one reason or another, was going to get out a little bit early, I understood that they perhaps were subject to recall for that period at a later date, or something along that line. And I thought it was unwise.

Mr. Jenner. Is this what you said to him?

Mr. Oswald. Yes, sir. I pointed out—I felt like since it was to be under the regular enlistment period very shortly thereafter, I believe September 11, 1959, that it would have been the wise thing to stay in.

Mr. Jenner. What did he say to that?

Mr. Oswald. I do not recall, sir.

Mr. Jenner. You were living in Fort Worth, married, and still you were having substantially little contact with your mother, is that correct?

Mr. Oswald. That is correct.

Mr. Jenner. Would you explain to the Commission the reasons for that, the conditions which brought that about?

Mr. Oswald. After my marriage to Vada M. Oswald, my mother on a number of occasions—I say a number—perhaps three or four occasions—made it quite difficult for my wife and myself when we were in her presence at her apartment there in Fort Worth.

Mr. Jenner. Now, please, Mr. Oswald—when you say your mother made it quite difficult, give us some examples. What do you mean by "made it quite difficult"?

Mr. Oswald. Generally, sir, it was the continuation that, even though I was married and apparently able to take care of myself and start my own family, she certainly wanted to—my mother certainly wanted to—still control my thinking, my actions, and my wife's actions.

Mr. Jenner. Can you give us one specific example?

Mr. Oswald. Sir, I cannot recall any specific examples.

Mr. Jenner. Indicate the nature of those incidents.

Mr. Dulles. Had she objected to your marriage?

Mr. Oswald. I don't believe she did, sir. At least I do not recall any time that she ever stated that, any objections to my marriage.

Mr. Jenner. Did you have the feeling that she objected?

Mr. Oswald. Yes, sir, to some extent I did.

Mr. Jenner. Did you have a conversation with her about your becoming married before you became married?

Mr. Oswald. Yes, sir, I did.

Mr. Jenner. And did she—what views did she express in that connection?

Mr. Oswald. I believe, sir, that would be generally that I was leaving her alone, that both Lee and John at this time were in the service, and she would be alone, and that she would like for me to live with her, that I would stay with her.

Mr. Jenner. When was your marriage again, please?

Mr. Oswald. I have never stated it before, sir. It was in November—November 20 or 21, 1956.

Mr. McKenzie. Off the record.

(Discussion off the record.)

Mr. Jenner. The question has been asked of you as to the date of your marriage.

Mr. Oswald. This was in November 1956, sir.

Mr. Jenner. Had you been courting your present wife prior to that time?

Mr. Oswald. Yes, sir.

Mr. Jenner. Was your mother acquainted with her?

Mr. Oswald. Yes sir; she was.

Mr. Jenner. Did she—did her objections to your marriage, in addition to those you stated—were there any personalities in the sense of her objecting to your fiance?

Mr. Oswald. None that I recall, sir.

Mr. Jenner. Did you have any feeling that there was any personality in the sense of objection on her part, or lack of approval of your fiance?

Mr. Oswald. If I might say, sir, I feel sure there was, and in my mind right now—I can think of really no one that she ever approved of to the extent of my friend, either boys or girls.

Mr. Jenner. Was that also true of your brother, John Pic? And I will also ask you about Lee Harvey.

Mr. Oswald. John very seldom, if memory serves me correct, ever brought any of his friends over to the house, to meet mother.

Mr. Jenner. Presented them to mother, you mean?

Mr. Oswald. Presented them to mother.

Mr. Jenner. Was that his choice?

Mr. Oswald. I would say so now that I believe it would have been his choice.

Mr. Jenner. He preferred not to?

Mr. Oswald. This would be my assumption, that he preferred not to.

Mr. Jenner. Not presenting his friends to your mother?

Mr. Oswald. Yes sir; that is correct.

Mr. Jenner. Would you answer the same question as to Lee, as to whether he brought his friends to your home?

Mr. Oswald. Yes, sir; I believe he did. He quite frequently played around the house with friends there in the neighborhood.

Mr. Jenner. They were children, however, in the immediate neighborhood?

Mr. Oswald. Yes, sir; that is correct.

Mr. Jenner. He is five years younger than you.

Mr. Oswald. Yes, sir. He would have been 13 in 1952, this period we are talking about.

Mr. Jenner. We are interested in this matter of the antipathy existing between you and John on the one hand and your mother on the other. Had that gone on for sometime? In order that I don't violate the same thing that I raise with you occasionally, let me take you back to the military school days, or to Bethlehem Orphanage. Did a measure of antipathy exist at that time?

Mr. Oswald. No, sir; I don't believe it did.

Mr. Jenner. When did it really arise in any marked degree?

Mr. Oswald. I believe after her divorce from Mr. Ekdahl.

Mr. Jenner. That was in June 1948.

Mr. Oswald. Yes, sir. And from the time that we moved to the Young Street address in Fort Worth.

Mr. Jenner. At or about that time?

Mr. Oswald. Yes, sir.

Mr. Jenner. Would you refresh my recollection as to when that was? Was that in 1948?

Mr. Oswald. Yes, sir; it was.

Mr. Jenner. Would you please indicate how that antipathy or that change was evident? What change of attitude was there, either on the part of you boys, or on her part, or on the part of all of you?

Mr. Oswald. Perhaps, sir, for the first time in any period, all of us were together. And perhaps, sir—I say perhaps this would be correct—she did not366 know myself and my older brother John at that particular time to any extent.

Mr. Jenner. You had been away at school pretty much?

Mr. Oswald. That is correct.

Mr. Jenner. But you had been home for three months in the summertime?

Mr. Oswald. That is correct. But still, searching my own mind, I certainly felt this way at that time. And John and I were not accustomed to her. Certainly I cannot speak for John. But for myself, on that point, I would say we were not accustomed to her. We had become—there again I say we—John and I—I feel like I certainly had become more disciplined and used to being disciplined by men, and not used to having a woman around the house. I believe this was perhaps my feeling at that time.

Mr. Jenner. All right. Now, if we can return to the events of April 1959, did your mother appear to you to have been injured?

Mr. Oswald. Yes, sir; she did.
Mr. Jenner. What evidence was there of her injury?
Mr. Oswald. There appeared to be a little swelling in the upper part of the nose.
Mr. Jenner. Any scratch or other skin break?
Mr. Oswald. No, sir; none that I recall.
Mr. Jenner. Did you form an opinion at that time as to whether her injury was major or minor?
Mr. Oswald. I asked her about it, or she volunteered the information of how the accident occurred, and that she had been seeing doctors, and so forth. And I did recall her stating to me that she had been to either two or three doctors, and none of them had said anything was wrong with her, and then she was insisting that there was definitely something wrong, and she was continuing to see other doctors.
Mr. Jenner. Had that sort of thing occurred prior thereto, in which your mother felt that she was ill and she went to physicians, and the physicians indicated otherwise?
Mr. Oswald. Not to my knowledge, sir.
Mr. Jenner. She was not chronic in that respect?
Mr. Oswald. No, sir, not to my knowledge.
Mr. Dulles. Was she hospitalized at any time in connection with this injury?
Mr. Oswald. Not to my knowledge, sir.
Mr. Dulles. Did she have to give up her work for a period of time, or did she continue working?
Mr. Oswald. I believe she did miss a short period of time when the accident occurred.
Mr. Dulles. Thank you.
Mr. Jenner. But she was at work on the day you visited her?
Mr. Oswald. Yes, sir, that is correct.
Mr. Jenner. Were you forewarned that your brother was returning from the service earlier than he was scheduled to return?
Mr. Oswald. No, sir, I don't believe I was.
Mr. Jenner. Were you forewarned that he was returning at all at this particular time—that is, on or about the 11th of September, 1959?
Mr. Oswald. If I may take a moment, please, sir.
Mr. Jenner. Yes, sir.
Mr. Oswald. No, sir, I was not aware that he was being released from the service earlier.
Mr. Jenner. Had you received any communication from him prior to his return—that is a communication that was reasonably near the time of his return?
Mr. Oswald. The only one that I have a record of, sir, is a letter dated—postmarked June 6, 1959, at Santa Ana, California, addressed to me at my Fort Worth address of 7313 Davenport, return address, Pfc. L. H. Oswald, Santa Ana, California. The letter itself is undated.
Mr. Jenner. You have made reference, Mr. Oswald, to a letter you received in an envelope postmarked June 6, 1959, from your brother. You have the original of that letter before you?
Mr. Oswald. Yes, sir; I do.
367 Mr. Jenner. Now, that letter—did you receive in addition to this letter until September 11, 1959, any other letter from your brother?
Mr. Oswald. Not that I can recall, sir, or that I have record of.
Mr. Jenner. Now, this letter in the third paragraph reads, "Well, pretty soon I will be getting out of the Corps, and I know what I want to be and how I am going to be it, which I guess is the most important thing in my life"—"in life." Have I read it correctly?
Mr. Oswald. You have, sir.
Mr. Jenner. Did you respond to that letter?
Mr. Oswald. Not to my recollection did I respond to the letter, sir.

Mr. Jenner. Now, when your brother was mustered out, on or about September 11, 1959, did you have a discussion with him with respect to this subject matter—that is what he wanted to be in life, and how he was going to go about it?

Mr. Oswald. No, sir, I did not—to this extent. He did, of course, indicate to me that he wanted to go to New Orleans, Louisiana, and live and find a job there, and he did not indicate what type of job or what type of work he wanted to do.

Mr. Jenner. For the purpose of the record, Mr. Chairman, this letter has been identified and is in evidence as Commission Exhibit No. 296.

How did you learn that your brother was in Fort Worth, upon his being mustered out of the Marines?

Mr. Oswald. I believe, sir, he called me on arrival at Fort Worth.

Mr. Jenner. That was the first notice or knowledge that you had that he had been discharged?

Mr. Oswald. I believe that is correct.

Mr. Jenner. Is that correct?

Mr. Oswald. Yes, sir.

Mr. Jenner. And his call to you was the first notice or knowledge you had that he was in Fort Worth?

Mr. Oswald. Yes, sir, that is correct.

Mr. Jenner. It necessarily follows, and I take it it is a fact, that your mother had not called you to advise you that he was being discharged or would be discharged at or about that time?

Mr. Oswald. Not that I can remember, sir.

Mr. Dulles. Might I ask you at this point whether your brother ever talked to you about his experience in the Marines. Did he tell you anything about that, give you any incidents? I think you only had one day—that would have taken place on that one day, between the three or four days between his return and going off again.

Mr. Jenner. Or may I add, Mr. Chairman, any correspondence he had in the Marines, and any leaves.

Mr. Dulles. We have no letters, have we, from the witness?

Mr. Jenner. No, but I thought there might possibly be some.

Mr. Dulles. I don't want to interrupt, but it seemed to me to fit in at this particular point.

Mr. Oswald. I do not recall, other than general discussion, about the Marine Corps. I recall—and I believe this was on his leave in 1958, when we discussed this—I had asked him did he know any of my drill instructors, and I at the time recalled a senior drilling instructor at Camp Pendleton, by the name of Sgt. Cobie. And he stated he did not. However, he did run across, while he was in boot camp, some other drill instructor, but he could not recall his name, who stated he recalled me, or asked him one day did he have a brother that had been in the Marine Corps a few years before. He said yes, he had. And apparently this man did remember me, because he asked was I the right guide in that platoon. And my brother Lee did not know that I was. I do recall that conversation.

Mr. Jenner. Did you have any other conversation with him or any correspondence from him in which the subject matter of his career in the Marines was discussed, or to which allusion was made?

Mr. Oswald. I certainly received other letters during the course of his enlistment in the United States Marine Corps. I do not recall any specific instance368 that reflected what his opinion was of the Marine Corps, nor that at any time I remember did he refer to any happenings or incidents while he was in the Marine Corps that perhaps might upset him, or might have made him happy.

Mr. Jenner. Nothing either way?

Mr. Oswald. No, sir.

Mr. Jenner. Completely bland in that respect?

Mr. Oswald. Yes, sir.

Mr. Dulles. Do you recall whether any of those letters are available now? Do you have those letters?

Mr. Oswald. No, sir; I believe I do not have those. I say I believe I do not. I have looked for just everything that I could possibly find on Lee's life, and letters and so forth, and I have not run across any others.

Mr. Jenner. I was about to ask you that. You have made a thorough search?

Mr. Oswald. Yes, sir; I have.

Mr. Dulles. If you should find them, you will make them available to us, will you not?

Mr. Oswald. Certainly, sir.

Mr. Dulles. Thank you.

Just one more question on that, if I may. I would gather that the correspondence you had during his stay in Russia was more voluminous than while he was in the Marine Corps, from what you tell me.

Mr. Oswald. Yes, sir; it certainly was. There was certainly a larger flow of letters from him, and from me to him, at this time than there was during his stay in the United States Marine Corps.

Mr. Dulles. Thank you.

Mr. Jenner. So while he was in Russia, he wrote you considerably more often, at least after the first year, I guess it was, or nine months, than he had theretofore?

Mr. Oswald. No, sir. If I might there again refer to the letters from Russia received from Lee Harvey Oswald and placed in evidence before this Commission, when he notified us in 1959 that he was no longer going to write or contact us, and did not want us to contact him in any way, it was until April of 1961 before I heard from him again, which was, of course, a period of time after one year.

Mr. Jenner. Had you written him in the meantime?

Mr. Oswald. No, sir; I did not.

Mr. Jenner. Did you know where he was in the meantime—that is, any particular town or city in Russia?

Mr. Oswald. No, sir; I did not.

Mr. Dulles. And you had the impression that he did not want you to write to him at that time?

Mr. McKenzie. Mr. Dulles, he says that in the letters.

Mr. Jenner. Yes—one of these letters I am about to examine him about so states. That is correct, is it not?

Mr. Oswald. That is correct.

Mr. Jenner. I take it, then, however, that in contrast, commencing with the letter in 1961, April I believe you said it was—from that time forward, there was, by comparison, a considerable number of letters, and a larger volume of correspondence than you had ever had from your brother?

Mr. Oswald. Yes, sir, there was a continuous flow. Realizing the period that it would take to make a complete cycle of the exchange of one letter to another, of approximately two weeks—the letters were quite regular.

Mr. Jenner. And this had not been the pattern even in prior years.

Mr. Oswald. No, sir; it was not.

Mr. Jenner. When he was in the Marine Corps, or when you were in the Marine Corps?

Mr. Oswald. No, sir; it was not.

Mr. Jenner. Confirmatory of that, Mr. Oswald, I note in Commission Exhibit No. 296, is the last paragraph which reads, "I know I haven't written in a long time. Please excuse me. Well, there really isn't too much news here. But I would like to hear from you and the family. Write soon. Your brother, Lee".369 I take it from that that there had been—this was the first communication you had had from him, as he says, in a long time.

Mr. Oswald. Yes, sir, that is correct.

Mr. Jenner. Does your memory serve you sufficiently now to define more clearly the period to which he refers as "a long time"?

Mr. Oswald. I would say in between the leave in 1958, and his letter received, postmarked in June 1959, I would not have received over two or three letters.

Mr. Jenner. His leave in '58 was when, again, please?

Mr. Oswald. I recall this to be in the early fall of the year—perhaps September.

Mr. Jenner. All right. Directing your attention now back to the letter of November 8, 1959, which is Commission Exhibit 294, I will ask you this: Is this the first letter you received from him from Russia?

Mr. Oswald. That is correct.

Mr. Jenner. Is it the first communication of any kind, at least directly from or initially by him, that you had from him?

Mr. Oswald. Yes, sir, that is correct.

Mr. Jenner. This is, then, the first time you heard from him from the day he departed to go to New Orleans, as he had stated to you, for the purpose of finding employment?

Mr. Oswald. Yes, sir, that is correct.

Mr. Jenner. You testified yesterday that you responded to this letter—that is, Commission Exhibit 294, dated November 8, 1959. Is that correct?

Mr. Oswald. That is correct.

Mr. Jenner. You were unable to recall particularly well yesterday your letter in response to Commission Exhibit 294. Has the reading of the letter of November 26, 1959, which is Commission Exhibit 295, and your re-reading of the letter of November 8, Commission Exhibit 294, served to refresh your recollection as to the contents of your letter which you wrote in response to Commission Exhibit 294?

Mr. Oswald. To some degree, sir, it most certainly has.

Mr. Jenner. All right. Would you now, having had your recollection refreshed, relate to us as near as may be, if you are able to do so, your letter in response to your brother's letter, Commission Exhibit 294?

Mr. Oswald. Which was the letter of November 8—is that correct?

Mr. Jenner. That is correct.

Mr. Oswald. To the best of my recollection, in my response to his letter, I asked him why he went to Russia, and for what purpose he went to Russia. And I believe, sir, that is to the best of my ability, in the remembrance of my letter, that would be the only two questions that I asked him.

Mr. Jenner. Now, in the letter of November 8, he says, "Do you know, for instance, that I have wanted to do this for well over a year"—that is, go to Russia. I take it from your prior testimony that you had not known, either well over a year or even for an instant, that he had any intention of going to Russia.

Mr. Oswald. That is correct.

Mr. Jenner. Had the name Albert Schweitzer College ever been mentioned by your brother Lee prior to this time—that is, let us say, prior to the middle of September 1959?

Mr. Oswald. No, sir; it was not.

Mr. Jenner. He also states in this letter of November 8—makes the rhetorical question—"Do you know that I speak a fair amount of Russian, which I have been studying for many months". Had that subject matter ever come to your attention prior to his uttering it in the letter of November 8?

Mr. Oswald. No, sir; it had not.

Mr. Jenner. You did not know, up until this time, that your brother had been studying Russian while in the Marines?

Mr. Oswald. That is correct. And again if I may elaborate on that, I was not aware that he ever studied any foreign language.

Mr. Dulles. Did your brother ever talk to you about what he was reading during this period?

Mr. Jenner. Or at any time, during his school period?

370 Mr. Oswald. No, sir. Of course, I have seen him read various books. I never did see him read a book—unless the covers—or perhaps if I picked it up—it didn't indicate anything about communism or socialism. He did like to read. He read quite a bit. And by this, I have observed him to read anything from funny books to novels, to westerns, the full scope. He liked American history. I have seen him read American history a great deal.

Mr. Jenner. Was he a voracious reader? That is, did he read a great deal, devote much attention to reading?

Mr. Oswald. Yes, sir, he was what I would term an assiduous reader.

Mr. Jenner. I am directing your attention to his—oh, say, from age, let's say, nine or ten to the time he enlisted in the Marines—maybe we better go back a little bit more, since you were away. I would like to cover his youth up to the time he enlisted in the Marines. Is that the period of which you speak?

Mr. Oswald. No, sir; I do not. I speak of a later period—my visit to New Orleans after I received my discharge from the Marine Corps.

Mr. Jenner. And before he enlisted in the marines?

Mr. Oswald. Yes, sir; before he enlisted in the Marine Corps. And of his moving to Fort Worth.

Mr. Jenner. Fix the time.

Mr. Oswald. With mother—in 1955.

Mr. Jenner. On these occasions you observed him reading assiduously?

Mr. Oswald. Yes, sir.

Mr. Jenner. And you had an opportunity, and you embraced it to some extent, just out of curiosity if nothing else, of observing the nature and character of the literature and the subject matter of the literature he was reading?

Mr. Oswald. Yes, sir; that is correct.

Mr. Jenner. And it is of the nature and the subject matter you already stated?

Mr. Oswald. Yes, sir.

Mr. Jenner. During any of that period, and any observation you ever made whether then or prior thereto, had you noticed him or seen any books—he uses the expression "Marxism", communism—or any books or works, or pamphlets of that nature?

Mr. Oswald. No, sir, I did not. I did not at any time observe him reading or have in his possession any type of pamphlet or book, should I say, of a political nature.

Mr. Jenner. Even American politics?

Mr. Oswald. American politics, of course—American history, of course, would go into some degree of American politics.

Mr. Jenner. I think you are probably right. But other than American history.

Mr. Oswald. No, sir, I did not observe him.

Mr. Jenner. Now, your brother states in this letter of November 8, the United States was a country that he hated. Taking the whole letter, we would like to have you state what your reaction to the letter was when you received it and read it, in view of the rather severe things he says, and startling things he says in this letter.

Mr. Oswald. If I may, sir, refer to my testimony yesterday in relation to this letter, and my reactions then, I thought more along that line. I have not come up with any other conclusions where my thinking as to my reaction at the time I received the letter—other than it was something that I expected, due to what I had read in the newspapers prior to receiving the letter of November 8, 1959.

Mr. Jenner. Your shock, if I may call it such, had been conditioned——

Mr. Oswald. To some degree it had; yes, sir.

Mr. Jenner. In other words, then, the letter, when you did receive it, with these utterances in it, did not surprise you?

Mr. Oswald. I feel, perhaps, if anything would have surprised me that did not appear, to my recollection, would be the statement "I will never return to the United States, which is a country I hate," particularly the latter part of that statement—"which is a country I hate."

Mr. Jenner. That did shock you despite your having read the newspaper clippings or articles?

371 Mr. Oswald. Yes, sir, I feel certain that it did.

Mr. Jenner. And in your response to your brother's letter, did you advert to that particular portion of his letter? To the best of your recollection?

Mr. Oswald. Yes, sir—I was just making a note on that. I didn't realize you would ask me that so soon. I do believe I asked him why he hated the United States.

Mr. Jenner. Now, have you given us—exhausted your recollection as to the content of the letter you wrote in response to the letter of November 8, Commission Exhibit 294?

Mr. Oswald. Yes, sir; I feel I have.

Mr. Jenner. Well, now, let us turn, if we might, to Letter No. 26, which is Exhibit 295, an eight-page letter.

Mr. Oswald. All right, sir.

Mr. Jenner. Mr. Chairman, to summarize this letter, if I may, for you, it is an eight-page letter. Lee Harvey Oswald sets forth in it extensively his philosophies, what they purport to be as of that time, the reasons why he has decided to defect to the Soviet Union.

He complained about the economic system in the United States.

Mr. Dulles. System?

Mr. Jenner. System—which he stated exploited all of its workers.

He complained of segregation and unemployment, and automation in the United States.

He stressed disapproval of American foreign policy, which he characterized as being one of imperialism. In framework, it is framed as a response partly to some questions that our present witness has posed in a letter, which Mr. Robert Oswald had written in response to the letter of November 8, such as a question as to why Lee Harvey Oswald and his fellow workers and communists would like to see the present capitalist system of the United States overthrown—he having made an indication to the witness in that respect.

Apparently in Robert's letter to Lee, he had couched it in terms of suggesting that apparently Lee Harvey Oswald thought he might have some advantage economically if he went to Russia, and Lee Harvey Oswald responded, "So you speak of advantages. Do you think that is why I am here, for personal material advantages? Happiness is not based on one's self, does not consist of a small home, of taking and getting. Happiness is taking part in a struggle where there is no borderline between one's own personal world and the world in general. I never believed I would find more material advantages at this stage of development in the Soviet Union than I might have had in the United States."

Mr. McKenzie. At this point, Mr. Chairman, I might also add, in connection with what Mr. Jenner has stated about this letter, that the letter appears, in answering questions that Robert may have posed in a previous letter to Lee Harvey Oswald—it appears to have been lifted in some respects out of a communist text, and it even appears to me—and this is pure supposition, that it could possibly have been written by someone else with Lee Harvey Oswald coming back in and adding other things to it. It is the longest letter received, consisting of some eight pages. A careful reading of the letter will show only one or two misspelled words, whereas in the other letters there are a number of misspelled words.

And I don't know what that adds or detracts from the record. But I do feel that there is a difference in the letters as you read all of them put together.

Mr. Dulles. I am glad you called that to our attention. It is an interesting observation.

Mr. Oswald. And I would like to, if I may, point out something I observed in between the letter of November 8, 1959, and the letter of November 26, 1959.

In the letter of November 8, 1959, towards the last paragraph on the last page, I quote, "I really don't see what we could talk about. If you want to send me money, that I can use. But I do not expect to be able to pay it back."

I now refer to the letter of November 26, 1959, on the last page, the second last paragraph, "I have no money problems at all"—underlined.

372 "My situation was not really as stable then as it is now. I have no troubles at all now along that line."

Mr. McKenzie. And, furthermore, he had moved from Room 233 in the Metropole Hotel to Room 201 in the Metropole Hotel. And marks on the letter of November 26th, "Note new room number."

Mr. Dulles. Could I get into the record here, just for clarification—when was this written in relation to his arrival in the Soviet Union? Do we have that on the record? Was it a month after? Was it before the other incident that has been described for the record, with regard to——

Mr. Oswald. If I may, sir; I believe I can answer that.

Mr. Jenner. I didn't want to hazard a guess. If you know, will you please state it?

Mr. Oswald. I believe Lee, as a matter of record, did arrive in the Soviet Union on October 13, 1959.

Mr. Dulles. Is it written then, roughly, a little less than a month and—a little over a month after his arrival—these two letters referred to?

Mr. Oswald. That is correct.

Mr. Jenner. I intended to draw your attention to that which you have already mentioned—that is, in the letter of November 8 he indicated that he would be pleased if you would send him some funds, whereas on the last page of the letter of November 26th he advises you that as far as funds are concerned—he is in good shape.

Mr. Dulles. And both of these letters were written, as I recall, before he was advised that he could not stay on in the Soviet Union the first time?

Mr. Jenner. That is correct, sir. They are written before he went to Minsk, as well.

Mr. Dulles. Thank you.

Mr. Jenner. Had you sent him any funds in the interim period?

Mr. Oswald. No, sir.

Referring to my testimony yesterday—at which time I replied to his letter of November 8, 1959, on his request for any money that I might send him, I stated to him I would gladly send him the necessary money for his return to the United States, and for that reason only.

I did not enclose any money in my answer.

Mr. Jenner. Now, that is an interesting factor about which I would like to inquire of you; also, as to its implication.

Later, your brother, as the correspondence we have now introduced in evidence discloses, desired to return to the United States. And he was having, according to the correspondence, some problem in raising the necessary funds to return to the United States.

Did he at any time write you requesting that you honor your letter in response to his letter of November 8th in which you said you would gladly send him money to return to the United States?

Mr. Oswald. No, sir; he did not request it directly. He had certainly indicated, as his letters do indicate, that he was having a little difficulty in raising the necessary funds to return to the United States. And I, in my reply to that letter, volunteered to raise the necessary funds to bring his wife and himself to the United States.

Mr. Jenner. Would you identify the particular letter to which you now refer?

Mr. Oswald. In reply to your question, sir, I am referring to the letter of February 15, 1962.

Mr. Jenner. Which, for the record, is Commission Exhibit 315.

Did you respond to that letter and offer to advance to him the funds necessary to bring about his return to the United States?

Mr. Oswald. Yes, sir; I did. And I also included an offer for him to stay with us on his return to the United States, he and his family, for any length of time that they so desired, until he was able to get settled himself.

Mr. Jenner. Did you ever receive from him a letter in which he responded directly to your offer to advance funds?

Perhaps I will put it this way. Have you produced all of the letters that you received from him while he was in Russia?

Mr. Oswald. To my knowledge this is all of the letters I received from him.

Mr. Jenner. Did you make it a practice during this period to keep, intentionally and deliberately keep, all letters that you received from him?

Mr. Oswald. Yes, sir; that was my intention.

Mr. Jenner. To the best of your knowledge you have produced all of those letters to the Commission?

Mr. Oswald. That is correct, sir.

Mr. Jenner. Did you ever report to your brother that it would be necessary for you to make a loan on your automobile in order to advance any funds to him?

Mr. Oswald. No, sir, I did not.

Mr. Jenner. Including particularly the $200 that you advanced to him when he returned in June of 1962?

Mr. Oswald. No, sir, I did not.

Mr. Jenner. Did you become aware at any time prior to November 22, 1963, that he made a representation to the New York welfare authorities that it would be necessary for you to make a loan on your automobile to advance the $200?

Mr. Oswald. No, sir, I have not.

Mr. Jenner. There was no discussion of that subject by him with you when he returned to Fort Worth and lived in your home, or thereafter?

Mr. Oswald. No, sir. This is the first knowledge I have of such a report.

Mr. Jenner. All right.

Now, returning to the letter of November 26—and keeping in mind, also, the letter—let's just stay with the letter of November 26th.

Prior to the time of the receipt of that letter, had your brother Lee ever in your presence uttered thoughts of that nature, or even spoken to you any thoughts of the nature contained in the letter of November 26th with respect to the United States, its economic system, Communist Russia, or countries of that character?

Mr. Oswald. No, sir; he did not.

Mr. Jenner. And what was your reaction to the letter of November 26, particularly those features of it dealing with his attitudes towards the United States and its political and economic and social system?

Mr. Oswald. Sir, I remember somewhat vividly my reply to him—my reply to his letter——

Mr. Jenner. You did reply to the letter of November 26th?

Mr. Oswald. Yes, sir.

Mr. Jenner. Would you please state what your reply was?

Mr. Oswald. I did reply to the letter of November 26, 1959, and it was—and I believe until this day remains to be the longest letter I ever wrote.

Mr. Jenner. All right—tell us about it.

Mr. Oswald. I answered all the questions as to—if I may refer to the first question.

"Do you remember the time you told me about the efforts of your milk company to form a union? Try to see why workers must form unions against employers in the United States."

I recall I did reply to that statement.

Mr. Jenner. What did you say?

Mr. Oswald. It was my opinion—and I am not anti-union or pro-union. I believe it should be taken on the basis of the individual companies. It was my opinion that I expressed to him at that time that in this country, the employees did have a right to vote yes or no whether or not they wanted a union, and in this particular instance, the union was voted out.

Mr. Dulles. Could we just have a moment's pause?

(Brief recess.)

Mr. Dulles. Will you proceed?

Is it all right to proceed?

Mr. Oswald. Yes, sir; please.

Mr. Jenner. You were reciting what you said in your letter of response to the letter of November 26.

Mr. Oswald. All right, sir, if I may pause a moment to locate the second question or some statement that perhaps I recall referring to directly in my 374 reply—I recall replying to the statement that was, that is contained, on the second page of the letter of November 26, to the latter part of this statement that I will quote from: "See the segregation, see the unemployment and what automation is. Remember how you were laid off at Convair?"

I am referring now to the last question of "Remember how you were laid off at Convair?"

Mr. Jenner. Yes.

Mr. Oswald. I believe I pointed out to him at that time that this was something I was aware of when I accepted the job at Convair in Fort Worth, Texas. It was a condition, perhaps an unspoken condition, because it was a government job in that when I was laid off, I did not have to go only to the government to look for employment but I was able to secure the type of employment that I was most interested in at that time or that he had a variety to choose from and that no one would say to me that, "You work here or there."

Mr. Jenner. Did you experience any bitterness in being laid off at Convair?

Mr. Oswald. No, sir.

Mr. Jenner. Resentful?

Mr. Oswald. No, sir; I do not.

Mr. Jenner. What was your reaction?

Mr. Oswald. My reaction since I have been laid off at Convair and when I was laid off at Convair I felt like it was the best thing that ever happened to me.

Mr. Jenner. When did that event take place?

Mr. Oswald. In August, 1957, sir.

Mr. Jenner. All right.

Proceed with your recollection of your reply to this letter.

Mr. Oswald. If I may, sir, continue to answer something along the question of how I felt or reacted to my layoff at Convair; the reason why I recall the date is because my daughter was born two or three days after I was laid off, and I knew I was going to be laid off before she was born and I did not tell my wife and I recall that quite vividly.

Thank you.

Mr. Jenner. I think I will ask you an additional question about that, if I may, please.

Mr. Oswald. All right, sir.

Mr. Jenner. Was there any discussion, at least in Lee's presence, regarding your being laid off at Convair and your attitude with respect thereto.

Mr. Oswald. No, sir; none that I recall.

Mr. Jenner. And where was he—let's see, 1957, he was in the Marines then.
Mr. Oswald. Yes, sir; that is correct.
Mr. Jenner. I take it then sometime along the line you had advised him that you were no longer with Convair.
Mr. Oswald. Yes, sir; I feel certain like I did.
Mr. Jenner. Perhaps you wrote him to that effect or you told him about it when he was on leave in 1958.
Mr. Oswald. I would feel like perhaps I wrote him about it.
Mr. Jenner. And to the best of your recollection did you indicate any resentment or bitterness in that regard?
Mr. Oswald. No, sir. As I have never been resentful to that or bitter about it.
Mr. Jenner. So that at least, as far as you can recall, any statement you made or any attitude you have with respect to your layoff which might have come to his attention, did not form a basis for his predicating the Convair comment, on which he might have predicated the Convair comment, in his letter of November 26?
Mr. Oswald. That is correct, sir.
Mr. Jenner. All right. Proceed.
Mr. Oswald. I also——
Mr. Jenner. Excuse me, if I asked you a similar line of questions with respect to the union question would your answer be the same?
Mr. Oswald. Yes, sir; It certainly would.
Mr. Jenner. You never expressed any dislike of unions. You never expressed to him, or in his presence, or members of your family, views that unions were exploited?
375 Mr. Oswald. No, sir; I did not.
Mr. Jenner. All right.
By the way, had there been any discussion in the course of your youth, as you boys grew up, expressions in your family of any of these attitudes that he is expressing in his letter of November 8 and his letter of November 26?
Mr. Oswald. No, sir. To my knowledge there was never any type of discussion that would reflect any of the statements or questions that he wrote in his letter of November 26, 1959.
Mr. Jenner. Would you say to the extent there were discussions among you, and your family life, that the contrary was expressed?
Mr. Oswald. I do not recall any discussions, sir, but if there was any discussion it would have been to the contrary.
Mr. Jenner. Your family was always a typical, loyal American family?
Mr. Oswald. That is correct, sir.
Mr. Jenner. That is, loyal to the Government of the United States and you thought well of it?
Mr. Oswald. Yes, sir.
Mr. Jenner. When I say, you, I mean all of the members of your family as far as you knew?
Mr. Oswald. Yes, sir; that is correct.
Mr. Jenner. All right.
Proceed with your recollection of your response.
Mr. Oswald. I refer to his statement in the letter of November 26 on the second page, "I can still see Japan and the Philippines and their puppet governments. More important, I can see the Americans in uniform, men who were there because they were drafted or because they were adventurers or unemployed in civilian life."
I referred to my own volunteering in the United States Marine Corps at that time, and I felt that nothing he pointed out there applied to my case, and I felt quite a few other men felt as I did, as to the reasons behind their joining the United States service.

Mr. Jenner. Had you expressed any dissatisfaction to him with your tour in the Marines, or was that subject discussed in family councils or visits on his part to Fort Worth?

Mr. McKenzie. May I for just a moment?

(Discussion off the record.)

Mr. Oswald. Would you repeat the question, I believe I had it; I want to be sure of it.

(The question was read.)

Mr. Oswald. I do not believe that at any time we discussed it. We might have mentioned my tour in the United States Marine Corps. He was very proud of my service record and it would so indicate that I conducted myself in the best tradition of the United States Marine Corps; not that I was any lily white, but I was never in any serious trouble and I progressed in rank in keeping with the period that I was in the United States Marine Corps.

Mr. Jenner. Had that thought been expressed, or at least that flavor left, with the members of your family?

Mr. Oswald. I feel that it was, particularly to Lee, because I——

Mr. Jenner. Would you elaborate on that, please; we are interested in that.

Mr. Oswald. Yes, sir. Because I feel very surely that the reason that Lee joined the United States Marine Corps was because of my service in the United States Marine Corps and he wanted to follow——

Mr. Jenner. And your reaction to it had been communicated by you to him?

Mr. Oswald. I feel like it was, sir.

Mr. Jenner. Many witnesses have a habit that you have when you feel like it was. Do you mean that you actually conveyed that thought to him?

Mr. Oswald. I believe I did, sir.

Mr. Jenner. All right.

Mr. Oswald. Thank you.

I believe I was stating that I believe that the reason that Lee joined the United States Marine Corps was to follow in my footsteps, in that same service, and frankly I believe that at that time in earlier years and later years that he 376 looked up to me, not only in that respect, but that eventually he wanted to follow in my footsteps.

I would say within the family relation that Lee and I were closer than Lee and mother or Lee and John during our entire lifetime. That if there was something that he was going to discuss with anybody, or say to anybody, within the family I would be the one that he would discuss it with.

I refer to his statement on the second page of the letter of November 26, 1959, "I will ask you a question, Robert, what do you support the American government for? What is the ideal you put forward. Do not say freedom because freedom is a word used by all people through all of time."

I did refer to the word "freedom" and I recall stating to him that the word "freedom" to me was something that was earned and not handed down.

I refer to the third page of the letter of November 26, 1959, and the brief statement, "America is a dying country."

I replied to him that perhaps, and I believe some great man said this statement at one time or the other, I do not recall who, that we were a sleeping giant, and that we were coming awake.

This was, of course, in reference to the Communist world.

Mr. Jenner. This was something you said in your letter?

Mr. Oswald. Yes, sir.

Mr. Jenner. All right.

Mr. Dulles. May I ask what is the date of this letter?

Mr. Jenner. It is in response to the letter of November 26.

Mr. Dulles. November 26, yes.

Mr. Oswald. I refer to the bottom of the page of the letter of November 26, "So you speak of advantages. Do you think that is why I am here for personal material advantages, happiness is not based on oneself, it does not consist of a small home of taking and getting."

I recall my reply to this series of questions as being—as to having that right to seek for oneself his own personal desires to the extent that the material advantages were something of a secondary nature, and was something of a reward for his efforts.

Mr. Jenner. While the witness is looking further, Mr. Chairman, this is a little tedious, but as counsel for the Commission, I suggest its importance and relevancy in that, if nothing else, it serves to demonstrate the response of the witness to the letter indicating the attitude of the Oswald family on these subjects and isolating these views to Lee Harvey Oswald.

Mr. Dulles. I think this is important, and the more I hear of this letter the more I get the impression that there was some help given in writing this letter.

Mr. Jenner. That is why I am spending so much time on it.

Mr. Dulles. Yes.

Mr. Jenner. With apologies to you, Mr. McKenzie, that is the only way we can go at it because we don't have the actual response itself.

Mr. McKenzie. Mr. Jenner, I commend you on the way that you are conducting this interrogation.

Mr. Jenner. Thank you.

Mr. McKenzie. Mr. Oswald, under no circumstances speculate on what you wrote in answer to these letters. State to the best of your recollection only what you did write, if you recall.

If you can't recall tell Mr. Jenner so.

Mr. Oswald. Yes, sir, this is what I have been doing, sir.

Mr. Dulles. In view of the importance of this letter of November 26 and certain other of these letters, as Chairman and in view of the absence of a number of my colleagues today for unavoidable reasons, I think it might be well to insert the entire letter in the record and possibly certain other letters on which you are going to interrogate the witness.

You see no objection?

Mr. McKenzie. None whatsoever, Mr. Chairman.

Mr. Dulles. I have in mind that other members of the Commission may not be able to read all of the exhibits but I think they should read these letters on which we are interrogating the witness.

377 Mr. McKenzie. Yes, sir.

Mr. Dulles. In order to get the full purport, flavor of this particular line of interrogation.

Mr. McKenzie. I couldn't concur more, Mr. Dulles.

Mr. Dulles. We will leave it then to your discretion with Mr. Rankin to decide what letters should go in, in connection with his testimony.

Mr. McKenzie. I might add in that regard, Mr. Chairman, that I have no objection, whatsoever to any or all of the letters going into the record.

Mr. Dulles. Thank you.

Mr. Jenner. They are already in the record. But you mean set forth in full in the record.

Mr. McKenzie. I would mark right now the spot in the record following the Chairman's remarks and my concurrence and, of course, Mr. Jenner's suggestion that the letter be in its entirety placed in the record, I would mark that place now so that it could go in at this spot.

Mr. Jenner. Also the letter of November 8. And November 26 letter.

Mr. Jenner. Proceed, Mr. Oswald.

Mr. Oswald. I do not recall any other statements that I would have replied to, or did reply to, in my reply to his letter of November 26, 1959.

Mr. Jenner. All right, sir.

Now, did you receive any direct response to your letter, and your next letter is Commission Exhibit No. 296, sometime during the summer of 1959, it is a short one-page letter.

Mr. Oswald. This is December, 1959, sir.

Mr. Jenner. No, it is in the summer of 1959, isn't it, or is that the one-page letter which you had written December 17, 1959.

Mr. Oswald. Yes, sir.

Mr. Jenner. And is that the next letter you received from your brother?

Mr. Oswald. That is correct, sir.

Mr. Jenner. Is there any reference in that letter to the response you made to the November 26 letter?

Mr. Oswald. No, sir. There is not.

Mr. Jenner. Did you receive any subsequent letter in which he made any direct response to your long letter which you wrote him in response to the letter of November 26?

Mr. Oswald. No, sir, he did not, and if I might say I wrote earlier and as a reminder to myself that I was concerned at the time I received the letter of December 17, 1959.

Mr. Jenner. That is Commission Exhibit 297.

Mr. Oswald. That Lee did not have time to receive my reply to his letter of November 26, 1959.

Mr. Jenner. I see.

Then the next letter you received, at least in the series you have produced, is May 5, 1961, a two-page letter, Commission Exhibit 298.

Mr. Oswald. Could I have that date again, please, sir?

Mr. Jenner. May 5, 1961.

Mr. Oswald. Yes, sir.

Mr. Jenner. He makes no response in that letter to your response to his letter of November 26.

Mr. Oswald. No, sir, he does not. Perhaps, sir, the only way that I can be aware that he received my letter in reply to November 26 letter, to his letter of November 26, 1959, I did enclose one photograph of my daughter Cathy Marie Oswald at the age of 2 years old in that letter.

Mr. Jenner. In your response to his letter of November 26?

Mr. Oswald. Yes, sir; and at a later date Lee was to tell me that he did keep this photograph, so he did receive my letter.

Mr. Jenner. Would you repeat what you just said, sir, or would you read it, Mr. Reporter?

(The reporter read the answer.)

Mr. Jenner. You said Lee was to tell you, did you mean by that expression that he actually acknowledged receipt of the photograph?

Mr. Oswald. Yes, sir, he did.

378 Mr. Jenner. Which leads you to believe necessarily then that he received your response to his letter of November 26.

Mr. Oswald. That is correct, sir.

Mr. Jenner. Did he state that he had received that photograph in a letter that he wrote you or was that orally after he returned to the United States?

Mr. Oswald. I believe this was orally, sir.

Mr. Jenner. After he returned to the United States?

Mr. Oswald. Yes, sir, that is correct.

Mr. Jenner. Now, returning to his short stay at Fort Worth upon his being discharged from the Marines, what do you recall, if anything, of any discussion respecting his financial status at that time, that is whether he was in funds and if so, what volume of funds.

Mr. Oswald. I was not aware of his financial situation at that time.

Mr. Jenner. Was it discussed?

Mr. Oswald. Not that I recall, sir.

Mr. Jenner. Did any member of the family, during that period of time, ever discuss with you, having in turn discussed that subject matter with Lee?

Mr. Oswald. No, sir, they did not.

Mr. Jenner. Did you ever have a conversation with your mother prior to November 22, 1963 respecting Lee's financial status at the period of time when he was immediately—right at the time he was discharged from the Marines?

Mr. Oswald. No, sir; I did not. I do not remember one.

Mr. Jenner. So that up to November 22, 1963, there was never any discussion in which you participated or which you overheard on that subject?

Mr. Oswald. That is correct, sir.

Mr. Jenner. Now, with respect to the remaining series of letters, were you ever advised while your brother Lee was in Russia how much money he was given or earned?

Mr. Oswald. While he was——

Mr. Jenner. Or he received?

Mr. Oswald. While he was in Russia employed?

Mr. Jenner. While he was in Russia.

Mr. Oswald. While he was in Russia.

Mr. Jenner. Either from his employment or by gift.

Mr. Oswald. Yes, sir; there is a reply in one of these letters that I received from Lee from Russia stating how much he was making while employed in Russia.

Mr. Jenner. The letter will, of course, be the best evidence of that. Did he say it in terms of dollars or in terms of rubles, what is your recollection?

Mr. Oswald. In both, sir. I believe he stated it in the words rubles and in parentheses in the amount of American dollars.

Mr. Jenner. I see, we will find that out.

Mr. Oswald. And I believe on a monthly basis.

Mr. Jenner. Did he ever write you as to whether he had received any money by way of gift from any agency in Russia?

Mr. Oswald. No, sir.

Mr. McKenzie. Mr. Jenner, I respectfully submit that the letters themselves would be the best evidence.

Mr. Jenner. You are undoubtedly correct and I will desist.

Did you have any discussion with him on that subject after he returned from Russia?

Mr. Oswald. No, sir, I did not.

Mr. Jenner. Or on the subject of his earnings in Russia?

Mr. Oswald. None that I recall, sir.

Mr. Jenner. Did you receive any packages or gifts from Russia while your brother was there?

Mr. Oswald. Yes, sir; I did.

Mr. Jenner. What did you receive?

Mr. Oswald. Well——

Mr. Jenner. And give the approximate times.

Mr. Oswald. There again, sir, there is a letter from Lee in Russia stating that he had sent a gift or gifts to us at my residence in Fort Worth, Tex. I379 recall that on two occasions we received gifts from Russia at my address in Fort Worth, Tex. I believe the first one consisted of Russian cigarettes, Russian candy, six place mats or six napkins that Marina had embroidered herself.

Mr. McKenzie. Or at least what they told you Marina had embroidered.

Mr. Oswald. Yes, sir. And also a Russian wooden doll, the type that pops open in the middle and has a smaller doll on the inside and so forth down the line until you end up with one approximately an inch high from one originating from one six or seven inches high. That was the first package that I recall receiving from Lee and his wife while they were in Russia.

Mr. Jenner. Approximately when was that?

Mr. Oswald. Prior to Christmas of 1961.

Mr. Jenner. There was a second occasion when you received a package?

Mr. Oswald. Yes, sir, that is correct.

Mr. Jenner. What was that?

Mr. Oswald. This was closer to Christmas of 1961.

Mr. Jenner. And it contained what?

Mr. Oswald. It contained one Russian children's book.

Mr. Jenner. In the Russian language or in English?

Mr. Oswald. In the Russian language, sir, and going by the cover of the book and as you open the book in the center section, a Russian rocket ship would unfold and be standing in the launch position, and was quite evident by the pictures, at least in the book, that this was a book for Russian children depicting the Russian efforts toward their space program.

Mr. Jenner. Do you still have that book?

Mr. Oswald. Yes, sir; I do. And there was also another children's book, and I believe this package only consisted of a present for Cathy Marie Oswald for Christmas, 1961 from her aunt and uncle, Lee and Marina.

Mr. Jenner. A child's gift?

Mr. Oswald. Yes, sir, and the second book was a child's coloring book, a Russian coloring book.

Mr. Jenner. Does that exhaust your recollection as to gifts you received from them or from Lee while they were in Russia?

Mr. Oswald. Yes, sir, it does.

Mr. Jenner. Did he ever send you a pair of boots?

Mr. Oswald. No, sir, he did not. And I might add we also still have the child's coloring book that was received at that time for Christmas, 1961.

Mr. Jenner. All right, sir.

Now, would you please relate to us everything that your brother Lee told you about hunting in Russia?

Mr. McKenzie. You mean other than in correspondence?

Mr. Jenner. I mean other than by the correspondence. I should precede that by the question did you have any conversation with him about hunting in Russia?

Mr. Oswald. Yes, sir, I did.

Mr. Jenner. And that occurred after he returned to the United States?

Mr. Oswald. Yes, sir.

Mr. Jenner. Fix the approximate date.

Mr. Oswald. Approximately the latter part of June, 1962.

Mr. Jenner. While he was residing in your home?

Mr. Oswald. That is correct, sir.

Mr. Jenner. What did he say? Excuse me, this occurred in your home?

Mr. Oswald. Yes, sir; it did.

Mr. Jenner. Was anyone present other than yourself and your brother?

Mr. Oswald. Perhaps Marina and my wife Vada. As I best remember the conversation, since our interest in hunting was mutual, that he had on two or three occasions gone bird hunting or duck hunting and that he had killed some birds and some ducks on two or three of these occasions that he had gone in, that he had only used a shotgun, that they were not allowed to have a rifle.

Mr. Jenner. Was there any discussion of that subject matter on any other occasion prior to November 22, 1963?

Mr. Oswald. I believe in his letters——

Mr. Jenner. No, discussions.

380 Mr. Oswald. Pardon me, no, sir; there was not, not that I recall.

Mr. Jenner. Did you have any discussion with him during the period from his return in June of 1962 up to November 22, 1963, of his membership in a gun club while he was in Russia?

Mr. Oswald. No, sir; I did not.

Mr. Jenner. Did any discussion occur between you as to his membership in any other group while he was in Russia, whether it was a gun club, a social club, a labor union or otherwise?

Mr. Oswald. None that I recall, sir.

Mr. Jenner. In one of the letters, your brother Lee asked you whether, to check to see if, the United States had any, lodged any charges against him.

Do you recall that?

Mr. Oswald. Briefly, yes, sir.

Mr. Jenner. What did you do when he made that request to you, if any?

Mr. Oswald. I recall replying to his letter and stated that to my knowledge, and I could see no reason why they would have any charges against him for going to Russia, because he was an American citizen, and he was free to do as he chooses as long as it was not harmful to the United States Government and I didn't feel like he had done anything harmful to the United States Government by going to Russia.

Mr. Jenner. Did you ever write in any of the letters that you wrote him, did you raise the question with him of whether he had in fact renounced or attempted to renounce his United States citizenship?

Mr. Oswald. I was advised that, at the time, that we became aware that Lee was in Russia by newspaper correspondents in Fort Worth, Tex., that the United States Embassy acting on their own accord, would not allow him to sign any final papers denouncing his United States citizenship. Whether he wanted to or not they were attempting to prevent him from doing this. I never did hear any more about that. Perhaps during the correspondence or on his return from Russia, this was certainly evident that he had not signed any final papers denouncing his United States citizenship.

Mr. Jenner. I take it from your response, sir, that you did not raise that matter with him in any letters that you wrote to him?

Mr. Oswald. Not to my recollection, sir.

Mr. Jenner. Did you have any discussion with him on the subject on his return to the United States?

Mr. Oswald. Possibly so, sir.

Mr. Jenner. Do you recall that distinctly at the moment?

Mr. Oswald. No, sir, I do not.

Mr. Jenner. Did your brother Lee raise again with you, following your response to his request that you investigate whether or not there were any other charges against him; did he raise again with you the question of whether you had made an investigation, whether there were charges?

Mr. McKenzie. When you say did he raise again——

Mr. Jenner. At any time subsequent thereto, that is apart from the correspondence which has been introduced in evidence.

Mr. McKenzie. There are several instances in the correspondence, Mr. Jenner, there are questions raised about this.

Are you talking about after he returned from—to the United States from the Soviet Union?

Mr. Jenner. Yes, sir; I am at the moment.

Mr. McKenzie. All right.

Mr. Oswald. No, sir; not to my recollection.

Mr. Jenner. When he returned to the United States and while he was living with you, was there or were there any occasions in which there was discussion of his trip back from Russia and the course they took in returning to the United States, the means and manner of return?

Mr. Oswald. Yes, sir; there was.

Mr. Jenner. Give us your recollection of what that discussion was and what your brother and/or Marina said to you and your wife Vada or either of them?

381 Mr. Oswald. I recall asking him how his trip was from Russia to New York City by boat. I asked him what route they had traveled, and he advised me then, that is as I believe he advised me in one of his letters, the first one, was to go from Minsk to Moscow and then from Moscow to Holland, I believe, to board a ship that touched at England, and from England to New York City.

Mr. Jenner. Did he or they——

Mr. Oswald. He.

Mr. Jenner. This is a conversation with him?

Mr. Oswald. Yes, sir, that is correct.

Mr. Jenner. Did you have any conversation with Marina on this subject or in her presence?

Mr. Oswald. Not that I recall, no, sir.

Mr. Jenner. But he did state specifically that they had gone to Moscow?

Mr. Oswald. Yes, sir.

Mr. Jenner. And from Moscow to where?

Mr. Oswald. To Holland, if my memory serves me correct, sir.

Mr. Jenner. Did he say, did he indicate, how they had traveled from Moscow to Holland, by what means of conveyance?

Mr. Oswald. No, sir, he did not.

Mr. Jenner. Was anything said about how long they stayed in Moscow before they took off for Holland?

Mr. Oswald. In this discussion, I do not recall that he did, sir.

Mr. Jenner. And did he say how long they stayed in Holland, if they stayed there at all?

Mr. Oswald. No, sir, he did not.

Mr. Jenner. But you do recall his stating specifically they touched England in the sense that the ship——

Mr. Oswald. Yes, sir; for supplies or for some other reason, it appeared not to be, I say appeared, I assume it was not a very long stay there and that they did not leave the ship.

Mr. Jenner. He did state that they did not leave the ship at that point?

Mr. Oswald. No, sir; this is an assumption on my part—the way he put it to me.

Mr. Jenner. And they proceeded from there directly to New York Harbor, New York City.

Mr. Oswald. Yes, sir; that is correct.

Mr. Jenner. By what means? And he did report that to you?

Mr. Oswald. Yes, sir.

Mr. Jenner. Did this series of letters you received in the early portion, period of his stay in Russia excite your suspicions as to whether he was or might be a Russian agent?

Mr. Oswald. If I understand the question correctly this was the early stay of his in Russia in 1959?

Mr. Jenner. Yes, sir, 1959 and let us say to the early part of 1961.

Mr. Oswald. No, sir.

Mr. Jenner. Did you have any occasion to discuss that subject during this period of time with your mother or she with you?

Mr. Oswald. Prior to his return in 1961 she did discuss this with me.
Mr. Jenner. All right.
Where did this discussion take place?
Mr. Oswald. If I may fix the date approximately, sir, if you could give me the date of her trip to Washington, D.C.
Mr. Jenner. You have me at a disadvantage because Mr. Liebeler has been called out and he can furnish that. I don't want to guess at it.
Mr. McKenzie. May I then ask if possibly the Chairman might recall?
Mr. Dulles. The date of that visit to Washington?
Mr. McKenzie. Yes, sir.
Mr. Dulles. No, I don't think I do.
Mr. McKenzie. Possibly Mr. Rankin might know.
Mr. Jenner. Our information was that that was January 26, 1961.
Mr. Oswald. Thank you, sir. If I may have, the question again, please.
(The question was read by the reporter.)
382 Mr. Jenner. Whether the suspicions, on the part of yourself or your mother, were that your brother was or might be an agent for the Russian Government.
Mr. Oswald. Pardon me, sir, I believe I misunderstood. I thought it was in reference to whether or not Lee might have been an agent of the United States Government.
Mr. Jenner. No. It was the Russian Government I asked about.
Mr. Oswald. I am sorry, sir. At no time was any discussion that I have been into indicated that in any way.
Mr. Jenner. Now, you have referred then to, or had in mind, a conversation with your mother as to whether your brother was an agent of the United States Government.
Mr. Oswald. Yes, sir; that is correct.
Mr. Jenner. And are you able to fix the time of that discussion now having been supplied with the date when your mother visited Washington?
Mr. Oswald. Approximately the spring of 1961.
Mr. Jenner. Several months following her visit to Washington in January, 1961.
Mr. Oswald. That is correct, sir.
Mr. Jenner. Where did that discussion take place?
Mr. Oswald. I believe this was a telephone conversation, sir.
Mr. Jenner. Did you call her or did she call you?
Mr. Oswald. She called me, sir.
Mr. Jenner. And you recognized her voice, did you?
Mr. Oswald. Yes, sir, I did.
Mr. Jenner. What did she say on the subject?
Mr. Oswald. That she told me briefly about her trip to Washington, and that she, as she put it, had seen various important people, and that she was reaching or coming to the conclusion that Lee was an agent of one sort or another for the United States Government.
Mr. Jenner. Did you respond to that?
Mr. Oswald. I do not recall, sir, that I did; if so, what my response might have been.
Mr. Jenner. You don't recall whether you responded, and if you did, you don't recall your response?
Mr. Oswald. That is correct, sir.
Mr. Jenner. All right, have you given us now all your conversations you had with your mother on the subject of whether your brother, that is up to November 22, 1963, as to whether your brother was or might have been an agent of the Government of the United States or an agent of any other government including that of Russia?
Mr. Oswald. Yes, sir, that is correct.
Mr. Jenner. As you received these letters, particularly the series of letters in 1961, up to the first of January, 1962, did there occur to you the thought that your brother was or might be an agent of the Russian Government?

Mr. Oswald. No, sir; it most certainly did not.

Mr. Jenner. And at any time thereafter up to November 22, 1963?

Mr. Oswald. No, sir; it has not.

Mr. Jenner. Did you have any contact with the State Department or did the State Department have any contact with you at any time while your brother was in Russia?

Mr. McKenzie. Mr. Jenner, I believe the record will show there was a previous telegram to Mr. Christian Herter who was Secretary of State at the time.

Mr. Jenner. Other than the telegram you testified about yesterday.

Mr. Oswald. No, sir.

Mr. Jenner. Did you have any conversations with your mother respecting her contacts, if any, with the State Department during the period of time your brother was in Russia?

Mr. Oswald. No, sir, I did not.

Mr. Jenner. Did you at any time prior to November 22, 1963, no, I will include that date, let's say at any time prior to December 1, 1963, have any view or suspicion that Marina Oswald was or might have been an agent of the Russian Government?

383 Mr. Oswald. No, sir; I did not.

Mr. Jenner. In the letter of July 14, 1961, being Commission Exhibit 301, your brother expresses or states, makes some derogatory comments respecting Russia. Is that the first information or knowledge that you had of any change of attitude on his part?

Mr. Oswald. No, sir, it was not.

Mr. Jenner. Indicate the prior event that gave you some suspicion in that connection.

Mr. Oswald. If I understand it correctly, sir, whether or not had I had any prior indication prior to receiving the letter of July 14, 1961, that Lee was becoming——

Mr. Jenner. Disenchanted.

Mr. Oswald. Disenchanted with the Russian way of life?

Mr. Jenner. Yes.

Mr. Oswald. When I received his first letter from Russia after a year or so of silence——

Mr. Jenner. Give the date of the letter.

There is a break between December 17, 1959 and May 5, 1961.

Is it the letter of May 5 of 1961?

Mr. Oswald. I am referring to the letter of May 5, 1961.

Mr. Jenner. All right. It is Commission Exhibit 299.

Mr. Oswald. It indicated to me, whether it so states in there or not, because he did start writing again that he was in fact disenchanted with the Russian way of life.

Mr. Jenner. This is the first letter you received after Lee had gone to Minsk, is it not?

Mr. Oswald. Yes, sir, that is correct.

Mr. Jenner. And it is the first letter you received following the undated letter of, in December, 1959, but that you have noted was received on the 17th of December, 1959.

Mr. Oswald. That is correct, sir.

Mr. Jenner. I take it then the subsequent letters heightened your impression of suspicion that he was becoming—either was completely or was becoming, disenchanted with Russia.

Mr. Oswald. Yes, sir, in his letter it certainly doesn't indicate that he was, but it was my opinion at that time and still is that he was then——

Mr. Jenner. After you had read that letter, meaning the letter of May 5, 1961, which is Commission Exhibit 299, you felt that, or you had the reaction that, he was becoming disenchanted with Russia?

Mr. Oswald. That is correct, sir.

Mr. Jenner. And that was later confirmed by subsequent letters in which he expressly stated——

Mr. McKenzie. Disenchantment.

Mr. Oswald. Yes, sir, that is correct.

(Discussion off the record.)

Mr. Jenner. There appears to be on some of the envelopes now in evidence some stamps. They are in Russian but they may indicate that they are stamps placed upon those envelopes by a censor, and we will now undertake to investigate that circumstance.

Mr. McKenzie. Would you like for me to tell you which ones?

Mr. Jenner. If you will give me the dates I will recite the exhibit numbers.

Mr. McKenzie. It is June 26, 1961.

Mr. Jenner. That is Commission Exhibit No. 300.

Mr. McKenzie. August 21, 1961.

Mr. Jenner. Is the envelope dated August 21?

Mr. McKenzie. Yes.

Mr. Jenner. Would you see if that contains a one-page letter; oh, yes, August 21, that is Commission Exhibit No. 303.

You need not do it.

Mr. McKenzie. And September 10, 1961.

Mr. Jenner. That is Commission Exhibit No. 305.

Mr. McKenzie. And I call the Commission's attention particularly to the word stamped on the envelope "recommende" for whatever it means.

Mr. Dulles. That is French.

Mr. Jenner. Would you please relate, Mr. Oswald, Marina's ability to speak or understand English at the time that she and your brother returned from Russia in June of 1962?

Mr. Oswald. Her ability to understand was far less than her ability to speak English words. I spoke to her on the telephone the night of June 13, 1962 from New York City, to my residence in Fort Worth, Tex., and her statement to me at that time was, "Hello, Robert." I replied but no answer, and Lee took the telephone over again.

Mr. Jenner. During the month they lived in your home, were you better able to form an opinion as to her ability to speak and understand English?

Mr. Oswald. I believe the best way to establish the degree of what she understood in English at that time and her ability to speak the English language would be very, very, very small, if anything at all.

Mr. Jenner. As to her facility in that regard—did her facility in that regard become better as the months and years wore on?

Mr. Oswald. Yes, sir.

Mr. Jenner. Was there any discussion which you overheard or with you, respecting her undertaking to study, learn to speak, English?

Mr. Oswald. Yes, sir; she most certainly wanted to learn to speak English at the time, and she was staying at my home in Fort Worth, Tex., and prior to their departure from Fort Worth, Tex., to Dallas, Tex., in the winter of 1962.

Mr. Jenner. What was your brother's attitude with respect to her desires in that respect?

Mr. Oswald. I do not recall him stating his desires in that respect either pro or con.

Mr. Jenner. You have no impressions on the subject either way?

Mr. Oswald. No, sir. I might have an impression, pardon me, that he wanted her particularly at the time we were staying, they were staying at my home in Fort Worth, Tex., to learn English.

Mr. Jenner. That was expressed in your presence during that period of time by him?

Mr. Oswald. Not in so many words, sir. It was perhaps implied, and he left me with the impression that he wanted her to learn English at that time or as soon as she possibly could, and I might add that on a number of occasions during the visit at my home in Fort Worth, Tex., that my daughter Cathy, with her childhood language in 1961, which would establish her age at 4 years old, would talk to her and it appeared that she would gather more English from Cathy than she would the adults in the family.

Mr. Jenner. Did the State Department or any agency of the United States, get in touch with you with respect to your supplying funds or the possibility of your supplying funds to your brother while he was still in Russia for the purpose of financing his return to the United States?

Mr. Oswald. No, sir; they did not.

Mr. Jenner. Did any agency of the United States or any public body located in New York City get in touch with you with respect to supplying him funds for his transportation from New York City to Fort Worth?

Mr. Oswald. Yes, sir, they did.

Mr. Jenner. Was that the initial request or knowledge to you that you received that funds were necessary, or would be needed for that purpose?

Mr. Oswald. Yes, sir, that is correct.

Mr. Jenner. Do you remember the name of the agency? Was it the one that you identified yesterday?

Mr. Oswald. Yes, sir, it was.

Mr. Jenner. All right.

In his letter of November 30, 1961, he makes a request for a football.

Did you send the football to him?

Mr. Oswald. No, sir, I did not.

Mr. Jenner. In the letter of December 14, 1961, which is Commission Exhibit 385 No. 311, he makes a reference to the fact that he had not received any letter with "certain" questions. Apparently questions that you had put to him.

Mr. Oswald. Yes, sir.

Mr. Jenner. Do you have that letter?

Mr. Oswald. The letter of July 14?

Mr. Jenner. No, this is December 14.

Mr. Oswald. Pardon me.

Mr. Jenner. That is Commission Exhibit 311. It is two pages.

Mr. Oswald. Yes, sir, I have the letter.

Mr. Jenner. Does that refresh your recollection as to some letter you had written him prior thereto?

Mr. Oswald. Yes, sir, I do.

Mr. Jenner. Will you state what the letter was and whether it was in response to an earlier letter?

Mr. Oswald. No, sir, it was not in response—it was a response to an earlier letter from Lee. I did in an effort to determine whether or not all my letters——

Mr. Jenner. The last prior letter was the letter of November 30, 1961, Commission Exhibit 308, and then immediately prior to that was the letter of November 1, 1961, Commission Exhibit 309.

Mr. Oswald. In reference to the question regarding that letter of December 14, 1961, at which time he stated "I did not receive any letter with 'certain' questions."

I did write him a letter at which time I recall raising two political type questions to see whether or not he would receive——

Mr. Jenner. He would respond?

Mr. Oswald. Sir?

Mr. Jenner. To see whether he would respond, did you say?

Mr. Oswald. To see whether or not he would receive the letter itself.

Mr. Jenner. I am sorry, I thought you said to receive.

Mr. Oswald. I believe, sir; if my memory serves me correct in some earlier letters he refers there to some Russian censors he felt like were censoring his mail and my mail also and I wanted to find out in my own way whether this was so or not.

I might say that was the only time I attempted to raise any type of political questions in my response to any of his letters or any other letters that I sent him, because I did want the letters to go through rather than be destroyed or not received by him.

Mr. Jenner. We can draw our own inference as to whether he received your letter.

Was there any discussion of the subject after return to the United States, that is, the subject whether he had received your letter?

Mr. Oswald. Not to my recollection, sir.

Mr. Jenner. Did you have any discussion with your brother on the subject of his undesirable discharge after he returned to the United States?

Mr. Oswald. Yes, sir; I did.

Mr. Jenner. And when was that? Was it more than one occasion?

Mr. Oswald. I believe, sir, only on one occasion did we discuss that matter.

Mr. Jenner. When was that? Where was it?

Mr. Oswald. Approximately June 1962 at my home in Fort Worth, Tex.

Mr. Jenner. Who was present?

Mr. Oswald. I believe just Lee and I were present in this one room which was the living room of our home.

Mr. Jenner. In your home?

Mr. Oswald. Yes, sir.

Mr. Jenner. What did he say?

Mr. Oswald. He said he wanted to go down the next day to the Marine Corps office in Fort Worth, Tex., and discuss with them and perhaps find out what action he needed to take to have this corrected to an honorable discharge.

Mr. Jenner. What did you say?

Mr. Oswald. My reply to him on that was that I thought that that was a good idea and that he might raise the question at the Marine Corps office in Fort386 Worth, Tex., if I could be of some assistance in writing the Marine Corps office directly on behalf of him. I do not recall if he made this trip to the Marine Corps office. I do not recall any further conversation in reference to his dishonorable discharge.

Mr. Jenner. Would you turn your attention now to the letter of May 22, 1962, shortly before he returned to the United States?

Mr. Oswald. Yes, sir.

Mr. Jenner. Commission Exhibit 318.

As I recall that letter, he refers to some things that you had said when he departed for Russia. Do you find that portion of the letter?

Mr. Oswald. Yes, sir; I do.

Mr. Jenner. Would you read it aloud, please, just that portion?

Mr. McKenzie. May I interrupt you at this point, Mr. Jenner?

Please, Mr. Chairman.

Mr. Dulles. Certainly, proceed.

Mr. McKenzie. The two letters of November 8 and November 26 which we should make copies of for the purposes of the record, if you will pull them out of your file there I will—do you want to take the originals?

Mr. Jenner. That will be the best way of doing it.

Mr. McKenzie. Except that yours are already marked with the exhibit number. I have no objection.

I will find out who I should see about making these.

Mr. Jenner. Why do you not make them on the Xerox machine?

I had asked you to read that portion of the letter so we can place the matter in context.

Mr. Oswald. "I know what was said about me when I left the United States as Mother sent me clippings from the newspapers. However, I realize it was just the shock of the news which made you say all those things. However, I will just remind you again not to make any statement or comments if you are approached by the newspapers between now and the time we actually arrive in the United States."

Mr. Jenner. Is he referring then to things that were reported in the newspaper clippings that you said or is he referring to something you said to him before he departed for Russia, or is he referring to something you said in a letter you may have written him when he was in Russia?

Mr. Oswald. He is referring, sir, to the clippings of newspapers that mother had sent him containing reportedly my statements to the newspapers at the time we were advised on October 31, 1959 that Lee was in Russia.

Mr. Jenner. Did you have occasion to make any comments to newspaper reporters when it became known that he was about to return to the United States?

Mr. Oswald. Yes, sir; I did.

Mr. Jenner. And did those come to your brother's attention?

Mr. Oswald. No, sir; they did not.

Mr. Jenner. Did you ever discuss them or he with you?

Mr. Oswald. When the newspaper reporters contacted me prior to his arrival in New York City, I did not divulge my knowledge of his departure as per this letter of May 22, 1962, the approximate date he would be in the United States. I did not give them any indication whatsoever at that time that he was leaving the Soviet Union.

Mr. Jenner. Did you ever respond to that particular letter?

Mr. Oswald. No, sir; I did not.

Mr. Dulles. May I ask a question here?

You indicated that your brother was disappointed when he arrived at Love Airfield and the newspapermen were not there when he came back from Russia.

Did the newspapermen thereafter talk with your brother at your house or elsewhere?

Mr. Oswald. They attempted to, sir. I say "they." It was, more specifically, one newspaperman.

Mr. Jenner. But he did not succeed in getting an interview?

Mr. Oswald. That is correct, sir.

Mr. Jenner. Reference is made in your brother's letter to you of November 17,387 1962, which is Commission Exhibit 320, to Thanksgiving dinner. Would you obtain that exhibit, please?

Mr. Oswald. Yes, sir; I have it.

Mr. Dulles. What Thanksgiving, 1962?

Mr. Jenner. 1962, sir.

Was the Thanksgiving dinner held at your home on Thanksgiving Day, November 1962?

Mr. Oswald. That is correct, sir.

Mr. Jenner. Would you tell us all of the circumstances preceding, leading up to and what occurred on that date and who attended the Thanksgiving dinner?

Mr. Oswald. Lee and Marina and their small child had moved to Dallas, Tex.

Mr. Jenner. Where in Dallas, Tex.? Do you recall?

Mr. Oswald. I did not have any address, sir. I had only a post office box, Box 2915, Dallas, Tex.

Mr. Jenner. All right.

Mr. Oswald. My older brother John had called me from San Antonio, Tex., prior to Thanksgiving 1962, indicating that he was going to be able to take a leave——

Mr. Jenner. Excuse me, Mr. Oswald.

Mr. Chairman, there is some confusion respecting this Thanksgiving dinner.

Mr. Oswald. Where John was stationed in the Air Force—he called me from San Antonio stating that he would be able to take a leave during the period of Thanksgiving of November 1962 and that they would travel from San Antonio, Tex., to my home in Fort Worth, Tex. I wrote Lee and asked him would it be possible for him to join us at that time with his family.

Mr. Jenner. Did you indicate in your letter that his brother John and wife were to join you on that occasion?

Mr. Oswald. Yes, sir; I did.

Mr. Jenner. Did you indicate that anyone in addition, to wit, your mother, was also to join you on that occasion?

Mr. Oswald. No, sir; I did not.

Mr. Jenner. All right.

Mr. Oswald. In reference to the letter dated November 17, 1962, from Lee Harvey Oswald——

Mr. Jenner. That is Commission Exhibit 320.

Mr. Oswald. It replied to my letter: "In answer to your kind invitation for Thanksgiving, we love to come and will be in Fort Worth Thanksgiving morning and we shall come by bus and give you a ring on the phone from the bus station (about 9:10). See you soon. Lee."

Mr. Jenner. Did he come to Fort Worth?

Mr. Oswald. Yes, sir.

Mr. Jenner. For that particular occasion?

Mr. Oswald. That is correct, sir.

Mr. Jenner. When did he arrive?

Mr. Oswald. Approximately nine to ten o'clock in the morning.

Mr. Jenner. Of Thanksgiving Day?

Mr. Oswald. Yes, sir; that is correct.

Mr. Jenner. Was he accompanied by anyone?

Mr. Oswald. Yes, sir; he was.

Mr. Jenner. Who?

Mr. Oswald. Marina N. Oswald and the baby June Lee Oswald.

Mr. Jenner. Did all of you have Thanksgiving dinner on that day?

Mr. Oswald. Yes, sir; we did.

Mr. Jenner. Did both Lee and Marina attend that dinner?

Mr. Oswald. Yes, sir; they did.

Mr. Jenner. And John Pic and his wife?

Mr. Oswald. Yes, sir; they did.

Mr. Jenner. You and your wife?

Mr. Oswald. Yes, sir.

Mr. Jenner. Your children?

Mr. Oswald. Yes, sir.

Mr. Jenner. The children of Lee and Marina?

Mr. Oswald. Yes, sir.

Mr. McKenzie. The child. There was only one at that time.

Mr. Jenner. That is right, the child June. Anyone else?

Mr. Oswald. The children of John and Marge Pic.

Mr. Jenner. But your mother did not attend the dinner?

Mr. Oswald. That is correct, sir.

Mr. Jenner. Had you invited her?

Mr. Oswald. No, sir; I had not.

Mr. Jenner. As far as you know, she was unaware of it?

Mr. Oswald. Yes, sir; that is correct.

Mr. Jenner. Was any comment made that she was not present, about the fact that she was not present at the dinner?

Mr. Oswald. No, sir; there was not.

Mr. Jenner. Was anything said about what your brother Lee was doing by way of employment in Dallas?

Mr. Oswald. Yes, sir; there was.

Mr. Jenner. What was said, and by whom?

Mr. Oswald. I feel like I had asked Lee what he was doing at that particular time, and his reply to me was that he was working for a traffic outfit in Dallas, the name of which I do not recall. However, he did state the name of the firm. I do not recall the name of the firm. And that it was to him very interesting work. He thought that he could perhaps learn this type of work and progress in it quite ably.

Mr. Dulles. How did he appear to you mentally and physically on this occasion of the Thanksgiving dinner?

Mr. Oswald. Very fit physically and very alert mentally.

Mr. Jenner. Discussion on that day occurred between you and your half-brother, John Pic, did it not, respecting your brother Lee's un-American beliefs?

Mr. Oswald. Yes, sir; it did.

Mr. Jenner. Would you relate that discussion between yourself—was it confined to a discussion between yourself and John Pic?

Mr. Oswald. Yes, sir; it was.

Mr. Jenner. Did you raise the subject?

Mr. Oswald. I believe I did, sir.

Mr. Jenner. You were concerned about his un-American beliefs, were you not?

Mr. Oswald. I was not concerned about them. I wanted to state to John, since he had not been in contact with Lee when Lee was in Russia, or when he was at my home in Fort Worth, that this conversation took place.

Mr. Jenner. You state it.

Mr. Dulles. Was John present?

Mr. Oswald. Yes, sir.

Mr. Dulles. He was present.

Mr. McKenzie. It was to John.

Mr. Dulles. Was he present?

Mr. Oswald. No, sir; he was not. I was about to say that this conversation took place on our way from my house to the bus station to pick up Lee, Marina and June the morning of Thanksgiving 1962. I do not recall the circumstances preceding this particular point of why I brought it up other than I do recall mentioning that the FBI had talked to Lee and apparently that everything was all right because they were not proceeding to discuss with him at any length and they were not holding him for any reason, so I assumed that everything was all right in that respect.

Mr. Jenner. I see.

Have you exhausted your present recollection of that conversation?

Mr. Oswald. Yes, sir; I have.

Mr. Dulles. How did you know that the FBI had talked with Lee?

Mr. Oswald. Lee had told me and I was aware that they had called my house and requested Lee to come down to their office in Fort Worth and talk with them.

389 Mr. Dulles. Did he report to you on that conversation at all? The details of it?

Mr. Oswald. A very small detail of it, sir.

Mr. Jenner. What details?

Mr. Oswald. I asked him when I returned home from work that afternoon how did it go. He said, "Just fine." He said they asked him at the last whether or not he was an agent for the United States Government. His reply was "Don't you know?"

Mr. Jenner. You recited that yesterday.

Mr. McKenzie. This was testified to yesterday. It is repetition.

Mr. Oswald. Yes, sir.

Mr. Jenner. Did you at that time say to John that the FBI had—excuse me—had assured you that Lee was all right and not dangerous to our country?

Mr. Oswald. No, sir; I had not.

Mr. Jenner. Did you say to John on that occasion or any other occasion that he need not worry about Lee in connection with possible danger to our country?

Mr. Oswald. Yes, sir; I did.

Mr. Jenner. When was that?

Mr. Oswald. This was on the same occasion on the trip to the bus station as I have so indicated, that I had assumed, since they were not holding Lee or questioning him to any frequency, because at that time they had only questioned him to my knowledge one time, that everything as far as un-American views that he expressed when he went to Russia, everything was cleared and they had no reason to hold him or suspect him of anything.

Mr. Dulles. Did you know about the Fair Play for Cuba incident in New Orleans at this time?

Mr. Oswald. No, sir; I did not.

Mr. Jenner. Did your brother Lee and Marina leave your home after Thanksgiving dinner?

Mr. Oswald. Yes, sir; they did.

Mr. Jenner. That same day?

Mr. Oswald. Yes, sir.

Mr. Jenner. Did you have occasion to see your brother at any time from that moment when he departed until sometime on the 22d of November 1963?

Mr. Oswald. No, sir; I did not.

Mr. McKenzie. Mr. Jenner, may I interrupt you one more time?

In response to your question, Mr. Chairman, it is my best recollection, and I may be wrong and stand to be corrected if I am wrong, that the Fair Play for Cuba or the pro-Castro leaflets that he was handing out in New Orleans was in the summer of 1963.

Mr. Dulles. I think you may be right.

Do you remember that?

Mr. Jenner. Yes, that is correct.

Mr. Dulles. That is correct. It had not taken place.

Mr. McKenzie. It had not taken place in November of 1962.

Mr. Dulles. Right.

Mr. McKenzie. To the best of our knowledge.

Mr. Jenner. Did the witness have any opportunity to respond to my last question?

Mr. McKenzie. You had finished your question and I interrupted you before you could make another question.

Mr. Jenner. You mean the witness had responded to it?

Mr. Dulles. No; I do not think he had.

Mr. Jenner. Would you read the pending question?

(The last question was read by the reporter.)

Mr. Jenner. Did you see Marina at any time subsequent to their departure on Thanksgiving Day, November 1962 and November 22, 1963?

Mr. Oswald. No, sir; I had not.

Mr. Dulles. Did you have any telephone conversations with either of them?

Mr. Oswald. Yes, sir; I had.

Mr. Jenner. In the interim period?

Mr. Oswald. Yes, sir; I had.

390 Mr. Jenner. Were there a number of those or were they infrequent?

Mr. Oswald. I recall only one, sir.

Mr. Jenner. When did that take place?

Mr. Oswald. Approximately two or three weeks after Thanksgiving of 1962.

Mr. Jenner. That would be sometime then in December of 1962?

Mr. Oswald. That is correct, sir.

Mr. Jenner. Did you call him or did he call you?

Mr. Oswald. No, sir; he called me.

Mr. Jenner. You recognized his voice?

Mr. Oswald. Yes, sir.

Mr. Jenner. And was it day or night?

Mr. Oswald. It was, I believe it was Sunday afternoon, sir.

Mr. Jenner. Sunday afternoon. And what was the occasion of his making that call as you recall it?

Mr. Oswald. That he was in town briefly.
Mr. Jenner. In Fort Worth?
Mr. Oswald. In Fort Worth, Tex., and that I asked would we see him; he said no, they were visiting some friends.
Mr. Jenner. "They" meaning he and Marina?
Mr. Oswald. Yes, sir, and that they would be leaving for Dallas very shortly.
Mr. Jenner. That was a social call?
Mr. Oswald. Yes, sir.
Mr. Jenner. You have given the full of the conversation?
Mr. Oswald. To the best of my remembrance; yes, sir. It was very short.
Mr. Jenner. Did you have occasion to talk to Marina over the telephone on that particular time?
Mr. Oswald. No, sir; I did not.
Mr. Jenner. Did he talk with any other member of your family on that occasion?
Mr. Oswald. No, sir; he did not.
Mr. Jenner. Other than that telephone conversation, had you had any other conversation with your brother Lee from the time on Thanksgiving Day, November 1962 to the time you saw him on November 22, 1963?
Mr. Oswald. I did not see him on November——
Mr. McKenzie. He did not see him on that day.
Mr. Oswald. On November 22, 1963.
Mr. McKenzie. He saw him on November 23, 1963.
Mr. Jenner. Then my question is November 23.
Mr. Oswald. No, sir; I had not had any conversation with him after November 1962, Thanksgiving Day, other than the one I have mentioned, up to the time of November 22, 1963.
Mr. Dulles. Did you make any attempts to get in touch with him in that period?
Mr. Oswald. Only through the mail, sir.
Mr. Jenner. I was about to come to that.
Did you have any correspondence with him in the sense of your dispatching a letter or note or he dispatching one to you?
Mr. Oswald. Yes, sir; I did.
Mr. Jenner. Did you retain the correspondence insofar as anything you received from him is concerned?
Mr. Oswald. Yes, sir; I did.
Mr. McKenzie. And that has previously been furnished to the Commission.
Mr. Jenner. It has previously been furnished and it is, I see, a postcard which is dated as I recall—you give the date.
Mr. Oswald. We are still referring to the period after November 1962, Thanksgiving Day?
Mr. Jenner. Yes, we are.
Mr. Oswald. All right, sir.
One postcard dated January 10, 1963.
Mr. Jenner. And that is Commission Exhibit 324.
Did you receive any other correspondence?
Mr. Oswald. Yes, sir; I did.
Mr. Jenner. And do you have it there?
Mr. Oswald. Yes, sir; I do.
Mr. Jenner. And it is a letter dated?
Mr. Oswald. Yes, sir.
Mr. Jenner. What date?
Mr. Oswald. March 16, 1963.
Mr. Jenner. And that is Commission Exhibit 322.
Did you receive any other correspondence from him?

Mr. Oswald. No, sir; I have not.

Mr. Jenner. Did you dispatch any to him?

Mr. Oswald. Yes, sir; I had.

Mr. Jenner. Did they have any relation to either of the exhibits you have now identified?

Mr. Oswald. No, sir; they did not.

Mr. Jenner. That is, neither Exhibit 322 nor Exhibit 324 was in response to any communication that you had dispatched to him?

Mr. Oswald. Pardon me, sir, I was incorrect on that.

The letter of March 16, 1963 was in response to a letter I had written him approximately the first week of March 1963.

Mr. Jenner. Did you retain a copy of the letter you sent him? And if you made one, did you retain a copy?

Mr. Oswald. No, sir; no copy was made and I did not retain it.

Mr. Jenner. Would you state the contents of your letter?

Mr. Oswald. It was, briefly, sir, that we had moved to Malvern, Ark. I informed him of my new address and advised him that I had placed my home in Fort Worth, Tex., up for sale, and I had been given an opportunity by the company for a better and higher position, and that I had taken this opportunity and moved to Malvern, Ark. and requested, if possible, we would like to have them visit us.

Mr. Dulles. When did you move to Malvern, approximately?

Mr. Oswald. The fifth day of March 1963, sir.

Mr. Dulles. And how long were you there?

Mr. Oswald. To September 13, 1963, sir.

Mr. Dulles. And then you returned to——

Mr. Oswald. No, sir. Then I moved to Denton, Tex.

Mr. Dulles. Denton, Tex.?

Mr. Oswald. Yes, sir.

Mr. Jenner. So that at the time of the event, November 22, 1963, you were residing in Malvern, Tex.?

Mr. Oswald. No, sir; I was residing in Denton, Tex.

Mr. Jenner. I should have said Malvern, Ark., anyhow.

Mr. Dulles. Let's see, you were then in Malvern, Ark., from March 1963, to approximately September 1963?

Mr. Oswald. Yes, sir; that is correct.

Mr. Jenner. That is where I misunderstood. I thought he said December.

All right, sir. I take it then at least from Thanksgiving Day, 1962, and the 23d day of November, 1963, you never had any discussions with Robert with respect to his desire, if any, to return to Russia, with Lee rather?

Mr. Oswald. No, sir; I did not.

Mr. Jenner. Did you ever have any discussion with him on that subject?

Mr. Oswald. No, sir; I did not.

Mr. Jenner. Did you ever have any discussion with him or he with you or with Marina or she with you on her return to Russia, whether he desired it or she did?

Mr. Oswald. During that period?

Mr. Jenner. Prior to November 23, 1963.

Mr. Oswald. Yes, sir.

Mr. Jenner. When did that discussion that you now have in mind take place?

Mr. Oswald. At my home in June of 1962, sir.

Mr. Jenner. Who was present?

Mr. Oswald. My wife Vada and Lee.

Mr. Jenner. With Marina I take it?

392 Mr. Oswald. And Marina was there.

Yes, sir; I was having a conversation or she was having something of a conversation with me.

Mr. Jenner. Before you give the conversation, was there ever any other occasion up to and including November 23, 1963 when you had a discussion with your brother or with Marina respecting the return of either of them to Russia?

Mr. Oswald. No, sir; I only recall this one occasion.

Mr. Jenner. State what was said, please, and by whom.

Mr. Oswald. This was said by Marina Oswald in June of 1962 in very broken English: "I never want to go to Russia again."

Mr. Jenner. Return to Russia?

Mr. Oswald. Yes, sir.

Mr. Jenner. And that was said in the presence of your brother Lee, your presence and your wife's presence?

Mr. Oswald. Yes, sir; I feel certain that all four of us were present.

Mr. Jenner. Did your brother say anything on that occasion?

Mr. Oswald. No, sir.

Mr. Jenner. As to that subject matter?

Mr. Oswald. No, sir.

Mr. Jenner. This took place in your home? How long after they had returned from Russia did this conversation take place?

Mr. McKenzie. What was that question?

Mr. Oswald. I would say 1 or 2 weeks.

Mr. Jenner. One or two weeks after they had returned from Russia?

Mr. Oswald. Yes, sir.

Mr. Dulles. That is when they were staying with you after their return?

Mr. Oswald. Yes, sir.

Mr. Jenner. At any time prior to November 23, 1962, were you aware or did any incident arise or conversation take place indicating any desire on your brother Lee's part to go to Cuba?

Mr. Oswald. No, sir; it did not.

Mr. Jenner. Or to Mexico?

Mr. Oswald. No, sir; it did not.

Mr. Jenner. Or any other country than the United States?

Mr. Oswald. No, sir; there was not.

Mr. Dulles. Was there any particular reason why you did not have some contact with Lee during the period November, Thanksgiving 1962, and your departure for Arkansas in March of 1963?

Mr. Oswald. No, sir; none that I was aware of. I did write him on two or three occasions asking him to advise me of his address in Dallas, Tex., so when I had an opportunity either on business or otherwise passing through where I could possibly stop and see him, if not Marina and the child.

His response to this was as it is stated in the letter of March 17, 1963, that generally he was moving and it was not settled and he would always retain the post office box in Dallas, Tex., where I might reach him through the mail and that I would not be able to see him or his family when I came through town.

Mr. Dulles. Did that surprise you?

Mr. Oswald. It did not at first, sir, because I realized he was not settled as to a stable job and to an apartment. However, it did concern me later, and I refer to my letter that I wrote him in March of 1963 which he replied to on March 17 or March 16, 1963.

Mr. Jenner. Which is Commission Exhibit 322.

Mr. Oswald. That I would like to have an address other than a post office box, and when again he did not furnish me this information, I did not respond to his letter of March 17, 1963. The last time I wrote him was in September 1963 when I returned to Texas and our moving into Denton, Tex., advising him of my new address, and still at that time requesting again an address where they were staying at in Dallas so that I might contact him, since again we were close together, approximately 30 miles away.

Mr. Jenner. And he did not respond to that?

Mr. Oswald. No, sir; he never responded to that letter that I wrote him in September other than on the day that I visited him at Dallas County Jail or393 Dallas City Jail on November 23, 1963, he did say before I had an opportunity to say anything to him, "Robert, you now are living in Denton, aren't you?" And I said yes.

In other words, he had received my letter of September 1963.

Mr. Jenner. This was elicited by Mr. Dulles' question, his failure to advise you in due course eventually here as late as September 1963 of his location in Dallas aroused some suspicions, doubts or a question in your mind?

Mr. Oswald. It did to this extent, that I thought perhaps——

Mr. Jenner. Keep in mind all this history also, Mr. Oswald.

Mr. Oswald. Yes, sir.

Mr. Jenner. That you testified about.

Mr. Oswald. That perhaps he was angry at us or did not want to have anything to do with us. However, it was also my thinking on this that this would be out of character for him because he normally would keep in contact with me and let me have his address and so forth, even though he had furnished a post office box at first and which I understood, but his failure to give me an address indicated——

Mr. Jenner. Despite your at least two requests?

Mr. Oswald. Yes, sir.

Mr. Jenner. Or three requests?

Mr. Oswald. Indicated to me that perhaps something of a different nature was going on that I was not aware of, whether he was having trouble with Marina and perhaps the baby, and they were not getting along and he did not want me to become aware of this situation; this would be my only speculation on that, sir.

Mr. Dulles. Did your wife have any contact with Marina over this period we are discussing from Thanksgiving of 1962 to November 1963?

Mr. Oswald. No, sir; she did not.

Mr. Jenner. Did she ever indicate to you that she made any effort to effect a contact with Marina?

Mr. Oswald. Did my wife?

No, sir; she did not.

Mr. Jenner. In the light, Mr. Oswald, of the fact that your brother, as you testified, you thought looked up to you in his youth at least, in the light of his departure for Russia, in the light of the correspondence that you had with him in Russia about which you have testified, in the light of the conversations that you had with him upon his return, did not the fact that you did not hear from him for as long a period as from Thanksgiving Day of 1962 to well into the fall of 1963 raise any question in your mind beyond that which you have now testified about?

Mr. Oswald. No, sir.

Mr. Jenner. That it might be something other than possible marital difficulties?

Mr. Oswald. No, sir.

Of course, I refer to the postcard of January 10, 1963, and the letter of March 17, 1963, which I would state other than the fact that he did not advise me of his residence in Dallas, Tex.——

Mr. Jenner. Despite the fact that you requested it?

Mr. Oswald. Right, that the infrequency of the mail at this time was going back to prior to the time that he was in Russia, to the extent that he was not writing frequently then when he was in the service and so forth, and then again I thought that he was returning to this, because I was also not writing him as frequently as we had while he was in Russia. And it is my opinion, sir, that Lee felt that he had caused me enough difficulty, that he did not want to in any way, even though I had offered my assistance after his return from Russia, in any way that I possibly could, that he did not want to burden me in case he was in any financial difficulty or any other difficulty.

Mr. Jenner. All right, thank you.

I am going to attempt to cover in general terms, Mr. Chairman, Representative Ford's questions and see if I can shorten up the examination in that respect.

Mr. Dulles. Could I have just a word with you for just a moment.

(Short recess.)

Mr. Jenner. You are acquainted at least by hearsay at the moment, are you394 not, with respect to an alleged attack having been made by your brother upon General Walker?

Mr. Oswald. Yes, sir; I am.

Mr. Jenner. It is that to which I wish to direct a question.

Did you have any knowledge or information of any kind or character at any time prior to November 24, 1963, of that incident?

Mr. Oswald. No, sir; I did not.

Mr. Jenner. No one had spoken to you about it?

Mr. Oswald. No, sir; they had not.

Mr. Jenner. When did it first come to your attention?

Mr. Oswald. In the newspaper. I believe this to be sometime in the latter part of December 1963 or January 1964.

Mr. Jenner. It was subsequent to your brother's death?

Mr. Oswald. Yes, sir.

Mr. Jenner. And you had no information direct or indirect of any kind or character, scuttlebutt, hearsay or otherwise, up to that moment?

Mr. Oswald. That is correct, sir.

Mr. Dulles. Did you know of any acts of violence that your brother had carried out or had contemplated or attempted during his life other than school boy antics?

Mr. Oswald. No, sir; I was not. I have never known him to attempt or indicate to attempt to carry out any type of violence other than a schoolboy——

Mr. Jenner. Was he given to tantrums?

Mr. Oswald. No, sir; he was not.

Mr. Dulles. Did he ever seem to you to be a man who repressed himself, that he was boiling inside and that there were a great many emotions that he had that he was holding in? Did you get that impression from your knowledge of him?

Mr. Oswald. No, sir; I did not. I would say that Lee's character was that he was more of a listener than a talker, not to the extent of being an introvert. I do not believe he was an introvert.

Mr. Jenner. I was about to ask you that question. There have been people who have been interviewed, teachers and others, a good many of them as a matter of fact, who have described your brother as an introvert. Your mother used the expression that he was a loner in a statement that she made to the authorities in New York City, and I think on this record.

Was he in your opinion, gathered from your actual experience with him during his lifetime, a loner, that is, a person who would tend to prefer to be by himself and not seek out friends, not necessarily repulse friends but not affirmatively seek them out?

Mr. Oswald. I would say yes and no, sir, to that question if I may.

Mr. Jenner. All right.

Would you expand then and explain your answer yes and no?

Mr. Oswald. I feel like in the late 1940s to about the time of my departure to the service in July of 1952, that he did seek out friends, and that he did have friends. However, after my release from the service in 1955, I do believe that he had become more grown to himself.

Mr. Jenner. That is during the interim he had become, while you were away?

Mr. Oswald. Yes, sir.

Mr. Jenner. You noticed a change in him when you returned from the service?
Mr. Oswald. Yes, sir.
Mr. Jenner. Is that what you mean to say?
Mr. Oswald. Yes, sir.
Mr. Jenner. All right, proceed and describe that to us.
Mr. Oswald. Still my contact with him was limited, but he did appear to be drawn within himself more than he had been prior, and I do not know of any friends that he had at that particular time.

One factor of course would be that he had moved quite frequently or a number of times during this period.

Mr. Jenner. Apart from the reason, for the moment, I seek to draw from you your personal reaction as to whether he had become more retiring and that you had actually noticed that difference in him?

395 Mr. Oswald. Well, to me, sir, he had become or appeared to become more drawn into himself to the extent that I noticed that he wanted to read more, and of course when he wanted to read he wanted to be by himself. However, to me personally at that time when we were together, if he did not wish to read, he seemed and appeared to be as he was prior to 1952, sir.

Mr. Jenner. Did that state of mind or his action, did you notice that that persisted when he returned from Russia?

Was he still of that retiring nature?

Mr. Oswald. No, sir; he was not. I felt that he was more of a gregarious type person that wanted to mix with people and wanted to talk to people.

Mr. Jenner. After he left your home and took residence with your mother and thereafter in various places in Fort Worth, did he seek you out?

Mr. Oswald. Yes, sir. He called me on a number of occasions at my office.

Mr. Jenner. Did he come by your home and visit you voluntarily without invitation?

Mr. Oswald. I do not recall of any time, sir. I usually was talking to him on the telephone quite frequently during the period that he had moved out of my mother's apartment into their own duplex, to the extent that I always told him that if he would like to come out any time just to give me a ring and I would gladly pick them up and bring them out to the house and return them to their home.

Mr. Jenner. Did he do so?

Mr. Oswald. No, sir; he did not.

Mr. Dulles. There has been some testimony here before the Commission to the general effect that in the latter period he broke pretty much away with some of the Russian group of friends in Dallas that Marina had developed or liked to be with, and that is because she could talk Russian. Did you see anything of that, and can you throw any further light on that?

Mr. Oswald. No, sir; I did not. I was aware or had become aware of this group or some other group of the Russian-speaking population in Dallas, and I was aware of Mr. Gregory in Fort Worth, Tex., who had come to my house before Lee and Marina had moved out, to speak in the Russian language to Marina and to Lee. I was not aware that—I was aware that he was talking with and becoming acquainted with this group of persons, and I was not aware of the fact that he was withdrawing from this group of people.

Mr. Dulles. Did you know anything about his relations with a certain man named De Mohrenschildt?

Mr. Oswald. No, sir; I did not.

Mr. Jenner. Is the name familiar to you?

Mr. Oswald. No, sir; it is not.

Mr. McKenzie. Off the record.

(Discussion off the record.)

Mr. McKenzie. Mr. Dulles, who is the Chairman of the session today, has asked Mr. Oswald if he knows or has heard of a man by the name of De Mohrenschildt. Robert Oswald's answer I believe is reflected on the record that he did not know Mr. De Mohrenschildt. I have stated off the record to Mr. Dulles and to Mr. Jenner that I know George De Mohrenschildt.

I became acquainted with George De Mohrenschildt in this manner. Shortly after the law was passed in Texas that we could have women jurors——

Mr. Jenner. Could you fix that time?

Mr. McKenzie. No, I cannot, but it has been within the last five years. I would say. But shortly after the law was passed that we could have women jurors sitting in our courts, my wife happened to be on a jury in Dallas, Texas, in one of our district courts. Sitting on that same jury with my wife, Sally McKenzie was a man by the name of George De Mohrenschildt. As a result of her jury experience in the trial of this case, in which he was a juror, I met George De Mohrenschildt. I have since come to know him briefly, and in no way intimately.

George De Mohrenschildt at one time was married to a lady from Pennsylvania by the name of Wynne Sharples. They were subsequently divorced in Dallas. Wynne Sharples is an M.D. by profession. She comes from a well-known396 Pennsylvania family, and her father has been engaged in the oil business under the name of Sharples Oil Company.

Wynne Sharples, following her divorce from George De Mohrenschildt, remarried and married another M.D.

Mr. Jenner. What is her married name?

Mr. McKenzie. I do not recall her married name, but I do believe that she and her then husband, and I presume her present husband, the doctor that she married, were engaged in medical research at some hospital in Philadelphia or Baltimore, looking to the cause and a cure of a children's ailment of a very serious nature, and I believe it was connected with some blood type ailment.

Mr. Jenner. Leukemia?

Mr. McKenzie. No, it was not leukemia. There was an article on Wynne Sharples in one of the magazine supplements of either the Dallas Times-Herald or the Dallas Morning News, within the past five years.

George De Mohrenschildt has subsequently remarried, and some time within the past two years there was an article on George De Mohrenschildt in one of the Dallas daily newspapers, telling of a trip that he and his new bride were going to take through Mexico and Central America walking. In other words, they were going to walk from Dallas or the Mexican-United States border through Mexico and through Central America. It is my understanding that such a trip was taken, and that George De Mohrenschildt has since that time returned to Dallas, Tex. In fact, I have seen him in Dallas, Tex., within the past 7 months.

I do not know of any relationship between George De Mohrenschildt and Marina Oswald or Lee Harvey Oswald, nor have I ever heard of any.

Mr. Jenner. Would you describe George De Mohrenschildt physically, his physical appearance, the one you have in mind?

Mr. McKenzie. The man that I know is a large man, approximately six foot one to three inches. He would probably weigh 205 to maybe 215 pounds.

Mr. Jenner. Age?

Mr. McKenzie. He appears to be between 45 and 50 or 51 or 52. He has got a dark complexion, and I would say a typically foreign expression or foreign look to him, from the standpoint of being either a Russian or of the Slavic races.

Mr. Jenner. Have you ever spoken with him, to give us your impression of whether he has a foreign inflection in his speech?

Mr. McKenzie. He does have a foreign inflection in his speech, and I have heard, I do not know this to be true, but I have heard that Mr. De Mohrenschildt has quite a way with the ladies.

Mr. Jenner. All right, thanks.

Mr. Dulles. Thank you very much.

Mr. Jenner. Mr. Oswald, I have asked you about the Nixon and General Walker incidents. Did you at any time prior to November 23, 1963, have drawn to your attention any incident of any kind or character of action on the part of your brother Lee similar to those which have been raised as to General Walker and Richard Nixon?

Mr. Oswald. No, sir, I have not.

Mr. Jenner. You have seen pictures of, and you have heard about, the rifle which was allegedly employed by the assassin of President Kennedy in that assassination?

Mr. Oswald. Yes, sir.

Mr. Jenner. And you have seen pictures of it?

Mr. Oswald. That is correct, sir.

Mr. Jenner. Did you at any time prior to November 23, 1963, ever see the rifle which is alleged to have been employed in the assassination of President Kennedy?

Mr. Oswald. I have not.

Mr. Jenner. Did you ever see at your home or any place a rifle of that character in the possession of your brother, Lee Harvey Oswald?

Mr. Oswald. No, sir, I have not.

Mr. Jenner. Did you ever see any rifle of that character in or about any premises that he might or was occupying or that Marina was occupying?

397 Mr. Oswald. No, sir, I have not. I might further state I never knew him to own but one firearm in his entire life, and that was a .22 caliber rifle that he purchased from New Orleans, La., and on my visit to New Orleans, La., in 1955 on my discharge from the service, I purchased this from Lee for a total of $10. He had given approximately $16 for the rifle. It would not fire. And I gave him $10 for it, and took it back to Fort Worth and worked on it and put it into working condition.

Mr. Jenner. Did you have any discussion, did any discussion take place between you and Lee, or in your presence, other than that which you have testified heretofore up to this moment, of his use of a firearm, be it a pistol or a rifle, during the period from June 1962 to, and including, the 23d of November, 1963?

Mr. Oswald. No, sir, I had not.

Mr. Jenner. Nothing of that character occurred between you or in your presence and his presence during all of that period of time?

Mr. Oswald. That is correct, sir. I might say what they were saying at my home in Fort Worth, Tex., on Davenport Street during the first week, Lee and I were discussing hunting and so forth out at my in-laws' farm, I did produce at that time all weapons in my possession in front of Marina and Lee. They made Marina Oswald nervous, and shortly after looking at my weapons, I returned them to their proper place, and that was the only time that I have ever seen him handle a weapon from the time that he returned from Russia in 1962 until the reports of present-day activities along that line that he handled a weapon.

Mr. Jenner. Just to nail down this subject, I take it then that at no time from the time of his return in June of 1962 to the United States to and including November 23, 1962, did you ever see him in the possession of a firearm of any kind or character?

Mr. Oswald. No, sir; I did not. If I may, sir, referring to the hunting trip that we did take at the farm in June of 1962——

Mr. Jenner. Other than that to which you have already testified?

Mr. Oswald. Yes, sir, that is correct, at no time.

Mr. Jenner. And you had that in mind when you answered my question in the negative?

Mr. Oswald. Yes, sir.

Mr. Jenner. I was excluding your prior testimony.

Mr. Oswald. Yes, sir. Thank you.

Mr. Jenner. Apart from newspaper photographs, have you ever to your knowledge seen Jack Ruby on television?

Mr. Oswald. No, sir, I have not.

Mr. Jenner. Or a person said to be Jack Ruby?

Mr. Oswald. No, sir, I have not.

Mr. McKenzie. Use his full name.

Mr. Jenner. Jack Rubenstein.

Mr. Oswald. No, sir, I have not.

Mr. Jenner. Have you ever been in any establishment allegedly operated by him or in which he has an interest, to your knowledge?

Mr. Oswald. Would you mind, sir, giving me the names of those establishments?

Mr. Jenner. I will do that from other papers later on, but to your present knowledge, without refreshing or stimulating your recollection, could you give me an answer?

Mr. Oswald. I have not, sir.

Mr. McKenzie. Now would you go on and ask him, or would you prefer to——

Mr. Jenner. Would you mind waiting? I am just taking care of Representative Ford's questions at the moment.

Your mother testified that an FBI agent had shown her a picture of some man on the evening of Saturday, November 23, 1963. She testified further that later, after your brother had been killed, she saw a picture of Jack Ruby or Jack Rubenstein alias Jack Ruby in the newspaper, and that she exclaimed in your presence that Ruby was the man whose picture had been shown to her on a Saturday night, November 23, 1963, by an agent of the FBI. Does that refresh your recollection?

398 Mr. Oswald. Yes, sir, that is correct.

Mr. Jenner. And did that take place?

Mr. Oswald. Yes, sir, it did.

Mr. Jenner. Would you please testify or tell us of where that took place, who was present and what the circumstances were?

Mr. Oswald. That took place at the Inn of the Six Flags in Arlington, Tex., during the week of November 25, 1963, in the presence I believe of two or more Secret Service agents, and perhaps an Arlington police officer in the rooms that were assigned at the Inn of the Six Flags, and I feel like at least one of the Secret Service agents that was present——

Mr. Jenner. Excuse me, sir, you used the expression "and I feel like". Do you mean you are speculating?

Mr. Oswald. I believe, is that a better expression, sir?

Mr. Jenner. Go ahead, and then I will ask you on what basis you base that belief.

Mr. Oswald. All right, sir. I believe that the Secret Service agents, at least one of them was Mr. Mike Howard.

Mr. Jenner. That is your best recollection?

Mr. Oswald. Yes, sir.

Mr. Jenner. That is what you mean by believe?

Mr. Oswald. Yes, sir.

Mr. Jenner. All right.

Mr. Oswald. I testify it was either two or three Secret Service agents present, and my best recollection, another Secret Service agent would be Mr. Charles I. Kunkel, and if my recollection serves me correctly, there was an Arlington police officer at the time. It would be either Mr. Bob Parsons or Mr. Jeff Gan.

Mr. Jenner. These were the persons present on this occasion?

Mr. Oswald. I believe this to be.

Mr. Jenner. And what occurred and what was said?

Mr. Oswald. I believe, to my best recollection, mother was in another room and she had received a copy of a newspaper which I cannot identify, that reportedly had a picture of Mr. Rubenstein or Mr. Jack Ruby, and mother exclaimed to me——

Mr. Jenner. Did she come into the room in which you gentlemen were?

Mr. Oswald. Yes, sir, she did.

Mr. Jenner. And she had the newspaper in her possession?

Mr. Oswald. Yes, sir, she did.

Mr. Jenner. And she walked among you and said something?

Mr. Oswald. Yes, sir, she did.

Mr. Jenner. Did she exhibit anything?

Mr. Oswald. Yes, sir, she did.

Mr. Jenner. What did she exhibit?

Mr. Oswald. A picture that I could recognize as a picture now of a man known as Jack Ruby.

Mr. Jenner. That was a picture in the newspaper?

Mr. Oswald. That is correct, sir.

Mr. Jenner. All right, proceed.

Mr. Oswald. And she stated to me——

Mr. Jenner. In the presence of the others?

Mr. Oswald. Yes, sir; that on Saturday night, November 23, 1963, that two FBI agents had gone to the Executive Inn in Dallas, to the rooms where mother and Marina and Baby June Lee Oswald were staying, and that at this particular time Marina was taking a bath or a shower, mother had just completed hers, she was in a robe, she did not open the door fully, that one of the FBI agents produced a picture that she stated was Mr. Jack Ruby, and that was the text of it.

Mr. Dulles. You did not see the picture that was shown by the Secret Service man?

Mr. Oswald. The FBI man?

Mr. Dulles. The FBI man.

Mr. Oswald. No, sir, I did not. I was not there.

399 Mr. Jenner. Assuming it was shown, it was not exhibited to you. Your mother stated that a picture of Mr. Jack Ruby had been exhibited to her by an FBI man.

Mr. Oswald. That a picture that an FBI man——

Mr. Jenner. On the Saturday night, November 23, 1963.

Mr. Oswald. Yes, sir, that the FBI man exhibited a picture, and mother said that she recognized from the newspaper to be Mr. Jack Ruby.

Mr. Jenner. Did any of the gentlemen present say anything when your mother made that statement?

Mr. Oswald. I believe they did, sir.

Mr. Jenner. All right. Give us your best recollection of what was said, and if you can identify the person, do so, but in any event tell us what was said, if you can identify them only by stating he was a police officer or a Secret Service man or an FBI agent, then do that.

Mr. Oswald. I believe Mr. Mike Howard of the United States Secret Service looked at the picture in the newspaper and said something to mother in the line or in the nature of "Are you sure" and so forth like that. It was very brief, and she was saying that she was positive.

Mr. Jenner. She responded that she was certain of it?

Mr. Oswald. Yes, sir, that she was certain that the photograph shown to her on Saturday night, November 23, 1963, was the man in the picture being identified as Mr. Jack Ruby, the killer of my brother, Lee Harvey Oswald.

Mr. Dulles. Did she say anything about what the officer who had shown her this photograph had said to her, or explained why he was showing that picture?

Mr. Oswald. I believe, sir, she did indicate that they wanted to show it to Marina for identification, and mother explained to him that she was in the shower and was fixing to go to bed, and they were very tired.

Mr. Jenner. Now would you give us please your opinion and judgment as to the stability of your mother?

Mr. Oswald. Prior to November 22, 1963——correction, prior to November 24, 1963, I believed her to be a stable average person. However, during the week of November 24, including the date of November 24, 1963, through Friday of that week, which was November 29, 1963, due to the happenings and the events that had ensued from the November 22d afternoon through Sunday of November 23d, it is my opinion that at first that her reactions were quite normal, and to be expected.

However, it is my opinion during the latter part of that week, from approximately Wednesday, November 27, 1963, that her reactions to other matters related to the events of November 22 and November 24, 1963, were abnormal reactions.

Mr. Jenner. Did those normal or abnormal reactions continue to the best of your knowledge thereafter?

Mr. Oswald. Since I have not seen her, sir, since Friday November 29, 1963, I have talked with her on telephone calls only, I have no opinion on that at this time.

Mr. Jenner. One way or the other?

Mr. Oswald. One way or the other.

Mr. Jenner. Whether continued or not continued?

Mr. Oswald. Yes.

Mr. Jenner. You have testified that you thought you had an influence on Lee's joining the Marines. That is an influence of an example rather than a direct influence, that is any direct contact by you suggesting that if he entered the service he should enter the Marines?

Mr. Oswald. That would be correct, sir. It would be as an example.

Mr. Jenner. You mentioned a Mr. Gregory having visited at your home. Will you identify him, please?

Mr. Oswald. I believe his given name, sir, is Mr. Peter Gregory, but I am confused a little bit about his son. His son's name is Paul Gregory, or vice versa.

Mr. Jenner. It is Peter.

Mr. Oswald. Thank you. Mr. Peter Gregory came to my residence in Fort Worth, Tex. on 7313 Davenport Street.

Mr. Jenner. Approximately when, please?

Mr. Oswald. Two occasions, the first occasion being approximately the last week in June, 1962.

Mr. Jenner. What was that occasion?

Mr. Oswald. He had come over to see Lee and meet Marina and talk with them in his native Russian language.

Mr. Jenner. Was he accompanied by anyone?

Mr. Oswald. Not on this first occasion, sir, if my memory serves me correctly. I believe he was by himself.

Mr. Jenner. Was anything said in your presence that you understood, having in mind that he spoke Russian at least in part of that occasion, as to how he became aware that Lee and Marina were residing with you temporarily?

Mr. Oswald. We were expecting Mr. Gregory to come by that night. The preceding 2 or 3 days, I understood from Lee, that when he inquired at one of the bureaus of the Texas employment agencies in Fort Worth, that someone that he had talked to about a job had set up an appointment with Lee to go see Mr. Gregory, since Lee could speak Russian and write the Russian language, they thought perhaps Mr. Gregory might know of some contact that he could place Lee with, where Lee might obtain a job speaking and writing the Russian language. I understood from Lee——

Mr. Jenner. That is the result of discussions in your presence in your home?

Mr. Oswald. Yes, sir; that is correct.
Mr. Jenner. By Lee and Marina?
Mr. Oswald. By Lee to me.
Mr. Jenner. Lee to you?
Mr. Oswald. Yes, sir. And I understood that——
Mr. Jenner. Mr. Oswald, if you could, if it is the result of Lee having told you, would you please state it in those terms rather than that you understood, because your understanding may be based on hearsay that is not the fact.
Mr. Oswald. Lee in our conversation told me that he went to Mr. Gregory's office on the first occasion to meet Mr. Gregory.
Mr. Jenner. And that would be before this last week in June when Mr. Gregory visited your home?
Mr. Oswald. That is correct, sir.
Mr. Dulles. What is Mr. Gregory's profession, do you happen to know?
Mr. Oswald. He was a consultant geologist. On this first occasion that Lee spent 1 or 2 hours talking with Mr. Gregory, and at the end of this occasion, Mr. Gregory gave Lee a letter to the effect, which I did read——
Mr. Jenner. Did your brother Lee exhibit this letter to you?
Mr. Oswald. Yes, sir, he did.
Mr. Jenner. Have you seen the letter from the time that you read it to the present time?
Mr. Oswald. No, sir, I have not.
Mr. Jenner. And as far as you know the letter doesn't exist. You don't know whether it exists?
Mr. Oswald. That is correct, sir.
Mr. Jenner. Would you please recite the content of it as you now recall it?
Mr. Oswald. That it stated that Lee Harvey Oswald was competent to speak and write the Russian language fluently. That is my general remembrance of this letter.
Mr. Jenner. Was it signed? Did it have a signature?
Mr. Oswald. Yes, sir, it did.
Mr. Jenner. Was it on a letterhead?
Mr. Oswald. I believe it was, sir.
Mr. Dulles. Was Mr. Gregory a Russian by origin as far as you know?
Mr. Oswald. Yes, sir, he was.
Mr. Jenner. Did your brother tell you that?
Mr. Oswald. Yes, sir, he did.
Mr. Dulles. Was he a naturalized American, or don't you know?
Mr. Oswald. This I do not know, sir. But during this conversation, he told me about Mr. Gregory to the extent that he had come from Russia approximately——
401 Mr. Dulles. This is your brother now?
Mr. Oswald. Yes, sir, talking to me. Approximately 40 years prior to that time.
Mr. Jenner. So he had been in this country for approximately 40 years?
Mr. Oswald. Yes, sir.
Mr. Jenner. It was not long after that conversation in which your brother Lee reported these things to you that Mr. Gregory visited at your home the last week in June of 1962, is that correct?
Mr. Oswald. Yes, sir, approximately the last week in June 1962.
Mr. Dulles. Did your brother tell you where he had gotten to know Mr. Gregory?
Mr. Oswald. Yes, sir, he had.
Mr. Jenner. Would you please relate that?
Mr. Oswald. Through the lady at the Texas employment agency.
Mr. Jenner. He had gone to the Texas employment agency and had an interview with that lady?
Mr. Oswald. Yes, sir.

Mr. Jenner. In charge of the agency?
Mr. Oswald. One of the personnel working within the agency.
Mr. Jenner. Did your brother say to you that she had suggested Mr. Gregory as a possible source?
Mr. Oswald. Yes, sir.
Mr. Jenner. With regard to employment?
Mr. Oswald. That she had volunteered to call Mr. Gregory on his behalf to set up an appointment where Lee could go by and see him and talk with him in relation to employment.
Mr. Jenner. Did your brother indicate that that was his first acquaintance or knowledge of the fact that a person named Peter Gregory existed?
Mr. Oswald. Yes, sir; he did.
Mr. Jenner. And he said that to you affirmatively?
Mr. Oswald. Yes, sir.
Mr. Jenner. In the course of that conversation, did your brother report to you any recommendations by the lady in charge of the agency with respect to his contacting any other persons who were of Russian derivation or who could or might speak Russian and be of possible assistance to your brother in obtaining employment?
Mr. Oswald. No, sir, he did not.
Mr. Jenner. The conversation was confined to a Mr. Peter Gregory?
Mr. Oswald. That is correct, sir.
Mr. Jenner. And have you now given us all you can recall as to that conversation?
Mr. Oswald. Yes, sir, I have.
Mr. Jenner. And Mr. Gregory visited your home the last week in June or at least approximately then?
Mr. Oswald. Yes, sir.
Mr. Jenner. He came alone to the best of your recollection?
Mr. Oswald. Yes, sir.
Mr. Jenner. And it was a visit, intended as a visit with Lee and Marina primarily?
Mr. Oswald. That is correct, sir.
Mr. Jenner. You were present when he came to your home?
Mr. Oswald. Yes, sir, I was.
Mr. Jenner. Did he exhibit any acquaintance, prior acquaintance with Lee or with Marina?
Mr. Oswald. He certainly recognized Lee. He did not recognize Marina.
Mr. Jenner. Was he introduced to her?
Mr. Oswald. Yes, he was.
Mr. Jenner. On that occasion?
Mr. Oswald. Yes, sir, he was.
Mr. Jenner. In your presence?
Mr. Oswald. Yes, sir.
402 Mr. Jenner. And it is your impression that he was not acquainted with her prior to that time?
Mr. Oswald. That is correct, sir.
Mr. Jenner. Or she with him?
Mr. Oswald. That is correct, sir.
Mr. Dulles. Could I ask one question here. Do you know of any other close friends of Lee's?
Mr. Oswald. At that time, sir, I was not aware of any others.
Mr. Dulles. The Fords you met later, I believe, did you not?
Mr. Oswald. Yes, sir, that is correct.
Mr. Dulles. And are they Russian or is one of them Russian?
Mr. Oswald. His wife is originally from Russia.
Mr. Jenner. How did you discover that, Mr. Oswald?

Mr. Oswald. That Mrs. Ford was Russian?
Mr. Jenner. Yes.
Mr. Oswald. I believe Marina told me.
Mr. Jenner. Representative Ford has asked that that subject be inquired into also, sir.
Mr. Dulles. Won't you pursue it then if you wish, in whatever way?
Mr. Jenner. Would you relate to us to the best of your recollection the names of Lee's friends or associates from his return to this country in June 1962 up to and including November 22, 1963?
Mr. Oswald. The only ones I was aware of, sir, other than members of the family, was Mr. Peter Gregory and his son, Paul Gregory.
Mr. Jenner. May I stop you at that moment. You say his son Paul Gregory. Did you come to meet Paul Gregory as well as Peter?
Mr. Oswald. Yes, sir; I did.
Mr. Jenner. On some occasion subsequent to this last week in June of '62?
Mr. Oswald. Yes, sir; I did.
Mr. Jenner. Had you known that there was a Paul Gregory at the time Peter Gregory visited your home in June of '62?
Mr. Oswald. No, sir. He might possibly have mentioned his son at that time, but I do not recall that he did.
Mr. Jenner. You don't have any specific recollection of it?
Mr. Oswald. No, sir; I do not.
Mr. Jenner. When did you meet Paul Gregory?
Mr. Oswald. Approximately 2 or 3 days later.
Mr. Jenner. Under what circumstances?
Mr. Oswald. Mr. Peter Gregory and Mr. Paul Gregory both came to the house.
Mr. Jenner. And this is the second occasion of Mr. Gregory being in your home, to which you have already alluded?
Mr. Oswald. That is correct, sir.
Mr. Jenner. And what was the purpose of their visit at your house on that occasion?
Mr. Oswald. To meet with Lee and Marina again, and to the best of my remembrance, for his son, Paul Gregory, who was attending either the University of Oklahoma or Oklahoma University, or Oklahoma State University, at which he was studying the Russian language.
And I believe at this time he stated he was a junior at the university, and that he wanted to be around others who spoke the Russian language, besides his father, to improve his language, or his knowledge of the Russian language.
Mr. Jenner. Was that stated in your presence?
Mr. Oswald. Yes, sir, it was.
Mr. Jenner. In this case, you now identified?
Mr. Oswald. Yes, sir.
Mr. Jenner. By Paul Gregory?
Mr. Oswald. That is correct.
Mr. Jenner. Did he attempt to converse, or converse with Lee, and/or with Marina in Russian on that occasion?
Mr. Oswald. He did with both.
Mr. Jenner. And on both occasions did Peter Gregory confer or talk with Lee and Marina or either of them or both of them in Russian?
403 Mr. Oswald. Yes, sir, they did.
Mr. Jenner. Were you forewarned or did you have notice that the Gregorys, Paul and Peter, were to visit you on the second occasion?
Mr. Oswald. I do not recall, sir.
Mr. Jenner. Do you recall any conversation you had with your brother in advance of that visit, or with Marina on that subject?
Mr. Oswald. No, sir, I do not recall any.

Mr. Jenner. Are those the only two occasions that you ever saw or talked with Peter Gregory?

Mr. Oswald. No, sir, it was not.

Mr. Jenner. When subsequent to the second visit to your home, the first time subsequent thereto, did you see or speak with Peter Gregory?

Mr. Oswald. I spoke again with Mr. Peter Gregory on Sunday morning, November 24, 1963.

Mr. Jenner. So it was an occasion subsequent to the death of President Kennedy?

Mr. Oswald. That is correct.

Mr. Jenner. Where did that take place?

Mr. Oswald. At Howard Johnson's Restaurant on the turnpike between Fort Worth and Dallas.

Mr. Jenner. How did that come about?

Mr. Oswald. I was to meet Mr. Gregory and two Secret Service agents at that establishment, to proceed with them from there to the Executive Inn at Dallas, Tex.

Mr. Jenner. Who had arranged that rendezvous?

Mr. Oswald. By mutual consent between myself and the Secret Service agent, Mike Howard.

Mr. Jenner. Mr. Howard suggested it?

Mr. Oswald. He suggested this as a point of rendezvous on our way to Dallas.

Mr. Dulles. I believe this is described in your diary, is it not?

Mr. Oswald. Yes, sir; it is.

Mr. Jenner. Did you see or speak with Peter Gregory—have you seen or spoken with Peter Gregory at any time subsequent to this occasion?

Mr. Oswald. Yes, sir; I have.

Mr. Jenner. Now, first—when was that? Is it recorded in your diary?

Mr. Oswald. No, sir, I do not believe it is in my diary.

Mr. Jenner. And when did that meeting take place? The one you now have in mind.

Mr. Oswald. On three or four occasions during the week of November 25, 1963.

Mr. Jenner. In what city or town?

Mr. Oswald. At the Inn of the Six Flags, in Arlington, Tex.

Mr. Jenner. And was he visiting there?

Mr. Oswald. No, sir; he was there voluntarily to act as an interpreter between the United States Secret Service and Marina N. Oswald.

Mr. Jenner. I see.

Subsequent to that time, have you seen or spoken with Peter Gregory?

Mr. Oswald. No, sir; I have not.

Mr. Jenner. All right.

Now, you were seeking to report to us the friends and acquaintances of your brother and your sister-in-law subsequent to their return to the United States in June of 1962. Now, who next in addition to Paul and Peter Gregory?

Mr. Oswald. None, sir.

Mr. Jenner. None?

Mr. Oswald. None.

Mr. Jenner. Were the Fords friends of your brother Lee and your sister-in-law Marina?

Mr. Oswald. Yes, sir.

Mr. Jenner. And you became acquainted with them, when for the first time?

Mr. McKenzie. Last Tuesday, a week ago this past Tuesday, on February 11, 1964.

Mr. Jenner. You were unacquainted with either of them prior to that time?

Mr. Oswald. That is correct.

Mr. Jenner. And you have already testified about the Paines. And you can recall none other—no other persons?

Mr. Oswald. No, sir.

Mr. Jenner. Friend or acquaintance of either Marina or of your brother Lee Harvey Oswald?

Mr. Oswald. Other than the ones I have described.

Mr. Jenner. All right.

Mr. Dulles. Plus, of course, the Paines, whom you have already discussed, and others you may have discussed.

Mr. Oswald. Yes, sir.

Mr. Jenner. Did you have any knowledge of your brother Lee's defection or alleged defection other than that which you read in the newspapers?

Mr. Oswald. No, sir; I had not.

Mr. Jenner. And other—other than there might be a reference to that subject in the correspondence you have produced for us?

Mr. Oswald. That is correct.

Mr. Jenner. Do you have any possible reason to believe that your brother Lee Harvey Oswald knew Jack Ruby, or Jack Rubinstein, alias Jack Ruby?

Mr. Oswald. Sir, are you asking for my opinion?

Mr. Jenner. I am asking if you have any knowledge first—anything upon which you can base an opinion.

Mr. Oswald. No, sir, I do not.

Mr. Jenner. That he did or might have had an acquaintance with Jack Ruby, or Jack Rubinstein?

Mr. Oswald. No, sir; I do not.

Mr. Jenner. I will ask you the same question as to Officer Tippit.

Mr. Oswald. No, sir. I do not.

Mr. Dulles. With regard to Jack Ruby, you hesitated a moment.

Do you have anything else in your mind about that that you wanted to add or could add?

Mr. Oswald. I just misinterpreted his question as to whether or not he wanted my opinion, rather than any facts that I might have.

Mr. Dulles. Well, let's ask for your opinion now.

Mr. Jenner. Now, we will go to your opinion.

Do you have an opinion?

Mr. Oswald. Based on the newspaper articles that appeared during the week of November 25, 1963, at which time two reported employees of Mr. Jack Ruby, a man and a woman, stated to newspaper reporters that they had seen Lee Harvey Oswald in Mr. Ruby's establishment, known as the Carousel Club, and also on one occasion either or both of these reported witnesses stated that they had seen Mr. Ruby speaking to Lee Harvey Oswald.

Mr. Jenner. And it is on the basis of that newspaper report and only that that you voice this opinion?

Mr. Oswald. No, sir.

I might further elaborate on my opinion that at various times through various magazine articles and television programs, indicating the route taken supposedly by my brother Lee from the place of his boarding house, or apartment, and prior to his capture, was in a direct or approximately a direct line to Mr. Ruby's apartment.

Mr. Jenner. Are you acquainted with the decision which your sister-in-law, Marina, reached not to reside with your mother?

Mr. Oswald. Yes, sir; I most certainly am.

Mr. Jenner. And did you take part in that decision, or were you present during the course of any event that resulted in her ultimate decision?

Mr. Oswald. I would say that that decision, sir, was 90 percent my decision, and only 10 percent Marina N. Oswald's decision.

Mr. Jenner. All right.

Now, as to that event, would you please tell us the course it took, your participation in it, where it occurred, and as much as you now recall about it?

Mr. Oswald. This took place at the Inn——

405 Mr. Jenner. Before you answer—it is not recorded in your diary, is it?

Mr. McKenzie. The diary would be the best evidence of that.

Mr. Jenner. In order that I don't try to examine over 20 pages——

Mr. Dulles. I have just read the diary, and I do not recall it.

Mr. McKenzie. I don't, either. I don't believe it is.

Mr. Jenner. Proceed.

Mr. Oswald. This occurred at the Inn of the Six Flags in Arlington, Tex.

Mr. Jenner. Fix the time.

Mr. Oswald. On Thursday morning, November 28, 1963, at which time I talked to Mrs. Marina N. Oswald.

Mr. Jenner. In whose presence, if anyone?

Mr. Oswald. If memory serves me correct, sir, in the presence of Mr. Jim Martin, and perhaps one Secret Service agent that I cannot recall vividly enough to identify by name. That Mr. Martin—if I may back up, sir. We did have a Secret Service agent there. I do recall he was Mr. Gopadze, who was acting as an interpreter. And I do believe that Mr. Gopadze acted as an interpreter at the time when we discussed with Marina the possibility of her moving to Mr. Jim Martin's home in Dallas, Tex., as a permanent guest or for as long as she wished to with her children, and I believe at this time she asked my opinion of this, whether or not I thought this was the thing to do, and my advice to her was that it was, and that she was going to abide by my decision that this was the thing to do at that time.

Mr. Jenner. This discussion occurred in the presence of these people you have mentioned?

Mr. Oswald. Yes, sir.

Mr. Jenner. Included in that discussion, was the alternative of her residing with your mother discussed?

Mr. Oswald. No, sir; it was not, because I did not look to that as an alternative.

Mr. Jenner. Do you know whether Marina—had there been any discussion prior thereto, to your knowledge, of any possibility or suggestion by anyone that Marina undertake residence with your mother?

Mr. Oswald. Not to my knowledge, sir, was there any discussion between me and Marina or myself and my mother that Marina was going to reside in her place.

Mr. Jenner. As a possibility?

Mr. Oswald. Not to my knowledge, sir. I might——

Mr. Jenner. Whether the discussion was directly with you or not, was the subject of the possibility—it is always possible—of Marina residing with your mother—was it raised during this period of time? Did you know of anybody ever suggesting it, or it being considered—apart from whether there was discussion with you directly?

Mr. Oswald. No, sir, to my knowledge I was not aware of any situation such as that.

Mr. Jenner. I forgot now.

Did you say Marina was present during the course of this discussion?

Mr. Oswald. That is correct.

Mr. Jenner. And did she say anything on the subject through the interpreter?

Mr. Oswald. If I may, sir, go to the preceding day of Thursday, November 28, 1963, to Wednesday, November 27, 1963, at which time I was advised by Secret Service agent Mike Howard of the offer of Mr. Jim Martin to take Marina and the children into the family, into his family, and raise them as he would his own members of the family. I did not discuss at first with Marina this offer. I did discuss with Mr. Jim Martin, prior to discussing with Marina N. Oswald, this possibility.

Mr. Jenner. This possibility being what possibility?

Mr. Oswald. Of Marina accepting this offer.

Mr. Jenner. Of Mr. Martin?

Mr. Oswald. Of Mr. Martin's, that is correct.

After my discussion with Mr. Martin on this question—

Mr. Jenner. In that discussion, were any alternatives discussed?

Mr. Oswald. No, sir, there was not. It was a discussion only about Mr. Martin's offer to her with me in the presence of two Secret Service agents at lunch on that day, Wednesday, November 27, 1963. At the end of that discussion. I considered in my own mind for a number of hours, perhaps three or four hours, at which time I spoke to Marina N. Oswald.

Mr. Jenner. At the Six Flags?

Mr. Oswald. At the Inn of the Six Flags, in a motel room.

Mr. Jenner. Anybody else present?

Mr. Oswald. No, sir.

Mr. Jenner. All right.

Mr. Oswald. They were present in the room, but we were in a separate room.

Mr. Jenner. They didn't take part in the discussion?

Mr. Oswald. That is correct.

At which time I pointed out Mr. Martin to Marina Oswald, and related to her as best I could at that time his offer to take Marina into his home, and the children into his home.

Mr. Jenner. Let me interrupt you.

You say you pointed out Mr. Martin to your sister-in-law, Marina?

Mr. Oswald. That is correct.

Mr. Jenner. I take it—am I correct from that that she had not theretofore become acquainted with him?

Mr. Oswald. No, sir, I believe she had, but at that time she had seen so many people come in and out of there, that she did not remember which man was Mr. Martin.

And, at this time, I did point out Mr. Martin, so that she would know him from then on.

Mr. Jenner. Was any question raised about her residing at the home of a person who was a complete stranger to her? And about whom you knew little or nothing?

Mr. Oswald. At this time I was considering this, and I believe this was my attempt to have Marina consider this, of moving into a home with a complete strange family.

Mr. Jenner. In other words, you were raising a question in your own mind on the subject?

Mr. Oswald. Yes, sir.

Up to that time of Mr. Martin's offer, not recalling anybody that I stated it to—I assumed it my full responsibility to have Marina and her children move into my home in Denton, Texas.

Mr. Jenner. Had you suggested that to her?

Mr. Oswald. No, sir.

Mr. Jenner. Or to anybody else?

Mr. Oswald. No, sir.

Mr. Jenner. Had the suggestion been made to you?

Mr. Oswald. No, sir, it had not.

Mr. Dulles. Was going back to the Paines in the picture at that time?

Mr. Oswald. To some extent, and that was excluded entirely by me, sir.

Mr. Jenner. For what reason?

Mr. Oswald. For my observations of Mr. and Mrs. Paine at the Dallas police office, as previously testified.

Mr. Jenner. The antipathy to them that arose, or that you had when you met Mr. Paine, and Mrs. Paine that evening?

Mr. Oswald. That is correct.

Mr. Jenner. Did Marina say anything to you on the subject, of her desire or possibility of her residing—returning to reside with the Paines?
Mr. Oswald. Yes, sir, she did.
Mr. Jenner. And what did she say on that subject?
Mr. Oswald. That she thought she could go back up to Mr. and Mrs. Paine and live.
Mr. Jenner. Did she indicate that that would be entirely acceptable to her?
Mr. Oswald. Yes, sir.
Mr. Jenner. Even desirable to her?
Mr. Oswald. Yes, sir.
Mr. Jenner. And what was your response to that?
Mr. Oswald. I indicated to her that I thought that that was not the thing to do.
Mr. Jenner. Did you say that to her?
Mr. Oswald. Yes, sir, I did.
Mr. Jenner. Affirmatively?
Mr. Oswald. Yes, sir.
Mr. Jenner. And what did she say in response to that?
Mr. Oswald. I believe, sir, to the best of my memory she wanted to know why I did not want her to return with her children to Mr. and Mrs. Paine.
Mr. Jenner. That is a normal response.
What did you say to that?
Mr. Oswald. As best I could I indicated to her I didn't think they were the proper or correct people for her to be associated with.
Mr. Jenner. Well, that is a term of conclusion, Mr. Oswald. Would you please tell us—were you more specific than that, or just say, "I don't think they are the proper people"?
Mr. Oswald. No, sir. It is very difficult.
Mr. Jenner. Try and reconstruct this conversation as best you can.
Mr. McKenzie. Mr. Jenner, he is trying his best to reconstruct the conversation, and I think he has testified to the best of his recollection.
Mr. Dulles. Are you tired at all?
Mr. Oswald. No, sir, I am not tired. Thank you, sir.
Mr. McKenzie. Let me ask you one question, if I may.
Mr. Jenner. Could he answer the question I have just put to him first?
Mr. McKenzie. Surely.
Mr. Oswald. May I, sir, in my own way?
Mr. Dulles. Do you object to the question?
Mr. McKenzie. No, I don't object to it, Mr. Dulles. I don't think that Robert being a layman knows what a conclusion is insofar as the way the question was framed or insofar as the way it was responded to. And I think he is trying to answer your question.
Mr. Jenner. I don't mean to suggest otherwise.
But the witness, as always—this is not criticism of this witness—they do tend to speak in terms of conclusions.
I am seeking as best you are able to do to reconstruct this event and recite what occurred.
Mr. Dulles. Would you restate the question, or rephrase it, whichever you wish to do?
Mr. Jenner. When Marina indicated to you her desire to return to the Paines and live with the Paines, and you responded as you have now testified, that you thought that that would be unwise, and they were not the kind of people with whom she should reside, would you please call on your recollection so as to state, to the extent that you can, exactly what you said to her in that respect?
Mr. Oswald. My recollection of that, sir—I stated to her, because of her limited knowledge of English, that no—perhaps with some hand signals accompanying my "no" that this was not the thing to do. And I perhaps pointed to myself and indicated let me help her on this line—something of that nature, sir.

That is the best I can do.

Mr. Jenner. Did you indicate to her by sign or by expression or statement that you were suspicious of the Paines or that your reaction of that—was that Saturday night, did you say?

Mr. Oswald. No, this was a Wednesday.

Mr. Jenner. Wednesday night—had led you to have some reservations about them?

Mr. Oswald. No, sir. I perhaps attempted to give her some more indication on that. But due to the difficulty at that time of the language barrier, and her limited English, and she, I believe, was agreeable in accepting my explanation, no matter how brief it was—because, at this time, she was certainly looking to me for advice in trying to follow my wishes as best as I could get them over to her.

Mr. Dulles. May I just add for the record that the Commission realizes408 that Mr. and Mrs. Paine were separated or were living separately, and it was probably going back to Mrs. Paine, although I understand Mr. Paine from time to time would visit there.

Mr. Oswald. That is my understanding, too, sir.

Mr. Jenner. And was that the understanding at the time you gave Marina this advice?

Mr. Oswald. Yes, sir; it was.

Mr. Dulles. Do you know whether Mr. Paine stayed there from time to time, or he just visited his wife? I understand they are separated, and not divorced. Isn't that correct?

Mr. Jenner. That is my understanding.

Mr. Oswald. That is my understanding, also.

And in answer to your question, sir, I became aware of this on Saturday night, November 23, 1963, at the Dallas police office.

Mr. Jenner. Aware of the separation?

Mr. Oswald. Yes, sir. As the Paines were about to depart with Marina and the children and my mother. And the statement was made by Mr. Paine that he would—I believe this to be my best recollection—that he would take them out there and return to his apartment, at which time the looks on both my mother's and myself's faces asked the question to Mrs. Paine, without saying anything, and she said, "Well, it is a difficult situation, I will explain it on the way."

Mr. Jenner. And that increased your antipathy?

Mr. Oswald. Yes, sir; it did.

Mr. Jenner. And the decision was made, as you have related then, that Marina would reside with the Martins?

Mr. Oswald. Not on Wednesday night, sir.

On Thursday, the ensuing night.

Mr. Jenner. The following day?

Mr. Oswald. Yes, sir.

Mr. Jenner. And you have told us about that.

Mr. Oswald. Yes, sir.

Mr. Jenner. Now, you had occasion to observe, did you not, the treatment of FBI agents of your mother, at least in your presence? Their attitude towards her and their treatment of her?

Mr. Oswald. Sir, I do not recall any FBI agents in the presence of my mother.

Mr. Jenner. You do not?

Mr. Oswald. If I may, sir—I believe you have reference to the United States Secret Service agents there.

Mr. Jenner. No. I was going to ask you that. But Representative Ford has a question which he has limited, however, to the FBI, so I did want to cover that.

You have no basis for an opinion, then, as to the treatment of your mother, Marguerite, accorded to her by the—by FBI agents?

Mr. Oswald. That is correct.

Mr. Jenner. You might have an opinion, but you have no—well, I will withdraw that. Now, I ask you, likewise, with respect to the Secret Service agents.

Mr. Oswald. There was some friction with one agent and my mother, whom she seemed to resent very harshly, any time this agent spoke to her.

Mr. Jenner. You used the word "harshly." Does that include "unjustly" in your opinion?

Mr. Oswald. No, sir; it would not.

Mr. Jenner. Did you share the opinion that the Secret Service agent you have in mind was treating her harshly?

Mr. Oswald. No, sir; I would not be of that opinion. And the Secret Service agent in question here is Mr. Charlie Kunkel.

Mr. Jenner. During this period, did you have a good impression of him?

Mr. Oswald. Yes, sir, I did.

Mr. Jenner. Having in mind all of the circumstances, and the stresses, and his duties, do you have an opinion as to whether he accorded her normal and expected courtesy and proper treatment?

409 Mr. Oswald. Only on one occasion I might have a hesitation to give a positive answer to that, sir. This occurred at the Inn of the Six Flags, in Arlington, Texas. As Mr. Kunkel was going out the front door one day—I do not recall the day—I would say this would be approximately Wednesday, November 27, 1963—there was a brief exchange at the doorway between Mr. Kunkel and my mother, of which I am attempting to recall, at which time my mother stated to him to the best of my remembrance, that "Please, sir, don't say anything to me at all."

And Mr. Kunkel's reply was—and he was irritated—that he would not unless he had to, and for her not to please say anything to him.

And that was the end of that.

Mr. Jenner. That is the only harshness, if you would call it harshness, that you observed occurring between any Secret Service agent and your mother?

Mr. Oswald. That is correct.

Mr. Jenner. Your mother has made an assertion before the Commission that she believes that the FBI should have interviewed her, and she asserts that the FBI did not interview her.

Do you have any information on that subject?

Mr. Oswald. Are we referring to the period of the week of November 25, sir?

Mr. Jenner. Yes.

Mr. Oswald. May I have your question again, please?

(The reporter read the pending question.)

Mr. Oswald. During the week of November 25, 1963, my mother, Mrs. Marguerite C. Oswald, was not interviewed by FBI agents.

I might add nor myself by the FBI agents.

And the only person out there, to my knowledge, that was interviewed by the FBI agents was Mrs. Marina N. Oswald.

Mr. Dulles. You had been interviewed, though, at a previous time by FBI agents, had you not?

Mr. Oswald. Yes, sir; that is correct.

Mr. Dulles. I think that is indicated in your diary.

Mr. Jenner. I will touch on that subject in due course.

But Representative Boggs' area of questioning is confined to your mother. Do you have any—do you know why the FBI did not interview your mother?

Mr. Oswald. The FBI did not arrive at the Inn of the Six Flags in Arlington, Texas, until, to the best of my memory, Wednesday, November 27, 1963. There is a possibility this might have been Tuesday, November 26th. But I do believe it was Wednesday.

And their purpose of coming out there at that time, as stated to me by a United States Secret Service man, Mike Howard, was to interview Marina N. Oswald.

Mr. Jenner. And did they do so?
Mr. Oswald. They did, sir.
Mr. Jenner. And did they interview your mother?
Mr. Oswald. No, sir, they did not.
Mr. Jenner. Did they interview you?
Mr. Oswald. No, sir, they did not.
If I may, sir—in reply to your question whether or not they interviewed Mrs. Marina N. Oswald at that time, they attempted to interview her at that time.
Mr. Jenner. Was there an interpreter present?
Mr. Oswald. Yes, sir, there was. It was Mr. Lee Gopadze of the United States Secret Service.
Mr. Jenner. And you emphasize the word "attempt". Would you describe the circumstances and what occurred?
Mr. Oswald. When the FBI agents arrived there—I can identify one of them as a Mr. Brown, even though I know there are two or three Mr. Browns that I have met in the FBI—I do not know his initials—the other man I cannot remember his name. When the two agents and Mr. Gopadze came in, Marina immediately identified or recognized one of the agents who she had talked to before, and it is my understanding now, at the Paines' home in Irving, Texas.
Mr. Jenner. When?
410 Mr. Oswald. It is my understanding some time in the early part of 1963, sir.
Mr. Jenner. And did Marina state that, or did someone state that in your presence?
Mr. Oswald. This came to my knowledge, sir, after the departure of the FBI agents on this particular day.
Mr. Jenner. Through what source?
Mr. Oswald. I believe, sir, through, to the best of my memory—through Mr. Lee Gopadze, who acted as an interpreter.
Mr. Jenner. Was Marina present when you were afforded that information?
Mr. Oswald. I believe she was, sir.
Mr. Jenner. And did she have an aversion to being interviewed by the FBI agent on this occasion?
Mr. Oswald. Yes, sir, she did.
Mr. Jenner. And she expressed that aversion?
Mr. Oswald. Yes, sir, she did.
Mr. Jenner. Was the reason given in your presence?
Mr. Oswald. That she did not——
Mr. Jenner. Was it—yes or no?
Mr. Oswald. Yes, sir.
Mr. Jenner. By whom; Mr. Gopadze, by interpretation, interpreting Marina?
Mr. Oswald. There, again, sir, this was knowledge given to me after their departure.
Mr. Jenner. Yes—but through what source did you obtain it?
Mr. Oswald. Through Mr. Gopadze, in the presence of Marina Oswald.
And other Secret Service agents.
Mr. Jenner. And what did he say as to her aversion?
Mr. Oswald. That Marina had recognized this one FBI agent as a man who had come to the Paines' home in Irving, Texas, and perhaps at another location where they might have lived in Dallas, or the surrounding territory, and had questioned Lee on these occasions.
Mr. Jenner. In the home?
Mr. Oswald. In or outside of the home. I do not know whether it took place on the inside—but within the immediate grounds of the home, at least.
Mr. Dulles. And was this early in 1963? Prior, anyway, to November 22, 1963, was it not?

Mr. Oswald. Yes, sir, that is correct. And that this particular one agent—not the Mr. Brown I have referred to, but the other gentleman that I do not recall his name—she had an aversion to speaking to him because she was of the opinion that he had harassed Lee in his interviews, and my observation of this at this time, at this particular interview, was attempting to start—I would say this was certainly so. His manner was very harsh, sir.

Mr. Jenner. Harsh towards Marina?

Mr. Oswald. Yes, sir, it most certainly was. And by the tone of conversation by Marina to Mr. Gopadze, who was interpreting——

Mr. Jenner. In your presence?

Mr. Oswald. In my presence. And the tone of the reply between this gentleman and Mr. Gopadze, and back to Marina, it was quite evident there was a harshness there, and that Marina did not want to speak to the FBI at that time. And she was refusing to. And they were insisting, sir. And they implied in so many words, as I sat there—if I might state—with Secret Service Agent Gary Seals, of Mobile, Ala.—we were opening the first batch of mail that had come to Marina and Lee's attention, and we were perhaps just four or five feet away from where they were attempting this interview, and it came to my ears that they were implying that if she did not cooperate with the FBI agent there, that this would perhaps—I say, again, I am implying—in so many words, that they would perhaps deport her from the United States and back to Russia.

I arose and called Mr. Mike Howard of the United States Secret Service into the back bathroom, and stated this to him. And I also stated that I realized there was some friction here between the United States Secret Service and the FBI to the extent that I was of the opinion that they did not want the FBI at that time to be aware of the tape recording that had been made of411 Marina N. Oswald, that she had been interviewed, in other words, by the United States Secret Service before the FBI arrived at the location.

Mr. Jenner. You mean that the Secret Service did not want the FBI to know that they had taped an interview with Marina?

Mr. Oswald. Yes, sir.

Mr. Jenner. What was his response?

Mr. Oswald. He said, "Robert, I cannot tell you what to do."

I did ask him if he would go over there to speak to him, and kind of tone it down—if they were going to get anything out of her, they would not get it that way.

And he said he would speak to her.

Approximately, at this time, the telephone rang, and he had to speak on the telephone.

I returned to my chair at the table where we were still opening mail, and again for the second time, the same implication was brought out.

Mr. Jenner. By the FBI agents?

Mr. Oswald. Yes, sir.

Mr. Jenner. To Marina?

Mr. Oswald. Yes, sir.

Mr. Jenner. In your presence?

Mr. Oswald. Yes, sir.

Mr. Jenner. They spoke English?

Mr. Oswald. Yes, sir.

Mr. Jenner. Was the interpreter whom you named—was he participating?

Mr. Oswald. Yes, sir. It was from the FBI agent, the other gentleman, not named Brown, to Mr. Gopadze, to Mrs. Oswald, from Mrs. Oswald back to Mr. Gopadze to the other gentleman.

Mr. Jenner. Proceed.

Mr. Oswald. On the second occurrence of this implication, of the same implication, I arose again, and Mr. Howard was walking across the room, and I stopped him, and I told him for the second time, or requested for the second time that he please say something to them about that.

Mr. Jenner. Did you speak loudly enough to be overheard?

Mr. Oswald. No, sir. I just asked Mr. Howard to please inform the FBI that she had, to the contrary, been very cooperative from the time she had been out there, up until their arrival. And, again, I referred to Mr. Howard the reference there of perhaps the friction, or the condition that I assumed, that they did not want the FBI aware of the tape recording at this time.

And his reply to me, he said, "Robert, do what you want to do. You certainly absolutely are free to say anything you want to say."

Mr. Jenner. And did you?

Mr. Oswald. I certainly did, sir.

Mr. Jenner. What did you say? You went over to the agent?

Mr. Oswald. Yes, sir; I went over to Mr. Brown, the agent I knew, who was sitting at the end of the coffee table—it was a large round coffee table. And I sat there, and I spoke to him without saying so much about—anything about the tape recording. I did say to him—and I was shaking my finger at him, sir, I might say that—that I resented the implications that they were passing on to Marina, because of her apparent uncooperative attitude.

Mr. Jenner. Supposed, you mean?

Mr. Oswald. Yes, sir.

And that I knew for a fact that she had been very cooperative and highly cooperative. And I returned to my chair at the table.

They attempted for another 5 or 10 minutes to interview Marina Oswald at that time, at which time Mr. Brown—he left the immediate area of interviewing there, and came over and started speaking to me.

I do not recall what our conversation was. I think perhaps it was on what had transpired out there prior to their arrival.

As the other gentlemen arose——

Mr. Jenner. Transpired where, prior to their arrival?

Mr. Oswald. Out at the Inn of the Six Flags, prior to the arrival of the FBI agents.

And as the other FBI agent arose rather disgustedly to end the attempted interview, he walked to the door, opened the door, and spoke very harshly to Mr. Brown, who was just kneeling down in front of me—he said, "Just cut it off right there, Mr. Brown."

Mr. Brown indicated he wanted to talk to me some more. He just motioned to him to cut it off right here.

Mr. Brown left and went outside with him.

About 2 minutes later Mr. Brown appeared again, and asked me to come outside, which I did. And then the agent apologized to me. He said he thought I was one of the police officers out there and not Robert Oswald—he was not aware of who I was. At which time we went into the adjoining set of rooms, in the presence of both agents, and Mr. Brown asked me if—it was his understanding that Marina had been interviewed and had been cooperative prior to their arrival out there, and I said this was so.

Mr. Jenner. Was the Secret Service mentioned as having interviewed her?

Mr. Oswald. No, sir; it was not.

Mr. Jenner. The only expression was that, had she been interviewed.

Mr. Oswald. I believe, sir, that is correct.

Mr. Brown did use the term had she been interviewed. And my reply, I believe, verbatim would be—my answer to that question, sir, is yes.

Mr. Jenner. And the Secret Service, as the interviewers, had been mentioned?

Mr. Oswald. Yes, sir.

Mr. Jenner. By you?

Mr. Oswald. No, sir.

Mr. Jenner. By Mr. Brown?

Mr. Oswald. Implied, sir, by Mr. Brown.
Mr. Jenner. Is that the end of that incident?
Mr. Oswald. Yes, sir.
Mr. Jenner. Representative Ford has a notation here to obtain from you all the details on when you knew that your brother Lee wished to return from Russia, and you have given us those details, have you not? The information and knowledge came to you through the correspondence which now has been identified and admitted in the record?
Mr. Oswald. That is correct.
Mr. Jenner. And you had no other source?
Mr. Oswald. No, sir, I did not.
Mr. Jenner. Did you have any discussion with your mother with respect to supplying funds—either her doing so or your doing so—to your brother Lee when he was in Russia?
Mr. Oswald. My mother did write me on one occasion, sir, requesting that——
Mr. Jenner. This is while he was in Russia?
Mr. Oswald. That is correct. I believe at this time she was residing in Crowell, Texas.
Mr. Jenner. She wrote you a note?
Mr. Oswald. Stating that if I wanted to help Lee in any way, that I had to go through her to do it to the extent that she was going to handle everything, and that she was demanding—and that was the word she used in the letter—that I do so.
Mr. Jenner. That you do what?
Mr. Oswald. Send any funds that I might want to send to Lee to her, to forward to Lee.
This I did not do, sir.
Mr. Jenner. Did you respond to that letter?
Mr. Oswald. No, sir, I did not.
Mr. Jenner. Can you fix, approximately, when you received that letter?
Mr. Oswald. Approximately July or August of 1961, sir.
Mr. Jenner. Other than that letter, did you have any—well, in addition to the letter, did you ever have a discussion with your mother on the subject matter of supplying funds for your brother while he was in Russia?
Mr. Oswald. No, sir, I did not.
413 Mr. Jenner. And she had none with you, and none occurred in your presence?
Mr. Oswald. No, sir, she did not.
Mr. Jenner. What part, if any, did you play in assisting, if you did assist, your brother Lee in his making of repayments of the funds he had borrowed from the State Department?
Mr. Oswald. I did not assist him in any way, sir.
Mr. Dulles. He did not request it?
Mr. Oswald. No, sir; he did not. He wanted to do this on his own.
Mr. Jenner. Did you discuss that subject with him?
Mr. Oswald. Yes, sir; I did.
Mr. Jenner. And did he so express himself?
Mr. Oswald. That is correct, sir.
Mr. Jenner. Did you offer to help him?
Mr. Oswald. Yes, sir; I did.
Mr. Jenner. And he refused?
Mr. Oswald. Yes, sir.
Mr. Jenner. At any time—let us confine it first to the period that your brother resided with you in your home, upon his return from Russia—did he express to you any opinion or make any comment on his regard for, or affection for, or lack of affection for, or regard for Marina?
Mr. Oswald. No, sir; he did not.

Mr. Jenner. Was the subject ever discussed between you during that month that he was at your home?
Mr. Oswald. No, sir; it was not.
Mr. Jenner. Was the subject ever discussed at any time thereafter?
Mr. Oswald. No, sir; it was not.
Mr. Jenner. Did you have occasion—obviously, you did—to observe the relationship between your brother Lee and your sister-in-law Marina, in their—as husband and wife?
Mr. Oswald. Yes, sir; I did observe that.
Mr. Jenner. And would you please state what you observed in that respect?
Mr. Oswald. I felt on two or three occasions that Lee's tone of voice to Marina—not understanding what was being said—but by the general tone of voice, that he was being overbearing or forceful.
Mr. Jenner. Inconsiderate?
Mr. Oswald. Sir?
Mr. Jenner. Inconsiderate?
Mr. Oswald. Inconsiderate.
Mr. Jenner. Of her?
Mr. Oswald. Of her—some little thing she might want to do. I say some little thing—something that she was going to do there at the house or something, or was doing—I don't recall any specific incident.
Mr. Dulles. Do you recall her reaction?
Mr. Oswald. Yes, sir; I do.
Mr. Dulles. What was it?
Mr. Oswald. It was usually silence.
Mr. Jenner. Usually what, sir?
Mr. Oswald. Silence.
Mr. Jenner. A silence that indicated resentment on her part, or rejection on her part, of comments your brother was making to her?
Mr. Oswald. Generally, sir, I formed my opinion by the expression on her face, and her reaction as indicated, that it was not very pleasing to her to be perhaps reprimanded.
Mr. Jenner. In the presence of somebody else?
Mr. Oswald. Yes, sir.
Mr. Jenner. Tell us, if you will, please, from your observation of your brother and Marina, during all of the period of time up to and through Thanksgiving of 1962, her attitude towards your brother in the normal course.
Mr. Oswald. I believe, sir, it would be described as just a normal attitude of a wife to a husband. They seemed affectionate—both of them appeared to be—and I believe this still to be so—very affectionate to the baby June Lee Oswald.
414 Mr. Jenner. And it is your opinion, based on your observation during this period of time, up to and including August of 19—Thanksgiving Day 1962—it is your opinion that they led a reasonably normal married life, having in mind all the problems that were facing them?
Mr. Oswald. Yes, sir; that is correct.
Mr. Jenner. Did your brother ever discuss with you any incident in which he thought that Marina had been guilty of some misconduct—I don't mean sexual misconduct, but did he complain about her conduct?
Mr. Oswald. No, sir; he did not.
Mr. Jenner. Any kind or character, at any time?
Mr. Oswald. No, sir; he did not.
Mr. Jenner. Was there ever a discussion in your presence by anyone, including your brother and/or your sister-in-law, on the subject of his having physically harmed her?
Mr. Oswald. No, sir; there was not.
Mr. Jenner. The subject was never discussed in your presence?

Mr. Oswald. No, sir; it was not.
Mr. Jenner. By anyone?
Mr. Oswald. No, sir.
Mr. Jenner. Did it come to your attention at any time prior to November 23, 1962, or November 22, 1963, that your brother had inflicted some physical harm on your sister-in-law?
Mr. Oswald. No, sir; it did not.
Mr. Jenner. Did you ever see her when she had darkened eyes, as though a black eye had been inflicted upon her?
Mr. Oswald. No, sir; I did not.
Mr. Jenner. Or any other physical injury?
Mr. Oswald. No, sir; I did not.
Mr. Jenner. Your mother, in her appearance before the Commission, has stated, and implied, at least, that your sister-in-law Marina could understand English and could read English—let's confine it to the period up to and including November 22, 1963.
What is your opinion on that subject?
Mr. Oswald. It is my opinion even now, sir, if I may go a little bit further, that her understanding of the English language is less than what it appears to be. She does not understand a considerable amount that she, by her actions, appears to understand. This has come to my attention since her visit to Washington.
Mr. Jenner. You mean since she appeared before the Commission?
Mr. Oswald. That is correct.
She does not grasp enough, and by this I mean, sir, to any extent—perhaps it might be best if I compared that with my experience with my children, approximately a three or four year old—if that much.
Mr. Jenner. In other words, do I fairly state that your testimony, even to the present time, and including all of the period preceding the present time, in your contacts with her, it is your opinion that she has a very limited command of the English language, whether you speak in terms of reading or understanding or speaking?
Mr. Oswald. That is correct.
I might further qualify that, sir—that she could perhaps speak more English words than she can read or understand.
Mr. Jenner. And you do not, therefore, share your mother's expressed view and opinion that she understands the English language to a greater extent than, to use the vernacular—than she lets on?
Mr. Oswald. That is correct.
Mr. Jenner. Did your mother mention to you or has your mother mentioned to you at any time any—or asserted any claims on her part, that there were any stolen documents, either stolen from her or stolen from anyone else, that would be relevant to this matter?
Mr. Oswald. No, sir; she has not.
Mr. Dulles. Has he spoken to you about the disposition of funds that415 might have come without a clear address or indication as to for whom they were intended as between herself and Marina?
Mr. Oswald. No, sir; she has not.
Mr. Jenner. Now, Mr. Oswald, when your brother returned from Russia, was there ever an occasion, to the time of his death, when he discussed with you the subject as to why he had returned from Russia? This is, apart from the correspondence. Did you ever have a discussion with him on that subject, or he with you, or a discussion that occurred in your presence?
Mr. Oswald. None, sir, that I recall.
Mr. Jenner. None whatsoever?
Mr. Oswald. None.

Mr. Jenner. Now, is that likewise true of your sister-in-law? Did she ever discuss it in your presence, or with you?

Mr. Oswald. No, sir; at no time has she.

Mr. Jenner. Did you ever inquire of either of them on that subject?

Mr. Oswald. No, sir; I do not recall at any time discussing it.

Mr. Jenner. Nor were you present at any time when anyone else ever inquired of either of them on that subject, up to and including November 23, 1963?

Mr. Oswald. No, sir; I was not.

Mr. Jenner. I take it from previous questions that you have no knowledge of Marina ever having had a black eye or being otherwise molested or beaten by your brother, or anyone else.

Mr. Oswald. That is correct.

Mr. Jenner. Were members of your family together, including Marina, to celebrate, to the extent it might have been celebrated, Christmas of 1963?

Mr. Oswald. Christmas of 1963, sir?

Mr. Jenner. Yes, sir.

Mr. Oswald. I am sorry—I misinterpreted that.

Christmas of 1963—Christmas Eve of 1963 my wife and I and my children traveled from our home in Denton to the Martin's residence in Dallas, Texas, and spent Christmas Eve, or the biggest part of that day, with Marina.

Mr. Jenner. Did you remain over to Christmas Day?

Mr. Oswald. No, sir; we did not.

Mr. Jenner. Was your mother present on Christmas Eve while you were there?

Mr. Oswald. No, sir; she was not.

Mr. Jenner. Do you know whether she was invited to attend?

Mr. Oswald. No, sir; she was not.

Mr. Jenner. As far as you know, she didn't know you were attending there on Christmas Eve, is that correct?

Mr. Oswald. That is correct, sir.

Mr. Jenner. Was there any discussion that occurred during the time of your visit on Christmas Eve, 1963, of your mother? Was she mentioned?

Mr. Oswald. No, sir; she was not.

Mr. Jenner. Do you have an opinion as to whether the Secret Service kept your sister-in-law Marina secluded against her will following November 22, 1963?

Mr. Oswald. I have an opinion, sir, that they did not keep her secluded.

Mr. Jenner. Then you do not—all right.

Representative Ford is particularly concerned as to how stable a person your mother is, which would be of interest, of course, I must tell you, to the Commission, in judging the weight they might give to her testimony. And while I did ask you some questions on that subject this afternoon, would you give us your opinion on that?

Mr. Oswald. I believe, sir, I would refer to my prior testimony on that.

Mr. Jenner. Nothing has occurred since that you would seek to elaborate upon that?

Mr. Oswald. Perhaps one thing, sir.

Mr. Jenner. All right.

416 Mr. Oswald. That occurred during the week of December 2, 1963. It came to my attention from my wife, during the latter part of that week, that my mother said on one occasion, when I talked to her over the phone, a phone call that she had originated from her home in Fort Worth, Texas, while the Secret Service agents were still present with her, as they were in my home in Denton, Texas, that she turned around at the end of the conversation and said that I requested that they leave her home. And this, to my knowledge, was the reason why they left my mother's home prior to the time they ever left my home. And, as a matter of fact, some of the agents that were at my mother's home came out to Denton to stay at my home. And one of them had conveyed to my wife what was said that night.

Mr. Jenner. And that is an additional factor affecting your opinion as to the stability of your mother?

Mr. Oswald. Yes, sir.

Mr. Jenner. Which leads you to the view that she, since this tragic event, she is not as stable as she was prior thereto?

Mr. Oswald. That is correct.

Mr. Jenner. Now——

Mr. Oswald. And I might add, sir—I don't believe I stated this. I, of course, did not request that the agents be removed from my mother's residence.

Mr. Jenner. All right, sir.

You have testified to ownership of rifles.

Mr. Oswald. That is correct.

Mr. Jenner. And do you still own a rifle?

Mr. Oswald. Yes, sir; I do.

Mr. Jenner. Did you own and possess a rifle—I will withdraw that.

Did you ever take a rifle to the Irving Sports Shop in Irving, Tex.?

Mr. Oswald. No, sir; I did not.

Mr. Jenner. Have you ever been in the Irving Sports Shop in Irving, Tex.?

Mr. Oswald. No, sir; I have not.

Mr. Jenner. Did anybody ever take any firearm owned by you or possessed by you and take it to the Irving Sports Shop in Irving, Tex.?

Mr. Oswald. No, sir; they have not.

Mr. Jenner. May I inquire of you, Mr. McKenzie—I have a question here dealing with the nature of Marina's contract—if there is still one between Robert, Marina, and Thorne.

Do we have that contract?

Mr. McKenzie. Yes, it is in evidence and has been given an exhibit number.

And I might also state that I have just left Mr. Rankin's office where I was contacted by long distance telephone from my office in Dallas, Tex., and had a letter read to me over the telephone that Mr. Thorne has sent to Marina Oswald at the home of Mr. Declan P. Ford, in Dallas. Tex., to the effect that he has had and received a letter from me, but regardless of my letter to him, that she cannot unilaterally cancel his contract, and that his contract is one that is coupled with an interest and that it would be to her best interest to immediately contact him directly in order that certain probate papers may be filed in connection with the death of Lee Harvey Oswald, to establish her community interest under the laws of the State of Texas in the estate of Lee Harvey Oswald; and, further that there was some $7,000 being held for Marina Oswald in Fort Worth, Tex., subject to the payment of $100 by Marina N. Oswald, and that likewise there were other business contracts needed to be affirmed or discussed with Marina Oswald by Mr. Thorne.

I might add in that connection that I have instructed my office to have Marina Oswald bring the letter to my office this afternoon or this evening, have a photostatic copy made of Mr. Thorne's letter, and I further instructed my office to contact Mr. Thorne by mail, certified mail, return receipt requested, and requesting in such letter to have Mr. Thorne contact me directly relative to the representation of Marina Oswald.

And I have directed a copy of that letter to be sent to the Grievance Committee of the Dallas Bar Association.

Mr. Jenner. I take it there at least was, and there is a dispute about it at the moment, as to whether it is still legally effective, an agreement between,417 or a contract between Marina on the one hand and Robert Martin and Thorne on the other.

Mr. McKenzie. Yes, Mr. Jenner. And all of those agreements are in the record, and have been produced.

And I might also say that Marina Oswald had placed both Messrs. Thorne and Martin on notice that she has discharged them as her attorney and business agent, respectively, and, further, that I have likewise notified them since Mrs. Oswald has turned the matter over to me.

And, further, for the purpose of the record, I will state that Mrs. Oswald has paid me the sum of $25, which is not my usual fee, to represent her as a retainer.

Mr. Jenner. And you do represent her?

Mr. McKenzie. And I do represent her, and do not desire one dime out of any contributions that she may have received by anyone for the benefit of herself or her children, nor would I accept same.

Mr. Jenner. Do you have a written contract with her?

Mr. McKenzie. I have no written contract with her.

Mr. Jenner. Do you know whether Marina knows or can use or understand any language other than Russian, and other than English, to the extent that she is able to use and understand it?

Mr. Oswald. No, sir; I do not. I do know that she knows a little French.

Mr. Jenner. And that is the extent of your information on the subject?

Mr. Oswald. Yes, sir.

Mr. Jenner. How do you know that she knows a little French?

Mr. Oswald. During her recent stay at my home in Denton, Tex.——

Mr. Jenner. How recent was that? Just a few days ago?

Mr. Oswald. Within the past 10 days to two weeks—I believe this was brought about, to the best of my recollection, due to a television commercial with a little French involved. I gave my total French vocabulary of parlez vouz Français, or something, and she replied to that. And we asked her did she speak French, and she said four or five other words, and she said that was about all of it.

Mr. Jenner. Did your brother ever speak to you or raise the subject of his jealousy or possible jealousy concerning Marina and any other man or men?

Mr. Oswald. No, sir, he did not.

Mr. Jenner. And did any discussion of that subject or possible subject ever take place in your presence by anybody?

Mr. Oswald. No, sir; it did not.

Mr. Jenner. Do you know any of the following members of the Russian emigré group? I will omit those you have already identified.

George Bouhe?

Mr. Oswald. No, sir; I do not.

Mr. Jenner. Have you ever heard of that name?

Mr. Oswald. No, sir; I have not.

Mr. Jenner. Teofil Meller?

Mr. Oswald. No, sir; I do not.

Mr. Jenner. Have you ever heard the name before?

Mr. Oswald. No, sir; I have not.

Mr. Jenner. Elena Hall?

Mr. Oswald. No, sir, I do not.

Mr. Jenner. Have you ever heard the name before?

Mr. Oswald. No, sir, I have not.

Mr. Jenner. Mrs. Frank H. Ray?

Mr. Oswald. Yes, sir, I have.

Mr. Jenner. Have you heard that name or know of it during the lifetime of your brother Lee?

Mr. Oswald. No, sir; I did not.

Mr. Jenner. You became acquainted with that name, with that person, subsequent to his death?

Mr. Oswald. Yes, sir; that is correct.

Mr. Jenner. Are you acquainted with her?

Mr. Oswald. Yes, sir, I am.

Mr. Jenner. What were the circumstances, and when?

418 Mr. Oswald. On February 19, 1964, I went to Mr. and Mrs. Declan Ford's home from Denton, Tex., on my way to Washington, D.C., to visit with Marina briefly, and on arrival there Mrs. Ray—and I feel like this is the same one—was babysitting with the youngest child of Lee Harvey and Marina N. Oswald. Also, Mr. and Mrs. Declan Ford's child and her own child. And I had a cup of coffee and waited on a taxicab.

Mr. Jenner. That is the extent of your acquaintance with her?

Mr. Oswald. Yes, sir.

Mr. Jenner. That is the first time you ever saw or met or heard of her?

Mr. Oswald. Yes, sir.

Mr. Jenner. To the best of your information, did Marina ever tease your brother Lee in public?

Mr. Oswald. Not to my knowledge, sir.

Mr. Jenner. Did she, in your presence, or to your knowledge, through other means ever make fun of his ideas? Deprecate his ideas?

Mr. Oswald. No, sir; not to my knowledge.

Mr. Jenner. Did she ever, in your presence, ever make any comments with respect to your brother's sexual power?

Mr. Oswald. No, sir; she did not.

Mr. Jenner. Was the subject of sex as between your brother and Marina ever discussed?

Mr. Oswald. No, sir; it was not.

Mr. Jenner. And do you know whether any remarks of that nature were made by anyone, including Marina, to or in the presence of your wife, Vada?

Mr. Oswald. No, sir.

Mr. Jenner. Has anyone or did anyone during the lifetime of your brother ever discuss or raise the subject with you?

Mr. Oswald. No, sir, they did not.

Mr. Jenner. Did you ever during all the period of your brother's lifetime, ever hear any discussion?

Mr. Oswald. No, sir; I did not.

Mr. Jenner. On that subject?

Mr. Oswald. No, sir.

Mr. Jenner. Do you record in your memorandum, diary, all of the course of events of November 22, 1963, in which you took any part? In particular, your visit to the police station on November 22d.

What I am getting at, Mr. Oswald—if what you have written in your memorandum represents your best and sharpest recollection of the course of events recorded there as of the time you wrote that—that may satisfy the gentleman who wished that inquiry to be made.

Mr. Oswald. Referring to the time I arrived at the Dallas police station?

Mr. Jenner. Yes.

Mr. Oswald. On the night of November 22, 1963?

Mr. Jenner. Yes, sir.

Mr. McKenzie. Is there anything——

Mr. Jenner. And any other visits that you made on the 23d or 24th.

Mr. McKenzie. Other than what is in your diary, is there anything else you could add to it in the way of expanding on what is in your diary?

Mr. Chairman, also in the interests of a chronological and connected record, having in mind the context of the record when it is read, may I suggest that the memorandum diary which we have identified and admitted in evidence, be set forth in full in the transcript?

Mr. Dulles. I think it would be useful to do that.

Mr. Jenner. I think this would be a good point to do that. I will ask Mr. Oswald a few things.

Have you recorded in your notebook how the assassination of the President first came to your attention, where you were, where you proceeded from that point on, and what occurred with respect to the subject matter really from minute to minute or hour to hour throughout the course of the day?

Mr. Oswald. Yes, sir; I have.

Mr. Jenner. And all of your conversations and your contacts with anyone419 during the course of the day having relation to the subject matter of the assassination of President Kennedy on that day?

Mr. Oswald. Yes, sir; I believe I do.

Mr. Jenner. And the subsequent arrest of your brother and your visit to the City Jail?

Mr. Oswald. Yes, sir; that is correct.

Mr. Jenner. And is that likewise true—that is a detailed recording of the course of events as you participated in them on the 23d and 24th of November?

Mr. Oswald. Yes, sir; that is correct.

Mr. Jenner. Now, Mr. McKenzie has kindly asked a question that I would wish also to join in and put to you.

Having glanced through the memorandum again, or read it—is there anything you wish to add to any of the recordings that you have made in your notebook?

Mr. Oswald. Well——

Mr. Jenner. That is that you might have been stimulated during the course of the questioning yesterday and today to recall, that you did not recall at the time you made those entries?

Mr. Oswald. No, sir—not to the entries or material that is already in here. Of course this is not complete to the extent it is my intention to complete at least as fully as I possibly can the entire week out at the Inn of the Six Flags—and possibly other events that has occurred to me since that time that would be more in the nature of a personal nature than anything that perhaps the Commission would be interested in. However, I might say that any time that I do complete this, I would certainly turn it over to the Commission, if they or my attorney deemed it necessary.

Mr. Jenner. If you elaborate further on your memorandum, as I understand, you will supply the Commission with a copy, and with your willingness also to exhibit the original of what you add to it?

Mr. Oswald. Yes, sir.

Mr. McKenzie. Yes, sir, we shall.

Mr. Jenner. Mr. Chairman, you have read the memorandum. It does purport to state in some detail and accuracy the course of events of the 22d, 23d, and 24th, and during that week.

Was there anything in the course of your reading that memorandum that might have led you to pose any further questions of the witness?

Mr. Dulles. No, I think not at this time. I would have to go over it again and I will do that. But, at this time—it seemed to me, as I read it, to cover the area you have indicated.

I, of course, cannot myself judge the completeness of it. But it seems to cover the points that I would have questioned the witness on if I had not had the diary available.

Mr. Jenner. There is this feature. Mr. Liebeler and I have not examined the memorandum in depth with a view as to whether any thing said in it would stimulate us to ask further questions. I read it last night, but not with a view in mind of asking additional questions.

Mr. Dulles. Well, I read it from the same angle. I read it during these proceedings, and, therefore, I was distracted from time to time. I think it is a very helpful memorandum from the point of view of the Commission.

Do you wish to—it has been introduced in evidence.

Mr. Jenner. It is in the record.

Mr. Dulles. But do you wish it put in this record?

Mr. Jenner. Yes, I would like to have it recited in full in the record. And as I recall, you agreed, Mr. Oswald, to dictate—to take the memorandum and dictate it aloud on a tape, and Mr. McKenzie will forward the tape to us.

Mr. Oswald. Yes, sir; I have so agreed.

Mr. Dulles. And when you do forward it, would you kindly advise us at that time if there is anything on a rereading of this memorandum which you would like to supplement or add which you feel will be essential for the Commission to have, or desirable for the Commission to have?

Mr. Oswald. I will certainly do so, sir.

Mr. McKenzie. And, further, Mr. Dulles, in the event that any of the attorneys420 representing or working with the Commission see fit to be in Dallas in the course of the investigation of the Commission, with a little notice Mr. Oswald will be glad to appear and talk with them at any time.

Mr. Dulles. Thank you.

And it is, of course, possible that we might wish to recall you. I am not at all sure, and I hope that will not be necessary. But we always have to reserve that for the Commission.

Mr. Jenner. There may be other witnesses who will say things upon which we would like your testimony.

For the period recorded in the memorandum, and the events recorded in the memorandum, the recordings are full and complete, is that correct?

Mr. Oswald. That is correct.

Mr. Jenner. And if you wish, or should determine to add to it, it will be with respect to matters that have occurred subsequently to those events recorded in the memorandum?

Mr. Oswald. Yes, sir, that is correct.

Mr. McKenzie. With one exception, Mr. Jenner. In the event there is some recollection or something that is recalled to his mind, he would likewise add that to the memorandum.

Mr. Dulles. I will direct that a photostat of Commission's Exhibit 323 describing the events of November 22, 1963, and immediately following days insofar as concerns the witness be incorporated in the record at this point.

(The document referred to was marked Commission Exhibit No. 323 for identification and received in evidence.)

Mr. Jenner. Have you spoken to any member of the Dutz Murret family in New Orleans since November 22, 1963?

Mr. Oswald. I have not.

Mr. Jenner. What knowledge do you have as to the cause of the split between your sister-in-law, Marina, and Ruth Paine?

Mr. Oswald. The cause of that split, sir——

Mr. Jenner. What knowledge do you have of the split, first?

Mr. Oswald. Full knowledge of the split, sir.

Mr. Jenner. All right.

Will you tell us about it? What led to it and——

Mr. Oswald. Under my advice to Marina Oswald I requested that she sever all connections with Mr. and Mrs. Paine.

Mr. Jenner. When did you give that advice and make that request?

Mr. Oswald. At the Inn of the Six Flags.

Mr. Jenner. Was this the same occasion about which you have already testified, and which consideration was being given, to whether your sister-in-law Marina would reside with the Martins rather than with the Paines?

Mr. Oswald. This was the first occasion, sir.

Mr. Jenner. I take it then from your present testimony, just answering my present questions, that the discussion went beyond the question whether Marina would reside with the Paines as distinguished from the Martins, and when I say beyond, it went to the question of whether Marina would have anything to do with the Paines thereafter.
Am I correct?
Mr. Oswald. Not fully, sir.
Mr. Jenner. All right. Will you please explain?
Mr. Oswald. To the extent that the question arose whether or not after our first agreement that she would not live with the Paines, that question never has been brought up again. The question has come up from Mrs. Marina Oswald. The time I fix this second query or inquiry from her was approximately December 20 or 21, 1963, at which time we were advised that Mrs. Paine had written her a letter or letters requesting that she contact Mrs. Paine.
Mr. Jenner. What was the date?
Mr. Oswald. Approximately December 20 or December 21.
Mr. Jenner. Marina advised you that Mrs. Ruth Paine had written her.
Mr. Oswald. That is correct, sir.
Mr. Jenner. Had written her, Marina?
Mr. Oswald. Yes, sir.
421 Mr. Jenner. Asking Marina to do what?
Mr. Oswald. To contact Mrs. Paine; that Mrs. Paine wanted to speak with her. I do not recall any specific reference as to what she had to speak to her about. She just wanted to speak to Marina Oswald. She did not reply to these letters. She asked me would it be all right in my opinion for her to call her on the phone.
I recommended that she did not talk to Mrs. Paine at all nor answer her letters and to my knowledge this request has been done.
Mr. McKenzie. To the best of your knowledge, is that right?
Mr. Oswald. To the best of my knowledge she has not contacted Mr. or Mrs. Paine.
Mr. Jenner. She has followed your admonition or advice to have no contact whatever with Mrs. Paine?
Mr. Oswald. That is correct, sir.
Mr. Jenner. Or to permit Mrs. Paine to have any contact with her, Marina?
Mr. Oswald. That is correct, sir.
Mr. McKenzie. May I ask a question right there, please?
Mr. Jenner. Yes.
Mr. McKenzie. Mr. Oswald, your testimony is from the best of your knowledge, is that correct, insofar as any contact with the Paines or Mrs. Paine is concerned?
Mr. Oswald. That is correct, sir.
Mr. McKenzie. And if the Paines have contacted Marina Oswald or if Marina Oswald has contacted the Paines, do you or do you not know of any such contact?
Mr. Oswald. I am not aware of any such contact.
Mr. McKenzie. All right, sir. Proceed.
Mr. Jenner. I direct your attention to the month of October, 1962 for a moment. Were you aware that your sister-in-law Marina was living with Elena Hall at that time?
Mr. Oswald. October, 1962, sir?
Mr. Jenner. Yes.
Mr. Oswald. One moment, please.
No, sir. I was not aware of that.
Mr. Jenner. Were you aware of where your brother Lee was living in the month of October, 1962?
Mr. Oswald. Only to the city in which he was living.
Mr. Jenner. And what city was that?
Mr. Oswald. Dallas, Tex., sir. If I might ask, sir, can you fix the date in October, 1962 when Marina Oswald was reported living with Mrs. Hall?

Mr. Jenner. No, I can't at the moment. But neither Marina nor your brother was residing in Fort Worth at that time?

Mr. Oswald. No, sir, they were not.

Mr. Jenner. From your previous testimony I gather that you did not know the whereabouts of your brother Lee other than that it was, you supposed, somewhere in Dallas?

Mr. Oswald. That is correct, sir.

If I might make one correction, sir.

Mr. Jenner. All right.

Mr. Oswald. Referring to the postcard received from Lee Oswald post dated October 10, 1962 in Dallas, Tex., I recall receiving this two days after he had moved from Fort Worth, Tex., so it would be the first part of October of 1962 they were residing in Fort Worth, Tex.

Mr. Jenner, All right, with the exception of that.

Mr. Oswald. Yes, sir.

Mr. Jenner. I take it you are not in the habit of retaining personal correspondence you receive from others?

Mr. Oswald. No, sir; I am not.

Mr. Jenner. I think you have explained why you retained the particular correspondence that you produced for us, that it was from your brother while he was in Russia.

Mr. Oswald. That is correct, sir.

Mr. Jenner. And after he returned you received some correspondence and you retained that as well.

422 Mr. Oswald. That is correct, sir.

Mr. Jenner. Did the somewhat abrupt change in the attitude of your brother Lee toward the United States come as a surprise to you?

Mr. Oswald. You are referring to the period in 1959?

Mr. Jenner. I am.

Mr. Oswald. Yes, sir; it did.

Mr. Jenner. That is the letters of May 5 and May 31 and those that followed. But that change, and his desire to return to the United States, did come as a surprise to you, is that correct, sir?

Mr. McKenzie. Are you asking about his return to the United States or his going to Russia?

Mr. Jenner. No, sir, his return to the United States, his change of attitude.

Mr. Oswald. It was quite a surprise to me that he wished to return to the United States from Russia.

Mr. Jenner. Was the change in attitude toward the United States as expressed first in the letters of November 8 and November 26, 1959, and then the series of letters that commenced in the spring of 1961 a surprise to you?

Mr. Oswald. No, sir; it was not a surprise to me.

Mr. Jenner. Would you explain both of your answers.

Mr. Oswald. There, sir, I felt like in the due course he would certainly change his mind and opinion of the U.S.S.R., and I felt very strongly that after a period of so many months or a year or two that he would change his mind and return to the United States.

Mr. Jenner. Now, prior to your brother's leaving Russia to return to the United States, that is actually a day or two before, if not the day before they left Minsk for Moscow, in May of 1962, your brother Lee outlined his projected route by return to the United States. He spoke in that letter of leaving from England and arriving in New Orleans.

Mr. Oswald. I beg your pardon, sir?

Mr. Jenner. There is a difference in the route actually taken. Did you ever discuss with Lee why that change in route occurred? Are you seeking that May letter?

Mr. Oswald. Yes, sir; I am.

Mr. Jenner. It is probably the 22d of May and that is Exhibit 318.

Mr. Oswald. Yes, sir; I have the letter before me. You are referring to the letter of May 22, 1962?

Mr. Jenner. Well, it would appear from the notation handed to me. Is there any discussion in that letter about the route of his return, projected return, to the United States?

Mr. Oswald. Yes, sir; there is.

Mr. Jenner. What does it say, please?

Mr. Oswald. "Well, we have finally gotten the word from the U.S. Embassy and shall leave for Moscow tomorrow. We will be 10 to 14 days in Moscow and then leave for England where we shall board a ship for America. The transatlantic trip will take another two weeks or so."

Mr. Jenner. Now, the fact is that they did go to Moscow and then to Holland, and boarded a ship at Holland, and as you say touched England and then went directly to the United States.

Did you ever discuss with your brother that change in route?

Mr. Oswald. No, sir; I did not. And I did fail to read further on down where it does refer to, as he put it, "will actually arrive in America probably in New Orleans."

Mr. Jenner. He actually arrived in New York City.

Mr. Oswald. That is correct, sir.

Mr. Jenner. That subject matter was never discussed by you with him?

Mr. Oswald. No, sir; it was not.

Mr. Jenner. Or by him in your presence?

Mr. Oswald. No, sir; it was not.

Mr. Jenner. Or by Marina?

Mr. Oswald. No, sir.

Mr. Jenner. With you or in your presence?

Mr. Oswald. No, sir; it was not.

423 Mr. Jenner. Have you related, during the course of the day and yesterday, called our attention to all of the correspondence between yourself and your brother from the time of his return to the United States in June of 1962 to and through November 22, 1963?

Mr. Oswald. Yes, sir; I have.

Mr. Jenner. According to our records you and your wife, Vada, or either or both of you, had the following contacts with the FBI during the lifetime of your brother Lee. I direct your attention first, to the possibility of refreshing your recollection, to the date of April 27, 1960.

Were you interviewed by an FBI agent on that day, and would the name Fain serve to refresh your recollection on that score?

Mr. Oswald. It certainly does, sir. I cannot recall the date of our interview or our conversation.

Mr. Jenner. This would be in the spring, let us say, of 1960. I have given you the date. Does that sound right to you, April 27, 1960.

Mr. Oswald. It sounds approximately right, sir, because I do recall I just started my employment with the Acme Brick Company in Fort Worth on the 18th of April, 1960.

I do not believe that it was that close to my date of employment with the Acme Brick Company. I feel like it would have been perhaps 20 or 30 days later.

Mr. Jenner. All right.

Subject to that, do you recall the interview, is the name familiar to you as being the gentleman who interviewed you?

Mr. Oswald. Yes, sir; that is correct.

Mr. Jenner. And what inquiries did Mr. Fain make of you? What subject matter, first.

Mr. Oswald. He was inquiring as to whether or not I had heard from my brother Lee Harvey Oswald recently, I believe that is the way it was put.

Mr. Jenner. Did he at that time inquire of you on the subject matter of your brother's defection?

Mr. Oswald. Not to my remembrance, sir.

Mr. Dulles. By subject matter, do you mean reason?

Mr. Jenner. Reason or the fact that he had defected or what he might have known about his defection.

Mr. Oswald. No, sir; I do not believe he did.

Mr. Jenner. He didn't discuss that. According to your recollection, there was no discussion of that subject?

Mr. Oswald. That is correct, sir.

Mr. Jenner. Was the subject of the possibility of your being contacted by any Soviet officials discussed?

Mr. Oswald. It was discussed not in the term of Soviet officials. In case any——

Mr. Jenner. Any representative.

Mr. Oswald. Any Communist Party member or so forth along that line contacted me, I assured him I would certainly, if necessary, take care of myself or if I had time report it to his attention.

Mr. Jenner. You would report all contacts to the FBI either directly to Mr. Fain or some other FBI agent or office?

Mr. Oswald. That is correct, sir.

Mr. Jenner. And you agreed to do that?

Mr. Oswald. Yes, sir; I most certainly did.

Mr. Dulles. Have you had any other calls from the FBI officers since that date?

Mr. Oswald. Yes, sir; I have.

Mr. Jenner. I think we will get to that.

Mr. Dulles. Are they pertinent?

Mr. Jenner. Yes, they are and I think I have them listed.

Was the subject of the possibility of your receiving any request by any such people for any item of personal identification of your brother discussed with Mr. Fain.

424 Mr. Oswald. No, sir; I do not recall that it was.

Mr. Jenner. You have no present recollection of that?

Mr. Oswald. No, sir; I do not.

Mr. Jenner. This is not—trying not to be repetitious but the author of this memorandum is highly desirous of inquiring of you as to whether the subject of personal identification of your brother was raised by Mr. Fain in any connection or in any aspect.

Mr. Dulles. I don't understand that question, what do you mean by personal identification?

Mr. Jenner. Some item of personal identification.

Mr. McKenzie. Marks identifying.

Mr. Dulles. Wound or anything of that sort?

Mr. Jenner. Yes.

Mr. Dulles. Physical marks really.

Mr. Jenner. Two classifications, physical marks how he could be identified; secondly any items of identification, such as registration cards, things of that nature. But first personal identification in the sense of physical properties. The person of your brother Lee.

Mr. Oswald. I believe Mr. Fain did at that time inquire as to any scars that might appear, that I was aware of on Lee's body. The only scar that I was familiar with was the one over one ear, I do not recall which ear it was, where he had a mastoid operation performed at an earlier date.

Mr. Jenner. That is his right ear, was it not?

Mr. Oswald. I still don't know, sir. I don't recall.

Mr. Jenner. I see.

In that connection, however, did Mr. Fain raise with you the subject that if anyone inquired of you as to any items of scars or other possible identification that you would in turn advise the FBI that such an inquiry had been made of you?

Mr. Oswald. That is correct, sir, and I might say it was my further understanding that I did agree if anybody inquired about Lee in such a nature that other than perhaps newspaper reporters, who were properly identified to me and I did know, I would inform him or his office of this inquiry.

Mr. Jenner. Your present recollection as to aspects of identification was limited, that is the only one you discussed with Mr. Fain was the fact that your brother had a mastoid operation on one of his ears.

Mr. Oswald. That is correct, sir.

Mr. Jenner. And you knew of no other scar or similar identification on his body?

Mr. Oswald. That is correct, sir.

Mr. Jenner. Now, do you recall being again interviewed by Mr. Fain on September 18, 1961? This would be a couple of months, two or three months after your brother returned—no, he is still in Russia.

Mr. Dulles. He is still in Russia.

Mr. Jenner. Perhaps I may refresh your recollection an interview by Mr. Fain with you respecting your then current knowledge of your brother Lee's activities in Russia.

Mr. Oswald. May I inquire, sir, was this a telephone conversation?

Mr. Jenner. All that is reported to me in this memorandum is that Mr. Fain again interviewed you on September 18, 1961 with respect to your knowledge of your brother Lee's activities in Russia.

Mr. Oswald. I do believe that he did, sir, and I believe this was over the telephone.

Mr. Jenner. By way of a telephone call?

Mr. Oswald. Yes, sir.

Mr. Jenner. You do not recall as of this time or approximately this time any personal interview that is as distinct from interview by telephone?

Mr. Oswald. That is correct, sir.

Mr. Jenner. Do you recall that during the course of that conversation you advised FBI agent Fain that your brother had been critical of the Russians.

Mr. Oswald. This was in September 1961, sir?

Mr. Jenner. Yes, sir.

425 Mr. Oswald. Yes, sir, I did, sir.

Mr. Jenner. And that you were surprised that the Russians would permit such criticism to be conveyed to you by letter?

Mr. Oswald. I do not recall that specific statement but I do not deny it.

Mr. Jenner. It is possible that you made that statement?

Mr. Oswald. Yes, sir.

Mr. Jenner. Now, the next date is May 18, 1962. Was to your knowledge or by report from your wife, was your wife interviewed by the FBI on that date or approximately that date?

Mr. Oswald. My remembrance on that, sir, is that she was on or around that date, and also by telephone.

Mr. Jenner. Did she report both occasions to you?

Mr. Oswald. Yes, sir, she did.

Mr. Jenner. All right.

Would you please recite those, taking them in the order, what she said to you and where and what the circumstances were?

Mr. Oswald. She was at our residence in Fort Worth, Tex., and she acknowledged that Mr. Fain——

Mr. Jenner. Did she tell you that, sir?

Mr. Oswald. Yes. I might add very courteously, inquired——

Mr. Jenner. That Mr. Fain was quite courteous in his inquiries of Vada?

Mr. Oswald. Yes. He inquired over the phone as to whether or not we had recently heard from Lee, and was there any indication about how his efforts to return to the United States were progressing from that end.

Mr. Dulles. How did it happen he called upon your wife, rather than you; were you away at that time, away on business or what?

Mr. Oswald. I don't believe I was, sir. I do believe Mr. Fain was courteous enough perhaps not to call me at my office, and it was of such a nature that he felt like perhaps my wife could certainly answer whether or not we had heard from him recently.

Mr. Dulles. I see.

Mr Jenner. Did she report to you as to whether any understanding had been made by her, that she or you or both of you would advise the FBI as soon as you had information as to when he might return to the United States?

Mr. Oswald. No, sir, I do not recall that.

Mr. Jenner. You don't recall her reporting that to you?

Mr. Oswald. No, sir, I do not.

Mr. Jenner. You had already agreed with Mr. Fain back in September, 1961, to keep him advised of the comings and goings of your brother in any event, did you not?

Mr. Oswald. Yes, sir, I do not believe it was my intentions, nor do I believe I conveyed it to Mr. Fain at that time, that I would, as soon as I did have notice that when, or approximately when, he was going to arrive, that I would notify them. This was certainly not my intention then. It perhaps didn't even occur to me at that time.

Mr. Jenner. Did you say anything to Mrs. Oswald, Mrs. Vada Oswald, when she stated she had agreed to keep the FBI advised, or to advise the FBI when you and she or either of you was further notified as to the time, if any, of your brother Lee's return to the United States?

Mr. Oswald. No, sir, my wife did not advise me that she made any type of statement to Mr. Fain of that effect. So, I certainly did not advise her to what we would do or convey to the FBI when we did have knowledge of it.

Mr. Jenner. To the best of your recollection then there was no discussion on that particular phase of your brother's presence in Russia on the occasion you are now testifying about?

Mr. Oswald. That is correct, sir.

Mr. Jenner. Now, you adverted to two occasions when the FBI interviewed your wife. Was the second one June 26, 1962, or thereabouts?

In other words, approximately five weeks later?

Mr. Oswald. The date was June 26, 1962, sir?

Mr. Jenner. Yes, sir.

Mr. Oswald. I believe that would be correct, sir, or approximately correct.

426 Mr. Jenner. Did you have a conversation with Mrs. Vada Oswald on that subject and did she make a report to you of any kind?

Mr. Oswald. Yes, sir, I believe this is the occasion that either Mr. Fain or some other agent called the house in Fort Worth, Tex., and requested my wife to pass on to Lee Harvey Oswald that they would like to see him at their office in Fort Worth, Tex., for an interview.

This is the only other time my wife ever conveyed to me that the FBI had called the home and spoke to her, nothing else was said about it.

Mr. Dulles. This was about a month after his return, wasn't it?

Mr. Oswald. Approximately 2 weeks.

Mr. Jenner. Was there any discussion on this particular occasion between you and your wife on the subject of her not advising the FBI of your brother's arrival in the United States?

Mr. Oswald. No, sir, there was not.

Mr. Jenner. No discussion on that subject at all?

Mr. Oswald. No, sir, not at all.

Mr. Jenner. Did she report to you that she had stated to Mr. Fain that your brother Lee and his wife Marina and their child had come to Fort Worth and were living with you and with her?

Mr. Oswald. No, sir; she did not state that to me.

Mr. Jenner. Would you give again the full conversation?

Mr. Oswald. On that date of June 26, 1962?

Mr. Jenner. Yes, between yourself and your wife Vada.

Mr. McKenzie. To the best of your recollection.

Mr. Jenner. Yes.

Mr. Oswald. To the best of my recollection, the full text of my conversation with my wife was that Mr. Fain or some other member of the FBI Bureau in Fort Worth, Tex., had called and spoke to her and requested that she pass on to Lee Harvey Oswald that they would like to speak to him at their office in Fort Worth, Tex. I would not say this was part of the conversation, I would assume at that time, as I would assume now, that perhaps he asked her was Lee and his family there.

If you know my wife, she didn't lie to Mr. Fain or any other FBI agent, and she said he was, and perhaps this prompted the request. I might say this, sir. If they did not know that Lee Harvey Oswald had returned in June, until June 26, 1962, somebody was asleep on the job.

Mr. Jenner. I would perhaps be inclined to agree with that, sir. But as far as your conversation with your wife Vada is concerned, she said nothing that she had advised the FBI that—she had discussed with Mr. Fain the fact that she had not advised the FBI of your brother Lee's return.

Mr. Oswald. That is correct, sir.

Mr. Jenner. Now, do you recall an interview with the FBI, or they with you, on August 14, 1962 or thereabouts in Fort Worth?

Mr. Oswald. Yes, sir, and I recall that this was by telephone at the general office of the Acme Brick Company and outside of my office as I was leaving the office to go to lunch that day.

The telephone call came through and I took it in another office and spoke to Mr. Fain briefly. He inquired——

Mr. Jenner. He identified himself as Mr. Fain?

Mr. Oswald. Yes, sir, that is correct.

Mr. Jenner. Had you become acquainted with his telephone voice at least by that time?

Mr. Oswald. Yes, I had.

Mr. Jenner. And that voice was the voice that you identified at that time as that of Mr. Fain?

Mr. Oswald. That is correct, sir.

Mr. Jenner. All right.

What did he say and what did you say?

Mr. Oswald. He inquired as to where Lee was living at at that time and to the best of my recollection my reply to him was that I did not know the house number. I knew the street not by name but by locale and I gave him this location.

427 Mr. Jenner. Would you please tell me what you said to him?

Mr. Oswald. That to the best of my recollection, that this duplex was located across the street from the side of Montgomery Ward located on West 7th Street in Fort Worth, Tex., approximately three or four blocks from West 7th Street.

Mr. McKenzie. Mr. Chairman, you have greatly inconvenienced yourself this evening and accommodated both myself and Mr. Oswald for which we thank you.

However, it is now 16 or 17 minutes of 8 o'clock in the evening, and Mr. Oswald has been testifying here for, to the best way I can——

Mr. Dulles. It will be 12 hours pretty soon, 11 hours.

Mr. McKenzie. Approximately 11 hours and by the same token Mr. Jenner has been questioning him for a like period of time, with the exception of the few questions you have asked and the few questions I have asked, and I submit maybe we should start again in the morning.

And I likewise say that he is perfectly willing to go forward but I do know that you have plans and if we can meet——

Mr. Dulles. We will have to do it tomorrow.

Mr. McKenzie. We can be here at 8:30, if it will suit the Commission's——

(Discussion off the record.)

Mr. Dulles. 9:30 tomorrow morning.

And we will adjourn at 11 o'clock, come hell or high water.

(Whereupon, at 7:45 p.m., the President's Commission recessed.)

Saturday, February 22, 1964

TESTIMONY OF ROBERT EDWARD LEE OSWALD RESUMED

The President's Commission met at 10 a.m. on February 22, 1964, at 200 Maryland Avenue NE., Washington, D.C.

Present was Allen W. Dulles, member.

Also present were Albert Jenner, assistant counsel; and William McKenzie, attorney for Robert Edward Lee Oswald.

Mr. Dulles. The Commission will come to order.

We will continue the hearing of Mr. Robert Oswald.

Mr. Jenner. Thank you, sir.

Have you now recited for us all of the occasions on which any agent of the FBI called or visited with you prior to November 22, 1963?

Mr. Oswald. Yes, sir; I have.

Mr. Dulles. And your answer would include any other Government investigatory bodies, would it? I mean you didn't have the Secret Service at this time?

Mr. McKenzie. In answer to your question, Mr. Jenner, and to Mr. Dulles' further question, Robert has told me there was one other agency that he does recall at this time.

Mr. Jenner. Why don't we have him recite it, and then see if it is pertinent.

Or, may I suggest, Mr. Chairman, we might go off the record and see what it was.

Mr. McKenzie. It was Immigration and Naturalization.

Mr. Jenner. Fix the date, please.

Excuse me.

There was one other Government agency that interviewed you?

Mr. Oswald. That is correct.

Mr. Jenner. Would you give the time, please?

Mr. Oswald. To the best of my recollection, this was approximately January or February of 1962, at my residence in Fort Worth, Tex., approximately 7 o'clock or 7:30 p.m. The gentleman had called my home from Dallas, Tex.

428 Mr. Jenner. Had he called you?

Mr. Oswald. No, sir; he had called my home, and my wife had talked to him, and he asked if it was satisfactory if he came over to ask us some questions and some background information in regard to Lee Harvey Oswald.

Mr. Jenner. Was this a week day or a Sunday?

Mr. Oswald. This was a week day, sir.

My wife——

Mr. Jenner. How did you become informed of this?

Mr. Oswald. My wife called me at my office, sir. And she advised the gentleman on the phone unless I said to the contrary it was certainly satisfactory for him to come that night, which he did, at approximately 7 or 7:30 p.m.

Mr. Jenner. And you were there?

Mr. Oswald. Yes, sir; I was there, and my wife was present.

Mr. Jenner. Did he give you his name, and do you recall what the name was?

Mr. Oswald. Yes, sir; I am sure he did give his name, but I do not recall what his name was.

It was a rather brief meeting and conversation that we had, and it was with regards to the possibility or inquiry into the possibility of having Lee's wife, Mrs. Marina N. Oswald, brought to this country, with Lee Harvey Oswald.

Mr. Jenner. As best as you can, would you reconstruct the conversation?

Mr. Oswald. This gentleman did take notes or perhaps he did have a form outlining various questions that he needed answers to. I do not recall any specific questions. However, I did state to him, after three or four questions, in regards to Lee Harvey Oswald being in the Soviet Union, and quite surprised, I do recall, myself that he was not aware of the reasons why—or the reported reasons why Lee had gone to the Soviet Union.

And I suggested to the gentleman at that time that he perhaps contact the FBI and I specifically mentioned Mr. Fain by name—he said he was acquainted with Mr. Fain of the FBI Bureau, and that he would get the background information from Mr. Fain in regards to Lee Harvey Oswald.

I believe, sir, to the best of my remembrance that he stated at that time he was not aware of the situation, and he thought this was just an "ordinary" case of bringing an immigrant in from the Soviet Union to the United States.

Mr. Jenner. And when he said that, what person did you have in mind?

Mr. Oswald. Marina N. Oswald.

Mr. Jenner. That is the person to whom you thought he was referring, was Marina?

Mr. Oswald. That is correct.

Mr. Dulles. And this was after, as I recall, your correspondence showed that they were planning to come back, was it not?

Mr. Oswald. That is correct, sir.

Mr. Jenner. Could you give us a little more of your recollection as to the thrust of his inquiries, the subject matter of his inquiries?

Mr. Oswald. I believe, sir, the best of my recollection on that would be directed to us at that time about Marina N. Oswald.

Mr. Jenner. Of what nature—her age?

Mr. Oswald. I do not recall any specific questions, sir.

Mr. Dulles. Did they inquire about the marriage? That would be one of the things they would inquire about. Because it would be the marriage to an American that would give her the preference. I was wondering if that might have been the subject of the inquiry—whether you had evidence that she was married to your brother.

Mr. Oswald. No, sir; I do not recall that specific question, but perhaps this ground was covered. It was just a general background on Marina N. Oswald.

Mr. Jenner. But it did relate to Marina N. Oswald? You recall that much?

Mr. Oswald. Yes, sir; it did.

Mr. Jenner. And the questions were directed toward her and about her specifically?

Mr. Oswald. More so than Lee Harvey Oswald. Some questions were addressed to me by the gentleman in relation to my brother, Lee Harvey Oswald.

Mr. Jenner. And the inquiries of the agent—he inquired of you as to whether you were the brother of Lee Harvey Oswald, did he?

429 Mr. Oswald. I am sure he did, sir.

Mr. Jenner. I am just trying to reconstruct the scene for you.

Mr. Oswald. Yes, sir.

Mr. Jenner. And whether your brother Lee Harvey Oswald was then in Russia, and had been in Russia?

Mr. Oswald. Yes, sir.

Mr. Jenner. Whether he was married, and married to Marina?

Mr. Oswald. Yes, sir.

Mr. Jenner. And was he familiar with Marina's name?

Mr. Oswald. Yes, sir; he was.

I might further add, sir, if I may, that the gentleman advised me he assumed that Lee was employed by the Government in some capacity in Russia, and not having any background or apparent background of Lee's reported reasons for going to Russia.

Mr. Jenner. And did you make any response to that, when his conversation was such as to indicate that he was not fully advised of the circumstances under which your brother had entered and remained in Russia?

Mr. Oswald. Yes, sir; I did—to the extent as I have already testified.

I believe perhaps at this point, if not this exact point, I referred him to the FBI Bureau and Mr. Fain.

Mr. Jenner. Did he ask you—did he inquire whether you had received correspondence from your brother, or the extent to which you had been in touch with each other?

Mr. Oswald. Not that I recall, sir.

Mr. Jenner. These are horribly leading questions—but I take it then his inquiries were largely directed toward, as a representative of the Immigration and Naturalization Service, obtaining information as to Marina, whom he understood to be the wife of your brother, who, in turn, was about to return to the United States with Marina, then a citizen of Russia?

Mr. Oswald. That is correct.

Mr. Jenner. How long did this interview last?

Mr. Oswald. Approximately 30 minutes, sir.

Mr. Jenner. And your mind's eye is that he had a form, or he had some set questions which he was asking from a sheet of paper?

Mr. Oswald. Yes, sir; I do.

Mr. Jenner. Rather than the typical FBI or Secret Service inquiry, in which the questions range, as mine have, for example, largely dependent upon what your answers to the previous questions were?

Mr. Oswald. That is correct, sir.

I believe the gentleman did have some type of set form as to questions he was referring to when he spoke to me.

Mr. Jenner. Did he go into your family background, your own age, your occupation, and that sort of thing?

Mr. Oswald. I believe, sir; he just went into my background, as to the extent of my relation to Lee Harvey and Marina N. Oswald at that particular time.

Mr. Jenner. Would you describe this gentleman, please—his physical appearance?

Mr. McKenzie. If you recall.

Mr. Jenner. Yes, of course.

Mr. Oswald. To the best of my remembrance, I would describe this man to be average build, rather short, approximately 5-foot 9 or 5-foot 10, perhaps in his middle forties or early fifties. I do recall, sir; if I might further add, as the gentleman was leaving the house that night, I requested of him if it was possible for him to notify me when and if Marina's visa would be accepted or not, and he replied to me at that time that he could not do that. And I replied back to him that I guess I would know about it from the extent that if she arrived over here, it was approved.

Mr. Jenner. Have you now exhausted your recollection of this particular incident?

Mr. Oswald. Yes, sir; I have.

Mr. Dulles. Could I ask a question there?

Do you recall that at any time the State Department was in touch with you430 over this general period—that is, the period of your brother's stay in the Soviet Union, or his prospective return here?

Mr. Oswald. No, sir; at no time was I aware of any member of the State Department being in contact with me.

And I might further add that at this particular time, after the Immigration and Naturalization agent was there, including my prior testimony as to the contacts with the FBI Bureau, these were the only times prior to his arrival I was in contact with any Government agency.

Mr. Jenner. Any agency of the Government of the United States?

Mr. Oswald. Yes, sir; that is correct.

Mr. Jenner. Now, were you consciously in contact during any of that period up to November 22, 1963, with any agent or agency of any other government?

Mr. Oswald. No, sir; I was not.

And I might further add that no one else other than perhaps my close friends inquired as to my contact with Lee Harvey Oswald during that period.

Mr. Jenner. All right.

You have related to us an incident of your brother being interviewed by the FBI, and he reporting back to you either that evening or that same day of that interview. That is the one in which your brother reported to you that inquiry had been made of him as to whether he was an agent of any agency of the United States, and you responded—I have forgotten now just how you phrased it.

Mr. Oswald. "Well, don't you know, sir?"

Mr. Jenner. Now, in addition to that particular occasion, were there any instances in which you were directly advised or advised by your brother or by Mrs. Vada Oswald of any other interviews by any agent of the United States Government with your brother, after his return from Russia?

Mr. Oswald. I believe, sir, to the best of my remembrance on that question, that I was advised by Lee Harvey Oswald, after he and his wife took up residence on Mercedes Street in Fort Worth, that the FBI had contacted him and held an interview with Lee Harvey Oswald in their car in front of their apartment on Mercedes Street.

Mr. Jenner. When you say in their car, you mean the automobile of the agents?

Mr. Oswald. That is correct, sir.

Mr. Jenner. And was that approximately the middle of October—I mean the middle of August?

Mr. Oswald. Yes, sir; it would have been approximately the middle of August 1962.

Mr. Jenner. Your brother reported that to you, did he?

Mr. Oswald. Yes, sir; he did.

Mr. Jenner. Is that the first information you had about it—that is, did it come through your brother initially to you?

Mr. Oswald. No, sir; I had indication from Mr. Fain, when he called me at my office, inquiring as to where Lee was residing at that time, that they did want to speak to him.

Mr. Jenner. I see.

And I take it, then, that Mr. Fain had called you at your office, as you testified yesterday, shortly before this interview took place with your brother.

Mr. Oswald. That is correct.

Mr. Jenner. Did you inquire of your brother about it, or did he volunteer it?

Mr. Oswald. He volunteered the information, sir.

Mr. Jenner. I have forgotten now.

Have I had you recite what your brother said to you about it?

Mr. Oswald. No, sir; you have not.

Mr. Jenner. Would you please state that—and who was present when your brother related this to you?

Mr. Oswald. To the best of my remembrance of that occasion, sir, it was in the presence of my brother, myself, and his wife, Marina N. Oswald.

Mr. Jenner. In their home, or your home?

Mr. Oswald. In their home, on Mercedes Street—either the afternoon or the following day of the interview. And he just simply stated to me, sir, that431 the FBI had been by and had held an interview with him in their car in the front of their residence on Mercedes Street.

Mr. Jenner. Did he tell you anything about the thrust of the interview, anything that had been said, what the inquiries were of him?

Mr. Oswald. No, sir; I do not recall any.

Mr. Jenner. Your recollection now serves you only to say that he did report to you that FBI agents had interviewed him in their automobile, in front of or near their apartment on Mercedes Street—2703 Mercedes Street—is that correct?

Mr. Oswald. I do not recall the number of the house, sir. I do recall it was at the Mercedes Street address, and I have exhausted my recollection of that particular occasion.

Mr. Jenner. Do you recall what you said or what others said—that is, others in addition to your brother—on that particular occasion, when he recited the event?

Mr. Oswald. No, sir; I do not recall any further comment about that particular event at that time.

Mr. Dulles. There is one question I would like to ask at this point.

This is slightly on a different subject.

Mrs. Marina Oswald, as I recall—and I don't know whether you were present, Mr. Jenner, when she gave this testimony or not.

Mr. Jenner. I think not.

Mr. Dulles. She stated that in the later period she had the impression that your brother was trying to break off a little with, I might call it, the Russian group in Fort Worth that he had had a good many contacts with. That is when they called, he did not seem to welcome their coming, and they slowly stopped coming. I think this was to the house on Mercedes Street.

Do you have any recollection of that? Did you know about that? Did Marina speak to you about that? Or did your brother speak to you about that?

Mr. Jenner. Or did you have any impressions about it?

Mr. Oswald. Yes, sir; I do have impressions about that—at that particular time when they were residing in Fort Worth.

If I may, sir——

Mr. Dulles. It was Fort Worth when this took place?

Mr. Oswald. Yes, sir.

Mr. Dulles. Mercedes Street is in Fort Worth?

Mr. Oswald. Yes, sir.

Mr. Jenner. Would you sort of start at the beginning, and give us what impressions you had, as to how this impressed you, as an incident?

Mr. Oswald. All right, sir.

During the period that they resided at the Mercedes Street address, I was of the opinion—and I was present on one occasion at the Mercedes Street address——

Mr. Jenner. Could you fix the time?

Mr. Oswald. This would be approximately the latter part of August 1962, sir.

Mr. Jenner. It would be subsequent to this interview by the FBI agents with your brother in the automobile near their home?

Mr. Oswald. To the best of my recollection, I would say that would be so, sir.

Mr. Jenner. All right.

Mr. Oswald. That Mr. Paul Gregory had retained Marina in the capacity of teaching him the Russian language, and he in return was paying her a certain amount per hour for this instruction.

Mr. Jenner. And how did you come by that information?

Mr. Oswald. On the night that I was present at the home or apartment on Mercedes Street, I was informed——

Mr. Jenner. By whom?

Mr. Oswald. By Lee Harvey Oswald—that Mr. Paul Gregory was due to arrive at any moment, to take him and Marina driving around Fort Worth, Tex. During this period Marina and Mr. Paul Gregory would converse in the Russian language, and that she would be paid by the hour for her time, and for the instruction.

Mr. Jenner. Who was present on this occasion when your brother told you that, in addition to yourself and your brother?

432 Mr. Oswald. Marina N. Oswald.

Mr. Jenner. And your brother spoke in English, did he?

Mr. Oswald. That is correct, sir.

Mr. Jenner. To the best of your knowledge and present recollection, did Marina understand what he was relating to you? Did he make it apparent to her?

Mr. Oswald. I believe, sir, to the best of my recollection that generally she was apparent to what he was saying to me. I do feel like she certainly recognized the name of Mr. Paul Gregory and was able more or less to fill in the conversation to the extent that she understood that Mr. Gregory was due to arrive, and that they were to converse in the Russian language for his benefit.

And it was my understanding at this time, either implied or stated to me, by Lee Harvey Oswald, that this was not the first occasion that this had occurred.

Mr. Jenner. I see.

Mr. McKenzie. Mr. Dulles, if I may interrupt at this time—you have brought here with you this morning a copy of the New York Times which you have very kindly allowed me to look at and read.

On page 22 of the New York Times, Saturday edition, February 22, 1964, there is an article there——

Mr. Dulles. I may add I have not read the paper yet.

Mr. McKenzie. There is an article here by Mr. Anthony Lewis, correspondent for the New York Times, dateline Washington, February 21, which I would like to put into the record.

Now, the reason I would like to put it into the record——

Mr. Jenner. Mr. McKenzie, would it suit your convenience if we finished this incident, and then you put this matter into the record, or is it pertinent to this particular point?

Mr. McKenzie. It is not pertinent to this line of inquiry, Mr. Jenner. But with the Chairman's permission, I would like to insert it into the record, or make a statement into the record at this time.

Mr. Dulles. It is all right—go ahead.

Mr. McKenzie. It is apparent to me, from a reading of this article, that someone other than Robert Oswald or myself has made a statement to the press. We have consistently stated to the press that Mr. Oswald was under oath before this Commission, and that being under oath before this Commission he was in no position, or that it would not be an appropriate time for any statement to be given to the press.

And yet in this article, Mr. Lewis has given some direct quotes, or what appear to be direct quotes, of Mr. Oswald's testimony before this Commission.

Mr. Dulles. I wonder if it would be agreeable to you, if we go off the record at this point.

Mr. McKenzie. If I may still be on the record for one more second, please, sir—I would like to further and say that some of the text of this article gives testimony in the same light, and nearly in the same manner in which Robert Oswald has testified.

Now, if there is a leak to the press, or if anyone on the Commission or its staff are giving articles to the press, then I want to know as soon as possible, because if that is so we will go down and have a press interview, and I just don't think it is fair to the witness, nor do I think it is fair to the Commission.

And if you feel that I am right in my statement here, then I would like to have this article inserted in the record.

Now, if you would like to go off the record, that is fine with me, sir.

Mr. Dulles. Just for a moment.

(Discussion off the record.)

Mr. Dulles. Back on the record.

Mr. McKenzie. Mr. Dulles, off the record we have discussed the New York Times article, and I have stated to you—the New York Times article referred to as the one by Anthony Lewis, of February 22, 1964.

Mr. Dulles. I think it is of February 21, but reported in the Times on February 22.

Mr. McKenzie. That is correct.

I have stated to you that at no time to my knowledge has Robert Oswald433 given any statements to the press as set forth in this article, particularly his testimony to the Commission.

And, further, that both Robert Oswald and his counsel have stated to the press that while Mr. Oswald was under oath to the Commission, and subject to recall by the Commission, that he would not issue any press statements, because I have likened it to a grand jury investigation, and I have stated this to the press.

And I did not deem it appropriate at any time for him to make any statements to the press of his testimony before this Commission.

And yet there are—I find in this article by Mr. Lewis, dateline February 21, certain excerpts from his testimony before the Commission—and it can come from only one place, and that is from someone on the Commission's staff.

Mr. Dulles. Well, I may wish to make an exception to that—having been in Washington a long time, and knowing that things have a way of leaking, and many ways of leaking.

Mr. McKenzie. Well, sir, I will state to you—maybe my statement is too strong.

But I will state to you, sir, that at no time has Mr. Oswald or myself made any statements giving testimony to the press which has previously been given to the Commission.

Mr. Dulles. I am very glad to hear that statement.

Mr. McKenzie. And, further——

Mr. Jenner. I have every confidence in that. As a matter of fact, I have been with both of you most of the time.

Mr. McKenzie. And, further, if it has been given to the press by someone other than the people in this room, and I feel confident it was not given to the press by anyone—because I have either been with you, Mr. Dulles, or Mr. Jenner. But I feel that the Commission should investigate this to see if there is a leak, and, if so, I feel that it is reprehensible.

Mr. Dulles. I will present your statement to the Chief Justice.

Do you wish to identify the statements to which you take exception?

Mr. McKenzie. I will identify it this way.

Let me just identify it this way: "His brother told the Commission that Lee seemed changed when he returned to the United States. He had lost a lot of hair, which Robert said was unusual for their family, and he appeared to be under a strain."

"Robert testified that the last time he saw Lee before the assassination was at Thanksgiving in 1962."

Now, I offer that, sir, for the record from the standpoint that that is testimony given to the Commission and quoted in this article.

There are other items or matters in the article which Mr. Lewis could have received from public records, or from newspaper morgues, or newspaper records. However, the two quotes that I have given from this article are direct testimony from the Commission, from the Commission's records.

Mr. Jenner. I think in fairness, Mr. McKenzie, they are with respect to subject matter. I don't think they are direct quotes of the witness' testimony.

Mr. McKenzie. But you will agree with me, won't you, Mr. Jenner, that they are in respect to subject matter, matters testified to before the Commission by Robert Oswald?

Mr. Jenner. The subject matter of the hair, yes. I recall specifically asking Mr. Oswald about that yesterday. We had not inquired of the witness about that prior to that time.

Mr. McKenzie. I might further add, sir, that I am familiar with the statements made to the press by you, Mr. Dulles.

Mr. Dulles. I think you heard both of them that I made yesterday before the morning, afternoon and evening sessions.

Mr. McKenzie. Yes, sir; I did. And I would be remiss if I did not add that I know that you—when you have made statements to the press, you have been most fair, both to the press, to the Commission, and also the witness.

And I am in full accord with the statements that have been made to the press by yourself, by Mr. Rankin, and by the Chief Justice.

I might also add, Mr. Dulles, if I may, sir, that the only reason I bring this434 up is that I do feel that Mr. Robert Oswald is under strict—the strictest of oaths to give his testimony only to the Commission, in the interests of finding out the truth, and that he has not given any statements to the press nor have I.

Mr. Dulles. On that latter point, I would say that I appreciate and respect the position that you have taken in this respect, that in the case of previous witnesses, the Commission itself has no authority to, as I understand it, and has not attempted to "muzzle" witnesses that have appeared before it as to what they themselves may say after the hearings.

The Chief Justice has enjoined them during the hearings not to discuss the proceedings.

Am I correct, Mr. Jenner?

Mr. Jenner. That is my understanding.

Mr. McKenzie. And that is exactly the position we are taking, sir. And that is exactly the position that we have taken, and will continue to take at all times while he is under oath to the Commission, and until such time as he is released from that oath.

Mr. Dulles. Well, I will see that your statement is brought specifically to the attention of the Chief Justice and Mr. Rankin.

Mr. McKenzie. Thank you, sir.

Mr. Dulles. Shall we proceed, Mr. Jenner?

Mr. Jenner. Yes, thank you, sir.

When the discussion of the Times article arose, you were in the process, Mr. Oswald, of relating to us an incident of one evening in the home of your brother, in which—with respect to which Paul Gregory, the son of Peter Gregory, was expected to arrive at your brother's home and then to drive about the city of Fort Worth with Marina, she talking to him in Russian and he likewise in Russian, as part of a course of instruction in conversational Russian between Marina and Paul Gregory, who was seeking to improve his command of the Russian language. And you had reached the point at which you related a conversation with you in the presence of Marina, which you thought she understood and she took sufficient part, in to lead you to believe she did understand it.

Mr. Oswald. That is correct.

Mr. Jenner. Does that refresh your recollection as to where we were?

Mr. Oswald. Yes, sir; it does.

Mr. Dulles. And I would like to add, as I understand it, it was indicated to you by your brother that this was to be on a financial basis—that is, she was in effect giving Russian lessons to Paul Gregory, and would be paid for it.

Mr. Oswald. That is correct.

Mr. Jenner. Was any amount of money mentioned? It was by the hour, I think you said.

Mr. Oswald. Yes, sir; a figure was mentioned. However, I do not recall the exact figure. I could perhaps to the best of my ability and remembrance of the occasion place the figure at over $3 an hour.

I do not recall any further conversation that I had with Marina and Lee Oswald on that occasion.

I did leave their residence before the reported time that Mr. Gregory was due to arrive.

Mr. Jenner. Did anything occur that evening, in the course of that interchange and conversation, that had a bearing upon, or led you to believe or have the impression, that your brother Lee was seeking to break off or lessen relations on his part and Marina's part with their Russian friends?

Mr. Oswald. No, sir; there was not.

Mr. Jenner. All right, proceed.

Mr. Dulles. Could I ask one question there?

Did your brother indicate whether these lessons were being given in his and Marina's home, or whether they were to be given at the Gregory home?

Mr. Oswald. No, sir. It was implied if not stated to me at that time that the lesson was to be given going around Fort Worth, Tex.

Mr. Jenner. This particular occasion?

Mr. Oswald. Yes, sir.

Mr. Jenner. Did you get any impression, Mr. Oswald, as to the course of procedure in that respect for any future occasions, or those that had occurred in435 the past, because I believe you indicated that your impression was that this was not arising for the first time that evening.

Mr. Oswald. No, sir; I do not recall anything being stated at that time or any other time where these lessons were to be given other than my impression of that one night that it was to be given as they drove around Fort Worth, Tex.

Mr. Jenner. Am I correct in my impression of your testimony that your impression in turn was that this relationship had existed at least somewhat before this occasion?

Mr. Oswald. That is correct.

Mr. Jenner. Then would you proceed to the next circumstance or event which led you eventually to the conclusion or impression that your brother was seeking to lessen the relations between themselves, he and Marina, and their Russian friends?

Mr. Oswald. To the contrary, sir, that was the only time that I recall that any people of Russian descent or interested in the Russian language was mentioned in my presence, and I base my opinion on that particular incident that they were not at the time seeking to lessen their relationship within this group of people when they did reside at the Mercedes Street address in Fort Worth, Tex.

Mr. Jenner. I see.

I had been under the impression, Mr. Oswald, from your first immediate response to Mr. Dulles' question on this subject, that you had stated or at least indicated—I had that impression—that you had noted somewhere along a point of time while they were on Mercedes Street, some effort on the part of your brother to lessen the intensity at least of the degree of intercourse between themselves, that is he and Marina, and their friends of Russian derivation. Am I correct in that?

Mr. Oswald. I believe you are incorrect in that, sir. I believe I stated to Mr. Dulles that to the contrary at that particular time they were not attempting to lessen their relations with this group of persons. And I cited the incident of that night as they awaited on the arrival of Mr. Paul Gregory as an example that they were still in contact at least with that member of Mr. Gregory's family, if not Mr. Gregory.

Mr. Jenner. I see.

Mr. Dulles. It may well have been that the testimony that we previously had related to a subsequent period.

Mr. Jenner. That may well be.

I was not here when Marina testified.

It does lead me, Mr. Chairman, however, to make some further inquiries on this subject.

Mr. Dulles. All right.

Mr. Jenner. How old, in your judgment, if you have an impression, was Mr. Paul Gregory?

Mr. Oswald. Yes, sir. I would place his age at that time approximately 20 or 21 years of age.

Mr. Jenner. And I believe you testified last evening that you had met Paul Gregory.

Mr. Oswald. That is correct.

Mr. Jenner. Did you gain any impression that evening that prior contacts between Paul Gregory and your brother and sister-in-law in this area had embraced other occasions when they, meaning Marina and Paul Gregory, had driven about the city of Fort Worth?

Mr. Oswald. Yes, sir; I was of that opinion—whether it was stated or implied, at that time.

Mr. Jenner. Could you state for us a little more in detail any remark that led to that conclusion?

Mr. Oswald. No, sir; I do not recall any specific remark that was made at that time. But I was, as I am now, of the opinion that there were or had been prior interviews or lessons between Marina Oswald and Lee Harvey Oswald and Mr. Paul Gregory.

Mr. Jenner. That is prior occasions when this method of conducting a lesson had been pursued—that is, just driving about the city of Fort Worth?

Mr. Oswald. Yes, sir; that is correct.

436 Mr. Jenner. Now, did there occur subsequently any further occasions in which the conducting of lessons by Marina with or for Paul Gregory arose?

Mr. Oswald. Not to my knowledge, sir.

Mr. Jenner. Up to the time that they had left Fort Worth, which, as I recall, was the day after Thanksgiving, 1962, did there come to your attention, either through your brother or Marina or some other source, the undertaking by Marina to give or participate in lessons to persons other than Paul Gregory, the teaching or increasing the facility of use of the Russian language on the part of someone else?

Mr. Oswald. No, sir. And if I may, sir, to understand the question fully—you referred to the day after Thanksgiving, 1962, as the day that they had left Fort Worth, Tex. They had given up their residence on Mercedes Street in the early part of October 1962, and moved to Dallas, Tex., address unknown to me. On the occasion referred to on Thanksgiving 1962, it was my understanding that they returned to Dallas when they departed from my home in Fort Worth, Tex.

Mr. Jenner. You are absolutely correct.

I did misstate your testimony. But up until the time they did leave, were there any further occasions on which you received the impression, at least, that Marina had been engaged, either for compensation or voluntarily in teaching conversational Russian or increasing the facility or use of the Russian language by someone else?

Mr. Oswald. No, sir; I am not acquainted with any other persons that perhaps she had pursued this line of employment with, or volunteered to instruct anybody else in the use of the Russian language.

Mr. Jenner. Does that exhaust this subject, Mr. Chairman?

Mr. Dulles. Yes. You may proceed.

Mr. Jenner. At any time before Marina and Lee left Fort Worth to go to Dallas, did you become aware of her, at least from time to time, living with others in the city of Fort Worth—that is, not living with your brother in their home?

Mr. Oswald. No, sir; I was not aware of that.

Mr. Jenner. Mr. Oswald; I anticipate that a series of names which I am about to put to you would in large part be strange to you, but one of the other divisions of the investigation staff desires me to inquire whether any of these names are familiar to you.

Prior to November 22, 1963, did you or your brother, Lee, or any member of the Oswald family—that would include your brother John and your mother—as far as you know hear of any of the following persons:

Mr. Chairman, may I withdraw that question and put it to the witness first.

Did you, at any time prior to November 22, 1963, know of or hear of any of the following persons:

One, George Senator?

Mr. Oswald. No, sir; I have not.

Mr. Jenner. And that name is unfamiliar to you?

Mr. Oswald. That is correct.

Mr. Jenner. Ralph Paul?

Mr. Oswald. No, sir; I did not.

Mr. Dulles. We will assume that each of those questions the name is also unfamiliar to you.

Mr. Oswald. That is correct.

If you would like, may I suggest that you read the entire list and if any of them are familiar to me I would stop you on that occasion.

Mr. Jenner. Thank you.

Andrew Armstrong; Karen Bennett, also sometimes known as Carlin; Bruce Carlin; Roy William Pike, alias Mickey Ryan; Robert Kermit Patterson, alias Bobby Patterson; Donald C. Stuart; Charles Arndt; Stanley or Katch Skotnicki; Larry Crafard; Eva Grant; Joe Bonds; Joyce Lee McDonald, also known as Joy Dale.

Mr. Oswald. No, sir; I have not heard of any of those people mentioned by name, nor am I familiar with any of their names.

Mr. Jenner. And as far as you know, none of the members of your family,437 including your brother Lee, and Marina, knew of, or were acquainted with any of these people?

Mr. Oswald. That is correct.

Mr. Jenner. And this likewise would include your wife Vada and your mother and your brother John?

Mr. Oswald. That is correct.

Mr. Jenner. Do you know whether or not your brother Lee ever visited any of the following night clubs, bars, or taverns or restaurants in the Dallas-Fort Worth area:

The Bullpen Drive-In; the Carousel Club.

Mr. Oswald. Pardon me, Mr. Jenner. This is prior to November 23, 1963—is that correct?

Mr. Jenner. It is, sir.

Mr. Oswald. Thank you.

Mr. Jenner. I will repeat the list.

The Bullpen Drive-in; the Carousel Club; the Vegas Club; the Sovereign Club.

Mr. Oswald. No, sir; I am not aware at any time that he did enter these establishments.

Mr. Jenner. Have you been in any of these establishments?

Mr. Oswald. No, sir; I have not.

Mr. Jenner. This leads me to ask you about your brother's drinking habits, if any. Did he take an occasional drink—I mean of intoxicating liquor?

Mr. Oswald. To the best of my remembrance, sir, on that particular point, I have never known him to take a drink of an alcoholic beverage.

Mr. Jenner. And have you been with him on occasion when you have had alcoholic beverage, whereas at the same time he declined to have any, or did not have any?

Mr. Oswald. No, sir; I do not recall any occasion such as that.

Mr. Jenner. Were there occasions on which you would have drawn to your attention the fact that your brother was not a drinking man—even a social drinker?

That is, were you present when others might have been having a social drink at which your brother either declined or just didn't have one?

Mr. Oswald. No, sir; I do not recall any such incident.

Mr. Jenner. But you do have a firm recollection or opinion, in any event, that your brother was not a drinking man, even a social drinker?

Mr. Oswald. That is correct.

Mr. Jenner. And am I correct that you did testify a moment ago that there was never an occasion when you saw your brother imbibe an intoxicating liquor?

Mr. Oswald. That is correct.

Mr. Jenner. What about Marina in that respect?

Mr. Oswald. There, again, sir, we are referring to the time prior to November 23, 1963, is that correct?

Mr. Jenner. Well, let's take that first.

Mr. Oswald. No, sir; I have not.

Nor was I present on any occasion that she did take a drink of any type of alcoholic beverage.

Mr. Jenner. Now, I will take the period from the 22d of November to the present time.

Mr. Oswald. Yes, sir, I have been in her presence on a number of occasions where she has taken a drink of an alcoholic beverage.

Mr. Jenner. And has it been just an occasional drink, purely social drinking?

Mr. Oswald. That is correct.

Mr. Jenner. And——

Mr. Oswald. If I may qualify one point of that statement, as to being a social drink—during the period that we was at the Inn of the Six Flags in Arlington, Tex., the baby, Rachel Oswald, being breast fed, and due to the nature that she was quite upset at that particular time, that she was not eating proper, and that they were having some difficulty—she was having difficulty maintaining the natural milk supply in her own body for the baby, that one438 six-pack of beer was brought in, and at no time did I see her drink other than one beer at a time or one beer per day to help fortify herself in this production of milk.

Mr. Jenner. Did you ever hear any conversation in which your brother participated or Marina participated with you or in your presence respecting the subject of his or her or their attendance at any night club, bar, tavern, or restaurant in the Dallas-Fort Worth area, and when I use the word restaurant, I am thinking of a restaurant in which intoxicating liquors or entertainment might be employed.

Mr. Oswald. I am sorry I keep referring to this point again, sir, but this was prior to November 23, 1963?

Mr. Jenner. Yes, sir.

Mr. Oswald. No, sir; I was not aware of that.

Mr. Jenner. All right. That is, your brother and Marina were not in the habit of—you know of no occasion on which they attended bars or restaurants with entertainment which might be described as night clubs and that sort of thing?

Mr. Oswald. That is correct, sir.

Mr. Jenner. And I take it that is not your habit, either?

Mr. Oswald. That is correct.

Mr. Dulles. To your knowledge, did he have any friends in this circle, the nightclub circle?

Mr. Oswald. Not that I was aware of, sir, prior to November 23, 1963.

Mr. Jenner. Do you know of any friends or classmates or associates, either of yourself or your brother Lee, who have become nightclub entertainers? And may I say that includes so-called stripteasers or musicians or singers, or masters of ceremony.

Mr. Oswald. If I may refresh my memory to the question, sir, you did include myself in that statement, did you not?

Mr. Jenner. Yes, sir.

Mr. Oswald. The only gentleman that I was ever in a remote way acquainted with who has become perhaps what might be determined an entertainer as you have outlined was a boy that attended high school with me in Fort Worth, Tex., and he is now known as, as then—I believe his correct name is Mr. Van Williams. If I might pinpoint the series of programs on television that he appeared in was Surfside Six, and other western and detective type series programs on television.

Mr. Jenner. Do you know whether your brother was acquainted with him?

Mr. Oswald. I would be of the opinion, sir, that he was not acquainted with Mr. Williams.

Mr. Jenner. Now, do you know of any friends, classmates or associates of either yourself or your brother Lee who have become waitresses, bartenders, or, to use the vernacular, bouncers?

You know what a bouncer is?

Mr. Oswald. Yes, sir.

To answer your question, sir, I do not know of any that are personally acquainted to myself or that I would be of the opinion that were acquainted with Lee Harvey Oswald.

Mr. Jenner. And the same question as to members or employees of any gun clubs or shooting ranges, rifle ranges.

Mr. Oswald. Yes; 1 am acquainted with at least two people who have joined or belonged to a gun club or something of that nature.

Mr. Jenner. Would you please identify them, and also state whether or not your brother Lee was acquainted with these people.

Mr. Oswald. Mr. Bill Harlan, formerly of the Acme Brick Co., in Fort Worth, Tex., and Mr.—I am quite sure that Mr. Harlan is not acquainted with my brother, Lee Harvey Oswald.

The other gentleman is Mr. Jewel Godi, of the Acme Brick Co., in Denton, Tex., who is not acquainted with my brother Lee Harvey Oswald.

Mr. Jenner. I take it these two gentlemen you have identified are fellow employees of Acme Brick Co.?

Mr. Oswald. Or ex-employees that have become my personal friends, sir.

439 Mr. Jenner. As far as you know—I will withdraw that, because it would be repetitious.

What kind of gun clubs—hunting clubs, or gun practice clubs?

Mr. Oswald. Yes, sir.

Mr. Harlan belonged to an archery club in Fort Worth, Tex., that I believe was also part of a gun club.

And Mr. Godi belongs to a Denton gun club of the nature of a practice range.

Mr. Jenner. Do you know of any possible homosexual tendency or activity of your brother, Lee Harvey Oswald?

Mr. Oswald. No, sir; I do not.

Mr. Jenner. Do you have any information as to whether he at any time met with suspected homosexuals or whether he went to the places reputedly frequented by homosexuals?

Mr. Oswald. No, sir; I do not.

Mr. Jenner. What was your brother's attitude toward sex in general?

Mr. Oswald. I do not have an opinion on that, sir.

Mr. Jenner. Do you have any opinion whether it was a normal, healthy attitude?

Mr. Oswald. I would say it would be a normal, healthy attitude, sir.

Mr. Jenner. Do you have, any—do you know what his attitude was, if he had one and you are acquainted with, toward homosexuality and homosexuals?

Mr. Oswald. No, sir; I am not of any opinion on that particular question.

Mr. Jenner. And this series of questions which I have been asked to put to you, I intended to include his entire lifetime. And were you answering the questions with that in mind?

Mr. Oswald. Yes, sir. I would not change my own answers on that basis.

Mr. Jenner. Do you know whether or not any of the persons whose names I read to you, that series of names, beginning with George Senator, and concluding with Joyce Lee McDonald, contacted any member of your family or friends subsequent to November 22, 1963?

Mr. Oswald. No, sir; not to my knowledge.

Mr. Jenner. Or any employer or fellow employee of yours?

Mr. Oswald. No, sir. Not to my knowledge.

Mr. Jenner. And I take it from your previous answer, which was that these names were unfamiliar to you, that they certainly did not contact you—at least you did not know consciously that they contacted you.

Mr. Oswald. That is correct.

Mr. Jenner. This is not, I anticipate, fully repetitious, Mr. Chairman, but an inquiry has been made—I just want to make certain of it.

Were you at all aware as to whether in October of 1962—aware of the fact, that for a short time Marina resided with Elena Hall?

Mr. Oswald. No, sir; I was not.

Mr. Jenner. And were you aware that there was for a short period of time some argument or fight between your brother and Marina which may have played a part in her visiting in the home of Elena Hall for a short time in October 1962?

Mr. Oswald. No, sir; I was not.

Mr. Jenner. I take it, sir, this is all completely new to you. You have no information on this subject.

Mr. Oswald. That is correct.

Mr. Jenner. You were not aware of anything of this nature at that time?

Mr. Oswald. That is correct.

Mr. Jenner. Mr. McKenzie described at length yesterday Mr. George De Mohrenschildt. As I recall it, your testimony was that you were unacquainted with this gentleman.

Mr. Oswald. That is correct.

Mr. Jenner. Did you ever hear either your brother—were you present when either your brother or Marina discussed, or may have discussed Mr. De Mohrenschildt?

Mr. Oswald. No, sir; I have not been.

Mr. Jenner. Are you aware of any threat that your brother uttered against or may have uttered against Mr. De Mohrenschildt?

440 Mr. Oswald. No, sir; I am not aware of any threat.

Mr. Jenner. You are now aware of the photograph of your brother with the pistol on his hip and holding the rifle and also holding a sheaf of papers, are you not?

Mr. Oswald. Yes, sir; I am.

Mr. Jenner. And did you see that photograph by any chance at any time prior to November 22, 1963?

Mr. Oswald. No, sir; I have not. Or did not.

Mr. Jenner. You were unaware that it had been taken?

Mr. Oswald. That is correct.

Mr. Dulles. Did you know that your brother had either the gun or the pistol?

Mr. Oswald. No, sir.

Mr. Dulles. Or had acquired the gun or pistol?

Mr. Oswald. No, sir; I did not.

Mr. Jenner. Did Marina, following November 22, 1963, herself also acquire the same antipathy that you have testified you had with respect to the Paines?

Mr. Oswald. I would be of the opinion, sir, that she has not or does not have the antipathy that I have to the Paines. However, I feel confident that she has followed my advice along that line, and not contacted Mr. or Mrs. Paine since November 23, 1963.

Mr. Jenner. All right, sir.

Mr. Dulles. Did you have the impression that Mrs. Paine had some ulterior motive, other than a good motive, desire to befriend Marina when she was in some distress, and to gain the chance to talk Russian with her?

Mr. Oswald. No, sir; I would not have an opinion of that, since I was not aware of the circumstances of how they did become acquainted, and consequently started living in her residence in Irving, Tex.

Mr. Dulles. I gathered from your previous testimony that your feeling, visceral feeling, related both to Mrs. Paine and to Mr. Paine.

Mr. Oswald. Yes, sir; it did. More so, if I might add, sir, to Mr. Paine than Mrs. Paine. But still I will include both of them in that answer.

Mr. Dulles. Did you know anything of Mr. Paine's background and affiliations?

Mr. Oswald. No, sir; I did not.

Mr. Dulles. You knew of Mrs. Paine's interest in learning Russian, did you not, and in Russian matters?

Mr. Oswald. Following November 22, 1963, this has been reported to me.

Mr. Dulles. By Marina?

Mr. Oswald. No, sir; I believe I read this in various reported news articles and magazines that she has stated this was her intention.

Mr. Dulles. And Marina did not talk to you about either of the Paines particularly?

Mr. Oswald. No, sir; not to any extent.

Mr. Jenner. Your information with respect to the Paines, other than your meeting them, I believe you said, the evening of November 22, and later in the Inn of the Six Flags, is based primarily—in addition to that—on items you have read in the newspaper and that sort of thing?

Mr. Oswald. Sir, to fully understand the question, you referred to a meeting of Mr. and Mrs. Paine at the Inn of the Six Flags?

Mr. Jenner. I thought you said that Mrs. Paine—or was it Mrs. Ford in the Inn of the Six Flags?

Mr. Oswald. No, sir; neither of the ladies you have mentioned were in the Inn of the Six Flags.

Mr. Jenner. Then your whole acquaintance with the Paines was your being introduced to them, is that correct?

Mr. Oswald. No, sir; that is not correct.

Mr. Jenner. Would you relate your acquaintance with the Paines, and when it first arose?

Mr. Oswald. The first occasion that I met Mr. and Mrs. Paine, was at the Dallas police station on the night of November 22, 1963.

Mr. Dulles. May I ask there—had you heard about them before?

441 Mr. Oswald. No, sir; I had not.

Mr. Dulles. Hadn't even heard about them?

Mr. Oswald. No, sir; I had not. And my subsequent second meeting with Mr. and Mrs. Paine—and I might add my last meeting with Mr. and Mrs. Paine—was at their home in Irving, Tex., on the day that Mr. John Thorne, Mr. Jim Martin and myself—for the purpose of picking up Marina N. Oswald's and Lee Harvey Oswald's personal belongings. This was the only time that I have met them since the night of November 22, 1963.

Mr. Dulles. Did anything transpire on that occasion, when you were taking up Marina's and your brother's belongings?

Mr. Oswald. Perhaps, sir, the only thing that I recall that would perhaps be of some type of significance was that Mr. Paine, at the approximate time we were ready to depart from his home, called me over to the side and stated that he would like to know where Marina was staying, and they would like to be in contact with her. And my comment to him was that Marina was leaving the area, and that she was to be well taken care of. And at that time we left.

Mr. Dulles. Do you know whether the Paines have been in touch with Marina since that particular time, when you left the Paine's home?

Mr. Oswald. To my knowledge, sir, they have not in person been in contact with Marina Oswald. However, it is my understanding from Mr. Jim Martin and Mrs. Marina Oswald that Mrs. Paine has written a number of letters to Mrs. Marina Oswald during her stay at the Martin's home in Dallas, Tex.

Mr. Dulles. Do you know the content of those letters?

Mr. Oswald. No, sir; I do not.

Mr. Dulles. Do you know whether Marina still has them in her possession?

Mr. Oswald. I would be of the opinion that she does, sir. And the only comment she had made to me directly, or Mr. Martin perhaps made to me, as to the contents of the letters was that they wanted to talk with Marina, they wanted to be in contact with Marina in person.

Mr. Dulles. Thank you.

Mr. Jenner. Off the record.

(Discussion off the record.)

Mr. Dulles. Back on the record.

Mr. Jenner. Mr. Oswald, during all of the time that your brother and your sister-in-law Marina resided in Fort Worth, Tex., were you aware of any occasion when your sister resided or visited with, and lived with, anyone else other than your brother Lee in their home?

Mr. Oswald. Sir, if I may correct you—you referred to her as my sister.

Mr. Jenner. I meant sister-in-law.

Mr. Oswald. No, sir; I was not acquainted at any time that she did.

Mr. Jenner. Do you have any knowledge or acquaintance with whether Marina did any shopping on her own?

Mr. Oswald. During the period that they were in Fort Worth, Tex., sir?

Mr. Jenner. Yes.

Mr. Oswald. Yes, sir, I am acquainted.

Mr. Jenner. Would you relate your knowledge in that respect?

Mr. Oswald. A conversation with my wife on return home from work one afternoon, approximately the latter part of June 1962—correction, sir.

It was not a conversation with my wife—it was a conversation with my mother, at approximately the latter part of August 1962, or the first part of October 1962. And, to the best of my recollection, the conversation was to the effect that Lee Harvey Oswald had gone downtown in Fort Worth, Tex., looking for a job, and that Marina wanted to find Lee while he was downtown, and even though reportedly from my mother that she insisted that she not leave the house, she did, carrying the baby, June Lee Oswald with her, and walked approximately 15 or 16 blocks into downtown Fort Worth.

It is my understanding that she became lost or needed assistance in her directions, in her attempt either to find Lee Harvey Oswald or return home,442 that she asked the assistance of a police officer, and that apparently she did not have any other difficulty.

It is my understanding at that time that she did purchase either some baby clothes or perhaps some clothes for herself.

Mr. Jenner. And this was all related to you by your mother?
Mr. Oswald. That is correct.
Mr. Jenner. And does that exhaust your fund of knowledge as to any shopping trips or visiting and shopping at a local shopping center or stores by Marina?
Mr. Oswald. Yes, sir—prior to November 1963.
Mr. Jenner. November 22, 1963?
Mr. Oswald. Yes, sir; that is correct.
Mr. Dulles. The diary, or memorandum, has considerable information, you may recall, with purchases that were made by others for Marina and the child, as I recall.
Mr. Jenner. That was afterward.
Mr. Dulles. That was afterward?
Mr. Oswald. If I may, sir, I do recall another instance.
In the presence of myself, Lee Harvey Oswald and Mrs. Marina Oswald and the baby June Lee Oswald, approximately the middle of June 1963—the occasion was a grocery shopping for my family and for——
Mr. Jenner. June of 1963?
Mr. Oswald. Thank you, sir. June of 1962. And this was to my knowledge——
Mr. Jenner. Your statement 1963 was a slip of the tongue?
Mr. Oswald. That is correct.
And there was, to my knowledge, at that time the first occasion that Mrs. Marina Oswald had ever been in a supermarket of the nature that is found in the United States.
Mr. Jenner. Tell us about the occasion.
Mr. Oswald. I remember the occasion quite vividly. If you ever have the opportunity, sir, to take a person of that nature into a supermarket or an average size store, and watch the expression on their face, as to the magnitude of the food and the variety of the food that was in her presence—and I believe for the first time to any extent—it was quite a pleasant observation, I might add, sir. She was quite overwhelmed.
Mr. Jenner. Surprised and overwhelmed?
Mr. Oswald. Surprised——
Mr. Dulles. There is nothing like it in Minsk.
Mr. Oswald. I feel certain, sir, there is not.
Mr. Jenner. Did you get the impression that her reaction was such to indicate that at least she had never seen anything of this nature?
Mr. Oswald. Yes, sir; I was of the exact opinion she had not seen anything anywhere comparable to that in the nature of a food store.
Mr. Jenner. Now, did you get the impression this was a spontaneous reaction on her part?
Mr. Oswald. Most certainly it was, sir.
Mr. Jenner. She was not putting on an act to impress you and Lee and anyone accompanying you?
Mr. Oswald. No, sir.
Mr. Jenner. This is of interest, Mr. Chairman, particularly the spontaneity.
Mr. Dulles. Was that in Dallas or Fort Worth?
Mr. Oswald. This was in Fort Worth, Tex.
Mr. Jenner. This is while they were living with you, Mr. Oswald?
Mr. Oswald. That is correct.
Mr. Jenner. How did this arise? Did you just decide—was this part of showing her Fort Worth, or was it developed from desiring to go to the supermarket to purchase something, or was it a combination of both?
Mr Oswald. Sir, I believe it was a combination of both.
If I might add, the store that I went into was not the store that I usually purchased groceries from.
Mr. Jenner. You were leading—you were doing the leading of this party?
Mr. Oswald. That is correct.

Mr. Jenner. And, in addition to yourself and Marina, who was present?
Mr. Oswald. Only the baby, June Lee Oswald.
Mr. Jenner. Just the two of you going, and you were showing her around the town?
Mr. Oswald. And Lee Harvey Oswald.
Mr. Dulles. And you made some purchases?
Mr. Oswald. Yes, sir; we did. And she made some purchases. Or she selected some items.
Mr. Dulles. Can you tell us whether Marina had from time to time a certain amount of money for her own disposition? Did your brother Lee leave her money?
Mr. Oswald. Not to my knowledge that he did, sir.
Mr. Jenner. Would it be your impression that he did not?
Mr. Oswald. It would be my impression that he did not.
Mr. Jenner. I would appreciate it if you would proceed to tell about your taking her around on this particular day, and her reactions, perhaps, to other things that you showed her in Fort Worth at this early stage of her being in this country.
Mr. Oswald. Her reactions in the supermarket, sir, as I have testified, I believe to be completely spontaneous, and certainly from all appearances it was entirely new to her. I do recall we started off in the section of the store—do you want me to name the store, sir?
Mr. Jenner. Yes; you might do that.
Mr. Oswald. It was a Safeway Grocery Store, located on Camp Bowie and Ridglea addition of Fort Worth, Tex.
Mr. Jenner. I take it Camp Bowie is the name of a street?
Mr. Oswald. That is correct.
Mr. Jenner. And you obtained any additional impressions as you made this tour of Fort Worth, that is, as to her reactions to her new surroundings?
Mr. Oswald. Yes, sir. She reacted to a walk that we took after leaving the grocery store and drove across the street to a suburban shopping center, with a large variety of different type stores. I do not recall going into any particular store. We were, as the term is applied, window shopping. And she was quite impressed at the articles of clothing, of jewelry, of shoes, and such items as might be displayed in this type of suburban shopping center which would more or less encompass a full variety of practically everything other than large appliances at this time.
Mr. Jenner. All right.
At any time prior to November 22, 1963, did you become acquainted with her habits, if any, with respect to independent shopping on her part—that is, shopping by herself for foodstuffs or articles of clothing for little June or for herself?
Mr. Oswald. None other than, sir, that I have already related as related by my mother to me.
Mr. Jenner. Is the name Hutch's Market familiar to you?
Mr. Oswald. It is not.
Mr. Jenner. You testified yesterday that, as I recall—and if I am incorrect, please correct me—that your impression at least was that your mother was opposed to your marriage?
Mr. Oswald. That is right.
Mr. Jenner. Am I correct up to that point?
Mr. Oswald. Yes, sir; that is right.
Mr. Jenner. Without the degree of that opposition. Was it quite affirmative? Did she make any scene? Did she talk—express to you unequivocally her opposition?
Give us those circumstances, please.
Mr. Oswald. No, sir; I do not recall any specific instance where she firmly stated that she was against my marriage. It might have been little things along that line she might have said to me that I do not recall formulated my opinion that she was to some degree at least having objections to my marriage.

Mr. Jenner. But did you have the feeling, and was it conveyed to you, that she was quite affirmatively opposed to your marriage?

Mr. Oswald. I would say generally; yes, sir.

444 Mr. Jenner. All right.

Did Marina and your mother stay at the Adolphus Hotel in Dallas?

Mr. Oswald. In what period?

Mr. Jenner. Before they moved to the Executive House?

Mr. Dulles. Right after November 22—maybe the night of November 22. I think they had a room and moved out.

Mr. Jenner. I thought the witness referred to the Adolphus Hotel yesterday.

Mr. McKenzie. He has not referred to the Adolphus Hotel.

Mr. Oswald. I believe that is right.

My first occasion to meet with my mother and Marina Oswald on November 23, 1963——

Mr. Jenner. That is a Saturday.

Mr. Oswald. Was at the Adolphus Hotel, rather than the Baker Hotel, as noted in my notes on page 10, in my diary.

Mr. Jenner. I had noted that, Mr. Oswald. And would you identify the page to which you have reference now?

Mr. Oswald. Page 10, sir.

Mr. Jenner. Page 10 of your memorandum?

Mr. Oswald. That is right. And I might point out at the time I wrote it down in parens—"I believe." In other words, my statement was "I received a call from mother while at the DA's office, and she advised she was at the Baker Hotel—I believe."

Mr. Jenner. And your recollection has now been refreshed that that was the Adolphus Hotel rather than the Baker Hotel?

Mr. Oswald. Yes, sir; I am of the opinion now it was the Adolphus Hotel rather than the Baker Hotel.

Mr. Jenner. And then the next day they were moved to or themselves moved to Executive House.

Mr. Oswald. No, sir; that is not correct. They were moved later on, on Saturday, November 23, 1963, to the Executive Inn.

Mr. Jenner. Executive Inn that is called?

Mr. Oswald. Yes, sir.

Mr. Jenner. Rather than Executive House?

Mr. Oswald. Yes, sir; that is right.

Mr. Jenner. They went from the Adolphus Hotel in Dallas to the Executive Inn?

Mr. Oswald. Yes, sir. That is my understanding, that they did.

Mr. Jenner. I see.

Mr. Dulles. Were those quarters, as far as you recall, retained for them by the Life people, Life, Time, Fortune people?

Mr. Oswald. In my conversation with my mother on Saturday, November 23, while I was at the district attorney's office in Dallas, Tex., she related to me at that time that they had furnished her and Marina Oswald and the babies three rooms at the Adolphus Hotel, and that Life magazine was paying for these rooms, and that they could keep these rooms as they wanted—as long as they wanted to be close to Lee and the situation that was erupting in Dallas, Tex., at this time.

Mr. Jenner. I see.

Did you, during this period of time, have occasion to visit them at the Adolphus Hotel?

Mr. Oswald. Yes, sir; I did.

Mr. Jenner. And is that recorded in your memorandum.

Mr. Oswald. Yes, sir; it is.

Mr. Jenner. Then I don't wish to burden the record by asking you about it again.

Did you have occasion to visit them at the Executive Inn?
Mr. Oswald. Yes, sir; I did.
Mr. Jenner. And is that recorded in your memorandum?
Mr. Oswald. Yes, sir; it is.
Mr. Jenner. Identify the page, please.
Mr. Oswald. That begins on page 14, at the bottom of the page, under the date of Sunday, November 24, 1963.
445 Mr. Jenner. And on that same day, did they move to the Inn of the Six Flags?
Mr. Oswald. That is right—later on in the afternoon, Sunday, November 24.
Mr. Jenner. Did you accompany them on that occasion?
Mr. Oswald. Yes, sir; I did. I was in a separate car, but they were in the same party.
Mr. Jenner. All three phases, Mr. Oswald—Adolphus Hotel, Executive Inn, and the journey to and living at the Inn of the Six Flags, they are recorded in your memorandum?
Mr. Oswald. Yes, sir; they are.
Mr. Jenner. Did there come a time when differences arose between Marina and your mother?
Mr. McKenzie. You have covered that.
Mr. Jenner. Are you sure?
Mr. McKenzie. I will submit it to the Chair.
Mr. Dulles. I would think so. I think that has been covered.
Mr. Oswald. Did you want me to answer that, sir?
Mr. Jenner. We don't want it if it is repetitious.
Mr. Oswald. I believe that has already been testified to, sir.
Mr. Jenner. During the course of the days immediately following November 22, 1963, whether at the Adolphus or the Executive Inn or the Inn of the Six Flags, did any time arise, any talk with you or in your presence, of a supposed possible conspiracy between the Secret Service men on the one hand and Marina on the other?
Mr. Oswald. No, sir; there was not.
Mr. Jenner. Nothing of that character arose, as far as you can recall?
Mr. Oswald. No, sir.
Mr. Jenner. And I may say to you, Mr. Oswald, that the purpose of asking you that question is a statement made by your mother that there was a conspiracy between Marina and the Secret Service to turn Marina against your mother and against your brother, Lee Harvey Oswald, or the memory of your brother.
Mr. Oswald. I would say to the best of my remembrance of all happenings at the Inn of the Six Flags that at no time, to my knowledge, was there any type of conspiracy of that nature, and at no time was I aware of any type of conspiracy that would even resemble that statement, sir.
Mr. Jenner. All right.
Mr. Dulles. As I recall, however, you have testified that you discussed with the Secret Service the type of interrogation that the FBI were carrying on, and that has been fully presented in the record.
Mr. Oswald. That is right.
Mr. Jenner. Following November 22, 1963, you saw a good deal of Marina, did you not in those few days? You were guiding her and advising her?
Mr. Oswald. That is right.
Mr. Jenner. And you already testified that on at least one occasion, or maybe two, that you had taken her to your brother's grave in the cemetery.
Mr. Oswald. Yes, sir; on quite a few other occasions also.
Mr. Jenner. In addition?
Mr. Oswald. Yes, sir.
Mr. Dulles. And in your memorandum or diary—I don't know how we described that, but I think variously as memorandum or diary.

Mr. Jenner. I would say memorandum, except the last pages a diary.

Mr. Dulles. In your memorandum you have recounted certain problems in connection with the funeral arrangements. Is there anything else you would like to add to that?

Mr. Oswald. No, sir; I would not.

Mr. Jenner. On the basis of your participating in the course of events subsequent to November 22, and your continuing presence at the Inn, and advising your sister-in-law, Marina, do you have an opinion as to whether the Secret Service or anyone else was overly influencing Marina? Or even that they were attempting to influence her?

Mr. Oswald. Yes, sir; I believe that—perhaps I did not get the full statement there. I believe you included anyone, including the Secret Service agents.

446 Mr. Jenner. Could we confine it to the Secret Service first?

Mr. Oswald. All right.

In answer to that part of the question, I would say I felt like they were not attempting to influence Marina.

Mr. Jenner. Would it be your impression that they were trying to be completely fair, even leaning over backwards? Or do you have any impression in that respect?

Mr. Oswald. Yes, sir; I do have an impression and opinion on that.

Mr. Jenner. Would you state it?

Mr. Oswald. That I felt at no time during our stay at the Inn of the Six Flags during the week of November 25, 1963, including Sunday, November 24, 1963, that the United States Secret Service agents that were present at one time or another did anything other than to be extremely helpful to Marina, and not to the point of attempting to affect her judgment or to, so to speak, put words into her mouth, or in any way lead her with relation to the events that had occurred on November 22, 1963, or prior events that she had recorded on her tape recording interview in the Inn of the Six Flags, or the events that happened Sunday, November 23, 1963, until the time she left the Inn of the Six Flags.

In other words, they conducted themselves in a highly admirable way at all times.

Mr. Jenner. Now, would you give us your same opinion with respect to the FBI?

Mr. Oswald. As I testified yesterday, sir; I was of the opinion on the first and the second interview—and I refer to the first interview as I did yesterday as an attempted interview, and I referred to the second interview, to the best of my recollection it was the second interview, at which time the FBI, in my opinion, kept Marina Oswald in an interview to the extent that it had almost entirely exhausted her.

Mr. Jenner. Is this the occasion you related to us yesterday, or is this another one?

Mr. Oswald. No, sir; this is the second occasion, when there was an interview.

Mr. Jenner. Would you please tell us about that, and when it occurred?

Mr. Oswald. This interview occurred approximately Wednesday night, November 27, 1963.

Mr. Jenner. Where?

Mr. Oswald. At the Inn of the Six Flags, at which time the FBI agents and Mr. Tom Kelley, of the United States Secret Service, left the room that we had been staying in with Marina Oswald and went to the adjoining set of rooms that was located, of course, right next to the room we had been staying, and commenced an interview. It is my understanding that Mr. Kelley was not present at this interview.

However, he was in the adjoining room to that set of rooms, and that he was not permitted to be within the immediate interviewing area.

I do not recall the exact length of this interview. But as the night progressed, it became at least apparent to me that due to the state of Marina Oswald at that time, considering all the things that had occurred, and the difficulty that she was having producing enough milk for the baby Rachel, that they were extremely disregarding her own personal welfare at this time.

And I did go to the adjoining rooms, and I believe Mr. Kelley opened the door. And at that time I related to him that the babies had awakened, and that they needed their mother, Marina Oswald.

He immediately informed the interviewers in the next room. And as my memory serves me, Mr. Kelley turned to me and stated he was glad I did that, and I stated to him that the babies were still asleep, and I did it on the very purpose of stopping the interview, too, to the length and the nature of Marina's welfare, and to the extent that that was quite late at night.

Mr. Dulles. Were you present during the whole interview?

Mr. Oswald. No, sir; I was not. I was in the adjoining rooms, keeping an eye just in case the babies did wake and so forth.

Mr. Dulles. Was there an interpreter present at that time?

447 Mr. Oswald. Yes, sir.

Mr. Dulles. Was that FBI or Secret Service interpreter?

Mr. Oswald. To the best of my memory, sir, that was Mr. Lee Gopadze of the United States Secret Service.

Mr. McKenzie. Mr. Gopadze was participating in the interview?

Mr. Oswald. That is right.

Mr. Dulles. But only as interpreter.

Mr. Oswald. That is right.

Mr. Jenner. Do you have an opinion as to whether Marina was or is involved in any plot or conspiracy in connection with this affair?

Mr. Oswald. May I have the first part of that question again?

(The reporter read the question.)

Mr. Oswald. No, sir; I do not.

Mr. Jenner. Do you have an opinion to the contrary?

That is, that she is not?

Mr. Oswald. I am of the opinion, sir, that she is not involved in any conspiracy or was involved in any way with the event that took place on November 22, 1963.

Mr. Jenner. Thank you.

Mr. Dulles. Could I ask a question there?

Do you have any opinion as to whether any American security service, Secret Service, FBI, CIA, were in any way involved in any conspiracy or plot or otherwise involved in this whole affair?

Mr. Oswald. Sir, you are asking me of my opinion?

Mr. Dulles. Only your opinion, yes—obviously if you have information or any evidence we would like to have it.

Mr. Oswald. No, sir; I do not have any evidence or information along that line. I do have an opinion, sir, qualified to this extent. That it is very difficult for me to feel that Lee Harvey Oswald acted entirely on his own without any assistance whatsoever.

Now, whether this assistance was from my—from any member of any government agency, or just individuals, I do not know. I do feel like he had assistance of one nature or another, sir.

Mr. McKenzie. Robert, that does not answer Mr. Dulles' question. And I want you to answer his question fully.

Mr. Dulles. My question was really directed toward any security agency of the United States Government.

Mr. McKenzie. If I may state your question, Mr. Dulles, to Mr. Oswald—his question was whether or not any security agency of the United States Government, whether it be the FBI, the Secret Service, the CIA, or any Government agency, had any part in a conspiracy or plot dealing with the events of November 22, and what your opinion is concerning the same.

Mr. Dulles. That is correctly stated.

Mr. Oswald. All right.

I would correct my answer to this extent, sir. I would be of the opinion that no agency of the United States Government was in any way involved with the assassination of the President of the United States on November 22, 1963.

Does that answer the question?

Mr. Jenner. Or in any way involved with your brother's, Lee Harvey Oswald. Would you go that far?

Mr. Oswald. When we say involved, sir—excluding the interviews that I am aware of and so forth. Yes, sir; I would be of that opinion.

Mr. Dulles. To which you have testified with regard to the FBI and the Immigration and Naturalization.

Mr. Oswald. That is right.

Mr. Jenner. Would you elaborate further, please, when you first undertook to answer Mr. Dulles question—you made some references to an opinion on your part that your brother, Lee Harvey Oswald, must have had some assistance.

Would you please state what you had in mind there? Assistance with what, sir?

Mr. Oswald. My opinion on that, sir, would be that, concluding that Lee448 Harvey Oswald did actually shoot the President of the United States and Governor Connally of Texas on November 22, 1963—I do feel that he did have assistance to the extent that perhaps some money was given to him, and that other types of assistance, such as perhaps training and orientations as to perhaps the method to be used.

I believe that would conclude my opinion on the assistance I had reference to.

Mr. Jenner. This is based, I gather from what you have just said, on the assumption or opinion—I will say assumption first—that your brother Lee Harvey Oswald did assassinate President Kennedy?

Mr. Oswald. That is right.

Mr. Jenner. And do you have that opinion?

Mr. Oswald. That he did assassinate the President of the United States?

Mr. Jenner. Yes.

Mr. Oswald. On his own, sir?

Mr. Dulles. Did he handle the gun and shoot the shots?

Mr. Jenner. Let's take it in alternatives. You state it in your own words.

Mr. McKenzie. He has stated this once before, but I am going to ask him to state it again.

Mr. Jenner. Yes, I would like to have that clearly stated.

Mr. Oswald. Sir, as I previously testified to that question, based on the circumstantial evidence that has been put forth and that I have read from the newspapers and general impression of the time that the event took place, and the subsequent following days of that event, that I would be of the opinion, purely based on these circumstantial points, that he did actually fire the rifle that killed the President of the United States and wounded the Governor of Texas, Mr. Connally.

Mr. Dulles. The same would apply to the attack on Officer Tippit?

Mr. Oswald. I would base my opinion on Officer Tippit's death, sir, on my conversation with the District Attorney of Dallas, Tex., on the morning of Saturday, November 23, 1963, at which time during our conversation he said in his mind and based on the evidence and the eye witnesses, that he was reported to have, that there was no question to him that Lee Harvey Oswald did in fact kill Officer J. D. Tippit in Dallas, Tex.

Mr. McKenzie. And you believe that would be correct?

Mr. Oswald. I believe that would be correct.

Mr. Jenner. Have you had any conversation with Marina——

Mr. Dulles. Just one point on that.

You have testified that you felt that your brother did have or would have required some outside help or assistance to do what he did—roughly to that effect, I believe.

Mr. Oswald. That is right.

Mr. Dulles. Have you any idea at all or any thoughts as to what kind of help, where that could have come from, who was involved.

I have in mind—was this in your opinion a rightist plot, a leftist plot, an anarchist plot?

Mr. Oswald. If I may take your question, sir; in the parts that you pointed out—I believe the first part was to where and how.

Mr. Dulles. And who.

Mr. Jenner. May have assisted.

Mr. Oswald. The where and the how, sir, I am not of any opinion. And as to who might have assisted him, as related in my diary, or memorandum——

Mr. Jenner. Identify the page, please.

Mr. Oswald. On page 6—and I quote—"I still do not know why or how, but Mr. and Mrs. Paine are somehow involved in this affair."

I am still of that opinion, sir.

And as to any other persons that I might suggest was involved in any way in this affair, I do not know of their names nor can I identify them in any way.

Mr. Dulles. As this covers two of my questions——

Mr. Jenner. Why don't you proceed.

Mr. Dulles. May I proceed at this time.

I will proceed with a couple of questions I have at this time.

449 Mr. Oswald. Pardon me, sir; may I interrupt you here? And I would like to add something to my previous statement there.

Mr. Dulles. Please, yes.

Mr. Oswald. Perhaps there is one other person that I feel like would be involved in this affair, and the subsequent death of my brother, Lee Harvey Oswald, and that was the man that actually shot Lee Harvey Oswald, Mr. Jack Ruby or Mr. Rubenstein. And that would be the only other party that I could possibly attempt to identify that I feel like would have been involved and perhaps assisted Lee in this assassination.

Mr. Jenner. Would you please give us the basis of your opinion?

Mr. Oswald. I am of the opinion, as previously stated, based on newspaper accounts and magazine articles of Mr. Ruby's activities, to the best of my remembrance, as reported in one newspaper I recall reading after November 24, 1963, that a period of a couple of months, 2 or 3 months, prior to Mr. Ruby's killing my brother, Lee Harvey Oswald, in a Dallas police station, that he appeared at the Dallas police station and started making acquaintances at the Dallas police station to the extent that he, from then on, appeared frequently and was able to move about the Dallas police station very easily.

Based on that and the shooting of Lee Harvey Oswald, I am of the opinion that Mr. Ruby did in fact know Lee Harvey Oswald prior to Sunday, November 23, 19— Sunday, November 24, 1963, and that he was in my opinion paid to silence Lee Harvey Oswald.

Mr. Dulles. This is based on—this opinion is based on what you have read in the press subsequent to November 22?

Mr. Oswald. November 24; sir, 1963, the day of my brother's death. Up until that time I had never heard of Mr. Jack Ruby.

Mr. Dulles. I was including all of the press accounts that carried through from the time of the assassination.

Mr. Jenner. Well, the witness has referred, of course, to events immediately preceding November 22—that is Mr. Ruby's apparent interest in—his frequent visits to the quarters—did you say the police department?

Mr. Oswald. Yes, sir; the Dallas police station.

Mr. Dulles. I was trying to get at also—to cover what you had previously said about possible aid in connection with the assassination of the President.

Is that based largely on what you have read subsequent thereto?

Mr. Oswald. That is right.

Mr. Dulles. This question of mine covers the whole period of your relationship with your brother.

Do you recall during that entire period, up to November 22, that your brother made any comments with regard to President Kennedy of a derogatory nature or character or of any other character? Did he ever discuss the President with you during the whole period? Of course, he was only President for the last 3 years.

Mr. Oswald. No, sir; I do not recall at any time that he ever mentioned President Kennedy's name or referred to him in any way, either pro or con.

Mr. Dulles. Governor Connally—the same question.

Mr. Oswald. No, sir; not as Governor Connally.

Mr. Dulles. Or as Secretary of the Navy?

Mr. Oswald. Yes, sir; to the extent that he had mentioned his letter to Governor Connally, his request for his assistance in correcting the dishonorable or undesirable discharge that he had received from the United States Marine Corps.

Mr. Dulles. What was his comment with regard to Mr. Connally, Secretary of the Navy, and later Governor?

Mr. McKenzie. If you recall, go ahead and tell him. But it is covered in some of the letters previously introduced into testimony.

Mr. Jenner. If there was any discussion, I would like to have that. And I take it, Mr. Chairman, you are interested in that as well.

Mr. Dulles. I am interested in that, because there has been some testimony here from Mrs. Oswald to the general effect that he had not expressed any antipathy to Secretary of the Navy and Governor Connally, but rather the contrary.450 I would like to get your impression of that, what he might have said to you on that subject.

Mr. Oswald. All right.

I do recall a conversation at my home in Fort Worth, Tex., between myself and Lee Harvey Oswald——

Mr. Jenner. Fix the time, please.

Mr. Oswald. Approximately the middle part of June 1962, at which time the subject was brought up by him about his efforts to have the discharge corrected to an honorable discharge, and that again he advised me that he had written to the then Secretary of the Navy, John B. Connally, and that Mr. Connally, or his office had replied that he was no longer the Secretary of the Navy, and that he had turned over the correspondence to the then Secretary of the Navy, Mr. Korth, I believe.

Mr. McKenzie. Mr. Fred Korth.

Mr. Oswald. I do not recall any further discussion on that subject. And he did not indicate to me the pro or con of any antipathy toward Mr. Connally.

Mr. Dulles. He expressed no antipathy?

Mr. Jenner. As a person?

Mr. Oswald. As a person, he did not make any comment, sir.

Mr. Jenner. And did he at any time, apart from this particular event you are now relating, at any time prior to November 22, 1963, ever express any antipathy toward Governor Connally as a person?

Mr. Oswald. No, sir; he did not.

Mr. Dulles. Did you ever hear Marina Oswald express any views about President Kennedy one way or the other?

Mr. Oswald. No, sir; I do not recall at any time that she has expressed any views on Mr. Kennedy.

Mr. Dulles. Do you recall at any time that Lee Harvey Oswald expressed antipathy to government in general, people in authority, leaders?

Mr. Oswald. No, sir; I do not recall.

Mr. Dulles. Did he express any—apart from the letters, what he said in his letters to you, which we have—but after he returned from the Soviet Union, and during the period you saw him, subsequent to his return, did he ever discuss with you the failures of government, that government itself was not good, or if the kind of government we had in the United States was not good, as was expressed to some extent in the letters?

Mr. Oswald. No, sir; I do not recall at any time other than in his letters during the period of the latter part of 1959, at any time that he made any derogatory remarks about any official or any particular leader or the government of the United States.

Mr. Dulles. And that statement would include General Walker, would it?

Mr. Oswald. Yes, sir; it most certainly would.

Mr. Dulles. He never discussed General Walker with you?

Mr. Oswald. No, sir; I never heard him mention the gentleman's name.

Mr. Dulles. Did your brother have any sort of pet hatreds, institutions, people or otherwise, that he disliked, apart from what he said in his letters?

I am talking now of the period after his return from Russia.

Mr. Oswald. No, sir; to my knowledge he did not.

Mr. Dulles. I have nothing further at this time. I may have one last question at the end.

Do you wish to follow up on any of these points?

Mr. Jenner. No; not right at the moment.

Would you take your diary. There are one or two items that I would like to clear up.

Page 1—you speak of the old Denton plant and the new Denton plant. Would you please locate those plants?

Mr. Oswald. They are both located at Denton, Tex., and they are located approximately a mile apart, sir.

Mr. Jenner. And they are the plants of the Acme Brick Co. by whom you are employed?

Mr. Oswald. That is right.

451 Mr. Jenner. And the reason I asked you about these is that you talk about going from the old to the new plant, and I wanted to locate them.

Mr. Oswald. Yes, sir.

Mr. Jenner. The incident in New Orleans in which your brother was distributing literature of the Fair Play for Cuba Committee—did that come to your attention at that time?

Mr. Oswald. No, sir; that did not.

Mr. Jenner. And when was the first time that you became—you ever heard of the Fair Play for Cuba Committee, or anything about it?

Mr. Oswald. I believe this to be, sir, to the best of my remembrance, on Friday night, November 22, 1963, at the FBI office in Dallas, Tex.

Mr. Dulles. You are referring there, I assume, to Lee Harvey Oswald's connection with the committee, aren't you? Or are you referring to the fact whether he knew there was a committee.

Mr. Jenner. Both.

I will separate those. Did you know there was such a committee at any time up to that occasion—had you heard of its existence?

Mr. Oswald. Perhaps I had read about it in the paper and not recalling any significant value to myself I perhaps had forgotten about it.

Mr. Jenner. Then I will ask you the other part.

Had you heard of any connection on the part of your brother with or any activity on his part with respect to the Fair Play for Cuba Committee, prior to November 22, 1963.

Mr. Oswald. No, sir; I had not.

Mr. Dulles. You knew nothing of his short arrest in New Orleans?

Mr. Oswald. No, sir; I did not.

Mr. Dulles. You didn't even know he was arrested?

Mr. Oswald. No, sir. I did not even know he had traveled from Dallas, Tex., to New Orleans, until that night of November 22, 1963.

Mr. Jenner. Page 2 of your memorandum—you recited there that an announcer—I assume a radio station announcer—called you. Did you find that?

Mr. Oswald. Yes, sir; I do find the area that you are referring to. The announcer did not call me, sir. It was the radio announcer on the radio.

Mr. Jenner. I see.

And what did the announcer say?

Mr. Oswald. To the best of my remembrance, sir, the announcer stated that a man identified as Lee Oswald had been arrested in connection with a policeman's death and possibly the death of the President of the United States on or about that approximate time.

Mr. Jenner. And was that the first intimation of any kind or character, or the first notice or knowledge to you, of the possible involvement of your brother, Lee Harvey Oswald, either in the murder of Policeman Tippit or in the assassination of President Kennedy.

Mr. Oswald. That is right.

Mr. Jenner. And where were you when that announcement was made?

Mr. Oswald. I was in the office of the new Denton plant when this announcement was made, or at least I first became aware of the announcement on the radio at that time.

Mr. Jenner. Now, would you give us your immediate mental reaction when you heard that?

Mr. Oswald. I believe, sir, my reaction to that would be somewhat stunned.

Mr. Jenner. Stunned in the sense of disbelieving? You just could not absorb it?

Mr. Oswald. No, sir; not to that extent. If I may say this. My own personal mental attitude, through my entire life, seems to react to trouble to the extent that I do not perhaps go to pieces, so to speak, that I react apparently calmly in the face of adversity.

Mr. Jenner. I take it with that disposition that you have that anything in life is possible—no matter how extraordinary it may seem at the moment—you retain a grip on yourself?

Mr. Oswald. Yes, sir; or at least attempt to.

Mr. Jenner. You were disbelieving, but it might have been—at least your452 thought was that it was possible, though, you were disbelieving at the moment?

Mr. Oswald. That is right.

Mr. Jenner. Then you state in your memorandum on page 2 that you immediately called your wife Vada.

Mr. Oswald. That is right.

Mr. Jenner. And you went directly to the phone and called her?

Mr. Oswald. That is right.

Mr. Jenner. What did you say to her?

Mr. Oswald. I asked her first had she been listening to the television or the radio set, and was she aware that Lee had been arrested. She stated she had not heard this, even though she had been listening to television. In her statement to me, to the best of my recollection at that time, was that they had not, over the television set, referred to Lee by name.

Mr. Jenner. And, as I recall in your memorandum, you immediately told her you were going to come right home.

Mr. Oswald. That is right.

Mr. Jenner. And you did depart for home?

Mr. Oswald. That is right.

Mr. Jenner. On page 3 of your memorandum, you make a reference to your brother's arrest.

Would you find that place on page 3? The report to you of his arrest.

Mr. Oswald. Yes, sir; I have it.

Mr. Jenner. And as I recall, that was a report to you that he had been arrested?

Mr. Oswald. That is right.
Mr. Jenner. By whom, and by what means?
Mr. Oswald. Over the telephone, by Mr. Dubose, the credit manager in our Fort Worth general office. And, "Bob, brace yourself, your brother has been arrested."
Mr. Jenner. What did you say?
Mr. Oswald. "Yes; I know. I just heard."
Mr. Jenner. Did Mr. Dubose elaborate? Did he say only your brother has been arrested?
Mr. Oswald. Yes, sir. To the best of my recollection that was his exact words.
Mr. Jenner. Did he add, if I may refresh your recollection, assuming it is so, that he had been arrested in connection with the assassination of President Kennedy, and the murder of Officer Tippit?
Mr. Oswald. No, sir; I believe I did not give him an opportunity, if he wanted to state that, to complete his statement.
Mr. Jenner. You have now given us the whole of that particular conversation?
Mr. Oswald. That is right.
If I might add—other than that as noted on page 3, that he did advise me that my mother was trying to reach me, and gave me a number to call.
Mr. Jenner. I wish to go to that next. You did call her?
Mr. Oswald. That is right.
Mr. Jenner. And where was she? To where was your call directed?
Mr. Oswald. To Fort Worth, Tex., to which address I am not acquainted, but the telephone number is her residence in Fort Worth, Tex. I believe that to be 1220 Thomas Place.
Mr. Jenner. And when you called that number, your mother was home?
Mr. Oswald. That is right.
Mr. Jenner. All right.
What did you say to her?
Mr. Oswald. My comment to her that this was Robert, and she immediately started advising me of what she had heard, and that she had been in contact with a Star Telegram reporter.
Mr. Jenner. That is the Star Telegram reporter for the Dallas Star Telegram?
Mr. Oswald. No, sir, for the Fort Worth Star Telegram, sir.
453 Mr. Jenner. Thank you.
Mr. Oswald. And that she was going to go to Dallas in the presence of this Fort Worth Star Telegram, and she asked me did I have enough money to fly down immediately.
I advised her I was 35 or 30 miles away from Dallas, Tex., that I was not in Arkansas, and that it was my intention to go to Dallas just as fast as possible. And she stated that she believed she would stay at the Baker Hotel, and asked me to meet her there.
I agreed to this. However, this meeting never did take place at the Baker Hotel.
Mr. Jenner. A meeting did take place at the Adolphus?
Mr. Oswald. No, sir. As prior testimony—at the Dallas police station, on the night of November 22, 1963.
Mr. Jenner. You referred to, on page 3—to a Fort Worth general office, and a gentleman by the name of Reger.
Mr. Oswald. That is right.
Mr. Jenner. And that is the Fort Worth general office of the Acme Brick Co.?
Mr. Oswald. That is right.
Mr. Jenner. You mentioned another gentleman there. I don't know if I read your writing correctly. Bill——
Mr. Oswald. Darwin.
Mr. Jenner. Did you speak with him on that occasion that you related in your notes?
Mr. Oswald. Yes, sir; I did.

Mr. Jenner. And what was the purpose of your talking with those gentlemen?

Mr. Oswald. The purpose of talking to Mr. Darwin was to advise him that I needed to go to Dallas, and his immediate reply was yes, he had just heard—I believe he did say—about Lee, or about my brother, and that I was to do just anything that I deemed necessary and not worry about the office.

And he did inform me at the latter part of this conversation that the FBI had called the Fort Worth general office in an attempt to talk to me or to locate me.

Mr. Jenner. Was any suggestion made by him at that time that you get in touch with the Fort Worth Office of the FBI?

Mr. Oswald. No, sir; I advised him that I would contact the FBI upon completion of our conversation.

Mr. Jenner. And you did so?

Mr. Oswald. I did so.

Mr. Jenner. And a reference to that——

Mr. Dulles. By telephone?

Mr. Oswald. That is right.

Mr. Jenner. A reference to that appears on page 4 of your memorandum.

Mr. Oswald. That is right.

Mr. Jenner. I won't go into that interview. But on that occasion, and all other occasions when you had interviews with, or were interviewed either by the FBI or Secret Service, you related the whole truth and nothing but the truth to the best of your knowledge and information at the time you were being interviewed?

Mr. Oswald. That is right.

Mr. Jenner. At this moment, had you contacted anyone other than those you have now mentioned?

Up to this point of the sequence of events?

Mr. Oswald. May I qualify that question—outside of my office in Denton, Tex., sir.

Mr. Jenner. The office in Denton, Tex., the call to your mother, the call to Mrs. Oswald, your wife Vada, the call to the FBI office.

Mr. Oswald. No, sir; I did not.

Mr. Jenner. Are all of the contacts that you had and all of the occasions of interviews during the period November 22, 1963, through the following week, November 25, recorded in your memorandum?

454 Mr. Dulles. I wonder if to save time we could ask him to review that memorandum and to report if he finds that there are other calls that were made.

Mr. Jenner. Will that be acceptable to you, Mr. McKenzie?

Mr. McKenzie. Fine.

Mr Dulles, it is a quarter of one. Being as how it is a quarter of one, I know you have a luncheon meeting to go to. Our plane does not leave until 5 o'clock. We have to leave here no later than 3:30. We will be glad to have lunch and come back, if it would suit your convenience.

Mr. Jenner. There are a couple of things, in the interests really of Mr. Oswald, that have turned up, when I studied the memorandum last night, that I am sure Mr. McKenzie would like to have.

Mr. Dulles. Yes; I would like to give Mr. McKenzie plenty of time.

If the car is there, I can wait another 5 or 10 minutes. But I think that it would be better if I were to come back.

We will recess at this time until 2 p.m.

(Whereupon, at 12:45 p.m., the President's Commission recessed.)

Afternoon Session
TESTIMONY OF ROBERT EDWARD LEE OSWALD RESUMED

The President's Commission reconvened at 2:30 p.m.

Mr. Dulles. The Commission will come to order.

Mr. Jenner. Returning to page 1 of your memorandum, as I recall your recording of the events of that day, November 22, 1963, you first learned of the assassination or attempted assassination as of that moment of President Kennedy while you were at lunch with some fellow workers.

Mr. Oswald. That is correct.

Mr. Jenner. And would you identify those fellow workers, please?

Mr. Oswald. If I might——

Mr. McKenzie. I ask you to withdraw that.

Mr. Jenner. All right. You don't like the expression "fellow workers"?

Mr. Dulles. You object to the whole question, or just the way it was phrased?

Mr. McKenzie. Let's rephrase it, Mr. Dulles, if I may, please.

Mr. Jenner. I will yield to you, Mr. McKenzie. Fellow employees.

Mr. McKenzie. That is fine.

Mr. Jenner. You were at lunch with fellow employees of Acme Brick Co.?

Mr. Oswald. That is correct.

Mr. Jenner. Would you please identify those gentlemen?

Mr. Oswald. They are Mr. Bill Darwin, the director of marketing of the Acme Brick Co., Mr. Burnett Henry, director of plants and transportation of the Acme Brick Co., Mr. Bob Oech, who is the Texas division plant manager.

Mr. Jenner. Of Acme Brick Co.?

Mr. Oswald. Of Acme Brick Co.

And Mr. Bud Adams, who is the plant manager of both the old and new Denton plants.

Mr. Jenner. And it was at this time and on this occasion at lunchtime that you first heard any intimation or otherwise of the assassination or attempted assassination of President Kennedy?

Mr. Oswald. Yes, sir. At the completion of our lunch, as we were departing from the restaurant, as noted in my memorandum, page 1.

Mr. Jenner. Now, you speak on that page of driving in an automobile, either all or some of you gentlemen.

Whose automobile was that?

Mr. Oswald. All of us were in one automobile, and we were in Mr. Burnett Henry's automobile.

Mr. Jenner. And I take it—did the automobile have a radio in it?

Mr. Oswald. Yes, sir; it did.

455 Mr. Jenner. And did you gentlemen have the radio in operation?

Mr. Oswald. Yes, sir; we did.

Mr. Jenner. And listening to it?

Mr. Oswald. Yes, sir; we were.

Mr. Jenner. Were you listening to anything in particular?

Mr. Oswald. Yes, sir.

Mr. Jenner. What?

Mr. Oswald. We were listening to a newscast of the events that had already taken place in Dallas, Tex., at approximately 12:30 that afternoon.

Mr. Jenner. And you record the time in your notebook?

Mr. Oswald. Yes, sir—as approximately 1 p.m., sir.

Mr. Jenner. I think we had reached page 6 of your memorandum.

You record on pages 4 and 5—I think towards the bottom of page 4, and the upper portion of page 5—your meeting that day or early evening with Marina and, I believe your mother—but at least Marina.

Is that correct?

In Dallas?

Mr. Oswald. That is correct.

Mr. Jenner. And just for the purpose of making sure of the record, I gather from your testimony yesterday that this was the first time that you had seen Marina since Thanksgiving Day of 1962?

Mr. Oswald. That is correct.

Mr. Jenner. And where did this visit take place—where did you meet her on this occasion?

Mr. Oswald. At the Dallas police station.

Mr. Jenner. Did she have either or both of her children with her?

Mr. Oswald. She had both of her children with her.

Mr. Jenner. That would include the infant Rachel?

Mr. Oswald. Yes, sir; that is correct.

Mr. Jenner. Were you advised at any time prior to this occasion that her second child had been born to her?

Mr. Oswald. No, sir; I had not been.

Mr. Jenner. And this was the first information you had on this subject?

Mr. Oswald. That is correct.

Mr. Dulles. You probably knew that a child was contemplated.

Mr. Jenner. Well, he might not.

Mr. Oswald. No, sir; I wasn't aware of that.

Mr. Jenner. Had you even up to that moment been advised directly or indirectly that Marina had been pregnant, from which pregnancy the child Rachel had been born?

Mr. Oswald. No, sir; I had not been advised.

Mr. Jenner. Was there an interpreter present at the time you visited with Marina; as I recall your mother was present, also.

Mr. Oswald. That is correct.

Mr. Jenner. Was there an interpreter there at that time?

Mr. Oswald. There was a Mrs. Paine there, who was acting as an interpreter.

Mr. Jenner. You have now named everybody present—yourself, Marina, and her two children, your mother, yourself, and Mrs. Paine.

Mr. Oswald. With the exception, sir, that there was a police officer, or my assumption that he was a police officer, in the room.

Mr. Jenner. Was he in uniform or plain clothes?

Mr. Oswald. Plain clothes.

Mr. Dulles. Mr. Paine was not there at this time?

Mr. Oswald. No, sir, he was not.

Mr. Dulles. He came later that day, did he?

Mr. Oswald. Just a very few minutes after this meeting.

Mr. Jenner. Mrs. Paine then acted as interpreter between yourself and Marina and between her and others in the party?

Mr. Oswald. That is correct.

Mr. Jenner. Did you say anything in the presence of everybody to her with respect to the birth of her second child, which came as a complete surprise to you?

456 Mr. Oswald. If memory serves me correct, sir, I did make some type of statement to that effect.

Mr. Jenner. Did you express surprise?

Mr. Oswald. I feel certain that I did, sir.

Mr. Jenner. Do you recall now—you walked into the room, and there was Marina with these others, but with two children, one an infant that you had not seen before. Was it immediately explained to you? Did you inquire as to the identity of the infant? Can you reconstruct that for us?

Mr. Oswald. To the best of my remembrance on that, sir, possibly during the preceding half hour, when I was talking with my mother, she possibly—this I am not clear—advised me of the second child. If she did not, I was, of course, much more surprised when I walked into the room where Marina was holding the infant. I remember looking at the infant, as Marina held the infant, and making some type of comment about whether or not it was a boy or girl and how old it was.

Mr. Jenner. I don't recall this recorded in your memorandum—and it may very well be—that the preceding half hour you had had a meeting or conference with your mother?

Mr. Oswald. That is correct.

Mr. Jenner. And was that—in whose presence was that conference?

Mr. Oswald. First in the presence of two or three FBI agents, and a Star Telegram reporter, Fort Worth Star Telegram reporter, at the Dallas police station.

Mr. Jenner. Do you record that event in your memorandum?

Mr. Oswald. Yes, sir; I do, on page 5.

Mr. Jenner. On page 6 there is a reference, I think I have interpreted your writing, to a Mr. Cummings. Would you find that place on page 6?

Mr. Oswald. Yes, sir; I have it.

Mr. Jenner. Do I interpret your writing correctly?

Mr. Oswald. That is correct. I believe his name to be a Lieutenant Cummings.

Mr. Jenner. That is what I sought. He was an officer of the Dallas police force?

Mr. Oswald. That is correct.

Mr. Jenner. I believe you record on page 6, that Mr. Cummings, Lieutenant Cummings, or some other—well, I don't want to interpret what you do record—but you received a report at that time, according to your memorandum, of the fact of the arrest of your brother, Lee, in connection with the murder of Officer Tippit.

Mr. Oswald. That is correct.

Mr. Jenner. Is that the first information you had that your brother had actually been arrested in connection with that incident?

Mr. Oswald. No, sir; it was not.

Mr. Jenner. When had you first received information in that respect?

Mr. Oswald. As my prior testimony stated, at the office, at the new Denton plant, when Lee's name was first mentioned, stating that he had been arrested in regards to the shooting to death of a police officer, and possibly the President of the United States.

Mr. Jenner. All right.

Page 7—did you, at the time of the events recorded on page 7, see or request to see your brother, Lee Harvey Oswald?

Mr. Oswald. Yes, sir; I did.

Mr. Jenner. And of whom did you make that request?

First I would put it this way: Did you see Lee Harvey Oswald on that day or evening?

Mr. Oswald. No, sir; I did not.

Mr. Jenner. But you did make a request? Of whom did you make that request?

Mr. Oswald. To a police officer. I cannot recall his name. He reportedly passed on my request to captain of police, Captain Fritz.

Mr. Jenner. And what was his response?

Mr. Oswald. The police officer who passed on my request asked that I stay around, that Captain Fritz was quite busy, that he would see me later.

457 Mr. Jenner. And did you see Captain Fritz later?

Mr. Oswald. I did see him, but I did not talk to him. By this, I mean he was in his glass office, within an office, and I did see him through the glass, but I did not talk to Captain Fritz.

Mr. Jenner. What was the disposition of your—at least as of that day—of your request to see your brother?

Mr. Oswald. None, sir.

Mr. Jenner. Not decided either way?

Mr. Oswald. I never did receive an answer either way, sir.

Mr. Jenner. I see.

And you eventually left the police station, did you?

Mr. Oswald. That is correct.

Mr. Jenner. You record on page 7 that you walked to your automobile, do you not?

Mr. Oswald. Yes, sir; I do.

Mr. Jenner. Now, would you trace your course from the time you left the Dallas City police office to the time you retired that evening?

Mr. Oswald. You are referring to the time that I first left the Dallas police office?

Mr. Jenner. Yes—start there, and trace your steps to the time you retired for the evening.

Mr. Oswald. Well, my departure of the Dallas police office—I walked to my car that was in a parking lot approximately seven blocks away.

Mr. Jenner. About what time of day or evening was this?

Mr. Oswald. To the best of my recollection, approximately 8 o'clock at night, sir.

Mr. Jenner. All right, sir. When you left the Dallas police office or station, did you then have a definite route in mind as to where you were going?

Mr. Oswald. No, sir; I did not.

Mr. Jenner. You had no arrangements with anybody, and no one had any with you, with respect to where you might or could go?

Mr. Oswald. That is correct.

Mr. Jenner. All right. Proceed, please.

Mr. Oswald. On arrival at my car in the parking lot in Dallas, Tex., I started to drive, I did drive to Fort Worth, Tex., by Highway 80.

Mr. Jenner. You were then—you then had in mind doing what—returning home?

Mr. Oswald. No, sir; that was not the direction of home, sir. I did not have anything in mind other than I wanted to drive and to arrange my thoughts at that particular time.

Mr. Jenner. All right.

Now, you do say, and I quote from your memorandum, "I was attempting to arrange my thoughts and my fears."

Do you find that expression on page 7?

Mr. Oswald. That is correct.

Mr. Jenner. Now, would you please explain to the Commission what was meant when you recorded the sentence, "I was attempting to arrange my thoughts and my fears"?

Mr. Oswald. What I meant by that statement, sir—not being disrespectful—I believe it speaks for itself in view of the happenings of the day. To further elaborate on that, I wanted to have some time by myself to think about the happenings of the day and the arrest of my brother, Lee Harvey Oswald, and the reference to my fears, whether or not he could have possibly done this. He had been up to that time either accused or arrested for the death of Police Officer J. D. Tippit, and the investigation that was now going on in Dallas as to the death of the President of the United States and the wounding of Governor Connally, of Texas.

Mr. Jenner. All right. You were then driving in your automobile.

Did you actually reach Fort Worth?

Mr. Oswald. Yes, sir; I did.

Mr. Jenner. And then what did you do?

458 Mr. Oswald. After driving through Fort Worth, to the west side of Fort Worth, I turned around and headed back toward Dallas.

Mr. Jenner. Excuse me. Up to this point it was continuous driving, except as you might have been resting or waiting a change of stoplight or something of that character?

Mr. Oswald. That is correct.

Mr. Jenner. Did anybody contact you, or did you speak with anybody during the period of this drive up to the moment we now have reached?

Mr. Oswald. No, sir; they did not.

Mr. Jenner. All right, sir. You reversed your course and then where did you go?

Mr. Oswald. When I reversed my course, I still did not have any idea as to exactly where I was going. But I did reverse my course, and I started driving on the turnpike between Fort Worth and Dallas.
Mr. Jenner. Does that have a highway number?
I notice you mentioned a Highway 80.
Is that the same as the turnpike?
Mr. Oswald. No, sir; it is not.
Mr. Jenner. Would you explain that, please?
Mr. Oswald. Highway 80 is on the old highway from Fort Worth to Dallas, the turnpike being a later and more modern trafficway.
Mr. McKenzie. And a toll road.
Mr. Oswald. And a toll road.
Mr. Jenner. Did you take Highway 80 in going to Fort Worth?
Mr. Oswald. Yes, sir; I did.
Mr. Jenner. But you returned by the toll road?
Mr. Oswald. That is correct.
Mr. Jenner. All right, sir.
I take it you continued your drive—continued to drive along, while you were attempting to rearrange your thoughts.
Mr. Oswald. That is correct.
Mr. Jenner. And you eventually arrived where?
Mr. Oswald. At Dallas, Tex., sir.
Mr. Jenner. Did you become a guest of a hotel; did you register anywhere?
Mr. Oswald. Yes, sir, I did.
Mr. Jenner. Where?
Mr. Oswald. At the Statler Hilton Hotel.
Mr. Jenner. In Dallas?
Mr. Oswald. Yes, sir.
Mr. Jenner. Now, up to that moment, having in mind your route, had anybody contacted you, had you spoken with anybody? Up to the time that you entered the Statler Hilton Hotel to register?
Mr. Oswald. Yes, sir; I had spoken to somebody.
Mr. Jenner. Who was that?
Mr. Oswald. A gas station attendant midway on the turnpike where I stopped to buy gas.
Mr. Jenner. But other than that incident, you had no contact with anyone?
Mr. Oswald. That is correct, sir.
Mr. Jenner. All right. You registered?
Mr. Oswald. Yes, sir.
Mr. Jenner. Did you go to your room?
Mr. Oswald. Yes, sir; I did.
Mr. Dulles. Approximately what time was this?
Mr. Oswald. Approximately 10:30 p.m., that night, sir.
Mr. Jenner. After registering, did you retire for the evening, or did you go somewhere?
Mr. Oswald. No, sir; I did not retire for the evening. I did, in fact, go into the coffee room of the Statler Hilton Hotel in Dallas, and have a ham sandwich and some milk, and shortly after completing this, I walked across the street, which was approximately a half a block down the street, to the Dallas police station again.
Mr. Jenner. All right.
459 Now, up to that moment, other than was necessary for you to register and your conversation with a waitress, in connection with your having some evening lunch, did you have any contact with anybody?
Mr. Oswald. No, sir; I did not.

Mr. Jenner. Did you have any contact at all of any kind or character up to this moment with anybody in connection with the events of the day?

Mr. Oswald. No, sir; I had not.

Mr. Jenner. All right.

You went across the street to the Dallas City police station?

Mr. Oswald. Yes, sir, I did.

Mr. Jenner. Had you had an appointment?

Mr. Oswald. No, sir, I did not.

Mr. Jenner. What was your purpose in going across the street for that visit?

Mr. Oswald. I wanted to speak to Captain Fritz, if possible.

Mr. Jenner. You record on page 8 that you entered the Dallas police station, you were interviewed or consulted by some FBI agents in a small office.

Mr. Oswald. That is correct.

Mr. Jenner. Do you recall their names?

Mr. Oswald. No, sir; I do not.

Mr. Jenner. I take it in any event, however, that they questioned you, did they?

Mr. Oswald. That is correct.

Mr. Jenner. And were all the answers that you gave the truth and nothing but the truth to the best of your information, recollection, and belief, at that time?

Mr. Oswald. It most certainly was, sir.

Mr. Jenner. All right, sir.

When did you learn, if you ever learned, that your brother, Lee Harvey Oswald, had in fact been charged with the assassination of President Kennedy?

Mr. Oswald. At approximately midnight or a few minutes before midnight, November 22, 1963.

Mr. Jenner. And is that recorded on page 8 of your memorandum?

Mr. Oswald. Yes, sir, it is.

Mr. Jenner. What was your reaction when that information was conveyed to you? What were your thoughts?

Mr. Oswald. I do not recall if I had any thoughts at that particular time, sir. I did not make any comment that I recall. I believe I just shook my head.

Mr. Jenner. I was going to ask you in connection with page 8, your opinion respecting the possible involvement of your brother, Lee Harvey Oswald, in the assassination of President Kennedy, but Mr. Dulles this morning in his questions has covered that subject, so I will skip it.

Now, did you see Captain Fritz that evening?

Mr. Oswald. No, sir, I did not.

Mr. Jenner. Did you attempt to see him?

Mr. Oswald. Yes, sir; I did.

Mr. Jenner. Did you inquire further with respect to an opportunity on your part that you wished to see your brother?

Mr. Oswald. No, sir; I had been told so many times that Captain Fritz was quite busy, and I realize, of course, he was, and I let it go at that.

Mr. Jenner. Now, following your visit to the police station, which you do record there, and therefore I won't go into it further, what did you do that evening?

Mr. Oswald. I returned to my hotel, sir.

Mr. Jenner. And retired?

Mr. Oswald. That is correct.

Mr. Jenner. Now, between the time you left the Statler Hilton Hotel and the time you returned there to retire, were you contacted by anybody or did you have any conversation with anybody respecting the course of events of the day, other than you have recorded in your memorandum?

Mr. Oswald. No, sir; I did not.460 And I might add I did register under my regular name at the Statler Hilton.

Mr. Jenner. I didn't even think to ask you that, because I assumed it was so.

On page 9, you record and report the following morning an occasion when you were in the barber shop of the Statler Hilton, obtaining a shave. Isn't that correct, sir?

Mr. Oswald. That is correct.

Mr. Jenner. And you also record an observation by one or both of the barbers, I think the gentleman who was shaving you, on the subject of your brother, Lee Harvey Oswald deserved a fair trial like anybody else.

Mr. Oswald. That is correct.

Mr. Jenner. And then you end up that comment, "but I did leave my barber a 50-cent tip."

That followed an observation on your part that you did not engage in that conversation, and you merely listened.

Mr. Oswald. That is correct, sir.

Mr. Jenner. Now, would you indicate to me the significance if there is any significance, of the expression "but I did leave my barber a 50-cent tip."

Mr. Oswald. The only significance, sir, that I put to it at that time was that for the first time I was listening to somebody other than police officers and FBI agents as to the past events of the preceding day, and I was more or less hearing again for the first time a reaction, either—pro and con, to these two gentlemen's opinions, who I would take at that time would be average people, as to whether or not Lee did have a right to a fair trial, regardless of what he had done or been accused of.

Mr. Jenner. And do I take it a fair interpretation of your comment is that you were pleased that average everyday people, that their reaction was that your brother, Lee Harvey Oswald, was entitled to, and they hoped he would obtain a fair and impartial trial when put to trial?

Mr. Oswald. That is correct.

Mr. Jenner. And your reference to a 50-cent tip was an emphasis in your own mind of your pleasure that a spontaneous reaction of ordinary people was that he was entitled to and they hoped he would receive a fair and impartial trial?

Mr. Oswald. That is correct, sir.

Mr. Jenner. Would you turn to page 10, please? You record events—you were then in the district attorney's office?

Mr. Oswald. Yes, sir; that is correct.

Mr. Jenner. You refer to a "H. Wade." Who is H. Wade?

Mr. Oswald. Mr. Henry Wade.

Mr. Jenner. And what office did he hold?

Mr. Oswald. Dallas District Attorney.

Mr. Jenner. All right.

I don't know as I interpret your handwriting clearly. It looks to me as though you have written reference to a Jim Bowie. Who was Jim Bowie?

Mr. Oswald. First assistant district attorney to Mr. Henry Wade.

Mr. Jenner. On page 10 you use—you make a reference to, or a comment with regard to a conversation which I take it took place between you and Mr. Wade and Mr. Bowie, either or both of them, which was "not too informative." Do you find that?

Mr. Oswald. Yes, sir, I do see the section that you are referring to—if I may elaborate on that.

Mr. Jenner. I would like to have you elaborate.

Mr. Oswald. "Not too informative on either side."

Mr. Jenner. Either side of what?

Mr. Oswald. Referring to the district attorney's office as one side and my side as the other side.

Mr. Jenner. On what issue?

Mr. Oswald. Of the conversations that we had in reference to the legal standing of Lee Harvey Oswald or to his guilt, of the accusations that had been—that he had been charged with.

Mr. Jenner. Would you turn to page 12?

Mr. Oswald. Yes, sir.

461 Mr. Jenner. There is a reference there to a conversation as to whether Lee Harvey Oswald would say anything to you when and if you interviewed him.

Mr. Oswald. That is correct.

Mr. Jenner. What did you have in mind as to the subject matter about which Lee Harvey Oswald might speak with you?

Mr. Oswald. To the amount of involvement, if any, with relation to the death of the President of the United States on November 22, 1963.

Mr. Jenner. You were then contemplating your prospective conversation with him?

Mr. Oswald. That is correct.

Mr. Jenner. And you use an expression also there that you would do your best. Do you find that?

Mr. Oswald. Yes, sir; I do.

Mr. Jenner. Now, you would do your best to do what, sir?

Mr. Oswald. To find out.

Mr. Jenner. From whom?

Mr. Oswald. From Lee Harvey Oswald, during our conversation or our——

Mr. Jenner. Your prospective interview?

Mr. Oswald. Our prospective interview, whether or not he did in fact perform the acts, either alone or with other people, that he had been accused of.

Mr. Jenner. I see.

Now, following that conversation that you do record on that page, did you see your brother?

Mr. Oswald. Yes, sir; I did.

Mr. Jenner. Where?

Mr. Oswald. Dallas police station.

Mr. Jenner. Will you describe the surroundings?

Mr. Oswald. I was taken up on the elevator by a Dallas police officer—Mr. Tom Kelley, inspector from Washington, D.C., U.S. Secret Service joined us, and one agent, Mr. Mike Howard. On arrival to the floor where Lee was being held, the police officer passed through a glass slot in the window to another police officer the pass, I believe signed by Captain Fritz, which authorization was for me to see Lee Harvey Oswald. Two or three minutes went by, and I was advised that he was now ready to see me, and I was taken to a small room to the left of the elevators on this floor, and no one else was in this room on his side, or my side of the glass partitions that separated the locked side from the unlocked side.

And Lee was standing there before me on the other side of the glass.

Mr. Dulles. Did you have the impression that the officers had told your brother that you were the one who was coming to see him?

Mr. Oswald. No, sir; I did not.

Mr. Dulles. Because you just said that the officer said he was ready to see you, and I gained the impression from that——

Mr. Oswald. Yes, sir—whether or not I meant by that that—I do not believe that was my full meaning on that statement, because I was not aware that they had actually told Lee that it was me he was about to see.

Mr. Jenner. Did you converse with your brother?

Mr. Oswald. Yes, sir; I did.

Mr. Jenner. By what means?

Mr. Oswald. By telephone, while looking at him through the glass partition.

Mr. Dulles. How far apart were you, roughly?

Mr. Oswald. Just a matter of inches.

Mr. Jenner. How long were you in that room, conversing with your brother?

Mr. Oswald. Approximately 10 minutes.

Mr. Jenner. And as near as you can recall, what did he say to you and what did you say to him?

Mr. Oswald. I do recall to the best of my ability his first statement to me was "How are you?"

My reply was "I am fine."

I asked him how he was—as I observed the cuts and bruises on his face. He said he was just fine, and that they were treating him okay. I believe his next statement was at this time "I cannot or would not say anything because the line is apparently tapped."

I did not comment on that, and he rather carried the conversation for 2 or 3 minutes.

Mr. Jenner. Would you repeat it to us as best you can recall it, please?

Mr. Oswald. Sir, I do not recall this particular part of the conversation.

Mr. Jenner. Just do your best.

Mr. Oswald. I am sorry, sir, I just cannot recall that particular part of the conversation. I might comment on that particular part to this extent. That I felt that it was rather a mechanical conversation from his standpoint. He seemed to be speaking very fast, and there was approximately 2 or 3 minutes of him speaking in this nature. Then I took the initiative and started speaking to him about the family.

Mr. Jenner. His family?

Mr. Oswald. About the family, including his family, my family. And, also, at this time, when we talked about his family in particular—I believe my question to him was "What about Marina and the children?"

His reply to me at that time was "Don't worry about them. The Paines will take care of them"—that his friends, the Paines, would take care of them satisfactorily.

Mr. Jenner. That Lee's friends, the Paines, would take care of them satisfactorily?

Mr. Oswald. That is correct.

My reply to him on that was what he considered to be his friends were not mine.

Mr. Jenner. Did he respond to that?

Mr. Oswald. Not to my recollection, sir.

Mr. Dulles. Were you the first member of the family to see him, or had Marina seen him the day before?

Mr. McKenzie. Both Marina and Marguerite had seen him before.

Mr. Oswald. Earlier that afternoon, sir. I was the last member of the family to see him.

Mr. Jenner. Did you say anything about the new child, Rachel?

Mr. Oswald. Yes, sir; I did.

Mr. Jenner. Did you raise that, or did he?

Mr. Oswald. I believe I did, sir.

Mr. Jenner. What did you say?

Mr. Oswald. I simply stated that I had seen the new baby and was not aware of it at that time.

Mr. Jenner. Not aware that the baby had been born?

Mr. Oswald. That is correct.

Mr. Jenner. Did he respond to that?

Mr. Oswald. Yes, sir, he did.

Mr. Jenner. What did he say?

Mr. Oswald. He smiled and stated he had hoped for a boy rather than a girl. His further comment was, "Well, you know how that goes."

Mr. Jenner. He said nothing, I take it, then, by way of apology or otherwise that you had not theretofore been informed of the birth of this child?

Mr. Oswald. That is correct.

Mr. Jenner. You record on page 13 of your memorandum—you use this expression: "I was not talking to the Lee I knew."
Do you find that?
Mr. Oswald. Yes, sir; I do.
Mr. Jenner. Would you read that full sentence?
Mr. Oswald. "He talked about the Paines as his friends and that they would take care of Marina and the children."
Excuse me—I started too soon.
Mr. Jenner. That is all right.
Mr. Oswald. "I stated who he considered to be his friends were not necessarily mine. I did this to try to get through to him. To me his answers were mechanical and I was not talking to the Lee I knew."
Mr. Jenner. Were you able to get through to him?463 Did you feel you got through to him?
Mr. Oswald. No, sir; I was not.
Mr. Jenner. And would you elaborate, please, on your expression "I was not talking to the Lee I knew"?
Mr. Oswald. I was referring more specifically to the first part of our conversation, where his conversation seemed to me, as previously stated, very mechanical.
Mr. Jenner. You had the feeling he was not exposing himself fully to you?
Mr. Oswald. That is correct.
Mr. Jenner. Was this the last time you ever saw your brother?
Mr. Oswald. Alive, sir?
Mr. Jenner. Yes.
Mr. Oswald. Yes, sir; it was.
Mr. Jenner. On page 14 you record a later conversation after you had left your brother—you have an expression there along the lines that you agreed with someone that if the conversation had been person to person, that things might have been different. Do you find that?
Mr. Oswald. Yes, sir; I do.
Mr. Jenner. Would you please elaborate on what you meant by that?
Mr. Oswald. By "we" in that paragraph, sir, on page 14, I am talking about Mr. Tom Kelley, Inspector from Washington, D.C., United States Secret Service, and agent, Mr. Mike Howard.
Our discussion was of the nature—I related to them as best I could remember my entire conversation with Lee Harvey Oswald on that afternoon of November 23, 1963, and I was of the opinion, or perhaps expressed, either by Mr. Kelley or Mr. Mike Howard, that had we been placed in a room facing each other, perhaps more could have been learned or something could have been learned about whether or not he was actually guilty or how much he was involved in the assassination of the President of the United States.
Mr. Jenner. Could I elaborate on that? If you talked person to person to him in a room, in which there was assurance there was no bugging, nobody listening to your conversation, that you might have been able to obtain more information from him?
Mr. Oswald. That is correct.
Mr. Jenner. Is that a fair summary?
Mr. Oswald. That is, sir.
Mr. Jenner. If you wish him to elaborate or expand or amend that, Mr. McKenzie, it is perfectly all right with me.
Mr. McKenzie. No—that is all right.
Mr. Jenner. Does Mr. Oswald wish to elaborate?
Mr. Oswald. No, sir; I do not.
Mr. Jenner. Mr. Chairman, I have concluded my examination.

On behalf of myself and the staff, I express to Mr. Oswald and to Mr. McKenzie our appreciation for the splendid cooperation that we have received, and the frank and direct answers that the witness has given to all of the questions I have put to him.

Mr. McKenzie. Thank you, sir.

Mr. Dulles. I am very glad that was put on the record. I entirely share it for the Commission.

Mr. Oswald. If I could, possibly, sir, at this time——

Mr. Jenner. Would you like to add anything?

Mr. Oswald. I would like to make one little statement in regard to my memorandum, on page 12.

Mr. Jenner. Proceed.

Mr. Oswald. In relation or reference to my intentions at that time, as it is now, as recorded on page 12, "Intentions then as now was to find out the truth and nothing else."

Thank you.

Mr. Dulles. Thank you.

I have one question, only one.

You testified, I believe, yesterday that when you met your brother at the airport,464 upon his return from the Soviet Union, that he seemed somewhat disappointed that the press was not there to meet him and talk with him.

Do you recall, in your relations with your brother, any other instances where he appeared to desire publicity?

Mr. Oswald. No, sir; it is my opinion that that was the only time that I felt like possibly he did want publicity. At later dates, at my home, in Fort Worth, Tex., where they stayed, on quite a few occasions, either by telephone call or the newspaper reporter actually coming to my home, he stated he did not want to speak to him, and he did not want to see them, and they did not, sir, while he was in the presence of my home.

Mr. Dulles. Thank you very much.

Mr. Jenner. May I ask one further thing?

What is your religion?

Mr. Oswald. I was raised in the Lutheran religion, sir.

Mr. Jenner. And were all three of you boys so reared?

Mr. Oswald. That is correct, sir.

Mr. Jenner. Were you steady churchgoers? Or were you churchgoers at all?

Mr. Oswald. Yes, sir, we were.

Mr. Jenner. All three of you?

Mr. Oswald. Yes, sir; we were.

Mr. Jenner. I have nothing further.

Mr. Dulles. I want to join Mr. Jenner in expressing to you and your counsel, Mr. McKenzie, our thanks for your full and I believe frank testimony. I think you have been very helpful to us. I wish to thank you for it.

Mr. Oswald. Thank you, sir. And we hope that we have been of some help.

Mr. Jenner. You have.

Mr. McKenzie. I thank you, Mr. Chairman, for that statement, and likewise, Mr. Jenner, I appreciate on behalf of myself and Mr. Oswald your statement for the record.

I only have a few brief questions, Mr. Chairman, if I may, sir.

Mr. Dulles. These are to be put to your client?

Mr. McKenzie. Yes, sir. Although I will say this at this time—that the Chair has very generously, and Mr. Jenner likewise, granted me the opportunity to question or ask Mr. Oswald questions as we proceeded along.

Robert, there is a contract which has been introduced into the record, and I believe it is Commission Exhibit No. 277, which contract is dated December 9, 1963, and it is signed by Marina N. Oswald and yourself, and approved as to form by John M. Thorne,

Attorney, and James H. Martin. In this contract, it provides that Marina Oswald has appointed you as an assistant business manager to Mr. Martin. And in the last paragraph of the contract there is a statement to the effect that she has employed the firm of Thorne and Leach, attorneys-at-law, and further agreed that their services will be available at all times to yourself and that you will use same as required by you.

Now, my question to you is this: Have you ever at any time employed Mr. John M. Thorne to represent you?

Mr. Oswald. No, sir; I have not.

Mr. McKenzie. Has Mr. Thorne ever represented you in any capacity?

Mr. Oswald. No, sir; he has not.

Mr. McKenzie. All right, sir.

Mr. Dulles. May I just ask one question?

Mr. McKenzie now is your appointed lawyer?

Mr. Oswald. He is my selected lawyer.

Mr. McKenzie. Did Lee Harvey Oswald ever tell you or advise you, or has Marina N. Oswald told you of any trips that Lee took, or cities that he visited in Russia, other than Moscow, Minsk, or the hunting trip he took while he was in Russia reported in your diary? Or reported not in your diary, but reported in the letters to you?

Mr. Oswald. No, sir; he did not.

Mr. McKenzie. Do you know of any cities or any places that he might have gone in Russia, other than the two cities that I have named, and the hunting465 trip that he took as reported in the letter to you, which has been introduced into evidence?

Mr. Oswald. No, sir; I am not aware of any other cities.

Mr. McKenzie. Did Marina N. Oswald have either June Oswald, her two-year-old child, or Rachel, her infant child, baptized, to your knowledge?

Mr. Oswald. Yes, sir; she has.

Mr. McKenzie. And where was that, sir?

Mr. Oswald. It is my understanding that this took place in Dallas, Tex., some time in the year of 1963, sir.

Mr. Dulles. You are speaking now of June?

Mr. Oswald. I am speaking now of June.

Mr. McKenzie. Has the baby Rachel been baptized as of this time?

Mr. Oswald. Not to my knowledge, sir.

Mr. McKenzie. Do you know what faith June was baptized in? By faith I refer to what particular church or denomination.

Mr. Oswald. I believe, sir, this was the Greek Orthodox Church.

Mr. McKenzie. From your acquaintance with Marina Oswald, and based on your discussions with her, both in your home and elsewhere, including cemetery visits which you have made with her, do you now consider and believe that Marina N. Oswald is a Christian and believes in the teachings of our Lord and Savior Jesus Christ?

Mr. Oswald. I do, sir.

Mr. McKenzie. Has she professed such faith to you?

Mr. Oswald. Not directly, sir—only by implication, sir.

Mr. McKenzie. Do you believe or have you formed an opinion now, based on your discussions and observations of Marina Oswald, as to whether or not Marina N. Oswald is a Communist or a Soviet agent, either now or at any time since you met her at Dallas, Love Field, in June of 1962?

Mr. Oswald. No, sir; I do not believe that she is any of those things.

Mr. McKenzie. Now, do you think she is a Communist?

Mr. Oswald. No, sir; I do not.

Mr. McKenzie. Do you have any opinion as to whether or not she is at this time or since she arrived in this country?

Mr. Oswald. I am of the opinion that she is not, based on my observations of her reactions and her conversations with me.

Mr. McKenzie. Mr. Oswald, have I or has anyone at any time coached or briefed you—and if you don't understand what I mean by the word "coached" please tell me so—as to what you should testify here before this Commission, other than my cautioning you not to speculate or use conjecture?
Mr. Oswald. No, sir; you have not.
Mr. McKenzie. Has anyone?
Mr. Oswald. No, sir; they have not.
Mr. McKenzie. Have you told the Commission——
Mr. Jenner. Excuse me—that anyone includes any member of the staff of this Commission?
Mr. Oswald. That is correct.
Mr. McKenzie. And likewise it includes, does it not, any member of the FBI, or the Secret Service or any other Federal agency?
Mr. Oswald. That is correct.
Mr. McKenzie. And the same would apply to any State agency of Texas?
Mr. Oswald. Sir, that would apply to anybody, no matter what his position with any government agency or individual.
Mr. McKenzie. Now, have you told the Commission during the hearings here, since you have been testifying, only the facts as you knew them, or the facts as you know them now?
Mr. Oswald. That is correct.
Mr. McKenzie. And have you expressed opinions or speculated only when the Commission or Mr. Jenner or myself have asked you to do so?
Mr. Oswald. Yes, sir, I have.
Mr. McKenzie. Have you testified, Mr. Oswald, truthfully to the best of your recollection in each instance?
466 Mr. Oswald. Yes, sir, I have.
Mr. McKenzie. And in the event you have inadvertently made any mistake on dates, addresses, or facts, do you now ask the Chairman's permission to change your answer and correct any mistakes which you might have made in the event a mistake is at any time hereafter called to your attention?
Mr. Oswald. Yes, sir; I do so.
Mr. Dulles. Well, could I supplement that? In the event that you, yourself, find any mistakes—I think you said if it was called to his attention——
Mr. McKenzie. Yes, sir.
Mr. Oswald. Yes, sir, I certainly will.
Mr. Dulles. May I just add here—I hope that that will be looked over, the record will be looked over fairly promptly, so that we can make any corrections within a reasonable length of time.
Mr. McKenzie. Yes, sir; as soon as we receive it, Mr. Chairman, we will do so.
Mr. Jenner. May I say in that connection, Mr. McKenzie, if you could have him dictate that tape covering his memorandum, we can perhaps actually incorporate that in the record, which you will receive.
Mr. McKenzie. We cannot do it today, because we won't get to Dallas until late this evening. And I am going to church tomorrow and teach Sunday school and be with my children.
Mr. Oswald. And I with mine, sir.
Mr. McKenzie. I will make arrangements the first of the week to have it done.
Mr. Jenner. Send it to Mr. Rankin.
Mr. McKenzie. I shall.
If you receive from any source any further documentary information or any type of information which might be considered as evidence by this Commission, do you now ask the Commission's approval and permission to deliver such documents or

information, if any, to the FBI, so that the information may be immediately forwarded to the Commission to assist in preparing its final report?

Mr. Oswald. Yes, sir; I do.

Mr. Dulles. Is that satisfactory to you, Mr. Jenner?

Mr. Jenner. Yes, sir.

Mr. McKenzie. Likewise, do you authorize me to deliver any like information or documents which I may receive, discover or otherwise have in my possession to the same agencies for the same purpose?

Mr. Oswald. Yes, sir; I most certainly do.

Mr. Jenner. Here, again, Mr. McKenzie, if anything is delivered, would you have it delivered to Mr. Rankin, rather than to me?

Mr. McKenzie. Yes, sir.

Have you ever applied for relief, unemployment compensation, or any other form of welfare aid?

Mr. Oswald. No, sir; I have not.

Mr. McKenzie. And I refer there, sir, to both the Federal Government aid programs and likewise any aid program of the State of Texas or the State of Louisiana.

Mr. Oswald. That is correct—or any other State of the United States.

Mr. McKenzie. I believe that you have previously testified to this, but I want to make it absolutely clear.

Do you now believe that Lee Harvey Oswald was at any time an agent of any agency of the United States Government, from the time that he departed for Russia, until the day of his death on November 24, 1963?

Mr. Oswald. I do not believe that he was an agent of any government.

Mr. McKenzie. Prior to November 22, 1963, did you know of any activities of Lee Harvey Oswald relative to the Fair Play for Cuba Committee or his arrest in New Orleans, La.?

Mr. Oswald. No, sir, I did not.

Mr. McKenzie. Mr. Oswald, what has been your position insofar as the press is concerned, since the unfortunate and tragic happenings of November 22, 1963?

Mr. Oswald. My position with any news media, whether it be the newspapers, magazines, television, et cetera, has been that—no comment, and the only comment I ever made to any of them, at a very early date, was that I would abide467 by the decision of the Commission which is now known as the Warren Committee.

Mr. McKenzie. Have you ever sought to elaborate or give any statement to the press at any time?

Mr. Oswald. No, sir; I have not.

Mr. McKenzie. Do you recall any statements made by Marina N. Oswald expressing sympathy for President's family?

Mr. Oswald. Yes, sir; I do.

Mr. McKenzie. And if you will, state the source of your recollection and where the statement was made, and if she has ever made any statement to that effect to yourself.

Mr. Oswald. Yes, sir; she did make a statement directly to myself. To the best of my recollection, this was first done on Monday, November 25, 1963, at the Inn of the Six Flags, at Arlington, Tex., as Marina and myself observed the beginning of the funeral for the President of the United States.

Mr. McKenzie. And was there anyone else present at that time?

Mr. Oswald. Yes, sir; there were other people in the room. Whether or not they overheard our conversation, I do not know, sir.

Mr. Dulles. You observed that on television, I gather?

Mr. Oswald. That is correct.

Mr. McKenzie. Were there any Secret Service agents there at that time?

Mr. Oswald. Yes, sir.

Mr. McKenzie. Were they in the room with you and Marina Oswald?

Mr. Oswald. Yes, sir; they were.

Mr. McKenzie. And did they overhear any expressions of sympathy which she might have said?

Mr. Oswald. It is possible that they did, sir.

Mr. McKenzie. Have you ever testified in a lawsuit or given a deposition before a court reporter prior to your appearance before this Commission?

Mr. Oswald. No, sir; I have not.

Mr. McKenzie. Now, you have testified that you have not given any statements to the press other than the statement to the effect that you would abide with and be satisfied with the report of this Commission.

Since arriving in Washington, and since you have been sworn under oath before the Commission, have you given any statement to the press, other than saying goodnight, or good afternoon, or good morning?

Mr. Oswald. I believe at one time I did say thank you. Other than that, sir, I have not.

Mr. McKenzie. Now, have you read an article here in the New York Times of Saturday, February 22, 1964, on page 22 of the first section, entitled, "Russian training of Oswald hinted"?

Mr. Oswald. Yes, sir; I have.

Mr. McKenzie. Do you know Mr. Anthony Lewis?

Mr. Oswald. No, sir; I do not.

Mr. McKenzie. All right, sir.

Have you ever talked with Mr. Lewis?

Mr. Oswald. No, sir; not to my knowledge.

Mr. McKenzie. Now, you have testified this afternoon following our lunch break that you visited Lee Oswald in the Dallas County Jail. Do you recall that testimony—the testimony of just a few minutes ago?

Mr. Oswald. Yes, sir; I do.

Mr. McKenzie. Have you previously testified to that before the Commission, to your recollection?

Mr. Oswald. To my recollection, I believe we at least touched on that during our first session on February 20, 1963.

Mr. McKenzie. When you were in the jail—and I believe it is in the sixth floor of the Dallas County Jail—I mean the Dallas City Jail—talking with your brother, Lee Harvey Oswald, did you ask him at that time if he had committed the crime?

Mr. Oswald. Yes, sir; I had.

Mr. McKenzie. You did ask him that question?

Mr. Oswald. Yes, sir; I did.

468 Mr. McKenzie. And what did he say?

Mr. Oswald. I put it to him as stated in my diary, sir.

Mr. Jenner. Identify the page, please.

Mr. Oswald. On page 12, "I do not recall everything he said. I did try to point out to him that the evidence was overwhelming that he did kill Police Officer Tippit and possibly the President. To this he replied 'do not form any opinion on the so-called evidence.'"

Mr. Jenner. Is that all he said? He said nothing else?

Mr. Oswald. To that——

Mr. Jenner. In response to you?

Mr. Oswald. That is correct.

Mr. Jenner. At no time when you interviewed him over the telephone while you were in that—the sixth floor—did he affirmatively deny either that he had shot Officer Tippit or that he shot the President?

Mr. Oswald. He did not admit to anything whatsoever.

Mr. Jenner. Nor did he deny it affirmatively—other than the remark that you have recorded in your memorandum?

Mr. Oswald. That is correct, sir.

Mr. McKenzie. In other words, Mr. Oswald, when you were talking there with your brother, in the city jail of Dallas, he did not deny that he had killed Officer Tippit, nor did he deny that he had assassinated President Kennedy?

Mr. Oswald. He did not admit to anything, sir.

Mr. McKenzie. And he didn't deny anything?

Mr. Oswald. That is correct.

Mr. McKenzie. Have you, or haven't you told this Commission that you believed a denial?

Mr. Jenner. Excuse me, Mr. McKenzie, I don't understand that question.

Mr. McKenzie. It says in this article that he told the Commission that he believed the denial.

Since there was no denial, there was nothing for you to believe.

Mr. Oswald. That is correct.

Mr. Jenner. Up to this moment he has never testified as to that, to my recollection.

Mr. McKenzie. That is correct.

Again, based on the evidence that you have read or heard in newspaper articles, whether it be evidence or not, but based on everything that you have heard or read, you now believe that your brother, Lee Harvey Oswald, did kill Mr. Tippit and assassinated President Kennedy, is that correct?

Mr. Oswald. Purely on the circumstantial evidence that has been brought to my attention or that I have read.

Mr. McKenzie. I believe that is all, Mr. Chairman.

Mr. Jenner. May I ask one question?

Mr. Oswald, until this afternoon, when you recalled orally here the circumstances and the event of your discussion with your brother on the sixth floor of the Dallas—is that Dallas County?

Mr. McKenzie. No; it is Dallas City Jail.

Mr. Jenner. Dallas City Jail—had I had any conversation with you at all on that subject?

Mr. Oswald. None that I recall, sir.

Mr. Jenner. Thank you.

Mr. McKenzie. That is all, Mr. Chairman.

Mr. Dulles. That will then conclude the testimony of Mr. Robert Oswald, with the understanding that the Commission might later wish to recall him if any facts are adduced that would make that desirable.

Mr. McKenzie. Mr. Dulles—is he now released from his oath to the Commission, subject to recall and being resworn?

Mr. Dulles. That is correct.

Mr. Jenner. That is correct. That is my understanding.

In any event, I so agree, Mr. Chairman.

Mr. McKenzie. Thank you, sir.

I would like to state to the Commission one further thing, Mr. Dulles, if I may. We very much appreciate, and by "we" I mean myself as counsel, and Mr.469 Oswald as a witness, the manner in which the Commission and its counsel have conducted the interrogation of Mr. Oswald. We further appreciate the opportunity to be in Washington and to be heard, and hope that in some manner that we may assist in shedding some light that will assist this Commission in making its final report, and that the true facts of this situation will be known to the President of the United States to use at his discretion.

Mr. Dulles. Thank you very much, Mr. McKenzie.

Mr. Jenner. May I ask one more question?

Up until this afternoon when I questioned you, possibly there might have been a question this morning on the subject of any opinion which you might have held dealing with whether your brother did or did not participate in the shooting of Officer Tippit or the assassination of President Kennedy, had I had any conversation with you on that subject?

Mr. Oswald. Yes, sir; I believe you had.

Mr. Jenner. When was that?

Mr. Oswald. I believe this was on the first session, during the first session on Wednesday, February 20, 1964.

Mr. Jenner. Was it in this room?

Mr. Oswald. Yes, sir; it was.

Mr. Jenner. That is all I meant. I had no separate—no conversation with you on the subject other than as I might have put a question to you in the presence of the Commission.

Mr. Oswald. That is correct.

Mr. Jenner. Thank you.

Mr. Dulles. And a part of the record.

Mr. Jenner. And as part of the record; yes, sir.

Mr. Dulles. We will adjourn.

(Whereupon, at 3:40 p.m., the President's Commission recessed.)

Thursday, February 27, 1964

Testimony of James Herbert Martin

The President's Commission met 9:25 a.m. on February 27, 1964, at 200 Maryland Avenue NE., Washington, D.C.

Present were Chief Justice Earl Warren, Chairman; Senator John Sherman Cooper, Representative Hale Boggs, Representative Gerald R. Ford, and Allen W. Dulles, members.

Also present were J. Lee Rankin, general counsel; Norman Redlich, assistant counsel; Paul W. Leech, counsel to James Herbert Martin; Charles Murray and Charles Rhyne, observers; and Dean Robert G. Storey, special counsel to the attorney general of Texas.

The Chairman. The Commission will be in order.

Let the record show that Mr. Martin, first that Commissioners Dulles and Ford and I are present.

Mr. Martin, the witness, is here with his lawyer; would you state your name for the record, please?

Mr. Leech. Paul Leech.

The Chairman. Mr. Leech, I understand you are a partner of Mr. Thorne who was here representing Mrs. Oswald.

Mr. Leech. Yes, sir.

The Chairman. Gentlemen, I will just read an opening statement to you that we make for the record and for the benefit of the witness each time we convene.

On November 29, 1963, President Lyndon B. Johnson issued Executive Order No. 11130 appointing a Commission "to ascertain, evaluate and report upon the470 facts relating to the assassination of the late President John F. Kennedy, and the subsequent violent death of the man charged with the assassination."

On December 13, 1963, Congress adopted Joint Resolution S.J. 137 which authorizes the Commission, or any member of the Commission, or any agent or agency designated by the Commission for such purpose, to administer oaths and affirmations, examine witnesses, and receive evidence.

On January 21, 1964, the Commission adopted a resolution authorizing each member of the Commission and its General Counsel, J. Lee Rankin, to administer oaths and affirmations, examine witnesses, and receive evidence.

On January 21, 1964, the Commission adopted a resolution authorizing each member of the Commission and its General Counsel, J. Lee Rankin, to administer oaths and affirmations, examine witnesses, and receive evidence concerning any matter under investigation by the Commission.

The purpose of this hearing is to take the testimony of Mr. James Herbert Martin who has acted as the business manager of Mrs. Marina Oswald, the widow of Lee Harvey Oswald, who, prior to his death, was charged with the assassination of President Kennedy. In view of Mr. Martin's close association with Mrs. Oswald it is the intention of this Commission to ask Mr. Martin questions concerning this association and any and all matters related to the assassination, and to the subsequent killing of Lee Harvey Oswald.

Mr. Martin has been furnished with a copy of this statement and a copy of the rules adopted by the Commission for the taking of testimony or the production of evidence. Mr. Martin has also been furnished with a copy of Executive Order No. 11130 and Congressional Resolution S.J. Res. 137 which set forth the general scope of the Commission's inquiry and its authority for the examining of witnesses and the receiving of evidence.

I should also like to read into the record at this time a copy of a letter dated February 22, 1964, to Mr. Martin from Mr. J. Lee Rankin, General Counsel of the Commission, which reads as follows:

"Dear Mr. Martin:

"Confirming discussions between the staff of this Commission and John M. Thorne, Esquire, your counsel, we hereby request that you appear before this Commission at 9:00 a.m., on February 27, 1964, at Room 400, 200 Maryland Avenue, NE., Washington, D.C., for the purpose of giving sworn testimony concerning your association with Mrs. Marina Oswald and your knowledge of the facts relating to the assassination of President Kennedy and the subsequent killing of Lee Harvey Oswald.

"You are hereby requested to produce before this Commission at that time any and all books, records, papers, notes, and documents pertaining to your association with Marina Oswald and your knowledge of the facts relating to the assassination of President Kennedy and the subsequent killing of Lee Harvey Oswald including, but not limited to, those books, records, papers, notes, and documents pertaining to (1) your business dealings with Marina Oswald, (2) your activities as Marina Oswald's business representative, (3) Marina Oswald's business dealings with others, (4) your dealings with Marina Oswald in connection with the preparation of any testimony, interviews, public appearances, story, article, or other narrative concerning her personal history or the assassination of President Kennedy and the killing of Lee Harvey Oswald, and (5) your dealings with Marina Oswald in connection with her appearance before this Commission.

"The Commission is authorized to reimburse you for your expenses in connection with your appearance before the Commission, and the necessary details will be arranged when you are here.

"Attached herewith are copies of Executive Order No. 11130, dated November 29, 1963, S.J. Res. 137—88th Cong., 1st Session, and the rules of this Commission in connection with hearings conducted for the purpose of taking of testimony or the production of evidence."

I assume, gentlemen, you did receive a copy of that letter?

Mr. Leech. Yes, we did.

The Chairman. I will not be able to be here at all times today because we have, we are hearing arguments in the Court at 10 o'clock and I must leave to be there, but Mr. Dulles anticipates being here all day so in my absence he will conduct hearings.

471 Congressman Ford has some unfinished business at the Congress as I have at the Court so he probably will not be here all through the day.

Mr. Martin, will you please rise and be sworn?

Do you solemnly swear in this proceeding before the Commission to tell the truth, the whole truth and nothing but the truth, so help you God?

Mr. Martin. I do.

Mr. Leech. Your Honor, who are these other gentlemen here. I haven't been introduced to them.

The Chairman. This is Mr. Charles Rhyne, who represents the American Bar Association.

Mr. Leech. Former president of the American Bar Association?

The Chairman. Yes, and Mr. Murray who is also in the Public Defender's office of the District of Columbia.

Mr. Rankin. He represents Mr. Walter Craig, too.

The Chairman. He and Mr. Rhyne represent Mr. Walter Craig.

Mr. Leech. Who is that?

Mr. Rankin. Mr. Craig is the President of the Bar Association and was asked to act in order to protect or advise the Commission as to any interests of Lee H. Oswald because of—you probably saw the notice in the paper and so forth.

Mr. Leech. You represent the man from Arizona?

Mr. Rhyne. Walter E. Craig, President of the American Bar Association.

Mr. Rankin. Mr. Storey is the representative of the Attorney General of Texas.

Mr. Leech. He is Dean of the Southern Methodist Law School.

Mr. Rankin. Yes.

The Chairman. Of course, this is Professor Redlich of our staff. And this is the reporter.

All right, Mr. Rankin will conduct the examination.

Will you proceed, Mr. Rankin?

Mr. Rankin. Mr. Leech, does the reporter have your full name?

Mr. Leech. Yes, sir; he does.

Mr. Rankin. Mr. Martin, will you tell us your name, please?

Mr. Martin. James Herbert Martin.

Mr. Rankin. Where do you live?

Mr. Martin. Dallas, Tex.

Mr. Rankin. How long have you lived there?

Mr. Martin. Since 1956.

Mr. Rankin. What is your occupation?

Mr. Martin. Hotel executive.

Mr. Rankin. Are you now connected with the Six Flags Motel?

Mr. Martin. No.

Mr. Rankin. Were you at one time?

Mr. Martin. Yes.

Mr. Rankin. And during what period?

Mr. Martin. From May of 1962 until January 1, 1964.

Mr. Rankin. What was your position with that institution?

Mr. Martin. Resident manager.

Mr. Rankin. While you were at the Six Flags Inn, did you become acquainted with Marina Oswald?

Mr. Martin. Yes.

Mr. Rankin. About when was the first time that you met her?

Mr. Martin. I guess it was November 24.

Mr. Rankin. Of what year?

Mr. Martin. 1963.

Mr. Rankin. And will you tell us how that acquaintance started?

Mr. Martin. Well, I was called by the Tarrant County sheriff on Sunday.

Mr. Rankin. Who was that?

Mr. Martin. Lew Evans.

Mr. Rankin. Yes.

Mr. Martin. About 11 o'clock in the morning, and they wanted a room where they could question the Oswald family. I told them they could have it, and about four o'clock, I guess, four or four-thirty, I don't know the exact time they472 came in with the whole family, and we gave them several rooms to accommodate the family.

Mr. Rankin. Were you introduced to Marina Oswald at that time?

Mr. Martin. Well, I don't believe I was ever really introduced to her.

Mr. Rankin. How did you come to know her then?

Mr. Martin. Well, just through association.

Mr. Rankin. I see. Did you know the county sheriff before that?

Mr. Martin. Vaguely, not to any great extent.

Mr. Rankin. Do you know of any particular reason why he chose your establishment?

Mr. Martin. Because of the central location between Dallas and Fort Worth and the isolation of it.

Mr. Rankin. At that time who came to stay with you at the Six Flags Inn, Marina and some of her family?

Mr. Martin. Well, Marina and the two children and Robert and Marguerite Oswald.

Mr. Rankin. Did they have several suites there?

Mr. Martin. They had one room, well, one suite, room 423 and 424 and then we gave them two other rooms for the Secret Service.

Mr. Rankin. Did anyone make arrangements with you besides the county sheriff about how this would be handled?

Mr. Martin. Yes, Secret Service.

Mr. Rankin. Who, for the Secret Service?

Mr. Martin. Let's see, Charles Kunkel, and Howard—I can't remember his first name.

Mr. Rankin. Secret Service man?

Mr. Martin. Yes.

Mr. Rankin. Where was this arrangement made?

Mr. Martin. Well, down in the room in the suite.

Mr. Rankin. There at the Six Flags Inn?

Mr. Martin. Yes.

Mr. Rankin. And the three of you were there together, were you?

Mr. Martin. Yes, there were also Arlington police officers and several other Secret Service men.

Mr. Rankin. Who participated in the conversation?

Mr. Martin. Well, I don't know who else was in the conversation. It was primarily between Kunkel and Howard and myself.

Mr. Rankin. What was said in regard to this arrangement at that time?

Mr. Martin. Well, they said that they would need these rooms to accommodate the family and they had no idea how long they would need it.

Mr. Rankin. Was anything said about the price and who would make payment?

Mr. Martin. Yes. They said that the Government would take care of the room rate on it.

Mr. Rankin. Did you have to submit this matter to any of your superiors or did you make the decision at that time?

Mr. Martin. No, I made the decision.

Mr. Rankin. Had you had any prior dealings with the Secret Service people before that?

Mr. Martin. No.

Mr. Rankin. How long did Marguerite Oswald stay there?

Mr. Martin. I believe she left on Friday.

Mr. Rankin. What day?

Mr. Martin. Or maybe Thursday. Would be the 28th or 29th, I am not certain as to the exact date.

Mr. Rankin. Do you recall any incidents where Marguerite Oswald sought to leave prior to the Thursday or Friday that she left?

Mr. Martin. No, I don't recall anything like that.

Mr. Rankin. Have you ever assisted the local police officers in any other way at your Six Flags Inn before that?

Mr. Martin. Yes.

Mr. Rankin. In a general way what was the nature of that assistance.

Mr. Martin. Well, of course, I can't recall any specific instances. I know473 we cooperate with the law enforcement officers in anything they have to ask us, and we cooperate with them, giving them information. I don't know of any particular incidents other than——

Mr. Rankin. Would you describe briefly just where these rooms were in your Inn and where the Secret Service were compared with Marina Oswald's rooms?

Mr. Martin. Well, Marina Oswald was in Rooms 423 and 424, which were connecting rooms, and the rooms faced away from the entrance to the motel. And then the Secret Service had 422 and 421 also. They were rooms next door to it, but not connecting.

Mr. Rankin. After Marina first came there did the Secret Service have someone on duty while she was at the Six Flags?

Mr. Martin. Yes.

Mr. Rankin. All the time?

Mr. Martin. Yes.

Mr. Rankin. Do you recall who that was?

Mr. Martin. Let's see—well, I remember his first name now, Mike Howard, and Charles Kunkel, Lee Gopadze was there part of the time. They seemed to change quite frequently.

Mr. Rankin. Did they have someone there 24 hours of the day?

Mr. Martin. Yes, sir.

Mr. Rankin. During this early period did you ever talk to Marina?

Mr. Martin. No, except to say hello.

Mr. Rankin. Do you know whether she talked English much at that time?

Mr. Martin. From all appearances, she didn't.

Mr. Rankin. Did anyone visit you while she was there at the Six Flags during this early period that you recall?

Mr. Martin. Not to my knowledge other than the FBI.

Mr. Rankin. Did you invite Marina and her family to come to your home for Thanksgiving?

Mr. Martin. Yes.

Mr. Rankin. Will you tell us how that happened?

Mr. Martin. Well, it just happened. I don't know, I think I asked Robert if he would like to come out for dinner, Thanksgiving dinner. They weren't going to have a very happy Thanksgiving, and living in those rooms was pretty cramped.

Mr. Rankin. When was this that you asked Robert?

Mr. Martin. I believe on Wednesday.

Mr. Rankin. Did you include Robert and his wife as well as Marina and her family in the invitation?

Mr. Martin. Well, Robert's wife wasn't there, but I included Robert. He came out to the house also.

Mr. Rankin. Did Marina then come to your house for Thanksgiving?

Mr. Martin. Yes.

Mr. Rankin. Who all came at that time?

Mr. Martin. Let's see, there were Marina and June Lee, and Robert, Charlie Kunkel, and one Arlington police officer. I don't recall his name.

Mr. Rankin. What time of the day did they come?

Mr. Martin. I believe it was 3 or 4 o'clock in the afternoon.

Mr. Rankin. Did you invite Marguerite Oswald to Thanksgiving dinner at that time, too?

Mr. Martin. No.

Mr. Rankin. Did you say anything to her about it?

Mr. Martin. No. As I recall I just asked, I believe I just asked Robert if they would like to come, they were welcome if they would like to come.

Mr. Rankin. You mean by that that you included Marguerite Oswald in your invitation?

Mr. Martin. I don't think I named her. I don't know if she had left by then.

Mr. Rankin. You didn't deliberately exclude her from the invitation?

Mr. Martin. No.

Mr. Rankin. Then did you at some time discuss with Marina the possibility of her staying at your home rather than at the Six Flags Inn?

474 Mr. Martin. No, I discussed it with Secret Service first.

Mr. Rankin. When was that?

Mr. Martin. Thursday or Friday.

Mr. Rankin. Before this Thanksgiving dinner or afterwards?

Mr. Martin. I don't recall. I know the Secret Service made a statement that they were quite concerned as to where Marina would go after she left the Inn. They had no place to put her and they had no idea where she was going to go.

Mr. Rankin. Do you recall when they made that statement?

Mr. Martin. No, it was Wednesday or Thursday.

Mr. Rankin. At that time did you say anything about that?

Mr. Martin. I told them that if they couldn't find any place for her that I would be glad to take them into my home.

Mr. Rankin. Was anything said about what compensation you would receive for that?

Mr. Martin. No. There was no compensation considered.

Mr. Rankin. You didn't suggest any and they didn't, is that right?

Mr. Martin. That is correct.

Mr. Rankin. Did you discuss that idea with Marina at all?

Mr. Martin. No. They, the Secret Service told Robert about it, and——

Mr. Rankin. How do you know that?

Mr. Martin. Because he told me they had. And then Robert thanked me and said that it would work out all right.

Mr. Rankin. Before you made that suggestion had you had any discussions about selling any rights to Marina's stories or anything of that character?

Mr. Martin. No.

Mr. Rankin. With any media?

Mr. Martin. No.

Mr. Rankin. How did you happen to make this offer?

Mr. Martin. I felt sorry for her.

Mr. Rankin. Did you limit the offer to Marina and her children?

Mr. Martin. Yes.

Mr. Rankin. Was there any talk at that time about Robert living at your home, too?

Mr. Martin. No.

Mr. Rankin. Anything about Marguerite living there?

Mr. Martin. No.

Mr. Rankin. Did you discuss this proposal with your wife before you made it?

Mr. Martin. No.

Mr. Rankin. Could you describe for the Commission briefly your home, how the layout of it was?

Mr. Martin. Well, it is a three-bedroom house, with a living room, dining room, den and kitchen, two baths.

Mr. Rankin. All of it on the same floor?

Mr. Martin. Yes.

Mr. Rankin. Could you give us an idea of where the bedrooms were from the rest of the house?

Mr. Martin. Well, as you come in the front door you go through one end of the living room, and then into a hallway, and the bedrooms are along the hall.

Mr. Rankin. And is yours and Mrs. Martin's bedroom at the end of the hall?

Mr. Martin. Yes.

Mr. Rankin. Does it have a private bath associated with that suite?

Mr. Martin. Yes.

Mr. Rankin. And all of the rooms of the house are on one floor, is that right?

Mr. Martin. Yes.

Mr. Rankin. And then where was Marina's bedroom from yours?

Mr. Martin. The next room.

Mr. Rankin. And where was the bath that she used?

475 Mr. Martin. Right across the hall from it.

Mr. Rankin. And then after Marina's room right next to hers?

Mr. Martin. Is a children's bedroom.

Mr. Rankin. That was the closest one to the living room, is that right?

Mr. Martin. Yes.

Mr. Rankin. About how large was your bedroom?

Mr. Martin. I think it is about 14 by, maybe 14 by 14, 16.

Mr. Rankin. How large was Marina's room?

Mr. Martin. About 11 by 13.

Mr. Rankin. And the children's room?

Mr. Martin. About the same size.

Mr. Rankin. What children do you have?

Mr. Martin. I have a 14-year-old boy and a 12-year-old boy and a 6-year-old girl.

Mr. Rankin. And they are all living at home?

Mr. Martin. Yes.

Mr. Rankin. And they have been throughout this period, have they?

Mr. Martin. Yes.

Mr. Rankin. Had you discussed the assassination with Marina at all prior to the time she came to live with you?

Mr. Martin. No.

Mr. Rankin. Had you discussed any financial arrangements with her or the idea that you should manage her affairs before she came to live with you?

Mr. Martin. No.

Mr. Rankin. When did the donations for Marina and her children start to come in, do you recall the date?

Mr. Martin. No.

Mr. Rankin. Was it before she came to live with you?

Mr. Martin. Not to my knowledge, I didn't—I think it started after she came into the house.

The Chairman. Mr. Rankin, if you will excuse me now, gentlemen, I am going to retire to my Court work and Mr. Dulles, will you conduct the hearing? If you are still in session I will be here this afternoon to see you, if not, gentlemen, I am very glad to have seen you, both of you. Give Mr. Thorne my regards, please.

(At this point, the Chief Justice Warren left the hearing room.)

Mr. Dulles. Will you proceed, please.

Mr. Rankin. When did the idea of your being Marina's business manager first come up.
Mr. Martin. It was after the first of December. She had been there about 3 or 4 days, I guess.
Mr. Rankin. That is 1963?
Mr. Martin. 1963.
Mr. Rankin. Will you tell us how it came up?
Mr. Martin. One of the Secret Service agents suggested that I get an attorney for Marina.
Mr. Rankin. Who was that?
Mr. Martin. Lee Gopadze.
Mr. Rankin. Where did this conversation occur?
Mr. Martin. In the den.
Mr. Rankin. Who was there?
Mr. Martin. I think Marina was there.
Mr. Rankin. Anyone else?
Mr. Martin. Not to my knowledge.
Mr. Rankin. About what time of the day, do you recall?
Mr. Martin. No.
Mr. Rankin. Mr. Gopadze made this suggestion, he made it to you, did he?
Mr. Martin. Yes.
Mr. Rankin. Did he say that in English?
Mr. Martin. Yes.
Mr. Rankin. Did you know whether Marina understood it?
476 Mr. Martin. Well, he had discussed it with her.
Mr. Rankin. How do you know?
Mr. Martin. Well, he was talking about it to her about something in Russian.
Mr. Rankin. And then he turned to you, did he?
Mr. Martin. Yes.
Mr. Rankin. Did he say anything about who you should get as a lawyer for her?
Mr. Martin. No.
Mr. Rankin. What did you say about that?
Mr. Martin. Well, I told him I would be happy to get one for her.
Mr. Rankin. Did you do that?
Mr. Martin. Yes. John Thorne.
Mr. Rankin. How did you happen to select John Thorne?
Mr. Martin. I had known him from association at the Inn.
Mr. Rankin. Had he ever acted as your attorney?
Mr. Martin. No.
Mr. Rankin. What was the nature of your acquaintance with him?
Mr. Martin. Just a passing acquaintance.
Mr. Rankin. Did you discuss with Marina the qualifications of this attorney?
Mr. Martin. No.
Mr. Rankin. Did you say anything about it to Mr. Gopadze?
Mr. Martin. I, like I probably mentioned, John had handled some movie work and he would probably know something about the area in which we were talking.
Mr. Rankin. After you had made the suggestion of Mr. Thorne as a lawyer did you do anything about it?
Mr. Martin. I called Mr. Thorne.
Mr. Rankin. On the telephone?
Mr. Martin. Yes.
Mr. Rankin. And then what happened?
Mr. Martin. He came over, I believe, the next day and talked to Marina and Lee Gopadze and myself.

Mr. Rankin. How did he talk to Marina?
Mr. Martin. Well, through Lee Gopadze.
Mr. Rankin. As an interpreter?
Mr. Martin. As an interpreter.
Mr. Rankin. Mr. Gopadze is fluent in both Russian and English?
Mr. Martin. Yes.
Mr. Rankin. Could you tell what Mr. Gopadze said to Marina?
Mr. Martin. No.
Mr. Rankin. Did you discuss the nature of this retainer with Mr. Thorne at that time?
Mr. Martin. I don't understand the question.
Mr. Rankin. Did you discuss what he would be doing if he was employed as her lawyer?
Mr. Martin. Handling all her legal work.
Mr. Rankin. Did you tell him that?
Mr. Martin. Yes.
Mr. Rankin. And did you say anything about what the legal work would involve, the kind of work it would be?
Mr. Martin. I don't believe so at the time. I may have mentioned something about her story or something like that. I don't recall the conversation.
Mr. Rankin. Was anything said about the donations at that time?
Mr. Martin. No.
Mr. Rankin. Did you discuss what he would be paid by way of compensation?
Mr. Martin. Not at that time. It was later.
Mr. Rankin. Was anything said by you or Mr. Thorne about his qualifications to act as her attorney?
Mr. Martin. Not that I recall.
Mr. Rankin. Were formal arrangements made about the employment of Mr. Thorne as counsel for Marina?
Mr. Martin. Yes.
477 Mr. Rankin. When was that done?
Mr. Martin. I believe that was December 6.
Mr. Rankin. Do you recall anything else that was said or done at this conversation when Mr. Thorne came over and talked to Marina through the interpreter and you were present?
Mr. Martin. No.
Mr. Rankin. Was there a formal contract executed between Marina and Mr. Thorne at some time?
Mr. Martin. Yes.
Mr. Rankin. You think that was December 6 to your recollection.
Mr. Martin. Either the 5th or the 6th.
Mr. Rankin. Now, before that contract was executed did you discuss it with Mr. Thorne?
Mr. Martin. Yes.
Mr. Rankin. Was Marina present when you did?
Mr. Martin. I don't believe so.
Mr. Rankin. Where did this discussion occur?
Mr. Martin. I believe it was at the Inn.
Mr. Rankin. Your office?
Mr. Martin. No, in the coffee shoppe.
Mr. Rankin. Who else was present.
Mr. Martin. No one.
Mr. Rankin. Did you then go over the terms of the contract with him?
Mr. Martin. No. I think I left that up to him.
Mr. Rankin. Were you then the manager of Marina's affairs?

Mr. Martin. No.
Mr. Rankin. Who were you acting for in regard to that arrangement?
Mr. Martin. Well, acting for Marina although I had no—I had no contract to that effect.
Mr. Rankin. You were still acting under this suggestion by Mr. Gopadze that some counsel be gotten for her?
Mr. Martin. Yes.
Mr. Rankin. And you did go over the terms of this contract at that time, did you?
Mr. Martin. Yes.
Mr. Rankin. Did you make any suggestions for changes?
Mr. Martin. That we delete it, on my contract, we deleted any gifts or contributions.
Mr. Rankin. That is on the draft of the contract for you to act as manager?
Mr. Martin. Yes.
Mr. Rankin. And when did that idea of your acting as manager come up?
Mr. Martin. Well, I believe it was the same day that John Thorne came out to talk to Marina and to Gopadze.
Mr. Rankin. Do you know who brought it up?
Mr. Martin. No.
Mr. Rankin. Did you suggest that you act as manager?
Mr. Martin. I don't believe I suggested it. We were discussing the need for a manager, and I don't know who brought it up as far as my being the one.
Mr. Rankin. At that time was there any discussion about what compensation you would have?
Mr. Martin. No.
Mr. Rankin. When you were talking to Mr. Thorne in the coffee shoppe was there a discussion about how much compensation he would receive for acting as attorney?
Mr. Martin. Yes.
Mr. Rankin. What was said about that?
Mr. Martin. Well, just that it would be 10 percent.
Mr. Rankin. Had you ever discussed that before with him?
Mr. Martin. Not that I recall.
(At this point, Senator Cooper entered the hearing room.)
Mr. Dulles. Senator, we welcome you.
Senator Cooper. Thank you.
Mr. Dulles. Would you proceed? Would you just resume for a moment where we are in the proceedings?
Mr. Rankin. We are discussing the contract between Mr. Martin and Marina and also how Mr. Thorne became counsel under the contracts that were made.
Senator Cooper. Yes.
Mr. Rankin. This 10-percent figure for John Thorne and the contract with regard to his appointment then was his suggestion so far as you know?
Mr. Martin. As far as I know. I think we had discussed it.
Mr. Rankin. You had discussed it?
Mr. Martin. I don't know exactly how we came to these figures as far as that is concerned.
Mr. Rankin. But you think you had discussed it before the meeting at the coffee shoppe that you described?
Mr. Martin. Probably so.
Mr. Rankin. Did you suggest the amount?
Mr. Martin. I don't know.
Mr. Rankin. You don't recall whether you did or he did?
Mr. Martin. No.
Mr. Rankin. Did you talk that over with Marina?
Mr. Martin. Yes.

Mr. Rankin. Who was present at that time?
Mr. Martin. I believe Lee Gopadze.
Mr. Rankin. Anyone else?
Mr. Martin. Well, there were several times we discussed it with Marina. One time Robert was there. He read the contracts. Let's see, he usually came in on Sunday so he read the contracts more at length.
Mr. Rankin. Did Robert come in before or after your conversation in the coffee shoppe that you referred to?
Mr. Martin. I believe after.
Mr. Rankin. After you had the conversation in the coffee shoppe with Mr. Thorne, did you make any changes in the draft of the contract.
Mr. Martin. Yes.
Mr. Leech. Excuse me, what contract are you talking about?
Mr. Rankin. Thorne contract.
Were you referring to the Thorne contract?
Mr. Martin. Yes.
Mr. Rankin. What changes did you make at that time?
Mr. Martin. We deleted gifts, contributions. He used a standard contractual form, and in that contractual form it includes gifts and contributions, and we deleted those.
Mr. Rankin. I hand you Exhibit No. 279 and ask you if that is a photostat copy of the contract you have been referring to?
Mr. Martin. Yes.
Mr. Rankin. And it has stricken out the words that you have just described with regard to donations and gifts?
Mr. Martin. Yes.
Mr. Rankin. It does give him an interest in collections, trust funds and bequests, according to the language of this Exhibit No. 279.
Do you know what was meant by that?
Mr. Martin. No. That was in the standard contract that this was drawn from.
Mr. Rankin. Did you ever discuss this contract, Exhibit No. 279, with Marina Oswald?
Mr. Martin. Yes, with Mr. Thorne and Robert Oswald present.
Mr. Rankin. When was that?
Mr. Martin. Between the 1st and the 6th of December 1963. I can't recall the dates.
Mr. Rankin. Do you remember where you were when you had that discussion?
Mr. Martin. At the house, my home.
Mr. Rankin. What did you say to Marina about it?
Mr. Martin. I don't recall any conversation at all.
Mr. Rankin. Was anything said about the 10 percent at that time?
Mr. Martin. Well, she knew it was 10 percent.
Mr. Rankin. How do you know she knew that?
Mr. Martin. Well, we explained it to her.
Mr. Rankin. Who explained it?
Mr. Martin. I don't know whether I did or whether John Thorne did or Robert.
Mr. Rankin. Did she understand English enough to understand what you were talking about?
Mr. Martin. Yes.
Mr. Rankin. How do you know that?
Mr. Martin. Because of her reaction to it.
Mr. Rankin. Did she react about the 10 percent?
Mr. Martin. No. I mean there was no reaction as far as her, a definite reaction but I could tell she understood it.
Mr. Rankin. Can you tell us what you observed about her that caused you to think that she understood it?

Mr. Martin. Well, I don't know. I think it was explained to her as 10 cents of a dollar.
Mr. Rankin. Was anything——
Mr. Martin. But she said she understood percents.
Mr. Rankin. How did she say that?
Mr. Martin. That way. "I understand percents" or something of that type.
Mr. Rankin. Was there any discussion with Marina about the effect of this contract on donations and contributions from the public?
Mr. Martin. Yes. We said that that would not be included in that 10 percent.
Mr. Rankin. Did you say anything to Marina about whether this was a good contract for her?
Mr. Martin. I probably did.
Mr. Rankin. Do you recall what you said?
Mr. Martin. No.
Mr. Rankin. You have no recollection about that?
Mr. Martin. No. Actually we left most of it up to Robert.
Mr. Rankin. So whatever explanation was made to Marina was really made by Robert, is that right?
Mr. Leech. Excuse me for just a minute.
(Discussion off the record.)
Mr. Rankin. Back on the record.
Mr. Leech. Mr. Martin's contract and Robert had a contract with her, too, and Mr. Thorne's contract were left with her. They were not signed that day.
Mr. Rankin. You tell us what you know about that, Mr. Martin.
Mr. Martin. Well, Robert wanted to read over the contracts and think them over, and I believe he took copies of them. Now, I am not sure, I am not certain, about that.
Mr. Rankin. When did Robert get involved here, of getting a share?
Mr. Martin. From the beginning.
Mr. Rankin. Were you present when that matter came up?
Mr. Martin. Yes. That was Marina's request that he participate.
Mr. Rankin. When was that request made?
Mr. Martin. Prior to the signing of the contracts, probably December 4—3d or 4th.
Mr. Rankin. Who was present at that time?
Mr. Martin. I believe John Thorne and Robert, Marina and myself.
Mr. Rankin. What did Marina say about that at that time?
Mr. Martin. She wanted Robert to have some of the money.
Mr. Rankin. What did Robert say about that?
Mr. Martin. As I recall he didn't say much of anything.
Mr. Rankin. Did he say anything to indicate that he thought that was a good idea, a bad idea?
Mr. Martin. No. I think he said, "Thank you," that is about it.
480 Mr. Rankin. Did Marina say anything about how much she wanted Robert to get?
Mr. Martin. Yes.
Mr. Rankin. What did she say about that?
Mr. Martin. Ten percent.
Mr. Rankin. She just said 10 percent, is that all?
Mr. Martin. Yes.
Mr. Rankin. Did Marina make any explanation of how she decided that Robert should get a share, too?
Mr. Martin. No, other than she wanted to give Robert something.
Representative Ford. May I ask a question?
Mr. Rankin. Surely.
Representative Ford. Was there any discussion at any time, Mr. Martin, as to whether Marguerite should have any benefits from it?
Mr. Martin. No.

Mr. Rankin. Did Marina discuss with you at that time what Robert was to do for his 10 percent?
Mr. Martin. No.
Mr. Rankin. Do you recall any discussion about what you were to do for your share?
Mr. Martin. Yes, to sell her story.
Mr. Rankin. And what would Mr. Thorne do for his 10 percent?
Mr. Martin. Handle all the legal work involved.
Mr. Rankin. Did you ever hear any discussion about what Robert was to do for his percentage?
Mr. Martin. We said that—let's see—we would discuss with him on various occasions any of these contracts, but that he was—he would take over the handling of Marina's affairs in case of my disability.
Mr. Leech. Off the record.
(Discussion off the record.)
Mr. Rankin. Was there anything more said than you have related about what Robert would do for his share?
Mr. Martin. No. I think I probably remarked to him that there would probably be plenty for him to do.
Mr. Rankin. Was there any dispute between any of you or with Marina at this time about the percentages?
Mr. Martin. No. The only thing that I recall was the terms of the contract, of my contract.
Mr. Rankin. Was something said about that?
Mr. Martin. Was 10 years.
Mr. Rankin. Yes.
Mr. Martin. And Marina thought that was too long.
Mr. Rankin. What did she say about that?
Mr. Martin. She said she thought 10 years was too long.
Mr. Rankin. What did you say?
Mr. Martin. Let's see, she wanted a 1 year contract and I told her that actually 1 year, there is no telling how this story would develop or anything, and that 1 year might interfere with the sale of the story.
Mr. Rankin. What did she say to that?
Mr. Martin. That they agreed to it.
Mr. Rankin. She agreed then to the 10 years?
Mr. Martin. Yes.
Mr. Rankin. Was any interpreter present at that time?
Mr. Martin. No.
Mr. Rankin. So whatever Marina understood about was from her understanding of English and communication with you and Robert and Mr. Thorne?
Mr. Martin. Well, Lee Gopadze had discussed it prior to that.
Mr. Rankin. Was that in your presence?
Mr. Martin. No. He just discussed it, the general terms, I assume.
Mr. Rankin. But you don't know.
Mr. Martin. Of course. I couldn't understand what he was saying. We left the contracts with her for several days.
Mr. Rankin. But you don't know what was done with them?
Mr. Martin. No.
Mr. Rankin. Because you weren't present.
Do you know whether she understood English enough to read those contracts at that time?
Mr. Martin. No. She couldn't have read the contracts at that time. But she said she understood it sufficiently, and that she would trust Robert's judgment on it.
Mr. Rankin. When did she say that?

Mr. Martin. Just before—I guess the same day she signed it.
Mr. Rankin. I will ask you to look at Exhibit No. 279 and tell us whether you recognize the signatures on that?
Mr. Martin. Yes.
Mr. Rankin. Whose signatures are they?
Mr. Martin. Mrs. Marina N. Oswald and James H. Martin.
Mr. Rankin. In the parts that are stricken out——
Mr. Martin. John M. Thorne.
Mr. Rankin. On Exhibit No. 279 were those stricken out before the discussion of the contract?
Mr. Martin. Yes.
Mr. Rankin. Was that done when you were there?
Mr. Martin. Yes.
Mr. Rankin. Did you observe the signing?
Mr. Martin. Yes.
Mr. Leech. They were not signed the date it says they were signed.
Mr. Martin. On the 5th.
Mr. Leech. The date it says they were signed that is the date they were drawn up but they were all signed the same time, weren't they, Mr. Martin?
Mr. Martin. Yes.
Mr. Rankin. Can you tell us what the facts are in that regard, Mr. Martin?
Mr. Martin. The contracts were drawn—let's see—the contracts were drawn and Robert wanted to go over them, so we held it in abeyance. I think he was there on a Sunday and he came back on a Tuesday, I am not sure about the days, and signed the contracts.
Mr. Rankin. Do you know the signature of Marina Oswald?
Mr. Martin. Yes.
Mr. Rankin. Will you tell us whether or not Exhibit No. 279 bears her signature?
Mr. Martin. Yes, it does.
Mr. Rankin. It appears to be witnessed by you, is that your signature?
Mr. Martin. Yes.
Mr. Rankin. And the acceptance at the bottom of Exhibit No. 279, do you know whose signature that is?
Mr. Martin. John Thorne's.
Mr. Rankin. And you say that the exhibit was, the contract, Exhibit No. 279 was executed on the 6th rather than the 5th day of December.
Mr. Martin. Well, I can't recall the dates on it.
Mr. Leech. Excuse me for just a minute.
(Discussion off the record.)
Mr. Leech. Counsel, for what it is worth, Robert's was executed at the same time as the other ones. I believe his is dated the 9th, isn't it? So it would have been the 9th or afterwards. They were all executed at the same time.
Mr. Rankin. Mr. Martin, do you know that?
Mr. Martin. I know they were all executed the same time.
Mr. Rankin. Whether or not it was the 9th or the 6th you don't recall at this time?
Mr. Martin. No. I am fairly certain it was not the 6th.
Mr. Rankin. Are you certain what date it was?
Mr. Martin. No.
Mr. Rankin. What is your best recollection in that regard?
Mr. Martin. Well, it was several days after the contracts were drawn that they were executed, and I believe the contracts were drawn, and the date that they were drawn was entered on the contract.
Mr. Rankin. You think that might have been December 5 that they were drawn then?
Mr. Martin. Yes.

Mr. Rankin. Mr. Chairman, that is already in evidence.

Mr. Dulles. It has already been admitted.

Mr. Rankin. Yes.

Mr. Dulles. Mr. Rankin, we would like to have a short adjournment at 10:30. The members of the Commission would like to speak with you.

(Short recess.)

Mr. Dulles. The Commission will resume. Mr. Rankin, will you please continue with the examination?

Mr. Rankin. Mr. Martin, I have been asking you about some of your contractual and financial arrangements with Marina Oswald and also Mr. Thorne's and Robert Oswald's. If you and your counsel won't object I would like to depart from that because I would like to have this information developed when some of the members of the Commission are here who might not be at other times during your examination.

Mr. Martin. One thing Mr. Leech brought to my attention was that he thought maybe you might be under the impression that these contracts were all drawn on the same date, December 5. They weren't drawn on the same date. I think it was the 5th, 6th and 7th, or the 5th, 6th, and 9th. Robert's was drawn on the 9th, mine was drawn the 6th, and Mr. Thorne's was drawn the 5th.

Mr. Rankin. Thank you.

I want to ask you about a particular incident that was referred to in the Houston Post, an article in the paper and the source was given as you and that is in regard to Mr. Nixon, Richard Nixon, former Vice President of the United States.

Did Marina ever say anything to you about Lee Oswald planning any violent action or assassination of Richard M. Nixon?

Mr. Martin. Yes.

Mr. Rankin. When did you first learn about that?

Mr. Martin. I don't remember the date. It was sometime in January, and she mentioned it, said that he had come home one night and said, one evening, and said that he had waited for Nixon to shoot him.

Mr. Rankin. Where was this?

Mr. Martin. In Dallas.

Mr. Rankin. What time was it that he came home that night?

Mr. Martin. I didn't question her too much about the time. I assumed that it was after work.

Mr. Rankin. At about what time of the day was it?

Mr. Martin. Five or six o'clock. She said they were living on Neely Street, and he came home that night, and told her about it. So the next morning he got up, Nixon had not come into town, so he said that he would be in the next day, and so he got up the next morning and got dressed with a suit, I believe she said, and she locked him in the bathroom and kept him there all day, they said.

Mr. Rankin. Did she say how she locked him in the bathroom?

Mr. Martin. No.

Mr. Rankin. Did you ask her how she could do that, whether there was a lock on the inside of the bathroom or outside?

Mr. Martin. No, I thought it was a little—I thought the story was a little far-fetched myself.

Mr. Rankin. What did you say to her about it?

Mr. Martin. Well, I said, "Don't go around telling people something like that."

Mr. Rankin. Did she say anything about whether it was true or not?

Mr. Martin. She said it was true.

Mr. Dulles. May I ask a question?

483 Mr. Rankin. Yes.

Mr. Dulles. Was this brought up in connection with anything in particular or just come out of the blue, blurted out?

Mr. Martin. It just came out of the blue.
Mr. Dulles. There was no prior conversation that led up to this or any background to it?
Mr. Martin. Not that I recall. It was just a statement that she made. I think she was talking about Oswald——
Representative Ford. Was she prone to come out with these kinds of comments or was this an unusual circumstance?
Mr. Martin. No. She at times referred to some particular incident in Russia or various things like that. And they would be completely unattached to anything that we had been talking about.
Mr. Rankin. What more did you say to her about this incident when she brought it up?
Mr. Martin. Well, the only time I recall Nixon being in Dallas was in November. Now, she was not living with Oswald in November, and——
Mr. Rankin. Did you say that to her?
Mr. Martin. No. I just let the thing go.
Mr. Rankin. You didn't even ask her how she locked him in the bathroom?
Mr. Martin. No. I thought about it, because I know the only bathroom doors I have seen lock from the inside and they swing in.
Mr. Rankin. Did you ask her what he did after he was locked in the bathroom?
Mr. Martin. Yes.
Mr. Rankin. What did she say about that?
Mr. Martin. She said he didn't do anything. When she let him out that night, and I suppose he would be pretty mad at her, and she said no, he wasn't.
Mr. Rankin. Did she say she kept him in the bathroom all day?
Mr. Martin. Yes.
Representative Ford. Was anybody else present at the time of this statement by her to you?
Mr. Martin. My wife.
Representative Ford. Did your wife make any inquiry?
Mr. Martin. No. We thought it was some kind of a story.
Mr. Rankin. You mean you thought it was an untrue story?
Mr. Martin. Yes, and why, I don't know. It didn't sound logical.
Mr. Rankin. Were there other conversations with Marina that you had where you thought she was telling you things that were untrue?
Mr. Martin. She would relate stories about Russia that I would listen to but they didn't sound right.
Mr. Rankin. Do you recall any?
Mr. Martin. Well, they mostly dealt with boy friends.
Mr. Rankin. What did she say in that regard?
Mr. Martin. Oh, she would talk about some individual boy friends, usually a non-Russian, someone from Rumania or Germany or from some other country.
Mr. Rankin. What did she say?
Mr. Leech. Is this going to be made public?
Mr. Rankin. This might be, yes.
Mr. Martin. Oh, I don't know about specific incidents. She would remark about she knew—I am trying to think of a specific—one was, let's see, she left Leningrad and went to Minsk because of an association with a married man there.
Representative Ford. In Leningrad?
Mr. Martin. It was either she left Leningrad to go to Minsk or vice versa.
Representative Ford. But she left one or the other to go to the other because of an association with a married man?
Mr. Martin. Yes.
Mr. Rankin. Where was the association, in Leningrad or in Minsk?

Mr. Martin. Well, it was in the city that she left.
Mr. Rankin. She was getting away from that association, was she?
Mr. Martin. Yes.
Mr. Rankin. By going to the other city?
Mr. Martin. Yes.
Mr. Rankin. Do you recall any other conversation when she told you something that you don't believe?
Mr. Martin. Oh, she remarked about people that she knew in Russia that had, we will say, lovers——
Mr. Dulles. Did she tell anything about a letter that she wrote to a boy friend in Minsk?
Mr. Martin. After she was here in New Orleans?
Mr. Dulles. Yes.
Mr. Martin. Yes.
Mr. Dulles. What did she say about that?
Mr. Martin. Let's see, she said she wrote the letter, and I believe what it was she told the boy that she wasn't—she wanted to come back to Russia, to him, she loved him, and the letter was returned, I believe, for lack of postage, and Oswald got hold of the letter, and he asked her about it, and I think he asked her either to read it or he would read it. I believe she read it to him. This caused quite a bit of difficulty. Now, that is when she was in New Orleans.
Mr. Rankin. When she was telling you about these people that had lovers in Russia, you didn't believe these stories? Is that what you are saying?
Mr. Martin. Well, of course, I know nothing about Russian life.
Mr. Rankin. Yes.
Mr. Martin. So I more or less took it with a grain of salt. I didn't put any credibility to it or any doubt to it. It was just something that was said and I didn't either accept it or reject it.
Mr. Rankin. How did she happen to tell you about going to Minsk to get away from a married man in Leningrad?
Tell us how that came up.
Mr. Martin. I think she was just talking about boy friends, I guess.
Mr. Rankin. Did she tell you she had quite a few boy friends?
Mr. Martin. Yes.
Mr. Rankin. Was that in Russia that she had the boy friends?
Mr. Martin. Yes.
Mr. Rankin. How many did she tell you about?
Mr. Martin. Oh, boy. Well, she didn't mention any names as such, and I don't know whether different stories got confused to being two different people or—I would say 10 or 12.
Mr. Rankin. Did she include Lee Oswald among those?
Mr. Martin. Well, you mean as a boy friend?
Mr. Rankin. Yes.
Mr. Martin. No.
Mr. Rankin. Did she tell you anything about her relations with these boy friends?
Mr. Martin. No.
Mr. Rankin. You say you didn't believe these stories?
Mr. Martin. Well, I didn't have any reason to disbelieve or to believe them. They were just conversation.
Mr. Rankin. Now, on the Nixon matter, when that came to your attention, did you tell anyone else about it?
Mr. Martin. I discussed it with my wife, and with John Thorne.
Mr. Dulles. Excuse me just a moment.

Mr. Martin, this is Congressman Boggs, a member of the Commission, and this is Mr. Leech, counsel for Mr. Martin.

Mr. Leech. I know Mr. Boggs, I met him in New Orleans years ago.

Mr. Rankin. Will you tell us about the conversation when you related this to someone else?

Mr. Martin. It was on the telephone, and I was quite shocked at first about it and then thinking it over, it didn't sound logical.

Mr. Rankin. You believed it at first?

Mr. Martin. Yes. I guess I didn't see any reason for it not to be true. But485 then I didn't see any reason for it to be a lie, either, and I supposed it was possible.

Mr. Rankin. When did you tell Mr. Thorne about it with reference to when Marina told you?

Mr. Martin. The same day. I don't recall the date at all.

Mr. Rankin. What did you say to Mr. Thorne about it?

Mr. Martin. I just related the incident, what she had told me.

Mr. Rankin. Did you say anything to him about telling the Commission about it?

Mr. Martin. No.

Mr. Rankin. Did he say anything about telling the Commission about it?

Mr. Martin. No, I don't believe so.

Mr. Rankin. Was there anything else said in this telephone conversation with Mr. Thorne except relating what Marina had said?

Mr. Martin. I remarked what a big bombshell that would be as far as publicity was concerned if the newspapers ever got hold of something like that.

Mr. Rankin. That it would be helpful in regard to Marina's story, did you say that?

Mr. Martin. No, I did think it would be harmful.

Mr. Rankin. Did you say that to him?

Mr. Martin. I believe so.

Mr. Dulles. Why would it be harmful?

Mr. Martin. Well, this purportedly took place after the Walker incident, and she had made a statement that if Oswald repeated anything of a similar nature as the Walker incident she would turn him over to the police, and this was a repeat or similar, he actually didn't shoot at him but threatened to, and she did not report it to the police.

Mr. Dulles. I see.

The Walker incident took place on April 10, 1963, according to our records.

Senator Cooper. I would like you if you can to repeat everything that Mrs. Oswald told you about the Nixon incident. What did Lee say to her?

Mr. Martin. This has been a very confusing 2 months——

Senator Cooper. I know that.

Mr. Martin. To me.

Senator Cooper. Do the best you can. Take your time and tell us about it.

Mr. Martin. I couldn't recall it verbatim, but she said he came in one evening, early in the evening, and said that he had tried to shoot Nixon but that he had not come into town that night as he was supposed to have, or that day, but that he would be in the next day, and he would take care of it then.

(Discussion off the record.)

Senator Cooper. I think you said that she did at least partly identify the time by saying at the time they were living on Neely Street.

Mr. Martin. Neely Street.

Mr. Dulles. May I just add there our records indicate they were living on Neely Street on March 2, between March 2, 1963, and April 24, 1963.

Senator Cooper. Did Mrs. Oswald tell you anything that he said about the way or means he intended to kill him or at what place?

Mr. Martin. No.

Mr. Redlich. Do you recall what weapon she mentioned at the time?

Mr. Martin. I don't know if I recall that she said shoot him or kill him.

Representative Ford. Could she speak English well enough to differentiate between shoot and kill?

Mr. Martin. At the time?

Representative Ford. Yes.

Mr. Martin. Yes.

Representative Ford. She could distinguish English that well?

Mr. Redlich. Did she mention a pistol or rifle?

Mr. Martin. No.

Mr. Redlich. Did she mention whether he was employed at the time or unemployed at the time?

Mr. Martin. I don't believe so.

486 Mr. Redlich. Did you ask her how it was possible for her to keep him in a bathroom for one whole day?

Mr. Martin. No.

Mr. Dulles. Did you ask her why Lee Harvey Oswald wanted to kill Nixon, any motive?

Mr. Martin. I think I asked, "Well, why would he want to do that?" And she shrugged her shoulders.

Senator Cooper. I would like to follow up on that. In this conversation with her, did he give any reason to Marina Oswald why he wanted to kill Nixon?

Mr. Martin. Evidently not. She didn't answer. She didn't answer me when I asked.

Mr. Redlich. Mr. Martin, you have said in your opinion the Nixon incident was after the Walker incident.

Mr. Martin. Well, that is what she said.

Mr. Redlich. Did she relate it to the General Walker incident in any way when she discussed the Nixon incident with you?

Mr. Martin. She just said it was after General Walker.

Mr. Redlich. Did she relate to you any conversation that she may have had with Lee Harvey Oswald relating the Nixon incident to the Walker incident?

Mr. Martin. No.

Mr. Redlich. Did she refer to any promise that he may have made at the time of the Walker incident that may have related to the Nixon incident?

Mr. Martin. No. I remember her saying after the Walker incident she told him that if he ever did anything of that nature again that she would report him to the police.

Mr. Dulles. How did you know the Nixon incident was after or supposed to be after the Walker incident? Did she say that?

Mr. Martin. She said it was.

Mr. Dulles. She said that?

Mr. Martin. Yes; I asked when it happened and she said after Walker.

Mr. Redlich. When she told you that she had threatened Lee Oswald with going to the police if there were another incident, did you ever ask her why she had not done so in light of the Nixon incident which subsequently followed?

Mr. Martin. I must not have because I think I would have remembered it if I had.

Mr. Redlich. Did you ever consider reporting the Nixon incident to any Federal authorities?

Mr. Martin. If it didn't come out in the hearing, yes.

Mr. Redlich. When Mrs. Oswald was preparing to come to Washington with you for the hearings before this Commission, did you discuss the Nixon incident with her?

Mr. Martin. I don't think so. I know I told her to be sure to tell the truth to the Commission. She had mentioned that she had lied to the FBI.

Mr. Redlich. With regard to what?

Mr. Martin. On a Mexico trip. She told the FBI she didn't know he had gone there or that he was going.

Mr. Redlich. To the best of your knowledge had she ever related the Nixon incident to the FBI or Secret Service prior to her trip to Washington?

Mr. Martin. I don't know. I was never in on any of the questions.

Mr. Redlich. Did you give her any advice in connection with any of those interviews?

Mr. Martin. No. I told her if she got tired to tell them so that they could come back the next day.

Mr. Redlich. You say when she was planning to come here you advised her to tell the truth?

Mr. Martin. Yes.

Mr. Redlich. Did you give her similar advice in connection with the FBI and Secret Service interviews?

Mr. Martin. I don't think the situation ever arose. She asked specifically about the Mexico incident.

Mr. Redlich. Throughout the many interviews with the FBI and Secret Service you never asked her, I take it, whether she had discussed the Nixon incident with the FBI or the Secret Service?

Mr. Martin. I think I may have asked her when she told me, if she had told the FBI.

Mr. Redlich. What did she say?

Mr. Martin. She said no.

Mr. Redlich. What did you say?

Mr. Martin. I don't recall if I said anything.

Representative Ford. Mr. Redlich. I wonder if we couldn't have Mr. Martin tell us the time of day and the circumstances that this conversation with Marina in the presence of your wife arose, not necessarily the date but the time of day, and the overall——

Mr. Martin. It was in the evening.

Representative Ford. You were sitting around the room?

Mr. Martin. Yes, in the den.

Representative Ford. Just the three of you?

Mr. Martin. Yes.

Representative Ford. Did she just start talking or did you prompt her or just how did the situation arise?

Mr. Martin. I don't recall. I think maybe—I think it just came into conversation as we were talking about the whole thing in general.

Mr. Dulles. Were you talking at that time about what her memoirs or any writings she might——

Mr. Martin. No.

Mr. Dulles. —she might produce would include?

Mr. Martin. No.

Representative Ford. What was your wife's reaction to this story?

Mr. Martin. Well, she couldn't believe it either.

Representative Ford. Did she ask any questions about it such as the ones you have indicated?

Mr. Martin. No, other than the ones I asked.

Mr. Redlich. Could you tell us with whom you have discussed the Nixon incident other than those that you have mentioned thus far, I believe thus far you have said Mrs. Martin and Mr. Thorne.

Is there anyone else you have told this to?

Mr. Martin. Don Levine.

Mr. Redlich. Who?

Mr. Martin. Levine.

Mr. Redlich. Who is he?

Mr. Martin. A writer.

Mr. Redlich. For what publication.

Mr. Martin. He is an author.

Mr. Dulles. Freelance writer and author, Isaac Don Levine for the record.
Mr. Redlich. When did you relate this incident to him?
Mr. Martin. Back in January.
Mr. Redlich. Could you tell us why you told him?
Mr. Martin. He is of the opinion that there is more to this than meets the eye, so to speak. He is——
Mr. Dulles. More to what?
Mr. Martin. More to the assassination.
Mr. Dulles. The Nixon story?
Mr. Martin. No.
Mr. Dulles. The whole assassination, Kennedy assassination?
Mr. Martin. And he—of course, he is quite familiar with Russian affairs, and he said the stories just don't match, and he was trying to tie in Oswald, I guess, with the Communist Party or some attachment there some place, and I mentioned that I thought he was just a nut.
Mr. Redlich. That who was.
Mr. Martin. Oswald. And I said, I told him I didn't know how true it was but then I related the story, and he—I cautioned him not to pass it around or anything like that, which he said he wouldn't.
488 Mr. Redlich. Were you or Marina Oswald compensated in any way for the release of this information to Mr. Levine?
Mr. Martin. No.
Mr. Dulles. Was Mr. Levine at this time trying to get the rights to the story or the right to write the story?
Mr. Martin. He wants to write the story, and through Meredith Press.
Mr. Redlich. Were you negotiating with Mr. Levine at the time concerning the rights to Marina Oswald's story?
Mr. Martin. Yes.
Mr. Redlich. And it was during the course of these negotiations that you revealed to him the Nixon incident?
Mr. Martin. Yes.
Mr. Redlich. And this, you say, was sometime in January?
Mr. Martin. Yes.
Mr. Redlich. Did you tell anyone else other than Mr. Levine?
Mr. Martin. Not that I recall unless it was Robert Oswald.
Mr. Redlich. Will you try to refresh your recollection with regard to Robert?
Mr. Martin. I beg your pardon?
Mr. Redlich. Do you recall whether you had a conversation in mid-January with Robert Oswald concerning the Nixon incident?
Mr. Martin. I don't remember. I was trying to remember that the other day to find out if I had mentioned it to him. And——
Mr. Redlich. Do you recall when Robert Oswald would come to visit your house?
Mr. Martin. On Sundays.
Mr. Redlich. And what would he do on these Sundays?
Mr. Martin. Usually take Marina and the baby to the cemetery.
Mr. Redlich. Do you recall whether on one of those Sundays you had a conversation with him concerning the Nixon incident?
Mr. Martin. I don't remember. I am not sure whether I did tell him or not. It seems to me that I did, but I can't recall the incident at all.
Mr. Redlich. Did Mrs. Oswald, Marina Oswald, ever indicate to you that she had discussed the Nixon incident with anyone else?
Mr. Martin. No.
Mr. Redlich. To be more specific, did she ever indicate to you whether she had discussed the Nixon incident with Robert Oswald?

Mr. Martin. No.
Mr. Redlich. With Mrs. Marguerite Oswald?
Mr. Martin. No.
Mr. Redlich. With any Federal authority?
Mr. Martin. No.
Mr. Redlich. Could you state again what your advice to her was with regard to the revealing of this incident?
Mr. Martin. Well, I told her it would be advisable just not to say anything about it.
Mr. Redlich. To anyone?
Mr. Martin. That is right.
Mr. Redlich. But you related the incident to Mr. Levine.
Mr. Martin. Yes.
Mr. Redlich. When you accompanied Mrs. Oswald to Washington for the hearings before this Commission, did the Nixon incident come up at all during your conversations?
Mr. Martin. Not that I recall.
Mr. Redlich. This incident which you regarded of such importance at the time you didn't discuss with her at all during the time she was appearing before this Commission?
Mr. Martin. I don't remember mentioning it to her.
Mr. Redlich. You didn't ask her whether she had told the Commissioners?
Mr. Martin. I think I asked John Thorne if she had mentioned it.
Mr. Redlich. What did Mr. Thorne say?
Mr. Martin. He said no, not yet. And I dropped it at that.
Mr. Redlich. You and Mr. Thorne didn't have any conversations concerning whether she should mention it?
Mr. Martin. No.
Mr. Redlich. At the conclusion of the testimony did you ask Mrs. Oswald whether she had mentioned it?
Mr. Martin. Not to my knowledge, no.
Mr. Redlich. Did you discuss with Mr. Thorne the question of whether she had mentioned the Nixon incident before this Commission?
Mr. Martin. I think so.
Mr. Redlich. What did Mr. Thorne say?
Mr. Martin. He said no.
Mr. Redlich. Did you and Mr. Thorne discuss whether she should have mentioned that incident before this Commission?
Mr. Martin. No.
Mr. Redlich. Did you think it was an important incident, Mr. Martin?
Mr. Martin. No. I don't know why—the credibility of it didn't sound logical. It didn't seem to me that it actually happened.
Mr. Redlich. Did you speak to any representative of the Houston Post or the Associated Press with regard to this incident in the last several days?
Mr. Martin. Yesterday morning.
Mr. Redlich. Could you tell us the nature of that conversation?
Mr. Martin. He came out and asked me.
Mr. Redlich. Who is "he"?
Mr. Martin. Let's see, his name is Creighton, I believe or the last name began with a "C", he is with the Houston Post, reporter. He came out and asked me what I knew about the Nixon incident and I said I know nothing about it. He said well he had it on good authority that there was a diary that Lee Harvey Oswald had written and it was mentioned in the diary.

Now, I have never heard of a diary involved. There are some 60 pages of manuscript that he is supposed to have written, but I have never heard of a diary.

Then—which I told him.

He asked me if I knew of anyone that he could contact to find more about it. And I said well, if anybody knows about it, it will be the Commission, and I told him that I had just heard about it the day before, and he asked if Marina knew anything about it, and I said I don't know.

Mr. Redlich. You didn't discuss with this reporter whether you believed the incident to be true?

Mr. Martin. No.

Mr. Redlich. At the time you first learned about the incident you thought it was of sufficient importance that you called Mr. Thorne the same day, isn't that right?

Mr. Martin. Yes. We discussed it back and forth and I don't—we couldn't think of how it could happen.

Mr. Leech. Could we go off the record?

(Discussion off the record.)

Mr. Dulles. Read this brief report into the record.

Mr. Redlich. I would like to read into the record a story which appears in the Washington Post February 22, 1964—27, 1964, dated Houston, Texas, February 26, Associated Press:

"The Houston Post quoted an associate of Lee Harvey Oswald's widow tonight as saying Oswald planned to kill former Vice President Richard M. Nixon. The Post quoted James Martin, until a few days ago Marina Oswald's business representative, as saying that evidence to this effect had been presented to the Warren Commission investigating the assassination of President John F. Kennedy. Martin is scheduled to testify before the Commissioners Thursday. Nixon was in Dallas the day before President Kennedy was killed. Oswald was charged with the slaying."

Mr. Martin. Now. I did not tell him—I told him exactly what I told you, that I had no knowledge of it. I had secondhand knowledge only of it. I said if anyone knew about it the Commission would know it.

490 Mr. Redlich. Did you tell him that this evidence had been presented before the Warren Commission?

Mr. Martin. No, I told him if anybody knew about it, you would know about it.

Senator Cooper. I think you said a minute ago that you only learned about it the day before?

Mr. Martin. That is what I told the newspaper reporter.

Senator Cooper. What is the significance of that? Did you talk to somebody the day before?

Mr. Martin. No, it was just a method of brushing him off.

Senator Cooper. Had you talked to Robert Oswald the day before?

Mr. Martin. No.

Senator Cooper. May I ask this: Now, Mrs. Marina Oswald told you about the Nixon incident?

Mr. Martin. Yes.

Senator Cooper. Had she previously told you about the Walker incident?

Mr. Martin. Yes.

Senator Cooper. General Walker?

Mr. Martin. Yes, after it came out in the newspapers. The first I heard about it was when I read in the newspapers.

Senator Cooper. Then she talked to you about it?

Mr. Martin. I asked her about it.

Senator Cooper. You have read somewhere, have you, that Mrs. Marina Oswald said that Lee Oswald gave her his reason for wanting to shoot at General Walker?

Mr. Martin. The reason she gave me was that Lee Harvey Oswald thought that General Walker was a Fascist.

Senator Cooper. Right.

Mr. Martin. And needed to be killed.

Senator Cooper. Did she tell you any statement that Lee Oswald made giving his reasons that he wanted to kill or shoot Richard Nixon?

Mr. Martin. No.

Senator Cooper. Didn't talk about that at all?

Mr. Martin. No.

Senator Cooper. Did she ever tell you of any other statements that Lee Oswald had made to her about his, any attempts that he made or any intentions that he had to kill any other person?

Mr. Martin. No.

Senator Cooper. You are sure of that?

Mr. Martin. Positive.

Senator Cooper. Did she tell you about any statements that Lee Oswald might have made about President Kennedy?

Mr. Martin. No. Anything that——

Senator Cooper. You must have talked to her a great deal about this assassination of President Kennedy.

Mr. Martin. Actually, I tried to avoid most of this stuff.

Senator Cooper. What?

Mr. Martin. I tried to avoid most of these things. I don't know, I figured they would be a sore spot with her, but I don't know whether they were or not.

Senator Cooper. It would be tremendously helpful to this Commission to know if she did talk to you about the assassination of President Kennedy and anything that Lee Oswald might have said about him before and tell us anything——

Mr. Martin. If she had said anything to me about it I would definitely tell you. I cannot recall any incident that—of the conversation between she and Lee about any other assassination or about the President.

Mr. Dulles. Had you ever met or heard of Lee Harvey Oswald prior to November 22, 1963?

Mr. Martin. No.

Representative Boggs. Mrs. Oswald lived in your home for how long?

Mr. Martin. About 2½ months.

Representative Boggs. You had many conversations with her in that period of time.

Mr. Martin. No, not really many. I was usually out of the house, and there weren't many opportunities that arose to have a conversation.

491 Representative Boggs. Did you ever have any reason to believe that she was anything other than what she appeared to be, namely an ordinary housewife who had come to this country as the wife of an American whom she married?

Mr. Martin. Looking back on the whole picture, she doesn't seem quite right. I mean she doesn't fit.

Representative Boggs. What do you mean by that?

Mr. Martin. As a mother and a housewife. She is too cold for one thing.

Representative Boggs. Cold in what way?

Mr. Martin. Emotionally. This thing, I don't know whether it is the Russian woman or what, but this thing would have terrifically upset an American woman, and she was not very upset at all.

Representative Ford. Not upset about the assassination?

Mr. Martin. About her husband.

Representative Ford. About her husband's subsequent death?

Representative Boggs. Well now——

Mr. Martin. She was to a degree. But it didn't ring true.

Representative Boggs. So what do you mean by that. Do you mean that because of her coolness under very terrific—very difficult conditions and a very difficult situation, that maybe she was not just what she appeared to be, and if not, what do you think she was?

Mr. Martin. I have no idea. It is the way she treated, the way she treated contributions, for instance; someone would send a dollar, I don't know, maybe it was her last dollar, and she would look at it and throw it aside and say, "Oh, it is just a dollar." And John Thorne and I kind of built up an image for her or of her, for the American public, and she is not exactly as we picture her in the news articles.

Mr. Redlich. Would you spell that out in more detail?

Mr. Martin. Well, for one thing, I recall instances that she read the Bible every day, she didn't crack a Bible. She got up between 10 and 11 o'clock every morning. The only household chores she did was wash the evening dinner dishes, and occasionally she would vacuum.

Representative Boggs. This may be attributed to lack of energy or laziness.

Mr. Martin. Well, yes, that is true. But she is not a humble person at all.

Representative Ford. Did you ever see her cry or show any comparable emotions?

Mr. Martin. No. The closest I ever saw her to really showing any emotion at all was when, it was about a week after she had been there, she saw a picture, of Jackie Kennedy's picture—a picture of Jackie Kennedy, I don't know whether it was Life Magazine or what.

Representative Boggs. Did she ever do anything or say anything that would give you any reason to believe that maybe she was part of an intelligence system?

Mr. Martin. No. Although I have wondered about it since.

Mr. Redlich. Since when, Mr. Martin?

Mr. Martin. Well, this whole thing, since I got into it. This whole thing seems to me like I have been kind of made a patsy. Robert Oswald wouldn't take her in right after this incident because he was afraid of what might happen, might or might not happen.

The Fords also expressed the same opinion.

Mr. Dulles. What do you mean by the same opinion?

Mr. Martin. That they wouldn't have taken her in at first. Mr. Ford expressed the opinion that he was afraid of what the public reaction might be and he didn't know what to think.

We took her in with the full knowledge that anything could happen, and anything might happen, and it was done strictly on an altruistic basis at first, and then this manager thing came in which I wish it hadn't at all.

But be that as it may, it has happened, and things have been turned upside down.

But then as soon as the Secret Service was pulled off then Robert insisted that she move from my home to his home, and start proceedings to cancel the contracts that are in existence. She was up there—she came back to the doctor on a Tuesday after she left our home, and stopped in at the house and said she wanted to come back to live with us.

492 Mr. Dulles. When was this approximately? Just after she moved to the Fords or how long after she moved?

Mr. Martin. No, she left my home on Sunday, went to Denton to live with Robert, came back to the doctor, Dr. Bishop, on Tuesday, and came over to the house to pick up some of her belongings, and——

Mr. Redlich. Excuse me, just so the Commission has the date straight, the Sunday you are referring to when she left is the Sunday after her appearance before this Commission?

Mr. Martin. Yes.

Mr. Redlich. That would be the 9th of February, is that correct?

Mr. Martin. Right.

Then on Tuesday, which would be the 11th, she came back to the house, and wanted to move back in.

Representative Ford. Who drove her, how did she get there?

Mr. Martin. Vada Oswald, Robert Oswald's wife.

Mr. Redlich. Are you finished with what you were about to say?

Mr. Martin. It just seemed strange to me that a sudden move should be made like that and then within two days after that, it was Tuesday, and Wednesday, Thursday and I received a letter from her discharging me as her manager or attempting to discharge me.

Representative Boggs. I was asking you about intelligence and that sort of thing. This would not indicate that sort of thing to you, would it?

Mr. Martin. No, but the whole thing seemed to be a kind of a preplanned thing.

Mr. Redlich. Will you spell that out in more detail because when Congressman Boggs asked you questions as to whether Mrs. Oswald might be part of Soviet intelligence you replied you are now beginning to wonder, and you also replied you wonder if you have been made a patsy.

Could you, in your own words, explain that answer in greater detail?

Mr. Martin. Of course, not knowing how a spy would work or anything, I have no knowledge of anything of this sort, this whole thing shows a lack of gratefulness or something, and actually she showed the same thing with Mrs. Paine. She lived with Mrs. Paine for quite some time. Then Mrs. Paine has been trying to contact her consistently for, well, ever since the assassination, and we have passed letters to her, letters from Mrs. Paine to Marina, wherein she has asked Marina to at least call her or do something, and Marina doesn't want to have anything to do with her.

Mr. Redlich. Has Marina given you a reason for that?

Mr. Martin. She said she doesn't like her.

Mr. Dulles. Do you know why it was that Robert Oswald advised her not to go back to the Paines or did you know that he did?

Mr. Martin. I knew that he did.

Mr. Dulles. Do you know the reason for that?

Mr. Martin. No. He said he just didn't like her.

Mr. Dulles. He gave no reasons?

Mr. Martin. No.

Mr. Redlich. And Mrs. Oswald, Marina Oswald, gave no reason to you as to why she didn't like the Paines?

Mr. Martin. No, I think it is because Robert didn't. That is a thought.

Mr. Redlich. You said that——

Mr. Martin. She has expressed that.

Mr. Redlich. You said that you were beginning to wonder whether this is a preplanned affair. What do you mean by that?

Mr. Martin. Well, I don't mean preplanned from the very beginning, but I think probably sometime in December from then on it might have been planned.

We have accumulated for her a considerable amount of money in story rights.

Representative Boggs. How much?

Mr. Martin. Well, on advances, this is not the ultimate or the end result, but just on advances, it is $132,000.

Mr. Redlich. Mr. Martin, you are reading from a document. Is that something——

493 Mr. Martin. This I brought for you. We don't have the money. But these are the contracts that have been negotiated.

Mr. Redlich. Is this something you are turning over to the Commission?

Mr. Martin. Yes, that is for your information.

Mr. Dulles. What is the nature of this document?

Mr. Martin. It is a handwritten——

Mr. Dulles. By whom?

Mr. Martin. By me, a handwritten list of the publishers, and the news media that I have contacted in Marina's behalf to sell her movie rights, the TV right, book rights and so forth.

Mr. Dulles. And the amount they have proposed to pay for them?
Mr. Martin. Well, these are just the advances.
Now, in the case of Texitalia Films, for instance——
Mr. Redlich. Could I interrupt and get this identified?
Mr. Martin. Certainly.
Mr. Redlich. With your permission, we would like to introduce this into evidence and take, a photostatic copy and leave you with the original.
Mr. Martin. Certainly.
Mr. Dulles. Would you describe this?
Mr. Redlich. This document lists various publications, media of communication, and indicating the amounts which have been the subject of negotiation, and the contracts, if any, which have been signed with these various media of publication concerning Marina Oswald's story.
Mr. Dulles. Mr. Martin has said this is written in his own hand, is that correct, Mr. Martin?
Mr. Martin. Yes, sir.
Representative Boggs. Mr. Chairman, I have to go to a meeting at the Speaker's office momentarily, I would just like to ask one further question of this witness.
Now, I understand about the business negotiations here and so forth, but I want you to be specific—anything that comes to your mind as to whether or not this woman, anything more than what I asked you about.
Mr. Leech. Can you give us about two minutes in that room?
(Discussion off the record.)
Mr. Redlich. Back on the record.
Mr. Dulles. Just one minute. This should go in the record.
Representative Boggs. Who is this individual?
Mr. Martin. I have been trying to remember his name. I can find out his name. It began with an "H".
Mr. Dulles. Would you repeat the story, please, and then we will continue with the examination.
Mr. Martin. I met a gentleman who is an executive with the Dinkler Hotel chain, and he related the story to me that was told to him by one of their engineers, a maintenance man in the Atlanta, in their Atlanta hotel. The maintenance man's wife was an, or is a long distance telephone operator, and on the night preceding the assassination there was an individual that called, well, the way I heard the story, that she said he sounded like he had been drinking, and that he mentioned to her to remember this telephone call because it would go down in history. He made a credit card call to Lee Harvey Oswald, and simply said, "Proceed as planned."
Then he made another telephone call to Jack Ruby and told him that if anything went wrong he knew what to do.
Now, I questioned this, I guess there are numerous rumors of this type or whatever it is, and he said no, that it was definitely the truth, and the reason she hadn't come out before with it was that it is a violation of Federal law to listen to a long distance telephone call, and that they finally did report it to the FBI.
Mr. Redlich. The person you were speaking to, as I understand this story, received the information from a maintenance man whose wife was the telephone operator who overheard the conversation?
Mr. Martin. Yes.
Representative Boggs. Was this a telephone operator in a Dinkler hotel?
494 Mr. Martin. I didn't get that whether it was in a Dinkler hotel or whether she was in the long distance or toll offices in Atlanta.
Representative Boggs. Did this person have the credit card number and so forth?
Mr. Martin. No. The person that I was talking to?
Representative Boggs. Did the telephone operator have it?

Mr. Martin. The telephone operator did, or the telephone company has the records.

Representative Boggs. Do you have any other information that would indicate that—

Mr. Martin. No, I know this doesn't indicate anything about Marina as far as—no, it is just a strange feeling as far as Marina is concerned. She is too cold.

Mr. Redlich. When did you hear about this story, Mr. Martin?

Mr. Martin. About a week ago.

Mr. Redlich. You haven't discussed it at all with Marina in that week?

Mr. Martin. No.

Mr. Redlich. I would like to question you again on Congressman Boggs point. You have said she is too cold, you have said you thought that all this was preplanned. Is there anything specific in anything that she told you or in any of her actions which would lead you to believe that she has withheld certain information from you, or this Commission, concerning her knowledge about the assassination?

Mr. Martin. No, except she made a remark to me one time that she didn't volunteer anything. She only answered questions.

Representative Ford. This was after the return from the Commission hearing?

Mr. Martin. No, this was sometime ago. That was before——

Representative Ford. Before the Commission hearing where she appeared?

Mr. Martin. Yes. And it was——

Mr. Dulles. Is that all you had on this particular point?

Representative Boggs. Yes.

Mr. Martin. I don't remember what brought it up even. She didn't like the FBI. She said that. And she didn't like to answer questions.

Mr. Redlich. Did she tell you why?

Mr. Martin. No. She just didn't like them. Boguslav in particular.

Mr. Dulles. But her remark was made before her hearing before this Commission?

Mr. Martin. Yes.

Mr. Dulles. And did not relate then to that hearing.

Mr. Martin. No.

Mr. Redlich. Did she indicate to you she had revealed everything that there was to reveal before this Commission?

Mr. Martin. Yes. There again I didn't question her about anything that she said in the Commission. I didn't feel it was any of my business for one thing, and all I asked her is how it went, and she would say fine, and that would be the end of it. That is the limit of my questioning her as far as testimony within the Commission was concerned.

Mr. Redlich. Will you tell us how you found out about the General Walker incident?

Mr. Martin. Read it from the newspapers.

Mr. Redlich. When you read about it did you talk to Mrs. Oswald about it?

Mr. Martin. Yes.

Mr. Redlich. Could you tell us the nature of the conversation?

Mr. Martin. Well, I asked her if it was true, and she said yes, and I also asked her who was with Oswald, and she said no one. He did things alone. And, let's see, she related the story as to the note he had written. He had left earlier in the evening, and he hadn't come home at the, we'll say, at an early hour, and she was getting quite upset with him, and she found this note on a bed table or somewhere in the bedroom, and read it, and it simply said that he might be gone for a time or he might be in jail, and instructions as to what to do in case he was gone.

495 Mr. Redlich. Did Marina tell you all about this?

Mr. Martin. Yes.

Mr. Redlich. In English?

Mr. Martin. Yes.

Mr. Redlich. She knew English well enough to be able to relate this type of story?

Mr. Martin. She learned very rapidly.

Mr. Redlich. Do you recall approximately when that was?
Mr. Martin. No. It was the same day it came out in the paper.
Representative Ford. Did she know of her own knowledge about General Walker? Did she indicate any background information about General Walker?
Mr. Martin. No.
Representative Ford. She only told what Lee told her about it?
Mr. Martin. Lee told her he was a Fascist.
Mr. Dulles. Did she recount to you, that is, did Marina account to you, what she said to Lee Harvey after this incident, after the Walker incident, after he told her about the Walker incident?
Mr. Martin. Yes, she said that she hid the note that he left in a cookbook and told him if he ever did anything like that again that she would turn that note over to the police and turn him over to the police also.
Mr. Redlich. Mr. Martin, were you aware that Marina Oswald had given this information voluntarily to the Secret Service or the FBI concerning the Walker incident?
Mr. Martin. No.
Mr. Redlich. Did you ever ask her about it?
Mr. Martin. Well, it was in the newspapers so I assumed they knew about it.
Mr. Redlich. And you assumed she had volunteered this information?
Mr. Martin. Well, of course now, I was a little concerned to begin with as to how it got out.
Mr. Redlich. Why were you concerned?
Mr. Martin. Well, if she had told it to the FBI and the FBI only then how did it get in the newspapers?
Mr. Redlich. What was the—you say you were concerned that certain aspects of her story were being released. What was the nature of your concern?
Mr. Martin. Well, I was just wondering how that information got to the newspapers?
Mr. Redlich. Did you ask her?
Mr. Martin. No, I didn't ask her because she didn't see any newspaper reporters at all.
Mr. Redlich. Did you ask any of the agents of the FBI or the Secret Service?
Mr. Martin. Yes, Mr. Heitman.
Mr. Redlich. What did Mr. Heitman tell you?
Mr. Martin. He said it didn't come from the Dallas office. He said it must have come from Washington. The Houston Chronicle brought it out.
Mr. Redlich. By Washington he meant the Washington office?
Mr. Martin. Of the FBI, the Justice Department.
Mr. Redlich. FBI. That was his opinion as to where this information could come from?
Mr. Martin. Yes.
Mr. Redlich. Did you ever ask Mrs. Oswald why she had not revealed this information prior to that time?
Mr. Martin. No. I tried to stay as far away from this investigation as possible, because I didn't want to get into it at all to be real frank about it. I figured there are people better equipped than I to ferret out information and they have methods of doing it that I have no idea about.
Mr. Redlich. At that time, however, you were acting as her business representative.
Mr. Martin. Yes. Because I had to refute something in the paper.
Mr. Redlich. Were you assisting her at that time in the preparation of any narratives that she was preparing in connection with her story?
Mr. Martin. No. She has never written anything other than the manuscript that she wrote for the Commission. And we have never pre-prepared anything.

496 Mr. Dulles. Has she had conversations with others, to your knowledge, who have been writing material, Isaac Don Levine, for example?

Mr. Martin. The only one would be Levine.

Mr. Dulles. The only one would be Isaac Don Levine?

Mr. Martin. Levine told me she told him that her husband was a Trotskyite. Now what that means, I don't know but he seemed to think quite a bit.

Mr. Dulles. Marina told Isaac Don Levine?

Mr. Martin. Yes.

Mr. Dulles. That Marina's husband?

Mr. Martin. Lee Oswald was a Trotskyite.

Mr. Dulles. He was a Trotskyite.

Mr. Redlich. Mr. Martin, in what way do you consider yourself a patsy?

Mr. Martin. Well, because this, for instance——

Mr. Redlich. May we introduce this in evidence so we know what we are talking about?

Mr. Chairman, I offer——

Mr. Dulles. Identify it.

Mr. Redlich. In the course of the witness' explanation of his business representation of Mrs. Oswald the witness has presented before this Commission a list of arrangements that he has entered into or is considering entering into concerning the sale of certain aspects of Mrs. Oswald's story. This document is, we are told, written in Mr. Martin's handwriting. I show the witness Commission Exhibit No. 325 and ask you whether this document is one that you have brought before the Commission and whether its contents are as I have described them.

Mr. Martin. Yes, it is.

Mr. Redlich. Mr. Chairman, I ask that Commission Exhibit No. 325 be admitted.

Mr. Dulles. It shall be admitted.

(The document referred to was marked Commission Exhibit No. 325 for identification and received in evidence.)

Mr. Redlich. It is understood that a photostat of this exhibit will be made part of the permanent record of the Commission, and that the original will be returned to the witness.

Mr. Dulles. I wonder if you wouldn't leave us the original in this case because this was prepared for the Commission?

Mr. Martin. You can have the original.

Mr. Dulles. We will keep the original and we will be glad to give you a photostat for your records.

Mr. Martin. I have it right up here.

Mr. Dulles. Do you want to read that into the record, it is quite short and it might make the record more intelligible.

Mr. Redlich. Since this is in the handwriting of the witness may I suggest that the witness read it?

Mr. Dulles. Right.

Mr. Martin. Texitalia Films, $75,000 movie and the TV rights, World Wide plus $7,500 plus expenses per film appearance, plus $1,500 per—plus expenses for personal appearance. Contract was signed February 11.

Life Magazine was $5,000, North American rights for Lee had photo with rifle and pistol.

Stern Magazine, $12,500, story serial rights for Germany and Italy only, with a 70–30 percent reciprocal for serial rights in Europe, 70 percent to Marina.

Stern Magazine, $2,650 picture rights on the seven photos with same arrangements as above.

Mr. Redlich. Finish the documents.

Mr. Martin. Meredith Press, $25,000 advance on world book rights.

London Daily Mirror $2,200 guarantee on 50–50 reciprocal for British Commonwealth rights on rifle photo.

Detroit Free Press stole photo and has sold it to foreign news media thereby leaving themselves liable.

This Week Magazine, $1,500 for 500-word article.

Total is $132,350.

497 Mr. Redlich. Mr. Martin, it is in connection with this document that you have referred to yourself as a possible patsy?

Mr. Martin. Yes.

Mr. Dulles. Could I ask just one moment before that, how much has been received and how much is——

Mr. Martin. $50,000 of it. The rest is being held, $75,000 in Texitalia Films they have the money.

Mr. Dulles. Who is they?

Mr. Martin. Texitalia Films. But they don't want to part with it until this is settled.

Mr. Redlich. Until what is settled?

Mr. Martin. Until there is an amicable settlement between Marina Oswald and myself.

Mr. Redlich. Concerning your representation of her?

Mr. Martin. Yes.

Mr. Dulles. You mean they are holding their own money and not paying it at the present time?

Mr. Martin. Yes.

Mr. Redlich. It hasn't been put in escrow or anything of that kind?

Mr. Martin. No. We have received $5,000 from Life Magazine. That is in an escrow account. I have a check for $2,400 from Stern Magazine, which is uncashed because the attorney McKenzie who has been hired by Robert wrote a letter to Stern Magazine saying that I had no authority to make any deals for Marina. So they stopped payment on the check. Of course, I haven't tried to cash the check, so it is sitting.

Mr. Redlich. At this time, rather than go into the details of these business arrangements, I would like to revert to the question posed earlier in connection with this document, you referred to yourself as a patsy.

Would you care to explain that?

Mr. Martin. Well, I have put in approximately 2½; months of good, hard work and grief trying in the first place, trying to keep the news media away from her and at the same time trying to sell her story.

Mr. Redlich. Don't assume we know anything, tell us everything.

Mr. Martin. I had to leave my job at the Inn of the Six Flags to properly handle this which was the first of the year. I could not keep going on both jobs. These contracts were negotiated on the basis of my contract with her, which states that I have full power to sign any contracts for her in these fields.

William McKenzie, who is, was hired, apparently, by Robert Oswald, and is acting in his behalf, I guess, although he is using Marina Oswald's name, has tried to cancel my contract retroactively, in other words, just like it was never there at all, and it just happened too suddenly for it not to have been planned.

Mr. Redlich. What would have been planned? What is the plan that you suspect?

Mr. Martin. Well, the dropping of it—as soon as the money starts to come in, then the first thing they want to do is get rid of the personal manager and the attorney who has been taking all, who have been the buffers for the 2½; months prior to that.

The Secret Service was pulled off, there is apparently no danger at all concerning her life or anyone connected with her. So they feel perfectly safe in taking off, carrying on where we left off, utilizing all the work that we had put into it.

This was not a decision that was made in two days.

Mr. Redlich. Could you be more specific in terms of your suspicions with regard to the plan which you have alleged here was designed to get you off this job?

Mr. Martin. Well, I have letters from—one from Marina and one from McKenzie, that requests my discharge from this contractual agreement.

Now they have actually no reason to cancel the contract. I have performed as far as these sales are concerned quite well, and, of course, those are just advance payments of $132,000. There would be more on royalties after that.

Mr. Dulles. Did you sign these agreements or Mr. Thorne or did Marina sign them?
498 Mr. Martin. I did.

Mr. Dulles. These agreements with the news media?

Mr. Martin. I did.

Mr. Dulles. You signed them?

Mr. Martin. According to the contract that I have with Marina, "You will authorize me and approve for and in my behalf and in your discretion and decision the following: approve and permit the use of my name, photographs, likeness, voice, sound effects, characters, persons for all publicity, advertising and the promotion of any and all ventures desired by you to be undertaken by me and for the performance by me of any appearance or service. You are authorized, empowered and directed by me."

Mr. Dulles. I think we have a copy of this, do we not?

Mr. Redlich. Yes. You are reading from——

Mr. Martin. My contract.

Mr. Redlich. Yes, just so the record is clear, the contract between James Martin and Marina Oswald is Commission Exhibit 276 which was introduced in connection with Robert Oswald's testimony. Mr. Martin, there has been introduced in a prior hearing what is now Commission Exhibits Nos. 274 and 275, a letter from William McKenzie to you and a letter from William McKenzie to Mr. Thorne concerning the discharging of your services.

Do you have any document which you wish to introduce at the present time concerning that—the reasons given for your discharge, because I would like to ask you questions concerning that?

Mr. Leech. May I ask the date of the letter please, sir? Give me the date. I think we have the originals, sir.

Mr. Redlich. There is one dated February 18, two of them dated February 18.

Mr. Leech. Yes, one to Jim Martin and one to Mr. John Thorne.

Mr. Redlich. One is addressed to Mr. James Martin and the other to Mr. John Thorne.

Mr. Leech. Yes, sir; we have the originals.

Mr. Redlich. Do you have with you any other letters in connection with the termination of Mr. Martin's services?

Mr. Martin. One from Marina Oswald.

(Discussion off the record.)

Mr. Redlich. Mr. Martin, you said earlier in your testimony that you were building a public image of Marina Oswald?

Mr. Martin. Yes.

Mr. Redlich. Would you tell the Commission what you mean by that?

Mr. Martin. Well, in this type of thing——

Mr. Redlich. May I interrupt and suggest you don't thumb through——

Mr. Martin. Excuse me. We were trying to create in the public mind an image of a bereaved widow and a simple lost girl. And I think we did actually. This was for her, as I say, for her benefit. She has received some $68,000 in contributions, and the image is not all true.

Mr. Redlich. Would you tell us in respect to which in your opinion the image is not true?

Mr. Martin. Well, as I mentioned before about the bible, this is a very small incident, she has received numerous bibles in the mail, and to my knowledge has never read the first page of one, and most of them are in Russian.

This is a small thing really but it is part of her image, that she is a religious person.

She wants to be thought of as we have built her now but she doesn't conform to that image.

Mr. Redlich. In what way, how?

Mr. Martin. Well, she is lazy, for one thing.

Mr. Redlich. Lazy in what respect?

Mr. Martin. Well, as far as even taking care of the children. The children bother her. I mean to her they are a constant upset. When she left our home to go up to Denton, my wife offered to keep the baby there at the house if she liked, and Marina took her up on it and then Robert told her she had better take the baby with her. She hadn't seen the baby for over a week. And the first day she was back she was willing to leave the baby again.

499 Mr. Redlich. Is there anything else?

Mr. Martin. Her lack of, well, humbleness as far as all these contributions are concerned. She takes it as a matter of—she takes it for granted. She is quite unhappy when the contributions slack off.

Mr. Redlich. Has she discussed the amount of contributions with you?

Mr. Martin. I have kept her informed all along on it.

Mr. Redlich. Has she indicated that there is some relationship between the story that she reveals to the public and the contributions which she will receive?

Mr. Martin. Yes.

Mr. Redlich. Would you be more specific about that?

Mr. Martin. Well, she has read newspaper articles, for instance, that I haven't written but I have directed.

Mr. Redlich. Directed?

Mr. Martin. By giving them information.

Mr. Redlich. What is the nature——

Mr. Martin. To build it up.

Mr. Redlich. What is the nature of these articles?

Mr. Martin. Well, I recall one, I wonder if I have it, I guess I don't have it, that was written by Bill Burrus of the Times Herald in Dallas. It was a very good article, and not quite true, we will say. It is shaded in truth.

Mr. Redlich. Do you have the article with you?

Mr. Martin. Here is one Bill Burrus did that is when she went to midnight mass.

Mr. Redlich. Mr. Martin has submitted to the Commission an article which does not carry a date or the name of the publication in which it appears, but is headed "Marina Oswald attended mass, had quiet Yule", by Bill Burrus.

Mr. Martin. That was the Dallas Times Herald.

Mr. Redlich. Since we would like to question the witness about this, I would like to label it Commission Exhibit No. 326 and ask it be introduced in evidence.

Mr. Dulles. It will be admitted with no objection.

(The document referred to was marked Commission Exhibit No. 326 for identification and received in evidence.)

Mr. Redlich. I hand you Commission Exhibit 326, Mr. Martin. Will you tell us in what respects this article is not true?

Mr. Martin. Well, I wouldn't say it is strictly not true. But it embellishes the truth.

Mr. Redlich. Could you be specific in terms of references to the particular article?

Mr. Martin. Well, for instance, let's see, is this where she went to church?

Mr. Dulles. Did she go to church?

Mr. Martin. Yes.

Mr. Leech. It is my partner's church.

Mr. Martin. Well, for instance, "she wandered around the secret quarters for long periods of time, sometimes she listened to Christmas carols over radio or television", which I believe is not true. I don't believe I told that; that was just added in there.

"Marina continued her studies of the English language and watched television, including her favorite Steve Allen show". She doesn't even like Steve Allen. And, of course, she is never studying English.

Mr. Dulles. Was this information that you gave to Mr. Burrus?

Mr. Martin. No. That is the trouble with newspapers. I have told Bill Burrus that she watches Steve Allen. She does but just for lack of anything else to do.

Now I didn't say anything about the Christmas carols nor about studying the English language.

Mr. Dulles. You say she has not been studying the English language?

Mr. Martin. No, she is learning it quite rapidly because she had to in her own defense in order to converse with people. When she was living with us, there was no one there that spoke Russian so she had to learn English in order to converse.

Mr. Dulles. Is there anything else in this particular article that you would either regard as unslanted or untrue?

500 Mr. Martin. No.

Mr. Dulles. Could you give us other examples where——

Mr. Martin. There is the first one.

Mr. Dulles. If you are planning to comment on that I would like to introduce it in evidence.

Mr. Martin. Yes. This will go with it.

Mr. Redlich. The witness has submitted to the Commission an article appearing in the Dallas Times Herald on Sunday, December 15, 1963, the headline reading, "Marina Oswald, all the pity in the world won't help", written by Bill Burrus. This has now been marked as Commission Exhibit No. 327, and I ask that it be admitted in evidence.

Mr. Dulles. This will be admitted, if there is no objection.

(The document referred to was marked Commission Exhibit No. 327 for identification and received in evidence.)

Mr. Redlich. Mr. Martin, I hand you Commission Exhibit No. 327 and ask you to tell the Commission in what respects if any there is material in this article which you regard as untrue or exaggerated or slanted?

Mr. Martin. Here is a sentence in here, "She pores over the letters reaching her more than a thousand so far and is choked with emotion by the compassion and support they express", the only thing she did actually was to open the letters and did not open all of them. The only letters she read or attempted to read were ones written in Russian.

Mr. Redlich. What was her reaction to those letters?

Mr. Martin. Acceptance of it but no real thankfulness. The further it went, the longer it went, it seemed the less she cared whether——

Mr. Dulles. Did Burrus get this slanted material from you?

Mr. Martin. Yes.

Mr. Redlich. Do you recall anything she specifically said in response to these letters that is leading you to the conclusion that you have reached?

Mr. Martin. That she specifically said?

Mr. Redlich. Yes.

Mr. Martin. Well, for instance, one day she opened a letter and there was a dollar in it and she said, "Oh, a dollar", and threw it on the table, and there are little things that living as closely as we did, you can't really recall the specific incidents but there is a general feeling, and there is a complete lack of compassion as to what all these people are doing for her or trying to do for her.

Mr. Redlich. But you can't recall anything specific that she said which would indicate this lack of compassion?

Mr. Martin. No, other than "the American people are crazy for sending me that money".

Mr. Redlich. Is that a quotation from Mrs. Oswald? She said the American people are crazy for sending this money?

Mr. Martin. Yes.

Mr. Redlich. Did she elaborate on it?

Mr. Martin. No.

Mr. Redlich. Did you reply to that?

Mr. Martin. I told her that they felt sorry for her and she didn't say anything.

Mr. Redlich. Did she make any other comments of that nature?

Mr. Martin. Other than that dollar bill. Those are the only ones I can remember specifically.

Mr. Redlich. Would you continue your examination of Commission Exhibit No. 327?

Mr. Martin. Well, let's see, "unlike her husband, Marina is devout. She is a member of the Greek Orthodox Church", that is not true. She was not a devout Greek orthodox. She was not devout anything so far as religion is concerned.

Mr. Dulles. Did she ever say anything about the baptism of her child in that church to you?

Mr. Martin. Well, now let's see, she was supposed to have gotten June baptized without her husband's knowledge.

501 Mr. Redlich. You say she was supposed to have, where did you get that information?

Mr. Martin. Well, I read it somewhere prior to this article. This article has it in there. I didn't give him this information. He got it from some other article, and I recall reading it. And when she read this, she commented on it. She said he did know that June was being baptized.

Mr. Redlich. Did she read that?

Mr. Martin. Yes.

Mr. Redlich. In English?

Mr. Martin. Yes.

Mr. Redlich. She knew English well enough to read this?

Mr. Martin. Yes. It took her a while to read it.

Mr. Redlich. I would like to call the attention——

Mr. Martin. This is December 15.

Mr. Redlich. I would like to call the attention of the Commission to the date which is Sunday, December 15. You say as of Sunday, December 15, which is a little over 3 weeks after she came to live with you, Mrs. Oswald knew English well enough to be able to read this and understand it?

Mr. Martin. Not to read it legibly, I mean not to understand every word of it but she understood the biggest part of the article. I was quite amazed at how much she could read. She can't read writing or says she can't, but she can read printing or typing.

Here is another one now, "she is poring over children's primary readers and studying the Russian-English dictionary attempting to understand all the words and talk about her."

She had one child's book that one of the Secret Service men brought her, and she looked at it and that was the end of that.

Mr. Redlich. Where did this information appearing in this story come from? Did you tell that to Mr. Burrus?

Mr. Martin. Yes.

Mr. Redlich. When Mrs. Oswald read this story and saw things that were not quite true, did she discuss that fact with you?

Mr. Martin. On one occasion, let's see, what was it—it may have been in this article. Oh, yes, about the baptism. She said that Lee did know about the baptism. This was gleaned from some place else.

Mr. Dulles. Before or afterward?

Mr. Martin. Well, she said before. Before the baptism.

"She washes clothes for herself and June Lee, she cooks her own meals favoring macaroni and other casserole dishes." She did not cook her own meals. She cooked twice while she was at the house in two and a half months.

Mr. Redlich. Is this fact one which you related to Mr. Burrus, the fact she cooked her own meals?

Mr. Martin. I didn't say she cooked her own meals but she cooked.

Mr. Redlich. Do you recall what reaction if any Mrs. Oswald had in reading this comment?

Mr. Martin. The only one she commented on was she doesn't like macaroni, it is noodles.

Mr. Redlich. But Mrs. Oswald voiced no objection to your giving this information to the newspapers which to use your expression was not quite true?

Mr. Martin. No. "Marina now has the first dish washer she has ever used and she thinks it is wonderful". Actually, she didn't like it but now in most of this stuff Bill Burrus would ask me a question like, "Does she have a dish washer", and I would say "yes", and he would elaborate on it.

This is quite a sympathetic article. "Marina gets up at about 9 a.m. every day." She always got up between 10 and 11. "She asked Secret Service men to read some of the letters to her". I don't recall any incident where she did.

Mr. Redlich. Was that also a fact which you gave to Mr. Burrus?

Mr. Martin. No.

"As the hours and days tick by Marina watches television and struggles with newspapers. These things bring tears to her eyes, pictures of President Kennedy, Jackie, Lee Oswald, Mrs. Tippit, the wife of the slain police officer. Sometimes she turns off the set." That is not true.

502 Mr. Redlich. Could you be a little bit more specific about that? Were there instances in which she saw these people mentioned and what was her reaction?

Mr. Martin. No real reaction at all. Just there on television.

Mr. Dulles. You started to describe earlier I think when she saw a picture of Mrs. Jacqueline Kennedy and she made certain remarks. I don't know that we finished that.

Mr. Martin. Well, yes; she did. She remarked, "Oh, Jackie, Jackie", and that was it. There wasn't—kind of shook her head. That is in this article, too, and that is true.

Of course, this last paragraph, "The agents speak through curtains and she feels hunted sometimes despite friendly letters and packages". I don't think she has ever felt hunted or in danger. She has expressed that opinion. She didn't feel that anyone was—anyone intended to harm her.

Mr. Dulles. Did she ever express any ideas about going back to the Soviet Union?

Mr. Martin. She said it once and I questioned her about it. She said she was just—what was it—just joking. She used a funny sounding word for joking. I don't remember what it was.

Mr. Redlich. Do you have any further comments with regard to this particular exhibit?

Mr. Martin. No.

Mr. Redlich. I suggest this would be a good time for recess, Mr. Chairman.

Mr. Dulles. All right. The Commission will be adjourned until 3 p.m., this afternoon. Would you report with your counsel at that time?

(Whereupon, at 12:35 p.m., the President's Commission recessed.)

www.ingramcontent.com/pod-product-compliance
Lightning Source LLC
Chambersburg PA
CBHW052005070526
44584CB00016B/1631